Professional Examination

Strategic Level

Paper E3

Enterprise Strategy

EXAM PRACTICE KIT

Published by: Kaplan Publishing UK

Unit 2 The Business Centre, Molly Millars Lane, Wokingham, Berkshire RG41 2QZ

Acknowledgements

We are grateful to the Chartered Institute of Management Accountants for permission to reproduce past examination questions. The answers to CIMA Exams have been prepared by Kaplan Publishing, except in the case of the CIMA November 2010 and subsequent CIMA Exam answers where the official CIMA answers have been reproduced.

Notice

British Library Cataloguing in Publication Data
A catalogue record for this book is available from the British Library

ISBN: 978 0 85732 992 9

Printed and bound in Great Britain

CONTENTS

Section

Key features in this edition

In addition to providing a wide ranging bank of real past exam questions, we have also included in this edition:

- Paper specific information and advice on exam technique.

- Guidance to make your revision for this particular subject as effective as possible.

- Enhanced tutorial answers packed with specific key answer tips, technical tutorial notes and exam technique tips from our experienced tutors.

You will find a wealth of other resources to help you with your studies on the following sites:

www.EN-gage.co.uk

http://www.cimaglobal.com

INDEX TO QUESTIONS AND ANSWERS

INTRODUCTION

For all strategic level papers (E3, F3 and P3), CIMA will release a "pre-seen" scenario approximately 6 weeks before the real exam. As part of section A of the exam you will then get further "un-seen" information relating to this case and question requirements. These will make up the whole of section A in the exam, worth 50%.

Section B questions will continue to be stand alone and hence the bulk of this exam practice kit consists of such questions. The majority of these are past CIMA exam questions. If changed in any way from the original version, this is indicated in the end column of the index below with the mark *(A)*.

KEY TO THE INDEX

PAPER ENHANCEMENTS

We have added the following enhancements to the answers in this exam practice kit:

Key answer tips

All answers include key answer tips to help your understanding of each question.

Tutorial note

Many answers also include more tutorial notes to explain some of the technical points in more detail.

Top tutor tips

For selected questions, we "walk through the answer" giving guidance on how to approach the questions with helpful 'tips from a top tutor', together with technical tutor notes.

These answers are indicated with the "footsteps" icon in the index.

Examiner's comments

For exams from November 2010 onwards, the examiner's post-exam guidance comments have been included. These have been reproduced with the kind permission of CIMA.

SECTION A-TYPE QUESTIONS

SECTION B-TYPE QUESTIONS

INTERACTING WITH THE COMPETITIVE ENVIRONMENT (20%)

Page number (header over Question / Answer columns)

IMPLEMENTATION OF STRATEGIC PLANS AND PERFORMANCE EVALUATION (30%)

ANALYSIS OF PAST EXAM PAPERS

The table below summarises the key topics that have been tested in the examinations since May 2011

	May 11	Sep 11	Nov 11	Mar 12	May 12	Sep 12	Nov 12	Mar 13	May 13	Sep 13
Evaluation of strategic position										
Rational model and alternatives							Q1			
Suitability of strategic model	Q2									
Evaluation of strategic options	Q1	Q1	Q1	Q1	Q1,3	Q1	Q1,3	Q1		Q1,4
Porters generic strategies	Q2			Q1		Q1				
Organisational structure							Q4			
Ansoff's matrix		Q3					Q3			
Scenario planning/foresight									Q4	
Mission and objectives		Q4							Q1	
Project management								Q3		
BCG matrix			Q1					Q1		
Strategic information				Q4						
Interacting with the competitive environment										
Customer analysis/CRM							Q1			
Information systems strategy	Q2	Q1							Q2	
Stakeholders	Q4	Q4			Q2		Q2			Q2
Corporate Social Responsibility and ethics	Q4	Q1, Q4	Q3	Q1, Q2	Q1, Q2	Q2			Q3	Q1
Porter's Value Chain						Q4				
E-business							Q1		Q2	
Porter's Five Forces			Q2							Q2
Porter's Diamond			Q2							
SWOT										Q4
Change management										
Problem identification			Q1		Q3		Q2			
Change management process	Q1		Q1	Q1	Q3	Q4	Q2	Q1		
Change agents				Q3				Q4		
Culture								Q4	Q1	

	May 11	Sep 11	Nov 11	Mar 12	May 12	Sep 12	Nov 12	Mar 13	May 13	Sep 13
Implementation of strategic plans and performance evaluation										
Critical success factors	Q3					Q3		Q1		
Balanced scorecard		Q2			Q4					
SMART				Q3						
Benchmarking				Q4					Q1	
BPR/PI										Q3
Knowledge management						Q3				
Evaluation of performance management			Q4							Q1
Controls				Q1						
Data mining						Q3				

EXAM TECHNIQUE

- Use the allocated **20 minutes reading and planning time** at the beginning of the exam:

    - read the questions and examination requirements carefully, and

    - begin planning your answers.

    See the Paper Specific Information for advice on how to use this time for this paper.

- **Divide the time** you spend on questions in proportion to the marks on offer:

    - there are 1.8 minutes available per mark in the examination

    - within that, try to allow time at the end of each question to review your answer and address any obvious issues

    Whatever happens, always keep your eye on the clock and **do not over run on any part of any question!**

- Spend the last **five minutes** of the examination:

    - reading through your answers, and

    - **making any additions or corrections**.

- If you **get completely stuck** with a question:

    - leave space in your answer book, and

    - **return to it later.**

- Stick to the question and **tailor your answer** to what you are asked.

    - pay particular attention to the verbs in the question.

- If you do not understand what a question is asking, **state your assumptions**.

    Even if you do not answer in precisely the way the examiner hoped, you should be given some credit, if your assumptions are reasonable.

- You should do everything you can to make things easy for the marker.

    The marker will find it easier to identify the points you have made if your **answers are legible**.

- **Written questions**:

    Your answer should have:

    - a clear structure

    - a brief introduction, a main section and a conclusion.

    Be concise.

    It is better to write a little about a lot of different points than a great deal about one or two points.

- **Computations:**

  It is essential to include all your workings in your answers. Many computational questions require the use of a standard format e.g. net present value, adjusted present value.

  Be sure you know these formats thoroughly before the exam and use the layouts that you see in the answers given in this book and in model answers.

- **Reports, memos and other documents:**

  Some questions ask you to present your answer in the form of a report, a memo, a letter or other document.

  Make sure that you use the correct format – there could be easy marks to gain here.

PAPER SPECIFIC INFORMATION

THE EXAM

FORMAT OF THE EXAM

	Number of marks
Section A	
A maximum of four compulsory questions all relating to a pre-seen case study scenario and further new unseen information provided within the exam.	50
Section B	
A choice of two from three questions worth 25 marks each	50
	100

Total time allowed: 3 hours plus 20 minutes reading and planning time.

PASS MARK

The pass mark for all CIMA Qualification examination papers is 50%.

READING AND PLANNING TIME

Remember that all three hour paper based examinations have an additional 20 minutes reading and planning time.

CIMA GUIDANCE

CIMA guidance on the use of this time is as follows:

> This additional time is allowed at the beginning of the examination to allow candidates to read the questions and to begin planning their answers before they start to write in their answer books.
>
> This time should be used to ensure that all the information and, in particular, the exam requirements are properly read and understood.
>
> During this time, candidates may only annotate their question paper. They may not write anything in their answer booklets until told to do so by the invigilator.

FURTHER GUIDANCE

We recommend that you take the following approach with your reading and planning time in respect of the E3 paper:

- **Skim through the whole paper**, assessing the level of difficulty of each question.

- **Decide which section B questions you wish to attempt.** In doing this it may be worth doing a brief answer plan to ensure you have enough ideas to score well. Do not be fooled into attempting question with an easy part (a) only to find that you know very little about part (b).

- **Decide the order** in which you think you will attempt the questions:

  This is a personal choice and you have time on the revision phase to try out different approaches, for example, if you sit mock exams.

  A common approach is to tackle the question you think is the easiest and you are most comfortable with first.

  Others may prefer to tackle the longest questions first, or conversely leave them to the last.

  Psychologists believe that you usually perform at your best on the second and third question you attempt, once you have settled into the exam, so not tackling the bigger Section A questions first may be advisable.

  It is usual however that student tackle their least favourite topic and/or the most difficult question in their opinion last.

  Whatever you approach, you must make sure that you leave enough time to attempt all questions fully and be very strict with yourself in timing each question.

- **Write down** on the question paper next to the mark allocation **the amount of time you should spend on each part.** Do this for each part of every question.

- **Either: Start analysing the new unseen information** for the section A questions. You are allowed to annotate the question paper, perhaps highlighting key issues, thinking about which models to use and so on.

  Or: For each question in turn, read the requirements and then the detail of the question carefully.

  Always read the requirement first as this enables you to **focus on the detail of the question with the specific task in mind**.

  For computational questions:

  Highlight key numbers / information and key words in the question, scribble notes to yourself on the question paper to remember key points in your answer.

  For written questions:

  Take notice of the format required (e.g. letter, memo, notes) and identify the recipient of the answer. You need to do this to judge the level of financial sophistication required in your answer and whether the use of a formal reply or informal bullet points would be satisfactory.

  Plan your beginning, middle and end and the key areas to be addressed and your use of titles and sub-titles to enhance your answer.

For all questions:

Spot the easy marks to be gained in a question and parts which can be performed independently of the rest of the question. For example, writing down due dates of payment of tax, due dates for making elections, laying out basic proformas correctly.

Make sure that you do these parts first when you tackle the question.

Don't go overboard in terms of planning time on any one question – you need a good measure of the whole paper and a plan for all of the questions at the end of the 15 minutes.

By covering all questions you can often help yourself as you may find that facts in one question may remind you of things you should put into your answer relating to a different question.

- With your plan of attack in mind, **start answering your chosen question** with your plan to hand, as soon as you are allowed to start.

DETAILED SYLLABUS

The detailed syllabus and study guide written by CIMA can be found at:
www.cimaglobal.com

APPROACH TO REVISION

QUESTION PRACTICE IS THE KEY TO SUCCESS

Success in professional examinations relies upon you acquiring a firm grasp of the required knowledge at the tuition phase. In order to be able to do the questions, knowledge is essential.

However, the difference between success and failure often hinges on your exam technique on the day and making the most of the revision phase of your studies.

The **Study text** is the starting point, designed to provide the underpinning knowledge to tackle all questions. However, in the revision phase, pouring over text books is not the answer.

Revision cards are designed to help you quickly revise a topic area, however you then need to practice questions. There is a need to progress to full exam standard questions as soon as possible, and to tie your exam technique and technical knowledge together.

The importance of question practice cannot be over-emphasised.

The recommended approach below is designed by expert tutors in the field, in conjunction with their knowledge of the examiner and their recent real exams.

The approach taken for the operational and management papers is to revise by topic area. However, with the strategic level papers, a multi topic approach is required to answer the scenario based questions.

You need to practice as many questions as possible in the time you have left.

OUR AIM

Our aim is to get you to the stage where you can attempt exam standard questions confidently, to time, in a closed book environment, with no supplementary help (i.e. to simulate the real examination experience).

Practising your exam technique on real past examination questions, in timed conditions, is also vitally important for you to assess your progress and identify areas of weakness that may need more attention in the final run up to the examination.

In order to achieve this we recognise that initially you may feel the need to practice some questions with open book help and exceed the required time.

The approach below shows you which questions you should use to build up to coping with exam standard question practice, and references to the sources of information available should you need to revisit a topic area in more detail.

Remember that in the real examination, all you have to do is:

- attempt all questions required by the exam

- only spend the allotted time on each question, and

- get them at least 50% right!

Try and practice this approach on every question you attempt from now to the real exam.

EXAMINER FEEDBACK

After each real exam CIMA publishes examiner feedback detailing the suggested approach and common candidate weaknesses.

The main problems relating to E3 are:

- "misallocation of time", "running out of time" and showing signs of "spending too much time on an earlier questions and clearly rushing the answer to a subsequent question". Proper time allocation is essential!

- Failing to answer the verb specified in the requirements. In particular examiners will ask candidates to "evaluate" or "analyse" something but receive answers at the lower level of "describe" or "list".

- Failing to relate points to the scenario given. Often examiners are faced with generic lists of issues that candidates have learnt. At the strategic level knowledge alone will score very few marks – application is vital.

Good exam technique is vital.

DETAILED REVISION PLAN

Stage 1: Assess areas of strengths and weaknesses

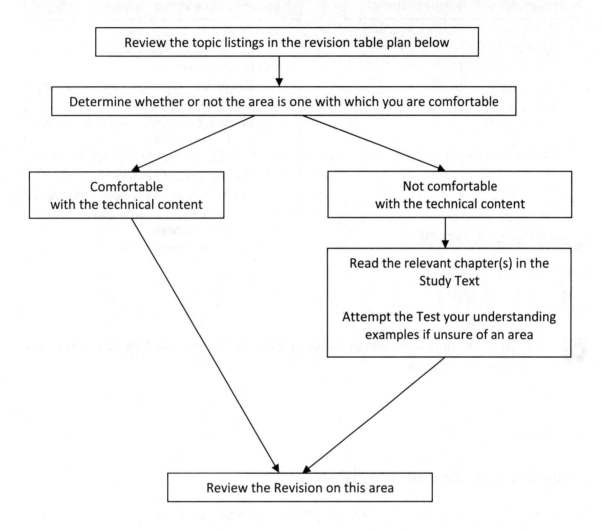

Stage 2: Practice questions

Follow the order of revision of topics as recommended in the revision table plan below and attempt the questions in the order suggested.

Try to avoid referring to text books and notes and the model answer until you have completed your attempt.

Try to answer the question in the allotted time.

Review your attempt with the model answer and assess how much of the answer you achieved in the allocated exam time.

Fill in the self-assessment box below and decide on your best course of action.

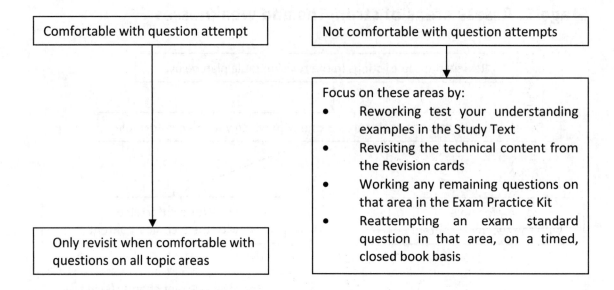

Note that:

 The "footsteps questions" give guidance on exam techniques and how you should have approached the question.

Stage 3: Final pre-exam revision

We recommend that you **attempt at least one three hour mock examination** containing a set of previously unseen exam standard questions.

It is important that you get a feel for the breadth of coverage of a real exam without advanced knowledge of the topic areas covered – just as you will expect to see on the real exam day.

Ideally a mock examination offered by your tuition provider should be sat in timed, closed book, real exam conditions.

THE DETAILED REVISION PLAN

Topic	Study Text Chapter	Question to attempt	Tutor guidance	Date attempted	Self assessment
Industry analysis	5	9	While industry analysis is more common in section A, it does come up in section B as this question illustrates.		
Country analysis	5	13	Porter's diamond is a possible exam topic – ensure you know when to use it instead of the more usual PEST, five forces, etc		
Competitor analysis	5	15	Competitor analysis is a more niche area. Try to learn the detail re Koetler.		
IT and e-business	11	19	This looks at the IT/IS/IM strategies for an organisation, which is a popular requirement in the exam.		
Knowledge management	12	20	An excellent but tricky question on CSFs, KPIs and knowledge management.		
Stakeholders	3	27	Mendelow's power-interest matrix is a framework that you must be comfortable applying.		
Ethics and CSR	3	26	An excellent question that focuses exclusively on ethics.		

Topic	Study Text Chapter	Question to attempt	Tutor guidance	Date attempted	Self assessment
Change – triggers	15	37	A good question on the triggers of change and Lewin's Force Field Analysis model, along with types of change.		
Change – management	16	Q38	Given its position in the syllabus, expect to see frequent questions on change management.		
The planning process	2	Q5(a)	Make sure you can evaluate the different approaches to strategic planning and suggest which is most appropriate to an organisation.		
Forecasting	4	10	Scenario planning, simulation and foresight are ignored by many candidates but may still come up.		
Value chain	6	47	A core topic that you must understand, along with criticisms and alternatives.		
BCG	8	49	The BCG matrix is highly useful for evaluating portfolios and developing strategy as this question illustrates.		
Product lifecycle	8	50	The PLC is often neglected in favour of the BCG matrix. However, question son this area are usually straightforward.		
Competitive strategy	8	53	A great question on Ansoff, with some evaluation mixed in.		

Topic	Study Text Chapter	Question to attempt	Tutor guidance	Date attempted	Self assessment
Control systems	10	61	A great question on the assessment of control systems.		
Evaluating strategies	8	57	An excellent question on using the SFA framework.		
Balanced scorecard	9	65	Make sure you can use the BSC to identify and evaluate relevant issues.		
Benchmarking	9	64	A comprehensive question on the different aspects of benchmarking		
Organisational structure	10	68	A tricky question on the appropriateness of a given structure for an organisation.		
Transfer pricing	10	70	A tough question linking transfer pricing and Porter's five forces model.		
Divisional performance	10	71	Divisional performance appraisal is an important area. You need to be aware of the underlying issues and problems connected with specific measures such as ROI and RI.		

In addition to the above questions you should attempt each section A style question.

Note that not all of the questions are referred to in the programme above. The remaining questions are available in the kit for extra practice for those who require more questions on some areas.

FORMULAE SHEET AND TABLES

FINANCIAL MATHEMATICS

Compound interest (values and sums)

Future Value S, of a sum of X, invested for n periods, compounded at r% interest

$$S = X[1+r]^n$$

Annuity

Present value of an annuity of one unit of currency per annum receivable or payable for n years, commencing in one year, discounted at r% per annum:

$$PV = \frac{1}{r}\left[1 - \frac{1}{[1+r]^n}\right]$$

Perpetuity

Present value of one unit of currency per annum, payable or receivable in perpetuity, commencing in one year, discounted at r% per annum:

$$PV = \frac{1}{r}$$

Present value table

Present value of £1 i.e. $(1 + r)^{-n}$ where r = interest rate, n = number of periods until payment or receipt.

Periods (n)	Interest rates (r)									
	1%	2%	3%	4%	5%	6%	7%	8%	9%	10%
1	.990	.980	.971	.962	.952	.943	.935	.926	.917	.909
2	.980	.961	.943	.925	.907	.890	.873	.857	.842	.826
3	.971	.942	.915	.889	.864	.840	.816	.794	.772	.751
4	.961	.924	.888	.855	.823	.792	.763	.735	.708	.683
5	.951	.906	.863	.822	.784	.747	.713	.681	.650	.621
6	.942	.888	.837	.790	.746	.705	.666	.630	.596	.564
7	.933	.871	.813	.760	.711	.665	.623	.583	.547	.513
8	.923	.853	.789	.731	.677	.627	.582	.540	.502	.467
9	.914	.837	.766	.703	.645	.592	.544	.500	.460	.424
10	.905	.820	.744	.676	.614	.558	.508	.463	.422	.386
11	.896	.804	.722	.650	.585	.527	.475	.429	.388	.350
12	.887	.788	.701	.625	.557	.497	.444	.397	.356	.319
13	.879	.773	.681	.601	.530	.469	.415	.368	.326	.290
14	.870	.758	.661	.577	.505	.442	.388	.340	.299	.263
15	.861	.743	.642	.555	.481	.417	.362	.315	.275	.239
16	.853	.728	.623	.534	.458	.394	.339	.292	.252	.218
17	.844	.714	.605	.513	.436	.371	.317	.270	.231	.198
18	.836	.700	.587	.494	.416	.350	.296	.250	.212	.180
19	.828	.686	.570	.475	.396	.331	.277	.232	.194	.164
20	.820	.673	.554	.456	.377	.312	.258	.215	.178	.149

Periods (n)	Interest rates (r)									
	11%	12%	13%	14%	15%	16%	17%	18%	19%	20%
1	.901	.893	.885	.877	.870	.862	.855	.847	.840	.833
2	.812	.797	.783	.769	.756	.743	.731	.718	.706	.694
3	.731	.712	.693	.675	.658	.641	.624	.609	.593	.579
4	.659	.636	.613	.592	.572	.552	.534	.516	.499	.482
5	.593	.567	.543	.519	.497	.476	.456	.437	.419	.402
6	.535	.507	.480	.456	.432	.410	.390	.370	.352	.335
7	.482	.452	.425	.400	.376	.354	.333	.314	.296	.279
8	.434	.404	.376	.351	.327	.305	.285	.266	.249	.233
9	.391	.361	.333	.308	.284	.263	.243	.225	.209	.194
10	.352	.322	.295	.270	.247	.227	.208	.191	.176	.162
11	.317	.287	.261	.237	.215	.195	.178	.162	.148	.135
12	.286	.257	.231	.208	.187	.168	.152	.137	.124	.112
13	.258	.229	.204	.182	.163	.145	.130	.116	.104	.093
14	.232	.205	.181	.160	.141	.125	.111	.099	.088	.078
15	.209	.183	.160	.140	.123	.108	.095	.084	.074	.065
16	.188	.163	.141	.123	.107	.093	.081	.071	.062	.054
17	.170	.146	.125	.108	.093	.080	.069	.060	.052	.045
18	.153	.130	.111	.095	.081	.069	.059	.051	.044	.038
19	.138	.116	.098	.083	.070	.060	.051	.043	.037	.031
20	.124	.104	.087	.073	.061	.051	.043	.037	.031	.026

Cumulative present value of 1.00 unit of currency per annum, receivable or payable at the end of each year for n years $\dfrac{1-(1+r)^{-n}}{r}$.

Periods (n)	Interest rates (r)									
	1%	2%	3%	4%	5%	6%	7%	8%	9%	10%
1	0.990	0.980	0.971	0.962	0.952	0.943	0.935	0.926	0.917	0.909
2	1.970	1.942	1.913	1.886	1.859	1.833	1.808	1.783	1.759	1.736
3	2.941	2.884	2.829	2.775	2.723	2.673	2.624	2.577	2.531	2.487
4	3.902	3.808	3.717	3.630	3.546	3.465	3.387	3.312	3.240	3.170
5	4.853	4.713	4.580	4.452	4.329	4.212	4.100	3.993	3.890	3.791
6	5.795	5.601	5.417	5.242	5.076	4.917	4.767	4.623	4.486	4.355
7	6.728	6.472	6.230	6.002	5.786	5.582	5.389	5.206	5.033	4.868
8	7.652	7.325	7.020	6.733	6.463	6.210	5.971	5.747	5.535	5.335
9	8.566	8.162	7.786	7.435	7.108	6.802	6.515	6.247	5.995	5.759
10	9.471	8.983	8.530	8.111	7.722	7.360	7.024	6.710	6.418	6.145
11	10.368	9.787	9.253	8.760	8.306	7.887	7.499	7.139	6.805	6.495
12	11.255	10.575	9.954	9.385	8.863	8.384	7.943	7.536	7.161	6.814
13	12.134	11.348	10.635	9.986	9.394	8.853	8.358	7.904	7.487	7.103
14	13.004	12.106	11.296	10.563	9.899	9.295	8.745	8.244	7.786	7.367
15	13.865	12.849	11.938	11.118	10.380	9.712	9.108	8.559	8.061	7.606
16	14.718	13.578	12.561	11.652	10.838	10.106	9.447	8.851	8.313	7.824
17	15.562	14.292	13.166	12.166	11.274	10.477	9.763	9.122	8.544	8.022
18	16.398	14.992	13.754	12.659	11.690	10.828	10.059	9.372	8.756	8.201
19	17.226	15.679	14.324	13.134	12.085	11.158	10.336	9.604	8.950	8.365
20	18.046	16.351	14.878	13.590	12.462	11.470	10.594	9.818	9.129	8.514

Periods (n)	Interest rates (r)									
	11%	12%	13%	14%	15%	16%	17%	18%	19%	20%
1	0.901	0.893	0.885	0.877	0.870	0.862	0.685	0.847	0.840	0.833
2	1.713	1.690	1.668	1.647	1.626	1.605	1.585	1.566	1.547	1.528
3	2.444	2.402	2.361	2.322	2.283	2.246	2.210	2.174	2.140	2.106
4	3.102	3.037	2.974	2.914	2.855	2.798	2.743	2.690	2.639	2.589
5	3.696	3.605	3.517	3.433	3.352	3.274	3.199	3.127	3.058	2.991
6	4.231	4.111	3.998	3.889	3.784	3.685	3.589	3.498	3.410	3.326
7	4.712	4.564	4.423	4.288	4.160	4.039	3.922	3.812	3.706	3.605
8	5.146	4.968	4.799	4.639	4.487	4.344	4.207	4.078	3.954	3.837
9	5.537	5.328	5.132	4.946	4.772	4.607	4.451	4.303	4.163	4.031
10	5.889	5.650	5.426	5.216	5.019	4.833	4.659	4.494	4.339	4.192
11	6.207	5.938	5.687	5.453	5.234	5.029	4.836	4.656	4.486	4.327
12	6.492	6.194	5.918	5.660	5.421	5.197	4.968	4.793	4.611	4.439
13	6.750	6.424	6.122	5.842	5.583	5.342	5.118	4.910	4.715	4.533
14	6.982	6.628	6.302	6.002	5.724	5.468	5.229	5.008	4.802	4.611
15	7.191	6.811	6.462	6.142	5.847	5.575	5.324	5.092	4.876	4.675
16	7.379	6.974	6.604	6.265	5.954	5.668	5.405	5.162	4.938	4.730
17	7.549	7.120	6.729	6.373	6.047	5.749	5.475	5.222	4.990	4.775
18	7.702	7.250	6.840	6.467	6.128	5.818	5.534	5.273	5.033	4.812
19	7.839	7.366	6.938	6.550	6.198	5.877	5.584	5.316	5.070	4.843
20	7.963	7.469	7.025	6.623	6.259	5.929	5.628	5.353	5.101	4.870

Section 1

SECTION A-TYPE QUESTIONS

M PLC (NOV 2011 & MAR 2012) – RELATES TO QUESTIONS 1 & 2

PRESEEN CASE STUDY

Introduction

M plc is a long established publisher of newspapers and provider of web media. It is based in London and has had a full listing on the London Stock Exchange since 1983. The company has three operating divisions which are managed from the United Kingdom (UK). These are the Newspapers Division, the Web Division and the Advertising Division.

Newspapers Division

The Newspapers Division publishes three daily newspapers and one Sunday newspaper in the UK. The Division has three offices and two printing sites. Between them the three offices edit the three daily newspapers and the Sunday newspaper. The Newspaper Division has two subsidiary publishing companies, FR and N. FR is based in France within the Eurozone and N in an Eastern European country which is outside the Eurozone. Printing for all the Division's publications, except those produced by FR and N, is undertaken at the two printing sites. FR and N have their own printing sites.

Web Division

The Web Division maintains and develops 200 websites which it owns. Some of these websites are much more popular in terms of the number of "hits" they receive than others. Web material is an increasing part of M plc's business. In the last ten years, the Web Division has developed an online version of all the newspapers produced by the Newspapers Division.

Advertising Division

The sale of advertising space is undertaken for the whole of M plc by the Advertising Division. Therefore, advertisements which appear in the print media and on the web pages produced by the Newspapers Division (including that produced by FR and N) and the Web Division respectively are all handled by the Advertising Division.

Group Headquarters

In addition to the three operating divisions, M plc also has a head office, based in the UK, which is the group's corporate headquarters where the Board of Directors is located. The main role of M plc's headquarters is to develop and administer its policies and procedures as well as to deal with its group corporate affairs.

Mission statement

M plc established a simple mission statement in 2005. This drove the initiative to acquire FR in 2008 and remains a driving force for the company. M plc's mission is "to be the best news media organisation in Europe, providing quality reporting and information on European and world-wide events".

Strategic objectives

Four main strategic objectives were established in 2005 by M plc's Board of Directors. These are to:

1   Meet the needs of readers for reliable and well informed news.

2   Expand the geographical spread of M plc's output to reach as many potential newspaper and website readers as possible.

3   Publish some newspapers which help meet the needs of native English speakers who live in countries which do not have English as their first language.

4   Increase advertising income so that the group moves towards offering as many news titles as possible free of charge to the public.

Financial objectives

In meeting these strategic objectives, M plc has developed the following financial objectives:

(i)   To ensure that revenue and operating profit grow by an average of 4% per year.

(ii)   To achieve steady growth in dividend per share.

(iii)   To maintain gearing below 40%, where gearing is calculated as debt/(debt plus equity) based on the market value of equity and the book value of debt.

Forecast revenue and operating profit

M plc's forecast revenue and net operating profit for the year ending 31 March 2012 are £280 million and £73 million respectively.

Extracts from M plc's forecast income statement for the year ending 31 March 2012 and forecast statement of financial position as at 31 March 2012 are shown in the appendix.

Comparative divisional performance and headquarters financial information

The following information is provided showing the revenue generated, the operating profit achieved and the capital employed for each division and the operating costs incurred and capital employed in M plc's headquarters. This information covers the last two years and also gives a forecast for the year ending 31 March 2012. All M plc's revenue is earned by the three divisions.

Newspapers Division	*Year ended 31.3.2010*	*Year ended 31.3.2011*	*Forecast for year ending 31.3.2012*
	£ million	£ million	£ million
Revenue external	91	94	94
Revenue internal transfers	90	91	96
Net operating profit	45	46	48
Non-current assets	420	490	548
Net current assets	4	8	(10)

Web Division	Year ended 31.3.2010	Year ended 31.3.2011	Forecast for year ending 31.3.2012
	£ million	£ million	£ million
Revenue internal transfers	55	60	66
Net operating profit	10	13	16
Non-current assets	37	40	43
Net current assets	1	1	(2)
Advertising Division	Year ended 31.3.2010	Year ended 31.3.2011	Forecast for year ending 31.3.2012
	£ million	£ million	£ million
Revenue external	162	180	186
Internal transfers	(145)	(151)	(162)
Net operating profit	10	18	19
Non-current assets	3	6	7
Net current assets	1	1	(2)
Headquarters	Year ended 31.3.2010	Year ended 31.3.2011	Forecast for year ending 31.3.2012
	£ million	£ million	£ million
Operating costs	8	9	10
Non-current assets	37	39	43
Net current assets	1	1	(1)

Notes:

1   The Advertising Division remits advertising revenue to both the Newspapers and Web Divisions after deducting its own commission.

2   The Web Division's entire revenue is generated from advertising.

3   The revenues and operating profits shown for the Newspapers Division include those earned by FR and N. The converted revenue and operating profit from N are forecast to be £20 million and £4 million respectively for the year ending 31 March 2012. FR is forecast to make a small operating profit in the year ending 31 March 2012. The Board of M plc is disappointed with the profit FR has achieved.

Additional information on each of M plc's divisions

Newspapers Division

FR is wholly owned and was acquired in 2008. Its financial statements are translated into British pounds and consolidated into M plc's group accounts and included within the Newspaper Division's results for internal reporting purposes.

Shortly after it was acquired by M plc, FR launched a pan-European weekly newspaper. This newspaper, which is written in English, is produced in France and then distributed throughout Europe. M plc's board thought that this newspaper would become very popular because it provides a snapshot of the week's news, focused particularly on European issues but viewed from a British perspective. Sales have, however, been disappointing.

N, which publishes local newspapers in its home Eastern European country, is also treated as part of the Newspapers Division. M plc acquired 80% of its equity in 2010. At that time, M plc's board thought that Eastern Europe was a growing market for newspapers. The subsidiary has proved to be profitable mainly because local production costs are lower than those in the UK relative to the selling prices.

The Newspapers Division's journalists incur a high level of expenses in order to carry out their duties. The overall level of expenses claimed by the journalists has been ignored by M plc in previous years because it has been viewed as a necessary cost of running the business. However, these expenses have risen significantly in recent years and have attracted the attention of M plc's internal audit department.

There has been significant capital investment in the Newspapers Division since 2009/10. The printing press facilities at each of the two printing sites have been modernised. These modernisations have improved the quality of output and have enabled improved levels of efficiency to be achieved in order to meet the increasing workloads demanded in the last two years. Surveys carried out before and after the modernisation have indicated higher levels of customer satisfaction with the improved quality of printing.

The increased mechanisation and efficiency has reduced costs and led to a reduction in the number of employees required to operate the printing presses. This has led to some dis-satisfaction among the divisional staff. Staff in the other divisions have been unaffected by the discontent in the Newspapers Division. Staff turnover has been relatively static across the three divisions, with the exception of the department which operates the printing presses in the Newspapers Division where some redundancies have occurred due to fewer staff being required since the modernisation.

Web Division

The web versions of the newspapers are shorter versions of the printed ones. There is currently no charge for access to the web versions of the newspapers. Revenues are generated from sales by the Advertising Division of advertising space on the web pages. Some of the websites permit unsolicited comments from the public to be posted on them and they have proved to be very popular. The Web Division is undertaking a review of all its costs, particularly those relating to energy, employees and website development.

The Web Division's management accounting is not sophisticated: for example, although it reports monthly on the Division's revenue and profitability, it cannot disaggregate costs so as to produce monthly results for each of the 200 websites. The Division is at a similar disadvantage as regards strategic management accounting as it lacks information about the websites' market share and growth rates. This has not mattered in the past as M plc was content that the Web Division has always been profitable. However, one of M plc's directors, the Business Development Director (see below under The Board of Directors and group shareholding) thinks that the Web Division could increase its profitability considerably and wants to undertake a review of its 200 websites.

Advertising Division

The Advertising Division remits advertising revenue to both the Newspapers and Web Divisions after deducting its own commission. In addition, the Advertising Division offers an advertising service to corporate clients. Such services include television and radio advertising and poster campaigns on bill boards. Advertisements are also placed in newspapers and magazines which are not produced by M plc, if the client so wishes. An increasing element of the work undertaken by the Advertising Division is in providing pop-up advertisements on websites.

Planning process

Each division carries out its own planning process. The Newspapers Division operates a rational model and prepares annual plans which it presents to M plc's board for approval. The Web Division takes advantage of opportunities as they arise and is operating in a growth market, unlike the other two divisions. Its planning approach might best be described as one of logical incrementalism. Increased capital expenditure in 2010/11 helped the Advertising Division to achieve an 11% increase in revenue in that year. The Divisional Managers of both the Web Division and the Advertising Division are keen to develop their businesses and are considering growth options including converting their businesses into outsource service providers to M plc.

The Board of Directors and group shareholding

M plc's Board of Directors comprises six executive directors and six non-executive directors, one of whom is the Non-executive Chairman. The executive directors are the Chief Executive, and the Directors of Strategy, Corporate Affairs, Finance, Human Resources and Business Development. The Business Development Director did not work for M plc in 2005 and so had no part in drafting the strategic objectives. She thinks that objective number four has become out-dated as it does not reflect current day practice. The Business Development Director has a great deal of experience working with subscription-based websites and this was one of the main reasons M plc recruited her in March 2011. Her previous experience also incorporated the management of product portfolios including product development and portfolio rationalisation.

There are divisional managing directors for each of the three divisions who are not board members but report directly to the Chief Executive.

One of M plc's non-executive directors was appointed at the insistence of the bank which holds 10% of M plc's shares. Another was appointed by a private charity which owns a further 10% of the shares in M plc. The charity represents the interests of print workers and provides long-term care to retired print workers and their dependents. Two other non-executive directors were appointed by a financial institution which owns 20% of the shares in M plc. The remaining 60% of shares are held by private investors. The board members between them hold 5% of the shares in issue. None of the other private investors holds more than 70,000 of the total 140 million shares in issue.

It has become clear that there is some tension between the board members. Four of the non-executive directors, those appointed by the bank, the charity and the financial institution, have had disagreements with the other board members. They are dissatisfied with the rate of growth and profitability of the company and wish to see more positive action to secure M plc's financial objectives.

Some board members feel that the newspapers market is declining because fewer people can make time to read printed publications. Some of the non-executive directors think that many people are more likely to watch a television news channel than read a newspaper.

Editorial policy

M plc's board applies a policy of editorial freedom provided that the published material is within the law and is accurate. The editors of each of the publications printed in the UK and France and of the websites have complete autonomy over what is published. They are also responsible for adhering to regulatory constraints and voluntary industry codes of practice relating to articles and photographs which might be considered offensive by some readers.

There is less scrutiny of the accuracy of the reporting in N's home country than in other countries. The Eastern European country in which N is situated has become politically unstable in the last two years. Much of this unrest is fuelled by the public distaste for the perceived blatant corruption and bribery which is endemic within the country's Government and business community. It is well known that journalists have accepted bribes to present only the Government's version of events, rather than a balanced view. There is also widespread plagiarism of published material by the country's newspapers and copyright laws are simply ignored.

Corporate Social Responsibility

A policy is in place throughout M plc in order to eliminate bribery and corruption among staff especially those who have front line responsibility for obtaining business. This policy was established 15 years ago. All new employees are made aware of the policy and other staff policies and procedures during their induction. The Director of Human Resources has confidence in the procedures applied by his staff at induction and is proud that no action has ever been brought against an employee of M plc for breach of the bribery and corruption policy.

M plc is trying to reduce its carbon footprint and is in the process of developing policies to limit its energy consumption, reduce the mileage travelled by its staff and source environmentally friendly supplies of paper for its printing presses. The Newspapers Division purchases the paper it uses for printing newspapers from a supplier in a Scandinavian country. This paper is purchased because it provides a satisfactory level of quality at a relatively cheap price. The Scandinavian country from which the paper is sourced is not the same country in which N is situated.

Strategic Development

The Board of Directors is now reviewing M plc's competitive position. The Board of Directors is under pressure from the non-executive directors appointed by the bank, the charity and the financial institution (which between them own 40% of the shares in M plc), to devise a strategic plan before June 2012 which is aimed at achieving M plc's stated financial objectives.

APPENDIX 1

Extracts from M plc's forecast group income statement and forecast statement of financial position

Forecast income statement for the group for the year ended 31 March 2012

	Notes	£million (GBP million)
Revenue		280
Operating costs		(207)
		——
Net operating profit		73
Interest income		1
Finance costs		(11)
Corporate income tax	1	(19)
		——
FORECAST PROFIT FOR THE YEAR		44
		——

Forecast statement of the group financial position as at 31 March 2012

	Notes	£million (GBP million)
ASSETS		
Non-current assets		641
Current assets		
Inventories		2
Trade and other receivables		27
Cash and cash equivalents		2
Total current assets		31
Total assets		672
EQUITY AND LIABILITIES		
Equity		
Share capital	2	140
Share premium		35
Retained earnings		185
Non-controlling interest		16
Total equity		376
Non-current liabilities		
Long term borrowings	3	250
Current liabilities		
Trade and other payables		46
Total current liabilities		46
Total liabilities		296
Total equity and liabilities		672

Notes:

1   The corporate income tax rate can be assumed to be 30%.

2   There are 140 million £1 shares currently in issue.

3   The long-term borrowings include £83 million of loan capital which is due for repayment on 1 May 2013 and the remainder is due for repayment on 1 April 2019.

End of Pre-seen Material

1 M PLC (NOV 11 EXAM)

Unseen material for Case Study

Web Division

M plc maintains 200 websites (Pre-seen page 2) and access to these is currently free of charge. M plc's most important website supports the 'Daily News' newspaper which is published seven days a week in the UK. This website has been operating for five years and normally receives 100,000 visits (hits) a day. The business model is that all M plc's websites generate income from advertising.

Current advertising revenue

The Daily News website currently carries 5 pages of advertising each day for which it charges advertisers £6,000 per page. M plc's Business Development Director, X, has identified a decline in advertising revenue from the Daily News website. X knows that the advertisers are attracted by the number of visits the website receives. However, the visitors come from a wide background with different social characteristics and economic resources. The advertisers would prefer to deal with a more tightly focused readership. This has led advertisers to reduce their spending to the current level of 5 pages per day, seven days a week.

X has commissioned market research which indicates that advertisers would:

(i)   increase the number of daily pages of advertising they buy if the Daily News website was subscription-only.

(ii)   not pay the current price per page if the number of subscribers was fewer than 60,000.

(iii)   expect to pay a decreasing amount per page as the number of subscribers decreased.

Move to subscription base

X believes it would be beneficial if the Daily News website ceased to be free and became available only by subscription. This would generate an additional revenue stream for the Web Division. She has discussed this idea with the Web Division's Managing Director, Y, who has asked her to provide detailed advice about the consequences of such a change.

Subscription revenue

X will offer subscribers a choice. They could either pay a daily subscription giving access for one 24 hour period or they could pay a weekly subscription giving access for 7 days. X has estimated the number of subscribers for three possible pricing strategies. Each strategy has a daily price and a weekly price. The strategies are totally independent. Details of the strategies are shown in the table below.

Strategy	Daily subscriptions Price per day	Daily subscriptions Forecast number of subscribers each day	Weekly subscriptions Price per week	Weekly subscriptions Forecast number of subscribers each week
1	£0.25	4,000	£0.50	17,000
2	£0.50	3,500	£0.75	15,000
3	£0.75	1,500	£1.50	6,000

Forecast advertising revenue

The pricing strategies for the subscriptions in the table above would give rise to the total subscriptions shown in the table below. In addition, the table below shows the expected advertising revenue for each page sold and the expected number of pages sold for each subscription strategy.

Strategy	Total number of subscribers each week	Forecast advertising revenue per page sold £	Forecast number of pages sold per day
1	45,000	4,000	7
2	39,500	3,750	9
3	16,500	2,500	10

Performance management

Although M plc has aggregate financial information for the Web Division it does not compute individual website's profit or loss. X believes that some of the 200 websites are profitable, should be invested in and could be candidates for changing to a subscription-only basis. X also believes that some of the 200 websites are unprofitable and should be closed down. She knows that the different websites consume different amounts of resources and activities. Under the current accounting arrangements the demands made on the division's activities by individual websites are not recognised.

X recognises that the task of reviewing the portfolio of 200 websites will be a complex one. Her previous experience indicates that better decisions are made when additional characteristics of products, besides their financial profile, for example, their relative market performance, are considered. However, X does not have detailed market information about the 200 websites. She is aware that the major search engines, such as Google, Yahoo and Bing can supply data relating to different market sectors and showing aspects such as market share and growth rates about individual websites. This data, which must be paid for, can be supplied for current and historic usage.

Strategic headcount reduction programme

M plc's Board of Directors is reviewing the company's competitive position (Pre-seen page 6).

Four of the non-executive directors are dissatisfied with the profitability of the company (Pre-seen page 5). As a response to this criticism, the three divisional managing directors have been instructed by M plc's Chief Executive to find ways of enhancing efficiency and reducing costs.

The Web Division's Human Relations Manager, Z, has been directed by Y to recommend how this instruction could be carried out. Z has suggested the Web Division carries out a strategic headcount reduction programme. The Web Division currently employs 380 people in 10 different departments. Not all departments employ the same number of people: the largest department, Web Development, employs 62 people; the smallest department, Web Security, employs 11 people. Z has recommended a reduction of 100 staff across the division which would cut the Web Division's costs by £2.5 million, thus, enhancing M plc's competitive position.

Z has suggested that the best way of implementing the headcount reduction programme is that each of the 10 departments should declare 10 redundancies. Z has suggested that each departmental manager should choose who will lose their job. The departmental managers will be responsible for notifying those members of their staff who will be losing their jobs. Z insists that preference for redundancy should be given to employees over the age of 50 who are earning high salaries. Z believes that the participation of the departmental managers in the programme will have a positive motivational effect upon them, and this could lead to savings in later years which would exceed the estimated £2.5 million saving each year arising from the strategic headcount reduction programme.

Required

(a) (i) Calculate the impact of each of the three possible pricing strategies suggested by X on the Web Division's weekly income. **(10 marks)**

(ii) Advise X of the other factors that should be considered before deciding to change the Daily News website to a subscription-only basis. **(10 marks)**

(b) Advise the Business Development Director, X:

(i) of the extent to which the proposed change to subscription-only usage of the Daily News website represents a conflict with M plc's strategic and financial objectives. **(7 marks)**

(ii) what arguments she could use to persuade the Board of M plc to agree to the proposed change. **(3 marks)**

(c) Advise X how she could use a portfolio analysis model, such as the Boston Consulting Group matrix, to review the portfolio of 200 websites to help her decide which to continue and which to discontinue. **(7 marks)**

(d) (i) Recommend, with reasons, three improvements to the strategic headcount reduction programme that has been proposed by the Human Relations Manager, Z. **(6 marks)**

(ii) Advise Z of approaches he could use to deal with any resistance to the changes resulting from the strategic headcount reduction programme from staff remaining in the Web Division. **(7 marks)**

(Total: 50 marks)

2 M PLC (MAR 2012 EXAM)

Unseen material for Case Study

M plc publishes three well known daily newspapers and of these the 'Daily Informer' is the longest established. The Daily Informer has positioned itself as 'the family newspaper with the broad focus.' It has sections on news, sport, politics, the arts, environment, fashion, technology, medicine, children's interests and world events. However, critics within the newspaper industry have stated that the Daily Informer has no clear identity and does not target any particular segment of the newspaper reading market. Its circulation has decreased by 38% during the last ten years. The Daily Informer made a loss in each of the last two years.

The Daily Informer is published six days a week: it is not published on Sundays. The daily sales of each edition of the newspaper amount to 150,000 copies and its selling price is £0.50 per copy. Each issue of the Daily Informer has 3 pages of advertising sold at £7,500 a page.

The Daily Informer employs 330 people made up of:

- 200 journalists and editorial staff: average salary £42,000

- 130 other staff: average salary £37,000

The Daily Informer

Forecast income statement for year ended 31 March 2013

	£000s
Revenue	
Circulation	23,400
Advertising	7,020
Total revenue	30,420
Costs	
Journalists and editorial staff	8,400
Other staff	4,810
Production costs:	
Fixed	3,180
Variable	5,180
Advertising costs	1,000
Distribution costs	4,680
IT	4,000
Third party pictures/photos	3,000
Total Costs	34,250
Loss	(3,830)

One of the Daily Informer's competitors, the 'Opinion', recently changed from being a paid-for newspaper to being free to its readers. This has resulted in a large increase in the newspaper's circulation and a reduction in journalists and editorial jobs and other staff. The general economic situation is bad for employment and many of the Opinion's former staff are unemployed.

It is noticeable that the Opinion has changed its character: it contains much more advertising, no in-depth reporting and the main content focuses on reporting the activities of footballers and other celebrities.

The Chief Executive of M plc, W, wants to investigate the possibility of the Daily Informer also becoming a free newspaper (hereafter referred to as 'FREE') and has asked S, the divisional managing director of the Newspaper Division, to examine the consequences of such a change. S has instructed the editor of the Daily Informer, E, to prepare a business forecast for FREE.

S has stated that the following criteria should be followed:

- FREE must target the same market segment as its competitor 'Opinion'

- Advertising space should be sold at £7,000 per page

- FREE's first financial objective should be to break-even within the next year

If the Daily Informer becomes 'FREE', it will, together with the 'Opinion' newspaper, form a new market segment of free newspapers. These will be the only such national UK newspapers.

E has stated that as FREE would no longer have a broad focus it would be possible to produce it with a smaller number of journalists and editorial staff. It is unlikely that FREE would continue to appeal to the Daily Informer's current readership. However, FREE would have a much greater popular appeal and achieve a higher circulation than the Daily Informer. E also believes that FREE would be able to sell substantially more advertising space, which was the experience of the Opinion when it changed its status.

The Daily Informer is currently distributed by its own staff using an in-house transport fleet. Most of the outlets which sell the Daily Informer are small retailers (that is, local newsagents and small shops). This means that currently the transport fleet has to make deliveries to 750 separate locations.

FREE would be available at 200 key points: for example, transport interchanges, such as train and bus stations and outside bars, restaurants, cinemas and sports centres. Each of these key points would distribute many more newspapers than the small retailers who are currently used for distribution. FREE would outsource the distribution to a transport specialist and this together with the reduced number of distribution points would lead to a substantial reduction in distribution costs for FREE as compared to the Daily Informer.

This new method of distribution would have an impact on the former distribution channel. The small retailers would no longer be able to sell the Daily Informer and this would lead to redundancies for some of the people in low paid jobs employed by the retailers. E knows from his previous experience working on another free newspaper that the readers are likely to only read FREE for a brief period of time, up to 30 minutes, and then they will throw away the paper. This could lead to a significant littering problem.

Predicted effects of changing the 'Daily Informer' to 'FREE' for year ending 31 March 2013

Forecast 'FREE' circulation	1,000,000	copies per day
All Savings/Increases below based on forecast income statement for the Daily Informer for the year ended 31 March 2013 and apply for the whole of the year to 31 March 2013		Comment
Saving: Reduction of journalists and editorial staff jobs	125 jobs reduction	Less requirement for journalists due to change in character of newspaper
Saving: Other staff	£2,600,000	Savings in other staff due to changes in production arrangements
Increase: Production costs	50%	Some costs rise but others fall due to economies of scale and use of recycled newsprint. The variable cost of one copy of FREE is £0.03. Fixed costs do not alter
Increase: Advertising costs	£500,000	Increase due to change in character of newspaper
Saving: Distribution costs	45%	Savings because of altered subscription
Saving: IT	50%	Savings due to change in character of newspaper
Saving: Third party pictures/ photos	25%	Savings due to change in character of newspaper

Competitive environment

The Daily Informer currently competes against ten other daily newspapers which cover various segments of the newspaper reading market. All of these newspapers contain between 7 and 10 pages of advertisements per issue. Some newspapers specialise in TV and sports coverage, others are directed towards women and one specialises in reporting financial markets and company news. Changes in reading habits and the growth of alternative news media have meant that the number of people in the UK who are prepared to pay for a newspaper is decreasing.

As the newspaper industry is a mature one, its technology is well-developed and production methods are similar across the industry. Since the Newspaper Division modernised its printing press facilities in 2009/10 (Pre-seen page 4) most of its competitors have followed suit.

Some journalists, often referred to as 'stars', are very important in UK newspapers and can command large salaries because they attract readers. These journalists often move between different newspapers.

When M plc is considering a major change to one of its businesses, it carries out a preliminary management accounting exercise. In the case of FREE, the exercise consists of calculating the number of pages of advertising it will be required to sell in order to cover all its costs and the implications of such a change. The result of this exercise, both qualitative and quantitative, will be used to inform any subsequent decision about whether or not to launch FREE.

Required

(a) (i)   Calculate the number of pages of advertising required to be sold in the year ending 31 March 2013 in order for FREE to break-even.

Base your calculation on 312 published days.   **(8 marks)**

(ii) Discuss the factors which could affect FREE's ability to achieve the sales of the number of pages of advertising you have calculated in (i).   **(6 marks)**

(iii) Advise S, the divisional managing director of the Newspaper Division, of the extent to which the publication of a free newspaper fits M plc's strategic and financial objectives (pre-seen pages 2 and 3).   **(7 marks)**

(iv) Advise S, the divisional managing director of the Newspaper Division, whether the effects of the proposed change to FREE are consistent with Corporate Social Responsibility principles relating to employment, the environment, and FREE readership.   **(8 marks)**

(b) Evaluate, using Porter's generic competitive strategy model, the likelihood of the proposed change to FREE giving the Newspaper Division a sustainable competitive advantage.   **(12 marks)**

(c) Advise E how he could use Lewin's three-step model of change to assist the staff to make the transition to the new working environment of FREE.   **(9 marks)**

(Total: 50 marks)

B SUPERMARKETS (MAY & SEP 2012) – RELATES TO QUESTIONS 3 & 4

PRESEEN CASE STUDY

Introduction

B Supermarkets (B) was founded as a grocery retailer in a European country in 1963. Its sales consist mainly of food and household items including clothing. B now owns or franchises over 15,000 stores world-wide in 36 countries. The company has stores in Europe (in both Eurozone and non-Eurozone countries), Asia and North America. B's head office is located in a Eurozone country. B has become one of the world's largest chains of stores.

B's Board thinks that there are opportunities to take advantage of the rapid economic growth of some Asian countries and the associated increases in demand for food and consumer goods.

Structure

The B Group is structured into a holding company, B, and three subsidiary companies which are located in each of the regions of the world in which it operates (Europe, Asia and North America). The subsidiary companies, referred to as "Regions" within B, are respectively B-Europe, B-Asia and B-North America.

Store operations, sales mix and staffing

B operates four types of store: supermarkets, hypermarkets, discount stores and convenience stores. For the purpose of this case study, the definition of each of these types of store is as follows:

A *supermarket* is a self-service store which sells a wide variety of food and household goods such as washing and cleaning materials, cooking utensils and other items which are easily carried by customers out of the store.

A *hypermarket* is a superstore or very large store which sells the same type of products as a supermarket but in addition it sells a wide range of other items such as consumer durable white goods, for example refrigerators, freezers, washing machines and furniture. Hypermarkets are often located on out-of-town sites.

A *discount store* is a retail store that sells a variety of goods such as electrical appliances and electronic equipment. Discount stores in general usually sell branded products and pursue a high-volume, low priced strategy and aim their marketing at customers who seek goods at prices which are usually less than can be found in a hypermarket.

A *convenience store* is a small shop or store in an urban area that sells goods which are purchased regularly by customers. These would typically include groceries, toiletries, alcoholic beverages, soft drinks and confectionery. They are convenient for shoppers as they are located in or near residential areas and are often open for long hours. Customers are willing to pay premium prices for the convenience of having the store close by.

B sells food products and clothing in its supermarkets and hypermarkets at a higher price than many of its competitors because the Board thinks that its customers are prepared to pay higher prices for better quality food products. B also sells good quality consumer durable products in its supermarkets and hypermarkets but it is forced to sell these at competitive prices as there is strong competition for the sale of such goods. B's discount stores sell good quality electrical products usually at lower prices than those charged in its supermarkets and hypermarkets, B only sells electronic equipment in its discount stores. Customers have a greater range from which to choose in the discount stores as compared with supermarkets and hypermarkets because the discount stores specialise in the goods which they sell. B's convenience stores do not have the availability of space to carry a wide range of products and they charge a higher price for the same brand and type of goods which it sells in its supermarkets.

Although B owns most of its stores, it has granted franchises for the operation of some stores which carry its name.

Nearly 0.5 million full-time equivalent staff are employed world-wide in the Group. B tries when possible to recruit local staff to fill job vacancies within its stores.

Value statement and mission

In recognition of the strong competitive and dynamic markets in which it operates, B's Board has established an overall value statement as follows: "We aim to satisfy our customers wherever we trade. We intend to employ different generic competitive strategies depending on the market segment in which our stores trade."

The Board has also produced the following mission statement:

"B practises sustainable investment within a healthy ethical and thoughtful culture and strives to achieve customer satisfaction by giving a courteous and efficient service, selling high quality goods at a reasonable price, sourcing goods from local suppliers where possible and causing the least damage possible to the natural environment. By this, we aim to satisfy the expectations of our shareholders by achieving consistent growth in our share price and also to enhance our reputation for being an environmentally responsible company."

Strategic objectives

The following objectives have been derived from the mission statement:

1   Build shareholder value through consistent growth in the company's share price.

2   Increase customer satisfaction ratings to 95% as measured by customer feedback surveys.

3   Increase commitment to local suppliers by working towards achieving 40% of our supplies from sources which are local to where B stores trade.

4   Reduce carbon emissions calculated by internationally agreed measures by at least 1% per year until B becomes totally carbon neutral.

5   Maximise returns to shareholders by employing different generic competitive strategies depending on the market segment in which B stores trade.

Financial objectives

The Board has set the following financial objectives:

1   Achieve consistent growth in earnings per share of 7% each year.

2   Maintain a dividend pay-out ratio of 50% each year.

3   Gearing levels as measured by long-term debt divided by long-term debt plus equity should not exceed 40% based on book value.

Governance

The main board comprises the Non-executive Chairman, the Chief Executive and nine Executive directors. These cover the functions of finance, human resources, corporate affairs (including legal and public relations), marketing, planning and procurement. There is also one executive director for each of the three regions, being the Regional Managing Directors of B-Europe, B-Asia and B-North America. There are also nine non-executive main board members in addition to the Chairman.

The main Board of Directors has separate committees responsible for audit, remuneration, appointments, corporate governance and risk assessment and control. The Risk Assessment and Control Committee's tasks were formerly included within the Audit Committee's role. It was agreed by the Board in 2009 that these tasks should be separated out in order not to overload the Audit Committee which has responsibilities to review the probity of the company. B's expansion has been very rapid in some countries. The expansion has been so rapid that B has not been able to carry out any internal audit activities in some of these countries to date. The regional boards do not have a committee structure.

Each of the Regional Managing Directors chairs his or her own Regional Board. All of the Regional Boards have their own directors for finance, human resources, corporate affairs, marketing, planning and procurement but their structure is different for the directors who have responsibility for the stores. In B-Asia, one regional director is responsible for the hypermarkets and supermarkets and another is responsible for discount stores and convenience stores. In B-North America, one regional director is responsible for the hypermarkets and supermarkets and another is responsible for discount stores (B does not have any convenience stores in North America). In B-Europe there is one regional director responsible for supermarkets and hypermarkets, one for discount stores and one for convenience stores. In all regions the regional directors have line accountability to their respective regional managing director and professional accountability to the relevant main board director. There are no non-executive directors on the regional boards. Appendix 1 shows the main board and regional board structures.

Treasury

Each of B's three regions has a regional treasury department managed by a regional treasurer who has direct accountability to the respective Regional Director of Finance and professional accountability to the Group Treasurer. The Group Treasurer manages the central corporate treasury department which is located in B's head office. The Group Treasurer, who is not a main board member, reports to the Director of Finance on the main board.

Shareholding, year-end share prices and dividends paid for the last five years

B is listed on a major European stock exchange within the Eurozone and it wholly owns its subsidiaries. There are five major shareholders of B, including employees taken as a group, which between them hold 25% of the 1.350 million total shares in issue. The major shareholders comprise two long term investment trusts which each owns 4%, a hedge fund owns 5%, employees own 5% and the founding family trust owns 7% of the shares. The remaining 75% of shares are owned by the general public.

The year-end share prices and the dividends paid for the last five years were as follows:

	2007	2008	2009	2010	2011
	€	€	€	€	€
Share price at 31 December	47.38	25.45	28.68	29.44	31.37
Net Dividend per share	1.54	1.54	1.54	1.62	1.65

Planning and management control

B has a very structured planning process. Each regional board produces a five year strategic plan for its region relating to specific objectives set for it by the main board and submits this to the main board for approval. The main board then produces a consolidated strategic plan for the whole company. This is reviewed on a three yearly cycle and results in a revised and updated group five year plan being produced every three years.

B's management control system, which operates throughout its regions and at head office, is well known in the industry to be bureaucratic and authoritarian. Strict financial authority levels for development purposes are imposed from the main Board. There is tension between the main Board and the regional boards. The regional board members feel that they are not able to manage effectively despite being located much closer to their own regional markets than the members of the main Board. The main Board members, on the other hand, think that they need to exercise tight control because they are remote from the markets. This often stifles planning initiatives within each region. This tension is also felt lower down the organisation as the regional board members exercise strict financial and management control over operational managers in their regions in order to ensure that the main Board directives are carried out.

Competitive overview

B operates in highly competitive markets for all the products it sells. The characteristics of each of the markets in which it operates are different. For example, there are different planning restrictions applying within each region. In some countries, B is required to operate each of its stores in a partnership arrangement with local enterprises, whereas no such restriction exists within other countries in which it trades. B needs to be aware of different customer tastes and preferences which differ from country to country. The following table provides a break-down of B's stores in each region.

	B Europe	B Asia	B North America
Supermarkets and hypermarkets	3,456	619	512
Discount stores	5,168	380	780
Convenience stores	4,586	35	

B is one of the largest retailing companies in the world and faces different levels of competition in each region. B's overall market share in terms of retail sales for all supermarkets, hypermarkets, discount stores and convenience stores in each of its regions is as follows:

	Market share
Europe	20%
Asia	1%
North America	1.5%

The following table shows the sales revenue and net operating profit earned by B in each of its regions for the year ended 31 December 2011:

	B Europe	B Asia	B North America
	€ million	€ million	€ million
Revenue	89,899	10,105	9,708
Net Operating Profit	4,795	743	673

B is constantly seeking other areas of the world into which it can expand, especially within Asia where it perceives many countries have an increasing population and strengthening economies.

Corporate Social Responsibility (CSR)

B is meeting its CSR obligations by establishing environmental targets for carbon emissions (greenhouse gas emissions), careful monitoring of its supply chain, undertaking sustainable investments and investing in its human capital.

Environmental targets for carbon emissions:

B's main board is keen to demonstrate the company's concern for the environment by pursuing continuous improvement in the reduction of its carbon emissions and by developing ways of increasing sustainability in its trading practices. A number of environmental indicators have been established to provide transparency in B's overall performance in respect of sustainability. These published measures were verified by B's statutory auditor and are calculated on a like-for-like basis for the stores in operation over the period measured.

In the year ended 31 December 2011, B reduced its consumption of kilowatt hours (kWh) per square metre of sales area as compared with the year ended 31 December 2008 by 9%. The target reduction for that period was 5%. In the same period it reduced the number of free disposable plastic bags provided to customers per square metre of sales area, by 51% against a target of 60%. Its overall greenhouse gas emissions (measured by kilogrammes of carbon dioxide per square metre of sales area) reduced by 1% in 2011 which was exactly on target.

B provides funding for the development of local amenity projects in all of the countries where B stores operate. (An amenity project is one which provides benefit to the local population, such as providing a park, community gardens or a swimming pool.)

Distribution and sourcing:

Distribution from suppliers across such a wide geographical area is an issue for B. While supplies are sourced from the country in which a store is located as much as possible, there is nevertheless still a requirement for transportation across long distances either by road or air. Approximately 20% of the physical quantity of goods sold across the group as a whole are sourced locally, that is within the country in which the goods are sold. These tend to be perishable items such as fruit and vegetables. The remaining 80% of goods are sourced from large international manufacturers and distributors. These tend to be large items such as electrical or electronic equipment which are bought under contracts which are set up by the regional procurement departments. B, due to its size and scope of operations, is able to place orders for goods made to its own specification and packaged as under its own brand label. Some contracts are agreed between manufacturers and the Group Procurement Director for the supply of goods to the whole of the B group world-wide.

B's inventory is rarely transported by rail except within Europe. This has resulted in lower average reductions in carbon emissions per square metre of sales area by stores operated by B-Asia and B-North America than for those stores operated by B-Europe. This is because the carbon emission statistics take into account the transportation of goods into B's stores.

Sustainable investments:

B aspires to become carbon neutral over the long term. The Board aims to reduce its carbon emissions by investing in state of the art technology in its new store developments and by carrying out modifications to existing stores.

Human Resources:

B prides itself on the training it provides to its staff. The training of store staff is carried out in store by specialist teams which operate in each country where B trades. In this way, B believes that training is consistent across all of its stores. In some countries, the training is considered to be at a sufficiently high level to be recognised by national training bodies. The average number of training hours per employee in the year ended 31 December 2011 was 17 compared with 13 hours in the year ended 31 December 2010. In 2011, B employed 45% more staff with declared disabilities compared with 2010.

Information systems and inventory management

In order to operate efficiently, B's Board has recognised that it must have up-to-date information systems including electronic point of sale (EPOS) systems. An EPOS system uses computers or specialised terminals that can be combined with other hardware such as bar-code readers to accurately capture the sale and adjust the inventory levels within the store. EPOS systems installation is on-going. B has installed EPOS systems in its stores in some countries but not in all its stores world-wide.

B's information systems are not perfect as stock-outs do occur from time-to-time, especially in the European stores. This can be damaging to sales revenue when stock-outs occur during peak sales periods such as the days leading up to a public holiday. In Asia and North America in particular, B's information technology systems sometimes provide misleading information. This has led to doubts in the minds of some head office staff about just how robust are B's inventory control systems.

As is normal in chain store groups, there is a certain degree of loss through theft by staff and customers. Another way that loss is suffered is through goods which have gone past their "sell-by" date and mainly relates to perishable food items which are wasted as they cannot be sold to the public. In most countries, such food items which cannot be sold to the public may be sold to local farmers for animal feed.

Regulatory issues

B's subsidiaries in Asia and North America have sometimes experienced governmental regulatory difficulties in some countries which have hindered the installation of improved information systems. To overcome some of these regulatory restrictions, B-Asia and B-North America have, on occasions, resorted to paying inducements to government officials in order for the regulations to be relaxed.

APPENDIX 1

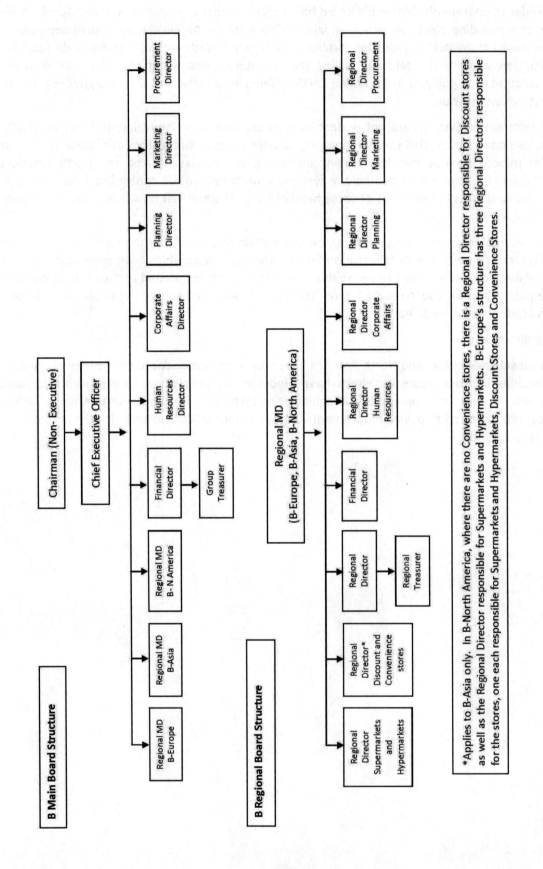

B Main Board Structure

Chairman (Non-Executive)

Chief Executive Officer

- Regional MD B-Europe
- Regional MD B-Asia
- Regional MD B-N America
- Financial Director
  - Group Treasurer
- Human Resources Director
- Corporate Affairs Director
- Planning Director
- Marketing Director
- Procurement Director

B Regional Board Structure

Regional MD (B-Europe, B-Asia, B-North America)

- Regional Director Supermarkets and Hypermarkets
- Regional Director* Discount and Convenience stores
- Regional Director
  - Regional Treasurer
- Financial Director
- Regional Director Human Resources
- Regional Director Corporate Affairs
- Regional Director Planning
- Regional Director Marketing
- Regional Director Procurement

*Applies to B-Asia only. In B-North America, where there are no Convenience stores, there is a Regional Director responsible for Discount stores as well as the Regional Director responsible for Supermarkets and Hypermarkets. B-Europe's structure has three Regional Directors responsible for the stores, one each responsible for Supermarkets and Hypermarkets, Discount Stores and Convenience Stores.

APPENDIX 2

Income statement for the year ended 31 December 2011

	Notes	€ million
Revenue		109,712
Operating costs		(103,501)
Net operating profit		6,211
Interest income		165
Finance costs		(852)
Corporate income tax		(1,933)
Profit for the year		3,591

Statement of financial position as at 31 December 2011

	€ million
Assets	
Non-current assets	57,502
Current assets	
Inventories	7,670
Trade and other receivables	1,521
Cash and cash equivalents	3,847
Total current assets	13,038
Total assets	70,540
Equity and liabilities	
Equity	
Share capital 1	2,025
Share premium	3,040
Retained earnings	18,954
Total equity	24,019
Non-current liabilities	
Long term borrowings	15,744
Current liabilities	
Trade and other payables	30,777
Total liabilities	46,521
Total equity and liabilities	70,540

Notes:

1   There are 1,350 million €1.50 shares currently in issue. The share price at 31 December 2011 was €31.37.

End of Pre-seen Material

3   B SUPERMARKETS (MAY 2012 EXAM)

Unseen material for Case Study

Franchising discount stores within Country P

B Supermarkets (B) is evaluating the possibility of expanding its business into Country P which is in Europe. Country P has an underdeveloped economy. However, it was described by a leading international bank as a 'Global Growth Generator': that is, one of the countries with 'the most promising growth prospects for 2010-2050'.

B does not currently conduct any business within Country P. B would like to test the market there. B's Marketing Director has suggested that one possible way of doing this would be to introduce discount stores within Country P by granting franchise agreements to local entrepreneurs (the franchisees) within Country P. This would also have the advantage for B of limiting its capital investment in Country P, as the entrepreneurs would be responsible for providing the premises so B will not incur any capital costs for buildings relating to any franchise. The equipment will be supplied by B.

B has had success when it has granted franchises in many countries. This experience has enabled B to establish the following fee structure which it would apply to franchises in Country P.

Country P fee structure: charged by B per franchise

'One-off' fees: charged at the start of the franchise	€
Franchise fee	60,000
Training fee	20,400
Equipment fee	150,000

Annual fees (payable at the end of each financial year)	€
Royalty fee	15% of revenue
Service fee	5% of revenue
Marketing contribution fee	5% of revenue

To justify the launch of discount store franchises in Country P, B's Marketing Director has set a minimum required income of €3 million per year for B, to be earned from the annual fees charged to the franchises (that is, from the royalty fee, the service fee and the marketing contribution fee).

B's Marketing Director estimates that the cost of capital for entrepreneurs in Country P is 12%.

In addition to the one-off fees and the annual fees, B has estimated the following average monthly operating costs and revenues for each discount store franchise:

Per month	€
Revenue	100,000
Fixed costs	2,000
Variable operating costs	65% of revenue

The variable operating costs are additional to the annual fees which are payable to B.

Sustainability

In its mission statement (pre-seen page 3) B claims to 'Practise sustainable investment'. B also aspires to '...enhance our reputation for being an environmentally responsible company'. B is also keen to demonstrate its concern for the environment by pursuing continuous improvement in the reduction of its greenhouse gas emissions and by developing ways of increasing sustainability in its trading practices. B has developed a number of environmental indicators to provide transparency in its overall performance in respect of its sustainability (pre-seen page 5).

If B does undertake expansion into Country P, 90% of its products will have to be imported into Country P: half by road, half by air. The distribution of the imported products within Country P will be done by road transport. If the discount stores are opened they will be in new purpose built premises which will be designed to be energy efficient. B's Marketing Director believes that it will be possible to operate the discount stores in Country P as 'carbon-neutral' businesses. B will expect the discount store franchises in Country P to comply with all aspects of its corporate social responsibility policy (pre-seen pages 5 and 6). Each discount store will be able to operate without giving its customers free disposable plastic bags.

Planning and management control

B has a very structured planning process. (pre-seen page 4). Its management control system is 'bureaucratic and authoritarian' (pre-seen page 4). B's Planning Director is aware of the internal tensions within the company regarding the planning and management control systems.

If the discount store franchises proceed within Country P, B's Planning Director sees it as an opportunity to introduce a substantial degree of reform to the planning and management control systems currently operating within B. Country P would function as a test site for planning and management control system reform for B. If this experience proves to be successful then the Planning Director would suggest to B's main Board that reform should be extended throughout the company. The Planning Director has suggested to B's Board that if the reform of the planning and management control systems is introduced then B Europe's Regional Director for Discount Stores (pre-seen page 7):

- could use a reformed planning and management control system in Country P.

- would be responsible for achieving a profit target for discount stores in Country P which would be agreed with B's Chief Executive Officer.

- would be able to employ whatever planning and management control systems he preferred in Country P. He would be required to submit a monthly return to the Finance Department at B's Head Office.

- could use whatever Information System he wanted in Country P. However, this would have to be compatible with B's management control system for data entry and reporting purposes. The design and operation of the reporting systems used within Country P would be the exclusive responsibility of the Regional Director for Discount Stores.

- would have the authority to decide which products are sold in Country P's discount stores and source them from anywhere.

- would have sole responsibility for making all decisions about the entrepreneurs in Country P; such as appointment, renewal and cessation.

The Corporate Affairs Director has reacted strongly against the Planning Director's proposals for reform of the planning and management control system. He said 'In my opinion this is not how we do things. Our procedures have served us well in the past. Tinkering with our culture in this way is a waste of money and could be dangerous.'

Required:

(a) Calculate the number of discount store franchises that need to be granted in Country P to earn the minimum required income of €3 million per year. **(4 marks)**

(b) (i) Advise the minimum period for which a franchise should be granted in Country P to make it financially worthwhile for an individual franchisee.

You should ignore the capital cost to the franchisee of providing the premises. **(4 marks)**

(ii) Advise which additional factors are likely to influence entrepreneurs about the desirability of investing in a discount store franchise in Country P.

Your answer should include factors under the following headings:

- Marketing/Branding

- Risk

- Franchise implementation and operation **(17 marks)**

(c) Evaluate how Country P's discount store business could assist B Supermarkets in achieving 'sustainable investment' and increased sustainability in its trading practices. **(10 marks)**

(d) Advise B's Chief Executive, of the advantages AND disadvantages for B which might arise if the reforms to the planning and management control system within Country P, that have been suggested by the Planning Director, were introduced throughout B Supermarkets. **(15 marks)**

(Total: 50 marks)

---

4 B SUPERMARKETS (SEP 2012 EXAM)

Unseen material for Case Study

Rationalisation in Country W

B's first venture to open stores outside Europe was in Country W in 1982. Initially, this was very successful but the current business environment is very competitive and the forecast results shown below have prompted questions about the continued viability of B's business operations in Country W.

B's business in Country W is organised into four sectors which cover the four different types of store which it operates there. Each sector has a sector manager who reports to the Regional Managing Director responsible for Country W. The individual store managers report to the sector managers who are senior to them.

Table 1: B's forecast sector profit/(loss) for Country W for year ended 31 December 2012

Sector	Super-market	Hyper-market	Discount stores	Convenience stores	Total	%
	€ million	€ million	€ million	€ million	€ million	
Revenue	330	450	300	120	1,200	100
Costs						
Trading	198	243	225	72	738	62
Establishment	33	18	30	12	93	8
Regional Office	68	204	34	34	340	28
Profit/Loss	**31**	**(15)**	**11**	**2**	**29**	**2**

Notes:

The amounts in Table 1 have been converted from Country W's currency to Euros.

Trading costs are all variable with revenue.

Establishment costs are all variable with revenue.

The regional office costs are all fixed. They comprise:

- Insurances of €35 million

- Property taxes of €100 million

- B Supermarkets' management charge of €205 million. This is a central charge imposed by B Supermarkets: its basis is not disclosed to sector managers and it is a non-negotiable charge.

The regional office costs are apportioned on the basis of the floor areas of the sector's properties as shown below:

Supermarkets	Hypermarkets	Discount stores	Convenience stores
%	%	%	%
20	60	10	10

The Regional Managing Director responsible for Country W is very dissatisfied with the forecast sector trading results and considers that the forecast profit of €29 million is unacceptable. The Regional Managing Director responsible for Country W proposes to close the hypermarkets which he believes should improve the profit to €44 million.

However, the Sector Manager of Country W's Hypermarkets has argued that:

1   The current apportionment base of the regional office costs is unfair because these costs are not directly related to floor area but are more closely associated with the revenues generated by each of Country W's four trading sectors;

2   In terms of its trading performance, the Hypermarkets sector is Country W's best sector;

3   If any sector is to be closed, it should be the discount stores and the convenience stores because their combined forecast revenues in the year ended 31 December 2012 is only €420 million which is €30 million less than the Hypermarkets' revenue;

4   The regional office costs are too high and they contain a lot of wasteful expenditure: The sectors should not have to pay costs which they do not understand and did not authorise.

Competitive strategy

The Regional Managing Director responsible for Country W has attempted to manage B's business in Country W within the spirit of the company's mission statement, particularly 'selling high quality goods at a reasonable price'. However, he realises that this strategy has not been successful for all of the business sectors in Country W. The Sector Manager for Country W's Convenience Stores has commented that 'B's business in Country W is going nowhere: we are stuck in the middle. We should develop different competitive strategies to fit the characteristics of each of our four sectors'. Country W's four sectors have the following characteristics:

Sector	B's Brand Characteristics	Customer Characteristics	Product Characteristics	Pricing	Competition	B's Market Share
Super-markets	Many well sited supermarkets enable B to operate with a very economical cost structure.	Live locally. Value 24 hour opening. Middle income.	Wide variety of food and household goods.	Price sensitive	Two well-established national chains each with 10% market share. Their super-markets are often in inconvenient locations.	30%
Hyper-markets	Very highly regarded. High reputation for quality.	Willing to travel up to 50 miles. Affluent.	Consumer durables, high value items such as televisions, furniture, computers. Many up-market brands some of which are exclusive to B	Customers value quality and are willing to pay a premium for it.	Hyper-markets are a new concept in Country W. Only one recently founded competitor which is trading at a loss.	85%
Discount Stores	Highly regarded for its specialist range of products	Expect prices to be lower than in hypermarket. Mid and lower income groups.	Limited range of branded and 'own branded' goods.	Customers are extremely price sensitive.	Competition is mixed: some is very profitable, innovative and efficient: some is trading at a loss and very badly organised.	15%

| Conven-ience Stores | No clear identity. Some stores are market leaders; others are market laggards. | Live locally. Mid and upper income groups. | Low value items. | Customers will pay a premium price if location conven-ient. | One national chain which has 65% of the market. Remaining 25% is fragmented. | 10% |

Required:

(a) (i) Calculate the forecast sector contribution margins and the forecast total profit or loss for Country W for year ended 31 December 2012.

You should assume that:

- The Hypermarkets sector is closed on 30 September 2012.

- The Hypermarkets sector's costs and revenues accrue equally throughout 2012. **(3 marks)**

(ii) Calculate the revised forecast sector profits and forecast total profit for Country W for year ended 31 December 2012.

You should assume that:

- The regional office costs are allocated on the basis of sector revenue.

- The Hypermarkets are not closed. **(3 marks)**

(b) Prepare a report evaluating the strategic proposal, made by the Regional Managing Director responsible for Country W, to close the Hypermarkets sector.

In your report you should:

(i) Discuss, in turn, each of the four arguments put forward by the Sector Manager for Country W's Hypermarkets. **(12 marks)**

(ii) Advise B of the strategic implications that closing the Hypermarkets might have on B's future operations within Country W. **(12 marks)**

Your report should consider both the financial and non-financial effects of the proposal by the Regional Managing Director responsible for Country W to close the Hypermarkets sector.

(c) Assume all four sectors of B's business continue in Country W.

(i) Recommend, giving your reasons, which competitive strategy B should follow in future, in each of Country W's business sectors.

You should use Porter's model of generic competitive strategies in your answer. **(16 marks)**

(ii) Advise B of TWO limitations of Porter's model of generic competitive strategy. **(4 marks)**

(Total: 50 marks)

V (NOV 2012 & MAR 2013) – RELATES TO QUESTIONS 5 & 6

PRESEEN CASE STUDY

V, a private limited company in a European country (SK), which is outside the Eurozone, was founded in 1972. The currency in SK is SK$. V is a travel business that offers three holiday (vacation) products. It has a network of 50 branches in a number of major cities throughout SK.

History of the company

V achieved steady growth until six years ago, when it found that its market share was eroding due to customers increasingly making online bookings with its competitors. Direct bookings for holidays through the internet have increased dramatically in recent years. Many holidaymakers find the speed and convenience of booking flights, accommodation or complete holidays online outweighs the benefits of discussing holiday alternatives with staff in a branch.

V's board had always taken the view that the friendly direct personal service that V offers through its branch network is a major differentiating factor between itself and other travel businesses and that this is highly valued by its customers. However, V found that in order to continue to compete it needed to establish its own online travel booking service, which it did five years ago. Until this point, V's board had never engaged in long-term planning. It had largely financed growth by reinvestment of funds generated by the business. The large investment in IT and IS five years ago required significant external funding and detailed investment appraisal.

Much of V's business is now transacted online through its website to the extent that 60% of its revenue in the year ended 30 June 2012 was earned through online bookings.

Current structure of V's business

V offers three types of holiday product. These are known within V as Package, Adventure and Prestige Travel. V only sells its own products and does not act as an agent for any other travel companies. It uses the services of other companies engaged in the travel industry such as chartered airlines and hotels which it pays for directly on behalf of its customers.

Package

"Package" provides holidays mainly for families with children aged up to their late teens. These typically are for accommodation in hotels (where meals are part of the package) or self-catering apartments (where no meals are provided within the package).

Adventure

"Adventure" caters for people aged mainly between 20 and 30, who want relatively cheap adventure based holidays such as trekking, sailing and cycling or who wish to go on inexpensive back-packing holidays mainly in Europe and Asia.

Prestige Travel

"Prestige Travel" provides expensive and bespoke holidays mainly sold to couples whose children have grown up and left home. The Prestige Travel product only provides accommodation in upmarket international hotel chains in countries across the world.

All three of these products provide holidays which include flights to and from the holiday destinations and hotel or self-catering accommodation. V has its own customer representatives available at the holiday destinations to provide support to its customers. All-inclusive holidays (in which all food and drinks are provided within the holiday price) are offered within each of the three product offerings.

Support products

V supports its main products by offering travel insurance and foreign currency exchange. The travel insurance, which is provided by a major insurance company and for which V acts as an agent, is usually sold along with the holidays both by branch staff and by staff dealing with online bookings.

Currency exchange is available to anyone through V's branches irrespective of whether or not the customer has bought a holiday product from V. A new currency exchange product is provided by V through which a customer purchases an amount of currency, either in SK's home currency (SK$) or else in a foreign currency and this is credited on to a plastic card. The card is then capable of being read by automated teller machines (ATM's) in many countries across the world allowing the customer to withdraw cash in the local currency up to the amount that has been credited on to the card.

Marketing of products

V relies for the vast majority of its business on the literature, available in hard copy and online, which it provides on the holiday products it sells. Exceptionally, V is able to offer some of its existing holiday products at discount prices. These may be offered under any of the three main products offered but they are mostly cut-price holiday deals which are available under the Package holiday product label.

Sales structure

Staff in each of the 50 branches accept bookings from customers and all branches have direct IT access to head office. Online enquiries and bookings are received and processed centrally at head office, which is located in SK's capital city.

Branch managers have some discretion to offer discounts on holidays to customers. V offers a discount to customers who buy holidays through its online bookings. The branch managers have authority to reduce the price of a holiday booked at the branch up to the amount of the online discount if they feel it is necessary to do so in order to make the sale.

Financial information

V's revenue, split across the holiday and support products offered, for the financial year ended 30 June 2012 is summarised as follows:

	Revenue *SK$ million*
Package	90
Adventure	60
Prestige Travel	95
Support products	5

The overall net operating profit generated in the financial year to 30 June 2012 was SK$35 million and the profit for the year was SK$24 million, giving a profit to sales ratio of just under 10%. V's cash receipts fluctuate because of seasonal variations and also because V's customers pay for their holidays shortly before they depart.

Further details, including extracts from V's income statement for the year ended 30 June 2012 and statement of financial position as at 30 June 2012 are shown in Appendix 1.

Financial objectives

V's key financial objectives are as follows:

1   To grow earnings by, on average, 5% a year.

2   To pay out 80% of profits as dividends.

Foreign exchange risk

V has high exposure to foreign exchange risk as its revenues received and payments made are frequently in different currencies. It normally settles hotel bills and support costs, such as transfers between hotels and airports in the local currencies of the countries where the hotels are located. It normally pays charter airlines in the airline's home currency. Scheduled airline charges are settled in the currency required by the particular airline.

V is exposed to fluctuations in the cost of aircraft fuel incurred by airlines which are passed on to travel businesses. It has often been necessary for V to require its customers to make a supplementary payment to cover the cost of increases in aircraft fuel, sometimes after the customer had thought that the final payment for the holiday had been made.

Board composition and operational responsibilities

The Board of Directors comprises five people: an Executive Chairman (who also fulfils the role of Chief Executive), a Finance Director, an Operations Director, an IT Director and a Human Resources Director. The Executive Chairman founded the business in 1972. He has three grown-up children, two of whom successfully pursue different business interests and are not engaged in V's business at all. The third child, a son, is currently taking a "year out" from study and is going to university next year to study medicine.

The branch managers all report directly to the Operations Director. In addition, the Operations Director is responsible for liaising with airlines and hotels which provide the services offered by V's promotional literature. The IT Director is responsible for V's website and online enquiries and bookings. The Finance Director is responsible for V's financial and management accounting systems and has a small team of accountancy staff, including a part-qualified management accountant, reporting to her. The Human Resources Director has a small team of staff reporting to him.

Shareholding

There are 90 million SK$0.10 (10 cent) shares in issue and the shareholdings are as follows:

	% holding
Executive Chairman	52
Finance Director	12
Operations Director	12
IT Director	12
Human Resources Director	12

Employees

V employs 550 full-time equivalent staff. Turnover of staff is relatively low. High performance rewards in terms of bonuses are paid to staff in each branch if it meets or exceeds its quarterly sales targets. Similarly, staff who deal with online bookings receive a bonus if the online bookings meet or exceed quarterly sales targets. V's staff, both in the branches and those employed in dealing with online bookings, also receive an additional bonus if they are able to sell travel insurance along with a holiday product to customers.

Employee development for staff who are in direct contact with the public is provided through updates on products which V offers. Each member of branch and online booking staff undertakes a two day induction programme at the commencement of their employment with V. The emphasis of the induction programme is on customer service not on details relating to the products as it is expected that new staff will become familiar with such product details as they gain experience within V.

Safety

V publicly states that it takes great care to ensure that its customers are as safe as possible while on holiday. To date, V has found that accidents while on holiday are mainly suffered by very young children, Adventure customers and elderly customers. There has been an increase in instances over the last year where customers in resort hotels have suffered severe stomach complaints. This has particularly been the case in hotels located in resorts in warm climates.

Executive Chairman's statement to the press

V's Executive Chairman was quoted in the national press in SK in January 2012 as saying, "We are maintaining a comparatively high level of revenues and operating profit. This is in a period when our competitors are experiencing very difficult trading conditions. We feel we are achieving this due to our particular attention to customer service. He cited V's 40 years of experience in the travel industry and a previous 99% satisfaction rating from its customers as the reasons for its success. He went on to state that V intends to expand and diversify its holiday product range to provide more choice to customers.

Board meeting

At the next board meeting which took place after the Executive Chairman's statement to the press, the Operations Director expressed some concern. He cast doubt on whether V was able to provide sufficient funding, marketing and IT/IS resources to enable the product expansion to which the Executive Chairman referred. The Operations Director was of the opinion that V places insufficient emphasis on customer relationship marketing. The Finance Director added at the same meeting that while V presently remained profitable overall, some products may be more profitable than others.

The Executive Chairman responded by saying that V's high level of customer service provides a sufficiently strong level of sales without the need to incur any other marketing costs. He added that since V achieved a high profit to sales ratio, which it has managed to maintain for a number of years, it really didn't matter about the profits generated by each customer group.

Retirement of the Executive Chairman

The Executive Chairman formally announced to the Board in July 2012 that he intends to retire on 30 June 2013 and wishes to sell part of his shareholding in the company. The Board members believe the time is now right for V, given its expansion plans, to enter a new stage in its financing arrangements, in the form of either debt or equity from new providers.

APPENDIX 1

Extracts from V's income statement and statement of financial position

Income statement for the year ended 30 June 2012

	Notes	SK$ million
Revenue		250
Operating costs		(215)
Net operating profit		35
Interest income		3
Finance costs		(4)
Corporate income tax	1	(10)
Profit for the year		24

Statement of financial position as at 30 June 2012

	Notes	SK$ million
Assets		
Non-current assets		123
Current assets		
Inventories		3
Trade and other receivables		70
Cash and cash equivalents		37
Total current assets		110
Total assets		233
Equity and liabilities		
Equity		
Share capital	2	9
Share premium		6
Retained earnings		60
Total equity		75
Non-current liabilities		
Long-term borrowings	3	50
Revenue received in advance		3
Current liabilities		
Trade and other payables		35
Revenue received in advance		70
Total liabilities		158
Total equity and liabilities		233

Notes:

1   The corporate income tax rate can be assumed to be 30%.

2   There are 90 million SK$0.10 (10 cent) shares currently in issue.

3   30% of the long-term borrowings are due for repayment on 30 June 2014. The remainder is due for re-payment on 30 June 2020. There are debt covenants in operation currently which restrict V from having a gearing ratio measured by long-term debt divided by long-term debt plus equity of more than 50%.

End of Pre-seen Material

5   V (NOV 2012 EXAM)

Unseen material for Case Study

Customer profitability

At a recent Board meeting the Executive Chairman stated that he was not concerned with the level of profitability generated by each customer as, overall, V has achieved a high profit to sales ratio for a number of years. However, the Finance Director believes that a more detailed understanding of V's product profitability should be carried out by V before making any decision about future product expansion. Also at this Board meeting, the Executive Chairman stated that V should focus on the increasing demand for Prestige Travel holidays and that this is backed up by the fact that V's Prestige Travel products are the best performing for the business, based upon revenue earned.

Following the Board meeting, the Finance Director instructed the Management Accountant to undertake an analysis of the revenues, cost of sales and administration costs associated with each of V's holiday products. The following information was identified for the year ended 30 June 2012.

	Package	Adventure	Prestige Travel
Revenue from in-branch bookings	SK$9,000,000	SK$3,000,000	SK$85,500,000
Revenue from online bookings	SK$81,000,000	SK$57,000,000	SK$9,500,000
Total Revenue	SK$90,000,000	SK$60,000,000	SK$95,000,000
Cost of sales as a % of Total Revenue	60%	65%	75%

The Management Accountant has also analysed the sales revenues earned from each type of holiday product.

	Package	Adventure	Prestige Travel
Average sales price of a holiday product booked in-branch	SK$3,000	SK$2,000	SK$5,000
Average sales price of a holiday product booked online	SK$2,700	SK$1,900	SK$5,000

Note: A 'holiday product booked' refers to a total holiday package and may vary in terms of the number of people booked onto each package. For example, a 'Package' holiday product may include 4 people (2 adults and 2 children). A 'Prestige Travel' holiday product may only include 2 people.

V's administration costs

In order to establish the net operating profit of each of V's holiday products, the Management Accountant has analysed the total administration costs of V. These administration costs are in addition to the cost of sales. He has identified that there are four administrative processes carried out by V's staff that make up the total administration costs, which are nearly all fixed. The Management Accountant has determined the average cost for each administrative process, which is shown below:

Administrative process	Average cost per process
1. In-branch holiday order processing	SK$600 per holiday product booked in-branch
2. Online holiday order processing	SK$200 per holiday product booked online
3. Late booking processing	SK$400 per late booking processed
4. After-sales queries/ complaints processing	SK$550 per after sales query/ complaint

Other information:	Package	Adventure	Prestige Travel
Late bookings processed as a % of total holiday products booked each year	35%	12%	6%
Number of after sales queries/ complaints as a % of total holiday products booked each year	27%	10%	75%

The administration costs of in-branch holiday order processing include the costs incurred in the time taken by branch staff discussing holiday options with customers and the subsequent completion of associated holiday ordering paperwork and administrative activities, including organising flights and hotel accommodation on behalf of the customer.

The administration costs of online holiday order processing are significantly less than in-branch costs due to less staff interface and the use of more automated order processing of hotel accommodation and flights.

Late booking administration costs are incurred if a customer books a holiday product within 2 weeks of departure. This requires administration time in processing accommodation, foreign currency and arranging flights at short notice. Late bookings, whether booked online or in-branch, are directed straight to a team at V's head office for processing. The costs are treated the same, whether booked online or in-branch. Late booking costs are in addition to the normal order processing costs.

After-sales queries administration costs result from customers changing their original bookings or making general enquiries after booking. This may include re-checking or making changes to flight or accommodation details. Sometimes errors occur during the booking process, for example due to staff in-branch processing orders incorrectly or due to customers using the website information incorrectly. Customers' complaints are dealt with by a specialist team at V's head office. Customer complaints are often due to customers being misled by customer sales representatives at the time of booking, largely due to the sales representatives not having sufficient product knowledge.

The Management Accountant has advised the Finance Director that the cost per administrative process identified in the table above are aggregate figures and give the average cost per holiday product booked.

Customer Relationship Marketing and E-business

V's Executive Chairman does not consider marketing to be a primary activity, as historically much of its business has come from word-of-mouth recommendations and repeat business. The Executive Chairman is confident that word-of-mouth recommendations have been successful in the past and will continue to be successful and that the high level of customer service offered by V is a key factor in this. However, the Operations Director, who is responsible for the marketing of V's products, considers that competitive forces have made customer retention more difficult. This is because customers are now more likely to shop around for the best holiday deals and are not necessarily loyal to one holiday tour operator. In particular, the main competitive threat to V appears to come from the proliferation of online holiday tour operators and travel agency services, many of which make use of sophisticated information systems.

The Operations Director believes that customer retention and loyalty could be improved by developing customer relationship marketing and by focusing more on 'e-business' and the use of V's information systems to transact more of its holiday product business.

Required:

(a) Discuss the benefits to V of following an emergent approach to strategy development rather than undertaking a long-term planning approach. **(5 marks)**

(b) (i) Analyse, for each of in-branch and online bookings, the net operating profit and the net operating profit percentage for (i) Package, (ii) Adventure and (iii) Prestige Travel holiday products. **(15 marks)**

(ii) Discuss how V could improve the product profitability of each of its three holiday product types.

Your answer should take into account the results of your analysis in (b)(i) and also consider any other information that would be relevant in helping V's Board determine how it could improve its product profitability. **(10 marks)**

(c) (i) Evaluate the strategic and competitive impact a Customer Relationship Marketing approach could have on V's customer retention. **(8 marks)**

(ii) Discuss TWO strategic benefits and TWO strategic barriers to e-business for V.

(12 marks)

(Total: 50 marks)

6 V (MAR 2013 EXAM)

Unseen material for Case Study

Review of V's product portfolio

In the statement to the press (pre-seen page 4), the Executive Chairman said that V intends to expand and diversify its holiday product range to provide more choice to customers. The current product range of V can be analysed as follows:

Package

The Package product has been the core product of V's business since it began 40 years ago. Growth in the package holiday market was rapid in the first thirty years of V's business, but this growth has slowed significantly in the last five years, largely as a result of the economic downturn which has impacted heavily on the package holiday market. Competition is strong for package holiday customers, as there is a large number of competing travel businesses operating both in SK and abroad. Despite this, V has maintained a strong competitive position, holding 25% of the package holidays sold in SK with its nearest competitor holding 15% of the market. Whilst good customer service is expected by V's Package customers, most are mainly interested in receiving good value for money.

Adventure

V has been offering Adventure holidays for the last 20 years. Demand for this type of holiday product has been high in the last 10 years as adventure activities have gained in popularity and more worldwide destinations have been made available to customers. However, there are a number of competitors in SK offering similar products. Two of these competitors specialise only in adventure holiday products and together hold a 65% share of the market. V currently has a 20% share of the market. When surveyed, Adventure holiday customers have stated that they value the number of destinations and activities offered by V. High demand in this market is expected to continue as more destinations are made available and as adventure activities gain greater popularity. However, competition is likely to become more intense and this will require further investment in adventure holiday products.

Prestige Travel

V was one of the first holiday businesses in SK to focus upon the prestige holiday market. V has seen the market for luxury holidays grow significantly in the last 15 years and V's Executive Chairman believes that there are still significant opportunities to develop these products, with more exotic destinations and a wider range of luxurious packages. Industry-wide, prestige holiday customers have been less affected by the economic downturn than package holiday customers. V has an excellent reputation in the prestige holiday market within SK for quality of service. V's Prestige Travel holiday customers value the level of customer service very highly and many prefer to book in-branch for a more personalised service, rather than online. V holds 35% of the SK prestige holiday market. However, it faces strong competition from another travel business specialising only in this type of holiday product. This competitor has attracted 25% of the market in just five years of operations. However, this competitor does not have the long standing reputation for high levels of customer service that V has achieved for its Prestige Travel products. In order to maintain its reputation, V invests heavily in staff training and marketing.

Expansion of V's Product Portfolio

The Operations Director is considering strategies to maintain or strengthen the market shares of its current products. The Executive Chairman has also asked the Operations Director to consider a proposal for product portfolio expansion into eco-holidays.

A recent development in the travel industry has been the introduction of 'eco-holidays'. These types of holiday have been designed to allow customers to engage in conservation and other community projects at a range of locations. Currently only a small number of SK travel businesses offer eco-travel holidays but recent market research indicates that there is a growing demand for this type of holiday product.

V-eco holidays

V is proposing to offer eco-holidays to its customers and these would be called 'V-eco holidays'. The introduction of these holidays would not require high levels of capital investment as the existing branches would sell these holidays alongside V's other holiday products. The Operations Director estimates that V-eco holidays could become operational from the start of July 2013 but V would have to secure contracts with hotels, transport organisations and other specialist companies before then. The Operations Director has discussed this proposal with the Finance Director who said she welcomed any proposal which would improve V's product expansion and impact positively upon V's environmental sustainability. However, she also stated that any proposal must also improve V's profit. She added 'because of the uncertainty of the proposal, it is unlikely to get the Board's approval unless it offers at least SK$2 million operating profit for the year ended 30 June 2014, that is, in its first full year of operation'.

Market research information and estimates for V-eco holidays

Forecast average price charged by V's competitors in the year ending 30 June 2014 for an eco-travel holiday product	SK$3,800
Forecast eco-travel holiday products sold in SK in the year ending 30 June 2014	33,000

It is proposed that V will charge the same price as the average price charged by competitors (as shown in the table above) for its first year of operating V-eco holidays. If V-eco holidays are introduced, SK$5 million of fixed operating costs will be incurred each year from the date of their introduction. This includes on-site staff, promotion costs and costs of contracting with transportation and accommodation providers.

It is anticipated that the contribution margin earned will be 35% each year. If V introduces V-eco holidays from July 2013 there will be:

- a 20% probability of achieving 25% market share in the year ended 30 June 2014

- a 30% probability of achieving 20% market share in the year ended 30 June 2014

- a 50% probability of achieving 10% market share in the year ended 30 June 2014

Proposed changes to improve customer services

Previous changes that have been made to V's products or to working arrangements have always been introduced gradually and have generally had a low impact upon V's branch staff. V's staff turnover within the branches is low and most of V's branch staff appreciate the high level of bonuses offered, which are based upon the number of products sold. Although V achieved a previous customer satisfaction rating of 99%, V's Board is concerned that a declining performance in V's customer service ratings over the last five years may affect its product expansion ambitions. It is therefore considering the following changes to assist V in improving its customer service levels:

- A change to the current bonus system (pre-seen page 4, under heading 'Employees'), whereby bonuses will be based upon achievement of targeted levels of customer service. This is designed to encourage a greater focus of branch staff upon customer satisfaction levels, rather than on the number of holiday products sold.

- Promotion of staff and annual pay increases will be based upon levels of qualification and training courses attended, rather than upon staff members' length of service.

- Branch staff will be expected to undertake placements in other branches and at head office in order to gain experience and a better understanding of other parts of the organisation as well as a greater awareness of V's overall operations and activities. This may involve branch staff having to travel considerable distances or to stay away from home for periods of time.

There have been a number of rumours circulating around V about these proposed changes. Many branch staff are very unhappy that they have not been consulted on these changes and some are considering if they wish to continue working for V.

Required:

(a)   (i)   Evaluate V's current product portfolio using the Boston Consulting Group (BCG) matrix.

Your answer should not consider the proposed V-eco holiday products.

(9 marks)

(ii)   Calculate the best and worst case outcomes, and the Expected Value, of V's operating profit in respect of its proposed V-eco holidays, for the year ended 30 June 2014.   **(7 marks)**

(iii)   Recommend, with your justifications, whether V should offer V-eco holidays. Your answer should consider the impact of your decision upon V's overall product portfolio.   **(12 marks)**

(b)   Recommend, with your justifications, one Critical Success Factor that V should consider implementing for each of the four holiday products of Package, Adventure, Prestige Travel and for the proposed V-eco holiday product.   **(12 marks)**

(c)   Advise V's Board how it might overcome the resistance to the proposed changes to improve customer services, using Lewin's three-stage model.   **(10 marks)**

(Total: 50 marks)

T RAILWAYS (MAY & SEP 2013) – RELATES TO QUESTIONS 7 & 8

PRESEEN CASE STUDY

Background

Country T is a small landlocked European country which is outside the Eurozone. Its currency is T$ which currently exchanges at GBP/T$ 1.5000 and EUR/T$ 1.2500, (that is, GBP 1 = T$ 1.5000 and EUR 1 = T$ 1.2500).

Unlike many other countries, Country T has a nationalised railway system known as T Railways. Before the system was nationalised two separate companies operated the railways.

The growth of road haulage transport and the increasing number of passengers wanting to travel by rail meant that by 1970 fare paying passengers replaced freight transport as the railway companies' main source of income. In 1975 Country T's Government took the view that the two railway companies were not operating in the public interest and they were nationalised; that is taken into public ownership. The Government bought out the two railway companies and established T Railways.

As the transport infrastructure developed, diesel trains gradually replaced steam trains and electric powered trains are now replacing the diesel trains as T Railways carries out electrification of its network.

In 1975, the Board of T Railways formed wholly owned subsidiaries which operated at arm's length from the Board. For example, it formed T Railways Engineering which was responsible for all the engineering works on the T Railways network. The T Railways Board retained a number of functions itself such as responsibility for the T Railways Transport Police Service and T Railways Property. However, this led to much duplication of resources and so in 1998 T Railways adopted a new management structure with T Railways as the holding company for three subsidiary companies as follows:

- T City-Link (TCL) to run passenger rail services.

- T Freight Railways (TFR) to run freight services.

- T Property and Track Services (TPTS) to manage the track, property, transport police and related services.

This structure still exists today with T Railways' corporate governance undertaken by the T Railways Board.

The activities of T Railways

Further details on the activities of each of the three subsidiary companies owned by T Railways is provided below.

TCL:

TCL is responsible for all passenger rail services within Country T and operates on average 1,800 passenger train services per day between Monday and Saturday with fewer services on Sundays. The services offered are between all towns and cities within Country T which are connected to the railway network. In addition, some of TCL's services cross national borders enabling travel from Country T to other countries, some of which are in the Eurozone. It also provides some services to remote country locations which originally were not accessible by road. Recent improvements in the road network have resulted in some of these country lines being discontinued by T Railways as demand for the railway service has diminished. Most of TCL's locomotives are now electric as the lines between the major cities within Country T have already been electrified.

TFR:

TFR is solely concerned with railway haulage of freight. In this context, freight is defined as goods transported in bulk, for example, coal, petroleum, industrial products such as steel and concrete, cars and, increasingly, retail goods for supermarkets and large retail shops. TFR does not offer any passenger services. It hauls freight right across the network within Country T and across national borders into other countries, some of which are situated within the Eurozone.

Most of TFR's trains are old diesel locomotives but it has recently invested in a number of electric trains which are less harmful to the environment. On average, TFR operates 600 freight services per day, including weekends but excluding national public holidays. In the year ended 31 December 2012, TFR provided 40% of T Railways' total revenue and its share of the freight haulage market in Country T was approximately 10%. Freight carried by road accounts for approximately 80% of the total freight haulage market in Country T. In the last 15 years, total freight carried by rail has increased by about 25% due to increased congestion on T's roads. T's Government considers that road congestion has had a major adverse impact upon the country's productivity.

TPTS:

TPTS replaced T Railways Property and has responsibility for all other services including maintenance and upgrade of track and all of T Railways' property. It operates 200 railway stations, rents space out within the stations for retail purposes as well as running some of its own cafes. TPTS also operates 11 maintenance depots.

T Railways' organisational structure

A strong bureaucratic culture has developed over time within T Railways. The T Railways Board uses a classical rational planning system in which strategic planning decisions are made in a regularised and formal way.

The Chairman of the T Railways Board reports to senior civil servants in T Government's Ministry of Transport. Ownership of T Railways rests entirely with the Government. There is a formal annual meeting with senior Government officials at which the financial statements of T Railways are approved. There are also occasional meetings between members of T Railways Board and Government officials, particularly when Country T's Minister of Transport needs to present information on railway transport to Country T's parliament.

Rail regulator

Country T now has a rail regulatory organisation whose senior staff are appointed by the Government. The Rail Regulator is empowered to make recommendations directly to the Minister of Transport in respect of all issues relating to the operation of T Railways.

The role of the Rail Regulator is to ensure that the railway service is delivered in Country T in a safe and efficient manner. It aims to help the T Railways Board meet future challenges in the provision of an efficient railway service which provides high levels of satisfaction to all rail users and the improvement of safety for staff and passengers. In essence, the Rail Regulator provides an independent review of T Railways' activities. Mindful of the need to show that T Railways fully recognises the role of the Rail Regulator, the Chairman of the T Railways Board recently said that:

"T Railways is committed to providing an excellent service to its customers and work is ongoing to improve our time keeping. Investment in improving railway stations is continuing and accessibility to railway services is increasing with new car parks being built at many stations in the network. Other service amenities are being improved such as better access ramps for disabled customers and the levelling of the height of platforms at many stations so that customers can access and alight from trains without having to a take a large step up or down to the platform. This will reduce the incidence of accidents which occur at stations where the platform infrastructure was developed for a bygone era of railway carriages."

Monitoring the levels of carbon dioxide emissions from rail transport is also an important area of work for the Rail Regulator. (See the section headed "Environmental considerations".)

T Railways' strategic objectives

T Railways' overall strategic goal is to deliver efficient, cost effective, safe and reliable rail services to help facilitate the Government's vision of sustained economic growth and the reduction of carbon emissions in the country as a whole. The T Railways Board has set two strategic objectives, following consultation with its stakeholder groups which are:

(i)   To deliver reliable, safe and punctual rail services to customers efficiently and cost effectively thereby helping to achieve economic growth in Country T by reducing congestion on its roads;

(ii)   To continually reduce its level of carbon emissions to help provide an environmentally friendly transport infrastructure.

Financial objectives for T Railways

The Government's aim and the T Railways Board's main financial objectives are that:

(i)   T Railways should at least cover its operating costs from the revenue it earns;

(ii)   T Railways should provide value for money.

Financial data for T Railways

The Government requires T Railways to prepare its accounts according to internationally recognised accounting principles so that it can show how it is performing in a commercial environment. The policy of the T Railways Board is not to re-value its non-current assets. Extracts from the latest set of financial statements according to internationally recognised accounting principles are shown in Appendix 1.

The revenue earned and operating costs of the three subsidiaries for the year ended 31 December 2012 are shown below:

	Revenue T$ million	Operating costs T$ million
TCL	680	630
TFR	516	494
TPTS	95	80

Notes:

(i)   The total head office operating costs of the T Railways Board are allocated and apportioned to the three subsidiaries.

(ii)   The total operating costs of TPTS was T$842 million in 2012 after the allocation and apportionment of head office operating costs referred to in note (i). All of these costs except for the T$80 million which relate to the revenue earning activities of TPTS, were allocated and apportioned to the other two subsidiaries.

Financing T Railways

The Government of Country T invested T$100 million when it formed T Railways in 1975. This is the only "share" capital that has ever been invested in T Railways. The financing model which has developed is that T Railways costs are guaranteed. This means that any overall operating deficit T Railways incurs on an annual basis is recovered by the T Railways Board through additional Government revenue funding.

Recognising that T Railways would need large amounts of funding to upgrade its infrastructure, the Government initially provided loans to cover capital expenditure. The loan facility was established to emphasise that any Government funding is a liability of T Railways and that T Railways must pay interest on the loan. The intention is that T Railways will also pay back the full amount of the Government loans in due course. The Government loans have no fixed repayment dates and are made to T Railways at a fixed rate of interest of 4% per year. This was the only source of capital funding for T Railways at its formation. However, following Government approval, the T Railways Board is now seeking to widen its sources of finance by, for example, obtaining loans from the banking and commercial sectors.

Key Performance Indicators (KPIs)

In order to plan their activities to meet T Railways' strategic objectives, its three subsidiaries operate a traditional accounting-led approach to strategic planning and management. All of the strategic planning and management activities of the three subsidiary companies are based upon meeting T Railways' strategic objectives. A number of Key Performance Indicators have emerged to evaluate T Railways' overall performance in achieving its strategic objectives.

Examples of KPIs relating to TCL:

- The results of the national customer survey of all forms of public transport in Country T.

- The number of customer complaints received. These are reported on T Railways' website every three months for the previous quarter.

Examples of KPIs relating to TFR:

- Train capacity utilisation, which measures the actual train load capacity utilised per journey against the total available load capacity for that journey.

- The number of trains arriving at their destination on time, measured as a percentage of total journeys made.

- Carbon emissions generated. The analysis of carbon emissions in freight transport is expressed in carbon dioxide emissions as a ratio of tonne per kilometre. That is, kilograms of carbon dioxide divided by weight transported multiplied by the distance travelled.

Examples of KPIs relating to TPTS:

- Number of delays per month to services due to signalling failure.

- Number of complaints per month relating to station cleanliness.

There are also KPIs relating to safety issues which are shown below under the heading of Health and Safety.

Health and safety

T Railways concentrates a great deal of effort on the management of particular risks such as Signals Passed at Danger (SPAD) and customer and staff injuries. T Railways has a Safety Committee which meets regularly and monitors performance against its annual safety targets which have been agreed with the Ministry of Transport. Examples of the KPIs specifically relating to safety which are used by T Railways are:

- The number of customer movement accidents per million passenger kilometres, for example accidents caused due to the motion of trains.

- The number of customer non-movement accidents per million passenger journeys, for example slips and falls while on T Railways' property.

- The number of accidents or injuries sustained by staff per million kilometres travelled.

The KPIs relating to safety issues are reported in T Railways' annual report which accompanies its financial statements.

Environmental considerations

The transport industry's carbon emissions are responsible for between 20% and 25% of all carbon emissions in Country T. In response to initiatives developed by the Rail Regulator, T Railways is increasing its efforts to reduce its levels of carbon emissions. T Railways is committed to reducing its carbon emissions by a third between now and 2015. In addition, all TCL and TFR drivers receive eco-driving training on an ongoing basis. (Eco-driving is driving in a manner that minimises fuel consumption.) TPTS is progressing work on making stations and depots energy efficient by improving lighting and heating systems including the use of intelligent lighting which automatically increases or decreases light output depending on the amount of natural light feeding into the sensors.

All three subsidiaries are keen to reduce waste and to increase the amount of waste they recycle. Each subsidiary is committed to helping to meet an overall target set by the T Railways Board of recycling 85% of T Railways' total waste by 2015.

Development of T Railways

The T Railways Board is constantly seeking ways of generating additional sources of revenue. Consideration is being given to a number of possible initiatives. Some ideas under consideration include:

- structural changes such as splitting T Railways up into its constituent parts and running the three subsidiaries as completely separate entities;

- expansion of the network;

- diversifying the portfolio through operating other forms of transport;

- outsourcing some or all of the current provision of passenger, freight, track, property or retail related services or privatising parts of the business.

The Government has considered privatising the whole of T Railways but so far has been wary of the British experience where ownership and operation of the rail network became very fragmented after privatisation and operations were split across more than 100 companies. However, possible privatisation of T Railways continues to be discussed within Government and Country T's Prime Minister has never ruled it out.

APPENDIX 1

Extracts from T Railways' statement of profit or loss and statement of financial position

Statement of profit or loss for the year ended 31 December 2012

	Notes	T$ million
Revenue		1,291
Operating costs		(1,204)
Net operating profit		87
Finance costs		(72)
Profit before tax		15
Tax	1	(5)
Profit for the year	2	10

Statement of financial position as at 31 December 2012

	Notes	T$ million
Assets		
Non-current assets	3	2,763
Current assets		
Inventories		12
Trade and other receivables		96
Cash and cash equivalents		202
Total current assets		310
Total assets		3,073
Equity and liabilities		
Equity		
Share capital from Country T's Government	4	100
Retained earnings		900
Total equity		1,000
Non-current liabilities		
Long-term borrowings from Government	5	1,800
Current liabilities		
Trade and other payables		273
Total liabilities		2,073
Total equity and liabilities		3,073

Notes:

1 The corporate income tax rate is 30%.

2 The agreement with the Government in Country T is that any losses after tax are charged back to the Government.

3 The non-current assets have not been re-valued.

4 The Government's initial investment in T Railways was T$100 million. Subsequent investment by the Government has been in the form of long-terms loans.

5 The long-term Government borrowings are undated.

End of Pre-seen Material

7 T RAILWAYS (MAY 2013 EXAM)

Unseen material for Case Study

TFR business sectors

T Railways has two strategic objectives (pre-seen pages 3 and 4). In order to assist in the evaluation of its performance in achieving these strategic objectives and to manage its operations effectively, TFR is split into three business sectors. These business sectors are based upon customer groups and the type of freight transported for each customer group. Each of these customer groups has different expectations of the service offered by TFR. The total revenue generated by TFR in the year ended 31 December 2012 was T$516 million.

1 Consumer and Heavy Goods (CHG):

This sector transports everyday consumer goods such as clothes, foodstuffs and electrical products for large retail companies throughout Country T. It also transports large industrial products for the construction industry, such as steel, cement and concrete blocks. This business sector currently provides 50% of the revenues of TFR's business. This sector transports freight to, and from, a number of large strategic rail freight warehouses located throughout Country T.

The delivery of retail goods is relatively simple logistically but often involves the movement of large numbers of small items. The delivery of construction goods is often complex, involving a range of different suppliers of the industrial products. It requires the use of specialist loading equipment and multiple drop-offs and pick-ups at a number of rail freight warehouses.

CHG freight transportation is undertaken by both diesel and electric trains. A number of Country T's large supermarket chains are currently considering the impact of their supply chain upon the environment and are looking for ways to reduce their carbon emissions. They are currently largely reliant on deliveries to their stores by road haulage and are evaluating the environmental benefits of switching more of their deliveries from road to rail freight. Many of the large construction companies in Country T take a different view and prefer the convenience of direct deliveries of construction materials to their construction sites, a service which is offered by road freight haulage. The main concern for many of the construction companies is the competitiveness of the price charged by road haulage providers and the punctuality of delivery.

2   **Energy:**

This sector transports coal to the nationalised power stations within Country T. TFR transports 90% of Country T's coal production used in its national electricity generation. This business sector currently provides 40% of the revenues of TFR's business. TFR operates dedicated tracks between coal mines in Country T and the national power stations and so is not reliant on using the main passenger track facilities. TFR uses its oldest diesel freight trains to transport coal supplies to the power stations. These trains have limited power availability to pull larger numbers of coal trucks. The power station operators are concerned that the number of journeys made by TFR is increasing their own staffing and management costs. The power station operators are putting increasing pressure on TFR to reduce the number of journeys made to the power stations because they are charged for each journey that is made by TFR.

3   **Automotive:**

This is a relatively new area of business for TFR, involving the transportation of new cars from car manufacturing facilities within Country T to ports in neighbouring countries. This business sector currently provides 10% of the revenues of TFR's business. TFR has recently invested in 20 new fuel-efficient electric freight trains, specially designed to transport cars. This type of freight haulage is a relatively simple process as it does not involve complex lifting or multiple loading operations nor does it require the use of TFR's rail freight warehouses. TFR has to meet tight deadlines for delivery times to ports. However, as the Automotive sector operates on the main passenger track facilities, its freight trains are sometimes delayed by passenger services which take priority on Country T's rail network. As the ports are in neighbouring countries, the Automotive sector's trains are reliant upon other countries rail networks to meet its deadlines.

Road freight haulage

Approximately 80% of Country T's freight haulage by volume is delivered by road and is carried out by many different private road haulage companies. The total revenue generated by the road freight haulage sector in the year ended 31 December 2012 was approximately T$3,770 million. Road freight haulage has been the main method of freight transportation within Country T for the last 40 years, largely due to the convenience of providing door-to-door deliveries. However, the demand for road freight haulage in favour of rail freight haulage has slowed recently, due to the introduction of road toll charges on Country T's major motorways and the ever worsening traffic congestion on Country T's roads. Also, recent legislation has been introduced by Country T's Government to restrict lorry drivers' hours of work and distances travelled per journey. In addition, Country T's Government is committed to reducing carbon emissions and has encouraged greater use of rail rather than road haulage for the transportation of freight.

Benchmarking

TFR undertakes an annual benchmarking analysis of its three business sectors, in order to compare their performance and to assess the performance of TFR in total against the road freight haulage sector. This benchmarking analysis involves the measurement of a number of Key Performance Indicators (KPIs) and is used by T Railways to assist in the evaluation of the achievement of its strategic objectives. Some of the information which TFR used to measure its KPIs in the year ended 31 December 2012 is shown below.

	TFR CHG	TFR Energy	TFR Automotive	Road Freight Haulage
	2012	2012	2012	2012
Journeys undertaken (actual)	83,000	115,000	15,000	1,000,000
Kilometres travelled (million)	10.2	10.2	2.0	145.0
Total operating costs (T$ million)	250	204	40	3,045
Average capacity utilisation (%) [1]	88%	82%	86%	92%
Journeys on schedule (actual)	74,120	109,250	12,300	650,000
Kg of CO2/ per tonne-kilometre [2]	0.04	0.06	0.03	0.13
Staff accidents (actual)	80	32	10	1,850
Number of goods damaged/ lost (actual) [3]	11,000	0	1,500	185,000

[1] This is the KPI and has already been calculated in the table above.

[2] This is the KPI and has already been calculated in the table above.

[3] Measured in terms of number of goods damaged/lost per 1,000 kilometres travelled.

As part of its annual benchmarking exercise, TFR also calculates the average operating cost per kilometre travelled and operating profit per kilometre travelled for each of the three business sectors and for TFR in total.

Privatisation of TFR

In other countries, such as the United Kingdom and Sweden, the privatisation of nationalised rail freight operations has been highly successful. A number of neighbouring countries of Country T have private rail freight operators. One organisation, Q Corporation, which currently owns and operates a private rail freight company in a neighbouring country, has approached Country T's Government with an offer to buy TFR. Q wishes to operate TFR as Country T's main rail freight operator, but as a private company. Q would invest significantly in TFR, and upgrade many of the current strategic rail freight warehouses, replace old diesel engines with electric engines and invest heavily in infrastructure and staff training.

Q is of a similar size to TFR but operates with only 60% of the number of employees compared to TFR. Q operates with a decentralised management structure where business sector senior managers are responsible for strategic decision making and also set their own strategic objectives. The emphasis of strategic management and planning is on core competences and critical success factors in each of its business sectors, unlike TFR which operates an accounting-led approach to strategic management and planning. Q plans to re-organise TFR into two separate companies:

- the 'Retail Freight Company' which would comprise the retail and supermarket customer business (currently part of the CHG sector) together with the 'Automotive' sector business

- the 'Industrial Freight Company' which would comprise the construction customer business (currently part of the CHG sector) and the 'Energy' sector business.

Q's shareholders are keen for this proposal to be accepted as they feel that the acquisition of TFR will have a positive impact upon their long-term shareholder value.

Required

(a) **Discuss the difficulties faced by T Railways, as a public sector organisation, in setting and measuring strategic objectives.** **(8 marks)**

(b) **Using the information presented in the benchmarking analysis for the year ended 31 December 2012,**

   Evaluate:

   - **the comparative performance of the three business sectors within TFR;**

   - **the performance of TFR as a whole against the road freight haulage sector.**

   Note: There are 10 marks available for calculation of the KPIs. **(28 marks)**

(c) **If TFR were privatised,**

   (i) **Discuss how the culture of TFR would be likely to change;** **(7 marks)**

   (ii) **Discuss how the strategic management and planning activities of TFR would be likely to change.** **(7 marks)**

   (Total: 50 marks)

8 T RAILWAYS (SEP 2013 EXAM)

Unseen material for Case Study

TFR business sectors

TFR is a subsidiary of T Railways and is solely concerned with the delivery of freight. In order to assist in managing its operations effectively, TFR is split into 3 business sectors. These business sectors are based upon customer groups and the type of freight transported for each group. Each business sector has to consider its own market conditions and respond to the needs of its customers but must also balance this with achieving the strategic objectives set by T Railways (page 3-4 of the pre-seen).

Consumer Goods (CG) sector: Stakeholder management

The CG sector transports consumer goods such as clothes, foodstuffs and electrical products for a number of large supermarkets and retailers throughout Country T. The transport of goods for supermarkets is a growing area of business for this sector, generating 15% of TFR's overall revenue in the year ended 31 December 2012, up from 9% in the previous year.

Country T's largest supermarkets are currently evaluating the impact of their supply chain upon the environment and are looking for ways to reduce the supermarket industry's carbon emissions. These supermarkets all use the CG sector to transport a proportion of their supplies around Country T to rail freight terminals. These supplies are then delivered by road to local stores. The supermarkets have recently formed a working party with officials from the Ministry of Transport and the Ministry for the Environment to work towards further reducing carbon emissions in the supermarket industry. As part of their discussions, the supermarkets are evaluating the environmental benefits of switching more of their deliveries from road to rail freight. The Government of Country T has already introduced a number of initiatives to encourage more companies to move their delivery of supplies to rail, not only to reduce carbon emissions, but also to reduce road congestion and improve the general productivity of Country T.

The senior managers of the CG sector have also recently met with the Rail Regulator, which reports directly to the Minister of Transport in Country T, to discuss the targets set by T Railways for TFR in respect of its own carbon emissions. Within the broader aim of encouraging T Railways to reduce the carbon emissions of the country as a whole, the Minister for the Environment and the Rail Regulator particularly wish to encourage greater collaboration between the CG sector and its stakeholders on the issue of carbon emissions within the supply chain of the supermarket industry.

CG's senior managers are concerned that the Government is trying to encourage more freight onto the railways but without providing the necessary investment in new trains and trucks to take on this extra volume of business. The CG sector will have to increase the tonnage carried by each delivery of its existing diesel and electric trains which will increase its own carbon emissions due to the increased number of trucks hauled by the engines.

Energy sector: Deliveries to Power station X

The Energy sector currently transports coal to several nationalised coal powered electricity generating power stations within Country T. These power stations provided 60% of the revenues of TFR's freight business in the year ended 31 December 2012. However, the Energy sector is the least profitable sector for TFR. Also, the Energy sector runs the oldest diesel trains owned by T Railways which emit high levels of carbon emissions.

The senior managers of the Energy sector are currently in discussions with the senior management of power station X, one of Country T's coal powered electricity generating power stations, regarding the frequency of its coal deliveries. Power station X requires between 7,300 and 7,400 tonnes of coal every day in order to maintain an uninterrupted power supply to its customers. Power station X's senior managers have proposed that the Energy sector could increase its load capacity to reduce the number of deliveries from its current level of 6 each day. The senior managers of power station X consider that this would help to improve the operating efficiency of the power station.

The senior managers of the Energy sector are aware that the diesel trains that it currently uses have very limited power, and the proposed extra coal trucks, which are owned by TFR, would significantly slow the trains down. In addition, the number of breakdowns is likely to increase due to the extra trucks being hauled by the trains. The trade union which represents staff in TFR is also concerned that operating at a greater level of capacity could compromise staff safety and could also lead to driver redundancies.

The Management Accountant for the Energy sector has presented some initial information relating to the proposal which is shown in the table below:

	Current	Proposed	Note
Coal trucks required per delivery	15	20	Maximum capacity of 100 tonnes per coal truck
Capacity utilisation per truck	82%	92%	The current 82% capacity has been the average capacity level of the Energy sector for over 30 years and management has until this point not considered it necessary to increase this.
Deliveries per day	6	4	
	Current	*Proposed*	*Note*
Energy sector Income			
Revenue earned per tonne of coal delivered	T$23.60	T$23.60	
Admin fee charged per delivery	T$500	T$625	Increase due to tonnage increase per delivery
Costs per delivery			
Direct Staff Costs	T$7,400 (per delivery)	Increase by 30% (per delivery)	Due to extra staff required to load the increased tonnage per delivery
Fuel Costs	T$10,000 (per delivery)	Increase by 40% (per delivery)	Due to increased tonnage and load capacity of each train and reduced speed
Variable Overheads	Approximately 70% of the direct staff and fuel costs (per delivery)	Approximately 70% of the direct staff and fuel costs (per delivery)	

Note: The direct staff are employed solely in the haulage of coal trucks to the power stations and cannot be deployed elsewhere within T Railways.

Automotive sector: Performance Measurement

This is a relatively new area of business for TFR, involving the transportation of new cars from car manufacturing facilities within Country T to shipping ports in neighbouring countries. The Automotive sector is a growing and profitable business area for TFR. The Automotive sector prices its transportation of new vehicles very competitively and it has doubled its market share to 30% in the last 3 years.

In order to improve its ability to compete with the road haulage sector in Country T, TFR has recently invested in 20 new fuel-efficient electric freight trains for the Automotive sector, specially designed to transport cars. These trains are able to operate at speeds in excess of those offered by road haulage firms and are designed to increase the speed and efficiency in loading vehicles onto and unloading vehicles from the trucks. Deliveries have to meet tight shipping deadlines or penalties for late delivery are charged to the Automotive sector. Drivers and staff working within the Automotive sector undertake regular training. Staff turnover in the Automotive sector is low and the rate of staff accidents is much lower than TFR's other two business sectors.

The senior managers of the Automotive sector are concerned that the strategic management focus of T Railways is based only on certain strategic and financial objectives (page 3-4 of the pre-seen) and that performance management activities are solely focused upon meeting those objectives. They believe that this is limiting the sector's ability to compete effectively against road haulage for new business. They strongly believe that this sector must take a competence based approach to strategic management and performance measurement. This would mean focusing upon its critical success factors which could then be used as a basis for introducing a balanced scorecard approach for performance management.

Required

(a)   For the CG sector only:

   (i)   Discuss the Corporate Social Responsibility (CSR) obligations which the CG sector has to any TWO of its stakeholders and the strategies it should adopt to manage these stakeholders.   (10 marks)

   (ii)   Evaluate the benefits to the CG sector of working with the Minister for the Environment and the Rail Regulator towards agreed carbon emissions targets.   (6 marks)

(b)   For the Energy sector only:

   (i)   Calculate the extra contribution which could be earned per delivery and per day by the Energy sector from the proposal made by power station X's senior managers.   (8 marks)

   (ii)   Discuss the additional factors which the Energy sector's senior managers should take into consideration before making a decision on this proposal. Your answer should consider the potential impact that this decision would have on the achievement of T Railways' strategic and financial objectives.

                                                                                 (10 marks)

(c)   For the Automotive sector only:

   The senior managers of the Automotive sector strongly believe that it must take a competence based approach to strategic management and performance measurement.

   (i)   Recommend, with reasons, ONE critical success factor for each of the four quadrants of the Balanced Scorecard for the Automotive sector, in support of a competence based approach to strategic management and performance measurement.   (8 marks)

   (ii)   Recommend, with justification, ONE key performance indicator that could be used to measure whether the Automotive sector is meeting each of the four critical success factors that you have identified in part (c)(i) of your answer.

           Note: Your answer should present one performance indicator for each critical success factor   (8 marks)

                                                                           (Total: 50 marks)

Section 2

SECTION B-TYPE QUESTIONS

INTERACTING WITH THE COMPETITIVE ENVIRONMENT (20%)

EXTERNAL ANALYSIS

9 GGM (SEP 13 EXAM)

GGM is a retailer of CDs, DVDs and computer games. At the beginning of 2013 it operated 50 stores in Country Q. It was set up by T in 1970 and he is the Executive Chairman. T currently holds 52% of the shares and 38% of the shares are held by family members, some of whom are members of the Board of Directors of GGM. The remaining 10% of shares are held by staff members of GGM.

In its stores, GGM sells CDs and DVDs and has in the last five years also sold electronic entertainment products such as computer games, MP3 players and gaming equipment. T has always had a very strong vision for GGM to be the leading high street entertainment retailer in Country Q.

Many of GGM's stores are very large and sell a vast range of entertainment products. However, high street customers have complained that it does not have the appeal of smaller, individual music and DVD shops, and that GGM's staff are not very knowledgeable. GGM's products, until recently, had always been cheaper on average than those sold by its high street competitors.

Throughout the 1970s GGM expanded its retail operations throughout Country Q, doubling the number of its stores. It faced competition from entertainment retailers throughout the 1980s and 1990s but its growth continued. However, by 2005, the arrival of online retailers meant that GGM was no longer the cheapest in this competitive market. The Internet created both price competition for physical sales as well as the introduction of a new format for music sales in the form of digital music downloads. This started the trend for customers to move towards accessing music through digital downloads. Developments in technology have allowed customers to hold huge amounts of digital music on small devices, such as MP3 players.

In 2009, following poor trading results, a business analyst wrote an article in the national press of Country Q, stating that the three greatest threats to GGM were:

1. online retailers,

2. downloadable music

3. the rising possibility of supermarkets entering the market and discounting loss leader products.

The business analyst also stated that if the GGM Board did not respond to these challenges appropriately the company would fail. T's public response to this article was "I strongly disagree with this assessment of GGM's position. I accept that supermarkets could potentially be a problem but not for the serious music, games or film customer. As for the other two, I don't ever see them being a real threat to GGM. Downloadable music is just a fad and customers will always want the atmosphere and experience of a music store rather than buying through online shopping."

In the following two years, GGM closed 10 of its stores, and also lost market share following a price war with the major supermarkets in Country Q, which were able to sell music and DVDs at highly discounted prices. Under T's direction, GGM's strategy continues to be to drive down operating costs rather than developing an online presence for the sale of physical or downloaded products.

For the last three consecutive years GGM has shown a loss. The Board of GGM is considering closing a further 20 stores, with the loss of over 400 jobs, as well as downsizing and relocating the remaining 30 stores   with the aim of focusing sales towards a more targeted group of music customers.

Required

(a)   **Evaluate the impact of information technology (including the internet) on GGM, using Porter's Five Forces model.** **(10 marks)**

(b)   **Discuss the role played by the Board of Directors and, in particular, the Executive Chairman, T, in allowing GGM to reach its current position.** **(6 marks)**

(c)   **Discuss the short-term and long-term impact of the Board's proposal to close 20 stores and to re-locate and downsize its remaining stores upon**

    (i)   **GGM's customers, and**

    (ii)   **GGM's employees.** **(9 marks)**

(Total: 25 marks)

10   NSF (MAY 13 EXAM)

The National Sports Foundation (NSF) for Country Z is a public body which operates within the central government department for Sport and Culture. NSF's role is to support and develop a sporting environment across all communities in Country Z and to increase the number of people participating in sport.

NSF is mainly funded by the Government of Country Z. Up until 2010, it employed several hundred staff and also relied upon thousands of volunteers throughout Country Z to run the various sporting clubs and associations, such as amateur football clubs and children's out of school sports activities. Following cuts in Government funding in 2010, NSF's level of staffing was considerably reduced. This resulted in NSF relying more on private sector partnerships and volunteers.

Until three years ago, the economic, social and technological environment in Country Z had been relatively stable, with NSF receiving guaranteed funding from the Government and the numbers of sports participants and volunteers being reasonably predictable. Therefore, the Board of NSF has not considered frequent and regular environmental analysis to be necessary.

NSF's Board has been taken by surprise by the changes that have occurred in the environment in the last three years. In addition to Government funding cuts, local administrative government bodies have been forced to sell off local community sports grounds and facilities to raise finance. Furthermore, the level of financial and operational support provided by private sector organisations has also declined due to similar economic challenges. Increasingly stricter regulations and rules have resulted in fewer volunteers throughout the country. The rapid growth in technology-based entertainment products has been blamed for the reduction in the number of young people participating in sports. In addition, NSF has failed to consider the changing demographics and ageing population of Country Z and the impact that this will have on sports participation in future years.

The Chairman of the Board of NSF has recently attended several conferences where the value of undertaking thorough 'environmental analysis' has been discussed. The Chairman now realises that there is a serious gap in NSF's knowledge about the environment in which it operates. He considers that if NSF is to continue successfully in the future then it must improve its foresight to actively plan for the future.

Required:

(a)   Evaluate the benefits to NSF of undertaking environmental analysis each year.

(8 marks)

(b)   Explain the concept of foresight and TWO techniques (other than scenario planning) which could be used by NSF in the development of foresight.   (5 marks)

(c)   Analyse each of the key stages that would be included in a scenario planning process which could be used by NSF.   (12 marks)

(Total: 25 marks)

11   CB (MAY 11 EXAM)

CB is a recently qualified CIMA accountant. He has just started a job as a Marketing Accountant for a newly built hotel, the Futurist. Currently, the Futurist has no marketing staff.

The hotel, which has not yet opened for business, intends to generate profit from its rooms and its restaurants. However, other hotels in the local area get much business by providing a 'wedding package'. A wedding package usually includes the provision of a venue for the wedding ceremony, a meal for the wedding guests, entertainment after the wedding and overnight accommodation for the bride and groom.

These competitor hotels market their weddings in a number of different ways. One hotel, the 'De Luxe', situated in a castle in a beautiful, rural setting, charges a minimum price of £50,000 for its wedding package which includes a meal for 100 guests and rooms for a bridal party of 10 guests for one night. The De Luxe has won many international awards for its food and for the high standard of its facilities and bedrooms.

In contrast, another competitor hotel, the 'Royal Albert' offers its wedding package for 100 guests for a total cost of £1,000, with no overnight accommodation provided in the basic price. The Royal Albert is a budget hotel situated next to a busy transport inter-change in the nearby town.

There are another five hotels which the Futurist regards as competitors: these other hotels charge between £35 and £50 for each guest attending a wedding at their hotel.

CB has been asked to join a team consisting of the hotel's General Manager and the Restaurants Manager to formulate a strategy for the Futurist to offer a wedding package.

Required:

(a) (i) Identify TWO models that the team could use to analyse the external environment. Briefly explain the models. **(4 marks)**

(ii) Explain how these models could assist the team in formulating a wedding package strategy for the Futurist hotel. **(6 marks)**

(b) (i) Explain how an understanding of Porter's three generic competitive strategies could help the team design a successful wedding package strategy for the Futurist hotel. **(9 marks)**

(ii) Advise the team how information systems strategies could support the three generic competitive strategies. **(6 marks)**

(Total: 25 marks)

12   BBB (NOV 11 EXAM)

BBB is an international bank with retail banking operations in many countries. BBB's retail banking is geared primarily towards individual customers and is provided through branches as well as the Internet. BBB offers a wide variety of retail banking products including savings and cheque accounts, debit and credit cards, insurances, mortgages and personal loans. BBB has a strong international brand image and a long record of success, particularly in Western countries.

BBB has offered retail banking services in country R since 2008. BBB decided to invest in R because R then had a rapidly growing economy and in 2008 BBB considered there were good retail banking opportunities as only 50% of the population of R had a bank account at this time. BBB initially invested $200 million entering R, establishing a branch network in 2008. It also purchased a local bank in R for $150 million just after the start of the global financial crisis in 2007.

R liberalised its economy in 1993 which means it now allows the free flow of capital into and out of the country. The banking sector contains some state-owned institutions that compete strongly for retail banking business. The largest state-owned bank, SB, has half of R's retail banking business and has a strong position of dominance. This has been strengthened recently due to a reorganisation in its senior management and the launch of some successful new retail banking products. These new products have proved to be very popular with customers and are very profitable.

One banking analyst has recently commented that "R's government has chosen to energise the banking sector through SB. It is less keen on foreign competition. The potential rewards for retail banking in R are great. There is plenty of growth left in this market and the margins are excellent. However, R's population is very conservative, they don't like change." Within R, mortgage and consumer lending has grown at 20% per year compound from 2007 to the present day. BBB's economic intelligence unit has forecast that this growth will continue for the foreseeable future because this reflects the policy of R's government.

There are a number of foreign banks which have been established in R for over 15 years and these are all profitable. They have 35% of R's retail banking market. Since the beginning of 2011, BBB has identified two foreign banks which entered R at the same time as BBB, but which have withdrawn from R. One of the foreign banks has stated its reason for withdrawal as being 'Our operations in R have reduced group profitability.'

Required:

(a)   Evaluate BBB's future potential for a profitable retail banking business within country R, using Porter's Five Forces model.   **(14 marks)**

(b)   Advise BBB, using your analysis from part (a) of your answer, whether it should continue its retail banking business in country R.   **(5 marks)**

(c)   Advise BBB how it could use Porter's Diamond in its preliminary analysis when considering future investment in new foreign countries.   **(6 marks)**

(Total: 25 marks)

13   D4D (MAY 05 EXAM)

D4D is a politically stable, developing country enjoying a temperate climate and a young, educated population, many of whom are educated to graduate level. Those who have studied at this level have tended to do so abroad since there are limited opportunities to do so in D4D.

The economy is mixed, based on agriculture and some light manufacturing but has enjoyed considerable revenue from oil exploration and production which is based offshore in its territorial waters. Some of this revenue is generated by providing services for the oil industry but the majority comes from a tax on every barrel of oil which the foreign oil companies extract.

The Government has used the revenue to keep personal and property taxes low and to support the largely uneconomic local industry. It now recognises that, although politically popular, this decision might not have been in the best long term interests of the country.

The Finance and Trade Minister of D4D is aware that the oil revenue may only last a further ten years. He wishes to build competitive advantage over the neighbouring countries. The Prime Minister is sceptical and has made the observation that 'companies have competitive advantages not countries'.

As a Management Accountant within the Ministry of Finance and Trade you have been asked to produce a number of documents, for both the Prime Minister and the Finance and Trade Minister, considering how competitive advantage could be achieved for D4D and examining the possibilities of attracting inward investment from foreign companies.

Required:

(a)   Using any models you consider appropriate, explain the factors which lead to competitive advantage being present in particular countries.   **(7 marks)**

(b)   Identify the aims that D4D should try to achieve in attracting appropriate investors into the country. You should also compare and contrast those aims with the likely aims of any company investing in D4D.   **(10 marks)**

(c)   Explain the steps that D4D should take to make the country more attractive to appropriate inward investment.   **(8 marks)**

(Total: 25 marks)

14   JURANIA (NOV 05 EXAM)

Introduction

The 222 Organisation (222) is a large information systems consultancy, based in the southern African country of Jurania. 222 was founded in 1987 and has become very successful, both within Jurania and in neighbouring countries, due to growth in the economies of those countries and the highly developed technology sector of the Juranian economy. 222 advises organisations on the development of Intranet and knowledge-sharing systems, and has many clients among the top 100 companies in Jurania.

222 employs over 500 staff in its very impressive modern office building on a business park near the capital city of Jurania. Also based on the business park are several IT hardware and software companies, and the country's largest internet service provider (ISP), JuraWeb. Many of 222's staff were trained at Jurania's university, which has an excellent reputation. Whenever 222 advertises for additional staff, it receives a large number of applications from suitably qualified applicants.

The internet strategy

Recognising that the growth of 222 is limited by the size of the local market for its services, the directors of 222 are considering the further development of its rather basic website. At present, the 222.com website only contains a description of the organisation and contact details. The site was designed by employees of 222 and is hosted by JuraWeb. The directors hope that a better website will allow the organisation to develop new business in other parts of Africa, but have no desire to become a global business at this stage.

The directors are considering using the services of a local specialist web design company to develop a sophisticated website with case studies of previous 222 contracts, and detailed descriptions of staff and services. The directors also believe that 222 should be hosting the website itself, and are considering the purchase of a powerful web server. They also want to upgrade the telecommunications infrastructure of the organisation by investing in a new fibre-optic broadband service, which is available from a recently formed company that has just opened its office on the business park.

Required:

(a)   **Evaluate whether the 222 Organisation might gain a competitive advantage as a result of being based in Jurania.**   **(13 marks)**

(b)   **Evaluate the risks to 222 if it decides to pursue its internet strategy as the directors have suggested.**   **(12 marks)**

(Total: 25 marks)

15   FFF COMMUNICATIONS (NOV 06 EXAM)

FFF is a manufacturer of specialist portable communications equipment, which is designed for use in hazardous and dangerous conditions. Developments of new technology in recent years, such as wireless mobile telephony, infra red thermal imaging and global positioning has allowed FFF to create new products.

The market for such equipment has grown significantly over the past five years. The customer base includes fire services, oil and chemical companies and the government. FFF now recognises that, during this period of rapid growth, the market has attracted a number of new entrants and may even be reaching a level of overcapacity.

The directors feel that they do not know as much as they should about the existing, and new, companies in the industry. The market is now maturing and, although FFF is managing to maintain its margins and leading market share (45%), it is likely that the characteristics of the industry will change.

Required:

As Management Accountant you are required to:

(a) advise the Board of the advantages of adopting a formal approach to competitor analysis
(10 marks)

(b) advise the directors of the stages in a formal competitor analysis process and identify any information that would need to be gathered at each stage for FFF.
(15 marks)

(Total: 25 marks)

16   G ELECTRONICS (NOV 07 EXAM)

G supplies electronic components to the automobile industry by exporting from the home country in which it is currently based. The company has recently set up a research facility in the home country to develop hydrogen fuel cells. The concept of hydrogen fuel cells has attracted a great deal of interest from the environmental lobby since it offers the prospect of very environmentally friendly vehicles. The market for these vehicles is in the development stage and there have been relatively few sales so far for this new technology. G hopes that the current pressure from environmental groups and governments will lead to large volume sales.

Increasingly, electronic component manufacturers are under pressure to manufacture close to the locations of their customers, the automobile manufacturers.

The research and development (R&D) director has decided that there is a need to open a research facility abroad, to work in partnership with the facility in the home country and capitalise on the benefits that a foreign base could offer. If this venture were successful, G would open a manufacturing facility next to the proposed overseas R&D base.

The Board of Directors recognises that different countries will offer different potential advantages and disadvantages. It has been decided that the ideal characteristics and factors for the chosen country should be determined, so that potential choices can be screened effectively before a final decision is made.

Required:

(a) Advise what ideal characteristics and factors should be present in the chosen country.
(15 marks)

(b) Recommend the nature and sources of information that G should use when evaluating potential countries.
(10 marks)

(Total: 25 marks)

E-BUSINESS, SCM AND INFORMATION MANAGEMENT

17   AAP (MAY 13 EXAM)

AAP operates an estate agency business in a northern European country, M. An estate agency business arranges the selling, renting or management of houses and other properties.

AAP has been in business for the last 30 years and has 10 offices located throughout Country M. It specialises in marketing and selling high value, exclusive residential properties in Country M. AAP has seen the number of its property sales decline steadily in the last five years. AAP's Board believes that this is due to the current economic downturn and its impact on residential housing sales rather than as a result of any underlying problems within AAP itself.

AAP uses a standard estate agency software package to manage its buyer enquiries, property viewings and marketing. AAP also uses the estate agency software package to automatically match buyer enquiry details against its database of properties. AAP does not have a customer database to record customer information.

AAP has a website on which it advertises all of its properties located throughout Country M. However, this website only allows customers to view the basic property details such as internal photographs and floor layout. In order to obtain more detailed information on each property, customers must visit one of AAP's offices or telephone one of the agents in order to be sent a printed version of the property details. AAP has an email system which allows customers to contact its offices. The email system is also the main form of internal communication between employees and is often used to transfer files from one office to another. The estate agency software package and the website are not linked. Therefore, if any changes are made to the information held on the estate agency software, this change has to be duplicated on the website. This has, in the past, led to incorrect information being viewed by customers on the website, as the information was not completely up to date.

Until now, investment in information technology has been minimal and the Board of AAP has not considered information technology to be a critical aspect of its business. AAP's Board has never considered developing an e-business strategy as it believes that its main strategic priority is enhancing AAP's reputation of high quality, face to face direct customer service. The Managing Director stated at a recent board meeting that 'we must retain our focus upon keeping our customers happy. Developing our website to sell our properties is merely a distraction from what we do and what our customers want.'

The Marketing Director is concerned that AAP is not keeping up to date with technological developments and that AAP should use its information systems more strategically. Having researched a wide range of websites, the Marketing Director has identified a range of Web 2.0 technologies that AAP could use to improve its own website. He is also aware of a new technology development which enables potential home buyers to receive property details whilst viewing a property, by using location-based applications on their mobile phones.

The Marketing Director intends to write a report to the Board of Directors outlining his research and his belief that AAP could benefit significantly from developing an e-business strategy.

Required:

The Marketing Director has asked you to provide him with a report in which you:

(a)   **Explain**

    (i)   **the criticality of information systems to AAP, using McFarlan's strategic grid;**

                    (4 marks)

    (ii)   **why the investment in information systems by AAP should be a strategic decision.**   **(5 marks)**

(b)   **Advise on the benefits AND problems of developing an e-business strategy for AAP.**

                    (8 marks)

(c)   **Recommend, with reasons, TWO different applications of Web 2.0 technology that AAP could adopt.**   **(8 marks)**

               (Total: 25 marks)

18   LM (MAR 11 EXAM)

LM a recruitment agency which has experienced very rapid organic growth since it was established in 2007. Currently, it has an annual revenue of £15 million and employs 90 staff, the majority of whom are recruitment consultants. LM is organised into three divisions: Executive Recruiting, Medical Consulting and Financial Services. Each of the divisions has a managing partner who is a member of the Board of LM. The three divisions operate in very different niche markets and each managing partner has a great deal of autonomy in the way he manages his own division. This autonomy is reflected in the information technology and systems (hereafter IT) used by each of the three divisions. As LM has grown rapidly and organically, so have its information requirements.

LM is managed by an Executive Board which consists of a Chairperson, a Finance Director and the three divisional managing partners. All the partners have an equity stake in the business. In 2010, LM appointed a new Finance Director with considerable experience of IT. The Finance Director decided to review LM's increasing reliance on IT. LM's spending on IT in 2010 was £1 million the same as its forecast profit for 2011.

Following the review of LM's use of IT, the Finance Director identified the following aspects of LM's IT provision:

- LM does not have a central IT department: IT is the responsibility of each managing partner within his own division and each managing partner has different levels of expertise and interest in IT.

- No member of LM's Board has a designated responsibility for IT.

- There is no recognition within LM of the potential strategic significance of IT for its business. LM does not have an IT strategy.

- Within LM and its divisions, there are very different standards for IT. This means that hardware, such as PCs and laptops are not standard and there are different replacement policies. LM does not use a common suite of software so there are often difficulties in transferring information within LM.

- LM has a corporate website which was designed by an external consultant in 2008. The front page of the corporate website displays LM's identity. However, if users navigate to the divisions' pages, these have a variety of styles and degrees of maintenance. For example, the Executive Recruiting pages are always up to date; however, the Financial Services pages are currently 'Under Construction'. No-one within LM has the responsibility for maintaining the corporate website.

Required:

(a) **Advise the Board:**

    (i)   **Why LM should have a common overall strategy for its Information Technology and Information Systems.**   **(8 marks)**

    (ii)   **What the strategy should include.**   **(7 marks)**

(b) **Recommend how LM should implement the strategy which you have suggested in (a) (ii).**   **(10 marks)**

    (Total: 25 marks)

19   Y (NOV 10 EXAM)

Y is the proprietor of a small business which provides gardening services. It has been established for three years. Y does not employ anyone in her business as she prefers to keep her business simple and to minimise the amount of administration. Y operates her business as a 'lifestyle business': A lifestyle business has been defined as 'A small commercial enterprise operated more for the owner's enjoyment and satisfaction than for the profit it earns'. Her business is not a high-growth business. It exists to provide her with an income sufficient to give her the lifestyle she desires.

Y has invested in her business so that she has all the machinery to enable her to provide a wide range of gardening services. She has established a list of ten key customers which together yield her sufficient income. She frequently gets requests from potential new customers because of her excellent reputation for creativity and reliability. However, she will only take on a new client if an old client leaves; this rarely happens.

Y has invested very little in information technology. She has a mobile phone which has all her customers' numbers entered in the memory. She also maintains a large diary each year which records the work she has done and which is the basis for her invoicing. Y writes her invoices by hand and thinks that all her customers pay her regularly, although she never checks if there are any amounts outstanding. Once a year she lends her diary to her accountant who deals with her tax affairs. Y has kept all the yearly diaries from the start of her business. Y does not own a computer.

Y was married six months ago and her husband is a full-time student so all of the family income comes from Y's gardening business. Y has recently learnt that she is having a baby and she is concerned that her income will be insufficient to support her family. Y is aware that a contract for the maintenance of a large luxury hotel's grounds will be up for tender in the near future. The hotel contract will run for the next two years, with the possibility of a rolling annual extension, dependent upon Y meeting the high levels of quality and service expected by the hotel. The hotel has a reputation for excellence and will be a very demanding client. However, the hotel pays premium prices to its suppliers which it monitors very closely for adherence to contract specifications.

If she secures the contract, Y's income would increase and become adequate for her new needs. However, in order to carry out the contract and continue to service the ten existing customers, Y would need to employ at least three gardeners and an administrative assistant to deal with the hotel's requirements.

Required:

Assuming Y secures the hotel contract:

(a)   **Discuss whether she will be able to maintain her lifestyle business strategy.**

(4 marks)

(b)   **Advise Y of the purposes and benefits of using in her business:**

(i)   **an information systems strategy;**

(ii)   **an information technology strategy;**

(iii)   **an information management strategy.**   **(12 marks)**

(c)   **Recommend what actions Y will have to take to implement each of the three strategies referred to in (b).**   **(9 marks)**

(Total: 25 marks)

20   HHH (SEP 12 EXAM)

HHH is a UK university. HHH's management board has identified student performance as a Critical Success Factor (CSF). HHH's management board has identified this CSF as it targets an area where it is currently underperforming compared to other UK universities.

HHH is aware of a nearby comparable university, SSS, which has had much success when several of its departments have worked together to improve their student performance. SSS has a culture of sharing knowledge and a knowledge management strategy. HHH does not have a culture of knowledge sharing. Within HHH, knowledge is regarded as the personal property of the individual and very few of its staff are prepared to share their knowledge with any of their colleagues. HHH has an abnormally high level of staff turnover compared to other universities. It is twice as high as that of SSS.

Student performance

Student performance is measured by HHH as the number of students successfully completing their courses. Those students who do not successfully complete their course are described as 'drop-outs'. The number of drop-outs is measured by the drop-out rate. HHH has access to data for all UK universities for student drop-out rates analysed by age and gender.

Drop-out rates vary greatly across HHH's academic departments. In some academic departments the drop-out rate is extremely high; in others it is very low, much better than the national average. Where the drop-out rate is much better than the national average, the departments have operated extensive schemes for student support. For example, students with personal problems can seek help from trained counsellors, students with financial problems have been helped to find part-time work and students with academic problems are given extra individual tuition from the academic staff.

In the departments where the drop-out rates are extremely high, none of these student support schemes is operating. The departments with the extremely high drop-out rates are not aware of how the departments with the very low drop-out rates support their students. The departments with the very low drop-out rates are unwilling to share their knowledge about how to reduce the drop-out rates as they have spent considerable time and effort developing their schemes and regard these as their own property.

HHH has not conducted any systematic analysis into its overall drop-out rate. Within its information systems, HHH has the following information about each of its students:

- Name
- Age
- Gender
- Address
- Educational record prior to joining HHH
- Educational record within HHH
- Academic department

HHH is aware that many universities have successfully used data mining to assist them in managing student performance.

Required:

(a) **Many organisations integrate their CSFs into their performance management systems by converting them to Key Performance Indicators (KPIs).**

Explain, using examples, the advantages that HHH would gain by doing the same.

(3 marks)

(b) **Advise HHH's management board:**

(i) **of THREE benefits the university and its staff could expect to receive from the successful implementation of a knowledge management strategy. (6 marks)**

(ii) **of a total of FOUR social and technical problems HHH might encounter in operating a knowledge management system.** **(8 marks)**

(c) **Explain data mining and how the outputs of the analysis could be used by HHH to improve the student drop-out rates.** **(8 marks)**

(Total: 25 marks)

21 JGS ANTIQUES (MAY 10 EXAM)

JGS is a long-established retailer which specialises in the sale of antiques*. JGS is owned by a married couple who both work in the business. They have no employees. Their premises consist of a large modern shop and there is an apartment above this in which the owners live. Over the last five years the local area has become very fashionable and the shop is now surrounded by smart restaurants, cafes and up-market fashion outlets. This area has also become a very popular place to live which has meant that property values have increased substantially. The owners believe that if they disposed of their premises they would make a substantial capital gain. The owners have noticed that the fixed costs of their property, including insurance, local tax, security and maintenance have risen very sharply during the last five years.

Since establishing the business the owners have developed their expertise. They now have a national reputation in the antiques trade and many repeat customers. They traded profitably between 1980 and 2008 but in the last year have made an operating loss for the first time. The owners are often consulted by other antique traders and collectors by letter and telephone and they have developed a considerable income stream by charging for their advice. However, they have found that their location is becoming increasingly problematic. Although the popularity of their area of town has increased and led to many more people living and visiting the area, unfortunately for the owners most of these people are not interested in antiques. They are young people who like the area but do not have the disposable income to spend on antiques.

A further problem is that the shop is not situated in a large city and it is very inconvenient for many antique traders and collectors to visit. The owners believe the location has recently restricted the success of their business. The owners know that a very popular development in the antiques trade has been the establishment of 'Antiques Fairs' where antiques are bought and sold. Some of these have established international reputations and have many thousands of visitors. However, because of JGS's location and the need to keep their shop open, the owners do not attend these. The owners recently set up a website which has basic information about their business on it such as their address, telephone number and the opening times of their shop. The website has received a large number of hits but it does not seem to have increased sales.

* Antique = 'a decorative object that is valuable because of its age'. (Oxford Concise Dictionary)

Required:

(a) **Analyse the strengths and weaknesses of JGS using the value chain model.**

Note: **You are not required to draw a value chain diagram in any part of your answer to this question.** **(8 marks)**

(b) **The owners propose to convert their website to facilitate e-commerce in order to increase turnover and profit.**

Advise the owners of JGS what they will have to do immediately, and also on a continuing basis, to carry out this e-commerce solution. **(8 marks)**

(c) **Evaluate how the introduction of e-commerce could affect JGS's value chain.**

(9 marks)

(Total: 25 marks)

22   BXA (MAY 05 EXAM)

The insurance industry is characterised by large organisations producing, packaging and cross-selling a number of different 'products' to their client base. Typical products include life insurance, health insurance, house insurance and house contents insurance. Therefore, cost efficiency, repeat business and database manipulation are of significant importance.

BXA is a medium-sized insurance company that has grown over the past 50 years by a number of relatively small mergers and acquisitions. Its business is focused on life, automobile and private property insurance. Over the last few years the insurance industry has undergone significant change with increasing consolidation and the squeezing of margins.

The Board of BXA recognises that it is quite old fashioned in its approach to business, particularly in its attitude to information technology. Much of the computing is done on personal computers, many of which are not networked, using a variety of 'user written' programs. There are a number of different computer systems in the organisation that have been inherited from the companies that have been acquired in the past. However, these computer systems have not been fully consolidated. It is recognised that this lack of compatibility is causing efficiency problems.

BXA has recently been approached by CXA, an insurance company of a similar size, with a view to a merger. Although BXA has never combined with an organisation of this size before, the Board recognises that this merger could present an opportunity to develop into a company of significant size but that this may also present further problems of system incompatibility. BXA has decided to proceed with the merger, but the Board recognises that this might only make the situation worse with regards to information management strategy of the resulting combined company.

The Finance Director has asked you, as project accountant, to investigate the potential of outsourcing the information technology function as part of the post-merger consolidation process.

Required:

(a) **Discuss the advantages and disadvantages of outsourcing the IT function for the merged organisation at each of the strategic, managerial and tactical levels of the organisation.** **(15 marks)**

(b) **Briefly describe the characteristics of the supplier that BXA will be looking for in the selection of the contractor to take on the outsourcing.** **(5 marks)**

(c) **Identify the factors which should be included in the service level agreement with which the contractor will be expected to comply in achieving the levels of performance that BXA will require.** **(5 marks)**

(Total: 25 marks)

23   EXTRANET (NOV 05 EXAM)

C is a large multinational car manufacturer. It has factories in five countries and sells its products through networks of independent dealerships throughout the world. As part of its strategy of reducing unit costs and improving quality, C has entered into a number of 'sole supplier' agreements. This means that, on a worldwide basis, C buys all of its requirement for a specific material or component from a single supplier organisation. Such contracts are normally for a five-year period.

S is a specialist manufacturer of safety equipment. It has recently been invited, by C, to submit a tender to supply all of the 'airbag' safety devices to be installed in C's cars. This will be the biggest order for which S has ever tendered and, if won, would require a 200% increase in production capacity (that is, to three times its present scale) for S. In return for this large order, S would have to agree to deliver the required parts to each C factory twice a day. Any failure to deliver on time would lead to S being liable for the cost of lost production.

As part of the contract, C would allow S access to its extranet. This would mean that S was able to see C's forecast production schedules on a real-time basis. C maintains detailed forecasts of the number of each model of car being produced in each factory. This information is available on an hour-by-hour basis for the next month, on a day-by-day basis for the following five months, and a week-by-week basis for the subsequent 18 months. This means that S would be able to view detailed production forecasts for a two-year period. The extranet also has a 'virtual trading room' where suppliers bid for new contracts. It also contains a lot of car industry information, some of which is not available to organisations that do not supply C.

Required:

(a)   **Discuss the advantages and disadvantages, to S, of the sole supplier arrangement described.**   **(15 marks)**

(b)   **Evaluate the benefits, to S, of access to the C extranet.**   **(10 marks)**

(Total: 25 marks)

24   C PHARMACEUTICALS MANUFACTURER (MAY 07 EXAM)

C is a major pharmaceutical manufacturing company producing and supplying a variety of prescription drugs in its home market. C currently uses its own fleet of vehicles to deliver to the wholesalers. There are six competitors who supply drugs that can be used to treat the same diseases as those produced by C.

Up until three years ago, the supply chain for the industry consisted of the manufacturers, and a group of ten wholesalers which covered the whole country and which supplied approximately 4,000 independent pharmacies. These independent pharmacies are all small companies which source their drugs from the wholesalers.

Traditionally, patients would see a doctor who would write a prescription for the correct dose of the required drug which the patients had to take to the pharmacy to get their supply. This was the only way they could obtain their medication. Because of a government subsidy, regardless of the medication prescribed, all prescriptions are charged at a fixed rate.

Three years ago, the legislation changed and for the first time supermarkets were allowed to employ a qualified pharmacist and to supply prescription drugs. Because of their size and buying power, the supermarkets are now refusing to deal with the wholesalers and are insisting on being supplied directly by the pharmaceutical manufacturers.

These changes have not been well received by the independent pharmacies. There has been a significant volume of comment in the press about pressure groups which see this as another encroachment by 'big business' on the small independent traders. Some government ministers have also expressed concern about the increasing market power of the supermarkets.

C is considering changing its distribution network so that it no longer supplies the wholesalers but will sell directly to all the independent pharmacies and will share the wholesalers' margin with them.

Although the transport manager has said that he believes the arrangements can be dealt with in-house, some of the Board of Directors feel that it might be better to outsource all the transport function.

The Board of Directors recognises that there would need to be significant changes in the way the company operates were either, or both, proposals to be implemented. These changes would also have a significant effect on the stakeholders of the business.

Required:

(a) Discuss the advantages and disadvantages, to C, of the proposal to supply directly to the pharmacies. (10 marks)

(b) Discuss the advantages and disadvantages, to C, of the proposal to outsource the transport function should the proposal to directly supply pharmacies be adopted. (8 marks)

(c) Advise the project team how C might best communicate the decision, to directly supply independent pharmacies, to each of its principal stakeholders. (7 marks)

(Total: 25 marks)

25   B (NOV 08 EXAM) *Walk in the footsteps of a top tutor*

B is a public company that operates 100 supermarkets in a European country. There are a number of other supermarkets operating in the country and the market is fiercely competitive. All of the supermarkets find it difficult to generate any customer loyalty and have found that customers are very price sensitive.

Like all other supermarkets in the country, B suffers a higher staff turnover than other retail outlets and this is recognised as one of the reasons for relatively low customer satisfaction and retention.

The marketing director has suggested that the company would benefit from introducing a credit card that its customers could use in its supermarkets and in other retail outlets within the country. At present, although all supermarkets in the country accept credit cards for payment for goods, no other supermarket offers its own credit card.

The marketing director claims that, in addition to the appeal to the customers, the credit card would allow B to gather large quantities of data about its customers. He feels this would offer advantages in terms of data mining, data warehousing and relationship marketing.

You are the management accountant for B. The finance director has said that she is unfamiliar with these techniques and has asked you to provide some explanations and advice in the context of B's business.

Required:

(a) Distinguish between data mining and data warehousing. (6 marks)

(b) Describe relationship marketing in the context of B's business applying the "six markets" model. (12 marks)

(c) Recommend, with reasons, three strategies that B can use to develop relationship marketing and improve customer loyalty. (7 marks)

(Total: 25 marks)

STAKEHOLDERS, ETHICS AND CSR

26   EEQ (MAY 13 EXAM)

EEQ is a multinational civil engineering company which undertakes a wide range of large projects around the world. EEQ employs over 20,000 staff worldwide. EEQ has to work with many other organisations and governments in order to manage complex construction and civil engineering projects.

EEQ's mission statement states that 'our company's foundation is built on the values of conducting business in a socially responsible and ethical manner. We respect the law, protect the environment and bring benefits to the communities in which we work.'

EEQ places strong emphasis on its ethical and sustainable business practices and the involvement of the local communities in which it operates as part of its strategic management processes.

EEQ's values are included within its Ethical Code of Conduct. All of EEQ's employees are fully trained in the Ethical Code of Conduct and they are expected to adhere to it. These principles provide a clear guide to staff in terms of expected conduct and standards of behaviour. EEQ also ensures that all of its suppliers are fully aware of its ethical principles, as EEQ provides ethical training to all of its suppliers before EEQ buys goods or services from them.

Country X highway construction project

EEQ is currently in the early stages of preparing a tender to bid for a project in Country X to construct a highway linking two of the country's major cities. Country X is an under-developed country and the construction of this highway should have major positive benefits to the economy of Country X and the living standards of its inhabitants. If EEQ were to win the bid for this contract, it would appoint a range of local contractors and suppliers from Country X and aim to ensure that the construction process minimises its environmental impact and social disruption.

During early negotiations of the tender with Government officials of Country X, it has come to light that the intended route of the highway, as set out by the Government, will pass through several remote villages which will be destroyed. The initial Government communications relating to the potential new highway development have provided no information to the people of Country X as to the proposed route. The Government intends to offer minimal compensation to villagers for the loss of their homes. In addition, the surrounding natural environment will also be damaged. The Government does not consider the damage to the natural environment to be as important to Country X as developing its economy. The Government has made it clear to EEQ and all other potential bidders that this information is confidential until the tender negotiations have been finalised and construction commences.

The Government has stated that it would require EEQ to buy goods and services from the Government's preferred suppliers if EEQ were to win the bid for this contract. However, EEQ has made it clear that all suppliers would need to be thoroughly vetted and would have to undertake its Ethical Code of Conduct training. A Government official has stated that if EEQ forgoes the thorough vetting and training procedure for the Government's own preferential suppliers then EEQ would almost certainly win the bid for this contract, as long as all other contract criteria are met.

Required:

(a) (i) Categorise, with your justification, which ethical stance EEQ follows.

(4 marks)

(ii) Discuss the importance to EEQ of incorporating business ethics and sustainability into its strategic management activities. (7 marks)

(b) Evaluate the ethical challenges faced by EEQ if it bids for the contract for the highway construction project with the Government of Country X. Your answer should:

- address the ethical principles being challenged;

- include your overall recommendation, with justification, as to whether EE should accept the contract if it is offered by Country X's Government.

(14 marks)

(Total: 25 marks)

27 PAS (MAR 13 EXAM)

PAS is a chemical manufacturing company which processes ingredients for a number of large food and pharmaceutical companies. The processes create non-harmful gases which do not smell and which are released into the atmosphere. PAS has always worked closely with the local government to ensure that it fully complies with all health and safety regulations, especially with regard to its emissions.

The company was founded over 80 years ago. At that time, the surrounding area where the factory is located was agricultural land. However, over the years, the surrounding area has gradually become urbanised and there is now a large residential area surrounding PAS's factory. Many of PAS's employees live within this residential area as there are a number of facilities located close by such as schools, shops and recreational facilities. There is little other industry in the area.

PAS is a large contributor to the local economy in terms of employment and in the past has contributed to local community events and sponsored local sporting teams.

PAS has been a successful and profitable business but in the last 10 years it has suffered a steady decline in its profit margins. The Board of Directors of PAS is considering the future direction of the company.

The company has recently invested in research and development activities to develop new processes in order to try to reduce its operating costs. The chemical engineers at PAS have recently developed and obtained the intellectual property rights (IPR) for a new process which could produce chemicals which could then be used in the cosmetics industry.

The cosmetics industry is very profitable and this new process would be an opportunity for PAS to gain a significant competitive advantage and generate new revenue streams. This new process can produce chemicals for use in cosmetic products far more efficiently and cost effectively than any of the existing processes used by other companies. However, although the process of producing these chemicals for the cosmetics market complies with all health and safety legislation, it would result in the emission of large quantities of non-harmful gases into the atmosphere, and these emissions would smell.

The majority of the current Board of Directors of PAS are members of the founding family and they have always taken an active part in the management of the business. Members of the founding family of PAS own 35% of the shares. The remaining shareholders are made up of institutional investors (30%), employees of PAS (25%) and the general public (10%).

Required:

(a) **In the context of the proposed process to produce chemicals for the cosmetics industry:**

    (i) **Advise the Board of Directors of PAS of the benefits it will gain from an analysis of its stakeholders.** **(5 marks)**

    (ii) **Analyse the main stakeholders of PAS using Mendelow's power/interest matrix.** **(12 marks)**

(b) **Recommend, with reasons, the actions that the Board of Directors of PAS could take to manage its stakeholders with respect to the smell emitted by the new process.** **(8 marks)**

(Total: 25 marks)

28 WWW (SEP 12 EXAM)

WWW is an international company based in Europe which trades principally in Asia and Europe. In its published Code of Ethics WWW has committed itself to 'being a company that will trade fairly and sustainably'. WWW has been following an expansion strategy which has led to the following three situations occurring:

Situation 1

At a recent presentation to investment analysts and financial journalists, WWW's Chief Executive Officer (CEO) gave a very optimistic forecast for the company's future, suggesting that revenue would double over the next three years and profits and dividends would increase by 50%.

However, the CEO had prepared his forecast in a hurry and had not had it confirmed by anybody else within WWW. He did not mention that WWW's home Government was considering taking legal action against WWW for underpayment of excise duties and had made a claim for large damages. If this claim was to be successful it would materially affect WWW's profit in 2013.

Situation 2

In connection with the legal case in 1, WWW's home Government had obtained a court order that all documents relating to WWW's export trade should be made available to the Government's lawyers.

However, many of the documents covered by the court order were the subject of confidentiality agreements between WWW and various entrepreneurs. These documents included details of patents and processes with a high commercial value and if knowledge of these became public it would destroy some of WWW's competitive advantage.

Situation 3

This situation, which is unconnected to situations 1 and 2, has also occurred. WWW has a joint venture agreement with a company, ZZZ. Under the terms of the joint venture agreement each company has to make regular returns of financial performance to the other. ZZZ is always late in making its returns, which are usually incomplete and contain many errors. ZZZ's accounting staff are very reluctant to co-operate with WWW's accounting staff and the working relationship between the two companies is poor.

WWW's financial controller has been involved in a review of the joint venture with ZZZ. Due to the many problems that ZZZ has caused him and his staff he has advised discontinuing the joint venture.

Required:

(a)   Advise, giving your reasons, whether each of the three situations is in conflict with CIMA's Code of Ethics.

   (i)   Situation 1.   **(4 marks)**

   (ii)   Situation 2.   **(4 marks)**

   (iii) Situation 3.   **(4 marks)**

(b)   Advise WWW of the stages of a procedure it could use to resolve ethical conflicts.

                                                                                                                      (7 marks)

(c)   Recommend, giving your reasons, TWO current ethical issues, other than those contained in CIMA's Code of Ethics, that could be included in WWW's Ethical Code.

                                                                                                                      (6 marks)

                                                                                                            (Total: 25 marks)

29   JJJ (MAR 12 EXAM)

JJJ manufactures electrical products. It is based in country Q which has a liberal developed economy. Since 2008 JJJ has suffered from decreasing profits due to increased competition from imported products which have reduced its market share. JJJ has always stressed that it has an 'ethical business' policy which is based on the following aspects:

- All of JJJ's products are sourced and made exclusively within Q.

- JJJ sells all its output within Q.

- JJJ pays high regard to its employees' working conditions and strictly adheres to all legislative requirements.

- JJJ has stated its commitment to the principles of fair trade although it does not currently trade with any developing economies.

Market research indicates that JJJ's customers and shareholders value its ethical business policy.

JJJ's chief buyer has identified several suppliers in country K, which is a developing economy. Suppliers from K could supply components to JJJ at a price which would undercut its existing domestic suppliers within Q by 40%. If JJJ bought from the suppliers in K, it would enable it to significantly reduce its product costs and compete on price against the imported products which have been reducing its market share.

JJJ's chief buyer believes the reasons for the low prices of the suppliers based in K are:

1   K's labour costs are 60% lower than those in Q. K' labour laws allow children from 10 years of age upwards to work in factories whereas in Q, no one under the age of 16 can work in a factory. K has a national minimum wage for adults which is only 10% of the national minimum wage for adults in Q. K has no national minimum wage for people under the age of 18.

2   Q has extensive health and safety legislation which, it is estimated by JJJ's Management Accountant, adds approximately 18% to its products' costs. K has little health and safety legislation.

Required:

(a)   **Advise JJJ whether the four aspects of its 'ethical business policy' could cause concerns for its shareholders.**

Assume that the components are not sourced from suppliers in K when answering this question.   **(9 marks)**

(b)   **Assume that JJJ has decided to source components from suppliers in K.**

Advise whether, and how, JJJ could continue with its ethical business policy in its relationship with the following interest groups:

(i)   **its suppliers in K**   **(4 marks)**

(ii)   **its suppliers in Q**   **(4 marks)**

(iii)   **its customers in Q**   **(4 marks)**

(iv)   **its shareholders**   **(4 marks)**

(Total: 25 marks)

30   HWS (MAY 11 EXAM)

HWS is a chain of shops which sells groceries. HWS was established in 1844 by a group of ethically motivated investors. Its mission was stated as '...to sell the best quality groceries at the cheapest prices'. Because of their religious beliefs the original investors restricted HWS from selling any alcohol or tobacco products. This restriction represented what was considered responsible business practice at that time. However, this restriction was an informal one and did not appear in the mission statement or the memorandum and articles of association of HWS.

HWS became a 'Public Limited Company' (Plc) and was floated on the London Stock Exchange in 2007. Its current market value is £450 million. It's most recent reported profit was £40 million. Its current shareholders are:

Shareholders	% of share capital	Number of investors	Motive for investing
HWS charitable trust	10	1	Uses funds to benefit health of the population
HWS employees	10	5,080	Part of remuneration
HWS directors	2	6	Part of remuneration
Pension funds	15	2	Long-term security for pensioners
Investment trusts	15	4	Medium/long-term investors
RCB : private equity fund	25	1	Seeks short-term profits
UK clearing bank	20	1	HWS is a client
Private investors	3	15,000	Many and varied

In 2010, HWS decided to become the '24/7/365 grocer'. This means that all its shops are always open, that is, 24 hours a day, every day of the year. Since then, HWS has found that many of its customers wanted to buy alcohol and tobacco products, particularly those customers using its shops between 2 am and 6 am. The Board of HWS has decided to implement a new retailing strategy and sell alcohol and tobacco products from 1 June 2011. HWS believes that this will give a substantial boost to its profits. HWS's Managing Director has announced in a statement to the Stock Exchange that '...this widening of our product portfolio should increase profits by at least £10 million a year by the end of 2012'. This announcement has attracted criticism from the HWS charitable trust which stated: '...this is against the whole ethos of HWS'.

Required:

(a)   Evaluate, using Mendelow's matrix, the levels of power and interest of HWS's shareholders in the decision to sell alcohol and tobacco. You should justify your evaluations.
(14 marks)

(b)   Advise HWS's Board of TWO other stakeholders who would be interested in the decision to sell alcohol and tobacco. You should state the reason for the interest of these stakeholders.
(4 marks)

(c)   Advise HWS's Board how it could respond to the increasing demands in society for responsible business practice.
(7 marks)

(Total: 25 marks)

31   LAS (SEP 11 EXAM)

LAS is a public company that has its corporate headquarters in Asia. It is listed on the London Stock Exchange. Its latest annual report was criticised in a leading international financial newspaper because of its 'exclusive focus on the interests of shareholders which ignored any other interested parties'.

LAS was established in 1851 and its purpose, at that time, was stated to be 'to trade in Empire commodities'. Since then, the nature of LAS's business has changed radically and it is now a property company with investments in many countries. In the year ended 30 June 2011, LAS managed properties valued at £800 million. LAS does not have a mission statement.

LAS's Financial Director, CR, is a CIMA member. He has suggested that the corporate headquarters be moved from Asia to London for the following reasons:

- London is a major international financial centre whereas its current host country is not. It would be easier for LAS to arrange finance from a London base and some of its transactions costs would be cheaper.

- LAS's business takes place in 28 different countries. None of these countries has more than 5% of LAS's business and there is no particular reason to site LAS in one of them.

The Board has agreed to this proposal and is considering using a change agent to help it in this process. LAS has decided that when the corporate headquarters is moved to London by the end of 2011, it would mean that 80 employees in Asia would lose their jobs. Their prospects for finding a replacement job are not good.

Required:

(a)   (i)   Identify which 'other parties', besides shareholders, are likely to be interested in LAS's annual report.   **(2 marks)**

       (ii)   Discuss how LAS could use Mendelow's matrix to classify these interested parties and rank their needs.   **(4 marks)**

(b)   Discuss the purpose of, and advantages LAS could derive from, a mission statement.   **(4 marks)**

(c)   Advise LAS of the benefits of using a change agent to help in the move of its corporate headquarters to London.   **(7 marks)**

(d)   Advise the Finance Director if his suggestion to move the corporate headquarters is a breach of CIMA's Code of Ethics.   **(8 marks)**

(Total: 25 marks)

32   WRL MINING (SEP 10 EXAM)

WRL is a multi-national gold mining company. Its mission statement explains that 'WRL exists to make the maximum possible profit for its shareholders whilst causing the least damage to the environment. WRL will, at all times, be a good corporate citizen'.

In 2007 WRL was granted a licence to mine for gold by the national government of Stravia, a small country whose economy is mainly based on agriculture. The national government of Stravia was very keen to develop its economy and saw gold mining as an important aspect of this. The area where WRL was granted the licence is very remote and has no towns or cities nearby. There are small villages near the site of the gold mine. One of the conditions of the licence is that WRL would employ local people wherever possible, which it has done. WRL is entitled under the terms of the licence to dispose of the waste from the gold mining wherever is convenient for it.

The terms of the licence granted a payment by WRL to the national government of Stravia, payable in US dollars, which in 2009 totalled $50 million. This is a significant amount of foreign exchange for Stravia's economy. Similar levels of payment by WRL to the national government are likely to continue annually for the foreseeable future. The mine has operated profitably since it began.

WRL's mine is in an area controlled by the Eastern state government. The Eastern state government was not involved in the negotiations to bring WRL to Stravia and is not entitled to any payment from WRL. However, Stravia's national government granted the Eastern state government $1 million in 2009 from the payments which it received from WRL.

The Eastern state government discovered that WRL's proposed mining techniques use a great deal of water which becomes polluted. The cheapest way for WRL to dispose of this polluted water is to dispose of it in a lake near the mine and it intends to do this.

The Eastern state government feared that if the polluted water was disposed of in the lake this would kill all the aquatic life in the lake and have a long-lasting adverse effect on the lake and the surrounding area. Therefore, the Eastern state government took legal action against WRL in the Eastern state courts to prevent the disposal of the polluted water in the lake.

During the court action, WRL argued that if it was not allowed to dispose of the polluted water in the lake its mining operations in Stravia would become uneconomic and the mine would have to close. A small number of WRL's shareholders argued that it was better to close the mine than to pollute the lake.

The state courts granted the Eastern state government's request to prevent WRL disposing of the polluted water in the lake. However, upon appeal to the National Supreme Court, WRL has been granted permission to pump the polluted water into the lake as its licence imposes no restrictions.

Required:

(a)   (i)   Categorise, according to Mendelow's matrix, any three of the stakeholder groups of WRL with respect to the decision about the disposal of the polluted water. You should explain what the power and interests of the three stakeholder groups you have categorised are likely to be.

Note: You are not required to draw the Mendelow matrix   (9 marks)

       (ii)   Advise the Board of WRL of the actions it should take to resolve the problem of its stakeholders' competing objectives.   (7 marks)

(b)   Discuss the extent to which WRL's mission statement is consistent with its plan to put the polluted water in the lake.   (9 marks)

(Total: 25 marks)

33   E MULTINATIONAL (NOV 08 EXAM)   *Walk in the footsteps of a top tutor*

E is a multinational organisation and is one of the largest global producers of chocolate, coffee and other foodstuffs. E categorises the countries in which it operates as follows:

1   Less developed countries, from which E sources raw materials, but where there is no established local market for the finished products.

2   Fully developed countries, into which E imports raw materials, manufactures, and serves the local and export markets.

In every country in which E operates, it follows the OECD (Organisation for Economic Cooperation and Development) guidelines for multinationals.

In the particular case of country F, a less developed country, E has helped the local farmers to organise themselves into cooperatives to produce their crops. E has also funded schooling for the children of both the farmers and their workers, built and staffed a hospital and has provided other welfare benefits. E considers itself to be a good 'corporate citizen' and is used as an example of good practice on the OECD website.

Although the farmers' cooperatives are free to sell to E's two main competitors, they tend not to do so because of the close and friendly working relationship that they have with E. Both of E's main competitors are multinationals, but both are smaller than E.

E has recently been receiving some bad publicity in country F. The management of E feels that this is being organised by the government and the national labour union of country F. The government of F is reasonably supportive of business, but won the last election with a narrow majority. The government is now under pressure to raise the standard of living of the population. An election is due within the next fifteen months. The national labour union, which is increasingly being supported by the main opposition party in country F, is extremely anti-business. It would like to see all foreign companies removed from country F and all foreign-owned assets, and co-operatives nationalised.

The government of country F has stated that the prices paid for cocoa beans are too low, and that country F is not gaining sufficient tax revenue from the exports. The government of country F has threatened to impose an export tariff on cocoa beans, unless prices are increased, and unless E opens a manufacturing facility in the country F. The management of E feels that it has been targeted by the government because it is the largest of the three multinationals operating in the country.

The national labour union of country F has argued that the farm workers are being victimised by the farmers, who have become too powerful because of the cooperatives. It states that the government of F should not allow the farmers to operate in this way.

The management of E does not want to build a factory because the transport costs from such a factory to the nearest market for finished products would force the company to operate the factory at a loss.

The Chief Executive of E is due to meet with government ministers from country F to discuss E's future operations and involvement in the country.

Required:

(a)   **Explain the advantages to E of conducting a stakeholder analysis of its operations in country F.**   **(4 marks)**

(b)   **Produce a stakeholder analysis for E's operations in country F.**   **(14 marks)**

(c)   **Evaluate the options available to E in its approach to the government of country F and recommend the option that you consider to be the most appropriate. (7 marks)**

(Total: 25 marks)

34   RGG (MAY 12 EXAM)

RGG plc (hereafter RGG) was incorporated in 1902 and operated as a pesticide manufacturer owned by a Western European Government. In 1992 RGG was privatised and its Articles of Association restricted its operations to countries within Europe.

This restriction is reflected in RGG's mission statement which states 'In accordance with our tradition RGG will only sell pesticides to customers in European countries'. In 1992 this stance was very popular with investors and many people bought shares in RGG because of it.

Since 2005, RGG has experienced declining profits, a depressed share price and its finance director believes it is vulnerable to a take-over. In the financial year ended 31 March 2012 it had revenues of £50 million, made a loss of £1 million and employed a total of 1,505 full-time and part-time staff.

RGG's managing director, S, who is a CIMA member, has received a suggestion from a member of staff of RGG that its mission statement is out-dated and restricts business expansion. S would like to abandon the mission statement and sell pesticides wherever it is profitable to do so. S believes that RGG could get a substantial amount of business from markets outside Europe which would mean better job security for RGG employees.

When S proposed, at a recent Board meeting, that RGG abandon its mission statement, a non-executive director objected because 'this is not what our shareholders want. They have bought their shares in RGG because of our mission statement and like the idea of restricted sales. It would be wrong for the Board to go against their wishes'.

S asserted 'We have over 5,000 shareholders, most of whom own no more than 250 shares. Nobody knows what our shareholders want or why they invest in us, but I doubt they want to artificially restrict our sales. Our mission statement reflects 1992 not 2012 and so it should be abandoned.'

Required:

(a) Explain TWO methods that S could use to form an understanding of RGG's external environment. **(4 marks)**

(b) Discuss if it is consistent with Corporate Social Responsibility for RGG to abandon its mission statement.

Your answer should address the following aspects of this proposal:

RGG's Economic, Legal and Ethical responsibilities. **(16 marks)**

(c) Recommend, using Mendelow's model, strategies that RGG could adopt to manage its relationships with different types of stakeholder with regard to the suggestion that it should abandon its mission statement.

Note: In your answer to part (c) you are not required to draw Mendelow's diagram.
(5 marks)

(Total: 25 marks)

35 XYZ (MAR 11 EXAM)

XYZ is a privately owned company which manufactures industrial chemicals. The manufacturing process produces large quantities of waste and is very noisy and smelly.

XYZ sources some of its raw materials from economically underdeveloped countries.

XYZ has an ethnically diverse workforce.

XYZ has always tried to stay within its country's laws.

However, recently there have been a number of accidents which XYZ's safety manager thinks were due to operator error.

XYZ would like to be listed on a stock exchange as this would provide access to capital which would assist XYZ's plans for expansion. XYZ does not have a policy for Corporate Social Responsibility (CSR). However, XYZ's auditors have advised XYZ that a CSR policy would be required if it is to be listed.

Required:

(a) Advise XYZ of the benefits of a CSR policy. **(10 marks)**

(b) Recommend the contents of a suitable CSR policy for XYZ dealing with its manufacturing process, procurement policy, labour force and compliance with the law. **(6 marks)**

(c) Advise XYZ how it could use Lewin's model of staged change to implement a CSR policy. **(9 marks)**

(Total: 25 marks)

CHANGE MANAGEMENT (20%)

36 RSS (MAR 13 EXAM)

RSS is a long established firm of lawyers. It undertakes a small range of legal work including family law, property law and criminal law. RSS was established over 40 years ago by three founders who are now three of the senior partners in the business. These three founding senior partners control all of the operational and strategic decisions in the firm. RSS has six other senior partners and employs a further 15 associate lawyers (who are qualified lawyers with varying degrees of experience) and 30 administrative staff.

RSS has a very strong local reputation for competence. However, there has been a significant increase in the level of competition in the last decade as many law firms have been set up in the same city. Many of RSS's competitors offer more competitive prices and also many offer a wider variety of legal services. Recently, RSS has also lost a number of its associate lawyers to rival firms, which have offered better pay and a greater variety of work experience. The number of legal cases dealt with by RSS has dropped by 10% each year for the last three years. However, the three founding senior partners are not concerned, as they believe RSS's reputation will ensure its continued success.

There is a very rigid hierarchy in place within RSS. The three founding senior partners have expensive company cars, large private offices and other partners and associate lawyers within RSS cannot contact them without prior arrangement. The other six senior partners also have large offices and drive expensive company cars. The 15 associate lawyers are ranked in terms of length of service, with those who have been with RSS the longest having superior office facilities and other privileges. Senior partners and associate lawyers work on their own legal cases and there is little collaboration or sharing of knowledge and experience. Additionally, associate lawyers must seek a senior partner's authorisation for most legal case decisions.

The administrative staff are required to wear a company uniform. Administrative staff are rewarded with an annual pay bonus. This bonus is based upon their commitment and loyalty to RSS and this is determined by the senior partner to whom the administrative staff member reports. In respect of the bonus, the senior partner will normally take into account sickness days, punctuality and general attitudes to work. Each administrative staff member is set regular performance targets and deadlines by the senior partners and if these are not met then disciplinary action is often taken. Staff turnover of administrative staff in RSS is high. Monthly newsletters are sent to all the staff of RSS, focusing mainly upon recent and past success stories and re-enforcing RSS's strong reputation for 'high standards, hard work and loyalty'.

RSS has recently appointed a highly experienced senior partner. The new senior partner is very experienced in property law but has also gained experience in environmental law and believes that there is a gap in the market in the city to offer environmental law services. This area of law would require some of the associate lawyers and senior partners to work more collaboratively on environmental legal cases. At a recent meeting of all of the senior partners, the three founding senior partners were very reluctant to consider offering this legal practice area and working more collaboratively, stating that 'this is not what RSS does'. However, the six other senior partners are interested in pursuing a change in the way RSS operates but do not feel that they have the necessary experience to manage a change process. The new senior partner stated 'even if RSS decides not to undertake environmental law cases, if RSS does not change its 'top down' culture, then it is likely that the firm will continue to decline and its existence will be threatened.' He also suggested that in order to facilitate any change then RSS should consider employing a change agent.

Required:

(a) Compare and contrast how a collaborative culture would differ from the existing 'top down' culture in RSS. **(6 marks)**

(b) Evaluate the factors which are likely to block cultural change within RSS. You should use Johnson's 'cultural web' model to assist in this evaluation. **(12 marks)**

(c) Advise the three founding senior partners of RSS of the benefits of appointing a change agent. **(7 marks)**

(Total: 25 marks)

37   PPP (NOV 12 EXAM)

PPP, an electricity generating company based in a European country, Z, was a monopoly supplier until 1995. Z's Government de-regulated the electricity market in 1995 and since then PPP has faced increasing competition from eight other electricity generating companies competing in Z.

PPP currently generates its electricity using only fossil fuels. However, the electricity generating companies' customers (which supply electricity to the final users within Z) are increasingly concerned about environmental issues. Many of these customers are willing to change to a different electricity generating company which generates some of its electricity from renewable sources.

Since 2010, PPP has lost 5% of its customers to competitors who generate electricity from a range of sources, including renewables.

PPP's organisational structure is hierarchical, its decision making is often slow, and its management style is bureaucratic. Many of PPP's employees belong to trade unions and there is usually much resistance to any new initiatives or changes to working arrangements.

In 2010, Z's Government agreed to conform to an overall European Union target of generating 20% of electricity production from renewable sources such as hydro, nuclear and wind generated power by 2020. In 2011, Z's Government announced plans for incentive payments to be awarded to those electricity generating companies investing in projects to generate renewable energy. Through a government initiative called the 'Renewables Pledge', Z's electricity generators are all now required by law to provide a proportion of their electricity generation from renewable sources or pay a penalty fee to the Government.

In January 2012, the Chief Executive Officer (CEO) of PPP, who had been with the company since the 1970's, retired. He had always been sceptical of the Government's drive towards renewable energy and he had often blocked any initiatives for the company to move towards renewable electricity generation. The new CEO is a strong supporter of wind based electricity generation and he recently stated to the Board of Directors 'if PPP is to survive and thrive, it must develop a strategy for wind powered electricity generation. However, this cannot happen overnight as the old style of management must change so that we remain competitive in the industry. We simply must not continue to lose customers'.

The new CEO wishes to exploit Z's windy countryside in the north of the country for wind powered electricity generation. However, gaining planning permission for wind powered generators has proved to be difficult so far in Z. Many proposals have been delayed in the planning system, often due to local residents' opposition. On average, the planning application for a wind powered generator in Z takes 2 years for a decision to be made by local government. The national Government is introducing new laws to force local governments to make decisions more quickly.

The new technology needed to operate and manage wind powered electricity generation will require extensive investment and training in new techniques and skills and require changes to PPP's culture. PPP's engineers have threatened strike action in order to gain large pay increases to compensate for the new working arrangements. Large pay increases would make PPP uncompetitive in the industry.

Required:

(a) Explain the internal and external triggers for change which have prompted the need for PPP to develop a strategy for wind powered electricity generation.

(6 marks)

(b) Evaluate, using Lewin's Force Field Analysis model, the forces which are driving and restraining change in PPP. (8 marks)

(c) Evaluate:

(i) the type of change, in terms of speed and extent, which needs to occur in PPP in relation to both the move to wind powered electricity generation and its management culture. (3 marks)

(ii) the methods of managing resistance to change for PPP. (8 marks)

(Total: 25 marks)

38 WAL (MAY 12 EXAM)

WAL is a manufacturer of biscuits which it sells to retailers. Its current year's revenue of £120 million represents approximately 3% of the UK market. WAL has a centralised marketing information system based on a software package bought in 2005. This package is financial accounts orientated: the only management information provided to support the marketing staff consists of reports showing revenue, profit, inventory value, receivables and payables balances. WAL's marketing staff and the Marketing Director, M, have complained that they are not provided with information such as customers' profitability, market share and market growth which would support their strategic decision-making. They consider the inadequacies of the current marketing information system to be so serious that they would like a Big Bang* change which would mean moving straightaway to a new marketing information system that would give them the information they need. They feel WAL is being left behind by its competitors and is losing customers.

The Company Secretary, R, manages WAL's IS/IT staff. R was responsible for buying the existing marketing information software in 2005 and he would also be responsible for the procurement of its replacement. R has identified three possible solutions to meeting the marketing staff's needs: the first two are evolutionary, the third would be a 'Big Bang'.

Solution 1

Modification: the existing marketing information system would be redesigned by WAL's in-house IS/IT staff to meet the needs of the marketing staff. Although WAL's IS/IT staff have limited experience of the type of work which would be required, they are confident the redesign could be done within a year. The IS/IT staff are unsure of the cost.

Solution 2

Development: WAL's in-house IS/IT staff would develop new bespoke software to meet the marketing staff's needs. The IS/IT staff have stated that 'because WAL's needs are unique, costs can only be roughly estimated. However, this solution is likely to be considerably more expensive than the 'Modification' solution. The final cost would be dependent upon the length of the project. It should take a minimum of six months to develop new software but it might take as long as two years. We have little experience of software development but are very enthusiastic about trying'.

Solution 3

Purchase: WAL could purchase the biscuit industry standard marketing information system software: this would be an expensive purchase but the product is well proven. Some of WAL's marketing staff have experience of using this software in other companies, are very appreciative of its benefits and believe it would help them considerably in their jobs. The software supplier claims that '90% of the biscuit industry uses our product and if you buy it we guarantee to have it working inside WAL within three months of you buying it'.

R believes that he represents the majority of opinion within the IS/IT staff who very much prefer that change should be evolutionary. They would be very resistant to change if it was carried out in any other way. R also pointed out that WAL has experience of 'Big Bang' organisational change in the recent past which failed because WAL's culture didn't change to reflect this.

R stated, 'It looks straightforward to go out and buy a software package but it's a lot more complicated than people think and it's my department that would have to do all the work.

* *'Big Bang':* *any sudden forceful beginning or radical change*

Required:

(a) Explain the circumstances in which it would be appropriate to use

   (i) evolutionary change.

   (ii) 'Big Bang' change.   **(4 marks)**

(b) (i) Evaluate each of the three solutions proposed by R.   **(9 marks)**

   (ii) Recommend, with reasons, which of the three solutions identified by R should be adopted.   **(3 marks)**

(c) Advise how WAL could overcome the resistance to change which would arise if Solution 3, the purchase solution, were to be adopted.   **(9 marks)**

                                                                (Total: 25 marks)

39   **JALL STATIONERS (SEP 10 EXAM)**   *Walk in the footsteps of a top tutor*

JALL is an independent retailer of office products selling 2,000 different items such as paper, stationery, printer cartridges, diaries and planners. JALL has been established for over 50 years and has successfully served the needs of its customers in the small town where it operates its three shops. The nearest competitor for JALL is ten miles away. JALL employs 50 staff and had revenue of €7,000,000 in the last financial year.

JALL has been owned by the same family since it began and many of its staff have worked in the shops all their lives. Staff turnover has always been very low and staff morale very good. JALL's managers know all their staff and major customers personally. JALL's managers are prepared to listen to suggestions and complaints and they like to 'keep a finger on the pulse' of the business. Staff appraisals are conducted informally once a year when the profit-sharing bonus is announced. JALL has paid its staff a bonus every year since it was established. JALL's customers benefit from competitive prices and a very high standard of service. JALL's suppliers are very pleased to work with JALL because its procurement procedures are very efficient and it always pays its accounts within the credit period.

Recently there have been a number of changes at JALL. Customers have noticed signs in the shop window stating 'Clearance sale: all items must go!' Suppliers have noticed that they are not always being paid on time. Within the shops, a manager is not always present and the staff have been told that JALL is to be sold to LNR, a large national chain of stationery retailers. When the staff enquired about the safety of their jobs they were told by their manager that there will be a meeting, at a future date, when they would be told whether or not they would be made redundant. However, the existing managers will keep their present jobs under the new ownership.

The effects of these changes are:

- Staff are very worried about their future with JALL and morale is at an all time low.
- Suppliers are thinking about changing their credit terms with JALL and are concerned about their future trading relationship.
- Customers are unsure about the future of JALL and some have switched their business to other retailers.
- JALL's revenue has fallen considerably and there is little inventory on display within the shops.

Required:

(a)   **Advise the management of JALL:**

    (i)   **Why it might encounter resistance to the change in ownership.**   **(6 marks)**

    (ii)   **How it could overcome this resistance to change.**   **(7 marks)**

(b)   **Advise the management of LNR:**

    (i)   **How it could use the Balanced Scorecard to manage its strategic performance.**   **(6 marks)**

    (ii)   **How it could construct targets for JALL's staff within an incentive scheme and use these targets to support the Balanced Scorecard.**   **(6 marks)**

(Total: 25 marks)

40   MMM UNIVERSITY (MAR 12 EXAM)

MMM is a university whose mission is 'to be the best'. It has a wide range of educational activities and is organised into six departments:

1   Arts

2   Medicine

3   Law

4   Engineering

5   Natural Sciences

6   Theology

Each of the six departments above is controlled by a senior manager, known as a Head, who has operational responsibility for their department's activities throughout the university.

On the advice of management consultants, it has now been decided to reorganise the University and establish the following three new departments which will replace the current six departments listed above:

1   Student experience: this includes teaching, welfare, progression, pass rates and quality for both undergraduates and postgraduates.

2   Research: this includes academic research and commercial research.

3   All profit-making activities other than commercial research.

Each of the new departments will be managed by one of the existing Heads. MMM wants to introduce a control system for its Heads and departments that will measure their performance against strategic and operational targets using quantitative and qualitative criteria. MMM's executive board has the following objectives for the new control system:

●   To develop the Heads' motivation

●   To encourage the Heads to accept responsibility for achieving strategic and operational targets

●   To encourage activities that generate income from external activities

MMM's executive board believes that the departmental reorganisation and the introduction of the new control measures will require cultural change within the university.

Required:

Advise MMM's executive board:

(a)   **how it could use the 'SMART' model to achieve the new control system's objectives.**   **(10 marks)**

(b)   **of the activities it must undertake to manage the process of:**

(i)   **changing the university's culture**   **(5 marks)**

(ii)   **introducing the new departmental structure**   **(5 marks)**

You must NOT use Lewin's three-step model of change as the basis of your answer to requirement (b).

(c)   **Discuss the role that a change agent could play in the change process in MMM.**
                                                                                            (5 marks)

                                                                                    (Total: 25 marks)

41   E CHARITY (MAY 09 EXAM)

E is a global environmental charity. E is internationally recognised for its work in the area of sustainable development and the protection of endangered species and habitats.

Some supporters of E have criticised the organisation for its lack of clear direction in an increasingly competitive environment. Donations to charities have been declining, year on year, for the past five years.

The structure of E is unusual in that there is an autonomous division in each country in which the charity operates. There are 45 autonomous divisions, each headed by a CEO. It is the responsibility of each divisional CEO to report to the Supervisory Board of 10 trustees, which is based in a European country. Four times a year, the 45 CEOs meet for two days to discuss performance and their plans for the future. The meetings usually finish with no clear decisions about a unified direction for the charity to take. The divisions act independently for the next three months. This has led to a number of crises, both financial and non-financial, in the past five years.

As a result, the Supervisory Board has recognised that the charity cannot continue with the existing lack of direction, control and accountability. The Supervisory Board has decided to introduce a performance measurement and control system which will help it to implement a clear strategic direction for the charity. The Supervisory Board recognises that this will be a significant change for the CEOs and managers, and the Board expects considerable resistance.

A consultant has suggested E should introduce a balanced scorecard system of performance measurement and control.

Required:

(a)   **Discuss the advantages and disadvantages for E of introducing a balanced scorecard system of performance measurement.**   **(12 marks)**

(b)   **Discuss four reasons why the CEOs of E might resist the proposed changes.**
                                                                                   (8 marks)

(c)   **Recommend the steps that could be taken to overcome the resistance to change.**
                                                                                   (5 marks)

                                                                          (Total: 25 marks)

EVALUATION OF STRATEGIC POSITION AND STRATEGIC OPTIONS (30%)

THE STRATEGIC PLANNING PROCESS

42   MNI UNIVERSITY (SEP 10 EXAM)

MNI is a university in a European country. It employs 350 academic staff and 420 other staff. It has 8,000 full-time students. Following a visit from government appointed auditors it was criticised for the following reasons:

- The university operated at a deficit; its expenditure exceeded its income.

- Student drop-out and failure rates were greatly in excess of the national average.

- It could not accurately produce a head-count of the number of students enrolled.

- Internal control of cash receipts was defective and in several areas there were discrepancies.

- The level of student complaints was very high and increasing.

- It had a large number of debtors, mainly ex-students, and was not doing anything to collect outstanding amounts.

- It had an abnormally high level of staff turnover.

- The quality of education provided by MNI had been given the lowest possible rating 'Poor'.

Following this visit, MNI replaced its Vice-Chancellor*. The majority of MNI's funding comes from central government which has instructed the new Vice-Chancellor to prepare a new Strategic Plan for the period 2011-2016. The new Strategic Plan will be required to address the criticisms identified in the audits.

The Vice-Chancellor is the University's Chief Executive Officer

Required:

(a) Categorise, under the headings, Operational, Management and Strategic, the recent criticisms made about MNI. Advise the Vice-Chancellor how control measures could assist in the successful implementation of the new strategic plan.

(7 marks)

(b) Recommend, with reasons, what controls the university could use to assist in the improvement of any three of the areas criticised in the recent audit. (9 marks)

(c) Advise the Vice-Chancellor how information systems could support the successful implementation of the new strategic plan. (9 marks)

(Total: 25 marks)

43 NNN (NOV 11 EXAM)

NNN plc, a transport company, has recently experienced a number of problems and trading conditions have become difficult in its business. NNN plc has invested very little recently in replacement vehicles, buildings and driver recruitment and training. As a result, its operational performance has declined and its unit costs per mile have risen to uncompetitive levels. Its financial report for the year ended 31 March 2011 was subject to a qualified audit opinion because the external auditors had serious concerns about NNN plc's ability to continue in business. The auditors had identified a number of causes for concern, namely:

Revenue: some customers paid by cash but this was not always recorded and the auditors felt that the declared revenue did not fully represent the actual revenue.

Cash: there were substantial discrepancies. The auditors identified a possible shortfall of £1,000,000 but they were unsure whether this was due to criminal activity or inadequate cash accounting.

Criminal activities: NNN plc employs 210 people. Following a police investigation in 2010, two directors, one manager and six drivers were prosecuted for people smuggling whilst using NNN plc's equipment. All nine employees were found guilty and sent to prison. During the trial of these employees the judge commented: 'There appears to have been a culture of criminality within NNN'. On 1 February 2011 NNN plc was fined £2,000,000 because of the actions of these employees.

The auditors noted that seven of the nine employees who started their employment with NNN plc in 2009 had not been subject to background checks or required to produce references. Two of these seven employees had criminal records. NNN plc does not have an internal audit department or an internal security department.

Financial results: although NNN plc had forecast a profit of £5,000,000 for year ending 31 March 2011 the outturn was a loss of £5,000,000.

In September 2011, NNN plc's bankers appointed a receiver and on 1 October 2011 NNN plc was sold to a venture capitalist, WGG. WGG plans to sell NNN plc for a profit by the end of 2013, but in order to do this NNN plc will have to satisfy the following conditions. It must

- have an unqualified audit report

- be making a profit

- not be engaged in any criminal activities

- have introduced an ethical code

Required:

(a) **Recommend the changes required to be made so that NNN plc satisfies the first three conditions set by WGG. Your answer should make recommendations under the following headings:**

- **Accountancy related changes**

- **Performance related changes**

- **Organisational related changes** (16 marks)

(b) **Recommend, with reasons, three principles that should be contained within an ethical code for NNN plc.** (9 marks)

(Total: 25 marks)

44 BBB ADVERTISING (MAR 12 EXAM)

BBB is an advertising agency, specialising in work for the hotel industry. BBB has no formal mission statement or strategy. However, BBB's management board agrees that it should grow and make profits as it always has done.

BBB's market niche is small and competition is intense. BBB is unaware of the total size of its market niche but believes that it is increasing. Within its market, BBB estimates it is the second or third largest company. BBB thinks it wins most of its work because of the high quality of its output, but thinks sometimes price is the determinant for securing a new client.

BBB which employs 15 staff has always found it difficult to attract sufficient staff. BBB sometimes has to turn down work due to a lack of staff. It passes such work onto other advertising agencies. When this happens BBB earns commission. However, due to the seasonal nature of the hotel industry, there are times when BBB has surplus capacity. The management board believes BBB could increase its profit if it increased the number of its staff in order to accept some of the work that it currently turns down.

BBB's accountant provides management accounting information to the management board to support planning and decision-making. This consists of budgetary control and standard costing information. The accountant produces budgetary control monthly reports which are very detailed and show every expenditure over £25. The annual budget is flexed each month to reflect that month's level of activity. The accountant produces very detailed monthly variance reports relating to labour, variable overheads and fixed overheads. The accountant produces a monthly profit figure.

Work undertaken for clients is priced by adding a standard uplift to total cost. A blanket overhead recovery rate is used in arriving at total cost. On occasions, some of BBB's clients have complained that they have been charged too much. However, on other occasions BBB believes that it may have undercharged its client.

The management board has stated that it 'urgently needs additional information to support its planning and decision-making'. A member of the management board attended a recent seminar which discussed benchmarking and is investigating whether this technique could assist BBB.

Required:

(a) Advise BBB's management board what additional information it needs to support its planning and decision-making. **(10 marks)**

(b) Recommend, with reasons, THREE improvements to the planning and decision-making information provided to BBB's management board. **(9 marks)**

(c) Advise the management board how BBB could benefit from the use of benchmarking. **(6 marks)**

(Total: 25 marks)

FORECASTING

45 B MEDIA COMPANY (MAY 07 EXAM)

B is a media company, publishing lifestyle magazines for the consumer market. These lifestyle magazines contain articles and advertisements about fashion, health and beauty products, homes, furniture and hobbies and are bought by people aspiring to a high standard of living.

Increasingly, consumers are turning to other media for the information and entertainment traditionally provided by this type of magazine.

Traditionally, 60% of B's revenue has been derived from selling advertising, the balance being provided by the cover price of each magazine. Over the last four years both the revenue and profits have declined as there has been a steady reduction in the sale of both advertising space and the number of magazines sold.

The industry is very dependent upon the level of discretionary disposable income. If this income is at a low level, fewer luxury goods are advertised. However, people still buy the magazines to read about these goods.

The company has tried to expand abroad but has failed, expensively, to achieve this. Similarly, attempts to enter other segments of the home market, particularly teenage magazines, have failed. Both of these failures have come as a surprise to the Board of Directors who thought that they understood the respective markets well enough to make the appropriate decisions.

New technology, in the form of digital media, has also affected the magazine industry. These changes have been felt in both production methods, such as broadband distribution of proof copies, and the choice of media, such as the Internet, available to consumers. To a large extent, the speed of these developments was a surprise to the directors of B.

Required:

As Management Accountant, you have been seconded to work with the organisation's forecasting and planning function, to improve its long-range planning.

(a) Evaluate the benefits to B of implementing a process of systematic environmental analysis. **(12 marks)**

(b) Describe the essential stages that should be included in a scenario planning process that could be introduced by B. **(13 marks)**

(Total: 25 marks)

46   BBB CHARITY (MAY 08 EXAM)

Based in a European country, BBB is a charity which raises funds to provide portable equipment to remove the poison arsenic from drinking water in villages, in less developed countries. Run by a Board of Trustees, the organisation operates on laissez faire management principles.   There are few full-time paid employees and BBB is heavily dependent upon the work of volunteers. Although these volunteers are dedicated, many have said that they do not feel the organisation knows where it is going and have said that they are not confident about the future of BBB.

Funding comes from appeals to the general population, which are made through newspaper advertisements. BBB does not use the Internet to promote or raise donations and, generally, does not use available technology to any extent in its organisation. Additionally, BBB receives corporate donations, most of which come from old school friends of the trustees. There is no government funding.

Recently BBB has had difficulty in attracting donations and is at risk of not being able to carry on its work. The charity industry has become more competitive and many other organisations within it have become more aggressive in their marketing and promotion.

None of the Board of Trustees has a commercial background. The Chairman of Trustees has recently been to a number of conferences where the value of foresight and the need to conduct a frequent and thorough 'environmental analysis' have been discussed.

The Chairman has accepted that there is a serious gap in the knowledge that the trustees have about the environment in which BBB operates. Recognising that BBB needs a more proactive approach to the environment in which it operates, your help as a management accountant has been sought.

Required:

(a)   **Discuss how conducting a frequent and thorough environmental analysis would help the Board of Trustees of BBB.**   **(14 marks)**

(b)   **Explain the concept of foresight and two techniques for the development of foresight.**   **(5 marks)**

(c)   **Discuss the difficulties that BBB might, as an organisation, experience in developing a process of environmental analysis.**   **(6 marks)**

(Total: 25 marks)

THE VALUE CHAIN

47   BBB FASHION (SEP 12 EXAM)

BBB is a fashion retailer with a chain of 20 shops, each with its own manager. BBB believes it can best compete by offering a wide selection of high quality products sold at a reasonable price. BBB has trained all its staff in customer care and prefers to employ staff who have worked for other fashion retailers.

As a large proportion of BBB's products are clothes which only remain fashionable for a short period, it is important that good inventory control is maintained. BBB has recently invested in a robotic system to improve materials handling in its warehouse.

As a service to its customers, BBB will deliver to their home, within 24 hours, any items bought from one of its shops. BBB's competitors do not offer such a service. BBB knows that it has demanding customers who appreciate the retail experience and after sales service which BBB offers. If a customer has any dissatisfaction with a purchase, BBB will make a refund without question. BBB frequently sends its regular customers special offers and invites them to fashion shows held in its shops.

BBB's head office is organised into departments which are responsible for the procurement of products, setting of personnel policies, investigating innovations in fashion retailing and general corporate administration.

BBB's management accountant has been investigating the acquisition of high-tech 'Smart Tills' which would provide the following information for each shop:

- Sales transactions and analysis

- Staff statistics (sales per staff member)

- Gross profit

- Inventory turnover and balances

- Audit information (a database recording all transactions)

If BBB replaces its existing tills with Smart Tills, it will be able to better manage cash and inventory and optimise its sales due to accurate real time information. This will have the benefits of identifying and controlling wastage and improve the accuracy of its forecasts.

The overall advantages offered by the Smart Tills are that BBB will be able to react more quickly to customer demand, ensure that it has sufficient stock in its shops, minimise wastage, reduce its investment in working capital and enable its head office to know, on a real-time basis, how well each of its shops is trading.

Required:

(a) **Explain how BBB could use Porter's Value Chain to achieve competitive advantage. Your answer should give examples from BBB of the NINE activities in the value chain and explain how each one of them could add value for BBB.** **(13 marks)**

(b) **Advise BBB how it could improve its profits by use of Smart Tills.** **(4 marks)**

(c) **Recommend FOUR key stages that BBB should include in a plan to introduce Smart Tills into all its shops.** **(8 marks)**

(Total: 25 marks)

48 C TEST EQUIPMENT (NOV 08 EXAM) *Walk in the footsteps of a top tutor*

C is a manufacturer of test equipment for electronic circuits. In the past, C was a dominant player in the international market. However, over the past three years, the company has found that its profits have declined as it has lost market share to other companies in the market.

C's business model consists of the following stages:

1   C's highly skilled engineers first visit client sites and, after discussions with the client's engineers, identify and design the appropriate testing equipment to meet the client's requirements. C's engineers are still recognised as the best in the industry, and customers agree that they produce the most effective solutions to the increasingly complex problems presented by C's clients. This stage of the process is seen as a very collaborative process between the engineers employed by C and the engineers employed by its clients.

2   In the laboratories at C, the equipment design goes through a fairly complicated process. Prototypes are developed, based on the discussions in stage 1. These prototypes are then tested. Once a final design is agreed, the plans are passed to the manufacturing department for production.

3   The manufacturing department of C then produces the appropriate equipment to the desired specification and installs it at the client's site.

4   After the equipment has been installed, C conducts maintenance on an annual basis.

It is standard practice within the industry for clients to pay a total price for design, manufacture and initial installation of the equipment and an annual maintenance charge after that. Total prices are quoted before design work commences. It is unusual for companies in the industry to maintain other manufacturers' equipment.

Although clients recognise the high quality of the solutions provided, they are increasingly complaining that the overall prices are too high. Clients have said that although other suppliers do not solve their problems as well as C, they do charge less. As a result, C has reduced its prices to compete with other companies. There is a suspicion that the manufacturing and installation stages of the business are not contributing sufficiently to the business because the costs may be too high.

Some of the Board of Directors of C have recognised that this situation cannot continue and have recommended that a value chain analysis be conducted, to identify the way forward for C. The Board feels that it is important that it identifies which activities in the current business model actually add value and whether all of them should be continued. One of the directors has suggested that C should actually be a solutions provider and not a manufacturer.

Although most directors are in agreement with the proposed value chain analysis, the managing director has argued that value chain analysis is a bad idea. He says that he has heard a number of criticisms of the value chain model.

You are the management accountant for C. The finance director has asked you to do the following.

Required:

(a)   **Explain the benefits that C might gain from conducting a value chain analysis.**

(12 marks)

(b)   **Explain the criticisms of Porter's value chain model that could be relevant to C.**

(8 marks)

(c)   **Describe an alternative form of value chain analysis which could be more appropriate for C.**   **(5 marks)**

(Total: 25 marks)

PRODUCT PORTFOLIO TOOLS

49   GC CONGLOMERATE (NOV 99 EXAM)

GC is a conglomerate which comprises five strategic business units (SBUs), all operating as subsidiary companies. Information relating to each SBU (and the market leader or nearest competitor) is given in the following table:

	Current market share			Market growth expected by GC
	GC %	Market leader %	Nearest competitor %	
Building brick manufacturer	3	25		Small
(Declining profitability)				
Parcel carriage service	1	6		Nil
(Long established, faces strong competition. Turnover and profitability over last three years have been stable but are expected to decline as competition strengthens.)				
Food manufacturer producing exclusively for household consumption	25		5	Slowly declining
Long established with little new investment. High levels of turnover and profitability which are being sustained.)				
Painting and decorating contracting company	0.025	0.5		Historically high but now forecast to slow down
(Established three years ago. Continuous capital injections from Group over that period. Currently not making any profit.)				
Software development and supply company	10		8	Rapid
(Acquired two years ago. Market share expected to increase over next two years. Sustained investment from Group but profitability so far is low.)				

Required:

(a)   **Comment on GC's overall competitive position by applying the Boston Consulting Group Growth matrix analysis to its portfolio of SBUs.**   **(10 marks)**

(b)   **Discuss how GC should pursue the strategic development of its SBUs in order to add value to the overall conglomerate group.**   **(15 marks)**

(Total: 25 marks)

50   3C PHARMACEUTICALS (MAY 06 EXAM)

3C is a medium-sized pharmaceutical company. It is based in Asia, but distributes and sells its products world-wide.

In common with other pharmaceutical companies, 3C has a large number of products in its portfolio, though most of these are still being developed. The success rate of new drugs is very low, as most fail to complete clinical trials or are believed to be uneconomic to launch. However, the rewards to be gained from a successful new drug are so great that it is only necessary to have a few successful drugs on the market to be very profitable.

At present 3C has 240 drugs at various stages of development; being tested or undergoing clinical trials prior to a decision being made whether to launch the drug. 3C has only three products that are actually 'on the market':

- Epsilon is a drug used in the treatment of heart disease. It has been available for eight months and has achieved significant success. Sales of this drug are not expected to increase from their current level.

- Alpha is a painkiller. It was launched more than ten years ago, and has become one of the leading drugs in its class. In a few months the patent on this drug will expire, and other manufacturers will be allowed to produce generic copies of it. Alpha is expected to survive a further 12 months after it loses its patent, and will then be withdrawn.

- Beta is used in the hospital treatment of serious infections. It is a specialised drug, and cannot be obtained from a doctor or pharmacist for use outside the hospital environment. It was launched only three months ago, and has yet to generate a significant sales volume.

The directors of 3C meet every month to review the product portfolio and to discuss possible investment opportunities. At their next meeting, they are to be asked to consider three investments. Due to a limited investment budget, the three investments are mutually exclusive (that is, they will only be able to invest in ONE of the options).

The three options are as follows:

- The directors can invest in a new version of Alpha, Alpha2, which offers improved performance. This will allow 3C to apply for a new patent for Alpha2, and maintain the level of sales achieved by Alpha for an additional five years. Alpha2 has successfully completed all its clinical trials, and can be launched immediately.

- The directors can invest in a major marketing campaign, to promote the use of Beta to specialist hospital staff. While this investment should lead to a significant growth in the sales of Beta, 3C is aware that one of its competitors is actively promoting a rival product with similar performance to that of Beta.

- The directors can invest in the final stage of clinical trials for Gamma. This is a 'breakthrough' drug, as it has no near rivals on the market. Gamma is used in the treatment of HIV, and offers significantly better success rates than any treatment currently available. The team of 3C specialists managing the development of Gamma is confident it can successfully complete clinical trials within six months. The team also believes that Gamma should be sold at the lowest price possible, to maximise the benefits of Gamma to society. However, the marketing department of 3C believes that it would be possible to earn very large profits from Gamma, due to its success rate and breakthrough status.

Required:

(a)   Briefly explain how the product life cycle model can be used to analyse the current product portfolio of 3C (that is, BEFORE the planned investment).   **(8 marks)**

(b)   Evaluate the potential impact of each of the three investment options (Alpha2, Beta and Gamma) on the product portfolio of 3C, referring to your answer to part (a) above.   **(9 marks)**

(c)   Discuss the social responsibility implications of each of the three investment options, for the directors of 3C.   **(8 marks)**

(Total: 25 marks)

51   D PRINTING (MAY 09 EXAM)

D is a printing company that was founded by three people 20 years ago. At that time, the company used a new technology which had been developed by one of the founders. Another founder member was a finance professional. The third person is Mr Z, who has a strong, dynamic, personality. Mr Z has been the driving force behind the development and growth of the business to its present size of 350 employees. With a charismatic leadership style, Mr Z was very proud of the fact that he knew all employees by their first names and considered everyone to be part of one big team. Everyone understood exactly what the company stood for and how things should be done.

As the company has grown, Mr Z feels he is not in touch with newer members of staff and that they do not understand his, and the company's, values.

In addition, the technology used by D is no longer considered innovative and there are a number of other competitors operating in exactly the same way. D is still market leader within the industry, but only by a few percentage points. Mr Z feels that the industry has reached the maturity stage of its lifecycle.

An acquaintance of Mr Z, a management consultant, has suggested that the company should have a published mission statement and a clear set of strategic objectives.

Required:

(a)   Identify the characteristics of the maturity stage of the industry lifecycle.   **(5 marks)**

(b)   Discuss the issues that the management of D would need to consider when creating an appropriate mission statement.   **(15 marks)**

(c)   Discuss the characteristics of strategic objectives that would be appropriate for D at this stage of the industry lifecycle.   **(5 marks)**

(Total: 25 marks)

STRATEGIC CHOICE

52   HFH (SEP 13 EXAM)

Help for the Homeless (HFH)

Help for the Homeless (HFH) is a charitable organisation in Country Z which works with members of society who have no home and require assistance in everyday activities, such as finding food and shelter. It employs over 100 staff but also operates with a further 150 volunteers throughout the country. Its funding mainly comes from business donations and local sponsorship but its profile in the public eye is low compared to other more publicised charities. It is well respected in the charity sector with an experienced Board of Trustees1 and has an excellent reputation for getting homeless people into permanent accommodation.

Due to the recent economic downturn in Country Z, donations to HFH have fallen in the last three years whereas the demand for its services is increasing. In the last three years, HFH has managed to retain its number of volunteers but they are struggling to cope with the rising level of demand for its services. In addition, the Board of Trustees believes that HFH should be developing the range of services it offers. The Board of Trustees considers that it should also assist those who need help in trying to find employment. This would then benefit the local communities and the national economy of Country Z. However, HFH's staff and volunteers currently do not have the skills or expertise to undertake this proposed development in the service

Care for the Community (CFC)

Care for the Community (CFC) is a much larger charitable organisation operating within Country Z, which employs over 500 staff nationwide. It focuses upon offering a wide range of facilities and support to the unemployed, elderly and also the homeless in Country Z. It receives funding from central government, large scale corporate organisations and also receives a large amount from public donations.

In recent years, the Board of Trustees of CFC has recognised the need to continually enhance its services to include helping people to acquire new competencies such as IT and life skills and to train and mentor them to prepare for job interviews. The Board of Trustees of CFC has always encouraged collaboration and partnerships with other organisations in Country Z, in order to develop and enhance the services it offers and to utilise the expertise and knowledge of other complementary organisations. CFC's management has also been highly innovative and has always analysed and kept up to date with changes in the environment in which it operates, in order to ensure that CFC is offering the services which best suit the needs of the people it serves. CFC has also always embraced new technology and operates a sophisticated website to promote its services and to keep in contact with suppliers, volunteers, sponsors and donors.

The Board of Trustees of CFC has recently approached the Board of Trustees of HFH with a proposal to merge their organisations. There is nothing in the governing constitution of either HFH or CFC which would prevent such a merger. The Board of Trustees of CFC believes that the reputation and skills possessed by HFH in helping the homeless would be very complementary to the services it offers to the community. In addition, the Government of Country Z has recently encouraged greater collaboration in its charitable sector which has resulted in some other charities merging.

Note 1:   A Board of Trustees directs the affairs of a charity or other form of non-commercial organisation in the same way that a Board of Directors directs the affairs of a business.

Required:

(a)   Produce a SWOT analysis for HFH.   **(8 marks)**

(b)   Explain TWO key attributes of CFC which can be used to demonstrate that it is a 'change adept' organisation.   **(4 marks)**

(c)   (i)   Discuss the benefits and difficulties for HFH of merging with CFC.   **(8 marks)**

(ii)   Recommend, with reasons, whether the Board of Trustees of HFH should agree to a merger with CFC.   **(5 marks)**

(Total: 25 marks)

53   GGG (NOV 12 EXAM)

GGG is a privately owned unlisted company which runs 20 residential care homes for the elderly. A residential care home for the elderly is a building where a number of older people live and receive care (that is, their physical needs are provided for), normally on a full-time basis. The elderly residents may pay the care home fees themselves or they may be paid by their relatives or by the local government authority.

The elderly residents of GGG's care homes are all capable of making decisions for themselves. All of GGG's care homes are located in and around two cities both located in the south of country X. GGG employs around 400 staff in the care homes, some of whom work part-time, and a small team of highly experienced administrators. GGG's care homes all have modern facilities and their staff are highly trained and dedicated. GGG has always been a profitable business, even though its care homes normally have a small amount of spare capacity. GGG has approximately 25% market share in the south of country X. The remainder of the market is shared by a small number of local government funded and operated care homes and some other small private businesses.

Due to the rising costs of operating care homes as a result of increased regulation and the general economic environment, a number of small privately owned care homes in the region have recently closed. The owners of some other privately owned care homes are considering closing or selling them. GGG is also aware that this trend is occurring nationally across country X.

A national shift in the demographics of the population in the last 30 years has resulted in a significant rise in the proportion of elderly members of society. Added to this, the increased social movement of families has resulted in an increasing demand for care home places for the elderly.   GGG undertakes limited advertising, relying more on word-of-mouth recommendations and referrals from local hospitals and doctors to obtain its customers.

The prices charged to care home residents by the local government authority run care homes are lower than those charged by GGG, due to central government subsidies. However, the Managing Director of GGG is confident that the services and facilities provided by GGG are superior to those offered by the local government funded care homes.

Although GGG currently offers only full-time care for its elderly residents, there is a growing need for the market to offer 'relief care' packages. This is where elderly people, who do not normally live in residential care homes, could use any of the 20 care homes' facilities for short periods of time (normally 1 week), in order to enable their normal carers (usually family members) to take holidays or rest periods.

A number of GGG's elderly residents are often referred to local hospitals by their doctors for treatments and therapies. Many of GGG's staff are fully qualified nurses and these treatments and therapies could be undertaken by the staff of GGG in each of its care homes. These hospital visits for treatments and therapies can be disruptive and upsetting for residents who often prefer to remain in GGG's care homes and be cared for by staff with whom they are familiar. However, if GGG were to offer these additional facilities within its care homes it will need investment in training and new facilities.

Required:

(a) Analyse the opportunities available to GGG, using Ansoff's strategic directional growth vector matrix. **(10 marks)**

(b) Evaluate the opportunities available to GGG in each of the four areas of the Ansoff strategic directional growth vector matrix using Johnson, Scholes and Whittington's Suitability, Acceptability and Feasibility framework. **(10 marks)**

(c) Recommend, with your justifications, which strategic directions, as set out in Ansoff's strategic directional growth vector matrix, would be most appropriate for GGG to follow. **(5 marks)**

(Total: 25 marks)

54 XZY (MAY 10 EXAM)

XZY, a publicly quoted company has expanded rapidly since its formation in 2005. Its rapid growth rate, based on a broad range of well-regarded products manufactured and sold exclusively within Asia, has led to high profits and an ever increasing share price. However, in the last year, XZY has found its growth rate difficult to sustain. XZY's core strategy has been described by its CEO as 'selling what we know to who we know'. However, this view has been criticised by a number of financial analysts and journalists who have warned that if XZY's growth rate is not maintained its share price will fall and the value of the company will reduce. XZY has a functional organisational structure and currently employs around 800 employees. The number of employees has grown by 20% since 2008.

Required:

(a) Evaluate, using Ansoff's product market scope matrix, the alternative strategies XZY could follow to maintain its growth rate in profits and share price.

Note: Ansoff's model is also described as the growth vector matrix. You are not required to draw this model. **(12 marks)**

The Human Resource Director of XZY has suggested that she carries out a review of XZY with the purpose of saving a significant amount of money by reorganising the company and reducing employee numbers. In this way, she considers she would be making a contribution towards maintaining XZY's profit growth rate. The CEO is interested in this idea but he is aware that changing organisational structure can be difficult. The CEO knows from his previous experience that such reorganisations do not always achieve their intended results.

Required:

(b) Advise the CEO of the difficulties which may be encountered in changing the organisational structure of XZY and reducing employee numbers. **(5 marks)**

(c) Recommend how the CEO could manage the process of changing the organisational structure. **(8 marks)**

(Total: 25 marks)

55 TKC (SEP 11 EXAM)

TKC is a publicly listed UK company consisting of three divisions: leisure, engineering and financial services. The three divisions have similar sized revenues and employ, in total, 900 people. The only division which is currently profitable is engineering, which has not been affected by the severe downturn in consumer spending which started in 2008 and is still continuing. The UK government has forecast that consumer spending will not recover to its 2007 levels until 2015. This reduced level of consumer spending has impacted very detrimentally on TKC's leisure and financial services divisions.

TKC's corporate strategy has been to 'buy any business where TKC's exceptional management skills give an opportunity to earn exceptional profits'. However, this strategy has recently been called into question, as since the start of the recession in 2008, TKC's cash reserves have been exhausted. It no longer makes a profit and its share price has declined by 80% from its historic high in 2007. TKC's Board is finding it difficult to manage its business because of the very different nature of the three divisions' activities, which means that they are subject to different external environmental influences.

Recently, the Board of TKC has been considering the future direction of its business. It has an opportunity to acquire a large engineering company, BAB, which is in financial difficulties. BAB currently employs 500 people. If TKC made this acquisition it would become the largest engineering business, in terms of revenue, in the UK. It would also have a substantial export business which it does not currently have.

The Board of TKC has been reviewing its current organisational structure and has decided to divest itself of the leisure and financial services divisions. The purpose of this corporate reorganisation is to achieve a more concentrated business focus and a return to profitability

Required:

(a) **Advise the Board of TKC of the future strategic directions available to it as indicated by Ansoff's product-market scope matrix. For each of the cells in the matrix give an example of a strategy TKC could use to carry out each of the future strategic directions.**   **(8 marks)**

(b) **Discuss the potential benefits and disadvantages of the possible acquisition of BAB.**
                                                                                                    (7 marks)

(c) **Recommend what things TKC should plan:**

   (i) **for the corporate reorganisation;**   **(5 marks)**

   (ii) **for the proposed acquisition of BAB if this proceeds.**   **(5 marks)**

                                                                                    (Total: 25 marks)

56 F PLASTICS (NOV 07 EXAM)

F is a leading manufacturer of plastics. Its major products are beer crates and small containers for food sold in supermarkets. Together these two product ranges constitute 90% of F's business, the remainder coming from selling more technologically sophisticated products.

The company is faced with a number of difficulties and may have to issue a profits warning in the coming year. Although the profit levels have been uneven for the past five years, this is the first time that F will have to report significantly reduced profits.

F has been adversely affected by the aggressive marketing of foreign companies importing beer crates into the market, such that F's market share has fallen from 80% to 60% in the past three years. Consolidation in the brewery industry has meant that profit margins for crate manufacturers have been squeezed.

The company is heavily dependent upon the home market, which accounts for 75% of its total sales. Exports have been mainly of food containers for supermarkets in neighbouring countries.

F has invested heavily in research and development (R&D) and, although there is one exciting proposition in electro-plastics, most expenditure has been on projects selected by R&D managers who have little commercial awareness. There is the possibility that some new products may be developed from the electro-plastics research.

F is highly centralised, with many decisions taken by the 20 members of the Board of Directors. The workforce is highly unionised, with a number of different unions represented. Each factory has several negotiating committees set up to agree pay and conditions. Negotiations are often time-consuming and confrontational. This has resulted in very precise job definitions, which are strictly adhered to. This has further resulted in considerable inflexibility, together with a complicated system of labour grades.

The Directors have had little communication with stock market analysts and investors, who have little knowledge of the company other than what is shown in the published accounts. An informal group of institutional shareholders has asked for a strategic review and has suggested that F should withdraw from the beer crate market.

Required:

(a) (i) **Discuss the main difficulties faced by F.** **(5 marks)**

(ii) **Identify and evaluate alternative strategies that F could adopt to address its difficulties and recommend those that are most appropriate.** **(12 marks)**

(b) **Explain why the failure to keep the shareholders more informed is a significant weakness for F.** **(8 marks)**

(Total: 25 marks)

57 DDD BIOTECHNOLOGY (MAY 08 EXAM)

DDD is a biotechnology company which develops drugs. It was founded seven years ago by three scientists when they left the university medical school, where they had been senior researchers. The Company employs 10 other scientists who joined from different universities. All of these employees are receiving relatively low salaries but participate in a share option scheme. This means that when DDD is successfully floated on the stock exchange they will receive shares in the company.

DDD currently has a number of new, innovative drugs in development, but the earliest any of these drugs might come to market is two years from now. It is expected that there would be one successful drug launched in most years after that for at least six years. However, successful drug launches are never guaranteed, due to the speculative nature of biotechnology and the long period of clinical trials through which any new drug must pass. DDD has to invest a significant amount of resources into the development of each potential drug, whether they are successfully launched or not. Currently, it has 12 drugs in development, a number of which may not be successfully launched. Due to the speculative nature of the industry, companies such as DDD are unable to obtain bank loans on commercial terms.

DDD is funded by an exclusive arrangement with a venture capital company. However, there is only sufficient cash in place to maintain the present level of activity for a further nine months. The venture capital company owns 15% of the equity of the company. The rest is owned by the three founders. It has always been the intention of the venture capital company and the founders that, once the company has a sufficient number of drugs in production and on the market, the company would be floated on the stock exchange. This is expected to happen in five years' time.

Recently there have been a number of approaches to DDD which might solve its cash flow problems. The three founders have identified the following options:

1   The venture capital company has suggested that it will guarantee the cash flow until the first drug is successfully launched in commercial quantities. However, it would expect its equity holding to rise to 60% once this offer is accepted.

2   A large pharmaceutical company has offered to buy DDD outright and retain the services of the three founders (in research roles) and a few of the staff.

3   Another biotechnology company has offered to enter into a merger with DDD. This company has also been established for seven years and has one drug which will be launched in six months. However, of the four other potential drugs it has in development, none are likely to be commercially viable for 5 years. This company would expect the three founders to stay with the newly merged company but feels a rationalisation of the combined staff would be needed.

As the financial advisor to the three founders you have been asked to comment on the approaches that have been made.

Required:

(a)   Describe the 'Suitability, Feasibility and Acceptability (SFA) framework as used for evaluating strategic options.   **(6 marks)**

(b)   Using the SFA framework, evaluate the strategic options identified by the founders.
                                                                                            (12 marks)

(c)   Identify and evaluate one other strategic option that the founders might pursue.
                                                                                            (5 marks)

(d)   Recommend the most appropriate strategic option based on your analysis above.
                                                                                            (2 marks)

                                                                             (Total: 25 marks)

58   JKL (NOV 10 EXAM)

JKL is a small European company based in the south of the UK which employs 35 people. It has an annual revenue of €9 million. One aspect of its recently formulated strategy is an aspiration to expand into a neighbouring country, France, by means of organic growth.

The reason that JKL's strategy for expansion is based on organic growth is due to JKL's past experience. Two years ago, the directors of JKL negotiated the purchase of a UK business, LMN, located in the west of the UK. At the time of this acquisition, LMN was regarded by JKL as having complementary capabilities and competences. However, within a short time after the acquisition, JKL judged it to have been a failure and LMN was sold back to its original owner at a loss for JKL.

JKL employed consultants to analyse the reasons for the failure of the acquisition. The consultants concluded that the failure had happened because:

1   JKL and LMN had very different accounting and control systems and these had not been satisfactorily combined;

2   JKL and LMN had very different corporate cultures and this had posed many difficulties which were not resolved;

3   JKL had used an autocratic management style to manage the acquisition and this had been resented by the employees of both companies.

The consultants recommended that JKL should consider the use of change agents to assist in any future acquisitions.

JKL has learnt that a French competitor company, XYZ, may shortly be up for sale at a price which would be very attractive to JKL. XYZ has a very good reputation in its domestic market for all aspects of its operations and its acquisition would offer JKL the opportunity to widen its skill set. None of JKL's staff speaks fluent French or is able to correspond in French. A small number of XYZ's staff speak English fluently but none of its staff are able to correspond in English.

Required:

(a)   Discuss, in the context of JKL, the respective advantages and disadvantages of pursuing a strategy of expansion by:

(i)   Organic growth

(ii)   Acquisition;   **(8 marks)**

(b)   Recommend what actions JKL should take to prevent the difficulties that occurred in the failure of the acquisition of LMN from happening if it acquires XYZ. (9 marks)

(c)   Discuss how a change agent could assist in the successful acquisition of XYZ.

(8 marks)

(Total: 25 marks)

59   CCC CONGLOMERATE (MAY 08 EXAM)

CCC is an established company in public ownership comprising the following divisions; construction and building, engineering and machinery, real estate. Although the company has traded profitably, its earnings have been subject to wide variations and some of the shareholders are concerned about the Board's policy of 'conglomerate diversification'

In the last year the company had the following earnings figures;

Division	Earnings
	$ million
Construction and building	50
Engineering and machinery	20
Real estate	30
	___
Group	100

Note: It should be assumed that the above divisional earnings are stated after tax.

Industry	Current average market sector PE
Construction and building	8
Engineering and machinery	13
Real estate	23

CCC is currently valued on the stock market at $1,000 million, and proposed/current dividends are approximately half analysts' expectations.

Construction and building

This activity represents the original business before CCC started to make acquisitions. The divisional management has described the business as 'mature, stable, offering the prospect of modest but sustained growth'.

Engineering and machinery

This activity represents the first acquisitions made by CCC whereby a number of small companies were bought and consolidated into one division. The divisional management has described the business as 'mature but offering the prospect of profit growth of 10% per annum'. Additionally the division has a broad customer base servicing a number of government agencies – minimising the risk of cash flow problems.

Real estate

This division represents the most recent acquisition made by CCC and has provided profit growth of over 20% per annum in the three years since it was formed. The divisional management, which is recognised as the most dynamic management team within CCC, feels that this rate of growth can be continued or surpassed.

HQ Organisation

Each division has its own headquarters office in a different town and the group headquarters, which has the responsibility for raising capital and operating a group treasury function is also separately located. The group headquarters is located in the capital, is quite luxurious and has a staff of 50 including the main board directors. Group headquarters, and the staff, is funded by a management charge on the divisions.

Investors

An informal group of institutional shareholders, which holds approximately 20% of CCC's equity, has requested a review of the Board's strategy and a rationalisation of the company's portfolio. These shareholders feel that the Board of Directors has destroyed value and that the company should take the opportunity to dispose of the real estate division, reduce costs by closing the group headquarters and relocate the board and treasury functions to one of the divisional headquarters. This, they have said, would allow the company to pay a large, one off, dividend to reward shareholders for their tolerance of poor past performance.

The Board of Directors feels that the suggestions are unreasonable and that its strategy has served the best interests of all shareholders.

Required:

(a) Explain the term 'conglomerate diversification'. (3 marks)

(b) (i) Evaluate the comments made by the institutional investors that the Board 'has destroyed value'. (3 marks)

(ii) Evaluate the suggestions made by the institutional investors that:

'the company should take the opportunity to dispose of the real estate division, reduce costs by closing the group headquarters and relocate the board and treasury functions to one of the divisional headquarters'. (7 marks)

(c) Identify and evaluate alternative methods available to the Board for the disposal of the real estate division, should it decide to do so, and recommend the method of disposal most appropriate to CCC. (12 marks)

(Total: 25 marks)

60 Y TELECOMMUNICATIONS (MAY 09 EXAM)

The telecommunications market in C, a developing country, has recently been deregulated and opened to foreign competition. The national telecommunication company was split into four separate companies, each of which has approximately 25% of the local market. The national telecommunication company was using old equipment and was in need of considerable capital investment. Each new company is individually quoted on the local stock market and the shares are held by both institutional shareholders and members of the general public.

The government of C made the decision to open the telecommunications market up to private investment to ensure that the country benefitted from the recent improvements in communications technology. There was some strong resistance to the privatisation from other stakeholders in C and the government is under political pressure to ensure that the country benefits from any foreign involvement.

Y is a successful and well established international telecommunications company. It has grown by acquiring companies in established markets. The company wishes to expand into C and is considering how to achieve this. If successful, this will be the first time that Y has entered a market at such an early stage of market deregulation.

The managing director of Y has stated that she would prefer to acquire one of the existing companies in C because this is the approach Y has always used.

However, other members of the Board of Directors have suggested that the best way forward may be to form a joint venture with one of the existing companies in the market. If Y were to adopt this strategy, this would be the first strategic alliance into which the company had entered.

The managing director of Y is concerned about the risks involved in joint ventures and has said that she is concerned about the reported lack of success of joint ventures.

Required:

(a) Explain the characteristics of a joint venture. (5 marks)

(b) Discuss the benefits to country C of a joint venture between Y and one of the telecommunication companies in C. (10 marks)

(c) Evaluate the risks that Y should consider before entering into a joint venture with one of the telecommunications companies in C. (10 marks)

(Total: 25 marks)

IMPLEMENTATION OF STRATEGIC PLANS AND PERFORMANCE EVALUATION (30%)

THE PERFORMANCE MEASUREMENT MIX

61   ZZZ (NOV 11 EXAM)

ZZZ is a manufacturing company employing 1,200 people which makes components for the automotive industry. ZZZ has had 'preferred supplier' status with a major car manufacturer MMM since September 2011. This means ZZZ is guaranteed a minimum amount of business with MMM each week. The preferred supplier status is reviewed annually. MMM insists on a year-on-year reduction of 4% in the prices charged by ZZZ. ZZZ's current level of guaranteed business with MMM is £2 million per week which constitutes 95% of ZZZ's revenue.

MMM operates a Just-In-Time production and purchasing system and it has a policy of not inspecting the components supplied to it by ZZZ. However, if there are two reports of any of ZZZ's components failing, either during production or later in a vehicle driven by one of MMM's customers, ZZZ would lose its preferred supplier status. ZZZ has a number of competitors which would like to replace it as MMM's preferred supplier.

ZZZ's Managing Director, H, has the following objectives, which have been imposed upon him by ZZZ's Board of Directors:

- Maintain ZZZ's preferred supplier status with MMM

- Keep ZZZ's expenditure within the limits set each year in the budget which is approved by its Board of Directors

- Develop the management skills of ZZZ's 32 operational managers

H is held responsible for the successful achievement of the objectives and he may lose his job if any are not met. H believes that the best way to achieve his objectives is by the use of a performance management system (PMS) which he has designed. H's PMS is based exclusively on budgetary control. This PMS uses quarterly reports prepared by ZZZ's budget accountant. These reports compare budgeted and actual expenditure for each of ZZZ's 2000 cost centres.

The quarterly reports are reviewed by H and later discussed with ZZZ's operational managers. The operational managers are shown the aggregate amount of under or overspending in the cost centres but are not allowed to know the detail underlying this. This is because H believes that the details of ZZZ's finances should only be known to members of the Board of Directors.

All ZZZ's investment in new capital equipment, amounting to £20 million in the previous financial year, was spent in two of the manufacturing cost centres. ZZZ's investment proposals are originated and prepared by H and submitted for approval to ZZZ's Board of Directors. The operational managers are not involved with the preparation of investment proposals. No investment proposal submitted by H has been refused by the board.

Required:

(a) Evaluate the effectiveness of ZZZ's performance management system in assisting H achieve his objectives. **(11 marks)**

(b) Recommend, with reasons, four improvements ZZZ could make to its current performance management system. **(8 marks)**

Note: In your answer to part (b), you must not include the balanced scorecard as one of your recommendations

(c) Recommend, with reasons, two performance measures that would show ZZZ's operational managers the progress they are making towards maintaining ZZZ's preferred supplier status with MMM. **(6 marks)**

(Total: 25 marks)

62 RCH HOTELS (MAY 10 EXAM)

In a widely published model, Johnson, Scholes and Whittington characterise the strategic management process as consisting of three inter-related elements:

- strategic analysis
- strategic choice
- strategic implementation

Required:

(a) Explain why strategic implementation is included in the Johnson, Scholes and Whittington model.

Note: You are not required to draw the model. **(5 marks)**

RCH, an international hotel group with a very strong brand image has recently taken over TDM, an educational institution based in Western Europe. RCH has a very good reputation for improving the profitability of its business units and prides itself on its customer focus. The CEO of RCH was recently quoted as saying 'Our success is built on happy customers: we give them what they want'. RCH continually conducts market and customer research and uses the results of these researches to inform both its operational and longer term strategies.

TDM is well-established and has always traded profitably. It offers a variety of courses including degrees both at Bachelor and Masters levels and courses aimed at professional qualifications. TDM has always concentrated on the quality of its courses and learning materials. TDM has never seen the need for market and customer research as it has always achieved its sales targets. Its students consistently achieve passes on a par with the national average. TDM has always had the largest market share in its sector even though new entrants continually enter the market. TDM has a good reputation and has not felt the need to invest significantly in marketing activities. In recent years, TDM has experienced an increasing rate of employee turnover.

RCH has developed a sophisticated set of Critical Success Factors which is integrated into its real-time information system. RCH's rationale for the take-over of TDM was the belief that it could export its customer focus and control system, based on Critical Success Factors, to TDM. RCH believed that this would transform TDM's performance and increase the wealth of RCH's shareholders.

Required:

(b) **(i)** Identify four Critical Success Factors which would be appropriate to use for TDM. **(4 marks)**

(ii) Recommend, with reasons, two Key Performance Indicators to support each of the four Critical Success Factors you have identified. **(16 marks)**

(Total: 25 marks)

63 DLC (NOV 10 EXAM)

DLC is a company which provides private telephone network services. It sells its services exclusively to business customers and, since its foundation in 2007, DLC has been very successful. DLC has been able to charge a premium price for its services and in financial years 2008 and 2009 achieved a Return on Capital Employed (ROCE) of 50% and 48% respectively. DLC's success has been built on excellence in two key success factors: Technological Innovation and Customer Service. DLC currently employs 80 people and in 2010 will have annual revenue of $24 million.

Technological innovation

DLC has been able to continually innovate its services based on the 'leading edge' skills of its founder and chief executive, X, who previously worked in a research institute. DLC's technological innovation also requires substantial, continued capital investment and DLC spent $6 million on this in 2009. X owns 100% of DLC's share capital. X has been able to attract several of her former colleagues to join DLC and they have contributed to the culture of research excellence and technological innovation.

Customer service

DLC's business has been the design, installation and maintenance of private telephone networks for large organisations. A recent contract completed by DLC was for a large media organisation to provide a network to support 7,000 current users, with provision for this number to be extended to 10,000 within three years. This type of business is very rewarding for DLC as it is not price sensitive. However, meeting the service requirements of the client is vitally important.

DLC's control system

DLC's only financial control system is a traditional one of budgetary control. Budgets are prepared using the actual levels of expenditure for the previous budget year together with an additional amount designed to reflect forecast levels of inflation. Monthly management accounts are prepared in which actual expenditure is compared to budgeted expenditure. DLC also computes monthly its overall Return On Capital Employed (ROCE) which X considers to be the best control measure available for her to use.

DLC has no system which explicitly sets targets and reports upon Technological Innovation and Customer Service. X considers DLC's performance in these two areas is best represented by the company's ROCE. DLC's sales achievement against budget is reported upon in total: there is no attempt made at sectional analysis. When X started DLC, she knew every detail about every customer and contract and their levels of profitability. However, as DLC has expanded she can no longer do this, which she feels is a weakness.

DLC's strategic aims

DLC has no formal written statement of strategy. However, X has expressed the following strategic aims: she wants the company to continue expanding within the same market/business segment, and to provide a rewarding lifestyle for herself and secure well-paid jobs for DLC's employees.

Required:

(a) Discuss the usefulness and limitations of DLC's control system. (12 marks)

(b) Advise X how non-financial performance measures could assist in the evaluation of DLC's two key success factors. (6 marks)

(c) Evaluate how Customer Profitability Analysis could assist in the achievement of X's strategic aims for DLC. (7 marks)

(Total: 25 marks)

64 E5E (MAY 05 EXAM)

E5E is a charity concerned with heart disease. Its mission statement is:

> To fund world class research into the biology and the causes of heart disease. To develop effective treatments and improve the quality of life for patients. To reduce the number of people suffering from heart disease. To provide authoritative information on heart disease.

E5E obtains funding from voluntary donations from both private individuals and companies, together with government grants. Much of the work it does, in all departments, could not be achieved without the large number of voluntary workers who give their time to the organisation and who make up approximately 80% of the workforce.

E5E does not employ any scientific researchers directly, but funds research by making grants to individual medical experts employed within universities and hospitals. In addition to providing policy advice to government departments, the charity's advisors give health educational talks to employers and other groups.

The Board recognises the need to become more professional in the management of the organisation. It feels that this can be best achieved by conducting a benchmarking exercise. However, it recognises that the introduction of this process may make some members of the organisation, particularly the volunteers, unhappy.

Required:

As Financial Controller:

(a) discuss the advantages and disadvantages of benchmarking for E5E (8 marks)

(b) provide advice on the stages in conducting a benchmarking exercise in the context of E5E (13 marks)

(c) provide advice on how those implementing the exercise should deal with the concerns of the staff, particularly the volunteers. (4 marks)

(Total: 25 marks)

65 CCC (MAY 12 EXAM)

T is the Chief Executive Officer of a motor car insurance company, CCC. T, together with the Board of Directors, developed a mission statement in 2011 following a detailed analysis of the company's operations and market place. The mission statement states that 'CCC wants to continually grow through its commitment to quality and delivering value to its customers'. CCC has developed a complementary vision statement which aspires to:

- Provide superior returns to our shareholders

- Continually improve our business processes

- Delight our customers

- Learn from our mistakes and work smarter in the future

CCC's overriding objective, also developed in 2011, is to double the size of its revenue by the end of 2015.

T has identified the following areas of concern:

- Poor customer service has led to CCC losing 15% of its customers in 2011/2012. The customer sales manager had sponsored an initiative to reward customers with a discount if they renewed their motor insurance. However, most of the sales executives were not familiar with the details of this scheme and did not mention it to customers considering renewing their insurance. The discount scheme had not affected the rate of loss of customers.

- The average age of CCC's personal computers (PCs) was five years. There have been many complaints from CCC's staff that their PC's are not adequate for the demands of 2012. The last time an initiative had been undertaken to bring PCs up to date was in 2009.

- CCC's internal auditors had conducted performance reviews in three departments during 2011. They found a common pattern in all three departments: many of the staff had only minimal educational qualifications which were inadequate for the jobs they were doing. This resulted in an unacceptable level of errors being made. No initiatives had been undertaken to address this problem.

- Investors have been critical of the low dividend yield on their CCC shares.

T is worried because, despite the time and effort put into the development of the mission and vision statements and the overriding objective, CCC is not making sufficient progress towards achieving its revenue target. Its revenue growth rate in 2011 was 10%.

CCC's shortfall against its revenue target was discussed at a recent Board meeting. The Corporate Affairs Director stated that "the Board is 100% behind our strategy and vision but it's just not happening. I have experience in my previous company of working with an integrated model, the Balanced Scorecard. Could the Balanced Scorecard help CCC?"

Required:

(a) Advise T how a Balanced Scorecard could assist in delivering CCC's vision and strategy. **(5 marks)**

(b) Assume that CCC has adopted a Balanced Scorecard approach to help it achieve its vision. Recommend FOUR perspectives and for each perspective show:

- An objective

- A measure

- A target

- An initiative **(16 marks)**

(c) Discuss briefly TWO drawbacks of the Balanced Scorecard. **(4 marks)**

(Total: 25 marks)

66   SAH (SEP 11 EXAM)

SAH is a family owned company employing 32 people, which builds and sells medium sized yachts which normally retail at £100,000. SAH operates in a very competitive market. SAH's yachts are usually bought by amateur sailors with high disposable incomes who value quality, reliability and performance. In 2011 it plans to sell 25 yachts. SAH's Managing Director, N, has a vision for the company to be 'regarded as the best yacht builder for the private owner'.

SAH has always emphasised the high quality of its yachts and knows that its customers are very knowledgeable. Each yacht is built to a specific order and there is usually a period of at least one year between an order being placed and the yacht being delivered to the customer. SAH's construction process is very traditional: most of its designs are at least 20 years old and much of the construction work on its yachts is done by hand. SAH regards its workforce as 'craftspeople' who have learned their skills through their work experience. SAH employs school-leavers and provides apprenticeships lasting seven years. However, most of its competitors employ university graduates who have studied yacht design and construction.

SAH designs all its yachts manually which is very time consuming, although most of its competitors now use CAD/CAM* suites for their designs. SAH does not have any staff with CAD/CAM experience. SAH uses natural materials: for example, cotton for the sails. However, recently some natural materials have become difficult to obtain and the prices of these have risen by as much as 40% in the last two years. Many of SAH's competitors have replaced natural materials with synthetic ones as these are easier to obtain, cheaper and give enhanced performance.

In 1985, SAH employed a consultant who designed a standard costing system for use in its manufacturing operations. This system is still in use at SAH today. N, relies on the standard costing system which is his only control system for the company. N knows that the manufacturing cost of a yacht amounts to 60% of its total cost and believes that if he is in control of 60% he is in control of the majority of cost. However, N has experienced some difficulty in his role as the control system only reports financial results. N would like a system that gives him integrated control over all aspects of the business and has been considering the use of a Balanced Scorecard.

SAH's business comes from repeat orders and recommendations. However, it has experienced criticism in the last year because it failed to meet the promised delivery time for 30% of its orders and has lost business because the potential customers said that SAH's yachts looked 'old-fashioned' and were 'too slow'.

Cash flow is particularly important for SAH, because of the long lead times for each yacht, and has been under pressure recently. SAH has had to increase its overdraft facility by £50,000 to £150,000 and this is nearly fully used. Every year since its inception SAH has reported a profit but in 2010 its Return on Capital Employed was 3% which N has stated is unacceptable.

*CAD/CAM: Computer-Aided Design, Computer-Aided Manufacturing

Required:

(a)   Evaluate the strengths and weaknesses of SAH's current control system.   **(9 marks)**

(b)   Advise N:

    (i)   how the Balanced Scorecard could be applied and used within SAH. You should also suggest and justify ONE measure for each of the balanced scorecard's perspectives.   **(10 marks)**

    (ii)   of THREE   potential problems he might encounter if he introduces the Balanced Scorecard.   **(6 marks)**

(Total: 25 marks)

67   JIK (MAY 11 EXAM)

JIK is a manufacturer, retailer and installer of domestic kitchens. It started business in 1980 and its market segment has been low to medium income earners. Until recently, its business model has been based on selling high volumes of a standard kitchen, brand name 'Value', with a very limited degree of customer choice, at low profit margins. JIK's current control system is focused exclusively on the efficiency of its manufacturing process and it reports weekly on the following variances: Materials price, Materials usage and Manufacturing labour efficiency.

JIK uses standard costing for its manufacturing operations. In 2011, JIK employs 40 teams, each of which is required to install one of its 'Value' kitchens per week for 50 weeks a year. The average revenue per Value kitchen installed is £5,000. JIK would like to maintain this side of its business at the current level. The Value installation teams are paid a basic wage which is supplemented by a bonus for every kitchen they install over the yearly target of 50. The teams make their own arrangements for each installation and some teams work seven days a week, and up to 12 hours a day, to increase their earnings. JIK usually receives one minor complaint each time a Value kitchen is installed and a major complaint for 10% of the Value kitchen installations.

In 2009 JIK had launched a new kitchen, brand name 'Lux-Style'. This kitchen is aimed at high net-worth customers and it offers a very large degree of choice for the customer and the use of the highest standards of materials, appliances and installation. JIK would like to grow this side of its business. A 'Lux-Style' kitchen retails for a minimum of £50,000 to a maximum of £250,000. The retail price includes installation. In 2010 the average revenue for each Lux-Style kitchen installed was £100,000. Currently, JIK has 2 teams of Lux-Style kitchen installers and they can install up to 10 kitchens a year per team. These teams are paid salaries without a bonus element. JIK has never received a complaint about a Lux-Style kitchen installation.

JIK's business is generated from repeat orders, recommendations, and local press advertising. It employs two sales executives who earn an annual salary of £35,000 each. It offers a twelve month money back guarantee and this has to be honoured for 1% of its installations. JIK has always been profitable but was surprised to see that in its results for 2010 it only made 0.1% net profit on its turnover.

Required:

(a) Evaluate the appropriateness of JIK's current control system. **(7 marks)**

(b) Recommend TWO Critical Success Factors (CSFs) which could assist JIK achieve future success. You must justify your recommendations. **(6 marks)**

(c) Advise JIK of the changes it will need to make:

(i) to its current control system following the introduction of the CSFs recommended in part (b) of your answer; **(4 marks)**

(ii) to its standard costing system, reporting frequency and information requirements to achieve improved control. **(8 marks)**

(Total: 25 marks)

BUSINESS UNIT PERFORMANCE AND ORGANISATIONAL STRUCTURE

68 DDD (NOV 12 EXAM)

DDD Ltd is a medium sized engineering and manufacturing company. DDD designs, manufactures and installs combined heat and power (CHP) generators. These CHP generators provide an emergency back-up heat and electricity source if the normal national grid service is disrupted. DDD manufactures a range of small off-the-shelf CHP units for offices and shops and these are priced at approximately £20,000 each. DDD also manufactures large bespoke CHP units for customers and these units are priced between £250,000 and £500,000. DDD also provides contract service, repairs and maintenance operations for all of the units it sells. DDD currently has three large bespoke jobs in progress:

* a CHP unit for a large city hospital in its home country;

* two large CHP units for an overseas hotel chain; and

* a CHP unit in a large central government building in its home country.

DDD is very reliant on the expertise and industry knowledge of its staff and DDD often requires them to be able to work on several designs and installations at the same time. However, some of DDD's highly respected senior engineers often complain about difficulties of communication and coordination with senior managers. These senior engineers have also expressed their frustration at their lack of input to decisions. DDD has a high staff turnover compared to other similar organisations.

DDD currently has a functional organisational structure. However, some members of the Board think that the functional structure has sometimes resulted in a lack of integration of the key activities of the company, resulting in job disruption and delays. This can be a significant problem if the customer's contract includes penalties for late delivery of the product or service. Despite having a functional structure, DDD has a highly centralised decision making process, as some of the Directors believe that decentralisation would lead to a loss of control.

The Board of DDD is considering moving towards a divisionalised structure in order to provide more focus. However, having worked for a divisionalised organisation previously, the Finance Director has concerns that this type of structure may adversely affect DDD's performance. The Finance Director has recommended that a more flexible structure be considered. She also believes that a move towards a more decentralised approach to management and control would facilitate flexibility and innovation.

DDD has recently learnt that it has won a large contract for several large bespoke CHP units which will be used to support a major international sporting event which will take place in six years' time. This contract will require DDD's staff to work alongside many different organisations including government agencies, service suppliers, energy and management consultants and other large engineering companies. It will require DDD to design and install a range of CHP products in collaboration with other organisations, working to a fixed deadline date. This is the largest contract that DDD has ever undertaken, estimated to represent about 60% of its total sales revenue for each of the next six years. The Board of Directors is hopeful that if it is successful in delivering this contract, then it could lead to other similar prestigious contracts in the future.

Required

(a)   Evaluate the benefits and drawbacks to DDD of having:

   (i)   A functional structure

   (ii)   A divisional structure   **(6 marks)**

(b)   Evaluate the benefits and drawbacks to DDD of having a centralised as compared to a decentralised decision making process.   **(6 marks)**

(c)   Recommend, with your justifications, an appropriate organisational structure for DDD to enable it to meet the needs of the large contract it has recently won.

(13 marks)

(Total: 25 marks)

69   NGV (MAR 11 EXAM)

NGV is a government department which researches biotechnology which has been defined as 'Any technological application that uses biological systems, living organisms, or derivatives thereof, to make or modify products or processes for specific use'. Source: United Nations.

NGV was formed in 1980 and since then it has been operated as a cost centre. Each year the Director of NGV agrees a budget with the government minister to whom he is responsible. If there is a deficit or a surplus at the end of the year this is not carried forward to the next year. NGV normally has a deficit at the end of the year. NGV receives no income other than its budget which in 2011 is £20 million. Within NGV there are 180 cost centres which spend the annual budget. NGV does not have a management accounting function but the Director knows approximately, on a monthly basis, the total spending which has taken place within NGV. There is no formal system in place for forecasting spending. The Director thinks that NGV will probably spend between £20 and £25 million in 2011. NGV has no record of its capital equipment as this is purchased, on its behalf, by a central government ministry and, therefore, appears on that central government ministry's balance sheet.

Often the work done by NGV results in an innovation which can be developed commercially. When this happens other government departments are responsible for patenting the innovation and its subsequent commercial exploitation. NGV does not pay any of the costs associated with patenting and commercial exploitation but neither does it receive any revenues generated from the patents or their commercial usage. Some of the past innovations developed by NGV have been extremely successful commercially and have generated significant revenues for other government departments and commercial organisations.

NGV currently employs 320 staff: 25% of these are regarded as being amongst the world leaders in their research expertise. In the past, when NGV staff have produced an innovation with commercial potential they have frequently left NGV a short time later and moved to a much better paid position in the private sector. Sometimes staff leave in the middle of a research project which cannot then be completed because of the loss of their expertise. The Director is worried about what he calls a 'brain-drain' and he is concerned that there is no system for capturing tacit knowledge i.e. the 'know-how of the individual member of staff. However, many of NGV's staff are long-serving employees who have not yet produced any significant research 'break-throughs'.

The Director of NGV has been told by the government minister to whom he reports that NGV is going to have to 'Join the real world, produce an adequate return on investment (ROI) and produce a strategy showing how this will be achieved'. From the next financial year NGV will not be allowed to run at a deficit but will be allowed to carry forward and use any surplus.

Required:

(a)   Discuss the extent to which the Director of NGV could use financial ratio analysis to exercise financial control and assist NGV in producing an adequate return on investment (ROI).   **(12 marks)**

(b)   Recommend how NGV should implement a knowledge management strategy.

(13 marks)

(Total: 25 marks)

70   FIVE FORCES MODEL (NOV 05 EXAM)

In the 'Five Forces Model', one of the conclusions reached by Porter is that firms or strategic business units (SBUs) compete with their customers and suppliers.

The same model can be used to evaluate the competitive environment of the SBUs of large complex organisations. In such organisations, some of the SBUs may be customer and supplier to one another. This leads to management accountants becoming involved in negotiations leading to the agreement of appropriate transfer prices between these SBUs.

Required:

(a)   Explain how the forces exerted in a customer-supplier relationship led Michael Porter to conclude that firms compete with their customers and suppliers.

Note: You are NOT required to explain the whole of Porter's model or draw the diagram.   **(10 marks)**

(b)   Discuss the issues to be considered when negotiating and agreeing transfer prices between SBUs within a large, complex organisation. You should make reference to Porter's model, and your arguments in part (a) where appropriate.   **(15 marks)**

(Total: 25 marks)

71 EEE DIVISIONALISED COMPANY (MAY 08 EXAM)

EEE is a divisionalised company, based in F, where it is quoted on the stock exchange. EEE manufactures and sells small electrical equipment products. As a country, F is more highly developed than the neighbouring countries. EEE has enjoyed a strong home market and has exported to the neighbouring countries.

EEE has had a reputation for producing high quality products. Recently, it has come under increasing competitive pressure from new, privately held, companies based in the neighbouring countries.

It appears that competitors based in these neighbouring countries have been selling lower quality products than EEE and have been undercutting it quite significantly in terms of price. Sales in both EEE's home and export markets have been badly affected by the actions of these competitors in the neighbouring countries.

EEE has looked at a number of possible solutions to this situation and has decided to acquire a manufacturing company in one of the neighbouring countries and move all of its production there, completely closing the manufacturing division in F. This would mean that EEE would purchase one of the companies that have recently become a competitor. EEE would maintain its present divisionalised structure within its home country F and treat the acquired company as a new division.

The Board of Directors recognises the need to carefully select a suitable acquisition target company. The Board also recognises that careful consideration will need to be given to the most suitable approach to performance management once the acquisition has been made. The Board is considering an approach based on either Return On Investment (ROI) or Residual Income (RI).

Required:

(a)   **Advise the Board on what information would be required to assess the suitability of an acquisition target.**   **(15 marks)**

(b)   (i)   **Discuss the difficulties that EEE may experience with the performance measurement of its divisions, post acquisition.**   **(6 marks)**

      (ii)   **Discuss the disadvantages that EEE may experience if it chooses to use ROI as its primary performance measure.**   **(4 marks)**

(Total: 25 marks)

OTHER IMPLEMENTATION ISSUES

72 SSS (SEP 13 EXAM)

SSS is a government-owned bank operating in Country W in Asia. It has over 100 branches and a large customer base. As a government owned bank it has traditionally been the first choice for customers when choosing a bank in Country W. In the last five years, the Government of Country W has permitted a number of foreign banks to operate within the country in order to open up foreign trade and develop its economy. This has been very positive for the economy of Country W.

The foreign banks have introduced a range of new products, including online banking and mobile and telephone banking facilities, and are delivering much better levels of customer service than SSS. In contrast, SSS does not offer any form of online banking facility. It does have a website but this can only be used by customers to review the products SSS offers.

SSS has very basic information systems, catering only for internal transaction handling and accounting activities. SSS operates an internal email system but most communications, both internal and external, are by telephone or post.

Many of the routine customer banking processes, such as cash and cheque deposits and cash withdrawals, are handled by SSS employees over the counter and are not automated. Often customers complain about the amount of time that they have to wait for service within SSS's branches. Other processes, such as loan applications or new account applications, are complex, requiring many documents to be completed and sometimes applicants need to have an interview with a branch manager before approval is considered. It can often take several weeks to handle loan applications. The paperwork frequently gets lost or is completed incorrectly by customers or SSS's staff. Replacement documentation then needs to be produced or corrections made which is time consuming.

Customer service evaluation has never been undertaken by SSS. Staff morale is very low in the bank, although there is little staff turnover. Many of SSS's employees have worked for SSS all of their working lives.

Since the introduction of the foreign banks in Country W, SSS has seen a significant reduction in the number of new customers and has lost some of its existing customers. This is despite the fact that, traditionally, customers in Country W have been very loyal to their own country's companies and products. The Board of Directors of SSS has recently met to discuss the shortfalls in its current service provision and the need to re-design the bank's business processes.

Required

(a)   **Explain the impact that Business Process Re-engineering (BPR) and Process Innovation (PI) would have on SSS.**   **(6 marks)**

(b)   **Discuss how SSS could use BPR to improve TWO of its current processes.**

         Note: You can choose any two of the current processes mentioned in the scenario.

                                                                                 (8 marks)

(c)   (i)   **Discuss the organisational cultural problems that SSS may face when implementing BPR;**   **(5 marks)**

                 and

         (ii)   **Recommend how these cultural problems could be overcome when implementing BPR.**   **(6 marks)**

                                                                         (Total: 25 marks)

73   MC (MAR 13 EXAM)

MC is the name given to an IT project currently being undertaken in Country Q to connect all of the medical centres[1] and hospitals to a national information system network for the health service. There are over 100 medical centres and 30 hospitals within Country Q, all of which are funded by the central Government. The MC project is also being funded by central Government.

A project team has been set up and the MC project commenced in January 2013. Until the MC project is complete, most information within the medical centres and hospitals is contained within manual paper-based systems and all data exchange is undertaken by means of telephone, post or fax.

Features of the MC information system

The MC project aims to provide a secure and dedicated information system network for all medical practitioners, managers and medical administrators in Country Q, in order for them to share and access healthcare information. The MC information system will include the following features:

- access to email facilities;

- medical centre and hospital appointment booking facilities;

- transmission of patient records electronically between medical centres and hospitals (from the patient databases held locally in each medical centre and hospital);

- automatic re-ordering facilities for drugs and medical supplies from external suppliers;

- access by medical centres and hospital authorised staff to online laboratory test results from hospital laboratory databases;

- access to a centrally-maintained medical diagnosis system.

MC Project Management

Q's central Government has placed a contract with the main large national telecommunications company (T), for T to project manage and implement the MC information system. T is contracted by the central Government of Q to provide all hardware and software systems support, training and maintenance for all medical centres and hospitals. No tendering process was undertaken.

The project team is mainly made up of managers and technicians from T, but also includes four doctors selected from a range of medical centres and four senior hospital managers. The project manager, a senior network technician from T, is required to report progress to the Government on a monthly basis and to report on any issues or difficulties which have arisen. All hospital managers and medical centre managers have been sent regular information about the MC project in order to encourage participation.

The Government has set the following objectives for the project team:

- To establish the technical requirements for each hospital and medical centre;

- To ensure that local users have access to technical guidance and training;

- To achieve a target of 80% of medical centres and 90% of hospitals connected to the MC information system and fully operational by July 2014;

- To track and monitor the use of the MC information system by medical centres and hospitals;

- To track and monitor costs in order to stay within the budget set.

Each medical centre and hospital has been authorised to discuss terms of its forecast usage of the MC information system directly with the MC project team for its own hospital or medical centre. Usage is defined for each medical centre and hospital as the hardware and software requirements, which aspects of the MC information system it will utilise and the timing of connection.

[1] *Medical centres are facilities in which local patients can have access to local medical care from doctors and nursing staff. The budgets for these medical centres are managed by the individual doctors, but funded by central government.*

Required:

(a) Evaluate how the features of the MC information system can assist in improving the services of the medical centres and hospitals in Country Q. **(8 marks)**

(b) Discuss the potential project management problems which might arise by allowing each medical centre and hospital to discuss its own usage directly with the MC project team. **(9 marks)**

(c) Recommend, with reasons, four performance measures which could be used to assess whether the project objectives, as set by the Government of Q, are being met. **(8 marks)**

(Total: 25 marks)

74   4D TEACHING HOSPITAL (MAY 06 EXAM)

4D is a large teaching hospital. While it offers a full range of hospital services to its local community, it also has a large staff of professors and lecturers who teach and train all kinds of medical students. 4D has a very good reputation for clinical excellence.

One of the areas in which 4D is very highly regarded is the training of surgeons. Three of the nine operating theatres in the hospital can be observed from a gallery, though only a limited number of students can watch any operation due to space constraints. This allows the students to watch an experienced surgeon carry out a procedure and then ask questions of their lecturer or the surgeon. Later in their training, students can use the same facilities to carry out operations while being observed by experienced staff and fellow students.

The IT department of 4D has just developed a new Information System for use in operating theatres. This system (OTIS – the Operating Theatre Information System) uses web technology to allow students anywhere in the world to videoconference with a lecturer during an operation. The students can observe the operation and the surgical team, and discuss the procedure with the surgeon and their lecturer. The system also works 'in reverse' so a surgeon at 4D can watch a student perform an operation elsewhere in the world, and provide guidance and support. The OTIS system is currently being tested, prior to introduction.

Required:

(a) (i) Distinguish between Business Process Re-engineering (BPR) and Process Innovation (PI), and explain the role of information technology in each of these techniques. **(6 marks)**

(ii) Discuss whether, in your opinion, the Operating Theatre Information System (OTIS) implementation is an example of BPR or PI. **(4 marks)**

(b) Evaluate THREE benefits to 4D and TWO benefits to society, of the Operating Theatre Information System (OTIS). **(15 marks)**

(Total: 25 marks)

Section 3

ANSWERS TO SECTION A-TYPE QUESTIONS

1   M PLC (NOV 11 EXAM)

Key answer tips

For part (a)(i) students were asked to calculate the impact of several pricing strategies on the Web Division's weekly income. This would have required the analysis of the division's current weekly income and a comparison with the new income under each strategy. As long as students read the requirement carefully this should not have been too challenging a requirement.

Requirement (a)(ii) asked students to take their analysis of moving to a subscription-based website business model further and consider any other factors that needed to be considered (beyond their analysis in (a)(i) above). There were no models required here – any reasonable suggestions should have been awarded credit.

Part (b)(i) asked students to link the proposed subscription strategy to M's strategic and financial objectives and identify any conflicts. Most of the pre-seen scenarios within E3 have contained information about the organisation's objectives and strategies and this requirement underlines the importance of making sure you have thought about them carefully before sitting the exam.

Part (b)(ii) asked students to examine the strategy from the other point of view and explain how the Board of M could be persuaded to agree to the proposal. This required students to focus on the positive aspects of the proposals. However, as this was only worth three marks, it was important not to spend too long on this section.

Part (c) should have represented relatively easy marks with the BCG matrix. Care was needed here as the question asked for **how** it could be used – rather than actually asking for an analysis to be undertaken.

Finally, part (d) asked for improvements to the proposed headcount reduction and how the company could deal with resistance to change. While the model answer uses Kotter and Schlesinger's approaches, other models would have been acceptable, such as Lewin's three-stage model.

(a) (i) The impact of the three possible pricing strategies suggested by X and financial effect of changing the Daily News website to a subscription basis is shown in the tables below:

(1) **Current advertising revenue per week**

Pages	Price per page £	Days	Total £
5	6,000	7	210,000

(2) **Forecast subscription revenue per week**

Strategy	Daily sub-scriptions: Price per day	Daily sub-scriptions: Forecast number of sub-scribers per day	Total daily sub-scriptions revenue per week £	Weekly sub-scriptions: Price per Week £	Weekly sub-scriptions: Forecast number of subscribers per week	Total weekly sub-scription revenue £	Total sub-scription revenue £
1	£0.25	4,000	7,000	0.50	17,000	8,500	15,500
2	£0.50	3,500	12,250	0.75	15,000	11,250	23,500
3	£0.75	1,500	7,875	1.50	6,000	9,000	16,875

(3) **Forecast advertising revenue per week**

Strategy	Days	Revenue per page £	Forecast number of pages sold per day	Total weekly revenue £
1	7	4,000	7	196,000
2	7	3,750	9	236,250
3	7	2,500	10	175,000

(4) **Total weekly forecast revenue from subscriptions and advertising**

Strategy	Subscriptions £	Advertising £	Total £
1	15,500	196,000	211,500
2	23,500	236,250	259,750
3	16,875	175,000	191,875

(5) **Comparison of subscription-based website and free website**

Strategy	Total forecast weekly revenue £	Current advertising revenue per week £	Incremental advantage/ (disadvantage) %
1	211,500	210,000	1
2	259,750	210,000	24
3	191,875	210,000	(9)

Examiner's comments

This question was well answered by most candidates. However, few candidates went on to actually calculate the impact of the strategies i.e. calculate the difference between the current revenue and the proposed revenues. Therefore, only a small percentage of candidates actually obtained maximum marks on this requirement by answering the question that had been set. Candidates must be aware that at this level of the examination and in this subject in particular, they could be asked to undertake a wide range of management accounting calculations and that they must be able and prepared to use a number of different financial and analytical techniques.

Although the requirement did not specifically state to undertake a comparison of the current revenue with the proposed revenue, candidates should have used their higher level knowledge and understanding of management accounting to have recognised that this would provide a clear indication of the impact of the proposed strategies. Candidates must have the higher level examination skills to interpret requirements and to identify the information which will satisfy the question.

Common Errors

- Not calculating the impact of the proposed strategies

- Failure to calculate the current advertising revenue of £210,000

(a) (ii) Table (v) shows that the results of changing to a subscription-based website per week. However, it would be useful for X, when considering the decision, to look at the aggregate effects of the change which is shown below:

Strategy 1 would give extra revenue of £78,000 a year (£1,500 × 52 weeks) which can be characterised as a slight improvement.

Strategy 2 would give extra revenue of £2,587,000 a year (£49,750 × 52 weeks), a substantial improvement.

Strategy 3 would give reduced revenue £942,500 a year (£(18,125) × 52 weeks) making this the worst strategy.

M plc has 200 websites and the Business Development Director, X, will be reviewing these. However, in her view, other websites of the 200 may be suitable for changing to a subscription-only basis. The experience which could be gained if the Daily News website changes could be usefully applied to the remaining websites.

A change to a subscription-based website might give M plc a temporary competitive advantage if this change puts the Daily News ahead of its competitors. Alternatively, this change may be necessary to keep the Daily News abreast of industry practice and readers' preferences.

The Daily News potential subscribers may prove to be loyal to the website and the website could exploit this by selling products to them.

The proposal to change to a subscription basis and the forecasted outcomes relies on a complex set of estimates namely:

- Subscription levels and their associated prices

- The ratio of daily to weekly passes

- The levels and prices for the advertising sales

These estimates originate from X, who has used her previous experience of subscription-based websites and the results of commissioned market research.

If any of these estimates were to be inaccurate, the final result would be affected: for example, if two fewer pages of advertising a day were sold at each subscription level the result would be substantial losses.

Summary

The financial results indicate that one of the proposed strategies would lead to significantly increased revenue and potential profit for M plc, one strategy would make little difference and the third would result in significantly reduced revenue and possibly lead to a loss.

The Web Division's Managing Director, Y, should be made aware that these forecasts rely on X's expertise and the results of market research. It would be prudent for Y to discuss the degree of confidence that X places in these forecasts before making the decision. The decision as to which strategy to adopt, if any, is likely to be made based on both financial and non-financial factors.

Examiner's comments

This question was reasonably well answered by most candidates. Most focused upon the reaction of customers and competitors and the technological requirements of the proposed strategy. A number of answers also correctly identified the need to ascertain the potential costs associated with the proposals as these were not included in the calculations in part (a)(i). The main weakness of answers to this question was the lack of discussion offered, as many answers were brief and covered too few factors. Also, some answers focused too much on the technological issues and incorrectly assumed that the web-based technology was not already in existence. Many answers overemphasised the potential technology impact and costs.

Common errors

- Brief answers with too few points of discussion
- Over focused upon discussions on technological impact of the strategies

---

(b) (i) The proposal to change the Daily News website to a subscription only basis should be evaluated against M plc's objectives as shown:

Strategic objectives

1 Meeting the needs of its readers for reliable and well informed news. The proposed change is neutral with respect to this objective.

2 Expanding the geographical spread of M plc's output to reach as many potential newspaper and website readers as possible. The proposed change is open to criticism because if the change takes place the maximum number of subscribers will be 21,000; a considerable reduction from the current level of 100,000 daily visits.

3 Publish some newspapers which help meet the needs of native English speakers who live in countries which do not have English as their first language. The proposed change is neutral with respect to this objective.

4 Increase advertising income so that the group moves towards offering as many news titles as possible, free of charge, to the public. The proposed change accords with the first part of this objective but conflicts with the second part.

Financial objectives

(i)   Ensure that revenue and operating profit grow by an average 4% per year. The proposed change would contribute towards this objective.

(ii)   Achieve a steady growth in dividend per share. The proposed change would contribute towards this objective.

(iii)   To maintain gearing below 40%. The proposed change could make a small contribution to this if strategy 2 is adopted and it fulfils its forecast.

Summary

The proposed change of the Daily News website from being free to being available only on a subscription basis contradicts two of M plc's strategic objectives and accords with one objective and is neutral regarding the other one. It could also contribute towards the achievement of the three financial objectives.

Examiner's comments

This question was reasonably well answered but many candidates did not evaluate all 7 objectives and therefore marks were limited. Most correctly recognised the conflict with the strategic objectives 2 and 4. Many candidates also correctly recognised that objective 4 both agreed and conflicted in different aspects of the objective. Those that did recognise this were awarded extra credit.

One of the main weaknesses of the answers to this question was that many candidates sat on the fence when evaluating the impact of the proposed strategies on the financial objectives. This was largely due to the fact that many candidates failed to identify that proposal 2 would be the chosen strategy, if the proposal was given the go ahead. Strategy 1 presented a much lower return and the strategy presented a negative impact, so the logical conclusion drawn by candidates should have been that strategy 2 would be chosen. However, many candidates stated that the financial objectives were not met because strategy 3 presented a negative impact. However, candidates should have recognised that quite clearly this strategy would not have been chosen and therefore its outcomes were irrelevant in this question. Candidates must learn to think for themselves more logically and make rational business based decisions within the examination room. It appears that far too often, candidates undertake calculations but do not really understand or really think about what these calculations mean or how they should be best used. It is no use merely undertaking the calculations; you must understand why you have undertaken them and how they can be used or not.

Common Errors

•   Only addressing a limited number of objectives

•   Failing to correctly evaluate the financial objectives due to evaluation based on Strategy 3

(ii)   X is likely to have to justify the change of the Daily News website to a subscription basis as it conflicts with two of M plc's strategic objectives. In this case, X may find that if the Divisional Managing Director takes a decision to implement this change, X will need to be able to defend the decision to the Board of M plc.

As regards Strategic Objective 2, X must concede that the proposed change does significantly reduce the readership of the website. However, she could point out that the subscribers may prove to be more loyal to the website than the current 'visitors' and they may be induced to buy other M plc's products through advertising directed at them through the Daily News website.

With respect to Strategic Objective 4 although the change means the website is no longer free it does increase the amount of advertising revenue which agrees with the objective.

The proposed change is also in broad agreement with one of M plc's financial objectives as it increases revenue and should increase operating profit and returns to shareholders.

The change has been put forward by X who has considerable experience of working with subscription-based websites. She has pointed out that the objectives were established in 2005 and that Strategic Objective 4 is outdated as it does not reflect current day practice. This view suggests that it could be time to change the objectives and that a slavish adherence to them may not be in M plc's best interests.

Summary

When the effects of the change are considered together, X could argue that the favourable ones outweigh the adverse. If the forecast results turn out to be accurate the subscription website will make a very significant addition to revenue and profit. This should be sufficient to justify the change despite the conflict with two of the objectives.

Examiner's comments

This question was reasonably well answered. Most candidates focused upon the previous experience of X and correctly recognised the potential positive impact of Strategy 2 on profitability. Many candidates also correctly recognised that objective 4 is outdated and therefore the conflict with this objective is not relevant

Common errors:

- Some answers were brief and focused only upon the outdated objective

---

(c)   M plc's 200 websites constitute a product portfolio. One well known example of a product portfolio analysis model was developed by the Boston Consulting Group (BCG). The BCG analysis takes the form of a matrix with two axes:

Relative market share: this is calculated as the firm's market share against its largest rival

Market growth rate: this is the annual percentage change in sales volume in the industry or market.

The matrix is illustrated below:

Relative market share	Market growth rate	BCG category	Recommendation
High	High	Star	Invest to build
High	Low	Cash Cow	Hold
			Harvest
Low	High	Question mark	Invest to build
			Divest
Low	Low	Dog	Divest

The above recommendations give guidance as to future action but it could be dangerous to use them in a prescriptive manner. Like all models, the BCG matrix offers a structured way of dealing with complexity but it is only a representation of reality: it is not reality.

The important aspect for X of the BCG matrix in analysing the 200 websites is that it will give her an alternative perspective, in addition to profitability, when making the decisions about continuance or cessation. The combination of website profitability allied to a BCG categorisation should lead to a deeper understanding of each website's potential. Thus, for example, a website which shows a loss might have a high relative market share and a high market growth rate which would make it a 'Star'. The BCG approach suggests that Stars receive investment. They may well become 'Cash Cows' in the future and yield positive cash flows.

It will be necessary to construct a number of BCG matrices for the 200 websites. It may be appropriate to group some websites together, perhaps by market segment or by the visitors' demographic characteristics. X 'lacks detailed information about the websites' so she will need to obtain market data from search engines such as Google and Yahoo. Some of this data is free whilst other data will have to be paid for.

M plc will need to use software to carry out a BCG analysis on its 200 websites.

Examiner's comments

This question was generally not well answered. Most answers were awarded marks only for the description of the BCG matrix and few of these obtained the maximum 4 marks for this. This was largely due to the inaccurate description of 'market share' and not 'relative market share' and some candidates also failed to correctly plot the four categories of product within the matrix. This is a basic strategic management accounting model and it was disappointing to see how many candidates could not accurately present it. Very few candidates attempted to discuss its application directly to M or to consider the complexity of the task for M.

Overall, answers to this question were superficial and merely descriptive. Once again, advice to candidates is that they must demonstrate a much deeper understanding of the tools and models within the syllabus and must not only be able to apply them but also to discuss the complexities of application.

Common errors

- Merely descriptive answers

- Inaccurate representation of the model

- Limited or no application to M

(d) (i) The Web Division's Human Relations Manager, Z, has suggested a strategic headcount reduction programme which would mean a loss of 100 jobs.

Z has suggested that each of the 10 departments should declare 10 redundancies. As the departments are of different sizes the effect of this proposal would be disproportionate within individual departments. If this was applied strictly some departments, for example, Web Security would be reduced to one member of staff and so be unable to function which is likely to be injurious for the business. Z should consult departmental managers as to an appropriate number of staff they could forego and be willing to modify his proposal.

Z's criteria for redundancy are related to salary and age. These criteria are not related to the needs of the business, other than increasing profitability, and are discriminatory and probably illegal. These criteria appear to be unethical. Z should ensure that the criteria are lawful. He should seek guidance from a specialist in employment law.

Z has imposed this reduction programme upon the departmental managers and given them the unpleasant duty of notifying the staff that will be made redundant. This raises the possibility that the departmental managers will carry out this task according to their individual preferences. It would be advisable if Z organised some training for the managers and if the notifications were a joint responsibility of the Human Resources Department and the departmental managers.

Z's programme is a response to the Web Division's Managing Director's instruction to examine ways of enhancing efficiency and reducing costs. The reduction of 100 jobs will reduce costs but may impede efficiency. The programme could offer short-term gains at the expense of long-term losses.

Examiner's comments

This question was well answered as most candidates identified the weaknesses of the current SHRP presented in the unseen material. Many candidates correctly identified three weaknesses and were then able to present a good range of relevant and well discussed improvements. Many answers were well structured and well argued. However, some candidates did present very limited answers and presented only one or two possible solutions which were not necessarily related to the problems identified. Some candidates presented alternative organisational structures and incorrectly discussed proposals as an alternative to the headcount reduction. This was not required and failed to answer the question that had been set.

Common Errors

- Only providing one or two relevant improvements

- Failing to answer the question set by providing answers as an alternative to headcount reduction such as re-organisation

---

(ii) Z could use any, or some, of the following approaches to deal with any resistance to change arising from the strategic headcount reduction programme (SHRP):

Participation and involvement: the Web Division's staff could be invited to influence the structure of the Division post SHRP;

Education and communication: the Web Division's staff could be given accurate and up-to-date information about the Division after SHRP which could help to reduce stress;

Facilitation and support: the staff who will remain after SHRP will be given help to adjust to their new environment;

Negotiation: Z could attempt to reach an agreement between M plc's objectives with respect to the SHRP and the wishes of the Web Division's staff remaining within it after SHRP.

Examiner's comments

This question was well answered by most candidates. Most candidates used the Kotter and Schlesinger framework to structure their answer, which was appropriate. Some candidates used Lewin's change management model which was equally valid if applied correctly and directly to the scenario information. Candidates who merely described these models were awarded very few marks. Also, answers which focused upon management of staff made redundant were also awarded no marks as this was not asked for in the requirement.

Common Errors

*   Limited application of the models used

*   Focus upon management of those made redundant and NOT those who were retained

---

2   M PLC (MAR 12 EXAM)

Key answer tips

For part (a)(i) students were asked to calculate the number of pages of advertising that would have to be sold in order to breakeven in 2013, while offering the Daily Informer newspaper for free. At this level, students can be asked to perform a range of different calculations and this should not have been too challenging.

Requirement (a)(ii) asked for a discussion of the factors that would affect the free newspaper's ability to achieve the level of advertising outlined in (a)(i). Any reasonable comments would have scored here. Don't forget that the requirement was for a discussion – meaning that the examiner would have expected students to look at the issue from a positive and negative viewpoint.

Parts (a)(iii) and (a)(iv) asked students to link the proposed strategy to M's strategic and financial objectives and its CSR principles. Most of the pre-seen scenarios within E3 have contained information about the organisation's objectives and strategies and this requirement underlines the importance of making sure you have thought about them carefully before sitting the exam.

Part (b) asked students to use Porter's generic strategies to analyse the proposed change in strategy. This is a fundamental model in E3 and should never catch out a well-prepared student.

Part (c) should have represented relatively easy marks with a question surrounding Lewin's 3-stage model. Care was needed here as students would have needed to apply this to the scenario. A generic answer would not have scored well here.

(a)   (i)   **Final projections for FREE newspaper year ending 31 March 2013**

	Daily Informer £000s	FREE newspaper £000s	Comment
Revenue			
Circulation	23,400	0	No sales revenue from
Advertising	7,020	26,224	FREE
Total revenue	**30,420**	**26,224**	
Costs			
Journalists	8,400	3,150	Reduction of 125 jobs
Other staff	4,810	2,210	Savings of £2,600,000
Production costs:			
Fixed	3,180	3,180	No change
Variable	5,180	9,360	£0.03 × 1,000,000 × 312
Advertising costs	1,000	1,500	Increase of £500,000
Distribution costs	4,680	2,574	Saving of 45%
IT	4,000	2,000	Saving of 50%
Third party pictures/photos	3,000	2,250	Saving of 25%
Total costs	**34,250**	**26,224**	
Loss	**(3,830)**	**0**	**Break even**

In order to break-even the FREE 'Daily Informer' (hereafter FREE) must generate sufficient advertising revenue to pay for £26,224,000 of costs.

The managing director of the Newspaper division, S, has stated that FREE should sell its advertising space at £7,000 per page.

Therefore, the number of pages of advertising required to be sold in order for FREE to break even is £26,224,000/£7,000 is 3,746 pages per year or 12 pages per day (3,746/312 days).

Examiner's comments

This question was well answered by many candidates. Most were able to calculate the revised costs correctly, although very few calculated the production costs correctly.

The most common mistake was where candidates calculated only a cost variance or occasionally mixed cost variances with revised costs to come to an incorrect revised cost total. However, in general this question was well answered by most candidates.

Common errors

• Only calculating variances

• No calculation of the breakeven pages undertaken

(ii)   The requirement to sell 12 pages of advertising per day is a significant increase from the Daily Informer's current total of three pages. FREE will be a different newspaper and it will target a different market segment. It will no longer have a broad focus and its content will be very different. FREE will not necessarily be a successful newspaper especially as it has to compete with 'Opinion'

However, the factors which could enable FREE to sell 12 pages of advertising a day are:

Circulation: this is projected to rise from the current level of 150,000 copies to 1,000,000 copies per day. This is a very significant increase which should be attractive to advertisers. Further, FREE is offering its advertising for £500 a page cheaper than the Daily Informer which is another attraction.

As FREE is aimed at a different market segment this could also be attractive to advertisers if, for example, the readers in this segment have high spending power.

It is in the balance whether FREE will be able to sell enough pages to breakeven.

Examiner's comments

This question was generally not well answered. Most candidates only discussed the adverse factors which would affect the number of pages sold. This obviously then limited the marks awarded. Although these adverse factors were generally well discussed, candidates must remember that a discussion requires a review of both positive and negative or adverse and favourable aspects of the point under discussion.

Common errors

•   Only reviewing adverse factors

•   Focus upon the readers and not the advertisers

(iii)   M plc established the following strategic objectives in 2005:

1   *Meet the needs of readers for reliable and well informed news.*

If the Daily Informer is changed to FREE its character will change from one with a small circulation of 150,000 copies to a much greater circulation of 1,000,000 per day. The nature of the content will also change. However, these changes do not preclude FREE from providing reliable and well informed news: albeit for a different segment of newspaper readers.

The change to FREE is capable of fitting well with this objective.

2   *Expand the geographical spread of M plc's output to reach as many potential newspaper and website readers as possible.*

The increase in circulation implies that FREE fits very well with this objective.

3   *Publish some newspapers which help meet the needs of native English speakers who live in countries which do not have English as their first language.*

The proposed change to FREE does not address this objective.

4   *Increase advertising income so that the group moves towards offering as many news titles as possible, free of charge to the public.*

The change to FREE will increase advertising income from £7,020,000 to £26,250,000: a significant amount. The change fits very well with this objective.

In addition to these strategic objectives M plc has also developed the following financial objectives

(i)   *To ensure that revenue and operating profit grow by an average of 4% per year.*

The Daily Informer is forecast to lose £3,830,000 in the year to 31 March 2013. If the change to FREE is made and the required level of advertising sold it will contribute to this objective.

Although the outcome of the change to FREE is unknown the proposal fits with this objective.

(ii) *To achieve steady growth in dividend per share.*

The proposed change to FREE does not directly address this objective.

(iii) *To maintain gearing below 40%, where gearing is calculated as debt/(debt plus equity) based on the market value of equity and the book value of debt.*

The proposed change to FREE does not directly address this objective but may have a marginal favourable effect.

Summary

The proposal to change to FREE does not contradict any of M plc's objectives and broadly fits with four of them.

Examiner's comments

This question was reasonably well answered by most candidates. Most attempted to evaluate all of the objectives which was a marked improvement from the last examination.

However, there was some misinterpretation of the information, particularly in the evaluation of strategic objectives 1 and 2, as nearly all of the candidates stated that strategic objective 1 and 2 were not met. Most of these made an incorrect assumption that because the focus of the newspaper's readership has changed this meant that the quality of the articles and news had decreased. Clearly the newspaper is now targeting a new audience of readers who would be interested in this form of news and there was no information in the scenario to suggest that it would be less well informed or of a lower quality. Similarly for strategic objective 2, many candidates suggested that because the distribution points had reduced that this reduced the geographical spread. However, this does not take into account the fact that circulation has increased dramatically and that the objective also considers the issues of 'reaching as many newspaper and website readers as possible', which many candidates ignored.

Common Errors

• Assumptions made regarding the quality of the newspaper

• Misinterpretation of geographical spread

• Omitting to discuss the financial objectives

(iv)   Corporate Social Responsibility has been described as the firm's obligation to maximise its positive impacts upon stakeholders whilst minimising the negative effects.

There will be a number of social consequences if the move to FREE takes place:

Employment

A number of people will lose their job against a background of poor economic prospects and unemployment amongst newspaper workers:

(i)   *125 journalists* – although some journalists may find work on other newspapers, their general job prospects are not good.

(ii)   *Other staff* – the Daily Informer has forecast a £2.6 million saving in this area which equates to 70 jobs. The employment prospects for these people are not good.

(iii) *Newsagents* – the new distribution arrangements mean that some low-paid jobs will be lost.

(iv) *FREE distribution staff* – jobs will be created when distribution is outsourced to the transport specialist. This will offset, to an extent, the job losses in the newsagents.

(v)   *Advertising* – as FREE will sell 300% more advertising than the Daily Informer, this implies some increase in advertising jobs.

Generally, the employment effects of the change to FREE are adverse. However, the Daily Informer was losing money, and its circulation had fallen in the last ten years. It is possible that if the newspaper is not restructured it may have to close and many more jobs will be lost.

Environmental

The change to FREE could have an environmental consequence of creating litter. On the credit side, FREE will use recycled newsprint instead of new newsprint.

Readership

The Daily Informer caters for the 'the family' and has a broad focus. With the change in the newspaper's character FREE will no longer appeal to these readers who may feel some sense of loss.

However, there are other newspapers in the UK which these readers can buy. Further, FREE will be serving the needs of an enhanced circulation, 1,000,000 daily readers as compared to the Daily Informer's 150,000.

The societal consequences of changing the Daily Informer to FREE are significant. The change will cause adverse consequences as well as favourable ones. As society is made up of diverse opinions some people will judge the change to be a bad one: others will think it is a good one. **Examiner's comments**

> This question was not well answered. Most answers were very limited in scope and only recognised the negative impact of redundancies and the littering problem. Very few answers considered the possible benefits of the proposal. Many candidates failed to recognise that the environmental impact was reduced by the use of recycled newsprint and many answers incorrectly focused upon extra trees being cut down to accommodate the extra pages. Many answers did not discuss the issue of readership at all.
>
> Common errors
>
> - Limited answers not covering all of the areas in the requirement

(b)   Porter's generic competitive strategy model suggests that a sustainable competitive advantage can come in the following ways:

Cost leadership

FREE will be operating in a very competitive industry. Production technology within the industry is mature and most competitors are operating with modernised facilities. So it is unlikely that this area will yield a cost advantage.

The move to FREE will cause an £8 million reduction in its total costs because of employing fewer journalists, and savings in other costs. This implies that FREE could achieve cost leadership but will this be sustainable?

All the innovations implied in the move to FREE can be imitated by its competitors which suggests that achieving a sustainable competitive advantage is doubtful.

Differentiation

This strategy depends upon customers believing that FREE is superior to its competitors. In its current form of the Daily Informer it has established itself as 'the family newspaper with the broad focus' which represents a differentiation strategy. If the change to FREE is implemented this form of differentiation will be lost.

FREE is envisaged as imitating a competitor 'Opinion' with which it will form a new market segment. These will be the only free national newspapers in the UK. This offers FREE the chance of being perceived as superior to its competitors which now fall into two categories:

- Opinion

- Nine other daily newspapers

FREE has the potential to differentiate itself from its competitors. However, it has to deal with two disadvantages:

- Opinion has first mover advantage

- If the move to FREE is successful and takes away business from the nine other daily newspapers, any, or all of them, could follow Opinion and FREE and become free newspapers

The remaining way FREE could persuade its customers that it is superior is by its content. If, for example, it employed some of the Star journalists from other daily newspapers these should help to build a perception of superiority and increase circulation. (This could increase the cost base and so require more advertising to be sold.) This policy is easily imitated by FREE's competitors.

A differentiation strategy could yield a sustainable advantage for FREE. However, as its competitors could replicate many of the aspects of this strategy FREE will find it difficult.

Focus (Niching)

This aspect of Porter's model relies on FREE addressing the needs of a particular segment of the UK newspaper reading market. S's insistence that FREE should imitate Opinion has limited its scope in following this strategy. The segment within which FREE will operate will consist of readers interested in: '....advertising, no in-depth reporting and .....the activities of footballers and other celebrities'. To be successful with a Focus strategy FREE has to:

- Achieve a good understanding of its customers' needs for which it will need to carry out research

- Ensure that the market segment is large enough to sustain FREE

- Thoroughly understand its competitors

FREE has the disadvantage that the market segment within which it will be operating is very different from the one of which it has extensive experience and it cannot be sure at the outset that the segment is big enough to ensure FREE's continued financial success. Further, there are no significant barriers to entry to stop any of the other nine daily newspapers following Opinion and FREE into this segment.

A Focus strategy could offer FREE a competitive advantage. However, the paradox which FREE faces is that such an advantage is likely to invite imitation and is unlikely to be sustainable.

Examiner's comments

This question was not well answered. This was most disappointing as this has been examined on a number of occasions before and it was expected that candidates would be able to apply it well to FREE. Even more disappointing was the number of candidates who failed to correctly define the generic strategies, with many confusing differentiation with focus and some poorly defining cost leadership as relating to low price.

As stated in the scenario, FREE would be operating in a very competitive industry, where production technology is mature and most competitors are operating with modernised facilities. So it is unlikely that this area will yield a cost advantage. Although savings would be made in the loss of journalists and other staff, most of the innovations implied in the move to FREE can be imitated by its competitors which suggests that achieving a sustainable competitive advantage through cost leadership is doubtful. Most candidates failed to recognise that a cost advantage is unlikely to be sustainable.

FREE has the potential to differentiate itself from its competitors. However, the Opinion has first mover advantage and any or all of the other 9 competitors could follow Opinion and FREE and become free newspapers, meaning a differentiation strategy could yield a sustainable advantage but its competitors could replicate many of the aspects of this strategy. Again, few candidates discussed the sustainability of this strategy. The Focus aspect relied on FREE addressing the needs of a particular segment of the newspaper market. S's insistence that FREE should imitate Opinion has limited its scope in following this strategy, which very few candidates recognised. There are no significant barriers to entry to stop any of the other nine daily newspapers following Opinion and FREE into this segment.

Overall, many candidates' answers were descriptive and very few addressed the question requirement directly as most missed the issue of sustainability.

Common errors

- Lack of knowledge of the model and inability to apply

- Application of Porter's Five Forces model

(c)   Lewin's model consists of the following stages:

- Unfreezing

- Change

- Refreezing

Unfreezing

In this stage E will have to make the need for change so obvious that the staff will be able to understand the reasons for the change and accept it.

E should point to the Daily Informer's decline in circulation over the past ten years and also that it is forecast to make a loss. This should show the staff of the undesirability of the newspaper carrying on as it is.

E can also point out that (s)he has been indirectly instructed by the Chief Executive to bring about the change.

E could also help the staff 'unfreeze' by increasing their knowledge about the competitive environment faced by their newspaper.

Change

E will need to help the staff through the process of change by identifying for them, or helping them to identify for themselves what their role will be in FREE. E needs to tell the staff what the organisation's expectations will be so that the staff can, in time, internalise them. E will need to make them aware of the character of FREE and the readership which it will address.

In the new environment FREE will employ fewer journalists than the Daily Informer did. It will also have fewer other staff. Therefore, E will need to establish new internal reporting procedures and relationships and train the staff in these.

E could also introduce new reward and incentive schemes which reinforce the new required patterns of behaviour and so assist the staff adjust to them.

Finally, E could review and possibly replace the management style within FREE. As FREE is a very different sort of newspaper to the Daily Informer it may be appropriate to have a different management style, for example, it will operate 38% less staff and there should be a consequent reduction in management numbers and possibly levels. If a new, possibly more informal style of management is introduced, part of its focus could be to help staff make the transition to their new environment.

Refreezing

This part of the change consists of consolidation so that staff do not revert to previous patterns of behaviour. One way of helping the staff in this regard is by way of incentives. It could be made clear to staff that their remuneration is linked to their acceptance of the change: this might be done through a bonus scheme.

Staff could also be made aware that future promotions will be linked to their acceptance of change.

E could also encourage the persistence of the new behaviour by publicising success stories of staff or parts of the organisation that have embraced the change and benefited from it.

Examiner's comments

This question was well answered by most candidates. Many displayed a sound knowledge of the model and most were able to apply it directly to the change in working in the new Free environment.

---

3 B SUPERMARKETS (MAY 12 EXAM)

Key answer tips

For part (a) students were asked to calculate the number of store franchises needed to earn a minimum income level. This should not have been a challenging calculation. However, students needed to take care not to spend too long on this requirement as it was only worth four marks.

Requirement (b)(i) asked for a further calculation examining how long the franchises should be granted for. Remember that the calculations in E3 are rarely complex, but will require you to think about how best they should be tackled.

Parts (b)(ii) asked students to advise which additional factors would influence entrepreneurs when deciding on whether or not to invest in a franchise. Students had to focus on the angle requested by the question – this is from the franchisee's point of view, not B's. In addition, the question gave three headings and students needed to make use of these.

Part (c) asked students how the discount store business could assist B in increasing its sustainability. Remember that sustainability is a key topic and has been examined relatively frequently in the exam.

Part (d) should have been relatively straightforward, requiring students to advise B's management about the advantages and disadvantages of rolling out the new control systems across the entire company. As usual, any reasonable suggestions should have scored well.

(a)

	Month	Year	Inflow to B per year
	€	€	€
Revenue	100,000	1,200,000	
Variable operating costs	65,000	780,000	
Royalty fee	15,000	180,000	180,000
Service fee	5,000	60,000	60,000
Marketing contribution fee	5,000	60,000	60,000
Fixed costs	2,000	24,000	
Total costs	92,000	1,104,000	
Profit	8,000	96,000	300,000

B's minimum return is €3 million.

Each Country P franchise will produce €300,000 per year.

Therefore, the number of franchises required to satisfy B's minimum return is 10.

Examiner's comments

This question was well answered by most candidates. This should have been a straightforward calculation, requiring candidates to identify the relevant information from the unseen material to undertake the calculation. However, it was disappointing to see that a number of candidates failed to calculate the number of franchises correctly. This was mainly due to not reading the unseen information carefully in order to identify the minimum required fees per franchise payable to B. A number of candidates over complicated the question by introducing unnecessary fees into the calculation.

Common errors

- Incorrect calculation of minimum required income to be earned from the annual fees charged to the individual franchises.

(b) (i) **Franchisee's costs and returns**

Year		€	Present value (PV) factor	€ PV
0	Franchise/Training/ Equipment fees	230,400	1	(230,400)
1 – 3	Yearly inflow	96,000	2.402	230,400
			Net Present Value	0

The estimated cost of capital for franchisees in Country P is 12%.

The Present Value annuity factor for 12%/3 years is 2.402

Therefore, the minimum period for which a franchise should be granted in Country P to make it financially worthwhile, in terms of wealth, for an individual franchisee is 3 years (to the nearest year).

Alternatively, this investment if evaluated in terms of Payback shows the payback period to be (€230,400/€96,000) 2 years 5 months.

Examiner's comments

This question was reasonably well answered. Most candidates correctly calculated the total investment cost of the franchise and the annual inflows. From this, most were then able to calculate a minimum investment period of 3 years. Many candidates used a payback calculation which was also credited. However very few candidates used a 3 year annuity on the cash inflows to calculate an accurate period of investment. However, overall, most candidates made a reasonable attempt at the calculation to identify a reasonably accurate minimum investment period.

Common errors

• Incorrect calculation of the yearly inflow.

• No/ incorrect calculation of the PV factor.

(ii)   If an entrepreneur becomes a franchisee within Country P he/she will be operating within the following context:

'A franchisee is an individual who purchases the rights to use a company's trademarked name and business model to do business. The franchisee purchases a franchise from the franchisor. The franchisee must follow certain rules and guidelines already established by the franchisor, and in most cases the franchisee must pay an ongoing franchise royalty fee to the franchisor.'

The factors which are likely to influence such an entrepreneur include the following:

Marketing/Branding

B Supermarkets (B) trademarked name and business model

B is a multi-national grocery business and has traded since 1963. B has a total of 5,168 discount stores within Europe. Therefore, B has extensive experience of discount store retailing which is a strength. However, B 'needs to be aware of different customer tastes and preferences which differ from country to country' (pre-seen page 4). B does not have any discount stores in Country P and so may lack the necessary awareness of tastes and preference which is a possible weakness.

B is 'one of the largest retailing companies in the world' which suggests that consumers in Country P should recognise B's trademarks and business model which is a strength. However, there is no information as to the reputation of B so this could be either a strength or a weakness.

Competition

'Country P's retailing sector does not have any discount stores'. This has several implications for the entrepreneur considering a franchise. B's approach to discount retailing will be innovatory within Country P which could give a competitive advantage. If this is the case, the entrepreneur will want to assess the benefit of such a competitive advantage and its likely durability. Therefore, the entrepreneur is likely to want to assess the strength and speed of competitive reaction to the introduction of discount stores. Alternatively, B's approach to discount retailing may not be popular within Country P. Therefore, an entrepreneur considering a possible investment in a franchise would want to examine market research findings about its attractiveness.

Exclusivity

As well as a franchise giving the right to use B's brand identity it would be normal for the individual franchise agreement to give some rights regarding exclusivity. Thus, for example, a franchise may be given the exclusive right to operate within a five mile radius. The wider the boundary is set for exclusivity the more attractive the franchise will be to the entrepreneur.

Risk

Franchise purchase

In order to purchase the franchise the entrepreneur will need to invest €230,400. In terms of investor wealth, the franchise must have a minimum period of 3 years to produce an NPV of €0.

The answer to (b)(i) shows that the minimum period for a franchise to payback is 2 years 5 months. However, an individual entrepreneur is unlikely to want to undertake such an investment merely to be 'Paid-Back'. Therefore, the length of the franchise is likely to be a crucial factor in the decision to invest. How many years after payback is the franchisee likely to continue earning €96,000?

A franchise period of 20 years will be significantly more attractive than one of 5 years.

Equipment

The entrepreneur will have to pay €150,000 as an equipment fee. Therefore, the expected lifespan of the equipment and whether it will have any disposal value will be an important consideration. The responsibility and arrangements for servicing the equipment may also be an influence in the franchise decision.

Opportunity cost

As well as considering the opportunity cost of financing a franchise, an entrepreneur in Country P is likely to consider this investment in comparison to other investment opportunities.

Franchise implementation and operation

Rules and guidelines already established by the franchisor

Franchisors take care to ensure that their brand and corporate identity is not compromised by any of their franchisees. To this end, B will require rules and guidelines to be followed by its franchisees within Country P. There may also be some regulations within Country P that are a government requirement. The entrepreneur will incur costs in complying with these requirements. If the requirements are too onerous this may deter the entrepreneur from the investment. However, if the requirements seem reasonable and justified the entrepreneur should accept these as a part of doing business with B.

Ongoing franchise royalty fee

As part of the franchise agreement, B imposes a 15% royalty on each franchisee's revenue in Country P. (This has been taken into account in the calculations above.) The royalty is incurred irrespective of the level of revenue attained by any franchisee who could regard it as a tax and this might prove a disincentive. However, it could be argued that this 'tax' is paid out of incremental revenue and the higher the 'tax' the higher the profit. The payment of a royalty based on revenue is a normal feature of franchised businesses.

Service fee and marketing contribution fee

These fees are directly related to revenue just as the royalty is. Therefore, the same arguments apply as did in the case of royalties. The entrepreneur is likely to want to ensure that he receives value for money from the 'Service' and 'Marketing' for which he will be paying. Therefore, he would expect that any agreement entered into with B should state the purpose and benefits of these two fees.

Examiner's comments

This question was reasonably well answered by many candidates. Most used the headings provided in the requirement, which helped the candidates to structure their answers. Most candidates scored well on branding and marketing factors, recognising the potential strengths and weaknesses of B's brand and reputation in country P. The risk issues were not discussed as well, as most candidates merely focused upon generic environmental issues such as political, economic and social factors. Most of these were discussed in general terms rather than with specific application of their influence upon the entrepreneurs' decision to invest. Again, candidates are reminded to always make sure that they are applying their answers as much as possible to the scenario information.

Common Errors

•   Incorrect focus of answers upon the desirability to B of investing in Country P, rather than the desirability of the entrepreneurs investing in a franchise.

•   Generic discussion of risk factors based around the PEST factors, rather than a specific focus on the risks considered by the entrepreneurs.

(c)   B states in its mission statement that 'it practises sustainable investment'. (pre-seen page 3). Sustainability has been defined as 'using resources in such a way that they do not compromise the needs of future generations.' Sustainability is about implementing strategies that contribute to long-term success. This includes not polluting the environment at a rate faster than the environment can cope with.

B has established a number of environmental indicators in respect of sustainability: (pre-seen pages 5 and 6).

Consumption of kilowatt hours

B has set a target to reduce kWh per square metre of sales area. The discount stores will operate from new purpose built energy efficient premises. This should contribute positively to sustainability.

Number of free disposable plastic bags

B has set a target to reduce the number of free disposable plastic bags given to customers. The discount stores will operate without plastic bags being given to customers which will contribute positively to sustainability.

Greenhouse gas emissions

B has set target to reduce greenhouse gas emissions. The discount stores should function as carbon neutral businesses. This will contribute positively to sustainability.

Local amenity projects

B provides funding for local amenity projects in all the countries where it operates. There is no mention of such funding within Country P. In this aspect of the discount stores there is not a contribution to sustainability.

Distribution/Transport

B sources 20% of its requirements locally whereas Country P's discount stores will only source 10% locally. The discount stores in Country P will import 45% of their requirements by road and 45% by air. The distribution of products within Country P will be by road transport. When B uses rail transport in Europe this leads to lower greenhouse gas emissions than that experienced in America and Asia which use road and air transport exclusively. Thus, because of its higher requirement for imports and the use of road and air transport the discount stores within Country P are unlikely to contribute positively to sustainability.

Examiner's comments

This question was not well answered. Many candidates failed to link the information provided in the pre-seen material relating to B's sustainability targets and practices with the relevant information relating to sustainability of the franchise operations provided in the unseen material. Many answers were generic and speculative, focusing upon possible sustainability practices of B, rather than those which were specifically referred to in the unseen.

Common errors

- Little/ no focus upon the sustainability targets and practices presented in the pre-seen material.

(d) **Advantages**

B's management control system is bureaucratic and authoritarian. The reforms will introduce a significant degree of delegation and counteract these tendencies. The essence of the reforms is localism which is the belief that decisions are best made by people closest to operations.

The reforms would be very empowering for B's Regional Director for Discount Stores and would contribute to his personal development. He would agree a profit target with B's Chief Executive Officer. This would give the Regional Director access to B's most important decision-maker and also enable the Chief Executive Officer to better understand the discount store operation in Country P and to build a relationship with the Regional Director.

If the reforms are introduced throughout B they could assist the management development of B's executives.

B's current inventory management system leads to stock-outs and sometimes produces misleading information. The reforms enable the Regional Director to opt out of B's generic systems and construct his own. These could provide more accurate information for the Regional Director which would be of benefit.

If the reform was introduced throughout B then other executives could implement their own information systems and avoid the problems currently experienced within B's generic system.

Currently, 'The main Board members ....often stifle planning initiatives within each region' (pre-seen page 4). The reforms might remove 'stifling' as local managers are given greater autonomy.

B currently has a complicated organisational structure: (Appendix 1, page 7). This structure emanates from the scope and size of its business. However, it may, in part, be due to its current arrangements for planning and management control. If the reforms are implemented throughout B it might be possible to simplify B's organisational structure. This could lead to lower costs, better decision-making and increased responsiveness to the external environment.

Disadvantages

Even if the reforms led to the successful operation of Country P's discount stores there is no guarantee that they could be successfully extended throughout B.

B Europe's Regional Director for Discount Stores may not have the personality and experience to thrive in the reformed environment.

As B's executives have operated in a bureaucratic and authoritarian environment they may not have the personal skills to flourish in the new environment.

Localism could lead to many different operating styles and B would lose uniformity and possibly control.

If the reforms were introduced B could find that a great number of diverse information systems were in use. This could lead to problems in co-ordinating and reporting on its global operations. If local information systems were introduced this would involve B in additional cost.

Due to the demands placed on the Chief Executive Officer's time it might not be possible to allow every executive of the Regional Director's standing the opportunity to agree a profit target with the Chief Executive Officer. If this is the case, the arrangement between the Regional Director and the Chief Executive Officer might cause resentment among other executives who could feel excluded.

'Regional board members exercise strict financial and management control over operational managers in their regions in order to ensure that the main Board directives are carried out'. If the reforms are implemented within B, the regional board members would find that their strict control had been reduced. This could cause anxiety to these board members: it might also mean that main Board directives were not carried out.

The Corporate Affairs Director believes that B's procedures have 'served us well in the past'. There is a risk that the introduction of the reforms throughout B could be costly due to extra expenditures on information systems and training. It is likely that a number of B's employees would not have the skills to work in the new environment and so there would be costs associated with redundancy and recruitment.

The Corporate Affairs Director has also pointed out that 'In my opinion this (the reforms) is not how we do things.' The introduction of the new practices would involve a degree of cultural change which has its own costs and is difficult to achieve.

Examiner's comments

This question was generally well answered, although a number of answers were generic rather than applied directly to B. Candidates must remember that limited marks are awarded to generic and unapplied answers. Most candidates identified and discussed a reasonable range of both advantages and disadvantages of a reformed planning and control system, although some answers lacked application directly to B's operations in Country P. Some answers incorrectly focused upon the information systems only, discussing the advantages and disadvantages of unique information systems for Country P. This should have only formed part of the answer and therefore was awarded only limited marks.

Common errors

- Lack of application of answers to B.

- Bullet point based answers with limited discussion of each point identified.

4 B SUPERMARKETS (SEP 12 EXAM)

Key answer tips

For part (a) students were asked to calculate contribution margins and profit or loss for Country W, based on various differing assumptions regarding the closure of the hypermarkets division and the allocation of central costs. These should not have caused students too many problems but, as normal, care had to be taken not to spend too long on the calculations as they were only worth six marks.

Requirement (b) asked for a report, so students were expected to format their answers appropriately. The report asked for a discussion of the four arguments put forward by the sector manager (which could be used as headings within the answer) and the implications of closing the hypermarkets on B's future operations within Country W. Students had to be careful to ensure that they answered the question set here – it wanted implications for hypermarket closures within Country W – not on B as a whole.

Part (c)(i) required students to use Porter's generic strategies and apply it to B's operations in Country W. This is a key model within E3 and any well-prepared student should not have found this to be a difficult requirement. Part (c)(ii) then asked for some limitations of Porter's model, which was a pure book-work requirement and should also not have troubled a well-prepared student.

(a)   (i)

After closure of Hypermarkets	Super-markets € million	Hyper-markets € million	Discount Stores € million	Convenience Stores € million	Total € million
Revenue	**330.00**	**337.50**	**300.00**	**120.00**	**1087.50**
Variable costs					
Trading	198.00	182.25	225.00	72.00	677.25
Establishment	33.00	13.50	30.00	12.00	88.50
Total variable costs	**231.00**	**195.75**	**255.00**	**84.00**	**765.75**
Contribution margin	**99.00**	**141.75**	**45.00**	**36.00**	**321.75**
Fixed costs					
Regional office					340.00
Profit					**(18.25)**

Examiner's comments

This question was reasonably well answered. Many candidates correctly identified the sector contribution margins but there were a large number of candidates who calculated profit instead of contribution. Candidates are reminded to make sure that they read each question requirement very carefully and only answer the question that has been set. Profit per sector was not asked for in requirement (a)(i) and therefore no credit was awarded to candidates who calculated sector profits instead of sector contributions. A number of candidates calculated the sector contribution incorrectly which was most disappointing and demonstrates a fundamental weakness of basic knowledge of management accounting principles. This is not acceptable at this level and all strategic level candidates are expected to be able to calculate contribution with no problem.

Common Errors:

- Calculation of sector profit and not sector contribution

- Incorrect calculation of contribution

(ii)

	Super-markets € millions	Hyper-markets € millions	Discount Stores € millions	Convenience Stores € millions	Total € millions
Revenue	330.00	450.00	300.00	120.00	1,200.00
Variable costs					
Trading	198.00	243.00	225.00	72.00	738.00
Establishment	33.00	18.00	30.00	12.00	93.00
Total variable costs	231.00	261.00	255.00	84.00	831.00
Contribution margin	99.00	189.00	45.00	36.00	369.00
Fixed costs					
Regional office*	93.50	127.50	85.00	34.00	340.00
Profit/(Loss)	5.50	61.50	(40.00)	2.00	29.00
* Allocated on revenue					

(b) **Report**

To: The Regional Managing Director of Country W

Subject: An evaluation of the proposal to close Country W's Hypermarkets

From: Management Accountant

Date: September 2012

(i) This report addresses the following arguments put forward by the Hypermarket's Sector Manager.

1 *The current apportionment base of the regional office costs is unfair because these costs are not directly related to floor area but are more closely associated with the revenues generated by each of country W's four trading sectors.*

The Sector Manager has not produced any evidence in support of his argument. However, with regard to the first cost, insurances €35 million, this is likely to have a relationship both to the sectors' floor areas and also their revenues. The second component of the regional office costs, property taxes €100 million, is likely to be related to floor area.

No basis has been given for the biggest proportion of the regional office costs, B Supermarket's management charge €205 million.

Summary

This aspect of the Sector Manager's argument is supported in respect of insurances and property taxes.

2 *In terms of its trading performance the Hypermarkets sector is Country W's best sector.*

Before closure	Super- markets		Hyper- markets		Discount Stores		Convenience Stores		Total	
	€m	%	€m	%	€m	%	€m	%	€m	%
Revenue	330	*100*	450	*100*	300	*100*	120	*100*	1,200	*100*
Variable costs										
Trading	198	*60*	243	*54*	225	*75*	72	*60*	738	*61.50*
Establishment	33	*10*	18	*4*	30	*10*	12	*10*	93	*7.75*
Total variable costs	**231**	***70***	**261**	***58***	**255**	***85***	**84**	***70***	**831**	***69.25***
Contribution margin	**99**	***30***	**189**	***42***	**45**	***15***	**36**	***30***	**369**	***30.75***

The table above shows that the Hypermarkets have:

- The lowest variable costs percentage of 58%

- The highest contribution margin percentage of 42%

- The highest aggregate contribution margin of €189 million

Summary

The criteria above demonstrate that the Hypermarket sector is the best performing sector in Country W.

If the Sector Manager's argument is accepted regarding the alternate apportionment base of revenue, the Hypermarkets also show the greatest aggregate profit and the highest profit margin. However, caution should be exercised in using these results as decision criteria as they combine operational performance with central cost allocations.

3   *If any sector is to be closed it should be the discount stores and the convenience stores because their combined forecast revenues in the year ended 31 December 2012 is only €420 million which is €30 million less than the Hypermarkets' revenue.*

The results in table 3 show that the Discount Stores have:

- The highest variable costs percentage of 85%

- The lowest contribution margin percentage of 15%

And the Convenience Stores have:

- The second highest variable costs percentage of 70% (the same as Supermarkets)

- The second lowest contribution margin of 30% (the same as Supermarkets)

Summary

The selection of revenue as the criterion for making a decision about closing a sector is a naïve approach.

The most appropriate criterion, from a financial point of view, to use in making this decision is the sector's ability to generate contribution which, other things being equal, leads to the highest profit. However, other strategic factors should also be taken into account and these are discussed below.

4   *The regional office costs are too high and they contain a lot of wasteful expenditure. The sectors should not have to pay costs which they do not understand and did not authorise.*

The Sector Manager has not expressed the reason(s) for his assertion about wasteful expenditure. In this regard his argument is not well-founded. There is a degree of validity to the criticism regarding the sectors bearing a cost over which they have no control. However, the Sector Manager should realise that the Regional office costs do have to be paid and the sectors are the obvious place where this should occur.

Summary

The Sector Manager's argument has a limited degree of validity.

Examiner's comments

This question was not well answered by most candidates. Many candidates merely repeated or agreed with the four statements presented in the material, with little further evaluation. For example, in argument 1, candidates were expected to evaluate the argument relating to the fairness of the apportionment of the overheads based upon floor space. However, many candidates merely stated that this argument was either correct or incorrect with little or no justification for this statement. A number of candidates merely stated that apportioning overheads based upon revenues would be preferable but provided no justification for this suggestion. Candidates must make sure that any recommendation made must be fully explained and justified.

Many candidates made very naïve suggestions that the Hypermarkets Sector Manager was correct in argument 3 to state that the Discount stores and Convenience stores should be closed as their combined revenue was lower than that of the Hypermarkets sector. Clearly, the most appropriate criterion to use in making this decision is the sector's ability to generate contribution which, in turn, leads to the highest profit. However, many candidates merely agreed with the viewpoint expressed in the statement without any additional financial or strategic considerations. Candidates must evaluate the information they are provided with in the scenario, not just accept that it is correct.

Common Errors:

- Limited evaluation of the four arguments presented

- Thin and unjustified arguments presented

(ii)   **Strategic implication of closure**

If the Hypermarket sector is closed in Country W, it will have a direct effect on the forecast trading results. Table 1 shows that the forecast trading profit of €29 million would become a loss of €18.25 million. This is due to the loss of the Hypermarket's contribution margin of €47.25 million which would have been earned by the Hypermarkets' sector if it had continued to trade throughout 2012. The proportion of the Regional office costs that had been allocated to the Hypermarket sector do not disappear if the sector is closed down: they are reallocated to the remaining sectors.

If the Hypermarket sector is closed down, this will impinge upon the remaining sectors' ability to pay the Regional Office costs. Unless economies can be made or profits increased in the three remaining sectors their viability will be called into question. The decision to close the Hypermarket sector is likely to precipitate the total closure of B's business within W. This would result in B having to forego any future profits which in 2012 are forecast to be €29 million.

There may also be an effect on the remaining sectors in Country W if the closure of the Hypermarkets sector is received badly by the consumers in Country W. This may dissuade consumers from purchasing products from B's remaining stores. Other stakeholders such as the suppliers and the government in Country W may react badly to the closure. The suppliers might be concerned about the credit-worthiness of B and reduce their willingness to extend credit. The government may ask for repayment of any grants or subsidies it has given to B and it may sour its opinion of B which could affect B's future business within Country W.

The Hypermarket concept is a new one in Country W and B's brand is highly regarded in W. Currently, this sector generates a contribution of €189 million and it is possible that this could increase in future years if the sector is developed. The Hypermarket sector may have the potential to profitably transform B's business in W. Without Hypermarkets, B's business prospects in W look less optimistic.

If the Hypermarkets are closed, B is likely to incur withdrawal costs which may have a further impact on its business in W for the future.

The effects of closing the Hypermarkets will affect B not only in 2012 but also in years to come.

Conclusion

The decision to close Country W's Hypermarkets should not proceed because:

(i)   It would damage B's profits

(ii)   It would impede B's future operations within Country W

Examiner's comments

This question was not well answered. Many answers were very thin and lacked sufficient depth of discussion. Some candidates failed to answer this question at all.

The main weakness of answers to this question was that many candidates only considered a very narrow range of implications, such as the impact upon the reputation of B and the effect upon shareholders and employees. Very few candidates considered the wider implications upon stakeholders and the impact upon the remaining sectors. In addition few candidates considered the financial impact and the loss of Hypermarkets contribution margin of €47.25 million which would have been earned by the Hypermarkets' sector if it had continued to trade throughout 2012. Also few candidates recognised that the proportion of the regional office costs that had been allocated to the Hypermarket sector do not disappear if the sector is closed down and that they will need to be reallocated to the remaining sectors. Therefore, there was a lack of consideration of previous analysis in requirement (b)(i) of the answer carried through into this answer, which would have been useful. The question clearly asked candidates to evaluate the strategic implications that closing the Hypermarkets might have on B's future operations within Country W. However, most candidates failed to do this.

Requirements (b)(i) and (ii) asked for a report format. Many candidates provided a correct header but the final conclusion or summary was missing in the majority of reports. Candidates must make sure that if they are asked to present a report format, they use an appropriate structure throughout the whole of their answer.

Common Errors:

•   A narrow range of factors considered

•   Limited evaluation of the impact of the factors identified

•   Poor/incomplete report structure

(c)   (i)   Porter's model of generic competitive strategies uses the following categories:

- Differentiation
- Cost leadership
- Cost focus
- Differentiation focus

Supermarkets

This sector has a 'very economical cost structure'. Therefore, it is reasonable to infer that B could attain a competitive advantage by following a **Cost Leadership** strategy: that is, it will thrive whilst charging industry average prices because of its reduced costs. It also has the option of trying to increase its market share by undercutting its two rival's prices but still make a reasonable profit because of its cost structure. This option could be successful for B because the sector is price sensitive. However, this option has the danger that it could provoke retaliatory action from the two rivals and lead to a price war which could prove to be disadvantageous to all three market participants. However, the Supermarkets' very economical cost structure should enable it to withstand a price war better than many of its competitors.

B's comparative cost advantage emanates from the position of many of its supermarkets and this gives it the potential for following an alternative strategy, **Cost Focus**. This implies that it could cater for niche markets within its supermarkets and charge differential prices according to location. However, this strategy would detract from the national brand identity of the Supermarkets sector and for that reason is not recommended.

Recommendation

The supermarkets sector should follow a strategy of Cost Leadership.

Hypermarkets

B's brand is highly regarded with a high reputation for quality. B currently has 85% of this market. The sector's customers are affluent and willing to travel a considerable distance in order to buy high value, up market branded items some of which are exclusive to B. The sector's customers value quality and are willing to pay a premium for it. B is already pursuing a strategy of **Differentiation** whether by design or by accident: that is, it is offering its customers products/services that are different from, or more attractive than, those of its competitors. B is in a powerful position because its offerings coincide with its customers' preferences.

The main problem with the sector is that hypermarkets are a new concept in Country W and B only has one competitor which is trading at a loss. Thus, it is reasonable to characterise demand as being unsophisticated and competition as weak. The stimulus for the maintenance of B's market dominance and improvement to its customer offerings will have to be internal to B.

Recommendation

This sector should follow a strategy of Differentiation.

Discount stores

This sector has a mixture of characteristics for B. Its brand is highly regarded and it has a limited range of branded and own branded products. Some of its competition is trading at a loss and is very badly organised. These characteristics suggest that a strategy of Differentiation could be successful for B in this sector and that it could charge a premium price for its products.

However, the sector's customers are extremely price sensitive and expect prices to be lower than in the hypermarkets. Further, some of B's competitors are strong; being very profitable, innovative and efficient. This is reflected in B's market share of 15%. For these reasons it is unlikely that B could successfully gain a competitive advantage over its strong competitors by following an overall strategy of Differentiation. This suggests that B, which does not have a cost advantage, should follow a Differentiation Focus strategy where it could concentrate on particular niches within the Discount Stores market, through its understanding of the market segment and the needs of those customers within it.

Recommendation

B's discount stores should implement a strategy of Differentiation Focus.

Convenience stores

The sector manager has referred to B being 'stuck in the middle'. When Porter developed his ideas about generic competitive strategy he cautioned against trying to satisfy customers in every possible way because this would lead to a lack of clear identity, the pursuit of competing strategies within the same organisation and a lack of success. This seems to be the position the discount stores have achieved. B has no clear identity, some of its convenience stores are leaders and others are laggards. This market segment is dominated by one national chain which with 65% of the market is dominant. B with a market share of 10% will find it difficult against this chain. However, the remainder of the market, 25%, is fragmented and this could be a most rewarding area for B in which to compete. Thus, B is probably constrained into adopting a **Differentiation Focus** strategy because it:

- has no cost advantages

- is unlikely to be successful competing nationally against the market leader

- has some local dominances

Recommendation

B's Convenience Stores should follow a strategy of Differentiation Focus.

Examiner's comments

This question was reasonably well answered. Candidates were expected to use the information provided in the table within the scenario to evaluate and recommend the most appropriate competitive strategy for each of Country W's business sectors. Most candidates adequately used the information provided in the scenario to recommend an appropriate competitive strategy for the Supermarket and the Hypermarket sectors. However, few candidates made correct recommendations for focus based strategies for the Discount and Convenience stores.

It was disappointing to see that there are some candidates who still do not understand the generic strategies model and who have great difficulties in applying this model to a scenario. This has been examined on several occasions in past examinations and candidates should be aware that this is an important strategic concept which will regularly be examined in E3.

Common Errors:

- Some candidates provided an overall competitive strategy for B instead of providing a competitive strategy for each sector

- Some candidates did not know /understand the model, making recommendations such as 'follow a cost differentiation leadership strategy'.

(ii)   Porter's model has received a wide degree of acceptance. It provides B with a structure which could help it achieve competitive advantage for its different sectors. However, the model has been criticised for the following aspects.

Stuck in the middle

Porter's assertion that this is not a viable strategy is belied, to an extent, by companies which have entered a market as niche/Focus participants and expanded successfully using a mixture of strategies

Simplistic

The presentation of the model with its two axes of competitive scope and competency are not rich enough to capture the complexity of modern business and consumer behaviour.

Restrictive

The dominance of the models may restrict strategists' thinking when other more innovative solutions could be more appropriate.

Market volatility and turbulence

These factors militate against Porter's model which might restrict managers' adaptiveness.

Topicality

The basic model was published in 1980 since when the business world has changed greatly. Strategic choice may be more complex in 2012 which inhibits the model's utility.

Candidates were required to give two limitations. More have been given in this answer as a teaching aid.

Examiner's comments

Most candidates could identify at least one limitation of the generic competitive strategies model but, in general, answers were very thin and often presented as bullet point lists. The question verb used was 'advise', which required candidates to do more than merely list the limitations of the model.

Many answers also failed to focus directly upon the direct limitations of Porter's model and instead identified areas which were not meant to be dealt with by the model. For example, some candidates stated that the generic strategies model failed to consider the PEST factors of the general environment. However, it was never designed to consider these factors. Candidates must make sure that they only consider the weaknesses of the actual model itself, not the fact that it does not do the job of other models that it was never designed to do.

Common Errors:

- Unexplained bullet point answers

- Inappropriate weaknesses not directly associated with the model itself

5 V (NOV 12 EXAM)

Key answer tips

For part (a) students were asked to looking at the benefits of emergent versus long-term strategic planning. This is not an unusual requirement, but the key here was ensuring that your answer was linked to V itself. Generic lists of points would have been unlikely to score well.

Requirement (b) asked for a calculation of the net operating profit and percentage for V's three main product types, followed by an analysis of how these could be improved. The E3 exam will typically have 10 to 15 marks for calculations within the A section question, so this requirement was not a surprise, but students would have needed to read the question carefully to identify all the figures that needed adding into the requirement. When commenting on how to improve the profitability of each product, students were expected to refer back to the figures they had calculated earlier. It was important to read the full requirement here – marks were also available for suggesting other information that was required to make a full analysis.

Part (c)(i) examined Customer Relationship Marketing. Students again needed to read the requirement carefully and look at the strategic AND competitive impact. In addition, note the word 'evaluate' in the requirement. A weighted argument was required here to get full marks.

Finally, (c)(ii) asked for two strategic benefits and two strategic barriers to e-business. This would have given three marks for each point made, so it needed carefully applying to V – students needed to explain WHY it's a benefit or drawback to get some potentially easy marks here.

(a) An emergent approach to strategy is one which tends to emerge over time rather than being the result of a rational and logical formal strategic planning process. An emergent approach is likely to evolve continuously and incrementally in response to the changing environment of the business.

Benefits to V of an emergent approach

V will be able to take advantage of emerging trends and therefore react more effectively to customer demands and tastes. For example, should the social or economic conditions change in a particular holiday region then V will be able to react to this and respond more effectively in terms of changing holiday destinations or the price of products.

An emergent approach also allows V to be more innovative and creative in the development of products and service delivery as it can react to the latest and most current trends in the holiday market. For example, the demand for online booking by customers drove the strategy to introduce the online booking facility in V.

V will also be able to try and test a strategy whilst it is being implemented and thus it can be adapted and changed where necessary over time. The holiday market is likely to be an evolving one where customer preferences and tastes for locations and activities will change and therefore an emergent approach allows V strategic flexibility.

Examiner's comments

This question was reasonably well answered. Most candidates could correctly define an emergent approach to strategy development and also identify a number of benefits of this approach. The main weakness of answers to this question was that some candidates spent too long discussing the drawbacks of a rational approach to strategic development which was not asked for and therefore awarded no credit. Candidates must make sure that their answers focus directly upon the question that has been set. In addition, some answers were very generic and did not apply the benefits of an emergent approach directly to V and its travel business. Candidates who presented generic answers were not awarded a pass mark.

Common errors:

- Generic answers not applied directly to V

- Discussion of rational planning instead of emergent approach

---

(b) (i) **Holiday product net operating profit calculation**

	PACKAGE	ADVENTURE	PRESTIGE
In branch administration costs			
Holidays ordered in branch	1,800,000	900,000	10,260,000
Late booking processing cost	420,000	72,000	410,400
After sales and complaints	445,500	82,500	7,053,750
Total in branch admin costs	2,665,500	1,054,500	17,724,150

In branch net profit calculation:	GP%		GP%		GP%	
Gross Profit (In-Branch Revenue x GP%)	40	3,600,000	35	1,050,000	25	21,375,000
Operating profit		934,500		(4,500)		3,650,850
Operating profit %		**10.4%**		**(0.2%)**		**4.3%**

On- line administration costs

Holidays ordered on line		6,000,000		6,000,000		380,000
Late booking processing cost		4,200,000		1,440,000		45,600
After sales and complaints		4,455,000		1,650,000		783,750
Total on line admin costs		14,655,000		9,090,000		1,209,350

On line net profit calculation:	GP%		GP%		GP%	
Gross Profit (On-line Revenue x GP%)	40	32,400,000	35	19,950,000	25	2,375,000
Operating profit		17,745,000		10,860,000		1,165,650
Operating profit %		**21.9%**		**19.1%**		**12.3%**

Weighted Profit					
	In branch	1%	0.0%	4%
	On line	20%	18%	1%
	Overall profitability	**21%**	**18%**	**5%**
	In branch admin cost per product	888.50	703.00	1,036.50
	On-line admin cost per product	488.50	303.00	636.50

Examiner's comments

This question was reasonably well answered by a large number of candidates. It was very encouraging to see that most candidates made a good attempt at this question even if they did not achieve the correct final answer. However, many candidates did so.

> Most candidates correctly identified the number of holiday products booked online and in-branch and this was the starting point for the rest of the calculations. The main weakness of answers was that some candidates made very basic calculation errors when calculating the apportionment of the late booking and after sales costs. Also, some candidates omitted cost of sales from the net operating profit calculations or made very basic addition and transcription errors when arriving at their final net operating profit calculations. Some candidates failed to split their calculations of profitability between online and in-branch bookings. Those candidates who took this approach were not awarded full marks as they failed to answer the question that had been set. Candidates must make sure that they read the question requirements carefully.
>
> Common Errors:
>
> * Basic addition and transcription errors
>
> * Not splitting operating profit and operating profitability between in-branch and online bookings
>
> * Using the incorrect cost of sales percentage or failing to calculate cost of sales at all in arriving at net operating profit and operating profitability.

(b) (ii) *Note: Candidates are not expected to provide any further calculations in answer to this question. These calculations are for additional information and analysis purposes.*

Administration costs	Package	Adventure	Prestige Travel	TOTAL V	
Holiday order per annum in-branch	1,800,000	900,000	10,260,000	12,960,000	28%
Holiday order per annum -online	6,000,000	6,000,000	380,000	12,380,000	27%
Late booking processing	4,620,000	1,512,000	456,000	6,588,000	14%
After sales and complaints	4,900,500	1,732,500	7,837,500	14,470,500	31%
Total administration costs	**17,320,500**	**10,144,500**	**18,933,500**	**46,398,500**	**100%**
	37%	22%	41%	100%	
Total products booked	**33,000**	**31,500**	**19,000**		
	SK$	SK$	SK$		
Admin cost per product booked	524.86	322.05	996.50		

Prestige Travel holidays

The Prestige Travel holiday products incur a significant proportion of the total administration costs of V (over 40%). A significant proportion (80%), of the in-branch services offered by V are taken up by the Prestige Travel customers, largely because 90% of Prestige Travel holiday products are being booked in-branch. The analysis in (b)(i) shows that the overall operating profitability of the in-branch services offered to the Prestige customers is only 4.3% which is significantly lower than the online profitability. Although online profitability is higher at 12.3%, this is still lower than the other two products due to the higher proportion of after sales queries and complaints by Prestige Travel customers. When the online and in-branch profits for Prestige Travel are weighted in terms of the proportion of holidays sold, it can be seen that the overall profitability of the Prestige Travel product is only 5%, which is significantly lower that the other two holiday products. Therefore, the assertion made by the Executive Chairman is incorrect.

V should try to encourage its Prestige Travel customers to use its online booking facilities more effectively, possibly by offering incentives or higher discounts for Prestige Travel online bookings and repeat bookings.

A major cost incurred by the Prestige Travel bookings is the after sales cost and complaints processing, as 55% of V's after sales and complaints costs are driven by Prestige Travel customers. It is not clear from the information if these are predominantly changes to bookings after the original sale or if they are complaints after the holiday but it is clear that these costs urgently need to be reviewed and managed more effectively. V must investigate the booking process to analyse why Prestige Travel customers are making after sales enquiries or changing their requirements after the sale. This could require improved customer sales representative training to ensure that customers' needs are fully addressed prior to booking.

Similarly, V must undertake a thorough investigation of its complaints processing so that all necessary activities are being carried out to ensure that customer needs are being met. The cost of each after sales/complaints process is SK$550 which is high and V must investigate not only how to reduce the number of complaints and queries but also the cost of handling them. Currently a specialist team deals with V's customer complaints and after sales and V should investigate how this team's activities could be improved or possibly handled more effectively in-branch. The use of IS/ IT systems in handling after sales issues should be considered.

As stated above, the weighted overall operating profit percentage for the Prestige Travel product is the lowest and is significantly lower than V's overall operating profit of 14%. This is driven by the high level of administration activities and costs incurred, which clearly must be reviewed. If V were to reduce these administration processes for the Prestige products, then this could significantly increase operating profit.

Adventure holidays

The Adventure holiday products are not causing V to incur administration costs at the same rate as the other two holiday products. Only 22% of the total administration costs incurred by V are caused by Adventure holiday products. 95% of the bookings are made online, thus reducing booking costs significantly compared to the Prestige Travel products. The net operating profitability of the online bookings for Adventure holidays is high at 19.1%. The operating profitability for the in-branch bookings is negative but not significant as they only account for a very small proportion of the overall activities of V. However, V should consider how it could encourage all of V's potential Adventure holiday customers to book online in future. They could consider only offering the Adventure holiday products online.

After sales and complaints are significantly lower for Adventure holidays, possibly due to most on these products being booked online and therefore potentially less sales rep errors or misinterpretation of requirements. The overall operating profit at 18% is high compared with Prestige Travel and it is recommended that V undertakes a thorough analysis of the Adventure holiday product booking processes in order to use these as a benchmark for the other two product types.

Package holidays

The Package holidays also incur significant administrative costs (37% of the total). However, the profitability both in terms of online and in-branch bookings is comparatively high against Prestige Travel holidays. In fact, overall, the Package holiday product is the most profitable for both online and in-branch bookings.

A significant proportion of its administration costs (27%) are due to late bookings, which occur at a rate of 35% of the total proportion of Package holiday products booked. V could consider either charging additional fees for late bookings or alternatively offer incentives such as discounts for early bookings. Costs associated with after sales queries and complaints are also high for Package holiday customers. There is not enough information to ascertain whether this is due to booking errors or complaints, but, either way, this is something that V must investigate and ensure that customer after sales queries are minimised and complaints eradicated or dealt with more effectively. Package holiday products achieve the highest level of absolute operating profit but, again, this could be significantly improved if late bookings and after sales queries and customer complaint costs were reduced.

Other information for consideration:

Branch closure

V could consider the closure of some of its branches, providing that fixed costs could be reduced as a result. Overall in-branch profit is considerably lower than operating profits earned online and that operating costs could be saved if some of the branches were closed. Clearly it would require further information on the viability of this option and the impact upon the staff and upon the image of the organisation. The closure of the branches could adversely affect the visibility of the organisation, and may adversely impact on the Prestige Travel and Package business. The Executive Chairman is also likely to resist this option as he appears to value the customer service offered by V most highly.

Late booking costs

More automation of late bookings to reduce this cost item. Of the 83,500 holidays booked by V, nearly 16,500 holidays are late bookings (20%), 70% of which are from Package holidays booked. The cost of handling late bookings is very high and improved IT systems and better procedures could reduce this cost.

Complaints and queries

V spends a total of nearly SK$15million on after sales queries and complaints. This is huge and represents nearly one third of the total administration costs incurred. Therefore V must improve the quality of its booking processes through better training of employees. It must have improved training of sales reps to reduce errors of misleading customers. Handling of complaints should be done more in-branch.

Examiner's comments

This question was reasonably well answered by most candidates. However, some candidates spent too long discussing the results of the previous calculations with limited discussion of methods to improve profitability. Some credit was given for analysis of the results of the calculations but this was not enough to pass this requirement as the question clearly asked for recommendations for improvements to product profitability for the three holiday products types. Most candidates correctly identified a number of improvements relevant to the scenario information such as improved training and discounts and incentives for early bookings. However, some candidates missed the point by discussing issues such as reducing cost of sales and offering different holiday products.

Common Errors:

- Too much analysis of the results of the calculations with limited focus on profit improvements

- Incorrect focus of improvements

(c)   (i)   **Customer Relationship Marketing**

Customer relationship marketing is the devotion of marketing resource to maintaining and exploiting the organisation's existing customer base, rather than using resources solely to attract new customers. It focuses on developing a long term relationship with a customer, and securing their loyalty.

Strategic impact

CRM should enable V to retain its customers which should result in it achieving competitive advantage over its rivals. If V were to undertake customer relationship marketing, this would involve V concentrating its marketing efforts upon increasing customer loyalty and demonstrating clear commitment to the customers' needs.

CRM would require V to reconsider its current approach of reliance on word of mouth based marketing and would have to consider a more direct marketing approach to ensure that customers' needs are satisfied.

CRM is likely to need a greater focus on customer care and service needed and this may involve additional costs in customer care training. However, in the long term, these costs should diminish and should result in improved customer loyalty.

CRM would require better training of customer sales representatives and regular updates on products and the use of product and booking software are necessary. V also needs to ensure that it focuses upon the quality of customer service.

Relationship marketing may involve more on-going costs for V but these may be outweighed by the benefits of improved customer retention.

However, any customer relationship marketing activities must be analysed to ensure that customers actually perceive the benefit they have received and remain loyal to V.

Competitive impact

CRM activities could include offering loyalty rewards for customers (such as discounts on the next holiday booking), as the retention of customers is a critical business issue. V is working within a competitive business environment and the Operations Director has recognised that competitive forces have made customer retention more difficult. Customers are now more likely to shop around for the best holiday deals and customers are not necessarily loyal to one holiday company or one travel agent.

The main competitive threat to V appears to be from the proliferation of online tour holiday operators and travel agency services. V needs to determine whether the online competitors offer incentives or discounts for online activity and, if so, V needs to develop its CRM activities to counter this. Many of V's customers do book online and, therefore, V needs to identify the CRM approaches which could target these customers. V also needs to consider how competitors may react to CRM approaches offered by V, particularly if CRM can be delivered more effectively online than in-branch.

Clearly, online competitors are a threat and V needs to decide whether to meet this competitor head on or to focus more upon its in-branch services and promote this as a differentiating factor. Either way, focusing upon high levels of customer service in order to obtain repeat business and loyalty will be a key factor in relationship marketing for V.

Examiner's comments

This question was generally not well answered. Although most candidates could define CRM, few could clearly discuss the impact it would have upon V and its ability to retain customers. Many answers focused largely upon the benefits of CRM without any consideration of the costs and impact upon V's way of operating. Most answers were largely generic and descriptive rather than directly applied and therefore marks were often limited. However, there were some very good answers, where candidates recognised the importance of CRM to V and the potential impact upon its competitive advantage.

Common Errors:

- Generic answers discussing only the benefits of CRM in general terms

---

(c) (ii) **Strategic Benefits of e-business to V**

V could benefit from increased revenues due to having more online sales and improved customer relationships which could lead to repeat business. V could reduce its costs and overheads due to improved procurement systems and linkages to the main suppliers such as airlines and hotels. Overall, this should enable V to achieve improved profitability.

V could benefit from better information for control and performance measurement purposes. V could use the online information to analyse sales data and customer performance to improve future decision making.

V could benefit from improved marketing to its customers via email with specific information targeted to specific customers with interests in specific holiday products. Again, greater targeted marketing should improve customer relationships and customer retention. V could achieve increased visibility through greater exploitation of its websites. This could lead to a much wider customer base for V, leading to greater market penetration.

Strategic Barriers of e-business to V

A barrier may be that V's customers may not want to transact online – particularly the Prestige Travel customers who prefer a more personalised service. For the higher-end expensive holidays, customers prefer to discuss options with in-branch customer representatives and may look elsewhere if the customer service is replaced by online business.

Security concerns may be an area of risk when V is holding confidential customer data which can be hacked or corrupted. Investment in security of its electronic systems will have to be a high priority and likely to be costly which could be a significant barrier to V.

The costs of setting up, running and enhancing an e-business may be prohibitive to V which is a relatively small tour operator compared to the large international chains.

The IT department of V is not likely to have the experience to sufficiently exploit the potential for e-business. V would have to invest in quality and highly trained staff, which is likely to be costly.

Note: Students were only required to present two strategic benefits and two strategic barriers.

Examiner's comments

This question was reasonably well answered. Most candidates correctly identified two benefits of e-business and were able to apply these to V. The main weakness of answers to this question was in discussing the barriers of e-business. Many candidates incorrectly focused upon the possible disadvantages of e-business such as competitors' reaction and price transparency. However, these are not considered to be real barriers to V implementing e-business, as they would not necessarily stop V from doing it. Competitors' reaction is likely to be inevitable but would not stop V from operating as an e-business if it meant survival. Overall, most candidates applied their answers well in this question but some answers were thin and lacked real discussion. This question was worth 12 marks, meaning that each benefit or barrier was worth 3 marks. However, many answers lacked sufficient depth of discussion to be awarded these marks.

Common Errors:

- Thin and poorly discussed answers

- Focus upon disadvantages rather than barriers to V of e-business

---

6 V (MAR 13 EXAM)

Key answer tips

In requirement (a)(i) candidates are expected to undertake a portfolio analysis of V's current three products, using the BCG matrix. This should be a straightforward question, using the information provided in the scenario to evaluate the market growth and the market share of the three product types.

Requirement (a)(ii) is a straightforward Expected Value calculation, identifying the different levels of profit which could be achieved by the proposed V-eco holidays, taking into account the probabilities of the market share achievable. Candidates should produce a final profit based upon the three different levels of market share achievable and calculate a final Expected Value profit. Candidates should only produce calculations in this answer. No discussion of the calculations is required.

Requirement (a)(iii) requires candidates to evaluate the results of their calculations and to use this, together with their evaluation of V's current product portfolio, to assess whether V should offer V-eco holidays. This requirement carries 12 marks and therefore a full discussion of both quantitative and qualitative factors is required. Candidates must present a final recommendation.

Requirement (b) requires candidates to present and justify a critical success factor for each of the holiday product types, including the proposed V-eco holidays. It is designed to examine the candidates' ability to analyse the information presented in the unseen material in order to identify those areas of V's business that it must get right. It is important that candidates clearly discuss the critical success factors chosen and their relevance to each of V's holiday products.

Requirement (c) should be a straightforward question requiring candidates to apply their knowledge of Lewin's 3 stage model to overcoming the possible resistance that may occur as a result of the proposed changes to improve customer services.

(a) (i) **BCG Matrix**

Relative market share

		High	Low
	High	**Star** **Prestige Travel** Cash Neutral	**Question Mark** **Adventure** Cash User
Market growth			
	Low	**Cash Cow** **Package** Cash Generator	**Dog** **None** Cash Neutral

Package

The Package products are likely to be classified within the BCG matrix as a cash cow, as they appear to have a high relative market share in a low growth market. The Package products also generated SK$90 million of V's revenue in the year ended 30 June 2012 which is nearly 36% of the total. The Package products have been a mainstay of V's business since it began and now have an advantage in economies of scale for V. Although not specified in the unseen material it is also likely that the slowing growth in the package holiday market implies that capital investment in these products is low and hence a cash surplus is occurring. It is important for V to maintain the Package product as it is likely to support the other products in the portfolio. Although growth may be low it does not mean that there is no growth and therefore there is still an opportunity for V to exploit further sales in this market. This may require additional promotion, advertising activities and offers which would appeal to the Package holiday customers overall preference for value for money.

Adventure

These are likely to be classified as Question Marks within the BCG matrix, as the growth in the adventure holiday market is high but V's relative market share is likely to be low as there are two other competitors in SK holding a 65% share of the market, with V holding a 20% share. The Adventure product only generated SK$60 million in revenue in the year ended 30 June 2012 (24% of V's revenue). However, clearly there is a growing opportunity for the development of V's Adventure products as demand is growing and more destinations are becoming available. However, it is likely that to turn these question marks into star products V will have to undertake significant investment. This is likely to be required in both the destinations offered and in the online booking facilities that V offers to its Adventure holiday customers. V must weigh up the costs of this investment with the anticipated benefits of increased market share in a highly competitive market place. Competition is currently intense and with high demand expected, this competition is likely to increase. Therefore, V needs to decide if it can continue to operate successfully by developing its available destinations.

Prestige Travel

These holidays are likely to be classified as Stars within the BCG matrix as V has a high relative market share in a growing market. V believes there are still significant opportunities to develop this product but this will require large amounts of investment to build and sustain this growth. Another competitor in SK could challenge the market leadership of V and therefore V must invest to ensure that it maintains its current strong position in the market and it maintains its high levels of customer service. V should ensure that its focus upon customer service and quality of product offered is maintained and improved upon. V should focus upon ensuring repeat business and exploiting its high customer service levels and reputation. This could be used as a key marketing and promotional tool. The main competitor is a real threat to V and therefore it must be aware of this challenge and be able to respond; possibly with in-store promotional activities and commitment to continued high levels of training for staff in customer service.

(a)   (ii)   **Possible outcomes**

Y/e 30/06/2014	Market share	**25%**	**20%**	**10%**
	Market	33,000	33,000	33,000
	V share	8,250	6,600	3,300
		SK$	SK$	SK$
Revenue		31,350,000	25,080,000	12,540,000
Variable costs		20,377,500	16,302,000	8,151,000
Contribution		10,972,500	8,778,000	4,389,000
Fixed Costs		5,000,000	5,000,000	5,000,000
Operating Profit		**5,972,500**	3,778,000	- 611,000
Probability		0.2	0.3	0.5

	Best Case		**Worst Case**	**Expected Value**
Operating Profit	1,194,500	1,133,400	- 305,500	**2,022,400**
Revenue	6,270,000	7,524,000	6,270,000	**20,064,000**
Profitability	19%	15%	-5%	**10%**

However, a significant proportion of the candidates either provided no attempt at the calculations or provided calculations which were very poor. Some candidates clearly do not understand what is meant by 'Expected Value' and incorrectly used the probabilities and market share information. More worryingly, some candidates made very basic management accounting mistakes, such as calculating the contribution margin after deducting fixed costs or omitting to include the variable costs at all. These kinds of basic mistakes around fundamental management accounting principles are unacceptable and should not be happening at strategic level.

Common Errors:

* Omitting to calculate the best and worst outcomes

* Incorrect use of the probability information

* Omission of variable costs from the calculation of operating profit

* Demonstration of a basic lack of understanding of contribution and operating profit

(a)   (iii)   Taking into account the market research information and the estimates provided, the V-eco holiday products would have an expected value of operating profit of just over SK$2million. The criterion set by the Finance Director was that unless the proposal offers at least SK$2million profit for the year ended 30 June 2014 it is unlikely to be accepted by the Board of Directors. Therefore, this proposal meets the criterion using an Expected Value calculation. However, V must also consider a number of other factors before making such a decision.

If V were to offer V-eco holidays, then this would provide V with an opportunity to expand its product range. As it is forecast that there is a growing demand for this type of holiday, then V could grab an early dominant market share if it chose to expand into this product now, rather than at some time in the future. However, the probabilities indicate that there is a 50% chance that V will only obtain 10% of the eco-holiday market, which would only amount to 3,300 holidays. The breakeven point is 3759 holidays ($5million/ $1,330), suggesting that there is a 50% chance that V will fall short of the breakeven sales, which clearly is a high risk.

This would also be a significant investment incurred for the sale of such a small number of holiday products. This is a high probability and, at this level, V would make a loss of over SK$ 600,000. This is therefore a very high level of risk for V. The best case is an operating profit of SK$5,972 million which is very high. However, there is only a 20% chance of the best case occurring.

However, there is a 20% probability that it could make nearly SK$ 6 million operating profit in the first year. Therefore the accuracy of the estimations and forecasts are critical to this decision. The predicted market share is also only an estimate based upon the current market data and predicted growth rates in the eco travel market. Therefore this also has to be taken into consideration before making any decision.

Considering V's current product portfolio, V is currently in a strong position in all of its three product areas. It currently has no dogs which are draining resources and has a cash cow and a star which has the potential for becoming a future cash cow. Should V undertake the V-eco holidays these are likely to become another problem child within V's product portfolio and are likely to require investment to ensure continued growth and future profitability for V. However, as stated in the unseen material they do not currently require significant levels of investment in the near future but this may change if V wishes them to become future stars and cash cows. V's current cash cow, the Package products are currently in a slowing market but this could be a temporary position due to the economic recession. It is very unlikely that V will allow these to become dogs and they are far more likely to invest in these holiday products to ensure their existence and to extend their life.

The Board is concerned whether the company has sufficient resources to expand into V-eco holidays as well as to maintain, or strengthen, its existing products. Its existing products face increased competition and if V expanded into V-eco holidays, then it may not have the resources to defend and invest in its existing products from the forecast increase in competitive forces. V needs to consider whether the introduction of the V-eco holidays could potentially cause a reduction in sales in any other areas of its business. For example, some of its current Adventure holiday customers may wish to try eco-holidays. Market research would need to be undertaken to assess the reaction of its current customers to the introduction of V-eco holidays.

Recommendation

It is recommended that V does not accept this proposal at the moment until more evidence is gathered on the eco travel market potential for V.

The V-eco holidays clearly have potential and there is evidence to suggest that they could be highly profitable. However, the current estimates also suggest that if V is not successful in gaining market share in the first year, then these products are likely to make a loss. Although the EV indicates a profitability of over SK\$ 2million, before making any final decision the estimates and probabilities must be reviewed more rigorously. Further justification is that the risk of only achieving a 10% market share for V-eco holidays is 50%, which is considerable, and this is forecast to result in a loss of SK\$(0.611) million. This could divert management attention away from the 3 existing products which are facing increased competition and need close management. The current portfolio is strong and balanced and it would be more appropriate for V to invest in its current product portfolio where it is already strong than invest in a product in which it has no experience.

Examiner's comments

This question was not well answered. Most answers to this question were very thin and poorly evaluated in terms of the current business context of V. Many candidates merely recommended that the V-eco product should be undertaken on the basis that it was above the target set by the Finance Director. However, this does not take into account a whole range of other equally important factors to consider before making this very important decision. Very few candidates questioned the basis of the calculations i.e. the probabilities and the range of estimates used in the calculation. It would seem a fundamental requirement to assess their viability before proceeding with a major business development such as a completely new product offering. However, most candidates did not consider this important.

Most candidates failed to evaluate the V-eco product offering at all, instead only considered the positive aspects of the decision, such as the low level of fixed costs, the positive impact upon sustainability and the addition to the product portfolio. Very few candidates truly evaluated the V-eco product, taking into consideration the current balance of the portfolio, the lack of experience of V in this type of holiday and the diversion of management attention away from the existing products in highly competitive environments.

Once again, some candidates failed to offer any recommendations, instead preferring to sit on the fence and recommend that more information is needed to make the decision. If you are asked to make a decision, then you must do so. Asking for more information is not a valid response.

Overall, it would appear that some candidates are unable to think for themselves or think within the business context of the scenario. If the answer does not involve the application of a model or a theory then some candidates just cannot cope with such a question. Yet, these are the challenges you will be facing every day as a management accountant i.e. reviewing your own business environment, gathering a range financial and non-financial information (and sometimes incomplete information) from a variety of sources and then being required to make sound business decisions appropriate to that situation. You must therefore be able to do this in the exam.

Common Errors:

* No recommendations made at all

* Poor recommendations made based upon very limited evaluation of financial information only

(b) Critical success factors are those areas that must go well to ensure the success of V, and represent those areas that must be given special attention to ensure high levels of performance. If results are satisfactory in these areas then this should ensure successful competitive performance for V. Basically, these are the areas that V 'must do right' and where it must outperform its competitors. Therefore it is important for V to identify the critical success factors for each of its holiday products, with reference to what it knows it must be good at within each specific holiday product.

Package: CSF Competitive pricing

The Package holiday customer is likely to be looking for the best value package holiday at an affordable price but of an appropriate standard. Therefore, V must ensure that it focuses upon its pricing policy and this ensures that it effectively matches the expectations of its customers for the product they are buying. Customers in the package market are likely to shop around and therefore an effective and competitive pricing strategy will be critical to V's business.

Adventure: CSF Variety of destinations offered or the variety of activities offered

The Adventure holiday customers clearly value variety of destinations offered. Therefore, V must ensure that it offers an extensive range of destinations to match the requirements of its customers. There is a high level of expected growth in this market and V has some strong competitors and therefore it must exploit the fact that its customers value the variety of its own products. These must be built upon as more destinations are expected to become available.

Alternatively, if V focused upon the range of activities, this could attract young people to unusual activities and 'extreme' sports. The location may be less important than what activities are on offer. The wider and the more unusual activities will play a key role in attracting customers to V's Adventure holidays over its competitors.

It is recommended that V should ensure that it offers a wide choice of unusual extreme sports and other activities to catch the attention and gain market share for its adventure holiday product.

Prestige Travel: CSF Customer satisfaction and high levels of customer service

V has built a very strong reputation in the market for its Prestige Travel products and therefore, to maintain and strengthen its position in the market, it must maintain its high levels of customer service. This is likely to be the most critical factor for the prestige holiday market as customers are less likely to be interested in value for money, rather quality of products and quality of service offered.

V-eco holidays: CSF Environmental impact

V-eco holiday customers are most likely to value the eco-sustainability of V's products offered and therefore V must ensure that the V-eco holidays have a sustainable impact upon the natural environment. As this is a new area for V, this is something that is likely to require investment in terms of finance and knowledge to ensure that V-eco holidays are appropriate to the market's needs.

However, it is difficult to set just one CSF as this proposed new range of holidays will have a different perception from different holiday users. Some may want improvements to the local community, some may want a reduction in carbon emissions whereas others may want protecting the planet as their top issue.

It is recommended that a survey is undertaken to establish what customers perceive they want to achieve on eco-holidays.

Examiner's comments

This question was not well answered. The main reason for this is a fundamental lack of understanding of critical success factors. This is a recurring area of weakness for candidates and an area which both candidates and tuition providers must clearly concentrate upon in the future. Candidates can provide a technically correct definition of a CSF, but the actual application in practice is very poor indeed. Many candidates merely stated outcomes such as 'increase market share' or 'improve profitability' which are clearly not CSFs, rather consequences of successfully applied and achieved CSFs. Candidates also confused CSFs with performance measures and many do not seem to know the difference between the two. For example, for the Prestige holiday product, several candidates stated that the CSF would be to undertake customer satisfaction questionnaires, which clearly is not a critical success factor, rather an activity which would assist in evaluating a performance measure. There is clearly much confusion and misunderstanding in this whole area of CSF's and performance measurement and therefore candidates are advised to spend more time getting to grips with these areas of the syllabus.

Common Errors:

- Candidates presented the outcomes of CSFs and not CSFs

- Performance measures presented

(c)   Using Lewin's three stage model:

Unfreeze

At this stage the Board of V needs to make the need for change obvious to the branch staff so that they can understand it and accept it. The Board must clearly demonstrate to the branch staff that the current levels of customer satisfaction are reducing as shown from the customer satisfaction forms. Also, within the competitive environment in which V operates, it is a situation that cannot continue. V could instigate a programme of education and consultation with branch managers to ensure that they are brought on board first so that they can create and promote a positive force for change within each branch. The appointment of a change agent could help V bring about the change and to make these communications to staff. A change champion should be identified within each branch to facilitate the change programme.

Change

The change process itself will involve:

- Establishing new patterns of behaviour. This would involve getting staff more involved in customer feedback evaluation.

- Creating new rewards/incentives – focus upon the benefit of using customer service reviews as a bonus system.

- Introducing a new style of management – involve staff in the changes and communicate with them. Allow the branch staff time to feedback to branch managers.

It is critical that V communicates directly with the branch staff on a regular basis and allows them the opportunity to participate in the change process. Involvement of staff is also critical at this stage. V could ask branch staff to put forward their own ideas for bonuses and staff training areas.

The change process does not need to be disruptive if handled sensitively. Costly placements to Head Office could be avoided or minimised by getting Head Office staff to undertake in-branch training or to have a road show and newsletters. Staff could be rewarded for ideas and input and weekly awards could be made to branches for highest levels of customer satisfaction achieved.

Refreeze

Refreezing or stabilising the change involves ensuring that the branch staff do not revert back to old ways of operating and thinking. This could be through offering 'employee of the month' awards based upon customer satisfaction ratings or through a positive attitude towards the new working arrangements. Best practice should be established and communicated throughout V. Regular training updates should be carried out in-branch by Head Office Staff and branch managers to ensure continued commitment and to gain feedback from staff and to get their continued input into improvements to the system. Staff bonuses should be set using a range of measures such as the use of the Balanced Scorecard that uses financial and non-financial data to measure performance. All targets should be fair and achievable in order to motivate staff.

Examiner's comments

This question was reasonably well answered, as would be expected, considering the number of times this area of the syllabus has been examined. Despite this, there were still a significant number of candidates who merely described the model, rather than apply it directly to V. Some answers were very general and largely ignored the detail in the un-seen material relating to the new bonus scheme and promotions policy, instead discussing general activities such as 'communicate', 'participate' and 'involve'. Marks were only awarded for these activities if they were directly applied to V and its proposed changes. Candidates are reminded once again that answers must be applied to the scenario material in order to pass.

Common Errors:

- Generic answers with limited application to the change situation proposed within V

- Use of Kotter and Schlesinger model instead of Lewin's three-stage model

---

7   T RAILWAYS (MAY 13 EXAM)

Key answer tips

In requirement (a) candidates are expected to use their knowledge and understanding of public sector organisations to consider the potential difficulties of setting and measuring strategic objectives. The scenario pre-seen introduces a range of strategic objectives and candidates should consider how the measurement of these can be difficult from a public sector perspective only. Answers should also focus specifically upon T Railways and not public sector organisations in general.

Requirement (b) is a complex requirement in which candidates are expected to produce a range of quantitative and qualitative analyses. Note that there are 10 marks for the calculations of KPIs and therefore 18 marks for the qualitative evaluation. Candidates should also consider that the requirement specifically asks for a comparative performance of the three business sectors and a separate comparative performance of TFR against the road freight haulage. Therefore, in terms of structure, candidates should plan and structure their answers carefully to ensure that all of the required information is addressed. Note that the verb used in the requirement is 'evaluate' and therefore candidates are expected to say more than 'this number is bigger than that number'. Rather, candidates must ensure that they attempt to evaluate why the performance of one business or one sector is better/worse than another.

Requirement (c) requires candidates to consider the potential impact on TFR of the proposed privatisation referred to in the unseen material, in terms of both the cultural impact and the changes to strategic management and planning activities. Therefore, candidates must consider the potential changes that are likely to occur as a result of the move from a public sector organisation to a private sector organisation, using a wide range of information contained in both the pre-seen and unseen material relating to the culture and strategic management activities of TFR.

(a)   As a nationalised industry, T Railways has a range of stakeholders and the focus of its performance has not been profit making as any losses have been covered by the central government of T. There has also been a lack of investment in new trains which will have adversely affected the performance of trains in the Energy sector. Therefore, it is difficult to compare different sectors as one has very old trains and another, the Automotive sector, has new trains.

T Railways has a range of conflicting objectives, as passenger services generate more revenues than freight (T$680 million versus T$516 million) and passenger trains take priority over freight trains. Additionally, the rail regulator is putting increasing pressure on T Railways to improve passenger services. This puts a lower emphasis on the performance of the freight division (TFR).

T Railways, and indeed TFR, has multiple stakeholders and this will mean it has multiple objectives to achieve. Each stakeholder will have different objectives, as can be seen from the strategic objectives set by T Railways which include reference to safety, reliability, cost effectiveness and environmental impact. Prioritising these objectives may be difficult as the achievement of one objective may directly impact upon another. For example, reducing carbon emissions may require increased investment in more modern fuel efficient trains but clearly this may impact adversely on the objective of cost efficiency. There is a conflict between safety, operating costs and carbon emissions and no clear direction as to what the priority in objectives is. Is it to reduce T Railways' carbon emissions or to maximise revenues or profits?

Conflict between stakeholders' objectives is inevitable. For example, for T Railways one of the objectives is to reduce carbon emissions, which is clearly a high priority for the regulators and some of the key customers such as the large supermarkets and retailers. However, this will inevitably impact upon costs if this involves investment in new facilities and trains. This will negatively impact upon other key stakeholders, such as the Government and its objective of cost effectiveness and efficiency. Therefore, managing stakeholder conflicts is likely to be a major activity for T Railways.

Many of the stakeholders will themselves have multiple objectives and will not only be looking at one aspect of T Railways' performance. For example, the CHG business sector is clearly considering the environmental issues but it will also be considering the punctuality and reliability of the delivery method. Therefore, this will be difficult when identifying and prioritising objectives as different customers may also have multiple objectives with different priorities.

Also it is often difficult to measure the achievement of objectives. For example, measuring punctuality may not be very easy to do, as there are likely to be many factors which impact upon this objective. For example, TFR may have increased its own punctuality but this may be negatively impacted upon by delays caused by passenger services or delays on other countries' networks. Similarly, measuring safety is likely to be far more complex than merely relying upon the measurement of accident statistics. Many complex factors play a part in all of the key performance indicators and these need to be taken into account before any action is taken.

Some stakeholders will hold greater power than others and some objectives may be more highly prioritised because of this. This may cause T Railways to focus incorrectly upon those objectives and KPIs most important to the key players, such as Government, and overlook those which are most important to its staff or its customers, as it may consider the Government to be its most important stakeholder.

This in turn could result in lost business if customers do not think that their objectives are being met. For example, reducing accidents may incur high investment costs in new trains and more training which may not be of high priority to the Government. However, T Railways' staff will be highly concerned with safety issues and may feel unhappy with T Railways if safety needs are overlooked in favour of cost efficiency measures.

Effective objectives should be SMART, that is specific, measurable, attainable, relevant and time-bound. These criteria for effective objectives may not always be easily achievable. The objectives set are not specific to any particular business subsidiary of T Railways. Neither of the objectives have a specific measurable aspect to them, such as reduce carbon emissions each year by x%. Without a defined measure it is difficult to evaluate progress towards the objectives. However, for T Railways, assigning SMART criteria may be difficult as it will be working with objectives which are not specific to one particular stakeholder group and it may also be difficult to put realistic time frames upon them. Also, some of these objectives are driven externally, such as the emissions targets which have been imposed by international agreements.

Measuring performance can always be undertaken. Even if it is not wholly accurate, it can indicate a trend. However, unless the key objectives are clearly defined and agreed, it can be difficult to know what to measure and which measurements are the most appropriate. For example, accidents – should this be expressed in the absolute number of accidents or as accidents per million kilometres or accidents per journey undertaken? The performance measures could be manipulated to make the figures appear better than they really are.

Examiner's comments

This question was reasonably well answered by most candidates. Most answers focused correctly upon multiple stakeholders and the conflicts that this may create between stakeholders. Many candidates also recognised the qualitative nature of public sector objectives and the difficulties this poses in measuring them. However, there were two main weaknesses of answers to this question. Firstly, many candidates merely described the process of setting and measuring objectives in a public sector environment, with a focus upon describing the three E's concept. However, this was not what was asked. Secondly, many candidates provided very generic answers with limited application to T Railways. Candidates should avoid repeating statements from the question scenario. In some cases candidates rewrote the current objectives of T Railways which were given in the question and failed to focus upon the specific difficulties faced by T Railways. Candidates are reminded that marks are maximised when answers are applied directly to the scenario organisation.

Common Errors:

- Focus upon a description of the concept of the 3 Es

- Limited application of the difficulties faced specifically by T Railways

- Generic answers

(b)   1   Evaluation of the performance of the three sectors in TFR

KPIs	CHG 50% 2012	Energy 40% 2012	Automotive 10% 2012	Total TFR 2012
Revenue per kilometre travelled (T$)	25.3	20.2	25.8	23.0
Operating cost per kilometre (T$)	24.5	20.0	20.0	22.1
Operating profit per kilometre (T$)	0.8	0.2	5.8	1.0
Operating profit (T$million)	8.0	2.4	11.6	22.0
Operating profit %	3.1%	1.2%	22.5%	4.3%
Average capacity utilisation %	88%	82%	86%	n/a
Punctuality %	89%	95%	82%	92%
Kg of CO_2 / per tonne-km	0.04	0.06	0.03	n/a
Accidents per million kilometres travelled	7.8	3.1	5.0	5.4
Damaged/ lost goods per 1,000 kilometres travelled	1.08	0.00	0.75	0.56

Cost Efficiency KPI - Operating Costs per kilometre travelled

Within TFR, the CHG sector has the highest cost per kilometre, indicating possible inefficiencies in operations. The scenario material does suggest that the delivery of industrial freight is complex and this complexity is likely to incur higher costs for this business sector. TFR needs to consider how these complexities could be reduced if it is to reduce these costs and improve the cost efficiency of industrial product transportation. Currently the CHG sector undertakes the longest journeys exclusively within Country T and it could be possible that if these were reduced in order to reduce complexity then costs could also be reduced. In terms of cost per kilometre, the CHG sector would appear to be uncompetitive compared to the road freight haulage sector with costs per kilometre being higher.

In total, the Energy sector incurs over 40% of the costs of the whole of TFR, and this is likely to be due to the number of journeys undertaken and the resultant high staffing costs and fuel costs. However, the costs per kilometre are relatively low. The Automotive sector has low costs per kilometre which may be driven by its use of modern, electric fuel-efficient trains.

Profit

The Automotive sector generates over 50% of TFR's total operating profit and the development of this business area needs to be focused upon in order to create continued growth in this business. The Automotive sector appears to operate at a level of profitability which is more competitive with the road haulage sector, which should indicate that this should be an area of business to pursue for TFR. An area of concern for TFR would be the CHG sector which is only achieving an operating profit of 3.1%. This is a significant concern as it currently accounts for 50% of TFR's business in terms of revenue generated. The complexity of some of this form of freight delivery service is incurring high levels of costs which are impacting upon the profitability of this sector and TFR in total. This needs to be investigated as clearly the costs are likely to be a significant concern for the industrial customers.

Although the Energy sector generates 40% of the total revenue for TFR, when considering the revenue generated per kilometre travelled, the Energy sector contributes the lowest revenue per kilometre. As TFR's most long standing form of freight business is to another nationalised industry, it may be that contracts are not regularly negotiated and prices are kept low in order to stabilise national energy costs. The revenue generated per kilometre by the Automotive sector appears to be in line with that of the Road freight haulage sector and therefore this business sector should be in a competitive position in its market.

Carbon Emissions KPI – Kg of CO2/ per tonne-kilometre

It is notable that the Automotive business which operates electric trains, generates significantly lower levels of CO2 emissions per tonne-km than the Energy sector operating with diesel trains. If TFR is to achieve T Railways' carbon emissions objective it needs to consider the increased usage of electric engines. However, this will require significant investment which may be cost prohibitive for TFR. The Energy sector in particular has a high number of kilometres travelled using old diesel engines. If the Energy sector could improve its capacity utilisation it could reduce the number of journeys it undertakes and thus reduce its emissions.

Staff accidents KPI - The number of staff accidents or injuries sustained by TFR staff per million kilometres travelled

A significant area of concern for TFR should be the level of accidents within the CHG sector where the number of accidents is significantly higher than the other sectors. The number of accidents per million kilometres is over twice that of the Energy sector. Therefore, TFR should consider investing in extra training and carrying out best practice analysis in order to reduce this. The Energy sector has the lowest number of accidents per million kilometres and therefore TFR could consider undertaking a best practice analysis on safety and accident procedures with this sector. However, this exercise may be limited as the mode of operation and delivery is likely to be very different.

Damaged Goods KPI - The number of incidents of goods damaged or lost in transit per thousand kilometres over which the goods are transported

There appears to be a significantly higher level of damaged goods occurring within the CHG sector than in the other sectors. This could be due to the fact that this sector transports large numbers of small value items for retailers that are more likely to get damaged or lost than the products transported by the other sectors. However, this may not be a significant area of concern for TFR as the CHG sector has a lower level of damage incidences than the road haulage sector which may be a positive factor in choosing rail versus road haulage for retailers and supermarkets. The overall damaged goods incidents per kilometre for TFR is rather skewed by the fact that the Energy sector has no incidences of damaged or lost goods.

Train Capacity Utilisation %

The Energy sector has lower capacity utilisation than the other sectors. This needs to be reviewed as this under-utilisation of total capacity of the Energy sector is significantly reducing TFR's overall capacity utilisation. This is also a concern of the power station operators which want to reduce the number of journeys carried out by the Energy sector in order to reduce their own costs.

Improvements in capacity could assist in the reduction of the number of journeys but this is currently hindered by the use of old and less powerful diesel trains. Investment in this area is likely to impact upon the costs of TFR.

Punctuality KPI - The number of journeys on time, measured as a percentage of total journeys made

This is likely to be a significant factor for TFR, particularly for the Automotive sector which has to meet tight shipping deadlines in neighbouring country ports. However, the punctuality for this sector is low compared to the other sectors. This is likely to be due to the distances travelled and the fact that automotive deliveries are reliant upon use of neighbouring countries' rail networks and the reliance on passenger track facilities. The Energy sector has a relatively good record of punctuality. Again, TFR could undertake a best practice exercise to assess if the Automotive sector could follow some of the practices undertaken by the Energy sector to improve punctuality. However, the effects of this could be limited due to the external factors which are affecting the Automotive sectors' punctuality and due to the nature of the Energy sector using its own dedicated tracks.

2 **Benchmarking analysis: TFR in total in 2012 versus the Road Freight Haulage sector**

KPI's	Total TFR 2012	Road Haulage 2012	Difference
Revenue generated (T$m)	516	3,770	-3,254
Revenue generated per km travelled (T$)	23.0	26.0	-3.0
Average kilometres travelled per journey	105.2	145.0	-39.8
Operating Cost per kilometre travelled (T$)	22.1	21.0	-1.1
Operating Profit per kilometre	1.0	5.0	-4.0
Operating Profit	22	725	-703
Operating Profit %	4.3%	19.2%	
Kg of CO_2 / per tonne-km	n/a	0.13	
Staff accidents	122	1,850	1,728
Staff accidents per million kilometres	5.4	12.8	-8.2
Damaged/ lost goods per 1000 kilometres	0.56	1.28	+0.72
Average Capacity utilisation %	n/a	92%	
Punctuality %	92.0%	65.0%	

Costs Efficiency

Overall, the costs per kilometre for TFR are higher than the road freight haulage sector by T$1 per kilometre. The lower total costs incurred by road freight haulage could be due to more efficient operations as a result of less bureaucratic and smaller structures than operated by TFR as part of a large public sector organisation.

Profit

TFR in total generates a total operating profit of T$22 million and an operating profit percentage of 4.3%. Road freight haulage generates a significantly higher level of operating profit at 19.2%. This may be due to the fact that, as stated above, private road haulage companies are likely to have less bureaucratic structures and operate in a more profit focused way. Road freight haulage businesses will be focusing upon increasing shareholder value whereas TFR's main focus is upon breaking even and ensuring that it achieves the goals set by T Railways.

There is a huge amount of revenue reduction that the road hauliers could make to try to keep customers using road transport by offering price cuts, before their margins are reduced to the level achieved by TFR. The average revenue per kilometre for road haulage is T$26 compared to T$23 for rail. Therefore, it appears as if rail prices are T$3 (12%) lower than road prices per kilometre. This may indicate that there is scope to increase rail prices or use this to incentivise customers to switch to rail freight haulage.

The income generated per kilometre for TFR is lower than road freight haulage and this is largely driven by the large proportion of business carried out by TFR in the haulage of coal to power stations by the Energy sector which has a very low level of income generated per kilometre compared to the other two sectors and which is a key driver in the overall income generated per kilometre for TFR in total in 2012.

Carbon Emissions KPI

Although the overall CO_2 emissions for TFR are not available, it would appear that the CO_2 emissions for the three TFR sectors are significantly lower than the CO_2 emissions generated by road freight haulage. This is likely to be a significant competitive advantage for TFR in terms of achieving growth in supermarket and retail customer business. The number of journeys, road congestion and idling time are likely to be significant factors in the carbon emissions for road freight haulage. This is a key competitive advantage for TFR and could help generate more rail freight business as companies try to reduce the level of carbon emissions in their supply chain. This is a key advantage for rail.

Staff accidents KPI - The number of staff accidents or injuries sustained by TFR staff per million kilometres travelled

TFR had 122 accidents in 2012, which equates to 5.4 accidents per million kilometres travelled. This is significantly lower than the road freight haulage business where accidents occur at a rate of 12.8 per million kilometres travelled. The Rail Industry regulator will be interested in this KPI and, once again, this could be used by TFR in order to gain customer confidence and support.

Train Capacity Utilisation %

Although the capacity utilisation in total for TFR is not available, it would appear that each individual sector has a lower capacity utilisation than the road freight sector. It is significant that the Energy sector has lower capacity utilisation than the other sectors. This needs to be reviewed as this under-utilisation by the Energy sector is likely to significantly reduce TFR's overall capacity utilisation. If TFR is to be competitive then it needs to consider increasing its capacity utilisation as this could reduce its overall costs. Capacity utilisation should reduce the number of journeys which need to be undertaken which should improve overall efficiency.

Punctuality KPI - The number of journey on time, measured as a percentage of total journeys made

TFR performs significantly better than the road freight industry in terms of punctuality. This is likely to be a significant competitive advantage for TFR particularly for the Automotive sector which has to meet tight shipping deadlines in neighbouring country ports. Clearly the congestion on Country T's roads is having an effect upon average speeds which is in turn impacting upon the ability of road haulage to meet its deadlines. For retail businesses such as supermarkets this is likely to be a significant factor in choice of delivery methods and if the CHG sector can deliver at a significantly better level of punctuality than road haulage then this should be highly attractive to the customers.

Overall, rail has several advantages over road haulage including better punctuality, lower carbon emissions, lower damage / loss rates and these factors should help persuade more customers to transfer to rail freight in future. These statistics should also help TFR to try to secure government funding for more investment in newer trains. More investment will improve punctuality and help reduce carbon emissions.

Examiner's comments

This question was reasonably well answered. The calculation of the KPIs was undertaken well by most candidates. However, some did make a number of basic mistakes, such as using the incorrect approach to calculate the KPIs (such as incorrectly calculating accidents per journey instead of accidents per 1,000 km). However, overall, most candidates scored well on the calculations, which was expected as they were not technically difficult.

However, the main weakness of answers to this question was in the evaluation of the KPIs. Candidates must remember that they are now sitting a strategic level paper and therefore the examiner is expecting somewhat more than 'X is bigger than Y' as an evaluative answer. Candidates were provided with more information in the unseen than ever before to assist them in this evaluation, but many candidates failed to use the information adequately (or at all, in some cases). What candidates must understand is that evaluation at a strategic level is much more than merely stating that one number is bigger or smaller than another. Those candidates who took this approach were awarded very few marks for their evaluation of the KPIs. For example, had candidates carefully read and understood the unseen material they would have seen that the Energy sector was using the oldest diesel trains which was likely to have a significant impact upon the carbon emissions KPI. Similarly candidates were told that the Automotive sector had invested in new electric trains, which would also impact upon this KPI. Candidates were expected to piece this information together from a range of sources and to then present a range of conclusions from this information; a skill which is a key requirement of a management accountant in practice. It was disappointing to see how many candidates were not able to demonstrate sound evaluation and judgement skills and it is an area which candidates and tuition providers must focus upon in the future.

Common Errors:

* Calculating inappropriate or unnecessary KPIs

* Limited evaluation based solely upon identification of one KPI being bigger or smaller than another

* Lack of evaluation and assimilation of the unseen material

(c) (i) TFR currently has a highly bureaucratic culture, where T Railways retains a tight control on strategic management and planning activities undertaken. Therefore, control systems are likely to be highly centralised and the structure bureaucratic. This is likely to result in a culture where change is not something that staff are used to or would accept easily. Power rests with T Railways' senior managers. The privatisation would have a major impact upon TFR's culture as it is likely that the current hierarchy would be reduced significantly.

The three business sectors would operate as two separate companies. This clearly would change the organisational structure and reporting which is an element of TFR's current culture. As they would now have a profit motive and their main influential stakeholders are the shareholders this would inevitably change the management focus and culture. The separate companies would operate in a competitive market against each other and other freight haulage organisations. The process of changing the structure could be a distraction from managing these businesses in the short term.

The paradigm – the 'way we do things' would be likely to significantly change. The power to make decisions would be released to senior managers within the businesses rather than the centralised decision making undertaken by T Railways. The old bureaucratic control systems and power systems would no longer exist.

The symbols and stories likely to exist within TFR concentrated upon its public sector and customer focus would be likely to be replaced with new symbols and stories to encourage the promotion of a profit focused business.

The number of staff used would likely be cut by Q. This would lead to resistance from TFR's current staff. This would require careful handling and good HR management to stop any de-motivation of employees after the company is privatised.

There would be a need for performance related pay or incentives to help motivate employees and to achieve goal congruence. Again, a culture, in terms of rewards to incentivise performance would need to be implemented. In a new privatised era, there would be a shortage of skilled management and new senior managers may need to be recruited to manage the change and to guide the companies. This happened when many of the UK nationalised industries were privatised in the 1980's and 1990's.

There would need to be much more focus on managing costs and achieving profit and shareholder returns. There would also need to be a greater focus on customers, the need to win more business and to retain customers by keeping them happy and meeting their needs, such as improved punctuality.

Examiner's comments

This question was not well answered. Many candidates correctly identified the current bureaucratic culture of T Railways but few adequately discussed the range of cultural changes which could take place if TFR were to become privatised. Most answers focused largely upon the impact upon staff and the issues relating to staff resistance and possible motivational issues. However, most discussions on this were largely irrelevant to the cultural changes. Many candidates used the cultural web as a framework to structure the answer, which was appropriate and useful. However, a number of answers were merely descriptive and presented limited application of the potential changes to the cultural web of TFR if it were to be privatised. Although many candidates did recognise the change in focus towards a competitive and profit driven environment this was not then followed up with a discussion of the potential impact of this upon the culture of TFR. Many answers were very thin and lacked sufficient depth of discussion to be awarded a pass mark. Some candidates merely mentioned structural and staff issues which clearly is not sufficient to be awarded a pass mark

Common Errors:

- Lack of focus upon the cultural impact of privatisation

- Lack of depth in the answers provided

(c)   (ii)   Q operates with a decentralised management structure where divisional senior managers are responsible for strategic decision making and setting their own strategic objectives. This is in contrast to TFR where strategic decisions are taken by T Railways and then passed down to the senior managers of TFR to manage through its KPI's. Therefore, the senior managers of TFR have little input in strategic decision making. This would be significantly different after privatisation as Q operates with a far more decentralised decision making structure.

T Railways currently operates an 'accounting-led' approach to strategic management and planning. The traditional accounting-led approach to strategic planning starts by looking at the stakeholders and their objectives. The emphasis is then upon formulating plans to achieve these objectives. This is currently the approach used by T Railways, which sets its strategic objectives and from these objectives, a number of Key Performance Indicators (KPI's) are set to measure TFR's overall performance in achieving these objectives. Therefore, TFR's management and planning activities are based upon measuring the KPIs in order to meet the strategic objectives set by T Railways. Objectives are clearly very important for TFR as its overall performance is assessed on the meeting of these objectives. However, this can be flawed as it can lead organisations to overlook market considerations. Even though TFR has no direct rail competitors, it still needs to consider other competitors such as road freight haulage companies.

In contrast, Q operates a more competence or resource led approach to strategic management, where the emphasis of strategic management and planning is focused on core competences and critical success factors. Q clearly focuses upon its core competences – what it is good at, and aims to ensure that these fit with market expectations. Therefore, there will be less focus upon stakeholder objectives and more upon its critical success factors in order to ensure that it achieves its objectives. Although the freight delivery market may be considered to be a relatively stable environment, there are clear market forces in operation, with strong competitors and opportunities for developments in some areas, such as CHG and Automotive. Therefore, this approach is likely to be more appropriate to a privatised organisation.

With the privatisation of TFR, Q would wish to prepare both top down and bottom up plans and see where the gaps are and what actions would need to be taken to achieve Q's goals.

Q would need to set guidelines of what levels of investment it is prepared to make and allow management to decide where the investment would achieve the best results for retaining customers and gaining new business. What would be the impact of increasing prices? With customers under pressure to cut carbon emissions in their supply chain, they may be willing to pay a slightly higher price to move freight by rail. Currently there is a T$3 difference between road and rail, with road prices being higher.

The level of capital investment and the required business resources and skills will need to be planned. Staff reduction and redundancies will also need to be planned. It is likely that there will be an inadequate level of senior management skills in respect of planning and IT, as these are areas which T Railways has neglected. This may result in consultants being appointed in the short-term to help with the planning process or for some of Q's more experienced staff being seconded to these two new rail companies. Once the strategic plans are agreed, then Q would require its management team to put detailed operational plans in place to ensure that they are met. The strategic plans and whether they are achievable will need to be discussed and agreed by the senior management team. Will management go for growth in volumes of rail freight or for better customer service with fewer late trains, or will it go for growth in profitability, with a price increase?

Examiner's comments

Again, answers to this question, as with (c)(i), were unsatisfactory. The final section of the unseen material provided a range of information to assist candidates in answering this question, so it was surprising to see how few candidates actually took note of and used this information in their answer. It was most disappointing that so few candidates recognised the difference between T Railway's current accounting- led approach, based upon setting and managing objectives versus the competence based and market driven approach used by Q. Most answers ignored this completely, instead focusing upon discussions on centralised versus decentralised decision making and upon shareholder wealth creation. Although these were relevant issues which were given credit, there were many other factors that could have been discussed by candidates. As with answers to part (c)(i), many answers were very thin and lacked sufficient depth of discussion to be awarded a pass mark. Answers to both (c)(i) and (c)(ii) were weak and there was a lot of overlap in these answers. Candidates are reminded that they must read the question carefully. Many did not appreciate the issue regarding accounting-led versus competency approaches to strategic management and instead just discussed the rational versus emergent approach.

Candidates must make better use of the information they are given in the unseen material. The information provided in the unseen material is given for a reason and should be used to assist in the formulation of answers. Yet it would appear that many candidates choose to answer questions with little or no reference to the scenario information at all. This would appear to be a significant contributory factor to the standard of candidate answers as many are inadequately applied to the scenario and largely generic. If candidates used the information in the scenario more effectively, then answers would be likely to improve. It appears likely that many candidates spend an insufficient amount of time studying the unseen material.

Common Errors:

- Poor use of the scenario information

- Limited focus upon strategic management activities using a competence based approach

8   T RAILWAYS (SEP 13 EXAM)

Key answer tips

For requirement (a)(i) candidates are required to discuss the CSR obligations of the CG sector to any two of its stakeholders. Candidates must make sure that they clearly discuss these CSR obligations AND the strategies CG should use to manage these two stakeholders. The strategies discussed must be specific to the stakeholder identified and not a generic discussion of stakeholder management strategies.

For requirement (a)(ii) candidates should not only identify a relevant benefit to the CG sector of working closely with the Minister for the Environment and the Rail Regulator on its agreed carbon emissions targets but they must also evaluate each benefit. This requires candidates to consider the relative impact of each benefit to the CG sector.

Requirement (b)(i) should be a straightforward question, requiring candidates to calculate the contribution earned per delivery and per day from the proposal information presented in the unseen material. Candidates should use the information presented in the table to undertake a calculation of contribution earned from the original number of deliveries and compare this to the contribution earned from the proposed number of deliveries in order to calculate the extra contribution earned.

Requirement (b)(ii) builds upon the answer to (b)(i) in that candidates should consider the additional factors which need to be considered, in particular the potential impact of this decision upon the achievement of the strategic and financial objectives set by T Railways. Candidates are not required to make a final recommendation in this answer.

Requirement (c)(i) should be a straightforward question, requiring candidates to apply their knowledge of critical success factors to the Automotive sector. Candidates are required to present only one critical success factor for each quadrant of the balanced scorecard. That is, only four critical success factors are required. However, candidates must clearly justify the critical success factors they have identified.

Requirement (c)(ii) builds upon the candidates' answers to (c)(i) as candidates are required to present and justify an appropriate performance measure for each of the critical success factors they have identified. Again, clear focus upon performance measures is required and each performance measure must be justified.

For all of the requirements for this question, candidates must make sure that they are answering each question from the perspective of the correct sector, as identified at the beginning of each question requirement.

(a) (i) The CG sector has multiple stakeholders which each has a different perspective upon the CG sectors CSR obligations. CSR refers to the firm's obligations to maximise its positive impacts upon stakeholders while minimising the negative effects.

The CG sector stakeholders affected by its CSR activities include:

Examiners Note: Candidates are only required to discuss two of the following stakeholders.

The Supermarkets

The supermarkets are a powerful stakeholder as they are large customers and very influential. They are positively encouraging the move to reduced carbon emissions and are in fact driving this through the working party which has been set up with the supermarkets in Country T, the Ministry of Transport and the Minister for the Environment. The supermarkets are trying to reduce the levels of carbon emissions in their supply chain and, therefore, they are considering switching more freight from road to rail, which will help them to achieve some reductions.

Thus the CG sector has a CSR obligation to work with the supermarkets to help them in reaching their own targets and the overall target for Country T in terms of carbon emissions. The CG sector needs to work with its customers to support and encourage this initiative which will generate higher revenues for the sector, as well as reduce carbon emissions in total. It can help the supermarkets by demonstrating the volume of carbon emissions produced for a given volume of freight per km travelled by rail compared to road.

However, if the CG sector is to convince supermarkets to switch more of their supplies from road to rail it must provide a viable and reliable service. Therefore it would need to invest in newer and more trains / trucks to be able to carry these increased volumes.

As key players in the CSR activities of the CG sector, CG must try to work with the supermarkets in developing strategies for reducing carbon emissions and optimising deliveries. From a business perspective this would be a good way to generate extra business and become more profitable and it offers competitive advantage against the road haulage firms. By working together, the parties can identify optimum delivery methods.

Rail Regulator

The Rail Regulator is both a powerful and interested stakeholder in the CG sector's CSR activities. It monitors performance of the rail industry in terms of carbon emissions and also set the targets with Government. The CG sector has an obligation to ensure that targets are met and that recommendations made by the Rail Regulator for improvements in CSR activities are made.

It is important for the CG sector to work closely with the Rail Regulator on emissions targets and on safety issues. It is in CG's interest if it can develop and work on targets together, rather than CG having targets imposed on it. The CG sector needs to work with the Rail Regulator to demonstrate the volumes of carbon emissions it currently generates, both in total as well as per freight km travelled. This should be compared to similar carbon emissions statistics for road transport to show how much better rail is versus road. Regular and ongoing communication must take place and the CG sector managers must make sure that they fully co-operate with the Rail Regulator.

If CG's capacity is increased to allow it to carry more freight, then ultimately this will lead to the CG sector producing more carbon emissions in total, although the volume per km travelled by rail should remain the same. However, the overall supermarket freight industry's carbon emissions should reduce as less freight will be transported by road. Therefore, statistics on carbon emissions should not only be measured in terms of absolute levels of carbon emissions but also carbon emissions per km travelled. The saving of road carbon emissions should be compared to the small increase in rail carbon emissions with more freight. The CG sector will have to also consider negotiating with T Railways' Board on the targets set for its own carbon emissions in the light of the impact of the increased capacity, for example some form of offset against the reduction in road transportation emissions.

Government / Minister of Transport

The CG sector has a CSR obligation to the national Government of T to meet the targets and expectations as set by the Government in terms of overall safety, reliability and efficiency of service to the whole country to ensure optimum productivity. The Government has recently been encouraging a move to rail haulage through its national transport and emissions policies, so it should be favourable towards encouraging and assisting in the CG sector's CSR obligations and activities. The Government of Country T is a powerful stakeholder, as ultimately it is the owner of T Railways and thus sets the agenda for investment and the overall direction and aims of the business. It is not likely, however, to be strongly interested unless there is bad publicity from the CSR activities of the CG sector. However, since the supermarkets have been working with Government officials then this may make the Government more interested in the CSR activities of the CG sector.

The CG sector must ensure that it keeps the Government satisfied and that it actively attempts to engage with the Government and implement government policies as directed. Open and regular communication with the Government must be undertaken. The strategies that the CG sector could adopt include attempting to persuade T Railways to obtain Government funding for the investment in more rolling stock / engines to increase its capacity so that it can help transport greater quantities of freight for the supermarket industry. This would meet the requirement to encourage more freight onto the railways and off the road. This will help the Government to improve the productivity of the country by reducing road congestion also.

Staff / unions

The CG sector has a CSR obligation to keep its staff safe which needs to be balanced with the need to keep its large supermarket customers happy. The staff of the CG sector are likely to be interested in the CSR activities of the business, in particular those relating to safety, but are not likely to be very powerful. However, staff could become very powerful with the backing of the unions, which have raised concern over the safety of increased capacity. The unions are likely to be very interested and powerful if staff conditions and safety are compromised. The CG sector could form a powerful alliance with the unions to press the Government for more investment.

The CG sector must keep staff and unions fully informed and communicate regularly and clearly to staff with regard to changes in working practices or updates on safety procedures. Training for staff in new methods of working or enhanced safety procedures must be undertaken.

Society

The CG sector has a CSR obligation to the wider public in that it should consider the impact that its overall carbon emissions have upon the general environment and the long-term impact this will have on society. The wider society of Country T is unlikely to have any power and little interest in the CG sector's CSR activities. Within this, the general road users of Country T are likely to be interested in reduced traffic congestion but will have limited power to influence the activities of TFR. Therefore, this stakeholder group requires minimum effort but some good publicity could be gained by the CG sector in the eyes of the wider general public in Country T through reduced carbon emissions. It may encourage more general train usage across T Railways. There will be less wasted time stuck in traffic and a better quality of life for road users due to less congested roads. This also has the effect of reduced fuel consumption due to less wasted fuel sitting in traffic.

Examiner's comments

This question was reasonably well attempted by most candidates. Most were able to correctly identify and map two relevant stakeholders and from this, together with the unseen material, were able to identify the CSR obligations of the CG sector to each. Most candidates used the scenario information very well and there was clear evidence of good application of answers for this requirement. Most candidates also made a reasonable attempt at identifying a suitable strategy to manage each stakeholder group, although answers to this part of the question were sometimes theoretical and not necessarily appropriate to the stakeholder being discussed. Some candidates missed the point of the question and discussed overall corporate level strategies such as investment in new trains, rather than considering stakeholder management strategies.

Common Errors:

- Some candidates omitted to identify a relevant strategy to manage each stakeholder group

- Generic discussions of stakeholder management strategies with limited application to CG

- Discussion of corporate strategy and stakeholder management strategies

---

(a)   (ii)   It is widely recognised that all companies need to monitor and report their carbon emissions. Most public companies include a section on carbon emissions in the CSR section of their annual report. T Railways has undertaken to reduce its carbon emissions by a third between now (2013) and 2015 (as per pre-seen material).

The CG sector not only needs to maintain close relationships with its customers, such as the supermarkets, but it can also obtain great benefits from maintaining close relationships with the Government and the Rail Regulator. The freight haulage industry is clearly directly affected by non-market forces such as the Government-led emissions targets and the Government-set regulations in terms of road charges and taxation levels. The Rail Regulator and environmental pressure groups are also likely to be influential in setting the agenda for carbon emissions targets. Therefore it is vital that the CG sector works closely with these influential parties.

Benefits to the CG sector

The managers of the CG sector can communicate their own position directly to the most influential decision makers and thus gain their direct support. This is an advantage that the individual road haulage firms are unlikely to have. The CG sector can gain a distinct competitive advantage by having access to the Government decision makers which the road haulage firms do not have.

The CG sector managers can be pro-active in the decision making and target setting, rather than being reactive if they are not involved in the process.

The CG sector should also have a better appreciation of the needs of the customers as the Government is currently working with the supermarkets in setting emissions targets for them. By working with the Government it can have a better understanding of the role and needs of its supermarket customers through communication with the Government.

Increase public perception and society opinion of the CG sector – if it is seen to be working closely with the Government on setting CSR targets and encouraging a commitment to staff safety, then this should result in good publicity.

As the CG sector increases the volume of freight carried, then the total volume of its carbon emissions will increase rather than reduce. Therefore, this is in direct conflict with the overall agreed objective that has been agreed with the Rail Regulator and this will conflict with the Government's wish to move more freight onto the railways. Therefore an alternative measure should be agreed and negotiated with CG and T Railways, aside from the total carbon emissions. Perhaps the new measure should be agreed with the Rail Regulator as the volume of carbon emissions per Km, the volume per journey or the volume per million kilogrammes of freight carried. There needs to be some link between carbon emissions and the volume of freight carried and the length of the journey for this freight, in contrast with the consequent reduction in carbon emissions from road haulage. By working closely with the Government and the Rail Regulator, the CG sector's managers will be able to identify the most appropriate and workable targets.

More openness, transparency and better understanding of carbon emissions and the targets set should help CG's managers to demonstrate to the Minister for the Environment and the Rail Regulator that carbon emissions are reducing. It would also demonstrate the CG sector's commitment in helping to meet the targets for a reduction in carbon emissions.

Examiner's comment

This question was reasonably well answered by many candidates. Most were able to identify a reasonable range of potential benefits of working with the Rail Regulator and Minister for The Environment and again, many answers were well applied to the scenario information. Most answers recognised the potential benefits of assisting in setting relevant and achievable targets and the potential public relations benefits for the CG sector. However, very few answers considered the potential impact upon competitive advantage, in terms of the advantage that the CG sector has over the road freight industry in being able to negotiate directly, as one organisation, with government.

Common Errors:

• Answers were sometimes brief and weakly developed. Candidates often identified benefits but failed to evaluate them

---

(b) (i) **Additional contribution**

	Per delivery *Based on 6 deliveries /day*	Per delivery *Based on 4 deliveries / day*	*Difference*
	T$	T$	T$
Revenue from coal delivered	29,028	43,424	
Admin fee charged per delivery	500	625	
Total revenue	29,528	44,049	
Costs:			
Direct staff cost	7,400	9,620	
Fuel costs	10,000	14,000	
Variable overheads	12,180	16,534	
Total costs	29,580	40,154	
Contribution per delivery	(52) loss	3,895	+3,947
	Per day	**Per day**	**Per day**
Contribution per day	(312) loss	15,580	+15,892

> **Examiner's comments**
>
> This question was reasonably well answered, although there were a number of sloppy errors made in many answers which meant that candidates lost marks where they should not have done. For example, a large proportion of candidates included the administration fee per delivery as a cost item rather than revenue, which clearly impacted upon their final answer. Candidates are reminded to read the detail of the questions and unseen material more carefully. In addition, several candidates also failed to answer the question that had been set, in that they did not calculate the additional contribution that could be earned per day and per delivery by the proposal. This was the actual final requirement, yet several candidates omitted this final calculation. Again, this was clearly not due to them not being able to do so, rather it was due to poor examination technique in that they failed to read the question requirement carefully.
>
> Common Errors:
>
> - Poor presentation of answers which were often illogically set out
>
> - Inclusion of administration fees as a cost item and not a revenue item
>
> - Failure to calculate what had been asked for in the actual requirement

(b) (ii) From the calculations undertaken in part (b)(i) above it can be seen that it would generate a much higher level of contribution for the Energy sector to operate at 4 deliveries per day to power station X . At the current level of 6 deliveries per day, the Energy sector generates a negative contribution per delivery of T$52. However, if it were to operate 4 deliveries per day, contribution per delivery would increase to T$3,895 towards covering fixed costs. On a purely financial basis, this proposal appears to be advantageous to the Energy sector as it would now generate a positive contribution towards covering part of the Energy sector's fixed costs.

However, as a public sector organisation, TFR and its 3 business sectors must also take into consideration the strategic and financial objectives set for T Railways. There are two main strategic objectives:

(i) To deliver reliable, safe and punctual rail services to customers efficiently and cost effectively thereby helping to achieve economic growth in Country T by reducing congestion on its roads;

(ii) To strive to continually reduce its level of carbon emissions to help provide an environmentally friendly transport infrastructure.

One of its financial objectives is that;

(i) T Railways should at least cover its operating costs from the revenue it earns from its customers.

With regard to the first objective, there is a requirement for reliable, safe and punctual rail services. However, the Energy sector managers have concerns that the proposal may compromise all of these factors.

Firstly, reliability could be at risk due to more breakdowns as a result of the extra capacity required to be handled by the old diesel trains. This is also a very high risk for power station X as it requires the coal to be delivered in order to ensure uninterrupted power supply. Breakdowns of trains could result in missed deliveries and therefore national power disruption.

Safety is also a concern of the unions as this may be compromised by the increased capacity per truck required by the proposal. Staff safety could be reduced by having to handle greater volumes of coal per truck.

Punctuality may also be at risk as the old diesel trains used are likely to be slower as a result of having limited power to cope with the increased capacity per train. If breakdowns occur, replacement coal may be slower to arrive, again risking the continuity of power production.

The second strategic objective refers to the reduction of the carbon emission targets, which clearly is an important issue for T Railways and the national Government. The carbon emissions are likely to increase as a result of inefficient and slower trains, meaning the Energy sector is unlikely to reach its emissions targets as set by the Rail Regulator.

The financial objective set by T Railways clearly does not place significant emphasis upon profitability, profit growth or contribution. As long as operating costs are covered from its revenues then the financial objective has been achieved. However, currently, each delivery to power station X makes a negative contribution of T$52 towards fixed costs. We do not know the level of fixed costs in the Energy sector, but it is likely to be high, due to the likely level of fixed operating costs such as infrastructure costs and staff costs and the re-charges from the TPTS division and Head office charges. Therefore, the current contribution of the deliveries to power station X towards these costs is marginally negative. With the reduced number of deliveries to 4 per day, there is a significant increase in the contribution towards fixed costs.

TFR's and subsequently the Energy sector's strategic planning and management activities are driven by these overall strategic objectives and the managers of the business sectors are evaluated against these. Therefore, although financially attractive, the Energy sector's managers must also consider the proposal's ability to satisfy the strategic objectives. It would appear that they will be compromised and therefore further discussion is necessary with the power station managers and T Railways' Board before any decision is made on this proposal.

Also, this is only one coal power station. There are other coal-based power stations in Country T and if the Energy sector were to focus more upon its efficiency and increased capacity it could significantly increase the capacity of its deliveries to all of the coal-based power stations which could positively impact upon overall reduced energy costs for consumers and increased profitability and efficiency for TFR.

Examiner's comments

This question was generally not well answered. Although most candidates correctly referred back to the strategic and financial objectives in the pre-seen material, few adequately evaluated the potential impact of the proposal on these objectives. Many candidates' answers were very brief and superficial, merely re-stating the information that had already been presented about the proposal in the unseen material, with little or no attempt at evaluation. Candidates were not asked to make a final decision on the proposal and therefore no credit was awarded to candidates who made a final recommendation.

> Common Errors:
>
> * Repeating of the unseen material with little or no added value analysis

(c) (i) The Automotive sector may wish to expand its operations as it has been successfully growing its business and has already increased its market share to 30%. If it is to expand, it will do so by using its key skills and competences. However, this expansion may be in conflict with T Railways' strategic and financial objectives. This is a very common problem in many businesses where divisions or subsidiaries have to 'toe the corporate line' and amend their strategic plans to fit in with imposed corporate objectives. This can adversely affect the individual division's performance. A competence based approach is where the emphasis of strategy formulation is to look at what the organisation is good at i.e. its core competences. For the Automotive sector, these should focus upon what the business must be good at in order to succeed in the automotive delivery market. Therefore, the Automotive sector must identify its critical success factors. Such CSF's will be difficult for its road haulage competitors to copy.

Critical success factors for the Automotive sector

Financial

Price competitiveness – a critical success factor in this market. It can be seen that pricing competitiveness has been a success factor for the Automotive business as it has doubled its market share in the last three years. Customers are clearly seeing price as an important factor and therefore it is an aspect of its business that is likely to continue to be critical for this sector.

Customer

Punctuality – this is a critical success factor for the customer as tight shipping deadlines must be met. Therefore, it is critical for the Automotive business to ensure that those deadlines will be met. This is a feature of its business that is likely to be difficult for the road haulage companies to easily copy as road congestion is becoming increasingly prevalent and therefore punctuality is an area of potential competitive advantage.

Internal Processes

Speed and efficient loading procedures – this is a critical success factor, as fast and efficient loading and unloading facilities will ensure efficiency and punctuality of delivery for customers. Again, this is likely to be a competitive advantage for the Automotive sector against the road haulage businesses.

Learning and Growth

Staff development – this is critical for the Automotive sector as well developed and trained staff in the complex logistics of loading and transporting large volumes of vehicles, will ensure the continued efficiency of the service delivered to customers. High levels of staff satisfaction should lead to better customer service.

Or

New designs or ways to increase capacity of freight trains - such as improved 'stacking' of new vehicles or better designed trucks to fit vehicles in more effectively. These new ways or designs could help to increase the efficiency of the trains which is likely to be critical in winning new business from the road haulage sector.

Examiner's comments

This question was not well answered. This was very disappointing indeed, as this area of the syllabus has now been examined in several recent diets, yet candidates appear to still not understand and more importantly, be able to apply, this area of the syllabus. There were a number of key weaknesses in both part (c)(i) and (c)(ii) which will be discussed below:

Firstly, many candidates got off to a bad start, as they did not know the four basic quadrants of the Balanced Scorecard. This is not acceptable at this level as it is a fundamental element of the syllabus and candidates MUST know these four key areas of the Balanced Scorecard. Clearly, those candidates who could not correctly identify the BSC found it difficult to score well on this question.

Secondly, candidates appear to have a poor understanding of a critical success factor for an organisation. There were so many clues presented to candidates within the unseen material, yet many candidates appeared not to see these. For example, candidates were told that pricing competitively was vitally important to the future growth of the market yet few candidates recognised this as a critical activity for the Automotive sector to get right. Instead, many candidates chose 'Profitability' or 'Market Share' as Financial CSF's which are both clearly wrong. How can market share be a critical activity? Market share and profitability are hopefully the outcome of a successfully applied and managed CSF, not the actual CSF itself.

Thirdly, many candidates confused CSF's with KPI's and in answer to part (c)(i) were providing KPI's and targets. For example, for the Learning and Growth Perspective, some candidates were providing examples such as monitoring the number of training courses attended by staff or the number of sick days taken. These are clearly NOT CSF's.

This area of the syllabus continues to be a real area of weakness for candidates and MUST be improved upon.

Common Errors:

- Poor knowledge of the Balanced Scorecard model

- Lack of understanding of CSF's

- Poor application to the Automotive sector

(c)   (ii)   **Financial**

CSF - Price competitiveness

Possible Performance Measures within the BSC could be:

- Profit growth per year (%)

- Growth in market share (%)

Profit growth and market share growth are both important indicators of the success of the pricing strategies of the Automotive sector. If deliveries are priced uncompetitively then the Automotive sector will fail to build upon its market share and the profit earned by the sector will also be limited.

Customer

CSF - Punctuality / on time deliveries

Possible Performance Measures within the BSC could be:

- Percentage of shipping deadlines met
- Number of penalties incurred / cost of penalties for late deliveries
- Customer satisfaction ratings

These performance measures are important to both customers (as they need the cars to be at the ports to meet shipping deadlines) and also to the Automotive sector as it will incur penalties for late delivery. The percentage of shipping deadlines met should be as close to 100% as is feasible.

Internal Processes

CSF - Fast and efficient loading procedures

Possible Performance Measures within the BSC could be:

- Number of deliveries per day
- Number of vehicles loaded / unloaded
- Time taken to load / unload per delivery on average
- Average number of staff required for each load delivered

These performance measures are justified as they will enable managers to compare the average time to previous time periods and between trains and even between different shifts / teams to encourage 'best practice'. It can also be used as a measure to see if any new designs for loading /unloading are speeding up the process or not. It may also indicate differences in loading for different types of vehicle.

This performance measure can also indicate whether there was a particular incident (such as an accident) which resulted in increased lead times, so that management action could be taken to stop such an incident occurring again.

Learning and growth

CSF - Staff development

Performance Measures:

- Staff turnover
- Number of training courses attended per annum

These performance measures are justified as they will identify any problems or weaknesses in any areas of staff training and ensure that staff are operating at the optimum levels of efficiency. It should also identify staff satisfaction levels if turnover is high. Therefore, weaknesses in staff levels of training or experience can be addressed or any issues with staff morale can be spotted before they affect the levels of service to customers.

Alternatively, a performance measure of learning and growth could be:

- Number of new cars transported per train

This measure could demonstrate whether any new operational methods or a new stacking system or truck design could help to increase the number of new cars transported per train. This measure will help to encourage innovation so that more cars can be transported by each train to maximise capacity.

Examiner's comments

As many answers to part (c)(i) were poor, unfortunately this had a knock-on effect on the answers to part (c)(ii), as these were equally as weak. However, credit was given to a sensible KPI which had been based upon a weak CSF in the previous answer. Again, the answers to this question were generally very weak and demonstrated a poor level of understanding and application. The main weakness of answers to this question was that few candidates adequately explained the reasoning for the KPI's they had chosen, as most merely presented a list of KPI's. The requirement clearly asked for a justification of your chosen KPI, yet most candidates failed to do so. If candidates are asked to justify an answer then they must do so, otherwise marks will be lost. As can be seen in the marking guide above, half of the marks in this requirement were for justification. Those candidates who merely listed the KPI's were therefore limiting their marks potential by ignoring the justification of the KPI's.

Common Errors:

- Weak KPI's following on from weak CSF's

- Poor or no justification of the KPI

Section 4

ANSWERS TO SECTION B-TYPE QUESTIONS

INTERACTING WITH THE COMPETITIVE ENVIRONMENT (20%)

EXTERNAL ANALYSIS

9   GGM (MAY 13 EXAM)

Key answer tips

Requirement (a) requires a high level of application of the scenario information and industry awareness to a recognised syllabus model, Porter's Five Forces. This is a difficult question as it requires candidates not only to apply the Five Forces model but also to do so in the context of the impact of IT (including the internet). Therefore it is not sufficient to pass this question with an application of the Five Forces model in general terms, with no reference at all to IT and the internet.

Requirement (b) should be a straightforward evaluation of the scenario information in the context of the role played by the directors of GGM in the company's current position. Candidates should focus their answers on both the role played by T and also the role and responsibilities of the other directors in managing the organisation. A high level of application of answers to the scenario information is required in this answer. A generic discussion of the roles and responsibilities of directors will not be awarded a pass mark.

Requirement (c) should be a straightforward question, requiring candidates to focus upon both the short and long-term impacts of the Board's proposal to close 20 stores and to re-locate and downsize its remaining stores. It is important that candidates clearly address all aspects of this requirement, with a clear focus upon the short and long-term impacts and how they affect the employees and the staff.

(a)   **Bargaining power of Suppliers**

The presence of powerful suppliers reduces the potential for high profits for GGM. The suppliers of GGM would mainly be the music recording companies, the film distributors and the technology manufacturers. Most of these are likely to be large businesses which themselves will be incorporating information technology into their own business processes. For example, the major film distributors will make use of the internet to advertise their products and will also be likely to use dedicated sites where customers can rent or buy films online. Music recording companies and artists will also make use of internet technology to advertise and promote their music online. This has therefore made suppliers more powerful as they are no longer wholly reliant on the traditional high street retailers such as GGM for the distribution of their products. Also the suppliers are likely to use technology to organise their supply chains and therefore use them to tie in distributors such as GGM.

Bargaining power of customers

Bargaining power of customers is another aspect which helps in assessing the industry attractiveness. Individual customers in the entertainment retail industry can be identified as the music and film buyers who purchase music either online or offline. The bargaining power of individual customers has been rising in recent years due to their ability to purchase music and films in downloadable digital formats which has forced the whole music and film retail industry to drive down prices. In addition, with intense competition from supermarkets and dedicated online sites, price cutting is evident especially in online music sales. Therefore, the bargaining power of customers can be assumed to be very high as their access to information technology grows and becomes less expensive. It is, therefore, a significant factor for GGM.

Threat of new entrants

The next force is the threat of new entrants which, to a great extent, depends upon the barriers to entry or the ease of entering the retail entertainment market. New entrants, in the form of online retailers, have grown significantly in recent years as there are no significant barriers to entry. In addition, the supermarkets, to some extent, can be seen as new entrants to the music and film sales market both off and online. Therefore, the threat of new entrants is high and this has largely been driven by the ease of access to the market through the use of information technology and has been a major threat to the existence of GGM.

Threat of substitutes

A substitute product or service can be identified as a rival product or service which meets the same customer needs approximately in the same way as the product or service of GGM. In the music and film retail industry the substitutes for paid music purchases or downloads can be identified as free streaming music online, pirated music downloads online and the TV & Radio channels playing 24 hour music. Free streaming music such as those on My-space allows customers to listen to tracks an unlimited number of times without purchasing them. Although customers don't have the luxury of downloading it for free and listening on the move, it still can be considered as a substitute as they are still being entertained. In addition, internet based film sites and catch-up television technology are substituting the need for purchased films. Therefore the threat of this substitute for GGM is very high.

Extra industry effects have a part to play when it comes to 24 hour TV & Radio music channels as the requirements for activating those services such as TV set top boxes and monthly subscriptions are quite expensive compared to the price of an album. But with added facilities of recording and choice of other channels on offer, they may have a better price to performance ratio when compared to a music album.

As part of the entertainment industry, music can also be substituted by other channels of entertainment such as movies and games. Although they may not be direct substitutes for music, they still provide similar services in entertaining the consumer. It may be said that compared to music, movies and games have a larger utility although the prices are set higher than music. In terms of gaming, the complementary products required such as game-stations are higher priced than a regular MP3 player, and the price to performance ratio is higher as the utility is considered to be higher. Therefore it can be said the threat of other entertainment sources are also posing a mid to low level of threat of substitution to the retail entertainment industry.

Industry rivalry

In terms of the attractiveness, the retail entertainment industry can be said to be highly attractive as more and more customers demand various forms of home entertainment products. The rivalry between online and high street competitors in the form of supermarkets has caused the problems evident in GGM.

Examiner's comments

This question was reasonably well answered. Most candidates demonstrated a sound understanding of the Five Forces model and most attempted to evaluate the impact of information technology upon GGM, using the model. Most candidates demonstrated a good degree of industry awareness and understanding. There was a degree of confusion in some answers between competitive rivalry and substitute products, but in general the model was well applied. Those candidates that scored badly on this question largely did so because they provided very generic answers with limited application to GGM or their answers failed to adequately consider the impact of IT and the internet upon GGM's competitive environment.

Common Errors:

• Theoretical answers with limited evaluation of the impact of IT and the internet

---

(b) The Directors of GGM are in a position of trust and must act in good faith in order to further the interests of the company, rather than their own. The Directors must always exercise due care and skill in carrying out their obligations as the key decision makers in GGM.

In the case of GGM, the Executive Chairman, T, has been a strong influence in the direction of the company. He has allowed his own personal beliefs and feelings about the business to sway the strategic direction of the business. Having founded the company in 1970, some 43 years ago, it is likely that T is aged between 60 and 70 years old. It would appear that he has been slow to react to change and perhaps not aware of what the new generation of 16 – 30 year olds demand in today's competitive music and entertainment market. T is not acting in the best interests of the company or safeguarding the jobs and long-term future of the employees. In addition, the Board is responsible as agents to look after the interests of its other stakeholders, such as banks, suppliers, customers and employees.

The current plan to close a few more stores and to relocate to smaller premises are still old-fashioned methods to cut costs. This plan does not address the change in the fundamental business model that GGM is operating, which is no longer a realistic model in today's instant world of music and film downloads. The requirements for success in this industry have moved permanently – so GGM has to change or not survive. It may already be too late. A real life example is HMV which ceased trading in January 2013 after over 100 years in the music business.

The Board has been weak and has allowed T to run the company as if it were his own. It has been unresponsive to warning signs of decline and profit reduction. It could be argued that the whole Board of GGM failed to exercise reasonable care, skill and judgement as it failed to consider the key environmental changes, in particular the growth of the internet and digital music, as a key threat to the business. It could be argued that, as a result, it also failed to promote the success of the company, as it undertook a highly risky price war with the supermarkets, which it lost. It could also be argued that T failed to exercise independent judgement as he was acting from personal interests and preferences rather than from strategic and market awareness.

In addition, the Directors have a responsibility to the wider stakeholders, in particular the employees. Redundancies are now likely if the rationalisation occurs which clearly affects a large number of employees. Again, had the Directors of GGM been more environmentally aware, they may have been able to safeguard more jobs by re-aligning the business to more online delivery.

Overall, the whole Board of GGM, led by T, has failed in a number of key duties as directors of the business.

Examiner's comments

This question was not well answered. Although most candidates did recognise T's overall influence in the current position of GGM, very few candidates adequately considered the role and responsibilities of the Board of GGM. Most candidates merely described the current situation, with little or no evaluation of the key failings of the Board of Directors and T in the past. Many candidates referred to the statement made by the business analyst but few adequately considered the impact of T's response. Very few candidates considered the responsibility of the Board to the wider stakeholders. Some candidates also incorrectly focused their answers upon a description of the structure of the Board.

Common Errors:

- Most answers were merely descriptive, repeating information provided in the scenario

- Poor evaluation of the wider role of the Board of GGM.

(c) **Short-term impact**

Customers

- The customers are likely to perceive GGM unfavourably as a result of the store closures.

- If they have not done so already, then they are likely to move to online or supermarket purchases or to the independent retailers.

- There will be fewer buying options for hard copy music and other entertainment products but, for most customers, the short-term impact is likely to be small. However, there is likely to be a feeling of negativity towards GGM from the customers as they will see GGM as a failed business.

Employees

- For some employees, the closures will mean immediate redundancy. GGM should consider strategies to lessen this impact on staff, such as redundancy packages, training and re-training and support for those staff remaining.

- There will also be a negative impact on those staff remaining. They may have to re-locate and also work different shift patterns or follow different working arrangements as a result of the rationalisation. Again, good communication and training is essential from GGM to lessen the impact upon remaining staff.

- Morale is likely to be low and staff turnover may increase as uncertainty about the future grows.

Long-term impact

Customers

- In the long-term, customers of GGM may perceive it far more favourably than now as it may become a highly specialised retailer.

- The reputation of GGM as a specialist, niche supplier of music should increase its reputation in the market.

- It is possible that GGM will build up a very loyal customer base for the products that it sells, providing that it survives in the long-term.

Employees

- In the long-term, the employees should develop a more focused and knowledgeable relationship with customers.

- They will have a better knowledge of the product they sell and this should improve staff morale.

Examiner's comments

This question was reasonably well answered. Most candidates were able to identify and discuss a range of factors impacting on both the employees and customers. Some answers were rather repetitive, merely re-stating the short term impacts for the long term impacts (for example, there will be redundancies in the short term and there will be redundancies in the long term.). However, very few candidates considered the possible long term benefits of the store closures and re-locations, as most answers were only focused upon the possible negative consequences, such as the immediate inconvenience to customers and the threat of redundancies for the staff. Candidates could also have considered the positive impact of more knowledgeable and focused staff concentrating upon a niche market, therefore providing better and more focused customer service to that group of remaining customers.

Common Errors:

- A degree of repetition in some answers between the short and long term impacts

- Lack of recognition of the potential for positive impacts

---

10 NSF (MAY 13 EXAM)

Key answer tips

Requirement (a) should be a straightforward question, requiring candidates to demonstrate their understanding of the benefits of environmental analysis for NSF. Focus specifically upon the benefits applicable to NSF is required and generic discussions of the benefits of environmental analysis will be awarded few marks.

Requirement (b) should also be a straightforward knowledge demonstration question, requiring candidates to demonstrate their wider knowledge of the syllabus area of foresight and planning.

Requirement (c) requires candidates to apply their knowledge of scenario planning to NSF. A high level of application of syllabus knowledge is expected in this answer.

(a)   NSF would benefit from a more formal, and systematic, approach to the gathering and analysis of information which is external to the organisation. This process of environmental screening would enable it to gather information under the broad categories of PEST: Political, Economic, Societal and Technological. Alternatively, it could use the categories described by one of the many other acronyms which exist for environmental factors. The benefits NSF would gain are:

- It would assist NSF in having a greater awareness of political priorities and their potential funding. Political policies tend to be cyclical and dependent on the views of the incumbent political party. By understanding the political context of the environment, NSF will be able to more effectively predict its future funding and therefore predict the potential threats that it could face.

- It would help NSF to identify and capitalise upon potential opportunities. It would, hopefully, be aware of the increasing importance of technology in society and could consider looking at ways to harness technology to increase awareness of sport. A greater exploitation of technology could be investigated. Similarly, an awareness of the ageing population could lead to directing more sporting activities towards this section of society. NSF could work in partnership with other public sector and voluntary bodies in health care to exploit this opportunity.

- NSF can acquire a base of objective, qualitative information. It would then have a deeper understanding of its market segments and its potential customers. This could avoid significant cost incurred in the developing of future strategies which are unsuitable. Understanding its changing market segments (such as the retired people) and their needs is critical for NSF and therefore having a reliable and up to date database of information would help this.

- By undertaking environmental analysis, NSF will have the capacity to be more sensitive to the changing needs of the population. Again, this should raise the company's awareness of the changing demographics. Exploiting technology to generate interest in the younger participants for example would help NSF to be more sensitive to its environment.

- Environmental analysis provides information for the strategy making process. This should improve the quality of strategy formulation and, as a consequence, reduce risk. NSF should be leading the sports in Country Z and not reacting to changes after the event. It must become more pro-active in its outlook and approach.

- NSF could be provided with a good, broad based, education and awareness of the sector in which it operates and the related industries. If NSF had been carrying out environmental analysis then the rate of societal change might not have been such a surprise.

- Regular environmental analysis, at least annually, will help the Board of NSF to identify and monitor new trends and changing interests in different sports. For example, newer sports (such as ultimate Frisbee) need to have an investment in facilities, trainers and coaches to try to introduce young people to the new sport. Awareness of different approaches to sport and fitness (such as low impact exercise for people with injuries or back problems) would help NSF to be fully aware of where funding needs to be considered and assistance focused on new trends and developments.

- All commercial businesses undertake SWOT analyses as part of their annual planning cycle and there is no reason why a not for profit government body such as NSF should not do so.

- Promotion and marketing of sport. Engaging in sport is a good way to meet people and to build a healthier lifestyle and combat stress. Health education and promotion of sports should be undertaken by the NSF as this will help it to achieve its overall goals. Environmental analysis will help NSF target areas where local people are less inclined to engage in sport.

Examiner's comments

This question was reasonably well answered. Most candidates were able to identify a range of benefits of environmental analysis, mainly by using the PESTLE model as a framework to structure their answer. However, some answers were once again largely generic, based mainly upon a general PESTLE analysis with limited reference to the benefits directly related to NSF. Answers taking this approach were awarded limited marks.

Common Errors:

- PESTLE analysis undertaken with little discussion of the benefits to NSF

- Generic answers

(b)   Foresight has been described as the 'art and science of anticipating the future'. For organisations such as NSF, foresight not only means predicting the future, but also developing an understanding of all potential changes which, if managed properly, could produce many new opportunities. There are a number of techniques which can be used to improve the foresight of an organisation. These include:

Visioning

A possible or desirable future state of the organisation is developed as a mental image by the management of the organisation. This vision may start off vaguely as a dream but should be firmed up into a concrete statement of where the organisation wants to be. The critical point is that the vision articulates a view of a realistic, credible and attractive future for the organisation, which is viewed as being an improvement on the current state of affairs.

Issues analysis

Issues arise through the convergence of trends and events. A trend is a trajectory that an issue takes because of the attention it receives and the socio-political forces that affect it. This convergence usually manifests itself because there are unfavourable events, which are sudden and unanticipated, public interest develops and becomes more important or there is increased political pressure. The issues should be analysed in terms of their impact on the organisation and their probability of occurrence.

Role Playing

This is where a group of people are given a description of a hypothetical future situation and are asked to behave as though they believe that the situation is true and happening.

Delphi Technique

This seeks to avoid the group pressures of conformity that are inherent in other group based forecasting methods. It does this by interrogating a panel of experts individually and sequentially and is based on the premise that knowledge and ideas possessed by some, but not all, of the experts can be identified and shared and this forms the basis of future interrogations.

Others which could be discussed are:

- Opportunity mapping
- Cross impact analysis
- Relevance trees

Note: Candidates were only required to explain two of the above techniques

---

Examiner's comments

This question was well answered by those candidates who obviously knew what foresight was. Many candidates had clearly read the article relating to this in a recent FM magazine. However, those candidates who did not know the term or the techniques of foresight performed very badly on this question.

Common Errors:

- Lack of syllabus knowledge of foresight and the associated techniques

---

(c) *Note: There is no one perfect method of producing scenario plans and the following answer is one of a number of ways in which scenarios can be developed. Candidates will be rewarded for appropriate stages which are applied to the NSF.*

Scenario planning, as a tool, will provide NSF with a better understanding of what could happen in the environment in which it operates and help to minimise surprises.

The stages could be as follows:

1 Define the scope of the scenario

NSF will need to decide what knowledge is most important to it. Consideration of its most important market segments and customers and the time frame it wishes to consider (i.e. how far into the future) should be paramount. It will need to decide whether the scenario is to be focussed on a specific issue e.g. the impact of the technology on the participation of children or a more blue sky approach where it asks a question such as; 'what is the future of community participation in sport in Country Z?'

2 Identify and map the major stakeholders

A consideration of who the main stakeholders are in the sporting environment should be undertaken and how they are likely to drive change over the period under consideration. For NSF this would most probably include the Government of Country Z (as the main funder), its volunteers and its customers. All of these stakeholders would need to be evaluated in terms of their impact and power to influence the future activities of NSF.

3 Identify the basic trends and uncertainties affecting the business

In assessing the trends and factors that would be identified in an environmental analysis and considering how they may change in the future, NSF would most probably want to focus upon the technological advances and the increasing use of the internet by children and young adults and its effect upon sport participation. Since it is very dependent upon the Government for its revenue it would also consider the trends in the economy which would affect its income. Also the changing demographics would be a major consideration for NSF.

4 **Identify the key trends and uncertainties**

Of the basic trends that have been identified NSF would need to decide which are the key uncertainties. These trends and uncertainties will be the 'drivers for change' which will require contingency planning activities and will shape the future of the industry. In the case of NSF this would certainly include the declining Government funding and societal and demographic changes. These will be the main drivers forcing change in NSF.

5 **Construct initial scenario themes, or skeleton outlines**

Possible future scenarios should then be created by forming the key trends and uncertainties into coherent themes. Usually two alternative scenarios are produced but more can be identified if necessary. NSF might develop one scenario where the economy continues to be depressed and funding continues to decline with sport becoming less important to society. This would be the 'negative' scenario. The alternative 'positive' scenario might feature a booming economy with many members of society both volunteering and actively participating in sport activities.

6 **Check for plausibility and internal consistency**

Effective scenarios are both internally consistent and plausible. This means that different directions that the trends have taken in the scenario could logically happen together and the events described could happen within the timescale chosen.

7 **Develop learning scenarios**

The next stage would be to 'flesh out' the scenarios so that they become full descriptions of the sector and conditions that are expected to prevail in the future timeframe. This is often done by writing a detailed piece of narrative. The managers of NSF would need to consider the detailed aspects of each scenario in terms of impact upon NSF's staff, possible plans for re-training, more detailed financial analysis and an overall view of the sporting environment in Country Z.

Examiner's comments

This question was very poorly answered. Many candidates demonstrated a poor level of basic knowledge and understanding of scenario planning. In addition many answers were very generic, merely listing or describing the basic scenario planning stages with little or no attempt to apply these stages directly to NSF. This appears to be an area of weakness in candidates' syllabus knowledge and understanding and must be addressed. Answers to this question were often very thin and lacked sufficient depth to be awarded a pass mark.

Common Errors:

- Poor syllabus knowledge

- Poor/no application to NSF

---

11   CB (MAY 11 EXAM)

Key answer tips

In part (a)(i), make sure you focus on explaining industry analysis and do not make the mistake of answering part (a)(ii) in this part of the question. When answering (a)(ii) don't forget that your answer MUST be applied to Futurist itself. A generic answer would not have scored well here.

Part (b)(i) examined Porter's generic strategies. This is a popular area and should be one any well-prepared student should be prepared for. Don't spend too long defining the terms – again the question clearly shows that the examiner is looking for application to the scenario and Futurist.

Part (b)(ii) has also been regularly examined in E3 – make sure you are able to discuss the three types of information systems strategies and again **apply them** to a scenario. Don't forget to answer the question set – the question clearly asked for how the information systems strategy could help with the generic strategies. If you haven't linked your answer to the generic strategies, you will be unlikely to pass this part of the requirement.

(a)   (i)   There are two main models used to analyse the external environment:

Porter's Five Forces model which examines:

1   the rivalry among the industry's existing firms

2   the threat of new entrants to the industry

3   the threat of substitute services and/or products

4   the bargaining power of the suppliers to the industry

5   the bargaining power of the industry's customers/buyers.

The other model is usually referred to by an acronym, PEST. This model analyses the external environment in terms of its:

Political influences: for example, taxation policy

Economic environment: for example, unemployment

Social and demographic factors: for example, age structure of the population

Technological factors: rate of innovation.

The PEST model has been supplemented by the addition of Ecological and Legal factors producing the PESTEL model.

Examiner's comments

This question was well answered. Most candidates correctly identified the above 2 models and were able to explain their main components. Some candidates however, incorrectly identified 'competitor analysis', the Ansoff matrix, scenario planning and Porter's Diamond within this answer. These were not considered to be relevant environmental analysis models and awarded no credit.

(ii)   The Five Forces model can be used by the team to assess how fierce the competition is likely to be if the Futurist decides to act as a wedding venue. This will then enable the team to appreciate how profitable this new strategy is likely to be and enable it to decide whether or not it should enter this market.

If the Futurist decides to enter the wedding business it will be competing against seven other hotels which are offering a range of different prices to different market segments. Therefore, an analysis of the industry via the Five Forces model could avoid the Futurist making a mistake with regard to its competitive position and enable it to exploit which of the five forces appear to be favourable.

The PEST model should assist the team in arriving at an informed understanding of the external environment which should enable the team to devise a strategy that better fits the needs of the market. It will also assist the team to understand how the various factors within the model are changing and also the direction of future trends. For example, an understanding of the likely future popularity of marriage, a Social factor, will be very important for the team's wedding venue strategy. The team may also find that some of the factors are inter-linked: if, for example, the popularity of marriage is linked to levels of unemployment. The team could refine its PEST analysis to identify key drivers for change: these are the factors which are likely to have a direct important bearing on whether the strategy will prove successful. An example would be trends in disposable income for people aged 20–30. If incomes are rising customers may be willing to spend more on their wedding which will influence the price the team will set for the wedding held in the Futurist.

Both of the models can be used by the team in the initial stages of formulating its strategy when it would form part of the rational approach to strategy. The models can also be used as part of a continuous process of environmental scanning. This would enable the team to be aware of opportunities and threats as they arise rather than having to wait for a formal strategic review as under the rational process. Environment scanning will be part of an emergent strategy approach.

Examiner's comments

This question was reasonably well answered by most candidates. Many answers were particularly strong in application of the PEST elements, in particular recognition of the economic and demographic forces which could affect the wedding business strategy. Porter's Five Forces model was generally less well applied, with many answers providing only a generic discussion of the forces.

However, overall most candidates demonstrated a reasonable ability to apply the model to the scenario context and were awarded pass marks for this part of the requirement.

(b)   (i)   Porter's model of three generic strategic approaches comprises the following:

1   Overall cost leadership

2   Differentiation

3   Focus

To achieve overall cost leadership the Futurist would have to be able to be the lowest cost producer in its market. In order to do this it would require some resource, competence or advantage not possessed by its competitors. It is a new hotel and so its equipment and layout should be modern. However, it is unlikely that this will give the Futurist a sustainable competitive advantage. In the absence of any other unique advantage a strategy of overall cost leadership will not be applicable for the Futurist.

A policy of differentiation should be based on providing a wedding package that its potential customers will perceive as being unique. This would mean that the customers would perceive that they are receiving premium value and so enable the Futurist to charge a premium price. This appears to be the strategy being following by the De Luxe hotel which is situated in a castle in a beautiful rural setting. This hotel has also won many international awards for its food and its rooms. These attributes of the De Luxe hotel, particularly its location, have enabled it to charge a premium price of £500 per wedding guest.

If the team is able to identify some attributes which would lead its customers to perceive that they were receiving premium value, then the team could pursue a differentiation strategy.

If the team wanted to follow a Focus or Niche strategy then it will have to follow a strategy which concentrates on one or more particular segments of its market rather than try to meet the needs of the entire market with a single service or product. As it seems unlikely that the Futurist will be the overall cost leader in its market, it could apply a Focus strategy to some sort of differentiated offering. Such a strategy appears to be being followed by the Royal Albert hotel which charges £10 per wedding guest. This suggests that it has targeted a market segment of people whom have low incomes or are very prudent with their money or do not like lavish wedding celebrations. However, depending on this hotel's capacity to cater for weddings, its margins and the number of weddings it attracts each year, it could be as profitable as the De Luxe which is serving a completely different market segment.

Therefore, a Focus strategy could be appropriate for the Futurist to follow.

Examiner's comments

This question was well answered by many candidates. It would appear that there has been a good degree of improvement in the candidates' knowledge and understanding of the generic strategies since it was last examined. It was encouraging to see that both the basic understanding of the model has improved, as too has the candidates' ability to apply the model to a scenario.

Most candidates correctly described the model and many were able to discuss its application to the wedding strategy of the Futurist hotel and its competitor hotels. It was particularly encouraging to see how many candidates attempted to present examples of how the generic strategies could be directly applied by the Futurist, although some candidates struggled to present a relevant discussion of the focus strategy. Some candidates still have difficulty in describing the focus strategy and there is some confusion between this and the 'stuck in the middle' approach identified by Michael Porter.

(ii)   Information systems can contribute to a generic competitive strategy by means of strategies for: Information Systems, Information Management, and Information Technology. The information strategies required to support the wedding venue strategy will be a sub-set of the hotel's information strategy. It may also be the case that if the hotel is part of a group its information strategy is a sub-set of a larger group information strategy.

Information systems strategy: this strategy is concerned with how the Futurist can use information to support its wedding package strategy. This strategy should describe the information needed to formulate the strategy and to maintain it. The Futurist would require regular management information reporting on the profitability of whichever wedding package strategy it decided to implement. This reporting should include internal information, for example, performance against budget, turnover and margins achieved. The management information should also take a strategic focus in placing the Futurist's performance in an external context. Thus, it should report on market growth and share and comparative information about competitors' performance. As well as the regular reporting there will be a need for 'ad hoc' reports, for example, when environmental scanning detects random events outside the internal environment of the Futurist.

Information management strategy: the Futurist will require this strategy to describe how the data and information relating to wedding business should be stored and accessed. As the hotel will have other strategies and information systems, the information management strategy should describe how these relate to the strategy for the wedding package. For example, there will be a requirement to calculate costs and margins for weddings. The hotel will also be calculating these for other aspects of its business. Therefore, the information management strategy should state whether there needs to be a separate system for calculating these for wedding business or whether the hotel's other systems can be used for this purpose.

The project team designing the wedding package strategy consists of CB the accountant, the hotel's General Manager and the Restaurants Manager. Once their strategy is being implemented they will have different levels of involvement and responsibility for it. With regards to the data and information associated with the strategy, their roles will need to be demarcated. This would be described in the information management strategy.

Information technology strategy: this strategy will specify the hardware and software required for the wedding package strategy. The wedding package strategy may not need a separate strategy for its technology as its needs are unlikely to be different from the needs elsewhere in the hotel, which will have been specified in an overall information technology strategy. However, it may require some specialist software in which case this would be stated in this strategy.

Examiner's comments

This question was not well answered. Most candidates merely described either the information required for each generic strategy or failed to correctly identify appropriate systems which directly supported the generic strategies. Most answers were unspecific and failed to correctly or directly apply to each generic strategy. Many answers discussed the use of the Internet and corporate websites but failed to clearly link these to the support of the generic strategies.

---

12   BBB (NOV 11 EXAM)

Key answer tips

In part (a), you needed to use Porter's Five Forces to evaluate BBB's market. This is a key model within E3 and you need to make sure you apply each force to the scenario and the impact it would have on BBB's profitability. Where possible try and conclude on whether each force is high or low.

Part (b) followed on from (a) – so as long as your answer was consistent with your analysis in the previous part of the question, you should have scored here. Remember again that at this level, if you are providing advice (which was asked for in the requirement), you must justify yourself.

In part (c) be careful not to undertake a Porter's Diamond analysis – the question simply asked how it could be used by BBB when considering future investment.

(a)   **Competitive rivalry within retail banking**

BBB has entered a market which contains state owned institutions that compete strongly for retail banking business. SB, which is the major state-owned bank has half of the retail banking business and has a position of dominance. There are also some well-established foreign banks that have 35% of the market. However, two foreign banks that entered country R at the same time as BBB have decided to withdraw from the country.

All of the above factors suggest that the competitive rivalry within R's retail banking market is intense.

Bargaining power of customers

The customers are the people of R who either have, or would like to have, a bank account. In 2008 only 50% of the population had a bank account. A citizen of R who wants a bank account in 2011 has the following possible providers:

- SB, the state owned bank, which has 50% of R's retail business

- Other state institutions

- Foreign banks who have 35% of the retail banking market

- BBB

- Any other banks or institutions which have a share of the 15% of the market and are not accounted for above

The choice of providers of retail bank accounts for the citizen of R is a wide one. This would not give the individual customer any power over a bank 'per se'. However the wide degree of choice will contribute to the degree of competitive rivalry.

Bargaining power of suppliers

As R has a Western style liberal economy, this would permit the free movement of funds so BBB should have access to cash both inside and outside of R. BBB should, therefore, be able to supply its capital needs subject only to normal financial market conditions.

There is no information given in the scenario about other inputs which BBB might require, so no judgement is given about this.

Threat of new entrants

Country R's economy is a liberal one which suggests that entry into the retail banking market should be possible for any bank able to meet R's regulatory requirements. However, the extent of the investment which BBB made to enter this market, $350 million, would constitute a barrier to entry for many businesses. The dominance of SB and the implied customer loyalty possessed by that bank would be further barriers. The recent experience of the two foreign banks which decided to withdraw from R could also dissuade other banks from entering R as does the conservatism of the citizens.

Threat of substitute products

This threat bears a relationship to the position of buyers who have a great degree of choice as regards a bank to supply them with a bank account. The way in which a bank account can be operated has changed lately with an increasing proportion being operated via the Internet. However, these are supplementary rather than substitute products.

Any innovation which BBB might introduce to differentiate itself is likely to be imitable by its competitors. Within a liberal economy, citizens are likely to become increasingly reliant on a bank account for which there is no equivalent substitute.

Summary

Porter's Five Forces Model attempts to describe an industry or market in terms of its competitiveness and resultant attractiveness.

The retail banking market within country R can be summarised thus:

Force	*Strength of force*
Competitive rivalry within retail banking	Strong
Bargaining power of customers	Weak
Bargaining power of suppliers	No judgement given
Threat of new entrants	Weak
Threat of substitute products	Weak

The aggregation of the Five Forces suggests that this market should be a profitable one. However, this does not imply that the market will be equally profitable for all the participants.

Examiner's comments

This question was not well answered. Many answers lacked depth and analysis and many were descriptive rather than applied. Most candidates adequately discussed competitive rivalry within the banking industry but few went on to discuss how this could affect future profitability for BBB. Many interpreted the power of the customers and suppliers incorrectly and there was also some confusion between the threat of new entrant and the threat of substitutes, with some candidates considering these to be the same force. The main weakness of answers was the lack of evaluation of the effect on profitability of each force for BBB. Many candidates could correctly describe the force and could adequately apply some to the scenario but they failed to then use this analysis to consider its effect on profitability for BBB.

> Common errors
>
> - Confusion of the forces
> - Lack of understanding of substitute products
> - Limited applications to BBB
> - Limited/no discussion of the effect on profitability of each force for BBB

(b)   The analysis in (a) suggests that the retail banking market in R should be a profitable one. Other favourable market attributes are the forecast of growth in the market which may be based, in part, on the consideration that in 2008 only 50% of the population had a bank account. As more of R's citizens acquire a bank account, then the amount of retail business in R will increase.

However, the earlier analysis indicated that this market has a strong degree of competitive rivalry. BBB faces competition from SB, a state owned bank which has 50% of the country's retail deposits. SB has been recently reorganised which has strengthened it. SB has shown it can innovate with its introduction of successful new products. SB will also benefit from the conservatism of R's population who don't like change. Although BBB has a strong international brand image, this may not be enough to overcome R's citizens' preference for the familiar. All these factors make SB a very formidable competitor. BBB also has to face competition from a number of foreign banks and possibly some more domestic banks.

In making a recommendation to BBB about the continuance of its business in R it is important to determine the sustainable competitive advantage(s) which BBB possesses with respect to its business in R. Given the dominance of SB and the strong competition within this market, there seems no obvious source of sustainable competitive advantage for BBB within R. This, presumably, was the conclusion also reached by the two foreign banks who decided in 2011 to withdraw from R.

BBB is advised to withdraw from retail banking in R. If this decision is implemented there will be exit costs to pay but there should also be some revenue resulting from the sale of BBB's assets within R.

> **Examiner's comments**
>
> This question was reasonably well answered. Most candidates presented a good range of positive and negative aspects of the analysis presented in part (a) of their answer and were then able to make a logical and reasoned recommendation to either leave, or remain in, Country R.

(c)   **Porter's Diamond**

BBB should find this model helpful because it examines the competitiveness of countries. It suggests that there are inherent reasons why some countries are more competitive than others and why particular industries within countries are more successful than others. If BBB is considering investing in a new foreign country it could use Porter's Diamond as a screening mechanism to reject countries where it seems investment will not be fruitful. On the positive side, the model will indicate countries where the business environment will be favourable.

The model implies that national advantage is due to the inter-relationship of the following:

Firm strategy, structure and rivalry: consideration of these factors will give BBB an appreciation of the likely competition it will face.

Factor conditions: this will inform BBB of the availability, within the country under consideration, of the factors it will need in order to do business, for example, the supply and skill levels of its potential workforce.

Demand conditions: this will reveal the sophistication of the country's consumers and how demanding they are. BBB will then be able to determine whether its product offerings will appeal.

Related and supporting industries: an understanding of this will enable BBB to determine if the country has the infrastructure to support its operations.

Porter also points out that two other factors may influence the ability of a country to produce world-class firms:

- *Government:* whose policies can impact on the four aspects of the Diamond given above.

- *Chance events:* for example wars and civil unrest or chance discoveries can also change the four aspects of the diamond unpredictably.

However, even if Porter's Diamond suggests a country is a good environment, the results of the analysis should be used advisedly.

Examiner's comments

Most candidates performed reasonably well on this question. Many demonstrated a basic knowledge of the Diamond and were able to apply it in some way to BBB. Those candidates who failed this question did so because they provided either descriptive answers or they demonstrated limited knowledge of the model.

Common errors

- Incorrect model or lack of knowledge of the model

- Limited application to BBB

---

13   D4D (MAY 05 EXAM)

Key answer tips

Part (a) should be a relatively straightforward application of Porter's diamond.

In part (b) ensure that you apply your points to the scenario. Also ensure that you answer the question and address the aims of D4D and those of the inward investing company.

In part (c) the question asks you to explain the required steps, so make sure your answer has the necessary depth and focus upon D4D.

(a)   **International competitive advantage**

To score extra marks here you could also look to discuss the role of government and the nature of clustering of firms within countries.

A popular model for discussing the link between competitive advantage and geographical location is Porter's diamond. Porter claimed that countries do not have an overall competitive advantage per se but that specific industries can exploit their location to gain a competitive advantage internationally. Porter identified four areas to consider:

Factor conditions

These include basic and advanced factors of production. Basic factors are unsustainable as they are easily copied (e.g. unskilled labour) whilst advanced factors can convey the advantage, as they are less easy to emulate (e.g. scientific expertise).

They include human, physical, knowledge, capital and infrastructure e.g. linguistic ability of the Swiss has provided advantage in the banking industry.

D4D's weather may give firms an advantage in growing certain crops. Similarly the young, educated workforce is likely to convey an advantage in high-tech industries.

Demand conditions

Sophisticated home demand can lead to the company developing significant advantages in the global market place. Fussy consumers set high standards for products whilst past experience of the product's progress through the life cycle in the home market can provide valuable input to new strategic initiatives. e.g. Japanese customers have high expectations of their electrical products which forces producers to provide a technically superior product for the global market place. They are so used to dealing with sophisticated customers that, when they come across unsophisticated markets, they excel way beyond the competition.

Related and supporting industries

An advantage can be conveyed by the availability of superior supplier industries e.g. Italy has a substantial leatherwear industry which is supported by leather working plants and top fashion and design companies.

Strategy, structure and rivalry

Different nations have different approaches to business in terms of structure and the intensity of rivalry that can take place. If a company is used to dealing with strong competition then it will have experience of rivals' attacks and so will be better able to fight them off.

Domestic rivalry can keep the organisations 'lean and mean' so that when they go out into the global market place they can compete more successfully with the less capable foreign competition e.g. Nokia and Finland's approach to the regulation of telecoms.

(b) **Aims**

*Be careful not to let your answer to (b) drift into part (c) territory by discussing how to attract inward investment – this section focuses on **why**, not how.*

The government of D4D will have the following aims:

- To attract as many foreign firms as possible to invest in D4D

- Protecting domestic firms from excessive competition – clearly there is a possible conflict between these first two aims

- To ensure that the foreign firms concerned are reputable and will invest in infrastructure such as education

- To maximise tax revenues

- To ensure compliance with relevant legislation re health and safety, pollution, etc

- Increased employment

- Reinvestment of profits by foreign firms to create growth and more jobs

- To develop clusters of similar firms, based on the Porter's diamond analysis. This will encourage competitive advantage and will attract yet more firms.

Companies seeking to invest in D4D will have the following aims:

- To maximise profit

- To minimise global tax liabilities

- Compliance with legislation

- To invest in countries with stable governments, a strong economy, good infrastructure and a skilled and well educated workforce

- To make the investment an attractive place for overseas posting of existing staff

- To reduce distribution costs by being near to other markets

- To develop strong relationships with government departments

- To get financial assistance, e.g. tax breaks, development grants and soft loans, from the government.

In most respects the aims of the D4D government are consistent with the aims of foreign firms seeking to invest in D4D:

- Both want to see profits, growth and jobs created

- Both want a country with a well educated workforce and strong infrastructure

- Both want political stability and an environment that encourages investment.

However, there are areas of possible conflict:

- Tax – the government will want to maximise tax revenue but companies will seek to minimise their liabilities through careful planning. They may also expect tax breaks as an incentive to invest in D4D (see below).

- Remittances – companies may want to take funds out of the country but the government will want to see them reinvested. This could affect dividend policy, for example.

- Competition – once established, a firm may not want to see competitors encouraged to invest in D4D.

- Employment – the government will be keen to see jobs go to locals but the firms may prefer to use staff from their domestic country.

- Finance – the company may want more 'sweeteners' than the government is happy to give.

(c) The government of D4D should focus on the following areas to make the country more attractive to outside investors:

Factor conditions

Porter suggested that the root of sustainable competitive success is 'advanced factors' so the government of D4D should focus on these.

- Government policy could be aimed at improving D4D's communications and transport infrastructure.

- Similarly, training and development policies could be focused on key industries to assist in enhancing the skills and knowledge required to achieve world-class excellence.

- Financial assistance could be offered to the unemployed to undergo retraining in certain key areas, and firms in certain industries could be incentivised to take on the unemployed.

- Additional government policies could be aimed at encouraging firms to invest more in R&D, such as tax incentives.

- Tax breaks and other assistance such as cheap loans should be offered to foreign firms seeking to invest in D4D.

- The government may make it easier for firms to raise capital by developing a strong capital market.

Demand conditions

- A second potential set of government policies might be to encourage consumers to be more demanding of product performance through increased spending on education and training and through consumer protection and product safety legislation.

- Similarly, government policies could be introduced to encourage best practice in:

    - product design and development

    - supplier and manufacturer partnership relations to deliver quality to consumers

    - marketing and selling overseas.

Firm strategy, structure and rivalry

- One potential government policy is to encourage, rather than discourage, competition at home. This can be achieved through less government intervention such as quotes to discourage foreign competition. It can be argued that increased rivalry among firms within an industry forces superior practice and, therefore, strengthens the industry.

Related and supporting industries

- The government could also acquire consultancy advice from experts within existing world-class industries overseas.

- Similarly, the government could set up development agencies in the key industries.

14 JURANIA (NOV 05 EXAM)

Key answer tips

Part (a) looks at the link between competitive advantage and location. Porter's diamond is a tool designed to explore such a link. To score well, each aspect of the diamond must be related to specific facts in the scenario and evaluated. Note that you would **not** need to draw the diagram within your answer.

In part (b) make sure you identify and evaluate risks.

(a) **Competitive advantage**

Michael Porter, in his book *The Competitive Advantage of Nations*, tried to isolate the national attributes that further competitive advantage in an industry. He argued that, for a country's industry to be successful, it needs to have the attributes and relationships shown in the diagram below.

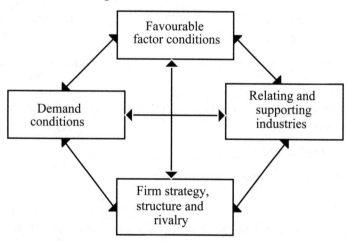

These can be applied to 222 as follows:

Favourable factor conditions

Industries can benefit from local factors such as physical resources, weather, capital, human resources, knowledge and infrastructure.

222 has clearly benefited from the local availability of suitably qualified staff, due partly to the excellent reputation of Jurania's university.

222 wishes to expand into other African countries so its factors need to be compared with those countries rather than globally. While it is doubtful whether the university at Jurania is producing better IT graduates than universities in the USA, for example, they will not demand such high wages either. There is more of a case, however, that 222 may have an advantage over firms from other African countries, with the possible exception of South Africa, provided 222 is not competing with any global foreign firms operating in those markets.

Overall, therefore, this should give 222 a competitive advantage in its chosen markets.

Demand conditions

There must be a strong home market demand for the product or service. This determines how industries perceive and respond to buyer needs and creates the pressure to innovate.

222 has benefited from the economic growth in Jurania and neighbouring countries in creating demand. Included within this demand are many top 100 companies who, presumably, put pressure on 222 to deliver better solutions than competitors. However, it is more doubtful that these firms will be as demanding as global customers encountered by global competitors.

As with factor conditions, it is likely that 222 has an advantage over indigenous local competitors but not against global players.

Relating and supporting industries

The success of an industry can be due to its suppliers and related industries.

222 has benefited from being close to several IT hardware and software companies and the country's largest ISP. However, there is little indication that any of these suppliers are world class and would have contributed to 222's competitive advantage.

Firm strategy, structure and rivalry

Porter found that domestic competition was vital as a spur to innovation and also enhanced global competitive advantage.

There is no indication that competition in Jurania has been intense so 222 will not have benefited in this way.

In conclusion, 222 has a basis for expansion into neighbouring countries but should be wary of becoming a global player.

(b) **Risks of proposed internet strategy**

Using the services of a local specialist web designer

The main risks here are:

- The local specialist may not produce a site as well designed as that from a major firm with more experience and expertise.

- The local specialist may go bust and not be able to service future changes to the site.

As long as the local specialist can demonstrate a proven track record and evidence of financial stability, these risks should not deter 222. The advantages of having a local expert to deal with issues when they arise should outweigh the risks.

Having a sophisticated website with case studies

The risks here include:

- The site may be too complicated for users.

- The case studies may disclose secrets to competitors, thus eroding competitive advantage.

- Previous customers may refuse to allow their details to be posted, reducing the effectiveness of the idea.

The first risk is not significant as 222 sells to organisations that in most cases will have more sophisticated buyers with some knowledge of the technology involved. The others can be managed by careful disclosure on the website.

222 to host the website

The main risks of 222 hosting its own website and buying a powerful web server are:

- 222 may not have the expertise that suppliers have, particularly to deal with problems. This could result in greater website downtime and lost business.

- There will also be the extra operating gearing risk due to investment in hardware, more expensive software licences, etc.

- There is also the risk of obsolescence regarding the server.

The first of these is the most significant risk and is unnecessary. All of them can be eliminated by using an external host. Competition to host is intense as firms could be based anywhere in the world and the cost of external hosting is low.

Fibre-optic broadband

Fibre-optic broadband is growing in popularity around the world so would appear to be a low risk option. However, there are risks associated with the choice of supplier:

- The supplier is a new company so may not have the experience required to develop a problem-free network.

- The supplier may not have the financial strength to ensure its medium-term future, so may not be around to service any problems as they arise.

These risks are significant so it may be more prudent for 222 to use a more established firm.

15 FFF COMMUNICATIONS (NOV 06 EXAM)

Key answer tips

This is an in-depth question on competitor analysis. The main problem is that many students will feel that they cannot generate enough (different!) ideas to ensure a pass.

However, as in many other questions the main weakness when this question was set was the lack of application to the given scenario. Some answers were mere descriptions of each stage and some were lists only. Most candidates failed to include the information that would need to be gathered at each stage again demonstrating an inability to read the question requirements properly

(a)   Competitor analysis can be defined as 'the systematic review of all available information (marketing, production, financial, etc) on the activities of competitors in order to gain a competitive advantage'.

The advantages of adopting a formal approach to competitor analysis are as follows.

Understanding relative competitive advantage

A detailed analysis of the value chains of existing competitors will allow FFF to assess the basis of competitive strategy used by itself and its competitors. This will enable FFF to assess whether its existing competitive strategy is sustainable and which aspects of the value chain need addressing to improve it.

Identifying potential new competitors

As well as analysing existing competitors, competitor analysis will help FFF identify potential new entrants to the industry and act accordingly – for example, by reviewing how barriers to entry can be strengthened.

Understanding competitors' current and potential strategies

By analysing competitors' past and current strategies, it may be possible for FFF to anticipate likely future moves and plan in advance, rather than having to react to competitor actions. This should reduce future levels of risk and uncertainty.

Understanding how competitors may react to FFF's actions

FFF will want to know which strategies to avoid because a particular competitor's response may be very aggressive.

Developing future strategies

Competitor analysis should allow FFF to decide with whom it should 'pick a fight' in the industry and in what way. This should increase the chances of success of such strategies.

Influencing competitors' future actions

By understanding how competitors assess whether particular market segments are worth targeting, FFF may be able be able to deter them from entering its markets – for example, by lowering prices.

Forecasting

An understanding of competitor behaviour will improve the accuracy of FFF's forecasts.

(b)   The key stages of a formal competitor analysis process are as follows:

Step 1: Identify competitors

The first step is to identify which competitors should be analysed.

Clearly all significant existing competitors need to be analysed, but even here the definition of a 'competitor' can be wide ranging.

Kotler identifies four types of competitors:

- *Brand competitors* include firms most like FFF with a similar product portfolio, of comparable size and targeting the same customers.
- *Industry competitors* offer similar products but in different segments – for example, firms who just make mobile phones or who just target oil company customers.
- *Form competitors* aim to satisfy the same customer needs but with different types of products – what Porter would refer to as 'substitutes'. For FFF this could include providers of land-line phones, for example.

- *Generic competitors* compete for the same income or budget as FFF. Thus armaments manufacturers could be seen as competing with thermal imaging products for government military budgets.

Forecasting potential new entrants is more difficult and could include the following:

- firms that are not in the industry but could overcome barriers relatively cheaply.
- firms that could gain obvious synergy if they entered the industry
- customers or suppliers who may wish to vertically integrate into the industry.

Step 2: Analyse competitors

Porter suggests that, once selected, competitors should be analysed with respect to the following headings:

Objectives/goals

It is vital to understand what drives competitors' behaviour. Knowledge of goals will allow FFF to understand whether competitors are satisfied with their current position and how likely they are to change that position. It will also enable FFF to predict likely responses to FFF's strategies.

For example, a competitor focused on short-term financial targets may not be willing to spend much to defend an attack.

Objectives can be determined from historical behaviour, investor communications and the chairman's statement in published accounts

Assumptions

This section looks at the assumptions a competitor makes about itself and its industry, even if these assumptions are unrealistic and outdated.

For example, a competitor may still see itself as the market leader despite problems over quality and falling sales. If it further believes that it still has high customer loyalty, then a speculative price cut by FFF to win customers may be met with little response. Identifying such blind spots can expose major opportunities for FFF.

Assumptions are more difficult to identify, but may include trying to understand the value systems of senior executives and main advisors.

Strategy

Analysis of strategy involves looking at where and how competitors are competing. Often what firms disclose in press statements is more revealing of how a competitor understands their strategy than looking at what they do.

Capabilities

This section looks at competitors' strengths and weaknesses and whether they have the competences and resources required for success in the industry. This can involve detailed analysis of financial statements (e.g. ratio analysis), scrutinising press reports and trade publications, discussions with ex-employees and discussions with customers.

Step 3: Develop competitor response profiles

The analysis of step 2 should allow FFF to create competitor response profiles that identify the strategic changes the particular competitor might initiate and also how they might respond to FFF's initiatives.

Competitors' goals, assumptions and strategies will indicate the nature, probability, strength and timing of a response but their strengths and weaknesses will indicate their ability to respond effectively.

Kotler suggests four typical response profiles:

- *Laid back* competitors are unlikely to respond to any initiatives.
- *Selective* competitors react to attack in selected markets only.
- *Tiger* competitors always respond aggressively.
- *Stochastic* competitors exhibit no predictable pattern of behaviour.

16 G ELECTRONICS (NOV 07 EXAM)

Key answer tips

In part (a) frameworks such as PEST, Porter's five forces and Porter's diamond can be useful for generating ideas but they need to be applied correctly to the scenario. For example, using Porter's diamond, strong domestic rivalry is viewed as a positive factor as it can result in highly competitive domestic firms but this would not make the market attractive to a new entrant such as G.

In part (b) you need to be careful to avoid repeating your answer to part (a).

(a) Given that G is planning to set up both research and manufacturing facilities, the ideal characteristics of a country are as follows:

Macroeconomic factors

- Strong growth in GDP and disposable income should ensure growth in demand for cars with a corresponding increase in demand for components.
- A stable currency reduces the perceived risk of the project and should facilitate better planning.
- Low inflation will also reduce the risk associated with the investment as well as generating consumer confidence.
- Low interest rates will give low cost finance for G, its potential customers and car purchasers.

Political environment

- A stable political environment will reduce the risk of the investment. For example, what is the likelihood of armed conflict, civil war or of employees being kidnapped by terrorist groups?
- The political attitude towards foreign firms is extremely important. For example, will G face protectionist measures regarding ownership structures and repatriation of funds?
- On the other hand some governments may be keen to encourage FDI via incentives such as soft loans and tax breaks.
- If the country is a member of a regional trade union such as the EU or NAFTA, then exporting components into neighbouring countries will be much easier and cheaper.

Social factors

- High standards of local education, especially to degree level and beyond, will ensure a good supply of suitable candidates to recruit locally for both the research facility and the manufacturing plant.

- Availability of labour and wage rates would be key factors for the manufacturing facility. Ideally G would want a developing country where education and skills levels are high but average wage levels have yet to catch up with its home country.

- A shared spoken language between G's home country and the target country will make communication easier.

Technological factors

- Is the communications infrastructure of the target country sufficiently developed? For example, some African countries still have very limited high speed internet access, which would make communication between the two research facilities more difficult.

Ethical issues

- G would want to check the country's record on human rights to avoid attracting negative publicity as investing there could be considered to be supporting the incumbent regime.

Competitive/market issues

- G would want to choose a country with a high number of major automobile manufacturers present. As well as providing potential customers for components, there may be scope for collaboration over research.

- Ideally there would also be neighbouring countries that are reasonably close with major car manufacturers.

- The presence of many rival components manufacturers could be a deterrent to G as it would make it much harder to earn high margins there.

(b) G could use the following sources of information when evaluating potential countries:

*The question asked for the nature **and** source of information, therefore you must identify and explain both **what** information is required (the nature) and identify **where** this can be obtained from (the source)*

- There are likely to be many publications regarding the state of the economy, GDP, average earnings, growth estimates and so on. The target country government is likely to produce many of these but international organisations such as OECD and the World Bank should also be contacted.

- Government departments in the target country could be contacted to determine government policy, both locally and nationally – for example, to see attitudes towards encouraging foreign firms to invest and/or what protectionist measures are in place.

- The published accounts of competitors and customers in the target country could indicate changes in the industry, growth profiles and provide useful information for benchmarking.

- Given the global nature of the automobile industry, there are likely to be many industry publications detailing the state of the industry in different countries and growth opportunities.

- Details regarding security risks and terrorism can be obtained from UN Departments and from the foreign offices of most developed countries. The latter will normally classify and assess the risks concerned.

- A country's environmental and human rights records can be assessed using Amnesty International and Greenpeace reports respectively.

- A target country's educational and skills standards will be the subject of UNESCO surveys and investigations.

- More specifically related to a potential research facility, G could contact local universities and examine their websites to see which areas of research they are involved with.

- The Internet can be an invaluable source of desk research with many websites, particularly US-based, who specialise in assessing country risk.

E-BUSINESS, SCM AND INFORMATION MANAGEMENT

17   AAP (MAY 13 EXAM)

Key answer tips

In requirement (a)(i) candidates should apply their syllabus knowledge of McFarlan's strategic grid to AAP's information systems. Candidates should consider bith the current information system used by AAP and the potential information systems that could be used.

In requirement (a)(ii) candidates shoals focus their answers upon the strategic importance of information systems. Again, application to AAP is required in this answer and therefore candidates should ensure that they explain why it is important for AAP specifically to consider investment in information systems at a strategic level. Both internal business and external industry factors should be considered.

Requirement (b) should be straightforward requiring candidates to discuss the benefits and problems for AAP of developing an e-business strategy. It is important that answers focus specifically upon e-business and not just upon the investment in information systems generally

In requirement (c) candidates are expected to demonstrate their wider syllabus knowledge of Web 2.0 technologies. A high level of application to AAP is required in this answer and generic descriptions of internet technologies would not be awarded a pass mark.

(a)   (i)

Strategic impact of future IT systems

		Low	High
Strategic impact of current systems	Low	**SUPPORT** Current Property Database Generic Estate Agency software.	**TURNAROUND** Mobile phone applications. Customer Databases Basic website
	High	**FACTORY** Improved property database with consistent information on properties.	**STRATEGIC** E-business - Website advertising and sales. Web 2.0 developments

McFarlan's strategic grid can be used to identify an organisation's current and future dependence on information systems. The model is based upon two axes which evaluate the strategic impact of the current systems used and the strategic impact of future systems.

Using this model, AAP's current information system is likely to be classified as 'Support'. The existing system used by AAP is not important to the organisation's strategic development and, as it stands, unless there are significant developments in bespoke software or investment in customer databases and mobile applications, then the current information systems are not likely to be a significant strategic impact on AAP. However, AAP is recognising the growing importance of its information systems as a means to improve its competitive position. The use of web technologies and e-commerce is likely to have a high potential to contribute to AAP's strategic objectives.

It could also be argued that the information systems in the estate agency business are 'Strategic' according to McFarlan's grid, as the current information systems are in fact critical to the smooth running of the business and its day to day activities. Future developments are vital to its success and should be a key part of its strategic objectives.

Examiner's comments

This question was very poorly answered, largely due to a lack of syllabus knowledge. Very few candidates had any knowledge of McFarlan's grid and therefore were unable to appropriately answer this question. These gaps in syllabus knowledge must be addressed. It is important to note that all areas of the syllabus are likely to be examined.

Common Errors:

*   Poor syllabus knowledge

(a)   (ii)   The investment in IS by AAP should be a strategic decision as the effect of not investing could have a significant long-term detrimental effect. Already AAP has experienced a slowdown in the growth of profitability and this decline could continue. Whilst face to face customer contact is important, it should no longer be the sole focus for the company. AAP needs to continue to be innovative and it cannot sit back and wait for customers to telephone its offices.

The cost of IT/ IS investment may involve high levels of expenditure for AAP. If this investment is not carefully planned and managed then there is a high risk of costly mistakes. Therefore, a strategic perspective is required to ensure that investment is carefully planned and resources are not wasted on information systems investment.

AAP must find a way to differentiate itself from its competitors. In the current economic climate the need for differentiation in order to win business from its competitors will be crucial for its survival. Strategic investment in information systems could give AAP a competitive advantage. As such, it should be part of AAP's strategic decision making process. This is not a decision that should be taken on an ad-hoc basis. The use of AAP's information systems could be a core driver of its competitive advantage and therefore is a critical part of its strategic decision making process.

Technology in this industry is rapidly developing, with the introduction of mobile applications for home buyers and the various Web 2.0 technologies which can be used. Therefore, AAP must continually monitor and develop its information systems to remain competitive and up to date. Although customers may want a good face to face service it is also likely that they will be increasingly moving towards a greater reliance on information systems to assist them in researching and reviewing properties. Therefore, the speed in the development in technology and the fact that key stakeholders are embracing this technology means that AAP must consider investment in information systems as a strategic decision.

The current developments in the use of systems within the industry are forcing AAP to reassess its operations. Leadership for the current developments is coming from the top of the organisation, via the Marketing Director. Information systems are opening up new possibilities for the estate agency industry. Without investment in new Information Systems, AAP may lose customers and see a further decline in profits. Therefore, investment in IS can be considered to be strategic as the long-term impact of not investing will threaten the future success of the company.

Information systems are likely to be highly complex, requiring the integration of many different forms of technology, such as internal estate agency software, customer and property databases, intranets, external links to other services and websites and website management. Therefore, this will require extremely careful planning and management which must be done at a strategic level otherwise it is likely that technology will become out of control and unmanageable. There are two further considerations for AAP, which are:

1   Does AAP have the funding to support the necessary expenditure?

2   Does AAP's management team have the necessary expertise to manage a more sophisticated IT system?

> **Examiner's comments**
>
> The answers to this question fell into two categories. This question was reasonably well answered by the candidates who correctly explained a number of relevant factors relating to investment in information systems being a strategic decision. However, most answers were largely generic and not directly applied to AAP.
>
> Common Errors:
>
> • Mostly generic answers provided

(b) E-business has been defined as 'the transformation of key business processes through the use of internet technologies'. The general estate agency business environment has clearly been affected by the development of e-business, with the recent technological developments identified by the Marketing Director.

Benefits to AAP

An e-business strategy ensures that information systems are considered by the organisation to be a critical and strategic aspect of its business survival. This will focus all staff and management attention on its importance and significance to AAP.

An e-business strategy would allow AAP to be more responsive to its customer needs and improve its customer relationship management through integrating and improving its business processes to focus on its customer needs both face to face and via technological interface. It will enable customers to gain information in a way they prefer, at a time they want, perhaps out of office hours, and this may result in customers recommending AAP to friends. Therefore, the customer experience will be improved.

Using e-business will present AAP with potential new business opportunities - including the advertising and selling of overseas properties. A global presence rather than just a national presence could be achieved if e-business was considered.

By using its website more effectively with the development of an integrated customer database, AAP can use e-business to understand customer buying behaviour more effectively and build up a detailed picture of customer requirements and needs such as popular locations, space requirements and individual customer tastes in types and styles of property required.

AAP would have a greater ability to interact with customers across a range of media - emails, blogs, social media, feedback forms; allowing greater dialogue with more customers via media that they are likely to use regularly.

Other competitors are likely to already be doing this, so AAP will be left behind if it does not follow an e-business strategy.

Sale and purchase of a property is a process that most people undertake infrequently, therefore their experience is vital if customers are to be satisfied. The ability to access AAP's website to get all the required information could result in a positive experience and repeat business at a later date.

Problems

The Board of AAP believes that the key to AAP's continued survival is excellent customer service, as it supplies a specialist service to a niche market. The nature of the business means that face to face contact is crucial in moving customer awareness into action. Therefore, this limits the ability of e-business to replace such personal contact, particularly with older, more traditional buyers.

Cost of investment in e-business may be prohibitive. However, as AAP already has an online presence and uses technology to some extent already with its estate agency software, additional e-business activities are therefore unlikely to be too costly for AAP.

A focus upon technology and not on customers' needs may reduce AAP's personal service which may put some customers off.

Currently, AAP is likely to have a lack of expertise in e-business. This is something which it must get right but currently is not likely to have the expertise to develop an e-business strategy. Lack of current expertise in AAP of e-business may cause resistance amongst AAP's staff who feel that they should be focusing upon the customer and not on e-business and technology.

The ability to effectively increase the customer base as house purchase and sales is an infrequent transaction for most home owners. There may be limited opportunity for repeat business for several years.

Some staff and managers may be sceptical about the benefits that e-business can offer AAP. However, conversely, many younger staff may welcome and embrace the change.

Examiner's comments

This question was reasonably well answered by many candidates. Most candidates identified a good range of advantages, mostly focusing upon increased business opportunities and in improved customer interaction through e-business. In addition, most candidates discussed the disadvantages of the impact upon staff and management morale and the potential for significant costs to be involved. However, once again, some answers were very generic and were focused more upon investing in information systems generally rather than specifically upon an e-business strategy. In addition, some candidates incorrectly discussed the customer database at length, which, although relevant as an opportunity for increased business development and customer focus, should not have been the main focus of the answer.

Common Errors:

- Largely generic with limited application to AAP

- Limited focus upon e-business specifically

(c)   Web 2.0 refers to the generation of web developments that facilitate communication, information sharing, interoperability and collaboration using the World Wide Web (WWW). It refers to the cumulative changes in the way that technology developers and end-users utilise the WWW.

The two Web 2.0 technologies recommended for AAP in the first instance are:

1   **'Mash-ups'**

This is where websites can now mix and match their web content and services to suit customer needs. For example, AAP can use interactive maps from geographical information programs from software providers such as Google Earth. These could be used together with links to local government information on school catchment areas or information on local planning application processes. Mash-ups allow individual websites to make use of a range of interactive technologies to enhance the website for optimum customer interaction, without heavy investment. For an estate agency business this is particularly useful as links to external geographical location or information sites are important informational and advice tools for potential customers.

2   Blogs - Information Sharing

An internal blog is a web log that any employee can view. Many blogs are also communal, allowing anyone to post to them. The informal nature of blogs may encourage:

- Employee participation

- Free discussion of issues

- Collective intelligence

- Direct communication between various layers of an organisation

- A sense of community

Internal blogs may be used in lieu of meetings and e-mail discussions, and can be especially useful when the people involved are in different locations, or have conflicting schedules. Blogs may also allow individuals who otherwise would not have been aware of or invited to participate in a discussion to contribute their expertise.

An external blog is a publicly available blog where company employees, teams, or spokespersons share their views. It could be used by AAP to announce new properties on the market or to announce new services or to explain and clarify policies, or to react on public criticism on certain issues. It also allows a window to AAP's culture and is often treated more informally than traditional press releases, though a corporate blog often tries to accomplish similar goals as press releases. In some corporate blogs, all posts go through a review before they are posted. Some corporate blogs, but not all, allow comments to be made to the posts.

In addition, other forms of Web 2.0 technology which could be discussed are:

Social media

By using popular social media network sites such as Facebook, Myspace, Twitter and YouTube, AAP could advertise its services. AAP could set up its own Facebook page where customers could access the latest company adverts and messages and also access message boards where they could contact AAP directly.

Peer to peer networking (P2P)

This is a technique used to share files over the internet or within a closed set of users. As AAP does not make use of an intranet, this could be a very useful form of Web 2.0 technology for AAP to adopt. Currently, email is the main form of communication and file transfer between staff in different locations. P2P would distribute files across many machines meaning that files would be accessible across the network and not just on one user's machine.

Competence syndication

AAP could open up a portion of its website for use by other firms of property related companies such as furniture removal companies, lawyers, interior designers and builders to advertise their services.

Examiner's comments

Some candidates provided excellent answers to this question and clearly had a detailed knowledge and high level of understanding of Web 2.0 technologies and applied this well to AAP. At the other end of the scale, there were numerous candidates who clearly did not understand the term and had very little knowledge of this area of the syllabus. This is clearly highlighted within the syllabus content of Section A of the E3 syllabus and therefore candidates are expected to be able to apply this to any given examination scenario.

Common Errors:

- Lack of syllabus knowledge

18   LM (MAR 11 EXAM)

Key answer tips

This is a tricky question surrounding IT and IS strategies. In part (a)(i) you are asked why LM should have an overall IT/IS strategy. Try to look at LM itself when answering this question. What problems is LM facing? How would having an IT/IS strategy help? Remember that IT/IS helps many businesses to gain competitive advantage in their markets and its successful use within the organisation can improve corporate image. Add in the fact that IT/IS is extremely expensive and it underlines how important it is for any organisation to have a formal strategy to enable them to monitor and control this area of their business.

There is no model to follow when answering (a)(ii). Try and be sensible here – if you were creating an IT strategy, what would **you** expect to include? Anything reasonable and practical should score here.

Part (b) again required you to logic through what you would expect to happen when implementing a strategy within an organisation. Again, the model answer is not completely comprehensive, so any sensible suggestions would have scored. However, try and talk through your suggested steps in chronological order to give your answer structure and ensure you explain your suggested steps.

(a)   (i)   **The case for an Information Technology and Information Systems strategy**

LM does not have a strategy for Information Technology and Information Systems (hereafter IT). It is spending a significant amount on IT. In 2010 this amounted to £1 million the same as its forecast profit for 2011. The Board of LM will be interested in the potential scope for any reductions in IT spending because, as equity holders, they would benefit from this. However, it could be the case that LM is not spending enough on IT and that this is restricting its growth and profitability. One of the deficiencies of LM is that it has not recognised the strategic importance of IT for its business. At the strategic level, this means that it has foregone the opportunity of using IT as a strategic variable which could give it a competitive advantage. Its use of IT could possibly distinguish it from other recruitment agencies and allow it to differentiate itself. As LM is organised into three divisions serving three niche markets it could be that IT could be tailored distinctively to support each of the divisions as their needs will be distinct.

At the management and operational levels LM's incoherent use of IT causes it difficulties, for example, it is difficult to transfer information within LM because of incompatible software and LM may not be getting the best prices when it buys hardware because this is done in an uncoordinated way. The appearance which LM presents to the outside world via its website is a variable one and probably detracts from LM's image and possibly its business growth.

All these are compelling reasons why LM should formulate an overall strategy for IT.

Examiner's comments

This question was reasonably well answered. Most answers correctly identified a good range of problems within LM and were then able to identify how an IT and IS strategy could overcome these problems.

(ii)   **Contents of the IT strategy**

The strategy should contain a statement of how LM intends to use IT to support its overall business strategy. Will IT be used as a source of competitive advantage or will its role be confined to being an enabler of LM's other strategies?

The strategy should state the timeframe with which it is concerned. As IT changes so quickly LM's IT strategy should state how often, and the means by which, it will be reviewed. The strategy should also articulate the resources and competences upon which it is based. It would be appropriate to state the amount of LM's spending on IT during the course of the strategy's duration. This may be stated in absolute terms or it may be stated as a proportion of revenue. The strategy should also state how and when the spending would be reviewed. The strategy should also state how the staff working in LM should use and be trained in the use of IT. The strategy should set some common standards for LM in its use of software, web design and hardware sourcing and acquisition.

Examiner's comments

This question was not well answered. Many candidates failed to answer this question correctly mainly due to the fact that most answers were based upon the process of strategy formulation and not upon the contents of a strategy.

Many answers were focused upon the rational planning model which was not required and considered to be an incorrect approach.

Common Errors:

•   Lack of focus on content of strategy

•   Too much focus upon process of strategy formulation

(b)   Once the strategy has been drafted LM has to implement it. As with any strategy before it is adopted, it could be subjected to the three tests (suggested by Johnson, Scholes and Whittington in 2008): Suitability, Acceptability and Feasibility.

On the assumption that the strategy passes these tests the first step would be to designate an LM Board member to be given responsibility for the strategy. There has to be, within LM, recognition that the implementation of the new strategy is a significant change. The Board member who is given the responsibility for the IT strategy will have to act as a change agent. One of the primary tasks he will have to deal with is how LM will reconcile its policy of divisional autonomy with its new overall IT strategy. The strategy will contain some centralised aspects, for example, in the use of software and this will have to be implemented sensitively. However, these common standards should not necessarily jeopardise divisional autonomy.

It is important that the change agent does not operate in isolation and it would be sensible to form a working group to introduce the strategy and implement it across LM and its divisions. Each division should be represented on the working party.

The working party should construct, within the parameters of the overall strategy, an implementation plan including a time-line. It is likely that the plan will have to make provision for some training and it should definitely contain a communication and dissemination plan. The working party should try to gain the support of influential people within the divisions for the new strategy. It is reasonable to assume that the new IT strategy may not be welcomed by everybody so the working party should have prepared tactics to deal with resistance to its proposed changes.

Finally, the working party should propose a protocol for its reporting to the Board. It should also put in place arrangements both for the review of its own activities and also for the operation of the IT strategy.

Examiner's comments

This question was reasonably well answered. Most candidates presented a practical and applied answer to this question, identifying and explaining a reasonable range of components and activities of an appropriate IT/ IS strategy. Some answers were too heavily focused upon the technological needs of the strategy i.e. they were over focused upon the hardware and software requirements. Some answers took an incorrect approach by again discussing the rational planning model here, i.e. focusing upon the process of strategy formulation rather than the activities required for the practical implementation of a designed strategy. This approach was awarded very few marks.

Common Errors

- Focus on strategy formulation and not strategy implementation

- Too much focus upon the IT aspects of the strategy and not enough focus upon the management of the implementation, i.e. training, resistance and management support.

---

19   Y (NOV 10 EXAM)

Key answer tips

In part (a), you needed to examine whether winning the new hotel contract would significantly change Y's approach her business. Given that it is currently run for her 'enjoyment and satisfaction' and the new contract would involve her hiring staff and monitoring quality, her approach is likely to change. Make sure that you apply your answer to Y's personal circumstances.

For part (b), make sure you answer the question fully. Use a separate heading for each strategy. Then, for each of the three strategies, you will need to define the strategy, explain its purpose and explain why it would be a benefit to her business, given that the new contract has been won. Remember that it only asks for benefits – identifying drawbacks would not score.

Finally, part (c) asked for how Y could implement each of the three strategies from (b). The trick here is to be practical. For instance, for Y's Information Technology strategy try suggesting actual pieces of IT infrastructure that Y may need to purchase.

(a) The opportunity offered by the hotel contract can be characterised as a transformational change. Johnson, Scholes and Whittington defined transformational change as change that is radical and will move the organisation outside its existing paradigm (way of thinking). This implies a significant cultural shift for Y which she is going to have to deal with.

Y has operated her business on a small scale in order to give her a particular lifestyle and she has not been interested in growth so she has turned away new business. As her personal circumstances are due to change, and she has no other options, she is trying to win the hotel contract. If she is successful she will have to employ at least 4 staff. She will then have responsibilities to, and for, four other people. Her business will, therefore, be more complex and her current administrative systems inadequate. However, her income will increase.

The lifestyle that Y has enjoyed will change if she obtains the hotel contract and she will no longer be able to maintain her lifestyle business strategy.

> **Examiner's comments**
>
> This question was reasonably well answered. Most candidates recognised that the change in Y's circumstances was likely to have a fundamental change on her lifestyle business strategy and that it would be unlikely that she would be able to continue as before if the hotel contract was successfully won.

(b) **Information systems strategy (ISS)**

An information systems strategy should define the long-term use of information within Y's business. The ISS will enable Y to specify the systems that will facilitate the use of information to support her in her new business strategy.

When Y has decided what her new long-term goals are then the ISS can express what systems (in the broadest sense of the word) are needed to support those goals. The ISS is a long-term approach expressing how information will be used to support Y's business strategy and/or create new strategic options. The process of defining her ISS will be an interactive one with that of defining her new business strategy: each strategy should inform the other. A benefit of Y looking at information strategically is that it may give her ideas about new ways of doing business and could lead to her securing a competitive advantage.

Y will also benefit from an ISS as she will have an overall context for the development of how she will use information within her business. Previously, although she had a number of sources of business information, for example, her diaries, she made no attempt to exploit this resource. She could, for example, have analysed the cost structure of different jobs and revealed her clients' profitability. When Y is operating the hotel contract she will have a need for real-time information to ensure she stays within the contract's specifications. An ISS should define how she will do this.

Information technology strategy (ITS)

Currently, Y has very little Information Technology (IT) to support her business. She, therefore, has to move from a position where she relies on her mobile phone to a much more complex business where she will have to have real-time control information regarding the hotel contract and also have to administer and pay her four employees. Clearly, Y's diary and mobile phone will be inadequate in these circumstances.

Y has little experience of using IT within her business and the acquisition of such technology will involve her in expense. She will benefit from developing an ITS rather than acquiring IT at random. As IT will become an important part of her business, Y needs to make sure that what she purchases is reliable, adequate for her needs and will be compatible with her client's requirements. The latter is particularly important in the case of software. Y's IT requirements will increase and by drafting an ITS, Y would define what computers, peripherals, communication links and software she would use in her new expanded business.

As the acquisition of IT will involve Y in increased investment in technology her ITS will enable her to define her technological needs and identify how and where these will be met. Part of her ITS will be a budget which she can use to control expenditure and provide 'feedforward' information for future acquisitions. This will benefit her in the future as lessons learnt from IT acquisition should help make better acquisition decisions.

Information management strategy (IMS)

An information management strategy will enable Y to define her approach to managing data and information within her business and how data and information should be stored and accessed. She will also use the IMS to describe the roles of the people involved in the use of information, systems and technology in the larger organisation. As Y will no longer be solely responsible for the business administration, she should use the IMS to demarcate responsibilities between herself and the new administrative assistant. Y could also use the IMS to guide her in the recruitment process for the administrative assistant.

Y will also require real-time information about the hotel contract and the IMS should specify who will collect this and how it will be done. Potentially, Y, her three gardeners, her administrative assistant and some of the hotel staff could be involved in this process. The benefit of an IMS is that it will bring clarity by stating the responsibilities of the different parties. On the assumption that Y buys a computer for her administrative assistant, the IMS should define who has access to it and who is responsible for maintaining and up-dating files and records.

The over-arching benefit of the IMS will be the clarity it gives to the roles and responsibilities regarding IT within Y's business.

Examiner's comments

This question was not well answered at all. Candidates demonstrated a lack of knowledge and understanding of the differences between these three strategies and most answers even failed to provide adequate definitions of each. There was much confusion between ISS and ITS and most candidates did not know what an IMS was at all. Many candidates failed to focus their answers upon each 'strategy' instead discussing issues such as what IT was required.

Common Errors

- Lack of understanding of the differences between ISS/ITS/IMS

- Poor definition

(c)   In the case of all three strategies Y may be unable to develop them herself due to her lack of experience. She could seek assistance from her accountant and she may find it necessary to use an IT consultant to help her develop the strategies.

Information systems strategy

In order for this strategy to be produced Y will have to articulate her new business strategy as she moves away from managing a lifestyle business. Although she does not have any employees who will be affected by the new strategy it would be appropriate to discuss it with her husband who will be affected by it. In producing the ISS she should examine how information could contribute to her long-term success. Y has details of all the work she has done in the past three years recorded in her diaries. She should analyse this data to discover for example, trends in customers' demands, profitability of customers, and seasonality of demand. Y's success has been built on creativity and reliability. In her ISS she should specify how these attributes could be recorded and acted upon as they will also be important for her future success.

Information technology strategy

In the future, as well as her current customer base, Y will be dealing with a demanding customer, the hotel, which expects very close adherence to its contract specification. Therefore, the scale and complexity of Y's business is going to change in such a way that her current information technology, a mobile phone and a diary, will be inadequate. Y will need to budget for her technological requirements.

Y will need to purchase at a minimum:

- A wireless enabled computer for her administrative assistant

- (Possibly) a laptop for herself

- A router

- A printer

- Software comprising programs for email, word processing, data base and spreadsheet

- A landline

It may be useful for Y to establish an Intranet.

Information management strategy

Y now has a number of information users to consider, herself, her administrative assistant, her three gardeners, her accountant and the hotel. She will need to specify the degree of connectivity for the various users: for example, instead of passing her diary over to her accountant at year end she could allow the accountant access to her information systems. Similarly, with her new customer, the hotel, which closely monitors performance against contract specification, she will have to establish how she will exchange information. It may be that the contract has provision for this in which case Y will have to follow the contract requirement and incorporate this into the IMS.

Y will also need to describe in the IMS the roles and responsibilities of herself and the administrative assistant.

Examiner's comments

This question was answered marginally better than part (b). Most candidates could offer some discussion of the actions that Y should undertake to implement the three strategies, even if there was some confusion as to where the actions should take place. Candidates were not penalised if they provided a suitable action for Y but placed it under the wrong heading. Many candidates provided a generic answer, listing a range of actions under no particular strategy heading. Again, candidates were not penalised if they took this approach but were able to demonstrate some ability to identify practical actions to implement these strategies.

Common errors

- Bullet point lists of actions provided with little discussion of why the actions should be carried out

- Over emphasis upon the IT implementation i.e. an over focus of answers on buying and implementing the IT solutions without considering the actions needed to manage her information system

---

20   HHH (SEP 2012)

Key answer tips

In part (a) you are asked to **explain** the advantages of converting CSFs into KPIs for HHH. Remember that even for three marks, you needed to apply your answer to the university in the scenario as requested in the requirement.

In part (b) was a slightly more unusual requirement, asking you to examine knowledge management and the benefits and problems that HHH might face when implementing it. This is a less commonly examined part of the syllabus, but is worth making sure you have revised.

The same can be said for part (c), which focused on data mining. This required a good working knowledge of data mining, but again this needed applying to the circumstances of HHH itself to score well.

(a)   Critical Success Factors (CSFs) are the limited number of areas which must go well if the university is to be successful. HHH's CSFs are abstract and it would be normal to translate them into the concrete form of Key Performance Indicators (KPIs). KPIs can quantify HHH's CSFs which enables them to be measured and performance can then be managed by means of targets, comparisons and feedback and feedforward.

Examples of KPIs for HHH are:

Student performance:

Number of first year students not completing their course;

Percentage of male students who drop out annually.

Examiner's comments

This question was reasonably well answered. Most candidates could define both CSF's and KPI's and most could also justify the link between the two. Many candidates correctly identified the importance of the drop-out rate for HHH and the need to convert this into a measurable KPI. The main weakness of some answers was the lack of application to HHH. Some candidates merely provided definitions without any attempt at applying these concepts to the advantages that could be gained by HHH.

Common Errors:

- Lack of syllabus knowledge of what a CSF is

- Weak understanding of the need to convert CSFs into measures such as KPIs

- Lack of application to HHH

(b)   (i)   Knowledge management has been defined as 'the management of the information, knowledge and experience available to an organisation'. A knowledge management strategy would enable HHH to build on its existing knowledge and extend it further. A knowledge management strategy would imply that the university would make deliberate efforts to gather, organise, share and analyse its knowledge to contribute towards the university's future success.

If a knowledge management strategy was successfully implemented, HHH could expect to benefit from the following:

- An increased level of motivation from its staff as they would have the opportunity of reciprocal knowledge sharing with colleagues. Based on the example of SSS, a comparable university, this could lead to HHH's staff achieving more external recognition in the form of prizes, publishing more books and articles and being awarded research contracts. These potential successes could increase the job satisfaction of HHH's staff.

- If HHH's staff achieves greater job satisfaction, greater external success and increased levels of motivation, it is likely to influence the value they place on working for HHH. This is likely to lead to a reduced level of staff turnover as staff will be happier.

- If HHH implements a knowledge management strategy, this should lead to staff having new opportunities to share their knowledge and to collaborate with colleagues across the university. The stimulation which these new opportunities provide may encourage the staff to become more innovative.

The increased level of shared knowledge may lead to greater efficiency. If knowledge is no longer regarded as a personal possession and collaboration becomes manifest, HHH's staff may benefit and be enabled to work 'smarter'.

Examiner's comments

This question was reasonably well answered. Most candidates identified a range of benefits including improved motivation and job satisfaction levels. However, few candidates considered the possibility of increased collaboration and innovation within HHH. Some candidates' answers incorrectly focused more upon the benefits of working together rather than specifically focusing upon the specific benefits of implementing a knowledge management system. Some candidates also provided very generic answers with little or no application of the benefits identified to HHH.

> **Common Errors:**
>
> - Answers focused upon benefits of collaboration rather than on a knowledge management system
>
> - Generic answers with limited application of the benefits to HHH

(ii) There are a number of areas where the introduction of a knowledge management system might encounter problems:

Social

- Within HHH there are barriers to sharing information because of the attitude of its staff. Sharing implies a different way of working and staff may be resistant to changing their existing work patterns. Staff may be unwilling to co-operate with an imposed knowledge management strategy.

- Some staff may become demotivated by the new strategy as they have previously regarded their knowledge as a personal possession, rather than something whose ownership is shared by the university.

- Some staff may feel that if they share their knowledge their status may be undermined within the university.

- If HHH's knowledge is to be shared, there will be winners and losers amongst its staff. The winners will be the staff who have little knowledge to share and will benefit from access to more productive colleagues' knowledge. The losers will be the staff with the most knowledge to share who may resent their hard-earned knowledge being shared with less productive colleagues.

Technical

- HHH may not have a comprehensive information system which would facilitate knowledge sharing.

- There may be incompatible systems and/or working methods within the university which will be an impediment to knowledge sharing and management.

- Not all data held within the university is necessarily held in digital form. This makes its sharing difficult: if such data is to be digitised, this will involve the university in extra expense.

- HHH will need to decide how its data is to be archived and how its archive is to be managed and accessed. HHH may not have the skills to deal with this issue which implies the knowledge management strategy will generate further expense.

Candidates were required to give only four problem areas.

Examiner's comments

This question was reasonably well answered. Most candidates recognised the problems of lack of staff willingness to share their knowledge and the potential demotivating effect. Many candidates also identified the possible technical problems of inadequate or incompatible systems. Once again, the main weakness of answers to this question was that many of the problems identified were generic, with little direct application of the impact of these problems on HHH. Some answers were also very thin and lacked explanation. The verb asked candidates to 'advise' HHH and therefore a mere list of problems without further explanation is not answering the question set.

Common Errors:

- Limited application of the problems directly to HHH

- Bullet point list answers

(c)   Data mining would allow HHH to analyse its data to discover previously unknown or unsuspected relationships, patterns and associations. Drop-out rates are a key factor in the ability to achieve its CSF of student performance. It would therefore assist HHH if it could analyse the performance of its best performing departments in this area in order to determine what the key factors are to learn from. HHH could use its data relating to its own students as well as data relating to students in other UK universities, which it could analyse and use to improve its drop-out rates.

Data mining will allow HHH to compare its results with other UK data. This would help HHH to identify potential solutions to drop-out rates in particular. Data mining could assist HHH in understanding what causes students to leave before completing their studies and make possible improvement to improve retention and student progression.

Data mining might be able to forecast the type of student that is likely to drop out. HHH could then use this to identify students most at risk of dropping out and offer them support and extra tuition and guidance. Data mining may permit HHH to identify associations, whereby one event can be correlated to another event. For example, poor performance in mock exams could result in failure in the final examination. Therefore, action could be taken to offer extra tuition and courses to these candidates.

Examiner's comments

This question was not well answered. This would seem largely to be due to the lack of knowledge of this area of the syllabus. The definitions were very often incorrect, focusing more upon databases than data mining. Therefore, many answers incorrectly considered the use of databases, which was not required and therefore awarded no credit. Candidates were awarded some credit for attempting to apply their answer to reducing the student drop-out rate, which many did.

Common Errors

- Defining databases, not data mining.

---

21 JGS ANTIQUES (MAY 10 EXAM)

Key answer tips

In part (a) you are asked to **analyse** the strengths and weaknesses of JGS, using the value chain. The easiest structure for your answer would be to use the various value chain headings. The question did not specify which part of the value chain to focus on, so you can use both primary and secondary activities in your answer.

Make sure you conclude for each one whether it is a strength or a weakness for JGS. Watch your timing here, too – there is a large amount you could write here, but you need to make sure you don't over-run.

In part (b) the key is to be practical. What would JGS need to do immediately and then on an ongoing basis to implement the proposed e-commerce project? As long as your points are sensible, they should gain credit here.

Part (c) asked for the effect of the new e-commerce system on the value chain. Again, look at both primary and secondary activities, but try not to over-run on your time.

(a) Strengths and weaknesses using the value chain

Porter's value chain is designed to help organisations analyse their activities and decide which ones add to their competitive advantage, either by improving quality or reducing costs.

For JGS, the model can be used to analyse the strengths and weaknesses of the business – both for the purchase and sale of antiques and the provision of specialist advice.

Primary activities:

Inbound logistics

For JGS this would involve the receipt and storage of antiques for sale as well as queries from traders and collectors.

Currently this is a weakness for JGS as these customers must contact JGS by letter or by telephone. This may be slower and less convenient than using email and may therefore put off some potential customers leading to a loss of sales.

Operations

Operations involve the conversion of inputs into a final product. For JGS this would involve placing antiques into their modern shop in order to sell them and deciding on appropriate answers to queries from other dealers and collectors.

This would appear to be a significant strength for JGS as both owners have achieved national recognition for their expertise, which they are using to provide a valuable additional source of income.

Outbound logistics

This is the delivery of the product or the provision of the service to the customer.

This area may also be a significant weakness for JGS. As the shop is located far from their customer base, it will be extremely difficult or expensive for customers to transport bulky antiques purchased from JGS. This may stop customers purchasing from JGS.

Marketing and sales

Given that the business is located far away from its customers, marketing and sales will be crucial to the success of the business. Customers are unlikely to "stumble across" the shop and will need to be persuaded to make the trip.

There is evidence that this is currently a weakness in JGS. They have a limited website which gives details of how to locate the store, but does little else to attract customers.

In addition, they do not attend antiques fairs. This would help to make the business highly visible to potential customers – especially other dealers and collectors who will then pay for advice later. Not attending these fairs is a major weakness in the marketing of JGS.

Service

After sales care is an important way of retaining customers in many businesses. Given that JGS has an excellent reputation and a large amount of repeat custom, this would appear to be a strength.

Secondary activities:

Technology development

This is a weakness for the business. With the exception of a basic website there is no evidence of any use of IT within the organisation – for example in emailing customers to inform them of stock - which may be holding back JGS's growth.

HRM

JGS is run by its two owners – there are no other members of staff. While the owners are extremely skilled, which will add to the reputation of the business, they seem to lack skills in other areas, such as the use of IT.

In addition, a lack of staff means that they are unable to attend the antiques fairs as well as keeping their store open, which means the business could be losing out on custom.

Infrastructure

The location of the business is currently both a strength and a weakness. As previously mentioned the store is not conveniently located for customers.

However, the premises have significantly increased in value, which would enable it to be sold at a significant profit. This would provide funds that could be reinvested in the business.

Procurement

This involves the acquisition of antiques for sale, amongst other things. This is likely to be a strength for the business, as they have managed to achieve good levels of repeat business.

(b) What is needed immediately and on a continuing basis to carry out e-commerce solution.

JGS is currently planning to upgrade its website to enable e-commerce. This will be a significant change to its current web presence. In order to do this successfully there are a number of issues that it will have to deal with.

Immediately:

The owners of JGS must decide exactly what features they want from their website. Will it be used for providing advice to dealers and collectors or do they want to begin selling antiques online, which could be more complicated. Discussions with existing customers would help JGS to decide which features are actually needed.

A decision will also need to be made on who will develop and run the website. While a basic website has been produced, JGS may lack the skills to create and manage an e-commerce solution. An appropriate design company may need to be contracted.

JGS must ensure they plan how customers will find their new website. The current site receives a large number of hits, so advertising may not be necessary. However, they may wish to ensure it can be found using search engines.

In addition, JGS will need to decide which markets they wish to operate in. Do they wish to start accepting orders and requests for advice globally or only orders from their current country?

Finally, JGS will need to ensure they set a budget for the development of their e-commerce facility. This is an area they have little current experience of and it will be easy for costs to increase rapidly if no controls are put in place.

Ongoing:

Going forward, the website will need to be maintained and redesigned periodically. If this is the case, JGS will need to ensure they have sufficient time and ability to do this themselves, or they will need to enter a maintenance agreement with an IT company.

If the website is going to be used to sell antiques, it will need to be regularly updated as stock is bought or sold. Again, the owners will need to decide if they have the time or skills to do this themselves.

(c) **Evaluation of the effect of e-commerce on the value chain of JGS**

E-commerce could have a dramatic effect on the value chain of JGS in the following areas:

Inbound logistics

E-commerce is unlikely to be able to significantly improve the initial handling of antiques, but it will enable JGS to increase the speed of processing requests for information from dealers and collectors.

These requests could be submitted through the website by email, which will be more convenient for many customers and may therefore attract more business.

Operations

Given that an e-commerce system could involve customers emailing queries to JGS – it would be possible for the owners to access these remotely – say, by laptop. This could mean that they will be more willing to attend antiques fairs as they will be able to continue with many of their day-to-day business activities at the same time.

An e-commerce system could also enable customers to place orders for antiques online rather than having to travel to the store itself.

Outbound logistics

Responses to customer queries could be sent by email, which may be faster and more efficient than the current method of replying by letter or telephone. This could improve our service and therefore increase customer satisfaction.

Marketing and sales

Use of e-commerce will allow JGS to gather information on customers, such as their email and home addresses, as well as tracking their buying habits. This could be undertaken for all customers – wherever they are based in the world.

This could allow JGS to advertise easily and cheaply to existing customers when new antiques that may be of interest to them come into stock. It may also enable JGS to ensure they only buy in antiques that are likely to be of interest to their main customers.

One weakness of using e-commerce is that many customers may not be willing to make such a major purchase without physically viewing the product. As JGS is far away from many of its customers, it may not help to increase sales – a problem that has been seen with the existing website.

However, JGS could upload photographs of all the antiques held in store along with a link to relevant information about that item. At the very least, this could help to attract customers to the shop, as it will reduce the chance a wasted trip if JGS does not have any items they would be interested in.

Service

JGS could improve its after sales service by having a section of frequently asked questions on its website, or information about how to care for items after purchase. This could help make customers more willing to buy products from JGS – in spite of the inconvenient location.

Favourable customer testimonials on the website may also help to prove the quality of the service provided by JGS.

Procurement

JGS could use their website as a way of attracting suppliers as well as customers. Details could be taken of antiques that individuals would like to sell – increasing access of JGS to new products.

E-commerce may also allow JGS to link its website to those of its suppliers, to allow it to locate items they have in stock which might be of interest to its customers.

HRM

New skills may be required to run the e-commerce system. JGS may need to consider the additional costs of running such a system. This would likely mean having to hire in new members of staff or sub-contracting.

Infrastructure

If the business is able to move many of its transactions onto an e-commerce basis, it will reduce any disruption to its activities if the owners decide to move the shop. Goods could still be shipped and queries could still be responded to as the move was taking place.

E-commerce will also allow JGS to expand its activities without needing to invest in any further infrastructure. If sales can be made online, it will reduce the need for any further shops.

Conclusion:

Overall, e-commerce seems like a reasonable approach for this business to take. It would appear to work particularly well for the advice and queries part of the business and could significantly improve efficiency of JGS's value chain. In addition, it has the potential to increase the visibility of the company.

However, it may be less appropriate for the sale of antiques, which customers are likely to want to see in person and does not solve the problem of the business being badly located, increasing the costs and time involved in shipping goods to the customer.

22 BXA (MAY 05 EXAM)

Key answer tips

In part (a) ensure that you distinguish clearly between the three managerial levels. In addition you should make sure you apply your comments to the scenario and use IT as an outsourcing example.

Similarly in part (b), it is essential that you apply your answers to the scenario. Providing only a generic list of supplier characteristics will not score highly.

Part (c) is more straightforward.

(a)   The advantages and disadvantages of outsourcing the IT function are as follows:

*Your answer should focus upon the advantages and disadvantages of outsourcing of IT for **each** managerial level, not a general discussion of the relative merits of outsourcing.*

Advantages	Disadvantages
Strategic level	
• The supplier will have economies of scale reducing BXA's cost base. This is particularly important given recent consolidation in the industry.	• Control of a vital part of BXA's business has been passed to a supplier, possible resulting in control problems.
• The supplier will have expertise and core competences in excess of BXA's, improving BXA's use of IT in the market place.	• It may not be cheaper to outsource, as the supplier will incorporate a profit element in their pricing.
• Together these should improve BXA's competitive advantage.	• BXA may become over-reliant on the supplier.
• This should also reduce BXA's risk exposure.	
• The supplier will have greater R&D competences and spend in the field of IT improving BXA's innovation.	
• There may be greater flexibility to respond to future industry advances	
Managerial level	
• Management can focus on other areas of the business where they have expertise.	• Problems implementing the changeover could seriously compromise BXA's competitiveness if the process is not controlled effectively.
• Existing bugs and incompatibilities will be eliminated quickly.	
• Problems integrating the two firms' IT systems will be avoided.	• Managing the merger and the IT changes simultaneously could prove very time-consuming for management.
Tactical level	
• Better information due to the possibility of networking systems, quicker systems and standardisation.	• Monitoring and controlling the quality of the service provided will be difficult.
	• Staff losses in IT need to be handled carefully to avoid loss of morale.
	• There will be extra training needed to educate staff in the new processes and systems.

(b)   BXA should look for a supplier with the following characteristics:

- Financial strength – BXA needs to ensure that the supplier is profitable and shows the ability for sustained growth. Credit reports should be sought and its financial statements analysed.
- Good reputation – BXA should see the supplier's existing client base and seek references where possible.
- Quality badges – has the supplier been awarded quality marks such as the ISO 9000 series?
- Strong technical support department.
- Strong innovation – particularly to deal with the challenges of the merger and the rapid changes in the industry.
- Size – BXA does not want to outgrow its supplier's capacity. One of the benefits of outsourcing is to gain from the supplier's economies of scale.

(c)   The following factors should be included in a service level agreement:

- A detailed explanation of exactly what service the supplier is offering to provide.
- The targets / benchmarks to be used and the consequences of failing to meet them.
- Specific targets / expected performance for handling the merger issues.
- Expected response time to technical queries.
- The expected time to recover the operations in the event of a disaster such as a systems crash, terrorist attack, etc.
- The procedure for dealing with complaints.
- The information and reporting procedures to be adopted.
- The procedures for cancelling the contract.

23   EXTRANET (NOV 05 EXAM)

Key answer tips

Make sure you analyse S's perspective, not C's. The question would be much more straightforward if you had to examine the benefits to C.

(a)   **Sole supplier relationship**

The advantages and disadvantages to S of the sole supplier relationship described are as follows:

Advantages

- Growth – The main advantage to S is the immediate 200% increase in volume. This should result in higher profitability and shareholder value.
- Low risk attached to earnings – the contract is for five years, giving stable earnings during that period.
- Economies of scale – manufacturing systems usually afford economies of scale in areas such as materials purchasing, improved scheduling and specialisation. These should reduce S's cost base giving it higher margins both for the C contract and other existing sales.
- Enhanced reputation – being an approved supplier for C may lead to other business opportunities.

Disadvantages

- Risk of penalties – S will incur cost penalties if it fails to deliver on time. What is not clear is whether this only applies to production schedules disclosed, say, a week ahead, or whether C could request extra parts at short notice. This will be a particular problem if C's production increases significantly, whether because of special promotions or extra demand for new number plates. Whatever the reason, S will probably have to hold some stock to act as a buffer, with the resulting holding costs.

- Systems and control – S will need to increase the scale of operations in production, probably resulting in considerable investment. Alongside this there will be the need for new control systems as S cannot afford for quality to be compromised.

- Human resources – S will have to recruit and train additional staff. This will take time and money and there is a danger of quality being compromised if it is not carried out effectively.

- Capacity constraints – S may not have the capacity to deal with large orders from C without displacing and losing sales to other customers.

- Over-reliance on C – while C is also tied in for five years, C will gain significant power when the contract is up for renewal. Losing such a major contract could compromise S's future viability. There is also the problem that S's prospects become over dependent on C's – if C's cars under-perform in the competitive car market, then S will suffer too.

- Working capital – the terms of payment by C and the enforcement of those terms are vital. If C delays payment or routinely takes too long to pay, then S's working capital position will be significantly affected.

Conclusion

Most firms would jump at the chance to treble turnover with one contract and S should seriously consider accepting the contract. However, S should ensure that the penalty clauses are not unfair, that acceptable payment terms are agreed and should also ensure that it pursues other customers over the next five years to reduce reliance on C.

(b) **Allowing S access to C's extranet**

*Make sure you **evaluate** the benefits as well as describing them.*

The main benefits to S of access C's extranet are as follows:

Planning

The main advantage to S is that it will be able to plan production better to match the requirements of C. For example, if C's volume is expected to increase in a particular month, then S can plan to arrange extra staff or overtime working to meet demand. The detail of information available on the extranet is vital to enabling S to do this without incurring penalties.

Working capital

S's ability to anticipate C's inventory needs and plan accordingly will also reduce delays in ordering and delivery. C appears to want to implement a JIT policy – the extranet may allow S to do the same. This should increase S's inventory turnover, reduce inventory holding costs and speed up cash collection.

Together this will give a significant benefit to S's working capital management. This particularly important given the huge growth the sole supplier agreement has brought to S.

Customer relationship management (CRM)

The ability of C to record details of support calls and problem resolution on the extranet will improve communication, collaboration and discussion between S and C. Ideally, this will reduce the likelihood of C moving to another supplier.

Other less significant benefits include:

Improved information

S will obtain access to C's buying preferences and tender specifications, enabling it to be more successful in meeting C's needs. Any changes by C will be highlighted on the extranet giving S quicker response times.

Critical information will not get lost in the mail or buried in an email in-box, and busy employees will not miss or forget key events.

S will also be able to access information not available to competitors, giving it an advantage in a changing industry.

Flexibility

By using the extranet, S can operate when and where it is most convenient. This self-serve approach frees S from unnecessary meetings and phone calls, and it cuts down on the costs associated with in-person information exchanges. For example, the extranet may allow S to process orders outside of regular business hours.

Administration savings

Once S's staff have learned how to use the new extranet, they will spend less time in the repetitive tasks involved in receiving and processing an order, thus reducing costs. The extranet should also lead to fewer errors in processing orders.

24 C PHARMACEUTICALS MANUFACTURER (MAY 07 EXAM)

Key answer tips

Parts (a) and (b) ask you to **discuss** pros and cons, so ensure that you explain your points, rather than simply listing them.

When discussing communication in part (c), you need to give details of the methods you suggest.

(a)   The advantages and disadvantages of supplying directly to pharmacies are as follows:

Advantages

- By avoiding wholesalers' margins, C will be able to charge more for its products. Subject to the cost increases detailed below, this will result in greater profits.

- C can build goodwill and customer loyalty directly with pharmacies by being seen to be responsive to their worries and concerns regarding supermarkets.

- C might also build greater brand awareness among end-users who may also be concerned about supermarket growth. This could give C an opportunity to differentiate itself from its six main competitors.

- By dealing directly with pharmacists, C will be 'closer to the customer' and thus better positioned to understand customer needs and respond accordingly.

- The move may win C some influence in government with ministers who are also concerned about supermarket power.

Disadvantages

- Pharmacists may be used to dealing with a single wholesaler who can provide all of their product needs – drugs, cosmetics, food and drink, for example – and may be unwilling to switch to C who can only supply drugs. C may thus lose customers.

- In order to meet pharmacists' needs, C will probably have to hold higher inventories of drugs. Previously wholesalers would have held buffer inventories.

- There will be much higher administration costs managing relationships with 4,000 pharmacies rather than 10 wholesalers. There is also the greater risk of irrecoverable debts.

- C may well incur higher packaging costs. Previously it would have supplied wholesalers with large boxes of drugs and relied on them to disaggregate. Now it may have to supply lots of small boxes to individual pharmacies.

- Unless outsourced (see below), distribution costs are likely to be much higher as C will have to deliver to 4,000 independent shops, rather than 10 wholesalers. This may mean, for example, that C will need more trucks.

- By focusing on supplying pharmacies directly, C could be missing out on the opportunity to supply supermarkets. This could be a major error should the supermarkets gain significant market share.

- If the supermarkets do gain market share, then it will be at the expense of the pharmacies that C is targeting.

(b) The pros and cons of outsourcing transportation are as follows:

Advantages

- The external supplier will have greater logistics expertise to handle deliveries to 4,000 pharmacies more efficiently than C.

- The external supplier may benefit from economies of scale allowing it to bid for C's contract at a lower price than the cost if C kept distribution in-house.

- Outsourcing avoids C having to buy more trucks for distribution to the 4,000 pharmacies. Completely outsourcing all deliveries would allow C to sell its existing trucks.

- C would be able to focus on its core skills of pharmaceuticals manufacturing without being distracted by distribution issues.

Disadvantages

- Outsourcing would make it more difficult for C to control its distribution function. Any problems with delays, for example, would impact on C's goodwill.

- The inevitable redundancies could damage C's reputation.

- Even though distribution is not considered core to C's business, outsourcing will result in lost competences and skills that may subsequently be useful.

- C is unlikely to have the skills required to manage subcontractors so may need to acquire these.

(c) If C decides to supply pharmacies directly, then it should ensure that key stakeholders are informed as follows:

Stakeholder group	Communication methods
Independent pharmacies	• A letter or an article in a trade magazine informing pharmacies of the proposed strategy and reasoning. Most pharmacists should be sympathetic to the reasoning concerning supermarkets.
	• Sales representatives should then arrange meetings with individual pharmacists to discuss their concerns and try to get customers signed up.
Wholesalers	• Senior staff from C should arrange a face-to-face meeting with wholesalers to explain their plans. This will minimise disruption in the period up to existing contracts ending.
Distribution staff	• Senior staff should arrange a meeting with all transportation staff as soon as a decision is made to discuss plans and outline the assistance that C may be able to offer (retraining, relocation, etc). Given that many staff will lose their jobs it is important that C acts responsibly as a caring employer.
The local community	• C should seek to generate good PR by trying to get articles in local newspapers, communicating with local chambers of commerce and business watchdogs. Throughout these the message should focus on protecting local businesses.
Doctors	• Letters should be sent to GP surgeries explaining the changes. Hopefully the doctors will support C's stand to support local businesses and may be willing to allow posters to be put up on notice boards to communicate to patients.

25   B (NOV 08 EXAM)   *Walk in the footsteps of a top tutor*

From your initial read of the scenario and requirements during the reading time you should have picked up the following points (and therefore annotated your question paper with it):

- ***What does the company do and where?*** *B is a plc operating 100 supermarkets in Europe.*

- ***What are the issues?*** *B's market is fiercely competitive. It is difficult to generate customer loyalty and customers are very price sensitive. The marketing director is suggesting introducing a credit card to help in carrying out some marketing techniques.*

- ***Which frameworks or theoretical knowledge are required?*** *Knowledge of data mining and data warehousing, the six markets model and relationship marketing.*

Based on this you could assess whether to attempt the question

- *Some students were put off by the 6 markets model but otherwise this is a straightforward looking question with parts a) and c) (13 marks in total) representing some of the easiest marks on the paper.*

(a)   **Data Mining v Data Warehousing**

As this question is only worth 6 marks, you are only expected to provide short explanations for each term. This is a requirement with no 'scenario content' and a good structure would be to split the answer into two sections, headed up Data Mining and Data Warehousing. This should represent very easy marks for the well prepared student.

Both data mining and data warehousing are techniques designed to utilise the large amounts of data held by organisations. This data may include customer details, regional sales information or spending habits for example.

Data Mining – Data Mining software looks for hidden patterns and relationships in large amounts of data. It looks for and discovers previously unknown relationships which can be used to help in decision making and predict future behaviour.

In a supermarket, data mining may uncover a previously unknown relationship between the purchase of two items, for example nappies and 'takeaway style food' or ready meals. The knowledge that customers are likely to buy these two items together can lead to focussed marketing campaigns or alteration of store layouts and product lines carried.

The identification of patterns and relationships is known as **classification** or **cluster,** the linkage of such patterns is **association** and the extrapolation of trends is **forecasting.**

Data Warehousing – A data warehouse consists of a database, containing data from various operational systems as well as reporting and query tools.

The data may originate from both internal sources (for example the sales system) and external sources (for example websites or market research agencies.)

The data warehouse is updated regularly, perhaps daily or weekly on an automated basis. Management therefore have a coherent set of information which can aid them in making decisions in the organisation.

Management also need the ability to access the information in whatever format they require and so the reporting and query tools are a key component of data warehousing. They allow data to be viewed in many different ways, for example by shop, product, region, price or time period.

(b) **Relationship marketing in the context of B's business applying the 'six markets' model**

Part (b) is easy if you know the model but difficult to make up otherwise!

Relationship marketing recognises the long term value to the organisation of keeping existing customers, rather than spending marketing resources constantly chasing new ones.

Through relationship marketing, an organisation attempts to enhance satisfaction by precisely meeting the needs of individual customers. It will therefore be necessary to use database systems to record customer details and preferences thus extending the principles of customer care and ensuring that when a customer purchases from an organisation repeatedly, anonymity is no longer present.

For B, with relatively low customer satisfaction and retention in a highly competitive industry, developing IT systems to enable relationship marketing to be carried out may be hugely beneficial.

The Six Markets Model in the context of B

The six markets model advocates that an organisation has 6 key markets, not just the traditional customer market. These six are customers, internal (employees), suppliers, referrals, recruiters and influencers. Marketing activity should be extended to build and manage relationships in all of these areas. This can be demonstrated in the context of B as follows:

Customer Market – As mentioned above, the focus here should be less on transactional or one off relationships and more on building long term relationships with customers.

For B, with high levels of competition from other supermarkets, finding a way to secure customer loyalty (as well as attract new customers from competitors) is important but difficult given the price sensitivity of its customers.

The introduction of a credit card which offers reward points or cash back on purchases from B may help to secure such loyalty. If the card can be used elsewhere, as appears to be the marketing directors plan, it is important to offer the customers 'more' as a reward for shopping in B than in competitors.

In summary, B must be seen to be looking after its customers and rewarding their loyalty.

Internal Market – for the customer care culture to work, staff must be committed to the idea of customer satisfaction.

Each member of staff should be encouraged to see other members of staff as internal customers and ensure that their role is carried out with sufficient attention to detail and quality to keep these internal customers satisfied.

In B for example, the staff members who are responsible for stocking the supermarket shelves should ensure products are neatly arranged and in date. This will make check out staff's job easier and they are likely to deal with fewer complaints.

Suppliers Market – It makes sense for organisations to see their relationships with suppliers as more of a partnership or collaboration than an exercise in power. Through co-operation and mutual concentration on quality, both supplier and customer can benefit.

For B it will be important to offer customers a wide variety of good quality produce to compete with other supermarkets. Without quality and low cost, they are unlikely to achieve the customer loyalty they wish for.

Therefore, flexible, long term agreements with farmers and processed food manufacturers will be crucial to B's success.

Referrals Market – An organisation may be able to use its own customers for referrals by getting them to introduce new customers to the business.

A mail order company may give a certain amount of credit for each new name and address to send a catalogue to for example.

It is also possible to work on achieving referrals from other company's like a bank referring customers to an insurance company.

For B, it may be possible to send out 'friends and family' discounts or offers to credit card holders and achieve referrals this way.

Recruiters Market – Skilled people will be needed to deliver customer service in the organisation and maintain levels of customer satisfaction.

It is therefore important to employ the right calibre of individual by ensuring that all recruitment literature, job descriptions etc. describe attributes that will promote customer care.

For B, ensuring that personable staff are present in each supermarket is important as well as incorporating the need to help customers and interact with them in job descriptions.

Like its competitors, B has a high staff turnover ratio and developing the recruitment market may go some way to remedy this.

Influencers Market – Organisations need to manage the relationship between themselves and the official bodies who can influence their operations.

These may include the government, regulators or even lobbyists and a great deal of PR will be required to market the positive attributes of the organisation and achieve favourable treatment from the relevant influencers.

For B, the European country's Competition Commission (or equivalent) will be an important body to be aware of, and developing relationships with local planning officials so that negotiations over new sites can take place easily may also be useful.

(c)   Three strategies that B can use to develop relationship marketing and improve customer loyalty

Use your own experiences to identify strategies such as loyalty cards, store credit cards, bonus point schemes, staff incentive schemes and customer retention initiatives. It is important to state clearly how each strategy will improve customer loyalty rather than just outline how the strategy will work. The requirement is however, only 7 marks so this can be done briefly for each strategy chosen.

1   **Target existing customers with a loyalty card**

In order to ensure that customers return to B and to gather information to populate a data warehouse and facilitate data mining, B could offer existing customers a loyalty card with which to collect points when they shop.

As the card will be used at each transaction, B will learn about customer preferences and can send out targeted offers to individuals. If people receive coupons for discounts off things they actually buy, they are much more likely to return to shop at B.

Periodically, the points can be 'cashed in' and the customer can be presented with credit to spend in B's shops (or even elsewhere.)

The benefits of this strategy will be two fold. B will learn a lot about their customers and can use this information to design future strategy, and the customers will feel valued and rewarded for their loyalty.

2   **Offer money off complementary products in return for significant supermarket spend**

B could offer customers who spend a significant amount vouchers to claim money off petrol, or food on sale in the supermarket cafeteria.

If these vouchers are valid at a later date, customers will be likely to return to spend a significant amount again whilst redeeming the voucher they received on their last shop.

Cheaper complementary goods will again, make customers feel valued and they will be less likely to take their custom elsewhere.

3   **Price check information**

B's market is predominantly price sensitive and so one of the most effective ways to secure customer loyalty is to point out that B is the cheapest amongst its rivals.

This can be done by conducting price check exercises and publishing the details on TV adverts, in newspapers and within the stores themselves. It will of course be necessary to adjust prices so that B is cheaper than its main rivals in the product lines advertised.

Customers will return to the supermarket they perceive to be the best value and they are likely to believe that B is looking after their interests through keeping prices low.

STAKEHOLDERS, ETHICS AND CSR

26   EEQ (MAY 13 EXAM)

Key answer tips

Requirement (a)(i) should be a straightforward application of the ethical stances in EEQ. A description of all the ethical stances is not required. Candidates' answers should focus upon the categorisation and justification of the ethical stance followed by EEQ.

In requirement (a)(ii) candidates are required to demonstrate their knowledge and application of business ethics and sustainability to EEQ. Candidate's answers should focus specifically upon the importance to EEQ of operating ethically and sustainably at a strategic level.

Requirement (b) requires candidates to evaluate the ethical challenges faced by EEQ in bidding for the new contract in Country X. Candidates are expected to demonstrate their knowledge and practical application of CIMA's Ethical Code of Conduct, through the evaluation of the ethical principles being challenged, the possible safeguards EEQ could incorporate and the overall recommendation of whether the contract should be accepted if offered. This is a challenging question which requires good planning and structure. An overall recommendation must be presented.

(a)   (i)   The definition of an ethical stance is 'The extent to which an organisation will exceed its minimum obligations to stakeholders'. EEQ is clearly an organisation which considers its ethical behaviour, sustainability and community involvement key factors.

Clearly, EEQ goes far beyond its minimal obligation to its stakeholders and society and therefore its ethical stance would be considered as one with 'multiple stakeholder obligations'. This ethical stance accepts that the organisation exists for more than making a profit for its shareholders. It takes the view that the organisation has a role to play in society and so it must take account of all the stakeholders' views. It explicitly involves other stakeholders and believes that it has a purpose beyond mere financial returns. EEQ has a strong focus upon community involvement and sustainability and therefore its obligations and expectations reach much further than purely short term financial gains.

Examiner's comments

This question was not well answered by most candidates. Very few candidates demonstrated any knowledge of the four ethical stances described in CIMA's Official Study Text. Most answers merely described EEQ's current mission statement. However, those candidates who recognised that EEQ focused upon its role within the wider community and its focus upon sustainability as core ethical principles were awarded credit. No marks were awarded for basic descriptions of EEQ's mission statement.

Common Errors:

• Lack of knowledge of the ethical stances

(a)   (ii)   Strong ethical principles that go beyond upholding the law can add value to EEQ in terms of improving its brand. Failure to act ethically can cause social, economic and environmental damage and undermine EEQ's long-term survival. Being such a large, multinational organisation, EEQ's ability to demonstrate strong ethical principles across its whole organisation will help to sustain its future viability. Ethics must be embedded in its business models, organisational strategy and decision making processes.

Often organisations which adopt strong ethical approaches will also see an improvement in profitability. Although this may not be the main driver for EEQ it is a consideration in a highly competitive global marketplace.

By having a range of suppliers which EEQ has trained in its ethical ways of operating, it is investing in the future and can work with them on repeated projects globally. This will tie these suppliers into EEQ and provide a stable working relationship which will deliver cost savings in the long-term. This is a complete contrast to many companies which operate a short term focus and change suppliers regularly or which are let down by non-delivery or poor performance of its sub-contractors. EEQ should not experience these problems and should gain a better reputation with its customers for on time delivery and good quality of work. All suppliers (services and products, such as building materials) will be at the standard that EEQ expects and requires as it has established a good working relationship with the companies it works with.

The ethical tone has to come from the top of the organisation. Therefore, it is at a strategic level that the ethical tone is set. The senior managers and business leaders of EEQ must demonstrate an ethical approach by example. This will show that middle and junior managers will be rewarded for taking an ethical stance and create the appropriate organisational culture.

Corporate communications and reporting on sustainability need to do more than just pay lip service to the sustainability agenda. They need to provide hard evidence of the positive impact on society, the environment and the strategic returns for the business, and how any negative effects are being addressed. EEQ places high regard towards ethical and sustainable business practices which appear to be clearly communicated to staff, customers and suppliers and by communicating its positive actions this should assist in achieving its overall business objectives.

It is important that the finance professionals within EEQ must also play an active role as ethical champions by challenging the assumptions upon which business decisions are made. They must do so while upholding their valued reputation for impartiality and independence when making business decisions and choosing appropriate strategic options.

Examiner's comments

This question was answered well by many candidates. Most were able to discuss the strategic impact of ethical behaviour upon EEQ's long term survival, its reputation and that it would be more attractive to investors and employees. Application in this answer was also good. Candidates demonstrated a sound understanding of the strategic importance of ethical behaviour in organisations.

Common Errors:

•   Generic answers provided

(b)   The first challenge faced by EEQ in its early contract negotiations relates to the destruction of the local villages and the natural habitat. The Government of Country X has stated that it intends to pay minimal compensation to villagers losing their homes and it would appear that it is not concerned about the damage that the highway construction will have on the surrounding habitat. Although we do not know the exact details of EEQ's Ethical Code of Conduct, we can base it upon CIMA's framework and its five guiding principles. From the point of view of EEQ, this is likely to challenge two of its main ethical principles; those of Integrity and Confidentiality.

Firstly, the principle of integrity implies dealing fairly and truthfully. Although the initial Government communication was nothing to do with EEQ, the threat faced by EEQ is that it could be associated with this communication if it was to win the contract. It could be seen that EEQ was complicit in hiding this critical information from the people of Country X. This would go against its mission statement of 'our company's foundation is built on the values of conducting business in a socially responsible and ethical manner. We respect the law, protect the environment and bring benefits to the communities in which we work.'

Possible safeguards to this ethical challenge could include EEQ trying to convince the Government to change the route to minimise destroying local villages and damage to the local environment and for the Government to agree to pay appropriate levels of compensation and landscaping costs to minimise visual damage.

The second ethical principle which is potentially being challenged is that of 'confidentiality'. The Government of Country X has stated that the information relating to the route of the proposed highway and the destruction of the villages and natural habitat should remain confidential until the contract is finalised. From CIMA's Ethical Code, the principle of confidentiality implies that information should not be disclosed unless there is specific authority or there is a professional duty to do so. However, this principle is challenged when it is required by law or there is a professional duty to disclose in order to comply with ethical requirements. In this case, there is no legal obligation to disclose the information but there may be an ethical one.

At this early stage of contract negotiations, EEQ should not disclose this confidential information to anyone outside EEQ. Currently, no construction has been undertaken and the bidding process is still in its early stages and therefore negotiations could still take place to lessen the impact of the route. However, EEQ should insist that the Government announce the plans for the road and the route it will take and take steps to invite comments from the local people and villagers affected by the route. The plans should be open and transparent. Whilst the Government cannot please everyone and there is bound to be criticism and some hostility to the new road, it should try to be open with the citizens of Country X and not keep plans confidential. This is not a good way to operate.

A third principle being challenged could be 'Objectivity', whereby the Government official has attempted to bribe EEQ to accept the Government's own suppliers, without undertaking EEQ's ethical training, in return for winning the contract. This challenges the basic principles of objectivity as EEQ is being asked to make a decision relating to its chosen suppliers based upon undue influence. This contract is likely to be worth a considerable amount of revenue for EEQ and thus this form of coercion is likely to be significant. However, EEQ clearly has a strict policy on the use of ethically trained suppliers and it must ensure that it continues with this policy on this contract even if this would mean losing the contract.

As a safeguard, EEQ should attempt to negotiate with the Government to allow EEQ to select its own suppliers based on its ethical principles and to try to select some local companies and employ some local labour, but only after they have agreed to undergo training in EEQ's ethical principles and when they meet EEQ's ethical requirements.

A final safeguard that EEQ should consider is to ask for an apology from the Government official in respect of the apparent bribery to win the contract. No coercion at all should occur during contract negotiations. If EEQ were to win the bidding process and asked to take the contract on, then this should be based on sound ethical principles.

Recommendation and justification

Overall, even if EEQ could get the Government to agree to some of the above actions, it is recommended that EEQ should reject the opportunity to bid for this contract, as the potential conflict between EEQ and Country X's Government seems to be irreconcilable.

Justification:

This contract impinges significantly on EEQ's ethical stance and the Government of Country X does not seem to meet the requirements of EEQ's beliefs at all. The short-term profit from this one contract could damage EEQ's long- term ability to compete on the global stage.

If, after negotiations, the Government refuses to change the route or increase its obligations to the displaced villagers and the natural habitat, EEQ should withdraw from contract negotiations, as to continue would be against its ethical stance and its mission statement. Moreover, unless the proposed route or the displacement of villagers is found to be illegal, then EEQ would be obliged to respect confidentiality as required by the Government.

A second aspect of the contract negotiations is the use of the Government's own preferential suppliers. EEQ must ensure that its business or professional judgement is not compromised because of some form of bias or inducement. Clearly, this is a form of inducement in order for the Government to get its own key suppliers into the project. EEQ must obviously NOT accept such an inducement. The negotiation team should take the matter to the senior management of EEQ who should explain to the Government officials responsible for the negotiations of the importance of its ethical training programme for its suppliers. EEQ must not undertake this project without following its normal procedures of supplier training based on its ethical code of conduct.

Examiner's comments

This question was not well answered. Very few candidates used CIMA's ethical principles which were of value in constructing their answer, although CIMA's approach was not necessary to pass this question. Some candidates merely listed and described CIMA's five ethical principles with little or no attempt at application to EEQ. Many candidates who did use the ethical principles tried to 'force' the challenges faced by EEQ into all five of the ethical principles, which was not necessary. Candidates must learn that they should only apply a model or theory wherever it is appropriate and not try to make the information fit the model or theory. For example, candidates tried to apply the principle of professional competence to the scenario, which was not appropriate or relevant to the scenario information provided. Similar to Question 1(a), there was no credit given for merely restating information from the scenario as candidates were clearly required to add value by evaluating why the issues faced were ethical challenges to EEQ.

Some candidates failed to consider the ethical dilemmas from the point of view of EEQ and instead discussed the view of the Government or focused more upon the residents of Country X. Many answers merely described the information that was already presented in the scenario, stating that 'this is an ethical challenge to EEQ' but failed to say how or why or what safeguards could be implemented.

The recommendations were largely satisfactory as most candidates recommended that EEQ should not undertake the project. However, some candidates, despite having recognised the serious ethical challenges to EEQ, recommended that EEQ proceed with the bid. Some recommended that EEQ should proceed on the grounds that if they did not, another organisation would do so. This is not a sound justification and it is quite disconcerting that a CIMA candidate should make such a recommendation.

Common Errors:

- Lack of application of the relevant ethical principles

- Descriptive rather than analytical answers

- Poorly justified recommendations

27 PAS (MAR 13 EXAM)

Key answer tips

Requirement (a)(i) should be a straightforward question, requiring candidates to advise on the benefits of stakeholder analysis. However it is important that candidates focus their answers directly upon the benefits to PAS and not a generic list of the benefits of stakeholder analysis.

Requirement (a)(ii) should be a straightforward application of Mendelow's power/interest matrix, using the information presented in the scenario relating to the various stakeholder groups. Therefore it is important that candidates clearly identify and discuss the different levels of power and interest of each stakeholder group and place them appropriately within the Mendelow matrix.

Requirement (b) requires candidates to recommend a range of actions to manage its stakeholder groups. This question clearly links to the analysis of the stakeholder groups identified in part (a)(ii) of the answer above. Candidates are specifically required to recommend actions to manage stakeholder groups which are directly appropriate to the decision being undertaken. A generic description of stakeholder management strategies is not required.

(a) (i) **Benefits:**

PAS has a number of interested stakeholder groups. Therefore it would benefit the Board of Directors to understand the power and interest of each stakeholder group, particularly when strategic decisions such as the chemical processing one, are being undertaken.

Any strategy that PAS wishes to undertake should have the agreement and support of those stakeholders with the most power and interest. Therefore, a stakeholder analysis will benefit PAS as it will assist in understanding which stakeholder group would be against its plans for the processing of chemicals for the cosmetics market and those stakeholders who would be prepared to support the decision.

It would be of benefit to PAS to determine the power and interests of the various stakeholder groups so that it can decide on the appropriate actions, such as to accommodate, negotiate, manipulate or resist the interests of the various stakeholders.

A further benefit is that PAS could use the support of those stakeholders who are in favour of the new chemical process to convince those stakeholders who are against it. In this decision, there is likely to be conflict between different groups over the new process. Some stakeholders, including the employees and institutional investors, will probably be in favour of the cosmetics chemical processing as it is likely to improve profitability and improve job prospects. Others, such as residents who do not work for PAS, will oppose it. Therefore PAS could look to those in favour to assist in persuading those against the process. The decision may allow PAS to be seen as a good corporate citizen which cares for its local community. This will maintain good relationships with its local community and the local Government which is important for an organisation employing so many local people. If PAS consults with its stakeholders it is more likely to gain consent from the stakeholders rather than face hostility.

Examiner's comments:

This question was well answered. Many candidates were able to identify a good range of benefits of stakeholder analysis and also applied these directly to PAS.

Common Errors:

*   Generic benefits of stakeholder analysis with limited reference to the benefits to PAS

(a) (ii) Using the Mendelow power/interest matrix, the main stakeholders of PAS can be classified by their power and interest in the decision to process the chemicals as follows.

High Power and High interest (key players)

The founding family is a powerful stakeholder as it owns 35% of the shares. It will have a high level of interest as it will have strong loyalties to the family business and is dependent on PAS for a living. It also makes up the majority of the Board of Directors and is therefore the key decision maker. Therefore it will have high power in making any decisions.

The employees of PAS own 25% of the shares, and therefore are quite powerful. They will also have a high level of interest as they depend on PAS for their employment which is likely to be more secure if the new chemical manufacturing process for the cosmetics industry is undertaken.

The local Government will be powerful as it could make the situation difficult for PAS if it decides to challenge the decision on behalf of the residents. Although the proposed process meets with health and safety legislation, it is likely to upset some of the residents, who may complain to the local Government. The local Government will have a high level of interest in PAS as the company contributes to the local economy in terms of jobs and to community events.

High Power and Low interest (keep satisfied)

The institutional shareholders will have a high level of power as they hold 30% of the shares of PAS. Their interest in this decision is likely to be low, as they are unlikely to be interested in local issues to do with the community. However, this decision needs to make a satisfactory return for PAS otherwise the institutional investors may become more interested in the decision if it reduces their shareholder returns.

Low power and high interest (keep informed)

The local community and the local residents who do not work for PAS are unlikely to have a significant degree of power unless they can convince the other residents who do work for PAS that the process is harmful. However, this is unlikely. Therefore, their power to influence the situation is likely to be low. They will have a high level of interest in the new process due to the emissions and their potential smell. They could, however, make things difficult for PAS in the future and, as such, they should be treated sympathetically and considerately by PAS.

Cosmetic industry customers. Although they will have no power to influence PAS's decision to undertake this chemical processing, they would be very interested in its production and would welcome the chemicals being produced more effectively as they could procure the chemicals from PAS at a lower price, therefore enabling them to price their end products more competitively or to reduce prices to gain market share and boost their profit margins.

Low power and low interest (minimal effort)

The general public who hold shares in PAS are not powerful as they are unlikely to act as a group. They are also unlikely to have any particular interest in this decision.

Examiner's comments

This question was well answered by most candidates. The stakeholders were very easy to identify and many candidates made a sound attempt at evaluating their levels of power and interest. However some candidates merely stated the position of the stakeholders within the power/interest matrix without any explanation of why they had placed them in this quadrant. Candidates must not merely state that the founding family, for example, are 'key players' without clearly justifying this categorisation. Some candidates stated that key players had high interest and high power but failed to justify why a particular stakeholder was considered to have this particular level of power and interest. Therefore, candidates are reminded that they must always justify why they have placed a stakeholder in a particular category – as the verb 'Analyse' should have made clear to the candidate.

In addition some candidates identified stakeholders which were unnecessary such as 'the media', 'suppliers', 'perfume customers' etc. There were plenty of relevant stakeholders directly identifiable from the scenario without introducing other, less relevant, stakeholders.

Common Errors:

- Poor or no justification of the categorisation of the level of power and interest of each stakeholder

---

(b)   **Recommendations:**

PAS must attempt to balance the interests of all of its stakeholders. As it has been operating in the area for 80 years, the Board of Directors must take a long term view of the situation. It will want to undertake the new cosmetic processing because of the positive impact that this would have on its profits and upon its continued existence. Therefore, it must attempt to manage the expectations of all of its stakeholders but it must concentrate on managing its key players and those stakeholders which it must keep satisfied and keep informed.

Employees have already been defined as key players in part (a)(ii) above. Although they depend upon PAS for their employment, they would also prefer the smell from this new process not to be there as they will also be living close to the factory. They are unlikely to directly oppose the process as this would jeopardise their livelihood, but they may feel unhappy about it, which could have a negative impact upon morale. Therefore, the Board of Directors of PAS must ensure that the staff are kept regularly informed and have a clear understanding of the impact of this new process upon the longevity of the business and therefore their own continued employment.

Also PAS should consult with the local government about the potential smell and other aspects of health and safety for the staff and local community. These consultations should provide information relating to forecasts of jobs created or retained and any future increase in jobs or community activities proposed which could benefit the local community.

The Board of Directors of PAS must actively engage with the local Government and wherever possible, with the local residents in order to reduce their concerns. Members of the local Government should be invited into the factory to see the process and should be kept fully informed and engaged as to how PAS will monitor the impact of the emissions upon the local area. The Board of Directors of PAS must actively engage with the local residents in order to reduce their concerns. PAS should hold consultation talks and open forums with the local Government and the local residents about the potential smell and all other aspects of health and safety.

Some residents may protest to the local Government and this may cause the local Government to look more closely at any future developments proposed by PAS and may be more inclined to refuse permission in the future. Whilst it may be an option to ignore the local residents and continue with the introduction of the new process, this would likely lead to future problems and local community resentment of PAS, which clearly it is not used to and would not want to deal with. Therefore, PAS could hold a number of events to engage with the local residents, such as open days to show how the business works and the value its products create for society, particularly as PAS supplies the food and pharmaceuticals industries. Increased sponsorship of local sports team, investment in local events, and possible financial assistance to local schools could be considered by PAS.

Regular communication with local residents should be undertaken in order to be open and honest and to clearly show residents that the benefit of the activities that it carries out are for the benefit of the community as well as the shareholders.

PAS should also monitor levels of the smell and other emissions to ensure statutory emission levels are not exceeded and these should be reported to the local Government regularly to ensure that compliance is fully transparent. PAS must also continually work towards the development of new techniques which could reduce or eliminate the smells produced by its chemical processing.

Examiner's comments

This question was reasonably well attempted, although many answers were rather generic. Some candidates merely discussed the options of 'keep informed' and 'keep satisfied' but failed to clearly apply these to the different stakeholders of PAS and the methods which could be used. Some candidates merely stated that PAS should 'communicate' with all of its stakeholders which again was not sufficiently applied to the individual stakeholder groups of PAS, all of whom would require different methods of communication. Candidates are once again reminded that generic answers are awarded few marks in E3 and all answers must be directly applied to the organisations and situations featured within each scenario.

A further weakness of answers to this question was that some candidates focused upon solutions to the problem of the smell rather than strategies to manage the stakeholders. For example, some answers included discussions relating to re-location of the factory and investment in new research and development to eliminate the smell. However, these are not stakeholder management strategies and therefore not awarded any marks

Common Errors:

- Generic answers which were not adequately applied directly to the stakeholders of PAS

- Focus upon managing the problem of the smell and not stakeholder management strategies

28 WWW (SEP 12 EXAM)

Key answer tips

This question requires you to have a strong working knowledge of the CIMA Code of Ethics and how to apply it to real-world scenarios. Don't forget that ethical issues are rarely 'black and white' so be prepared to discuss the issues the company will face when applying the Code to the situations it is facing.

Make sure you have thoroughly revised ethics before you sit your exam as it is a common and very important topic.

(a) CIMA's Code of Ethics (the Code) for professional accountants has five fundamental principles:

- Integrity

- Objectivity

- Professional competence and due care

- Confidentiality

- Professional behaviour

(i) **Situation 1**

This situation contains a possible conflict with the fundamental principle of Integrity. This principle imposes an obligation to be straightforward and honest in all business relationships.

The Code amplifies this principle to include communications that:

(a) *contain a materially false or misleading statement*

The very optimistic forecast may be misleading in view of the possible outcome of the legal action being taken against WWW.

(b) *contain statements or information furnished recklessly*

The CEO prepared his forecast in a hurry and did not consult anyone else within WWW. He may lack significant information about WWW. These factors combined may have resulted in the forecast being a reckless one.

(c) *omits information where such omission would be misleading*

The CEO omitted to tell his audience about the possible legal action with WWW's home government. As the outcome of this legal action could materially affect WWW's profit in 2013, this is potentially misleading.

In respect of Situation 1 the CEO's behaviour appears not to have been straightforward and honest. There is a conflict with CIMA's Code.

(ii) **Situation 2**

The Code's principle of Confidentiality imposes an obligation to 'refrain from disclosing outside the firm confidential information acquired as a result of business relationships'.

The information which WWW's home government wishes to be disclosed is covered by the Code's principle of confidentiality.

However, the Code modifies the restriction of confidentiality when disclosure is required by law: 'for example, production of documents in the course of legal proceedings'. As this is the case in Situation 2, WWW should disclose the documents and this is not in conflict with the Code.

(iii) **Situation 3**

Clearly, WWW accounting staff do not have a good working relationship with the accounting staff of ZZZ. This may have led WWW's financial controller to have an unfavourable opinion of the joint venture and this may have led him to advise against its continuance even though the joint venture is a profitable one. The Code has a principle of Objectivity and this imposes an obligation 'not to compromise business judgement because of bias'. It may be that the financial controller has become biased in his judgement of the joint venture because of the operational problems it has caused him and his staff. This situation does represent a conflict with the Code.

Examiner's comments

This question was reasonably well answered by some candidates. The question clearly required candidates to apply their knowledge of CIMA's Code of Ethics to the three given situations in order to determine whether or not there was an ethical conflict. Most candidates correctly identified the correct ethical principle in each case, although some candidates took rather a scatter gun approach and discussed all of the ethical principles within the code for each situation. A recurring weakness within a number of answers was that candidates confused the principles of integrity and objectivity in both Situations 1 and 3. In Situation 2 many candidates concluded that there had been a breach of confidentiality which suggested a lack of knowledge of the Ethical Code. Overall, most candidates demonstrated a sufficient knowledge of CIMA's ethical code to be awarded a pass mark but very few candidates were awarded high marks for this answer by demonstrating a real depth of understanding and application of the Code.

Common Errors:

• Too much time spent describing the ethical principles

• Lack of knowledge of some aspects of the Code including the modification of the restriction of confidentiality when disclosure is required by law

• Confusion between objectivity and integrity and between professional competence and professional behaviour

(b) WWW could use the following procedure to resolve ethical conflicts:

1 Assemble all relevant information.

2 Identify the ethical issues which are involved in the conflict.

3 Refer to fundamental ethical principles. These could be contained within CIMA's Code, WWW's Ethical Code, Mission Statement and Published values.

4 WWW should apply its internal procedures in enquiring into the ethical conflict.

5 WWW should investigate potential future courses of action and ask the following questions:

• What alternatives exist?

• Can the conflict be ameliorated?

• What is the degree of conflict?

• What are the consequences if the conflict is not resolved?

• Which stakeholders will be affected by the conflict?

6 Carry out an internal consultation with affected parties.

7 If appropriate, obtain advice from professional institutes, for example CIMA.

8 Achieve a resolution.

Conclusion

WWW should be aware that there is not necessarily an optimal solution to all ethical conflicts as their resolution will consist of trading off the interests of one group of stakeholders against another. The best outcome which WWW may be able to achieve is a 'least worst' one.

Examiner's comments

This question was very badly answered by most candidates. This should have been straightforward, requiring candidates to demonstrate their knowledge of the stages of a procedure required to resolve ethical conflicts. However, very few candidates were able to identify the required stages to resolve an ethical conflict. Some answers incorrectly referred to dealing with resistance to change, using the Kotter and Schlesinger framework, which failed to answer the question that had been set. A number of candidates stated that the participant should 'resign' if the ethical conflict could not be resolved, but the question asked for a procedure for WWW to resolve ethical conflicts, not advice for an individual. Candidates must make sure that they answer the question that has been set.

Common Errors:

• Not answering the question set.

(c) The following fundamental principles represent aspects of contemporary thought which could be incorporated in WWW's ethical code. The first two principles reflect the aspiration in WWW's published Statement of Values '...(to) trade fairly and sustainably'.

Fair trade: defined as enabling producers in developing countries achieve better trading conditions. WWW could include this principle in its ethical code because it recognises that the needs of stakeholders, other than its shareholders, are of importance. The implementation of fair trading policies might also help towards the achievement of sustainability (see below). This principle might also be included in an ethical code because the company believes that there is an unequal and unfair division of the benefits of international trade and fair trade attempts to rectify this.

Sustainability: which can be defined as an aspiration to follow strategies that contribute to long-term success. The rationale for this recommendation is due to a growing social awareness of the importance of sustainability, that is, conducting business in a renewable manner. An example of this is businesses which endeavour to conduct their activities in a 'carbon-neutral' fashion. If business activities are not conducted in a sustainable fashion the lifecycle of the company will be limited.

As the awareness and appreciation of sustainability increases with consumers a company which has this principle in its ethical code may find that it leads to increased business.

Equality of opportunity: this could be embodied within WWW's ethical code as a commitment to treat all people equally. The inclusion of this principle recognises that all societies have some disadvantaged groups which suffer from discrimination. A company might embrace this principle because of the moral values of its key stakeholders. Another reason for its inclusion is that a company may wish to be perceived as being socially progressive and this principle is a concrete example of that motivation.

Environmental integrity: which expresses the desire to minimise the company's impact upon the natural world. The reasons for this recommendation are the same as those for 'sustainability'.

Candidates were only required to recommend two principles. The others are given as a teaching aid. Any other appropriate fundamental principles given by candidates were credited.

Examiner's comments

This question was not well answered. This was most surprising as the information provided in the scenario relating to WWW's mission statement should have given the candidates a strong indication of the ethical principles of WWW. Yet most candidates did not use this information to help them to answer this question. Many candidates included issues not considered to be ethical issues, such as 'legality' and 'contract terms'. Some candidates merely restated the principles already covered in the answer to requirement (a) even though the question specifically asked for ethical issues not contained within CIMA's ethical code. Again, candidates are reminded to answer the question that has been set. Some candidates did correctly identify two correct issues but failed to adequately justify these. Again, the requirement asked for recommendations with reasons. Therefore, in order to obtain maximum marks, candidates should have fully explained and justified any ethical issue identified.

Common Errors:

- Not answering the question set – identifying ethical principles already discussed within CIMA's Ethical Code

- Not considering ethical issues at all e.g. legality and supplier contract terms

- Limited justification of the ethical issues identified

29   JJJ (MAR 12 EXAM)

Key answer tips

This question is heavily focused on ethics and ethical policies. Make sure that you try and be as practical as possible and apply it to JJJ's circumstances whenever you can.

(a)   JJJ's policy of ethical business consists of the following aspects:

All of its products are sourced and made exclusively within Q

The chief buyer has identified suppliers in country K which could undercut its existing domestic suppliers by 40%. If JJJ insists on sourcing all its requirements from within its home country this might reduce its profitability. However, the outcome of using imported components would depend on the attitude of its customers towards the policy of ethical business.

Thus, this aspect of JJJ's ethical business policy could conflict with shareholder wealth maximisation.

Fair trade

This is associated with a change in the terms of trade designed to adjust the balance between developed economies and developing ones. Currently, all of JJJ's inputs are sourced within Q and would not be affected by a Fair Trade policy. However, if JJJ was to become an exporter to developing economies, a Fair Trade policy might imply that JJJ sells exports to these countries on terms which are more advantageous than those it would offer to developed economies.

Thus, this aspect of JJJ's ethical business policy could conflict with shareholder wealth maximisation.

Legislative requirements

JJJ's policy with regard to this aspect should be one of compliance: that is, it obeys the law. JJJ is carrying out what is required of it which is the same as any other organisation in Q.

Therefore, this aspect of JJJ's ethical business policy does not conflict with shareholder wealth maximisation.

Employees' working conditions

JJJ pays 'high regard' to these. However, it would have to observe legislation within Q regarding these. If its policy does not extend beyond compliance it would not conflict with shareholder wealth maximisation.

However, if JJJ supplies employees with working conditions which exceed legal requirements this would conflict with shareholder wealth maximisation.

Summary

In addition to the judgements above, the overall effects of JJJ's ethical business policy should be evaluated. Even if the policy makes JJJ's products more expensive and/or leads to reduced margins, this may not necessarily reduce shareholder wealth. This is because JJJ may attract customers it would otherwise not have because these customers share the values of the ethical business policy.

Examiner's comments

This question was well answered by most candidates. Most recognised the potential conflicts within JJJ's ethical policies with the needs of the shareholders in terms of restricting the company's profit and growth opportunities. Most candidates correctly recognised the conflicts within the first two aspects of the ethical policy and most also recognised the need for compliance with the law and high standards of working conditions. A number of candidates also correctly recognised that even if the policy makes JJJ's products more expensive, this may not necessarily reduce shareholder wealth as it attracts customers it would otherwise not have done because they share the values of JJJ's ethical business policy.

(b) It is obvious that business standards in K are different to those in Q: for example, the employment practices regarding children are very different in the two countries. JJJ could easily find itself in a position, if it decides to import components from K, where it is infringing its own ethical business policy. Thus, although this could reduce its product costs this may be at the cost of alienating some of its customers. If JJJ wants to avoid this it will have to modify its behaviour as regards:

(i) **Suppliers in K**

JJJ needs to point out to the suppliers in K the different business practices in Q. Although these suppliers may be operating entirely lawfully within K if JJJ's customers became aware of the differing practices this could be very damaging for JJJ's business. In order to more closely align its ethical business policy with practices in K JJJ could initiate the following:

Child labour

JJJ could make it a condition of doing business with suppliers in K that these suppliers did not employ anyone under the age of 16 in their factories. However, this could erode the cost advantage associated with K. Alternatively, JJJ could take a position of acceptance of K's legislation whilst insisting on some minimum standards in K's factories for the children, perhaps, with the eventual aim of parity between the two countries.

Health and safety

Similar arguments apply here as to child labour. JJJ could insist that its suppliers in K work to the same health and safety standards as Q. However, this may be unrealistic and could erode the cost advantage. JJJ could take a position of acceptance of K's position whilst insisting on some minimum standards in K's factories for the children.

Fair trade

As this is an integral part of JJJ's ethical business policy it should influence the prices that JJJ (situated in a developed economy) is willing to pay suppliers in K.

(ii) **Suppliers in Q**

If JJJ sources components from country K this implies that some or all of its suppliers in Q would lose all or some of their business with JJJ. Importing from K is an obvious conflict with JJJ's existing ethical business policy which prescribes that all of its products are sourced exclusively within Q. This may be a factor that JJJ suppliers will be quick to point out.

However, although suppliers in Q will be damaged by this change, suppliers in K will benefit. As JJJ is situated in a liberal developed economy it will recognise that its import of components from K is an aspect of international free trade. Therefore, JJJ could justify its actions on this basis.

Although JJJ's new policy damages suppliers in Q, because of the benefits to suppliers in K and its shareholders it is still an ethical policy albeit a different one. Such a justification is unlikely to be acceptable to JJJ's suppliers in Q.

(iii) **Customers in Q**

JJJ should point out to its customers that sourcing components from K confers the following advantages:

Price: because of K's cost advantage JJJ is able to keep its prices down for its customers

Necessity: JJJ has to find cheaper inputs in order to compete against the imports which have been taking market share from it. Some of its competitors are probably sourcing components from K already so if JJJ follows suit they will be competing on an equal basis.

Employment: if JJJ buys components from K this will create/sustain employment within K. If JJJ does not import from K it may be forced to close which could cause unemployment in Q and JJJ's customers in Q would be deprived of a source of supply.

Child labour: JJJ has the opportunity to improve conditions for these children by imposing some minimum standards on its suppliers in K.

Health and safety: JJJ has the opportunity to improve conditions for workers by imposing some minimum standards on its suppliers in K.

JJJ should acknowledge that there are areas which could compromise its ethical business policy. However, it should be assertive and insist on some minimum standards from its suppliers in K. JJJ should state that, on balance the positive factors outweigh the negative and it is possible to trade with K and maintain its ethical business policy.

(iv) **Shareholders**

JJJ's shareholders 'value its ethical business policy' although the extent of this feeling is unknown. However, it is likely that some shareholders will be offended if they learn of the revision to the policy. As the sourcing of components is not a transparent activity JJJ must decide whether it will inform its shareholders of the revision. CIMA's ethical code provides a good guide here: 'professional accountants....(should be)...straightforward and honest in all business and professional relationships'. Therefore, if JJJ accepts this guidance it should inform its shareholders of the change to its ethical business policy.

JJJ should also point out that its change of policy has been prompted by its decreased profitability and declining competitiveness. JJJ has a duty to act in the best interests of its shareholders and balance the two aspirations: shareholder wealth maximization and its ethical business policy. JJJ is also trying to improve the working conditions of the people working for its suppliers in K. Its new policy is a compromise between the two, in this case, competing aspirations.

Examiner's comments

This question was not well answered. Many candidates recognised that sourcing components from suppliers in K was a conflict with the current ethical business policy but few considered the nature of the conflict in relation to each of the interest groups. Many answers went little further than recognising that a conflict existed, with either little or no discussion of how JJJ could manage its future relationships with each interest group. Some answers merely stated that the ethical business policy should be re-written, but this was not asked for and therefore awarded no credit.

Common Errors

- Limited answers stating only that the ethical policy had been breached

- Limited focus upon managing future stakeholder relationships

---

30 HWS (MAY 11 EXAM)

Key answer tips

This is a relatively straightforward question on stakeholder analysis. Part (a) asked for you to analyse HWS's **shareholders** and assess the level of power or interest. Remember that for each shareholder you will need to justify their position on the matrix (which you did **not** need to draw). This involves explaining why you think they have high/low power and interest.

Part (b) asked you to identify two other stakeholders that would be interested in HWS's decision to sell alcohol and tobacco. To do this, you would need to think practically of the possible interested parties in the real world. Any reasonable stakeholders would have earned credit here, but make sure you justify their interest.

Finally, part (c) looked at how HWS could ensure it acts responsibly towards society. Note that this does not necessarily mean reversing its decision and deciding not to sell alcohol and tobacco. Again, try to be practical!

(a) Mendelow's matrix measures the power and interests of stakeholders:

Low power/low interest

Private investors: on average each investor has a shareholding worth less than £1,000. It is unlikely that most of these shareholders would take an active interest in HWS's affairs. Collectively, as they only hold 3% of the equity, they have little power to affect any of HSW's decisions.

Low power/high interest

HWS charitable trust: although this holds 10% of HWS's share capital, on its own it has a very limited amount of power as regards the company's decisions. However, as its recent criticism of the decision to sell alcohol and tobacco demonstrates, it has a high degree of interest in the company's affairs.

HWS employees: like the private investors, the employees have little power to affect any of HWS's decisions. However, as their jobs are associated with their shareholdings, which are worth almost £9,000 on average, they are likely to have a high degree of interest.

High power/low interest

Pension funds and investment trusts: there are six of these which have 30% of the equity. If they act collectively they have a high degree of power. Their investment is worth £135 million at the current market price which suggests they would have a high degree of interest. However, these investors have not traditionally been interested in the day-to-day running of the companies in which they hold investments. They are more likely to be passive rather than active investors.

High power/high interest

HWS directors: these have a disproportionate, in relation to their shareholding, amount of power. It was their decision which is now being criticised and they are able to change it or withdraw it instead of implementing it.

RCB: private equity fund: this holds a significant proportion of HWS's equity, 25%. If it held another 5% it would be obliged to make an offer for the company which may be its intention. This puts RCB in a powerful position. Its motive for investing is to see short-term profits, so it is likely to have a high degree of interest in the decision.

UK clearing bank: this will be interested in the decision because it has both a substantial shareholding worth £90 million and because HWS is its client. This shareholding gives the UK clearing bank substantial voting power and it will also have power arising from its position as HWS's bank.

Examiner's comments

This question was well answered. Most candidates made a sound attempt at identifying the levels of power and interest for most of the stakeholder groups and were also able, in many cases, to evaluate the levels of power and interest. Those candidates who failed to clearly explain and evaluate the levels of power and interest for each stakeholder were awarded a fail mark for this question.

(b)   Stakeholders are defined by CIMA as 'Those people and organisations that have an interest in the strategy of the organisation. Stakeholders normally include shareholders, customers, staff and the local community'.

Among the stakeholders who are likely to be interested in this decision are HWS's customers. This is because the decision to sell alcohol and tobacco products is in response to unsatisfied customer demand. However, other customers of HWS may also be interested in this decision but not be in favour of it. This is because some people view alcohol and tobacco products as being injurious to health and/or unsuitable for young people and may not want HWS to offer an additional distribution channel.

Politicians at local and national level, with a particular interest in public health and health promotion, may also be interested in HWS's new retailing strategy because of its possible side effects on the health of HWS's customers.

Medical doctors may also have an interest in the new retailing strategy for the same reasons as politicians.

As the new retailing strategy is forecast to increase profits by 25% to £5 million it will be of interest to potential investors.

Although the requirement only asked for two other stakeholders this answer has given four for the sake of completeness. Candidates received marks for any other stakeholders if these were supported by a cogent argument.

Examiner's comments

This question was reasonably well answered. However many candidates failed to recognise that this decision by a chain of retail shops is unlikely to be of any significance to the national government or the national health authorities as, clearly, alcohol and tobacco are already currently on wide scale sale and one more retailer is not going to come to the attention of the national government. This decision is clearly more likely to have a local impact and therefore candidates were rewarded for recognition of this.

(c)   The first response that HWS could make to these demands is to acknowledge that they reflect current social concerns and should be taken seriously. This acknowledgement is implicit in the recognition of the concept of the stakeholder which covers a broader constituency than that of shareholders.

A set of guidelines describing principles and standards for responsible business conduct has been published by an international organisation, the Organisation for Economic Co-operation and Development (OECD). These guidelines are designed to ensure that companies operate in accord with government policies and strengthen the basis of mutual confidence between companies and society. The guidelines are voluntary but if HWS adopted them it would show a commitment to responsible business practice.

HWS could also demonstrate its commitment to responsible business practice by modifying its mission statement to explicitly state, for example, 'HWS is committed to responsible business practice' and/or 'HWS has adopted the OECD guidelines'.

HWS could operationalise these guidelines and incorporate them into its strategic decision-making process. For example, every important capital investment decision should include an assessment, perhaps in the form of a checklist, to measure the decision's compliance with the guidelines.

HWS could designate a director to periodically report on their responsible business practice and the report could be published externally. This would be a suitable responsibility for a non-executive director. (See the Higgs report 2003).

HWS could provide training for its employees on the application of 'responsible business practice'.

Examiner's comments

This question was reasonably well answered. Most candidates' answers were focused upon how HWS could operationalise responsible business practices through activities such as donations to charity, staff training, responsible sales practices and investment in local community schemes.

Very few answers focused upon the OECD guidelines which was not a problem, if instead the answer focused directly upon how HWS could improve its socially responsible practices. Most answers were very practical and well applied to HWS.

---

31   LAS (SEP 11 EXAM)

Key answer tips

Part (a)(i) should have been a very straightforward couple of marks. Remember that we normally analyse **stakeholders** – these are *any interested parties*, rather than just shareholders. Try and mention parties that would actually be linked to a business like LAS!

Part (a)(ii) should also be relatively easy to answer. Make sure you discuss how the matrix would be used. The question does **not** ask you to perform a stakeholder analysis for LAS, so be careful to not do too much here!

The easiest way to tackle part (b) is to break the question down into two parts – what is the purpose of a mission statement and what are the advantages a mission statement may bring to the organisation? Try mentioning LAS in each point you make – it will help ensure you are applying your answer as the requirement demands.

Part (c) looks at the use of a change agent. Focus on the benefits as far as possible, as requested in the question. Change agents do appear relatively frequently on the exam, so make sure you can talk about what they do.

Finally, part (d) looks at the CIMA Code of Ethics. This is vital knowledge for a CIMA student and is something the examiner will expect you to be fully conversant with. Make sure that you actually refer to the Code's ethical guidelines by name. You will likely be marked down if you do not.

(a)   (i)   A leading international financial newspaper has criticised LAS because its annual report has focused exclusively 'on the interests of shareholders and ignored 'any other interested parties'.

These parties are analogous to 'stakeholders' which CIMA has defined as 'Those persons and organisations that have an interest in the strategy of the organisation. Stakeholders normally include shareholders, customers, staff and the local community'.

> **Examiner's comments**
>
> This question was well answered. Most candidates identified two relevant stakeholders. However, some candidates merely listed a range of generic stakeholders without any real consideration of stakeholders directly relevant to LAS.
>
> Common Errors
>
> - Generic list of stakeholders

(ii)   In addition to the stakeholders identified by CIMA, LAS could consider also the needs of the financial press, both national and international and any other appropriate interest group which it could identify through an exercise in stakeholder analysis and mapping.

It could also employ a categorisation of:

Internal stakeholders: for example, management

Mixed internal and external stakeholders: for example, trade unions

External stakeholders: for example, Governments.

When LAS has identified its stakeholders it could use the Mendelow matrix, which has two axes denoting factors of 'Interest' and 'Power'. This matrix identifies 'High' and 'Low' levels of these two factors and demonstrates the potential influence of stakeholder group. Thus, a stakeholder with high levels of power and interest is ranked as a 'Key Player': a stakeholder with low levels of power and interest is ranked as one on which only 'Minimal Effort' should be expended.

> **Examiner's comments**
>
> This question was reasonably well answered. Most answers focused correctly upon the key elements of Power and Interest and most also correctly identified the key categorisations within the matrix. Some candidates also went on to apply the matrix directly to those stakeholders identified in part (a) of the answer, which was also awarded credit, if undertaken correctly.
>
> Common Errors
>
> - Limited discussions of only interest and power
> - No categorisations attempted / discussed

(b) **Purpose**

LAS's original purpose was stated to be 'trade in Empire commodities'. This has become outdated and misleading. LAS is now an international property company carrying on its business in 28 different countries. It shortly plans to move its corporate headquarters to London. The purpose of a mission statement for LAS is that it would accurately convey to the outside world 'the fundamental objective of an entity' CIMA.

In order to do this, LAS would have to carry out a process of self-analysis which may prove beneficial for the company. In coming to a decision about its fundamental objective it could learn much about the organisation and its stakeholders and might suggest new future strategic directions for LAS.

Advantages of a mission statement

When the mission statement has been drafted and published it may have a motivating effect upon its employees and give them an increased sense of ownership of their organisation.

The mission statement will communicate to the outside world the current identity and purpose of LAS and those of its stakeholders.

Examiner's comments

This question was reasonably well answered. Most candidates were able to identify both the purpose and a range of advantages of mission statements. The main weakness in some candidates' answers was a tendency to provide a generic list of the benefits of mission statements rather than focusing upon the benefits to LAS, which does not currently have a mission statement.

Common Errors:

• Limited / no application of benefits to LA

(c) Change agents are a response to the experience reported by Michael Jarrett that 'organisational change is exceedingly difficult and expected benefits are rarely realised'. Academic research suggests that 70% of change management programmes fail. A practice has developed in change management of involving an independent third party, a change agent, to facilitate change. The value of using a change agent is that he or she will help members of the organisation to:

• Define problems associated with the change

• Examine the problems and diagnose how they can be overcome

• Arrive at alternative solutions

• Implement solutions

• Transmit learning so the organisation can apply this to future changes

However, a contrary view about the benefits of using a change agent has been put forward by Jarrett who identified 'seven myths of change management'. Two of these myths are:

• Change can be managed: Jarrett contends that change agents might stimulate or even steer through change but this does not constitute managing it.

• The change agent knows best: Jarrett's view is that 'Ultimately, an organisation will find its own ways of responding to change'.

Therefore, although a change agent may be useful in facilitating the corporate move this should not be regarded as a panacea. Change will continue to be difficult and the use of a change agent will not be the answer to all the problems which change presents.

Examiner's comments

This question was not well answered. Many candidates merely listed the skills/ attributes of a change agent or identified the activities that they undertook. Other answers were focused upon project management activities rather than change management activities. Answers should have been directly focused upon the benefits to LAS of using a change agent within the current change activity being undertaken. Many answers were far too theoretical to be awarded a pass mark.

Common Errors:

- Discussions of skills / attributes of change agents
- Discussions of project management activities

(d) When LAS moves its corporate headquarters, 80 employees will lose their jobs. Unfortunately, their prospects of finding a replacement job are not good. This decision has some obvious bad consequences for these LAS employees.

Although the decision to move the headquarters was made by the Board of LAS, the Finance Director, CR, bears some responsibility for it taking place because he made the original suggestion and because, as a member of the Board, he shares in its collective responsibility.

As a CIMA member, the Finance Director should ensure that his behaviour complies with CIMA's Code of Ethics. The Code has delineated fundamental principles dealing with Integrity, Objectivity, Professional Competence and Due Care and Confidentiality. However, the Code does not exempt a CIMA member from making difficult decisions. A breach of the Code would only take place if CR infringed one of the fundamental principles described above.

As a member of LAS's Board, CR has a fiduciary responsibility towards the company's shareholders. As CR has identified some cost savings which would result from the move it is arguable that he would be in breach of his responsibilities, and possibly the Code, if he did not suggest it. Another consideration is that although jobs will be lost in one place, new jobs will be created in London. However, CR should ensure that when the move happens the employees who will lose their jobs are treated in accordance with legal requirements as regards their period of notice and redundancy pay.

Conclusion

Although CR is implicated in a decision which has some bad consequences for 80 employees this does not necessarily involve a breach of CIMA's Code of Ethics.

Examiner's comments

This question was not well answered. Although most candidates could correctly list and describe the elements of the Code of Ethics, it was most disappointing that the level of understanding of the Code was very poor. Many candidates presented very weak arguments to suggest that the move of headquarters was a breach of the Code, without any recognition or understanding of the difference between an ethical dilemma and a difficult business decision. Many organisations have to make difficult commercial decisions involving re-location and redundancies but this does not make them unethical.

There was nothing in the scenario information which suggested any unethical behaviour and candidates are not expected to assume information that is not there or to create their own information to support a viewpoint.

Common Errors:

- Listing and description of Ethical Code rather than application

- Inappropriate / incorrect application i.e. concluding that the FD was in breach of the Code

32 WRL MINING (SEP 10 EXAM)

Key answer tips

Part (a) (i) is a straightforward stakeholder analysis. Make sure that you stick to only discussing three stakeholders. Try to justify their position on Mendelow's matrix. Remember that as long as you can justify your conclusion you should get credit for your answer.

Part (a) (ii) is more complicated to answer. You may find that in some cases it is simply not possible to completely resolve stakeholder conflict – especially in this scenario, where the needs of some stakeholders is in direct conflict with the needs of others. For each of your suggestions, try and offer **advice**. You can do this by discussing how feasible each of your proposals are.

The easiest way to tackle part (b) is to break the mission statement down into its three main parts and use each one as a heading. The question asks for a discussion here, so you'll need to talk round the issues and explore ways in which the mission statement is consistent and inconsistent with WRL's actions.

(a) (i) **Categorisation of three stakeholder groups in WRL**

Eastern State Government/Local residents – High Interest, Low power (keep informed)

The Eastern state government, representing the local population of the area around the mine has proven it has high levels of interest in the project.

On a positive note, the mine will provide local employment as well as a payment from the central government of $1m. However, it will also have a significant adverse effect on the local environment, which has caused the state government to take legal action against WRL.

The Eastern state government seems to have low levels of power. It was not part of the negotiations and it appears that after its unsuccessful legal action against WRL it has no further power to prevent the mine from going ahead

Central Stravian government – Low Interest, High Power (keep satisfied)

The central government seems to have been unconcerned with possible effects on the environment as they have not built any controls into the licence with WRL. After the initial negotiations were concluded, the central government seems to have taken relatively little interest in the problems that have arisen with the project.

Should they decide to take an active interest in the future, however, they would undoubtedly have significant power over the project and could ultimately decide to close it down.

The Central government's interest may increase if the impact on the environment is a concern for local residents – meaning that it is possible they may become **key players** in the future.

WRL Shareholders – Low Interest, High Power (keep satisfied)

WRL's shareholders ultimately own the company and therefore they have significant control over its actions. Should a significant number of shareholders become unhappy with the operations in Stravia, it would put pressure on the company to withdraw.

In addition, as the investors in the company, they will also have a great deal of interest in WRL providing them with sufficient return on their investment. However, only a small number of shareholders have indicated any concern over the potential pollution of the lake in Stravia. The majority seem uninterested in the pollution, as long as their returns are sufficient.

(ii) **Advice on the actions needed to resolve competing stakeholder objectives**

The key conflict here is between the needs of the bulk of WRL's shareholders to make a profit and the concerns of the Eastern state government and a small minority of shareholders over pollution in the surrounding area. Unfortunately, this conflict is not easily resolved.

Reduction of environmental impact – One possible method is to investigate ways of treating the polluted water before it is pumped into the lake. While this may be more expensive, it may allow a compromise position to be found whereby the damage to the lake is minimised but the project is still economically viable for WRL.

Publicity – Failing this, WRL may need to attempt a damage-limitation exercise. This could involve the publicising of the positive effects of the mine on the local economy and residents. The Eastern state government presumably represents the needs of the residents, so highlighting the benefits of the new mine may go a long way towards calming their fears.

Withdrawal – Alternatively, given WRL's insistence on being a good corporate citizen, it could opt to pull out of Stravia completely and look for alternative investments that will not pollute the environment to such a degree.

It is unclear whether many alternatives are available for WRL to pursue. If not, this may not be acceptable to shareholders, who for the most part seem to support the Stravian mine. There may also be financial penalties for WRL withdrawing from its agreement with the central government.

WRL could use the model proposed by Cyert & March, who examined possible ways to deal with stakeholder conflict. These include:

- Satisficing – this would involve keeping the most powerful stakeholders happy – presumably in WRL's case, this would be its shareholders.

- Sequential attention – this involves WRL taking turns prioritising stakeholders needs. This would be unlikely to be useful in this scenario due to the conflicting nature of the stakeholders needs.

- Side payments – if WRL is unable to deal with the Eastern State Government's needs, it could look at other ways of compensating them. Perhaps offering additional payments would appease the local government.

- Exercise of power – ultimately if, as in this case, no agreement can be reached, the most powerful stakeholders can exercise their influence and force a settlement.

Conclusion – It should be noted that ultimately there may be no way to completely resolve this stakeholder conflict. In these cases, stakeholder analysis would indicate the need to side with the most powerful groups – the 'key players' – who in this case would be the shareholders.

(b)   Discussion of the extent to which WRL's mission statement is consistent with its plan to pollute the lake.

WRL's mission statement breaks down into three key statements. The proposed strategy in Stravia should be analysed to see whether it conforms to these.

To make the maximum possible profit for its shareholders

WRL obviously feels that this project is profitable for investors. After negotiations with the local government it has decided to proceed and feels it will only become uneconomic if the waste water has to be disposed of in an environmentally friendly way.

Causing the least damage to the environment

WRL would appear to not be meeting this requirement due to the damage about to be done to the lake and local environment.

However, given the vague nature of the mission statement, WRL may argue this is the least possible damage to the environment, given the nature of their business.

The damage to the lake could be seen as the least damage they can do whilst still meeting their other goal of maximising investor returns.

Be a good corporate citizen

Again, the answer to whether WRL is meeting this part of its mission statement is more complex than it might initially appear.

Certainly the effect on the local environment of the polluted water would not be consistent with good corporate citizenship.

However, it could be argues that WRL is also providing significant investment in the local area – with jobs for local workers as well as the $1m payout that the Eastern state government received.

Contributing to the local economy could be seen as meeting the requirement for good corporate citizenship.

33   E MULTINATIONAL (NOV 08 EXAM)   *Walk in the footsteps of a top tutor*

From your initial read of the scenario and requirements during the reading time you should have picked up the following points (and therefore annotated your question paper with it):

- *What does the company do and where? E is a multinational and one of the largest global producers of chocolate, coffee and other foodstuffs. It sources raw materials from less developed countries and imports and manufactures in fully developed countries. It follows OECD guidelines for multinationals in every country of operation.*

- *How big is it? E is the largest multinational operating in country F.*

- *What are the issues? E has recently been receiving some bad publicity in country F, a less developed country where E has provided many welfare benefits for farmers and their families. The government of F has been supportive of E in the past but is now under pressure to raise the standard of living and so is threatening to impose an export tariff on cocoa beans unless prices are increased and E opens a manufacturing facility in country F. The management of E are due to meet with the government to discuss the future of the business in F.*

- *Which frameworks or theoretical knowledge is required? Stakeholder analysis and strategic options for part c)*

Based on this you could assess whether to attempt the question

- *one of the easier questions on the paper, should not have caused any issues.*

(a)   **The advantages to E of conducting a stakeholder analysis of its operations in country F**

For 4 marks, you must explain the advantages to E of conducting a stakeholder analysis of its operations in country F. It is clear from the scenario that E has many stakeholders in country F and it would have helped if you had annotated these as the scenario was read.

Time is limited here but try to make comments relating to understanding and support gained through stakeholder analysis, preparation for the upcoming meeting and dealing with multiple stakeholders. Despite the few marks on offer, the requirement is to explain and so lists of brief points will not be sufficient. Be careful about writing too much and going over time.

- Through conducting a stakeholder analysis E will gain a greater understanding of the potential influence of stakeholder groups, particularly the government and national labour union (who E suspect are behind the negative publicity recently directed at E in country F.) An understanding of the threats from these groups is crucial if E is to avoid operating a loss making factory in country F.

- Whatever strategy E adopts in country F, it is unlikely to work without the support of its most powerful stakeholders. Through stakeholder analysis, E can ensure that stakeholder views are taken into account before strategies are devised and implemented. Protests against E's actions are consequently less likely.

- Conducting an analysis will prepare the CEO for the upcoming meeting with F's government ministers. The CEO can be ready with responses to the government's concerns, particularly in respect of their belief that the prices paid for cocoa beans are too low. An understanding of the issues, gained through stakeholder analysis, may aid E in reaching a compromise over the export tariff threatened by the government if E does not pay suppliers more and open a factory in F.

- E has multiple stakeholders in country F, amongst them the government and labour union. In addition however, there are the people of F whom E has behaved as a 'good corporate citizen' towards. With such a diverse set of stakeholders, analysis is crucial to ensure the needs and claims of stakeholders are not overlooked. If E wishes to continue to follow OECD guidelines and be used as an example by that organisation, it must treat all stakeholders fairly. Analysis will help E to do this.

(b) **A stakeholder analysis for E's operations in Country F**

An alternative to the 7 stage model described here is to use Mendelow but you need to make sure you actually carry out an analysis and don't just draw the model and categorise the stakeholders (this wouldn't be enough for 14 marks anyway.) The idea is that by the end of a stakeholder analysis, E would know exactly who their stakeholders were and which ones to prioritise..

There are seven stages in carrying out a stakeholder analysis:

1 **Identification of stakeholders**

Internal stakeholders include the management and staff of E.

Mixed internal and external stakeholders include the national labour union, the local farmers in their co-operatives, their workers and the local communities who have benefitted from E's corporate citizenship (via funding schools and hospitals.)

External stakeholders include the government of country F, the main opposition party (who may be in government within 15 months), E's two main competitors (both multinationals), the OECD, the press and other foreign companies operating in country F.

2 **Identification of their interests, values and concerns**

Internal stakeholders will be concerned with E's ability to operate in country F without hindrance from the government and labour union and continue to be a 'good corporate citizen'. Their interests will also be in keeping the price they pay for cocoa beans low, avoiding the export tariff and not being forced to bow to government demands and build an unprofitable factory in country F

Mixed internal and external stakeholders comprise various different groups. The national labour union is interested in taking power away from E and the farmers' cooperatives and, in fact, removing E from country F altogether. The union is concerned that farmers have become too powerful within their cooperatives and as a result farm workers are being exploited.

The local farmers' cooperatives on the other hand are likely to value their close and friendly relationship with E and will have concerns if this is threatened. The farm workers may be concerned about losing their jobs if F is forced out of the country but also interested in how F may respond to allegations that their actions have resulted in exploitation of workers.

The local communities will value F's contribution to their society, providing hospitals and schools and may fear for the future of such infrastructure if foreign companies are driven out of E

External stakeholders include the government who are interested in increasing tax revenue from exports and basically receiving more money directly from E in order to help fulfil their objective of raising the standard of living in F. The main opposition party is concerned with supporting the labour union in their quest to rid F of foreign companies.

E's competitors are likely to have similar interests, values and concerns to E; the OECD will be interested in promoting the benefits of good corporate citizenship and continuing to use E as an example of this; and other foreign companies will have a significant interest in whether E is able to continue to operate in country F.

3   **Identification of sources of stakeholder power**

Internal Stakeholders include management who have formal authority to make decisions regarding E's future strategy. This, combined with the benefits they have brought to country F makes them a very powerful stakeholder. They could presumably pull out of the country and source the undifferentiated raw materials from other less developed countries.

Mixed internal and external stakeholders include the national labour union, whose power comes from the fact they have the backing of the opposition party within F and are able to put pressure on the government as a result. The local farmers have more power in their co-operatives, however they are still much less powerful than customers like E and cannot influence the behaviour of large multinationals.

For similar reasons, workers and local communities will have very limited power.

External Stakeholders: In theory, the government of country F has the power to impose tariffs on E or seize assets but in reality, they are unlikely to risk the tax revenues they currently receive. The main opposition party has little direct power at present but as already noted they may be in government within 15 months. The OECD, although a respected supranational organisation, has no real power and can only hope to influence organisations and governments through its work.

4   **Identification of claims stakeholders can make on the organisation**

E's stakeholders will have expectations which must be managed.

Claims on E will come from the OECD and population of F, who will expect the company to behave in an ethical manner (paying a fair price for cocoa beans for example.) The responsibility that E has towards the local community is to an extent discretionary, since there is no legal obligation to provide schools and hospitals. E's global reputation may suffer however if this behaviour were to stop.

The other main claims on E will come from the government and labour union. E has a legal responsibility to obey relevant laws in country F and if the government demands money via an export tariff on beans, in the short term this claim will have to be met.

5   **Identification of the most important stakeholders from the organisations perspective**

According to Mendelow, the most important stakeholders are those with the highest levels of power and interest in an organisation.

From the analysis done above, high power and interest would appear to be held by the management of E, the government and the labour union. Mendelow's matrix would classify these as key players. This means that a successful strategy will only result if their objectives are considered and in addition they should participate in strategy formulation.

The OECD, farmers and community and other organisations have high levels of interest but low power and according to Mendelow would be merely kept informed of decisions made by E.

6   **Mapping of the relationships between stakeholders**

The management of E has to date had a good relationship with the government in country F but now is being threatened by them and suspects they are responsible for bad publicity directed at the organisation. It is unlikely that this relationship can be salvaged and the objectives of both groups are likely to be polarised.

The labour union similarly has a poor relationship with E at the moment which is unlikely to be remedied and will be under greater threat if the opposition party win the next election.

7   **Identification of the resultant strategic challenges**

The strategic challenges facing E are continuing their operations in F without being penalised by the government for doing so. In particular, E does not want to build a factory in country F as demanded by the government.

The meeting between the government ministers and the CEO is an opportunity for E to show that it understands the concerns of key players.

(c)   Evaluation of options available to E in its approach to the government of country F and recommendation of the most appropriate

---

Here you are asked to evaluate options available to E in its approach to the government of F and also to recommend the most appropriate option. For 7 marks, it is important to present a range of options and then a clear choice at the end. Provided sensible suggestions are outlined and one of these is then clearly chosen (not something new as an afterthought at the end!) marks should be relatively easy to pick up here.

Some kind of negotiation is the best solution however it is likely that any reasonable suggestion swill score marks.

As a key player, the government of country F can be a major driver of change and a major opponent of E's strategy. At the present time, there is a conflict of objectives between the government and E.

Cyert and March suggest some ways in which competing objectives can be resolved:

Satisficing – Through negotiation, a solution could be found which keeps all, or the most powerful, stakeholders happy. The government is under pressure to increase standards of living and is threatening export tariffs on cocoa beans unless E pays more for them and opens a factory in F. The management of E do not want to open the factory and may be able to avoid this if they offer to compromise and pay a higher price for the raw materials. Such negotiation could take place at the meeting between the CEO and government ministers.

Sequential Attention – the management of E could agree to the government's demands this time, on the basis that the next objective of the government in respect of E will not be met. Key stakeholders thus take turns in getting their objectives realised.

Side payments – The CEO of E could refuse to pay the higher prices for cocoa or build the factory but instead offer to compensate the government in another way. Since the government is under pressure to raise the standard of living of the population, further welfare benefits provided by E could persuade them not to impose the export tariff. Such benefits would also continue to enhance E's reputation as a 'good corporate citizen'.

Exercise of power – the management of E could simply refuse to pay the extra money and set up the factory. They could then use their power as a large multinational to prevent the government imposing the export tariff. The most obvious way to do this would be to threaten to leave country F altogether and switch support to another suitable less developed country.

The most appropriate option:

Practically speaking, the negotiation involved in option 1 (satisficing) is probably most appropriate. If this could be combined with the idea of side-payments, to fit in with the government's objective to raise the standard of living and E's wish to be a good corporate citizen then an acceptable outcome may be achieved.

34   RGG (MAY 12 EXAM)

Key answer tips

Section (a) asks you to explain two methods that RGG could use to understand its external environment. Application was important here (as normal), so try and pick external analysis methods that would be useful to RGG Itself, such as SWOT or PEST. Make sure you don't spend too long explaining them, as this requirement is only worth four marks.

Part (b) asks for a discussion on whether abandoning the existing mission statement shows good corporate social responsibility. Remember that a discussion requires you to look at both sides of the argument and then, where possible, come to a conclusion.

In part (c), you were asked to suggest strategies for managing stakeholders, based on Mendelow's model. Given the number of marks, this mainly involved explaining Mendelow's four possible stakeholder management strategies, with some basic application to the scenario where possible.

(a) There are a number of approaches that could be used to assist in forming an understanding of the external environment.

One well known model used for environmental analysis is SWOT: the acronym refers to Strengths, Weaknesses, Opportunities and Threats. Threats and weaknesses are defined in relation to the external environment. RGG plc (hereafter RGG) is threatened by a take-over and has an opportunity to expand its business into other countries.

There may be other threats and opportunities in RGG's external environment and RGG could form an understanding of these by the use of market research which also could be used to investigate shareholders' views about pesticide sales.

RGG could use the PEST model to examine its macro-environment and identify key drivers of change, sources of risk and opportunities and threats. RGG could research whether there would be any Political obstacles to widening its area of sales. An analysis of RGG's Economic environment could support the belief that the removal of the restriction would lead to increased sales. RGG could examine Social attitudes towards pesticide sales to establish if these have changed since 1992 when the Mission Statement was formulated. An awareness of developments within pesticides related technology would also enhance RGG's understanding of market opportunities. All the factors explored within PEST could be influential in RGG's shareholders' investment decisions.

Examiner's comments

This question was reasonably well answered. Most candidates identified two relevant methods but very few correctly explained how these could be used by RGG. Again, application rather than mere description was required to obtain maximum marks.

Common Errors

• Descriptive answers only.

(b) Corporate Social Responsibility (CSR) has been defined as the firm's obligation to maximise its positive impacts upon stakeholders while minimising the negative ones. Although CSR has not been uniquely defined It is usual to consider the economic, legal and ethical aspects of a business as falling within the scope of CSR.

With regard to the proposed abandonment of the mission statement, RGG has the following responsibilities to consider:

Economic

The primary motivation for the discarding of the mission statement is economic in that RGG's managing director, S, believes that the mission statement restricts business expansion. He believes that RGG could get a great deal of business from selling pesticides to countries outside its current area. RGG has been in slow decline since 2005 and in its most recent financial year it made a loss of £1 million. Therefore, S has a duty within CSR to try to reverse the decline.

If S is right then the economic performance of RGG will be improved when the mission statement restriction is removed. This means that the economic welfare of RGG's shareholders will be enhanced and is, therefore, socially responsible.

Legal

RGG's Board of Directors, which includes S, has a duty to act in the best interests of its shareholders. The proposed abandonment of the mission statement has been discussed by the Board and at least one non-executive director was not in favour of the new strategy.

The Board is not obliged to consult with the shareholders about every decision it makes: this would not be feasible. The shareholders have appointed the Board to run RGG and the Board is accountable to them. If the shareholders have a substantial disagreement with any of the Board's policies the shareholders have the right to replace the Board. What S has proposed; to sell pesticides to a wider market, is legal and because of its positive economic impact upon the shareholders could be considered as socially responsible behaviour.

Ethical

S, as a member of CIMA, must have regard to CIMA's Code of Ethics as regards his personal behaviour. The main sections of the Code are concerned with:

- Integrity
- Objectivity
- Professional competence
- Confidentiality
- Professional behaviour

However, the proposal which he is considering does not fall under any of these headings and so, from a professional point of view he is acting ethically.

As far as RGG is concerned, it would be legal to widen its area of sales and so, to this extent, the new policy would be ethical. However, an ethical issue arises because the shareholders have not been consulted. Given that the Board is supposed to act in the best interests of the shareholders, if the majority of shareholders were opposed to the removal of the restriction the new policy is clearly not in their best interests. In these circumstances, to persist with the abandonment of the mission statement would not be socially responsible corporate behaviour.

The argument could be widened further because, although increasing the area of sales would be legal for RGG, it could have bad effects if its customers used the pesticides irresponsibly. If RGG was to facilitate the irresponsible use of pesticides by its customers, for example, by selling pesticides to totalitarian states or to politically unstable countries this would not be socially responsible behaviour. As such, RGG would be acting unethically.

Examiner's comments

This question was not well answered by most candidates. Answers to this question were generally very thin and lacked sufficient depth of discussion of the three CSR aspects of RGG's responsibilities. Most candidates correctly identified and discussed RGG's economic responsibility to its shareholders reasonably well. However, the main weakness of answers was in discussion of the legal and ethical aspects of the decision. Most candidates incorrectly focused upon the general ethical and legal issues relating to the sale of pesticides in general business terms, rather than the specific legal and ethical issues relating to the abandonment of the mission statement.

Common Errors

- Poor focus – answers not correctly focused upon the abandonment of the mission statement.

(c)   Stakeholders are any individuals or groups that have an interest in the organisation. RGG could classify its stakeholders in relation to the power and interest they hold in relation to S's proposal. Mendelow has provided a model which suggests the following strategies:

Low power/Low interest:

Minimal effort: their lack of power and interest makes these stakeholders open to influence. They are more likely to accept what they are told and follow instructions.

High power/low interest

Keep satisfied: this group needs to be kept satisfied so that its interest is kept low and it does not move into the key players quadrant. This could involve these stakeholders being reassured about the outcome of S's proposal well in advance.

Low power/high interest

Keep informed: although these stakeholders are interested in S's proposal they do not have the power to impact upon it. However, efforts should be made to persuade any opponents of the proposal of its merits to avoid them seeking power by joining with stakeholders with high power but low interest.

High power/high interest

Key players: these stakeholders have the ability to thwart S's proposal. Their consent is vital if the proposal is to be implemented. S needs to communicate well with the key players and take their views into account.

Examiner's comments

This question was well answered by most candidates. Many correctly identified a relevant stakeholder and most also correctly identified a relevant range of strategies to manage the relationship with its stakeholders. However, a small number of candidates provided largely descriptive answers relating to the Mendelow matrix rather than the identification of stakeholder management strategies advised by the model.

Common Errors

- Mapping the stakeholders without discussing relevant strategies to manage the relationship.

---

35   XYZ (MAR 11 EXAM)

Key answer tips

This question has a strong focus on Corporate Social Responsibility (CSR). This is a highly topical area and one that you can expect to see being examined on a regular basis.

Part (a) asks for the benefits of CSR to XYZ. If you found yourself struggling with this requirement, make sure that you review the model answer carefully for ideas. Note that only benefits were requested in this requirement, but also be prepared to discuss drawbacks and problems with adopting CSR for companies as well. The model answer includes some detail about CSR indexes. While these are useful background to the answer, they would not be required in order to get full marks.

For part (b), as ever, try and use the question to structure your answer. Setting up a separate heading for each part of the policy detailed in the question would have really helped your answer to flow. Try to be practical with your ideas here and make sure they are relevant to XYZ itself. A list of generic points would be unlikely to score well here.

Finally, part (c) should have been relatively straightforward for a well-prepared student. Lewin's three-stage model is popular in the exam. For each stage, outline what the stage involves in theory and then discuss what XYZ itself would have to do.

(a) If XYZ produces a policy for Corporate Social Responsibility (CSR), there are a number of possible benefits it could receive. XYZ wishes to be listed on a stock exchange because this would give it access to capital and XYZ's auditors have advised it that a CSR policy is a requirement of listing.

In addition to this direct benefit, XYZ could benefit because companies with an active CSR focus are ranked by two major indexes. The 'FTSE4GOOD' index series measures the performance of companies that meet globally recognised CSR standards and is 'designed...to facilitate investment in these companies' (FTSE 2010). The 'Dow Jones Sustainability Indexes' track the financial performance of the leading 'sustainability driven companies worldwide'. These indexes provide asset managers with 'reliable and objective benchmarks to manage sustainability portfolios'. (2010 SAM Indexes). If XYZ has a CSR policy, it would enable it to be ranked on these two influential Indexes which could increase its attractiveness to ethical investors.

Research studies conducted in the late 1990's have indicated that companies investing in CSR have good financial performance. One view of company performance suggests this depends on the amalgamation of physical, human and organisational assets it offers to the external environment. XYZ, by following a CSR policy, can nurture and develop sustainable relationships with its stakeholders. If these relationships are difficult for other companies to imitate, then XYZ will have created competitive advantage for itself.

XYZ, in its pursuit of CSR, is acknowledging the needs of a wide group of stakeholders; that is, it regards itself as having responsibilities which are wider than those which it owes to its shareholders. This acknowledgement should bring two benefits to XYZ: it should foster good relationships with its stakeholders and this should enhance XYZ's reputation. Investing in stakeholder relations will promote loyalty to XYZ from its suppliers, staff and customers. This can lead to further benefits, for example, loyal staff are likely to want to stay working for XYZ so staff turnover will reduce which, in turn, reduces costs. If XYZ establishes a good reputation for its CSR policy, this will make it an attractive place to work and help it recruit high quality workers.

In order to implement a CSR policy, XYZ will have to acquaint itself with its stakeholders' preferences. This implies that XYZ will inform itself of changes in external regulations, technology and social attitudes. This awareness will be of assistance to XYZ's management of both internal and external risk.

Examiner's comments

This question was well answered by most candidates. Most answers were focused correctly upon the benefits to XYZ and most candidates presented a sound discussion of a range of potential benefits

(b) In its formulation of a CSR policy, XYZ should include sections dealing with the following matters:

Waste: As XYZ's manufacturing process produces large quantities of waste it should consider how this is disposed of and the extent to which any of the waste is recyclable. The production of the waste will have involved the use of resources, such as energy, so XYZ should ensure that there is no unnecessary waste.

Noise: XYZ's CSR policy should acknowledge the existence of the noise which it creates and describe how noise will be managed. Noise may not only affect XYZ's employees but noise pollution may contribute to environmental degradation in the area surrounding XYZ's premises.

Smell: the same considerations which apply to noise pollution apply to the odour pollution created by XYZ's process.

Raw material procurement: As XYZ sources some of its materials from economically underdeveloped countries, XYZ's CSR policy should delineate the terms upon which this business is conducted. The CSR policy should state XYZ's desire for equitable trading relationships with its suppliers and might include the aspiration to be a 'Fair Trade' partner.

Workforce: XYZ's CSR policy should include a statement about how it deals with equality of treatment for its workforce. Additionally, because XYZ has experienced a number of accidents recently, XYZ should make a commitment to workplace safety.

Compliance: XYZ has always tried to obey its country's laws which is commendable. CSR implies that companies will exceed their legal responsibilities if necessary. However, it would be appropriate for XYZ's CSR policy to acknowledge its willingness to comply with the law.

Examiner's comments

This question was well answered, as was expected with such a straightforward question. Most candidates identified a good range of contents covering the key areas of waste, noise, procurement, workforce, legal compliance and health and safety measures. Most answers were suitably applied to the scenario information. Some candidates provided a number of KPI's to measure compliance with these aspects and although this was not required some credit was awarded.

(c) Kurt Lewin (1975) proposed a three stage model of change which could be applied to the implementation of a CSR policy.

Unfreezing: This would involve XYZ finding methods of making the need for a CSR so obvious and compelling that its workforce will readily understand why a change from no CSR policy, is necessary. Unfreezing will also assist the workforce in accepting the change. There are a number of arguments which will help XYZ in 'unfreezing'. One strong motivation for the change is related to a bigger change, that of a listing on the stock exchange. If the workforce accepts the desirability of a listing then it should accept the need for a CSR policy.

On a more personal level, the employees will realise that many aspects of the CSR policy deal with their working lives, for example, noise, smell and safety. Thus, when the CSR policy is implemented, the employees may find that aspects of their working lives improve which will give them the motivation to 'Unfreeze'.

Changing: XYZ will want employees to change their patterns of behaviour so that the values expressed within the CSR policy become accepted by the employees and form part of their normal way of thinking. In this transitional stage, XYZ could facilitate the change by encouraging its employees to identify their own behaviour with that of role models who are expressing/demonstrating new behaviour patterns. For example, senior managers, such as the Managing Director, could attend safety training courses with production operatives to demonstrate commitment to the new CSR policy. XYZ could also place employees in situations where they have to adopt new behaviours if they are successful. For example, XYZ may commit itself in its CSR policy to a reduction in noise levels and this would compel manufacturing and engineering managers to investigate different production techniques.

Refreezing: Once the behaviour patterns within XYZ have been changed, then 'Refreezing' will ensure that the new patterns become the norm and there is not a regression to previous behaviour. Refreezing will aim to consolidate the new behaviour so it becomes the accepted way of doing things. Some refreezing will be organic in that the more often the new behaviour is repeated the more familiar it becomes until it attains the status of habit. XYZ could also make positive interventions to support the new behaviour. For example, the staff responsible for reducing noise levels could show their performance against targets linked to XYZ's appraisal system: staff who suggest CSR improvements might also be rewarded.

Examiner's comments

This question was reasonably well answered by most candidates. Most answers demonstrated a sound knowledge of Lewin's model. However, far too many answers were largely generic and descriptive rather than being applied directly to XYZ.

Common Errors

- Lack of application to XY

CHANGE MANAGEMENT (20%)

36   RSS (MAR 13 EXAM)

Key answer tips

Requirement (a) should be a straightforward question, requiring candidates to compare and contrast a top down culture with a collaborative form of culture. Candidates are required to apply their understanding of these two types of culture directly to RSS.

Requirement (b) requires candidates to apply their knowledge of the cultural web to the information presented in the scenario. The scenario contains a great deal of information directly related to aspects of RSS's cultural web, which candidates are expected to identify and apply correctly to the different aspects of the cultural web.

Requirement (c) requires candidates to demonstrate their knowledge and understanding of change agents. Candidates are expected to examine the benefits to RSS of employing a change agent. Again, application of the benefits directly to RSS is required.

(a) A top down culture in RSS is one based upon hierarchy and power structures. It is a rigid culture where the management hierarchy is not questioned and the senior team sets and imposes decisions. This is typical of an old-fashioned hierarchical organisation which is slow to change and which does not have a consultative management style. In a top down culture, the senior partners discourage challenges to the way things are currently done as is the case with RSS. In RSS, the lawyers are dependent on senior partners to make the final case decisions, and this is likely to lead to blame and lack of risk taking. Similarly, in RSS, appraisals are unilateral i.e. the senior partners set the targets for staff with no input from the staff themselves. This is likely to be demotivating.

In contrast, a collaborative culture encourages working together and the sharing of knowledge and experience of the senior partners and associate lawyers in order to develop synergy and encourage commitment and the creation of ideas. Lawyers and other staff would support each other to improve knowledge. A collaborative culture is one in which there is a free exchange of information and all employee input and suggestions are considered and valued. Ideas are shared and, as one person builds on another's ideas, a new synergy develops. This results in better job satisfaction, a good open exchange of ideas (to achieve best practice) and more experienced employees who contribute to their organisation. This results in a management structure that listens and is open to new ideas and suggestions for improvement. Typically, this type of organisation has a low staff turnover and 'grows' its own future managers. Appraisals would be done with the input of the staff members themselves. They will be involved in setting realistic and motivational targets.

Examiner's comments

Very few candidates answered this question but those that did had a reasonable understanding of a collaborative culture. Answers were well applied to RSS. Candidates were less knowledgeable of a top down culture and some candidates ignored this altogether in their answers. Again, candidates are advised to use the information within the scenario to help them answer questions as the clues to the features of a top down culture could be clearly found within the scenario. Most answers focused more upon hierarchical structure rather than culture in this answer.

Common Errors:

- Lack of knowledge/understanding of top down culture

- Poor use of scenario information

(b) The concept of the cultural web was first devised by Gerry Johnson to explain why organisations failed to adjust to environmental change. He identified that many organisations developed a 'paradigm' which is a way of understanding how their organisations worked and that some found it difficult to react to change if the paradigm was particularly strong.

The concept of the cultural web helps organisations to map out 7 main aspects which drive its culture to determine the elements of culture which need to change and to determine those factors which are likely to block cultural change. If we consider all aspects of RSS's cultural web we can identify a range of issues which are likely to block cultural change.

The key aspects of the cultural web for RSS are as follows:

Stories and myths

RSS relies heavily on its reputation. It uses its monthly newsletter to promote the stories and history of RSS and to 'reinforce' the organisation's beliefs and values. The stories and myths will play a strong part in re-enforcing the culture of conformity and commitment to RSS and its current way of operating, thus blocking a change of culture in RSS.

Routines and rituals

The formal staff appraisals and the need to make appointments to see the three founding senior partners are examples of routines and rituals. The formal appraisals do not appear to involve any input in terms of targets and performance measures from the administrative staff themselves and therefore these are likely to be very demotivating (as is evidenced by the high staff turnover). Also, the requirement to seek senior partners' agreement on decisions by associate lawyers is a routine which stifles creativity and independence and again is likely to lead to dissatisfaction and associate lawyers feeling undervalued. This high staff turnover and dissatisfaction, although not necessarily blocking cultural change, will be a factor, as high staff turnover will lead to lack of staff continuity and therefore no momentum for change to happen amongst the staff.

Organisational structure

RSS's organisational structure is very hierarchical and does not encourage collaboration. The structure is rigid and inflexible and compounded by the three senior partners being rather isolated from the rest of the staff and by the decision making routines. This rigid organisational structure is not conducive to flexibility or collaboration.

Control systems

The appraisal systems and reward systems are largely based upon punctuality and commitment to RSS, rather on high levels of individual performance or team work. This seems to have a negative effect as administrative staff turnover is high. The rigid control systems reward conformity and commitment and not creativity and collaboration. Thus the current control systems are likely to stand in the way of change in RSS.

Power structures

There is a hierarchy based on power and influence and decision making is only undertaken by senior managers in RSS.

The three founding senior partners have very strong beliefs about what RSS should be and do and these beliefs are the main blockers for change as clearly no strategic decisions can be made without their final agreement.

Symbols

The best offices and privileges for senior partners are clear symbols of power and hierarchy in RSS. The wearing of uniforms by administrative staff creates conformity and creates a 'them' and 'us' barrier in RSS. This is a clear block on collaboration and a re-enforcement of a top down culture.

The organisational paradigm

There is the general view amongst the three founding senior partners of 'the way we do things' in RSS. They have a strong view about the areas of law which they practice and the way in which the firm operates. This view and the culture which has been developed over the last 40 years will be difficult to change. It is clear that these three senior partners are not at all willing to release their decision making power and work towards a more collaborative culture. However, the other senior partners seem more willing to change and they may be the main facilitators.

(c)   The first task of a change agent would be to persuade the three founding senior partners of the importance of change and how they can make change happen. The change agent will also reassure the founding partners about any fears they have.

The main benefits to RSS of appointing a change agent would be as follows:

Identifying the restraining forces within the cultural web

Clearly, a need for a more collaborative culture is likely to be necessary for RSS to survive in the future and therefore appointing a change agent would help RSS to identify from the cultural web, which aspects were the most restraining towards a collaborative culture.

A change agent would identify the restraining forces to change in RSS and assist the senior partners in understanding these forces. Currently, the attitude is one of 'this is the way we do things'. A change agent would help to bring new ways of thinking to the senior management team, most of whom are interested in changing the way RSS operates.

Selection of appropriate change actions

A change agent would propose ways in which the problems identified by RSS can be overcome and to help the 3 founding senior partners to decide the most appropriate solutions. It is clear that a more collaborative approach to working is necessary, not only for current work but also should RSS decide to move into the environmental law area.

Therefore the change agent would help RSS to identify methods which could be used by the senior partners and associate lawyers to encourage more collaborative working. For example, team building exercises could be encouraged and carried out on a regular basis. Also, the six other senior partners could mentor associate lawyers and work together on legal cases and work through decisions together. RSS has never been open to these ways of working and has no experience of it, therefore a change agent will bring in external knowledge and experience to RSS.

Encourage Participation

Once the senior partners have made their decision as to which course of action is most appropriate, the change agent would then have to implement this. The change agent would talk to staff, encourage participation and understanding and actively move towards a collaborative culture. Administrative staff would also need to be involved and the change agent would assist in organising this for RSS. Staff are more likely to want to participate if it is led by someone who is not part of the current senior management team of RSS, as clearly there are difficulties in communication between the different levels of staff in RSS

Transmit the learning process to others and the whole of RSS

The change agent would document the learning process and all of the discussions and actions taken within the change process. This would be presented to all of the senior partners.

Examiner's comments

This question was reasonably well attempted. Most candidates appeared to have a good understanding of the role and benefits of a change agent and most were also able to apply these directly to RSS

Common Errors:

• Limited application - a generic list of the benefits of change agents

• Answers focused upon the role of a change agent and not the benefits of a change agent to R

---

37 PPP (NOV 12 EXAM)

Key answer tips

Requirement (a) should be a straightforward question, requiring candidates to identify from the scenario a number of change triggers. It is important that candidates clearly explain why these are considered to be change triggers.

Requirement (b) should be a straightforward application of Lewin's Force Field Analysis model. Candidates are required to identify, and more importantly, evaluate the driving and restraining forces in relation to the change occurring in PPP. Candidates will be awarded very few marks if they merely describe the model. Direct application to PPP is required to pass this requirement.

Requirement (c)(i) requires candidates to demonstrate their knowledge of the types of change and apply this directly to the scenario, using the Balogun and Hope Hailey classifications. This should be a straightforward question.

Requirement (c)(ii) should be a very straightforward question requiring candidates to demonstrate their understanding of the methods of managing resistance to change. This has been examined several times before and therefore candidates are expected to be able to apply their knowledge of this area of the syllabus directly to PPP without any difficulty.

(a)   A change process normally begins as a result of a trigger for change, which can be either external to the organisation or it can be an internal event or action from within the organisation. Internal and external pressures often make organisational change inevitable. There have been a number of change triggers affecting PPP, including the following:

Internal Change triggers

New CEO.

The new CEO is clearly a strong proponent of wind powered electricity generation and, therefore, his introduction to PPP is a significant internal change trigger. He has made it clear to the Board that not only does PPP need to undertake wind powered electricity generation but has also suggested that the old style of bureaucratic management must also change. Therefore, his introduction to the organisation has been a significant change trigger for PPP. His questioning of the old ways of doing things will result in major changes at all levels within PPP.

Impact on performance

The loss of customers in recent years to competitors offering renewable energy is likely to impact upon PPP's profitability and may mean PPP is increasingly uncompetitive. This has been recognised by the new CEO in his recent statement and he clearly considers this to be a significant internal trigger for change.

External Change Triggers

PPP is operating in a dynamic and complex business environment. The electricity generating market is changing and customers are also demanding more environmentally friendly forms of electricity production. Therefore, the main external triggers for change are as follows:

New EU environmental policies and directives

Z's Government has recently agreed to a European Union target of generating 20% of the EU's energy supply from renewable sources by 2020. This is clearly a significant change trigger as PPP will have to ensure its compliance with this directive or become uncompetitive and go out of business.

Fees and incentives from the Government

In 2011, Z's Government announced plans for incentive payments to be awarded to those companies investing in renewable energy supplies. In addition, a government initiative called the 'Renewables Pledge', requires, by law, all energy suppliers to provide a proportion of their sales from renewable sources or pay a penalty fee. Clearly, this is a significant change trigger as incentive payments could help PPP to invest in these new technologies. Secondly, a penalty fee would make PPP more uncompetitive and affect its profitability. In addition, the national Government is forming new laws to increase the speed of planning applications.

Customer attitudes

The generating companies' customers within Z have become increasingly sensitive to environmental issues and the impact of energy production on the environment and many are willing to switch generating companies to obtain some electricity which is generated from renewable sources. In fact, since 2010, PPP has lost 5% of its customers to competitors offering renewable energy production. This is a significant problem for PPP as its current reliance on fossil fuels is likely to be unpopular with more customers in the future and therefore, if it is to remain competitive, it must react to customer needs.

Examiner's comments

This question was reasonably well answered by most candidates. Most candidates recognised three obvious change triggers such as the arrival of the new CEO and the Government pledge and the associated incentives and penalty payments, making change inevitable for PPP. However, some candidates clearly did not understand a change trigger and discussed issues such as deregulation, trade unions and management style in their answers to this question. However, these are forces and not change triggers and should have been discussed in answers to part (b) of the question. Also, some answers were rather thin and lacked explanation. List-based answers are not appropriate at this level and all points made should have been clearly explained.

Common Errors:

- Incorrect focus upon forces for change

(b)   Lewin argued that organisations should consider change in terms of:

- Those factors which encourage and facilitate change (the driving forces)

- Those factors that inhibit change (the restraining forces)

Change can only happen successfully if the driving forces are greater than the restraining forces. Therefore, PPP needs to evaluate both the restraining and driving forces and ensure that the driving forces are strengthened and the restraining forces are weakened or removed.

The diagram on the following page highlights the main driving and restraining forces, with the arrows indicating the forces exerting the main pressure on the change process.

Driving Forces

The new CEO is a key driving force behind the change to wind based electricity production as, without him, the old ways of operating would have continued. It will require his continued drive, commitment and leadership to ensure that this change occurs and is successful. Therefore, his commitment to the strategy and drive should be a major force for change.

In addition, the Government and EU directives and legislation are a major driver of change as it would appear that PPP has little alternative but to ensure that it undertakes renewable electricity delivery. In addition, the Government is trying to drive though change more effectively through improved processing of planning applications, which should increase the success of the planning process. Therefore, as a driving force, the Government and EU directives are likely to be the strongest force for change.

A further driving force is PPP's customers. They are increasingly demanding renewable energy sources and, should PPP not provide this, then they are willing to move to other energy generators. This is clearly not sustainable for PPP and it must make sure it retains its customers in such a highly competitive market. It is likely that their strength as a driving force will grow and become more significant as competitors move more towards renewable energy production.

Restraining Forces

The attitude of the engineers and the unions could be a major restraining force for PPP. Should strike action occur, this will be very costly, but increased wages would make PPP uncompetitive. This will be a significant opposing force as the unions are clearly not afraid of taking strike action. However, PPP needs to manage this force carefully in order to reduce its impact by clear and open communication with staff regarding the future viability of PPP.

The current bureaucratic management structure may also make change difficult as management is likely to resist any changes to working arrangements and 'the way we do things'. Cultural change is always likely to be very difficult and a slow process to change. However, as a restraining force, this should be something that PPP can manage if it clearly communicates the importance of the change to staff.

The slow planning processes are not likely to be highly significant as the Government is introducing legislation to speed up the application process. However, local residents concern for their local environment could be a major concern for PPP as they may become powerful stakeholders who could lobby Government to relocate wind farms elsewhere in the country. Therefore, local residents could become a powerful restraining force if they form alliances and lobby Government.

Management of the Forces

PPP is trying to move towards its ideal state of being a wind powered electrical generating company. PPP must ensure that it strengthens its driving forces and weakens or eliminates the restraining forces. Therefore, it must ensure that all legislation is adhered to and that staff are fully communicated with in regard to the benefits of training and restructuring. In addition, customers must also be made fully aware of PPP's strategic development towards generating electricity from renewable sources.

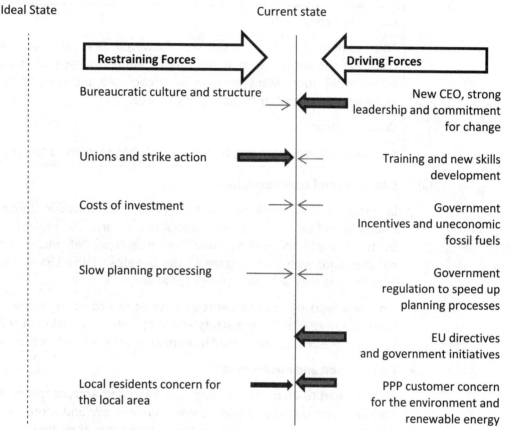

Note: **Candidates were not required to present their answers in diagrammatical form.**

Examiner's comments

This question was generally well answered by many candidates. Most answers correctly identified a range of appropriate driving and restraining forces. However, the main weakness of answers was that candidates failed to evaluate these forces i.e. discuss the relative strength of these forces for change in PPP. The question clearly asked for an evaluation and not a description and therefore those candidates who did correctly evaluate the forces were awarded high marks.

Common Errors:

- Limited or no evaluation of the strength of the forces identified

---

(c) (i) Change can be classified in terms of the speed of change (i.e. whether it is a 'big bang' all at once change versus an incremental, step by step approach) and the extent of change (i.e. it results in an overall transformation of the organisation's paradigm or merely a realignment of its existing operations and assumptions). Balogun and Hope Hailey identified four main types of change based upon these classifications:

		Extent of Change	
		Realignment	*Transformation*
Speed of	**Incremental**	Adaptation	Evolution
Change	**Big Bang**	Reconstruction	Revolution

The changes currently occurring in PPP could be classified as Evolutionary as the nature of change is likely to be incremental and occur over a period of time. It will result in a change of paradigm for PPP as it will transform PPP.

Examiner's comments

This question was generally not well answered. Few candidates used the correct classifications and those that did often identified a type of change without any sound justification. Many answers were confused and contradictory and syllabus knowledge appeared to be lacking in this area.

Common Errors:

- Lack of understanding of the types of change referred to in the E3 syllabus

---

(ii) **Education and communication**

In order to overcome resistance, PPP should consider communicating both internally and externally to key stakeholders. Clearly, the engineers feel threatened by the changes to working conditions, therefore PPP must educate them and communicate with them regarding the benefits of the change and the personal benefits that they will gain through retraining.

The new working arrangements and conditions could in fact work out to be far more favourable to the engineers and, if so, this information may encourage them to accept the change more readily. Communication should be regular and honest.

Participation and involvement

Through participation, PPP should gain increased acceptance, particularly as staff may feel that ownership gives them a greater say and more motivation. As the engineers are the key experts in the organisation, then their involvement in the development over wind powered energy is likely to be critical. Gaining local resident acceptance through participation may be more difficult and time consuming but PPP could consider involving local residents in user groups and forums in order to seek their guidance on local issues.

Facilitation and support

Training has already been offered to the engineers but this has been resisted. However, this does not mean that training should not be pursued and continued as it will be a necessary part of the change process. Additional training could be considered in non-technical areas to include training in management and other business skills to encourage motivation of the employees to see opportunities for growth and self-development. Counselling services could be offered to those staff experiencing difficulties with the change. However, this is likely to be an expensive option for PPP.

Negotiation and Agreement

As the engineers are unionised then some form of negotiation seems inevitable for PPP. Although PPP has stated that increased wages would make them uncompetitive, some form of pay settlement may be essential to ensure the changes to new working arrangements. Negotiations are likely to include discussions on new methods of working, use of new technologies, new activities and working arrangements and new qualifications required. PPP may need to offer incentives such as paid leave for training courses or additional payments for overtime.

Manipulation and coercion

Manipulation and coercion are seen as the last resort to overcoming resistance to change. If staff feel that they are being manipulated, then they are more likely to increase resistance. Coercion, whereby management force staff to accept change by means of using threats of redundancy, for example, is not an acceptable form of managing resistance for PPP.

Overall, a combination of methods to overcome resistance is likely to be the most appropriate approach. Clearly, some form of negotiation and agreement with unions and staff will be necessary, even if this costs PPP money to do so. In addition, regular and open communication with staff and local residents will be necessary to gain acceptance and some degree of participation should assist the feeling of involvement in, and therefore acceptance of, the proposed change.

Examiner's comments

This question was reasonably well answered. However, it was disappointing to see how many candidates provided very generic answers with little or no attempt at application to PPP. This is not acceptable at this level and candidates must understand that few marks are awarded for general and unapplied answers. They must also understand that this means REAL application to the scenario and not merely mentioning the name of the scenario organisation as many times as possible throughout their answer!

Common Errors:

- Limited application to PPP

---

38 WAL (MAY 12 EXAM)

Key answer tips

Part (a) examined when an organisation would need to use evolutionary or 'big bang' change. Remember that rapid, major changes tend to be forced on an organisation by environmental changes. Keep your answer relatively short here – as this is only worth four marks.

Part (b) was not based around any particular model. You were asked to evaluate the three solutions proposed in the scenario and then recommend which should be adopted. Remember that 'evaluate' is a common exam verb in E3 and requires you to look at the good **and** bad points relating to each solution.

> Part (c) asked you to advise how WAL could overcome resistance to change. Kotter and Schlesinger would be the clear choice here. However, to score well, it had to be applied to WAL's circumstances.

(a)   The case for change to WAL's software-based marketing information system seems to have been accepted by the two main parties which will be affected by the change: the marketing staff and the Company Secretary, R. What is in dispute is the speed of the required change. The marketing staff want change to be revolutionary: to happen straightaway. R is opposed to revolutionary change and has suggested three possible solutions: modification, development and purchase. The first two of these would be evolutionary, i.e. not be immediate: purchase would be revolutionary, i.e. quick, but R is sceptical about its effectiveness.

   (i)   **Evolutionary change** is appropriate when it's a proactive response to anticipated changes in the environment. However, in the case of WAL's marketing information system the changes in the environment have already happened: WAL is 'being left behind by its competitors and is losing customers'. Further, according to the software supplier, 90% of WAL's competitors are using biscuit industry standard software which implies that WAL is at a competitive disadvantage.

   (ii)   **Big Bang/Revolutionary change** is likely to be forced and reactive because of changing competitive conditions which is the situation in which WAL finds itself.

         The case for revolutionary change to WAL's marketing information system seems to be dominant, that is, it should happen. However, a caveat needs to be noted because of R's opposition and WAL's previous experience of failed change.

Examiner's comments

This question was reasonably well answered. Most candidates correctly described the two types of change but few correctly explained the circumstances appropriate for these types of change. Candidates must make sure that they answer the question that has been set as the question clearly asked for the circumstances when these types of change would be appropriate.

Common Errors

- Description of the type of change with no focus upon circumstances when appropriate.

(b)   (i)   The three solutions proposed by R are:

         Solution 1 – Modification

         This solution relies upon WAL's in-house IS/IT staff who have limited experience of the work which would be required and they are 'unsure of the cost.' Despite their lack of relevant experience the IS/IT specialists are confident that they could complete the work within a year.

         The judgement that this project could be completed within a year is questionable because of the staff's lack of experience. The staff's uncertainty about the cost means that WAL may pay excessively for this project's completion.

         As this solution relies upon modifying what is an inadequate system, the final result may not meet WAL's marketing staff's needs: neither will it present them with a quick enough remedy to the current system's inadequacies.

An important advantage of this solution is that it would fit the preference of R and the IS/IT staff for evolutionary change. As these are people who would be closely affected by the change to the marketing information system their views should be taken into consideration.

Summary

This solution is not recommended because the lack of certainty about its duration, cost and ability to meet its users' needs.

Solution 2 – Development

WAL's IS/IT staff would like the opportunity to develop new bespoke software themselves to meet the marketing staff's needs. If this solution was adopted it could have a positive motivational effect on the IS/IT staff. This solution would also meet the preference expressed by R for evolutionary change although it would not satisfy the marketing staff's need for a rapid change.

They have stated that 'because WAL's needs are unique, costs can only be roughly estimated. However, this solution is likely to be considerably more expensive than the 'Modification' solution. The final cost would be dependent upon the length of the project. It should take a minimum of six months to develop new software but it might take as long as two years. 'We have little experience of software development but are very enthusiastic about trying'.

Summary

This solution has an uncertain duration and cost. It is dependent upon WAL's IS/IT staff who have little experience of software development. For these reasons, this solution is not recommended.

Solution 3 – Purchase

WAL could buy the biscuit industry standard software. This software is expensive but there would be a boundary put upon its cost which would be its contractual price. This provides WAL with certainty.

The software is a proven product and some of WAL's marketing staff have experience of using this software in other companies, are very appreciative of its benefits and believe it would help them considerably in their jobs. The software supplier claims that '90% of the biscuit industry uses our product'. This suggests that this software would be readily accepted by its users. If the supplier's claim about having the software working within three months is a valid one, this solution would meet the need of the marketing staff for a revolutionary, rapid change.

As WAL does not currently use the biscuit industry marketing information software it may be operationally at a competitive disadvantage: the Purchase solution would put WAL on an equal footing, in this respect, with its competitors.

However, R is resistant to the Purchase solution and has indicated that the majority of IS/IT staff prefer evolutionary change and would be resistant to this solution. R was responsible for buying the current marketing information system and may feel that its proposed replacement is a criticism of the decision he made in 2005.

As R would make the decision about Purchase he would not want to be responsible for a failure. Although there is a high failure rate for software projects this would be a consideration for all three options so it should not preclude the Purchase option.

R also believes that many of his staff would be resistant to this option and he would have to deal with the problems this would create.

Summary

The Purchase option would give WAL the biscuit industry standard marketing information software. It would have a known cost and a guaranteed time span for implementation. This software should be readily accepted by marketing staff and would remove a possible source of competitive disadvantage.

Examiner's comments

This question was very well answered by most candidates, most of whom evaluated the information provided in the scenario for each of the 3 proposed solutions. Candidates who performed badly on this question did so largely because they failed to evaluate the information provided and instead merely re-wrote the information given in the scenario.

Common Errors

- Little/ no evaluation of the solutions.

(ii)   Although the Purchase solution is likely to provoke some resistance to change within WAL it is the recommended solution because of its speed, known cost and its proven ability to meet the needs of WAL's marketing staff.

Examiner's comments

Most candidates performed well on this question, largely as a result of a good level of evaluation in the previous answer. It was encouraging to see that there has been an improvement on previous diets in candidates' ability to make well-reasoned and justified recommendations.

(c)   R, who has an influential position as Company Secretary, appears to be resistant to change, in general, unless it is done slowly and incrementally. He claims that this view is shared by a sizable body of opinion within WAL. He has also pointed out that WAL has experience of change in the recent past which failed because WAL's culture didn't change and also that it would be his department that would have to do all the work. R has expressed serious anxieties based on his past experience, the amount of work a new software package represents and, if he is right, some of these anxieties are shared by others within WAL.

Unless R's views are taken into account he may prove a serious obstruction to the change process and prevent it happening. Two of the solutions which R has proposed, Modification and Development, may not be genuine responses to the marketing staff's requirements but may be ways of postponing change.

Kotter and Schlesinger proposed the following six point approach for dealing with resistance to change.

1   **Education and communication**

R and his IS/IT colleagues need to be convinced that the limitations of the existing software package are a serious constraint upon WAL. Given that R and his staff are likely to be concerned for WAL's success, if they can be persuaded that the old software is obsolete then they might be prepared to accept a faster rate of change, and, purchase the industry standard software. R's point about the need for cultural change is also valid and WAL needs to take this into account.

R's concerns, and those of people who think like him, should be acknowledged and provision made within the replacement project plan to deal with the issues raised by them.

2 **Participation and involvement**

Because of R's position he would be intimately involved in the Purchase solution. This means he would have every opportunity to be involved with the project. R could use his position to involve other members of his staff. The impetus for the change has come from outside R and his IS/IT colleagues: such a change cannot be imposed but will necessarily require the active participation and involvement of R and the IS/IT staff. If they are given opportunities to participate in the purchase of the new software this should increase their commitment to the change and make it more likely to work.

3 **Facilitation and support**

R was responsible for buying the original software program in 1985 and will be responsible for buying the replacement one. It could be that the source of R's resistance is because he anticipates he will have problems implementing the new software and adjusting to the new demands inherent within it. R may be helped by having some of the responsibility for the project being shared with other staff within WAL. He may also need to be reassured that his personal position will not be jeopardised. Similarly, support could be offered to any of the IS/IT staff who need it, if, for example, they lack skills to deal with the new software. In such a case they could be offered training.

4 **Negotiation and agreement**

R's resistance could be reduced if he is allowed to negotiate the degree of his involvement in the project. If R can be made to feel empowered rather than threatened his attitude could change. The IS/IT staff may also feel threatened by the forthcoming change: R has reported that a majority of these staff prefer change to take place incrementally. The Purchase solution represents revolutionary change but it may be possible for IS/IT staff to be reconciled to this change. For example, based on what R has reported there is a minority of IS/IT staff who are not opposed to revolutionary change: perhaps these could be tasked with the introduction and implementation of the new marketing information system software. The majority of staff who prefer evolutionary change could be used in parts of WAL's business where either no change or gradual change is contemplated.

5 **Manipulation and co-optation**

This approach can be used when other approaches won't work or are too costly. However, CIMA members should be very cautious in case this conflicts with CIMA's 'Code of Ethics' or with general business ethics. Further, WAL may be trying to conduct its business ethically and may feel that manipulation and co-optation lie outside the scope of ethical business.

This approach may work in the short-term but may have adverse long-term consequences.

Further, although it might be possible to manipulate R into accepting the changes this could rebound on WAL later if R realises he has been manipulated.

6   **Explicit and implicit coercion**

This method relies on the use of power, or the threat of force to enforce change. This method would not generally be recommended for a CIMA member as it conflicts with the spirit of the Code of Ethics although not any particular written section. However, there may be occasions where coercion is justifiable as with any ethical dilemma a choice has to be made between the lesser of two evils.

Kotter and Schlesinger published their model in 1979 since when it is arguable that what is acceptable business behaviour has changed.

Examiner's comments

This question was well answered by most candidates, many of whom used the Kotter and Schlesinger framework to structure their answers. Other candidates used Lewin's change management model, which was credited if applied directly to methods of overcoming resistance to change. The main weakness of this answer was lack of application to the scenario. Candidates clearly have a sound knowledge and understanding of the Kotter and Schlesinger framework but some candidates failed to adequately apply this to WAL. Some candidates also incorrectly discussed the Lewin framework often with very little application to its use in overcoming resistance to change.

Common Errors

•   Limited/ no application to WAL.

•   Lewin's change management model used but not applied to overcoming resistance to change.

---

39   **JALL STATIONERS (SEP 10 EXAM)** *Walk in the footsteps of a top tutor*

From your initial read of the scenario and requirements during the reading time you should have picked up the following points (and therefore annotated your question paper with it):

What does the company do and where? JALL is a small stationery company which operates three stores in one small town.

What are the issues? JALL is about to be taken over by a large national stationery retailer. This is causing some serious concerns for the workforce and the operations of JALL seem to be suffering because of this. JALL are losing staff, customer and supplier confidence.

Which frameworks or theoretical knowledge is required? Change management for part (a) and the balanced scorecard for part (b).

Based on this you could assess whether to attempt the question

(a)   (i)   **Reasons for resistance to change in ownership**

Part (a) (i) should be a very straightforward section to answer. Factors causing resistance to change is a common question within the change management section of the syllabus and is something you need to learn carefully. Even if you failed to use the three headings suggested, you should be able to come up with enough practical reasons from reading the scenario.

Resistance to change is normally caused by three factors.

Job factors

Staff have reason to be uncertain about their future employment. Managers have been unable to confirm whether they will become unemployed or not. This is likely to be a major source of resistance.

In addition, they may be worried about changes to their jobs. It is clear that the new owners do not have the same emphasis on quality service as the previous owners, given the failure to pay many suppliers.

Finally, they may worry that if business performance suffers, which it currently appears to be, they may lose out on the bonus that they have come to expect every year.

Personal factors

Employees may take the changes to the business as an implied criticism of the way the company has been run to date. Given the long service of many employees, they may well not see the need for change – especially as the business has been performing well to date.

In addition, staff seem to have been used to being consulted about key decisions being made within the organisation. This has clearly not happened with the changes that are currently being made and this may lead to further resistance.

Social factors

While employees seem to have traditionally had a good relationship with their managers, this may not continue. The fact that managers are no longer consulting them, as well as the fact that only managerial jobs are secure, may lead to friction.

Employees are far more likely to resist change if they dislike the people who are trying to implement it.

(ii)   **Methods of overcoming resistance to change**

For Part (a) (ii), you could have referenced Kotter & Schlesinger's model on methods of overcoming resistance – although there were unlikely to be any marks specifically available for 'name-dropping' here. If you can't think of a model to use, just be practical. What could be done to help the staff through the change process?

There are a number of possible approaches that managers could use to overcome this resistance.

One of the most effective is likely to be communication. The main reason for resistance by staff members in JALL is likely to be the uncertainty they face in their jobs. If possible, they should be told as soon as possible of the effect the takeover will have.

As employees are used to being consulted in the running of the business, managers could allow staff to participate in the change process. For example, if staff were informed about the changes to the payment terms for suppliers, they may be able to suggest ways of accomplishing these without upsetting suppliers. Staff are more likely to accept change if they are involved in the process.

Management could adopt a manipulative approach by stressing the benefits that staff will receive after the takeover. For example, if the annual bonus is to be increased under the new owners, this could be explained to staff. Doing so may make staff more eager for the change. However, any promised benefits of the takeover would, of course, have to be honoured.

Finally, managers could adopt a coercive approach. This would involve telling staff what is expected of them and insisting that will be punished if they do not go along with the changes that are being made. This is extremely risky as staff morale is already low. Using this approach may cause a total breakdown of the manager-staff relationship.

(b)   (i)   **How LNR can use the balanced scorecard to manage its strategic performance**

Part (b) focussed on the balanced scorecard and its usefulness as part of an incentive scheme. This may have taken a bit more thought than a normal balanced scorecard question. Make sure you briefly define the scorecard in part (i) before looking at how it would be useful for LNR. Part (ii) focuses more on its usefulness as part of an incentive scheme for JALL staff members. Try to avoid repeating yourself!

The balanced scorecard is a methodology that can be used to help measure performance in an organisation.

Rather than focussing on one area, the balanced scorecard looks at four key perspectives that are essential to the long-term success of the company. For LNR, these four are:

- **Financial perspective** – how can we create value for shareholders?

- **Internal business perspective** – what business processes must we excel at?

- **Customer perspective** – How do customers view us?

- **Innovation and learning perspective** – How can we keep our competitive advantage through improvement and change?

LNR can set itself detailed, measurable targets in each of these areas that support its overall strategy. If these targets are not met, corrective action can be taken to ensure LNR continues to meet its strategic performance targets.

This may be particularly useful for a company like LNR which expands by acquisition. The balanced scorecard will provide useful in providing detailed targets for newly acquired businesses.

If LNR follows this approach, it is important that they keep their measures in each perspective up to date, as they will change over time.

(ii) **How the balanced scorecard can be used within an incentive scheme to construct targets for JALL staff.**

The balanced scorecard, as mentioned above, is used by businesses to set performance targets for the organisation.

This can be easily adapted to set performance targets for employees. Doing so is likely to be especially useful for LNR as these targets can be used to form the basis of a new incentive scheme.

Potential targets could include:

- **Customer retention** – some of JALL's customers are currently moving their business elsewhere due to uncertainty over JALL's future. By setting targets in this area, LNR will aid the **financial perspective** in its balanced scorecard.

- **Staff turnover** – LNR could set JALL's managers targets for retention of staff. Given their long service and experience, LNR is likely to want to retain key staff to help maintain customer relationships. This target will aid LNR in its **customer perspective.**

- **Supplier payments** – it is not clear from the scenario why suppliers have not been paid on time. This will destroy JALL's relationship with its suppliers and could cause serious problems if LNR wish to continue using any of them. As such, it can set targets in this area to ensure that JALL pay their suppliers on time. This may help the **internal business perspective.**

In addition, the JALL staff are currently used to receiving a bonus annually, so ensuring that there is still an incentive scheme after the takeover is completed is likely to reduce resistance.

JALL's managers could also ensure that the targets set are agreed with workers. Involving them in the design process could reduce their resistance to the major changes that the company is seeing.

40 MMM UNIVERSITY (MAR 12 EXAM)

Key answer tips

Part (a) requires you to apply the SMART model. This is a useful model within E3 and should be easy to use in the scenario. As usual, the key here is to make sure that you apply your answer to MMM itself.

Part (b) required you to identify the activities required to change the university's culture and structure. The answer specifically didn't want you to use a model – instead it wanted focus on the activities themselves. Any sensible comments should have scored here.

> Part (c) asked for a discussion of the role of a change agent. Make sure you have thoroughly revised this, as it should represent easy marks in the exam – as long as you remember to link your answer back to MMM.

(a)   The SMART model is an approach designed to make aspirational objectives explicit. The objectives which have been set for the new control system are:

- To develop their the Heads' motivation

- To encourage the Heads to accept responsibility for achieving strategic and operational targets

- To encourage activities that generates income for external activities

However, as drafted, they are statements of intent which are open to multiple interpretations. The SMART model could help, for example, as follows:

Specific: the objectives should be stated in a clear way so everyone understands them. For example, the first objective is concerned with 'motivation': but what does this mean?

It could be made specific by attaching criteria to it. For the Head in charge of student experience 'motivation' could be defined, for example, as 'increasing the pass rates on all courses to the national average'.

Measurable: the objectives need to be quantified to enable control to take place. For the Head managing profit-making activities the third objective could be enhanced to state: 'new activities should be introduced to raise an extra £1 million profit a year'.

Attainable: any objectives which are set should be within the reach of those trying to achieve them. If unachievable objectives are set it will demotivate the managers and be a waste of time and money. This would also cast doubt on the process of objective setting.

For example, an additional £1 million profit a year may be attainable for MMM if it currently makes £10 million from these activities: £100 million is very unlikely to be attainable.

Relevant: the objective should be one that is appropriate to the organisation's mission statement and its stakeholders. As regards MMM, its mission statement is very vague so arguably almost any objective would be relevant for it and the three that have been set for the new control system are relevant. For example, 'to develop the Heads' motivation' in achieving strategic and operational targets would contribute towards the mission 'to be the best'. In this sense the objective is relevant.

However, when the context of its stakeholders is considered some objectives could be seen to be irrelevant. For example, an objective 'eliminate world poverty' is outside the scope of a university's concerns being more properly an objective for governments and international organisations. Such an objective would not be relevant for MMM.

Time-bound: the objectives need to have a time boundary; a date should be set for their achievement. For example the objective 'to encourage activities that generate income from external activities' and 'raise an extra £1 million profit a year' needs to state when this is supposed to happen. Without a boundary the objective is meaningless and control over it cannot be exercised. The objective needs to be modified, for example by adding '.......by the end of 2012'.

Examiner's comments

This question was not well answered. This was most disappointing as this should have been a very straightforward question. Many candidates scored well on the description of the SMART criteria, although it was surprising to see how few candidates actually described all five aspects accurately. However, few answers went further than this.

Most candidates were let down by their application of the SMART criteria to the objectives of MMM. For example, for the 'Specific' criteria, candidates could have suggested that for the first objective of 'motivation' this could be made more specific by stating this objective in a way such as 'increasing the pass rates on all courses to the national average'. Similarly for the 'Measurable' criterion, the third objective could be enhanced to state 'new activities should be introduced to raise an extra £1 million profit a year'. Most candidates failed to make an attempt at application of the criteria to the scenario objectives. Therefore marks awarded were limited.

(b)   The executive board is faced with the complex task of changing the university's culture and introducing the new department structure. It will have to deal with the following:

(i)   **Culture**

The executive board does not own the university's culture and there is no simple or quick way of changing culture. However, the executive board does have the ability to influence the culture and it could do this in a number of ways by:

- *Its announcements:* for example, communicating with its staff to explain and emphasise the importance of the new control system.

- *Its reward system:* for example, by orientating its staff's personal objectives to those of the university and paying staff for achievement.

- *Its symbols:* the university could allocate money for new signage; it could improve some of the buildings that the new departments will occupy.

(ii)   **New department structure**

The departments are going to reduce in number from six to three. This implies a reorganisation of resources. MMM currently employs six Heads to manage its six departments: in the new structure it only requires three. MMM will have to make a decision about the future of the surplus Heads.

The staffing establishment of all the new departments will have to be reviewed as six departments are decanted into three. This important task will require a separate personnel strategy.

The changes will need to be planned within the context of a budget which delineates both the resources allocated to the tasks and the timescales for their completion. Thus, the budget should state what money is to be spent, how, where and by whom.

Communication

As the university is to be organised into three bigger departments, consideration will need to be given as to the internal communications within and between these departments. This theme could be developed within training.

Training

As the university is adopting a new organisational structure it will be necessary to inform its staff what this implies for them and how the university will function in future. Therefore, training will need to be organised.

Resistance to change

It is likely that the changes proposed by MMM will encounter some resistance. MMM will have to plan for ways of dealing with this. It may wish to use the six-fold approach suggested by Kotter and Schlesinger. However, it should be mindful that two of these approaches, manipulation and coercion are ethically dubious.

Examiner's comments

This question was answered very badly. Candidates clearly had a poor understanding of changing culture and treated the process as a purely mechanistic one rather than an abstract one. Many answers focused upon a structured approach such as 'Plan, Organise, Monitor, Implement' and some answers merely re-wrote the Kotter and Schlesinger approach, but with little consideration of the specific difficulties of cultural change.

Part (ii) was also not answered well. Although this was more amenable to a mechanistic approach, very few answers recognised the details of the scenario. Again, the Kotter and Schlesinger framework was often used but once again, application was poor.

Common Errors

- Poor appreciation of the difficulties of cultural change

- Knowledge dumping of change management frameworks with little/no application

---

(c) **Change agent**

In order to progress these changes MMM will need to assign the responsibility for implementation to a person or a group of people. The person/people with this responsibility could be assisted by a change agent. The change agent could come from within the university or could be an external person or organisation, for example, a management consultant could be employed. However, the change agent's role, 'per se', would not be the implementation of the changes: rather it would be the facilitation of them.

A change agent would normally be able to assist in the change process in MMM by:

- *Defining the problem:* for example, what to do with three 'surplus' Heads.

- *Examining the causes of the problem(s):* the reduction in the number of departments.

- *Diagnosing how this can be overcome:* offering redeployment.

- *Offering alternative solution:* severance terms.

- *Devising implementation strategies:* when, how, where the surplus Heads will be redeployed.

- *Disseminating what has been learnt from this change process:* MMM could use this experience to help it with future changes.

41   E CHARITY (MAY 09 EXAM)

Key answer tips

A straightforward question on a well-tested area of the syllabus (BSC). Students should be familiar with the different aims and objectives of Not for Profit organisations.

Part (a) does not ask for contents of a balanced scorecard for E and candidates need to be certain to answer the requirement set.

Resistance to change should represent an easy 13 marks provided that reference to E is made throughout.

(a)   **Advantages and disadvantages for E of balanced scorecard**

Advantages:

The balanced scorecard (BSC) translates an organisation's mission into objectives and measures four different perspectives (financial, internal business process, customer and learning and growth). The 10 trustees and 45 CEO's are likely to agree on the overall mission of the charity which has been set up to promote sustainable development and the protection of endangered species. This agreed mission would be the starting point of a BSC, with objectives in each perspective relating back to it, for example the customer perspective could be measured by enhanced communication, perhaps providing potential donators to the charity with more information on their activities. The advantage of the BSC is that it can begin from an agreed starting point (the mission). If CEO's can see that all performance measures link back to that point, they are more likely to accept the BSC. Also the BSC forces CEOs to consider non-financial issues, particularly important for a charity

It can be used to inform stakeholders about E's activities.

If the balanced scorecard were to be used externally by E, for example if it were published on E's website, stakeholders would be able to see both what E is measuring (for example, number of endangered species helped) and their success in achieving those objectives (they may have helped numerous species which could all have their current populations listed and compared with previous numbers in existence). This would encourage support for E's work and help them to gain a competitive advantage.

The BSC will promote goal congruence

The 45 divisions may be autonomous but they all exist with the same objectives. A single BSC could therefore be devised with targets for all divisions to work towards. This would promote goal congruence and help to give E the unified direction it lacks. Slight adaptations may be required to the measures, for example in some countries E may rely more on volunteers and so measures relating to internal business processes (collecting money or awarding grants) may need to reflect this.

A BSC will help to give structure to the quarterly meetings

The contents of the BSC will give the quarterly meetings an agenda, with the agreement of performance measures the main topic of discussion. The fact that CEO's meet every 3 months means that review of BSC achievements (have the targets been met) can happen on a timely basis and CEO's will be motivated, knowing that review will occur. They can be held accountable for targets which have not been achieved at these reviews.

However, the inclusion of longer term targets, for example increasing donations by 10% within 3 years will ensure that long term strategies are still worked towards.

Disadvantages

Lack of CEO commitment – The CEO's may not see the need for a BSC, particularly if their division is doing well and they are committed to the causes which E promotes. It may be difficult to get them to 'buy in' to performance measurement and control which a BSC would bring. This problem will be intensified by the geographical split of the divisions. Aside from the 3 monthly meetings, it will be difficult for the trustees to keep track of the CEO's activities.

Measures may confuse management – Donations to charities like E have been falling over the last 5 years and the CEO's may be attempting to cut costs as a result of less funding being available. Cost reduction targets could be included under the 'financial perspective' in the BSC but if 'increase public awareness' is included within the 'internal business perspective', the CEO's may be unsure of which of these objectives should have priority. The CEO's may not have a finance background and may be unable to identify both value-adding and cost-adding activities.

Cost-benefit – The cost of devising a BSC for E may be seen as unnecessary, particularly given the reduction in charitable donations over recent years. It could be argued that E would be better off spending money on protecting endangered species.

Charitable objectives – The introduction of a BSC will not enable E to directly save endangered species or promote sustainability. Stakeholders could see the BSC as an exercise best suited to a profit making company, since improvements of performance can be directly linked to an increase in income

(b) **Four reasons why the CEO's of E may resist the proposed changes**

The CEO's may be fully committed to E's objectives and see the introduction of the BSC as somehow undermining that commitment by giving them an alternative focus

The objectives of E may be very clear in the minds of the CEO's, who are likely to be especially committed to them since each CEO is the figurehead for the charity in their country (and so effectively runs their own charity.) They may see the balanced scorecard as an unnecessary expansion on simple (and long held) objectives.

The CEO's may perceive the introduction of new performance measures as criticism of past performance

The trustees are signalling that change is necessary by proposing a balanced scorecard. The CEO's may be hard working and committed and not appreciate the implication that their performance has not been up to standard.

The CEO's may be too busy dealing with financial and non financial crises to begin work on the BSC targets

The lack of a coherent strategy has led to problems within the divisions over the last 5 years. It will be difficult to implement new objectives and performance measures into an environment where staff feel they already have enough to deal with.

The CEO's may not perceive their charity to have a 'lack of direction, control and accountability' as maintained by the Supervisory Board

The fact that the CEO's are geographically isolated from the trustees means they will only have a view of their division and may find it difficult to see the 'bigger picture'. They therefore may not see the need for a new system of performance measurement, or for the charity to be judged as a whole, rather than on a divisional basis.

(**Note**: other factors could include fear of the unknown and/or lack of knowledge throughout the business)

(c) **Steps to be taken to overcome the resistance to change**

Trustees will need to 'Unfreeze' the existing culture amongst CEO's.

The CEO's will need educating about the falling donations and the lack of direction, control and accountability. If the trustees can communicate exactly why there is a need for a balanced scorecard, the CEO's are much more likely to accept the current way of doing things could be improved.

In addition, if the CEO's are able to participate in the setting of objectives for the balanced scorecard, they are much more likely to accept it as a new way of measuring performance. The CEO's and their staff will not be motivated to improve areas they do not see as crucial to their success, therefore if they are able to suggest measures and objectives for inclusion in the BSC it will be a more successful tool. Such participation is likely to lead to negotiation regarding disputed areas.

As a last resort, the trustees could use coercion to persuade the CEO's to accept the BSC. This may take the form of incentives for hitting the targets laid out in the scorecard. However, given that E is a charity and donations have been falling, there may be limiting funds available for such coercive strategies

EVALUATION OF STRATEGIC POSITION AND STRATEGIC OPTIONS (30%)

THE STRATEGIC PLANNING PROCESS

42   MNI UNIVERSITY (SEP 10 EXAM)

Key answer tips

Part (a) is a very technical question on the different levels of strategy. Remember the definitions of each level of strategy and it should help you to list the points into a sensible order.

In part (b) you need to suggest controls that would have helped solve any of the three problems identified by the auditors. There are a huge range of potential problems and solutions to choose from, so anything practical would have scored well here.

In part (c) you need to outline how IS could help with the new strategic plan (which is predominantly a plan to fix the problems found by the auditor.) Again, any sensible, practical ideas would have scored well here.

(a)   **Categorisation of the recent criticisms made about MNI**

Operational – day to day management issues

- Lack of head-count of students

- Internal cash receipt control problems

Management – issues with the competitive advantage of the university

- Level of student complaints

- High levels of student drop-outs and failures

- University operating at a deficit

- Large numbers of outstanding debtors

- High level of staff turnover

Strategic – issues with the long-term, high-level direction of the university

- Overall quality of education classed as 'Poor' by auditors

How control measures can assist in the implementation of the new strategic plan

MNI requires control systems to be put in place to monitor the implementation of the strategic plan and determine the action and resources required to ensure that targets are being met. They will ensure that employees actually follow the new plan and help to identify any unexpected problems that may arise during its implementation.

Strategic plans may not always work well in practise. Controls will identify any areas that are not being solved by the strategic plan, which can then be adjusted to deal with these problems.

(b)   **Recommendation of the controls that should be used by the university**

University operating at a deficit

This could be solved by the setting of budgets. For MNI to be running at a deficit may imply a simple lack of financial control, with the university overspending without being aware of it until the end of the year.

By setting budgets and then regularly reviewing MNI's actual performance against them, MNI will be able to identify potential deficits early and take corrective action by reducing expenditure in non-essential areas.

This will also ensure that the university's resources are used to the best possible effect.

High level of staff turnover

This is likely to have a serious effect on the quality of the tuition for students at MNI. Employee surveys should be regularly undertaken and reviewed in order to ascertain the key areas that staff are currently unhappy with. This could also take the form of exit interviews for staff who decide to resign which will enable MNI to analyse any common issues between them and implement appropriate solutions.

By discovering the reasons for staff dissatisfaction, MNI will be able to look at ways of improving morale and retaining staff. It will also be able to use the surveys to judge whether the new strategic plan is having any effect once implemented.

Student complaints

It is not clear what issues students are complaining about. However, it should be possible to give someone within MNI responsibility for monitoring and dealing with student complaints. It may be that many of the complaints are caused by a few key problems.

By logging the details of the complaints, MNI may be able to understand the problems students are facing and achieve real change. It can also use this to monitor, and deal with, any problems that students may have with the new strategic plan.

(c)   **How information systems could support the implementation of the strategic plan**

Information systems could be vital in supporting the new strategic plan in several key ways.

Firstly, information systems can be used to **inform all members of staff** about the detail of the new strategic plan. Given the large number of staff in the university, communicating new plans could be time-consuming and complex.

Using an information system, such as an intranet or email, will enable the rapid spread of this vital information.

Information systems can be used as **a control system** for the new strategic plan. The government auditors noted a number of key failings within MNI. The new strategic plan will need to deal with these.

Information systems can be used to monitor these important areas, enabling MNI's managers to get feedback on whether the strategic plan is effective. If not – it may be down to poor implementation by staff (which can be investigated) or a failure of the strategic plan, which can then be updated.

Information systems may even be the **direct solution** to some of the university's problems.

For example, IS can be used to log student details as they enrol on courses. This would enable MNI to get an accurate headcount of students – a major criticism of the current systems.

IS could also be used to create aged debtor reports which will aid in collection of outstanding balances from students. In addition to this, it should be possible to use IS to develop a detailed budget program to help ensure MNI does not run at a loss. This could be easily updated for actual results to provide a powerful financial control tool.

Overall, IS could help speed up the effectiveness and the efficiency of implementing the new strategic plan, as well as providing a number of solutions to MNI's problems.

43 NNN (NOV 11 EXAM)

Key answer tips

There is no model that you need to follow in order to score well in this question. Any reasonable changes that can be recommended to enable NNN to meet the conditions set out by WGG should earn credit. However, you need to remember to justify your suggestions and explain why your proposed changes would help.

(a)   WGG, the new owner of NNN plc, plans to sell it by the end of 2013 and requires NNN plc to satisfy the following conditions:

- It must have no more qualified audit reports

- It must be making a profit

- It must not be engaged in any criminal activities

- It must have introduced an ethical code

As WGG's planning horizon for NNN plc is only a little over two years, any changes which need to be made will need to be made quickly. Due to the numerous causes for concern identified by the auditors NNN plc will require comprehensive change and what amounts to a 'turn-around' strategy.

The causes for concern can be categorised as:

Accountancy related: incorrect accounting for revenue and cash, inaccurate forecasting, unreported revenue, cash discrepancies.

Performance related: loss of £5,000,000 in year ended 31 March 2011

Organisation related: criminality

These categories are not mutually exclusive. NNN plc will need to devise strategies and set objectives for each of the areas of concern.

Accountancy

As the auditors revealed the causes of concern and NNN plc needs to give an unqualified audit report by the end of 2013, this would be a good place for NNN plc to start. If the management of NNN plc enter into discussions with the auditors it should be able to receive guidance as to the auditors' priorities and requirements. It could also be that colleagues from the auditors' firm could be hired as consultants to remedy some of NNN plc's problems. As the large accountancy firms usually have specialists in IT, Human

Resource Management and Project Management, NNN plc could find this a useful way of achieving a quick turnaround.

NNN plc will have to review its accounting systems and procedures to ensure both revenue and cash are accurately accounted for. NNN plc has a problem with its cash accounting as it has a shortfall of £1,000,000. NNN plc needs to investigate this, determine as far as it is able the causes of the shortfall and institute robust systems to prevent this reoccurring. This may involve NNN plc devising new systems for revenue and cash comprising both physical security and accounting systems. However, it could be that the existing systems are adequate as long as NNN plc ensures that they are complied with.

NNN plc's forecasting system proved to be very inaccurate in 2011. Forecasts are important for investor and creditor confidence as well as for internal managerial motivation. When the actual results were declared in 2011 this would have badly affected a number of parties' confidence. Part of the large discrepancy between the forecast and actual achievement would be due to the fine. However NNN plc needs to analyse the reasons for the rest of the shortfall. This may not be straightforward because the forecast may have been inaccurate because:

1   the forecasting procedure is flawed

2   NNN plc's performance fell short of expectations

3   a combination of both these factors

In order to rectify 1, NNN plc will need to examine its forecasting methodology and it might benefit from some specialist external consultancy to help it do this.

Performance

It is likely that NNN plc's performance did fall short of expectations as it made a loss of £5,000,000 only part of which might be attributable to the fine. WGG plans to sell NNN plc in approximately two year's time when it must be making a profit and so there is a pressing need to improve its operational efficiency. NNN plc's operational efficiency has declined due to a lack of investment and this has impaired its competitiveness. NNN plc will have to address the deficiencies in its vehicle fleet, infrastructure and driver recruitment and training. It will need to formulate a capital budget and subject investment proposals to proper scrutiny and appraisal, for example, Net Present Value calculations where appropriate.

Organisation

Several of NNN plc's activities give rise to concern: people smuggling, revenue and cash discrepancies. There are a number of procedures NNN plc should implement to prevent future occurrences. NNN plc should examine its recruitment processes to ensure that any future staff it employs are honest. The employees who were convicted of criminal activities came from different levels of the company: they were two directors, one manager and six drivers which indicates that the criminality was widespread. As well as the obvious precaution of severely tightening up its recruitment procedures, possibly using specialist outside consultants to do so, NNN plc may need to review its internal culture and seek to change it to a more ethical/honest one. The introduction of an ethical code would be one step in this direction.

NNN plc could set up an Internal Security Department to monitor employee behaviour and to safeguard its cash transactions. Given that there was a possible shortfall of £1,000,000, this implies that NNN plc has a substantial number of cash transactions and the auditors also noted that not all cash revenue was recorded. The Internal Security Department could employ ex-police officers to monitor any employees whose behaviour gave cause for concern. Other physical security methods could be used as appropriate, for example, closed circuit TV, safes, searches of employees and specialist security couriers to move large amounts of cash.

NNN plc should also establish an Internal Audit Department which could work in conjunction with the Internal Security Department. The Internal Auditors should establish a programme to verify compliance within NNN plc with its procedures. The Internal Auditors could also carry out 'ad hoc' investigations as required.

Examiner's comments

This question was reasonably well answered by candidates. Candidates generally scored well on the 'performance' and 'organisational' related changes required, with most recognising the need for training, investment and revised HRM policies and procedures. Disappointingly few candidates performed well on recommending 'accountancy' related changes as recommendations were often vague and not well explained in this area. However, most candidates did correctly identify the need for an internal audit function and improved accounting controls. Candidates were not penalised if their recommendations were not included within the appropriate heading but were still relevant.

Common errors

- Generic recommendations not specific to the details of the scenario

- Over emphasis on corporate governance issues and Board structure

---

(b) In drafting its own ethical code, NNN plc could draw upon CIMA's Code of Ethics. This describes a number of fundamental principles which are applicable to NNN plc.

NNN plc's code could state that the company and its employees should comply with the following principles because they constitute best practice:

Integrity: NNN plc should be straightforward and honest in all business relationships.

Objectivity: NNN plc should not allow bias, conflict of interest or undue influence of others to override business judgements.

Confidentiality: NNN plc should respect the confidentiality of business relationships and not disclose information to third parties without proper authority.

Legality: NNN plc must comply with the law.

NNN plc could also consider a broader scope for its ethical code than that adopted for CIMA's Code which is orientated towards the professional behaviour of its members. NNN plc could include the following principles which reflect contemporary ethical concerns, for example:

Sustainability: NNN plc will aspire to implement strategies that contribute to long-term success.

Fair trade: NNN plc will contribute towards enabling producers in developing countries to achieve better trading conditions.

Non-discriminatory/equality of opportunity: NNN plc will treat all people equally.

Environmental: NNN plc will endeavour to minimise its impact upon the natural world.

Examiner's note: more examples of ethical principles have been given than asked for in the requirement to assist teachers and candidates.

> **Examiner's comments**
>
> This question was not well answered. Most candidates were awarded the marks for identifying the principle (mostly from CIMA's ethical code) but few further marks were awarded for many candidates. It was disappointing to see how many candidates could not provide adequate definitions and there was much confusion between professional behaviour and professional competence and due care and between objectivity and integrity.
>
> This should be straightforward knowledge demonstration but there were a number of candidates who clearly lacked sufficient depth of knowledge in this area of the syllabus. It was also disappointing that so few candidates were able to go on to apply the principles to the scenario by explaining correctly why these were important to NNN specifically. Candidates must be aware that at this level they must always be able to apply their knowledge of any aspect of the syllabus to the scenario. This was the first time that the examiner had required a high level of application of the ethical code and candidates unfortunately did not perform well.
>
> Common errors:
>
> * Limited knowledge of the principles
>
> * Poor application of the principles

44 BBB ADVERTISING (MAR 12 EXAM)

> **Key answer tips**
>
> Part (a) asks you to advise the board on the additional information it needs to support its planning and decision-making. Remember to try and say **why** the additional information you have suggested would be useful to the business.
>
> Make sure you don't answer (b) at the same time. Part (b) asked for how BBB could improve the information provided to the board. These could have been based on some of the issues you've identified in (a).
>
> Finally, part (c) asks for you to look at the benefits of benchmarking to BBB. Be careful here – a generic list of advantages would not have scored well. You had to link each benefit to BBB itself.

(a) BBB currently has budgetary control and standard costing information to support planning and decision-making. This is inadequate because the "management board has stated that it 'urgently needs additional information to support its planning and decision-making'".

The current information has a number of inadequacies:

Internal focus

The current output concentrates on what is happening within BBB. The budget reporting is very detailed, probably too detailed. The variance analysis may yield some control information but given the nature of BBB and its business much of this reporting may well be not 'relevant'.

Although the accountant produces a monthly profit figure this is not analysed or compared to historical or forecast performance. This means it is without context which restricts its usefulness for planning and decision-making.

Deficiencies

There are many deficiencies in BBB's current information and these relate to the absence of an external focus. Thus:

- BBB is unaware of the total size of its market niche

- It does not know its market share (BBB estimates that 'it is the second or third largest company')

- BBB is unsure why it wins new business: high quality or price

- BBB is unaware of market prices: 'sometimes... clients complain they are overcharged'

These deficiencies inhibit BBB's ability to meet the needs of its present and future customers.

Costing/Pricing

When pricing work for clients, BBB uses:

- A standard uplift

- Absorption costing

- A blanket overhead recovery rate

This approach is very introspective and inhibits flexibility, for example, in quoting for marginal work/new products/promotional work/'one-off' situations. It has led: to complaints of over-charging, possible undercharging.

BBB's current uniform approach to costing and pricing may not be the best foundation for interacting with its market. It reflects an internal focus rather than an external one: What do our customers want? What are our competitors doing?

Summary

The usefulness of BBB's current information provided to support planning and decision-making is restricted because of:

- Its internal focus

- A lack of information about its markets, clients and competitors

- Its approach to costing and pricing

Therefore, additional information addressing these deficiencies is required.

Examiner's comments

This question was not well answered. Candidates seemed to have a basic lack of understanding of planning and decision making information and many answers merely listed a range of possible information and information sources. For example, a number of candidates suggested SWOT analysis, PEST analysis and mission statements but failed to explain their role in planning and decision making for BBB. Many candidates merely listed all of the aspects of the scenario where it had stated that there was a lack of information currently, but again, made no attempt to explain its relevance to assisting in planning and decision making. Overall, candidates demonstrated a lack of understanding of the basic information needs of organisational decision makers.

Common Errors

• Generic list of organisational information requirements

• Focus upon activities rather than information

(b)   The information available to the management board would be improved by addressing the drawbacks identified above: the internal focus, the lack of market, client and competitor information and BBB's costing and pricing strategies.

Internal focus

BBB should adopt the external approach advocated within Strategic Management Accounting. It should critically review its current management accounting output and evaluate whether the resources devoted to it could be better employed seeking information about its external environment. The current budget reports are very detailed and the variance analysis may be of limited value. For example, calculating labour rate variances when BBB only employs 15 staff, who work on creative and support activities and are salaried may not give any information that could not be gleaned by 'Managing by Walking Around'.

The tenor of BBB's variance analysis seems more suited to a traditional manufacturing organisation not an advertising agency. There appear to be grounds for abandoning it, i.e. to save management time and money. As an alternative BBB could invest in, from time to time, an   analyses such as Five Forces and PEST which could add to their understanding of its external environment. The results of such analysis could be reported within the normal management accounting cycle or on an 'ad hoc' basis as necessary.

Markets, clients and competitors

Currently BBB is unaware of the size of its market and its relative market share. BBB could commission market research or it may be able to buy research reports which would inform it of both of these: market size and relative market share could form a part of the monthly reporting package.

BBB is unsure of the reasons it wins business: is it because of 'high quality' or 'price'? This indicates that BBB is unaware of its competitors' strategies and its customers' preferences.

It could attempt to overcome this first deficiency by carrying out competitor analysis which CIMA defines as the 'Identification and quantification of the relative strengths and weaknesses (compared with competitors or potential competitors) which could be of significance in the development of a successful competitive strategy'. Key findings from competitor analysis could be made available as and when required. Similarly, competitors' costs could be reported on.

BBB could also research and report upon the attributes which customers value. These could assist BBB to understand why it wins business and would help its planning and decision-making.

All these innovations could be reported upon:

- Periodically

- Occasionally

- A combination of both

BBB's management accounting reporting should be driven by the needs of its users not its provider.

Costing and pricing

BBB's approach to both of these important matters seems stereotyped and may be leading to sub-optimal decisions. Although absorption costing is a suitable method for external reporting it may not be the best method for decision-making. Alternatives which could be used to advantage include Activity Based Costing, Target Costing and Marginal Costing. These methods could underpin alternative pricing policies.

BBB should recognise that pricing (an external orientated decision) should not necessarily be subordinated to costing (an internally orientated decision).

In order to improve the management accounting information available for planning and decision-making BBB should recognise that it can use different costs (and prices) for different purposes. BBB should also be willing to incorporate reporting on qualitative factors, such as Quality, Innovation and Customer Satisfaction which may prove to be more relevant for planning and decision-making purposes than traditional quantitative reporting.

Examiner's comments

This question was not well answered, largely as a result of the weaknesses of answers to part (a). Candidates were expected to focus their answers upon information which would address the drawbacks identified in part (a) of the answer, including the internal focus, the lack of market, client and competitor information and BBB's costing and pricing strategies. A number of candidates incorrectly focused upon the methods of collecting and using information and sources of information, rather than improvements to the information. For example, a number of candidates discussed the need to undertake rational planning and others discussed the need for a mission statement. Neither of these is specifically related to the information needs of planning and decision making. A number of candidates merely re-wrote their answers to part (a) in answer to this question.

Common Errors

- Repeat of information from part (a) of the answer

- Poor focus upon planning and decision making information needs

---

(c)   CIMA has defined Benchmarking as 'The establishment, through data gathering of targets and comparators, through whose use relative levels of performance (and particularly under performance) can be identified. By the adoption of identified best practices it is hoped that performance will improve'. There are four ways that BBB could carry out benchmarking: internal, functional, competitive and strategic. The essence of all the approaches is that BBB will have comparative information against which it can judge its performance.

If BBB commits to a benchmarking system its planning and decision-making will be widened to include an external dimension. Post-benchmarking BBB may find that it is able to reduce its costs and, possibly, increase its clients' satisfaction.

By gathering information from outside itself BBB will increase its awareness of its competitors' behaviour and strategy. This would give BBB the opportunity of imitating successful strategies and avoiding ones which could be harmful.

Benchmarking could also help BBB overcome any complacency it has about its performance. It could also help the management board better understand its business model and how BBB creates value.

Examiner's comments

This question was reasonably well answered, although it was disappointing that more candidates did not score highly on this requirement. Most were able to define benchmarking and most also made an attempt to highlight a number of benefits of benchmarking. However, most answers were generic and descriptive, with limited reference to the benefits which could be obtained by BBB specifically.

FORECASTING

45 B MEDIA COMPANY (MAY 07 EXAM)

Key answer tips

Section (a) asks for an evaluation of the benefits of a system of environmental analysis and NOT an explanation or application of the technique. Therefore you were NOT required to undertake a detailed PEST analysis or Porters' five forces analysis. Furthermore, you do need to **evaluate** benefits rather than simply list them.

Part (b) is standard bookwork but needs to be related to B to get full marks.

(a)   **Environmental analysis**

Systematic environmental analysis would benefit B in the following ways:

- More comprehensive information available for decision making

    A number of B's recent strategic decisions, such as overseas ventures have failed due to insufficient information. A more detailed environmental analysis would have helped B identify key factors to consider. This is perhaps the most important aspect – systematic environmental scanning will improve the planning and decision-making process.

- Anticipating opportunities and threats sooner

    B seems to have been slow to appreciate the growing importance of the Internet for advertising and, more specifically, as a media type with the development of online magazines. As a consequence, this appears to have become a threat to B's business model rather than an opportunity to exploit. A PEST-style analysis would have revealed this technological development sooner.

- Be able to evaluate opportunities more thoroughly

  B recently failed in an attempt to enter the domestic teenage magazine market. A PEST style analysis would have indicated the extent and drivers of growth in this segment and a Porter's five forces analysis would have revealed key competitive forces. This information may have resulted in a decision not to enter the market or a different strategy for entry. Either way, the considerable costs of failure would have been avoided.

- Quicker response to changing customer needs

  The directors of B are being forced into a reactive style of management as they are being surprised by the rate of change in some markets. Systematic market analysis would allow them to identify changes sooner and hence change products to more quickly match customer needs.

- Lower risk

  The net result of all of the above is that systematic environmental analysis will reduce B's downside risk exposure but should increase its ability to exploit opportunities.

- More accurate budgeting

  A greater awareness of forecasts regarding the advertising industry and the mix of paper versus e-advertising would allow B to budget its future advertising income more accurately.

(b) **Scenario planning**

Scenarios are detailed and plausible views of how the business environment might develop in the future based on groupings of key environmental influences and drivers of change about which there is a high degree of uncertainty.

Scenario planning involves the following steps:

1   Identify high-impact, high-uncertainty factors in the environment

    Relevant factors and driving forces could be identified through a strategic analysis framework such as a PEST analysis. Once identified, factors need to be ranked according to importance and uncertainty.

    For example, for B three key factors could be the speed of development of e-magazines, consumers' attitudes to e-magazines and the cost of paper.

2   For each factor, identify different possible futures

    Precision is not possible but developing a view of the future against which to evaluate and evolve strategies is important. For example:

Factor	Possible futures
Development of e-magazines	• Rapid
	• Slow
Consumer attitudes to e-magazines	• Good substitute
	• Poor substitute
Cost of paper	• Rising
	• Stable

3   Cluster together different factors to identify various consistent future scenarios.

This process usually results in between seven and nine mini-scenarios. For example,

Scenario 1:

Consumers still prefer conventional magazines, partly because of the limited growth in e-magazines offered to the market.

However, the future does not look positive, due to rising paper costs. If these are passed on to customers, then it might encourage them to consider e-magazines more seriously.

Scenario 2:

There is rapid growth in the availability of e-magazines and associated marketing costs.

Together with increasing acceptance of e-magazines as an alternative to paper-based products, this has resulted in many potential customers switching to electronic media.

4   'Writing the scenario'

For the most important scenarios (usually limited to three), build a detailed analysis to identify and assess future implications.

As part of this, planners typically develop a set of optimistic, pessimistic and most likely assumptions about the impact of key variables on the company's future strategy.

The result of this detailed scenario construction should include:

- financial implications – anticipated net profits, cash flow, and net working capital for each of three versions of the future

- strategic implications – possible opportunities and risks

- the probability of occurrence, usually based on past experience.

5   For each scenario identify and assess possible courses of action for the firm

For example, possible strategies for the two alternative scenarios outlined above:

Scenario 1: A possible strategy would be to cut paper costs by the increased use of recycled products.

Scenario 2: A possible strategy would be to develop ranges of titles aimed at older customers, who will (presumably) be slower to accept e-magazines.

Some strategies make sense whatever the outcome, usually because they capitalise on or develop key strengths of the firm. For example, B could look to strengthen its relationship with key advertisers.

However, in many cases, new resources and competencies may be required for existing strategies to succeed. Alternatively, entirely new strategies may be required. For B this could be the development of on-line versions of its magazines, accessible by subscription.

6   Monitor reality to see which scenario is unfolding

7   Revise scenarios and strategic options as appropriate

46 BBB CHARITY (MAY 08 EXAM)

Key answer tips

Part (a) asks for a discussion of how environmental analysis would help the trustees of BBB, not a discussion of environmental analysis itself. Reference to the practical benefits needs to be made, chiefly by picking up on the weaknesses in the scenario and how the use of PESTEL and 5 forces could improve how BBB deals with them.

Part (b) asks for an explanation of the concept of foresight, together with two techniques to develop it. With only 5 marks, even the most knowledgeable student needs to keep this brief.

Part (c) is a practical problem solving requirement, discussing difficulties the charity may face in implementing techniques which were designed to help formulate corporate strategy.

(a) The usefulness of frequent and thorough environmental analysis in BBB

Environmental analysis is carried out by organisations as a preliminary stage of strategic planning. Through careful study of the competitive environment, firms can not only identify the threats and opportunities they face but can go on to prioritise them, ensuring that key issues are targeted. Ultimately, thorough environmental analysis will lead to strategies which guard against these threats and exploit opportunities.

For BBB, this would clearly be beneficial. The volunteer's perception that the organisation does not know where it is going is de-motivating at best and indicative of a bleak future for BBB at worst. BBB could use both the PESTEL framework and Porters 5 forces to help assess their current position within the charities 'industry'.

PESTEL analysis

If BBB researched the current political stance on charitable donations they could find themselves considerably better off. They receive no government funding at present, but such funding may be available to them and could prevent their work from being threatened in the future as it is now. There is likely to be significant competition for government funding but with the right campaign, BBB are just as likely to receive it as other charities in the European Country.

Political donations will largely depend on the strength of the economy and BBB will benefit from knowing as much as possible about the current economic situation in their country. In strong economic conditions, donations are more forthcoming and companies are often looking for charities to 'adopt' and fundraise for.

Should there be a downturn in the economy, BBB will need to put more resources into promoting their work, to 'win' the smaller amount of funds available. Unless BBB understands more about the current economic situation, they will lose out to those charities which do target their fundraising towards the most likely source.

BBB's appeals to the public are made through newspaper adverts. This is despite the fact that social habits have changed and people are more likely to keep up with the news on line or via the television. The trustees of BBB should change their appeals process to reflect current social habits. A TV advert aired during the day may be more effective and not prohibitively expensive. In addition, people may well prepare to donate on line and technological advances like this must be considered. BBB's inability to receive donations online means it misses out on funding and internet advertising.

The board of trustees do not use technology at all within the organisation but with the right promotional activity (geared towards social habits), the ability for people to both donate and contact the charity on line would lead to more people volunteering and more funding to further the work of BBB.

BBB carries out projects of great humanitarian benefit which impact on the environment of the countries they operate in. In Europe, general awareness of environmental issues has improved and social habits have developed to protect the global environment. If BBB publicises the benefits of their work to the environment as well as to the people within developing countries, this could lead to more donations.

BBB must keep up to date with charitable legislation in its home nation or be at risk from closure. Organisations like BBB use public money and as a result are very much in the public interest. Their compliance with the law will be closely scrutinised and any departure from good corporate governance on their part will have significant consequences. Laws and regulations in this area are always changing and being updated and it is imperative that BBB stays abreast of this.

Porters 5 Forces

Competitive Rivalry – It makes sense for the trustees to understand their competitors. Given the difficulties they currently face in terms of funding, they need to quickly understand how available donations are being won and by whom. In particular the charities which have a more 'aggressive' marketing stance need to be benchmarked against.

Power of Suppliers – If the suppliers are those who donate to BBB, then it is clear that the more the trustees understand their needs the more likely they are to source future funding from them. Companies for example are likely to want positive publicity in return for giving and are in a powerful position with so many charities vying for their donations.

Power of Customers – BBB must perform effectively and efficiently. The charities' 'customers' may not be traditionally powerful but still their needs dictate BBB's overall objectives. If BBB get their objectives wrong and attract negative publicity, it could affect their survival as a charity.

Threat of New Entrants – this is ever present in the charities industry. As the media develops and people become more aware of new crises around the world, more and more charities are formed to try and alleviate suffering. The trustees need to ensure they are aware of potential competitors in their particular area i.e. the provision of equipment to clean drinking water.

Substitutes – again, other charities are substitutes for BBB's services.

This kind of environmental analysis would obviously help the trustees to establish their overall direction for the future. It cannot be seen as a one off exercise however, the environment of any organisation changes all the time and so producing an analysis of it must be seen as an ongoing exercise.

(b) **The concept of foresight**

For organisations, foresight means not only predicting the future but developing an understanding of all the potential changes, which if managed properly could produce many new opportunities.

By carrying out techniques to develop foresight, management try to shape the future, rather than 'wait' for it to happen and become a victim of changes they are unable to adapt to. The concept is crucial in the global commercial environment, where technological changes for example, or non-traditional competition can erode a company's dominant position overnight.

Techniques for the development of foresight

1   **Scenario Planning** involves management pulling together plausible future scenarios for their organisation. The do this by conducting environmental analysis and identifying uncertainties facing their business. They can then plan to deal in a positive way with changes which may occur.

2   **Visioning** involves management developing a 'mental image' of the organisation in the future. This should be realistic, attractive and better than the company's' current state. Management can then devise ways to reach this future ideal.

(c)   **Difficulties for BBB in developing a process of environmental analysis**

The process of environmental analysis involves obtaining up to date information about an organisation's environment and structuring it, via frameworks, in a way that is helpful to strategy formulation.

BBB may find it difficult to access the information required to carry out PEST and 5 forces analysis. This is particularly given the lack of use of available technology in the organisation. Without good management information and access to the internet, environmental analysis will be challenging.

The trustees may lack the expertise needed to carry out environmental analysis. None of them has a commercial background and so they will be unused to the idea of strategy and the role that frameworks like PEST and 5 forced have in its formulation.

It may be difficult to justify spending money on the services of a management accountant or a consultant to help the trustees with the analysis process. Public perception may well be that the charity's money should be spent on the charitable cause and any other use of it represents a departure from its purpose.

The charity relies on volunteers who may not accept or wish to be involved in the process. Incentives in terms of financial rewards cannot be used and so alternative ways of securing the volunteers commitment will need to be sought.

THE VALUE CHAIN

47   BBB FASHION (SEP 12 EXAM)

Key answer tips

Section (a) asks for a Porter's value chain analysis of the firm. This should be relatively straightforward as long as you apply your comments to the scenario and justify how a given activity adds value. Note that drawing the value chain is **not** required.

Parts (b) and (c) both focus on the new Smart Tills and the improvements they will provide to BBB as well as the stages needed in order to introduce them into the company. There are no models for you to use here – rather, you needed to make sensible comments that were applied to the scenario. Any reasonable suggestions should have scored.

(a)   Porter's Value Chain is shown below:

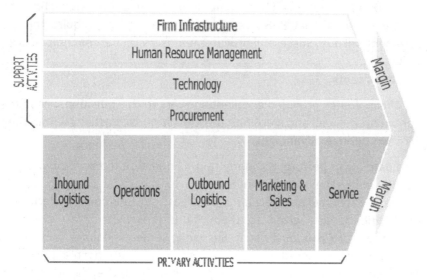

BBB's activities are categorised as follows:

Primary activities consisting of:

Inbound logistics: BBB has invested in a robotic system to improve its material handling. This should reduce wastage and contribute to a greater margin. BBB should be able to improve its service to its customers which will contribute to competitive advantage.

Operations: BBB has trained all its staff in customer care and prefers to employ staff with experience gained from other fashion retailers. This ensures that, in this aspect of its operations, BBB is at least as good as its competitors and possibly better.

Outbound logistics: BBB offers its customers the service that it will deliver their purchases to their home within 24 hours. Not all customers will take advantage of this but some will and it provides a distinguishing feature of BBB's retail experience.

Marketing and sales: BBB sends its regular customers special offers and invitations to fashion shows. In this way, it keeps its customers informed about BBB's business which should enhance its competitiveness.

Service: BBB will refund, without question, a customer's money. This aspect of its after sales service should placate any dissatisfaction from its customers and contribute to competitiveness.

Support activities consisting of:

Firm infrastructure: For BBB this consists of general corporate administration, management accounting and its management structure. All these aspects need to be in place and successful for the primary activities to be successful. If BBB is able to organise any aspects of its infrastructure better than its competitors, then it will have a potential source of competitive advantage.

Human resource management: These are BBB's personnel policies and training programmes. If these are successful BBB's staff will offer their customers a good retail experience which will help BBB to outperform its competitors.

Technology development: BBB carries out investigations of innovations in fashion retailing as retailing technology and customers' preferences are quick to change. One result of these investigations has been the potential acquisition of 'Smart Tills' which should enhance BBB's overall performance and competitiveness.

Procurement: BBB believes it can best compete by offering a wide selection of high quality products. It is essential that BBB's procurement activity can acquire the products that BBB's customers will buy. Successful procurement is a vital part of competitive advantage.

Examiner's comments

A number of candidates provided excellent answers to this question. Those that did, used the scenario material well and identified the impact of each activity within the value chain upon BBB's competitive advantage.

Those candidates who performed poorly on this question did so for two reasons. Firstly, they failed to apply the scenario information to the value chain model. A significant number of candidates merely speculated on areas that BBB could undertake, rather than use the activities clearly given to them by the examiner. You are given scenario information, therefore you must use it. Secondly, some candidates failed to consider the impact of the activities identified upon BBB's competitive advantage, so although they may have applied the scenario factors to the value chain, they failed to fully answer the question that had been set.

Common Errors:

- Limited use of the scenario information given

- Not considering the impact of each factor in the value chain upon BBB's competitive advantage

---

(b) **Smart Tills**

The Smart Tills will give BBB real-time information about its inventory turnover and balances. This offers BBB the opportunity to reduce its investment in working capital and to increase its responsiveness to its customer demand. Both of these aspects should improve profits.

The Smart Tills can provide an analysis of BBB's sales transactions. This will enhance BBB's understanding; for example, which dress is selling well, which shop has sold the most jackets last week? This greater and more timely knowledge will enable BBB to better understand and to meet its customers' requirements which should improve its competitiveness.

The Smart Tills will report sales per staff member. BBB might use this information as the basis of an incentive scheme which could improve its profitability. It could also indicate areas where staff could benefit from training which could lead to better customer service and improved profitability. BBB could also use this information for internal benchmarking purposes which could lead to improved profitability.

BBB will be able to effect these improvements because the Smart Tills will give it detailed real time information about each of its shops. With this new understanding of its business, BBB will be enabled to review, improve and possibly change its competitive strategy.

Examiner's comments

This question was well answered by most candidates. This was encouraging as it required candidates to consider the scenario information provided and to advise upon the impact upon profits of the introduction of the proposed Smart Tills. Most candidates were able to explain a range of relevant improvements. The main weakness of this answer was candidates providing only bullet point answers, with unexplained improvements listed. Even though the requirement was only worth 4 marks, candidates were required to 'advise' on, albeit briefly, the improvements to profits. List based answers are not sufficient to be awarded a pass mark.

Common Errors:

* Unexplained lists

(c) **Project leader/team:** BBB should appoint one or more people to lead the project. This could be either an internal or external appointment. BBB should ensure that the leader has experience in managing change and understands both the Smart Tills technology as well as BBB's fashion business.

Consultation: BBB should consult the individual shop managers and explain why it is introducing Smart Tills. This is a significant change and not all of the 20 managers can be expected to welcome it. Therefore, BBB should be prepared to encounter some resistance to its introduction of the Smart Tills.

Training: the shop managers and their staff will need to be trained to use the Smart Tills. BBB should receive help from the supplier of the Smart Tills in familiarising its staff with the new technology. BBB's project leader will have to plan over what period the Smart Tills are to be introduced and how this will happen: simultaneously or sequentially?

Performance management: the management accountant should revise reporting structures to use the information generated by the Smart Tills. Previously, it had not been possible to calculate the profitability of each individual shop. With the introduction of Smart Tills, this becomes possible and so the management accountant should take advantage of this and could, in future, produce a league table of shop profitability to help performance management.

After sales service: BBB should ensure it will be given adequate after-sales service by the supplier of the Smart Tills. BBB's future business will be orientated around the Smart Tills and any breakdown could be critical for BBB. BBB should negotiate a service contract for the Smart Tills which cover response times for breakdowns.

Examiner's comments

This question was generally not well answered. Again, many answers were list based with limited explanation or justification for the recommended stages of the proposed plan. Most candidates did identify the need for training and communication and for the appointment of a project team. However, overall, answers to this question lacked application to the project to implement Smart Tills and most answers were very generic and lacked real depth of understanding of the stages of project planning.

Common Errors:

- Answers lacked depth and application directly to the Smart Tills project

- List based answers with unexplained and unjustified project stages

---

48 C TEST EQUIPMENT (NOV 08 EXAM) *Walk in the footsteps of a top tutor*

From your initial read of the scenario and requirements during the reading time you should have picked up the following points (and therefore annotated your question paper with it):

- *What does the company do and where? C is a manufacturer of test equipment for electronic circuits. It operates in international markets.*

- *What are the issues? In the past C was a dominant player but over the last 3 years profits have declined and market share has been lost. C provides the most effective solutions to clients' problems but not the cheapest. Lowering prices to match competitors has lead to a loss of competitive advantage.*

- *The directors are of the view that the situation cannot continue and are considering using a value chain analysis to help.*

- *Which frameworks or theoretical knowledge is required? The value chain and the Value Shop as an alternative for service organisations.*

Based on this you could assess whether to attempt the question

- *Very straightforward as long as you knew the value shop alternative. When this question was set there was no excuse for not knowing this as it had appeared in an article beforehand.*

(a) **Benefits that C might gain from conducting a value chain analysis**

Part (a) asks for an explanation of the benefits that C might gain from conducting a value chain analysis. A common mistake would be to spend time outlining the value chain model itself in detail. A short paragraph to put the model into context will suffice, mentioning the splitting of the organisation into 5 primary and 4 support activities and the study of which add value and which do not.

The approach after this initial paragraph should be to use information from the scenario about C's business model to illustrate every possible advantage. For example, management suspect that manufacturing and installation are not contributing to the business. This may be confirmed by value chain analysis showing excess costs in these areas combined with customer feedback suggesting they are not valued anyway. These areas could then be scaled back giving C the benefit of reduced costs.

For 12 marks, students should look to explain at least 4 benefits in detail. This will be difficult without a real in depth read of the scenario. Porter's value chain was designed in 1985 as a systematic way to examine how competitive advantage develops and identify where value is added in an organisation. In using the model, the organisation splits itself into 5 primary activities and 4 support activities, all procuring and consuming resources in a certain order. How well the value chain activities are performed determines costs and affects profits.

C is a manufacturer of test equipment for electronic circuits although it would seem from its business model that the real value to clients is in problem solving and designing complex solutions to problems. C may gain the following advantages from using the value chain model:

1   Over the last three years, C has lost market share to competitors. Using the value chain, C will examine all of its activities and may be able to pinpoint the weakness in its business model that has allowed this to happen. Ultimately, use of the value chain will allow C to remove or reduce non value added activities.

In order to remove activities, C will need knowledge of the costs and benefits that go with each one. Management may find that the suspicion that manufacturing and installation are not contributing to the business is confirmed by the excessive costs within these activities combined with customer feedback which shows the activities are not valued anyway. These activities can then be scaled back or removed.

2   C has highly skilled engineers, recognised as the best in the industry and customers agree they provide the most effective solutions to the complex problems they face. C is therefore a differentiator, able to provide a better quality service when compared to its competitors.

Despite this, customers believe that C's prices are too high and compare them to other suppliers who do not solve problems as well as C. The value chain will allow C to identify why their image as a differentiator is not sufficient to allow them to charge a premium.

It may be the case that customers do not need such accurate solutions to problems and can in fact settle for less. On the other hand, C may not be adding value in their marketing and sales activities through not communicating the extra benefits to clients that their solutions bring.

3 C charges a total price to each customer before the design phase begins. The value chain will enable C to study each primary and support activity and remove any inputs, processes or outputs which represent unnecessary costs.

Fewer engineers may suffice at the discussion stage perhaps or management may discover that the prototype development frequently involves purchasing raw materials which are never actually used.

The removal of non value adding costs will increase C's profits since the total price is fixed at the outset of each project.

4 Once C 'wins' a new client, there is ongoing revenue from annual maintenance charges. Since it is unusual for companies to maintain other manufacturers' equipment, loss of a new order to a competitor offering poorer quality solutions actually means a loss of revenue going forward as well. The management of C must, however, try to establish whether profit is actually made from this ongoing maintenance work and the value chain analysis will help to do this.

If profit is not made on the ongoing maintenance, this may add further weight to the argument made by one of the directors that C should actually be a solutions provider and not a manufacturer.

5 Overall, the fact that value chain analysis, if done properly, would force C to consider every cost in the business would be extremely beneficial to the organisation. Even the most valued design stages in the process may have unnecessary costs which can be reduced. Since C has already reduced its prices to compete with other companies this is likely to be the only way that margins could be saved.

(b) **Criticisms of Porter's value chain model that could be relevant to C**

Part (b) asks for an explanation of criticisms of the value chain which could be relevant to C. If students are familiar with the complete text, they will know that one of the main criticisms is that the value chain cannot easily be applied to service organisations. C is predominantly a service organisation with highly skilled engineers providing solutions to complex problems and so the issues in the examiners article will apply here.

The question does however ask for criticisms and so wider points will score marks and candidates should try and put down as many relevant points as possible. Ultimately the value chain may not help C to gain a competitive advantage.

Students must remember that the CIMA qualification is ultimately about management accounting, and the role of management accountant will always be examined (here you are told that you are the management accountant). The main thing to achieve in parts a) and b) is an explanation of the value chain which is tailored to C, showing how the analysis would benefit them but also its drawbacks. The drawbacks in b are only worth 8 marks and so 2 or 3 explained points will suffice.

C charges a 'total price' for all of the activities it offers customers including design, manufacture and installation. A criticism of the value chain is that it assumes non-value adding activities can be removed or reduced but for C, the removal of activities which do not appear to generate profits may lead to loss of clients who expect to deal with a 'one stop shop' type organisation.

It is unusual for companies in C's industry to maintain other manufacturers equipment and so C may be forced to still offer these services (value adding or not) in order to keep business. The value chain assesses value in terms of whether an activity affects profits but it may be too simple to look at C in that way on an activity by activity basis.

The value chain cannot be applied easily to service organisations. There is an argument that given the level of personal service and bespoke products that C provides, it is actually a service organisation. (If the director's suggestion that C should become a solutions provider and not a manufacturer gains support, this will certainly be the case.)

In service organisations, the value-creation process deals with unique situations and the linear linkages between primary activities present in the value chain may not be seen. An example can be found in C's business model where a design may pass to the laboratories at C, a prototype may be developed but testing of this prototype may lead to the engineers going back to the design stage to alter the solution.

This means C will find it difficult to categorise activities using the value chain model, for example does design and problem solving fit into operations or service? In addition, C may need to call on experts from other organisations, one in particular being the engineers actually employed by the client. It is difficult to see how their input could be factored in as a value adding activity or assessed.

(c) **An alternative form of value chain analysis which could be more appropriate for C:**

Application is not expected here so it should be very straightforward as long as you know the value shop model

The value shop is an alternative representation of a value chain for a professional services firm which was developed in 1998 by Stabell and Fjelstad.

A value shop is considered to be a workshop which mobilises resources to solve specific problems. This may involve repeating a generic set of activities until a satisfactory solution is reached. The shop model applies to many organisations, particularly those whose main purpose is to identify and exploit specific opportunities like designing a bespoke product.

Since C is mainly involved in providing solutions to complex problems presented by clients, they may be much better off using the value shop model.

The model has the same support activities as Porter's value chain but the primary activities are described differently. In the value shop they are: problem finding and acquisition, problem solving, choosing among solutions, execution and control/evaluation. The management in the value shop organisation therefore focuses on areas such as the assessment of problems and opportunities, the mobilisation of resources, project management, the delivery of solutions, the measurement of outcomes and also learning.

The value shop primary activities are arranged in a circle showing that they are cyclical, with an organisation often moving back and forth to develop or reject theories before reaching a conclusion. Since C collaborates with client staff to find a solution before developing prototypes to be tested, it is easy to see how they might find the value shop to be an easier model to apply and use.

PRODUCT PORTFOLIO TOOLS

49   GC CONGLOMERATE (NOV 99 EXAM)

Key answer tips

This question presents the market share and market growth position of the five strategic business units that comprise a conglomerate group. Additional information is provided regarding the level of profitability of each SBU. The application of the BCG Growth/Share matrix to analyse the performance of each SBU is required together with a discussion as to how strategic development could be pursued.

(a)   The BCG matrix uses short emotive titles to illustrate how a portfolio of products/SBUs can be analysed for strategic planning purposes by using two important criteria of attractiveness. Market growth is shown on the vertical axis and market share by the horizontal axis. In this framework the 'Star' is the software development company because it possesses the attributes of high market share and expected high market growth. The food manufacturer is a steady cash generator and is termed a **'Cash cow'**. It posses the attributes of high market share but low/declining market growth. The top right-hand quadrant describes the characteristics of the **'Problem child'** .The parcel carriage business has low market share and no prospects for growth. Lastly the two companies in the building and allied trades are identified as **'Dogs'** in that they have low market share and low market growth.

(b)   The management of GC faces a problem that is typical of any conglomerate, which is to devise a strategy that provides value to the shareholders in the long term and thus enable the combined business to improve its chances of long-term survival. The strategy must focus on the following issues:

- Should we dispose of the companies in the building and allied trades ('Dogs')?
- How do we exploit the food manufacturer (Cash cow)?
- What resources need to be injected to develop the software business (Star)?
- How do we retain the position of the parcel business in an increasingly competitive market (Problem child)?

Divestment strategy

The declining profitability of the building brick SBU and the loss-making aspect of the painting and decorating business make them prime targets for divestment. Both companies serve a volatile business sector and require a degree of specialist management skill, which may not be available in a conglomerate. The Board could formulate plans to sell them off. The building brick company may fit into the portfolio of an organisation that is a supplier of material to the building and civil engineering sector. The painting and decorating company could fit into the portfolio of a company that provides support services like office cleaning and laundry. In the short run profits may be boosted by disposal surpluses and by elimination of trading losses. The cash generated by the sale could be used to finance the software development company as well as to support the parcel carriage service.

Improvement strategy

The food manufacturer activity is a steady cash generator but in the long term this cash generation could reduce. The Board could review their investment strategy. Will further investment in new technology improve their product range and prolong the ability to generate cash?

The development of new products could reverse the trend of declining market growth and improve the position of the business.

A profit improvement plan could examine the issue of reducing infrastructure costs and thus improve the profit in the medium term.

Promotion strategy-parcel carriage

The cash released by the disposal of the 'Dogs' could be invested in the parcel carriage business where the market place is becoming increasingly competitive. The increase in market entrants with a proven record in quality service provision (e.g. Fedex) and the possibility of the privatisation of public sector services makes investment a critical issue if the business is to survive. The fragmented nature of the market (the market leader holds 6% only) makes this business viable in the long term if an aggressive strategy of promotion is backed up by the necessary investment.

Investment strategy – software development

This SBU is likely to be the 'trump card' in the years to come but it will absorb considerable amounts of cash in product development in order to improve market share and generate value for the shareholders. The absence of a market leader is a good sign as well as the fact that the market share of 10% is higher than that of the nearest competitor. This SBU will therefore make a more pressing claim for the largest amount of any funds released by the divestment strategy outline above.

50   3C PHARMACEUTICALS (MAY 06 EXAM)

Key answer tips

Part (a) asks for application of the product lifecycle to 3C (many students completed a BCG analysis, which was not required!). It is vital that you comment on each product in terms of the overall portfolio and not just in isolation.

In part (b) it is again vital that your comments concerning each option are put in the context of the impact on the portfolio as a whole.

In part (c) ensure that you discuss each option, explain why there is an ethical issue and conclude.

(a)   The product life cycle model classifies products into four main phases:

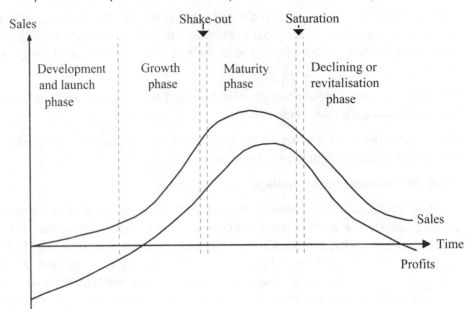

The model is normally used to assess the overall balance of the portfolio with respect to:

- growth – e.g. new products replacing those at the end of the life cycle

- cash flow – e.g. positive cash flows from some products can help finance those that are currently cash negative

- other resource requirements

- risk – e.g. having some stable low risk products to compensate for other high risk ones.

The model can be applied to 3C as follows:

3C has 240 drugs at various stages of development, either being tested or undergoing clinical trials. All of these fall into the 'development and launch' phase of the product life cycle. While being a significant drain on company resources, they are an essential part of the portfolio as they are needed to ensure the firm's future profitability by replacing older drugs that have come to the end of their life cycles.

- Epsilon is at the end of the 'growth' phase and is entering 'maturity', as high sales growth has come to an end. As such it should be a net cash generator to help finance other products in the portfolio that are currently cash negative. However, it will not contribute to future growth.

- Beta is at the latter stages of the 'development and launch' phase as significant growth in sales has yet to occur. As such it is unlikely to have reached breakeven sales and is still a drain on the firm's resources.

- Alpha is coming to the end of the 'maturity' phase and will be entering 'decline' in 12 months' time when patent protection expires and generic copies flood the market. At present it is likely to be cash positive, helping to finance product development but will neither contribute to cash flow nor future growth beyond the next year.

Overall the portfolio is reasonably balanced in terms of future growth potential and cash flow. Beyond the next year it is vital that Beta becomes cash positive and further products move from development to launch.

(b)   The three options will affect the portfolio as follows:

You must conclude, for each option, whether the portfolio is strengthened or weakened and recommend which option to pursue.

Alpha2

Alpha2 has already completed clinical trials so is ready to launch. This would effectively allow the patent protection for Alpha to be extended a further five years, thus preventing Alpha from entering the decline phase and lengthening the maturity phase.

This should prevent the portfolio from becoming unbalanced with respect to cash flow as the revised Alpha2 will generate cash to finance other products in the portfolio. It will also reduce the risk of the portfolio as sales for Alpha2 will be more certain than estimated returns for other products currently in development.

Beta

Investing in a marketing campaign for Beta would move it into the growth phase and improve the immediate growth prospects of the portfolio.

However, the presence of a close substitute in the market increases the risks attached to Beta and may result in lower growth than expected and even delay Beta breaking even as extra funds would be required to establish Beta ahead of its rival. In the short term Beta may place greater demands on the portfolio cash flow rather than helping it.

Gamma

If Gamma completes the final clinical trials successfully, then it will quickly move from development and launch into the growth stage. Even if prices are set at a high level, expected demand should result in very high growth, improving the overall growth balance of the portfolio. However, there is no guarantee that Gamma will be successful and, on balance, is the most risky option presented.

The impact on overall portfolio cash flow will depend, to some extent, on the price set. While a low price may still generate positive contribution and cash flow in the immediate future, when Gamma is viewed over its whole life cycle a loss and negative cash flow may result.

A higher price will enable 3C to finance many more other drugs that are still in the development phase.

Recommendation

On balance, investing in Alpha2 appears to offer the safest way to balance the portfolio in terms of cash flow whereas Gamma offers the highest growth and profit potential. The final decision will depend on the risk aversion of the directors.

(c)   Social responsibility is the idea that an organisation should behave responsibly in the interests of the society in which it operates.

Answers to this requirement could be structured either 'option-by-option' or 'issue-by-issue'.

The social responsibility implications of the three options given are as follows:

Alpha2

Extending the patent in the way described would delay competitors from producing cheap generic copies. The ethical argument here is that, if 3C invests, then customers would not have access to cheaper pain killers so, in effect, 3C is increasing the pain of many sufferers.

However, there are many alternative pain killers on the market, including generic drugs, so the comparison is really between cheap pain relief and more expensive but better pain relief.

Beta

The ethical position with Beta is the other way round – one could argue that 3C has a moral duty to invest in Beta as this will increase the availability of drugs dealing with serious infection. However, if 3C does not invest in Beta, then there are equivalent drugs on the market for patients and hospitals are likely to prioritise such treatments anyway. What investment in Beta would achieve is a likely fall in the price of such drugs due to extra competition. It could be argued that this should allow health trusts' funds to go further, thus treating more patients.

Gamma

The situation with Gamma is very different. Millions of people around the world are infected with HIV/AIDS and, although progress is being made with anti-retroviral drugs, Gamma would be a major step forward in treatment.

A separate ethical issue is the price that 3C should charge for Gamma. Selling Gamma at the lowest price possible would ensure greater access to sufferers, particularly in poorer countries in Africa where the situation is at its worst. A high price would effectively exclude such people from treatment.

There is thus a major ethical conflict between the higher profits that 3C could earn for its shareholders verses increased treatment for people in the developing world. While it could be argued that 'the business of business is business' and that it is up to governments to make funds available to pay for drugs, the ethical argument here is compelling.

Conclusion

On ethical grounds further investment should be put into Gamma. In fact, the key ethical argument against investing in Alpha2 or Beta is that they preclude investment in Gamma. The pricing issue is more complex.

51   D PRINTING (MAY 09 EXAM)

Key answer tips

Part (a) should provide an easy 5 marks to the well prepared candidate and in addition, should generate ideas for the rest of the question, since D is in an industry at the maturity stage of its life cycle.

Part (b) requires a sound knowledge of the 'usual contents' of a mission statement. It is important to then tie these 'contents' to D, as issues management must consider.

(a)   The characteristics of the maturity stage of the industry life cycle

Like the product lifecycle, the industry life cycle has four stages: introduction, growth, maturity and decline. The two forces which drive the industry life cycle are growth in demand and the diffusion of knowledge (investment in research and development.)

At the maturity stage of the lifecycle, the following assumptions can be made:

- The products made by the industry are standardised and of superior quality. Since they are well established, consumers know exactly what to expect.

- The product innovation involved in the introduction and growth stage has slowed, and instead organisations are looking to exploit process innovation, with the aim of seeking cost advantage and improved product reliability to give them the edge over the many competitors who entered the market in the growth phase.

- Due to the intense competition and no longer innovative product, margins will be falling at the maturity stage. Organisations like D must therefore look to increase volume if they are to survive.

(b)   Issues for the management of D to consider when creating an appropriate mission statement

The mission of an organisation can be defined as its 'fundamental objectives expressed in general terms'. When creating an appropriate mission statement, D will need to consider the following issues:

The nature of D's business – Management will need to ask themselves not only what business are they in, but what business should they be in? For example, D's founders may consider the company to be in the printing industry, but ought they to consider it to be in the client service industry?

The printing technology is no longer innovative and so unlikely to 'hook in' prospective customers on its own. A description of the business as client focussed, offering essential printing services, may convey D's objectives much more effectively in a mission statement.

Stakeholders (i.e. who the business exists for) – D must exist for its customers, and asking what business they should be in, as outlined above, will help to clarify this. It is essential that they consider the client perspective when formulating the mission statement since it will be a public relations tool with which to communicate with prospective customers.

It is also clear however, that D has historically valued its employees with Mr Z knowing all employees first names and considering them to be part of a team. If this team spirit has been lost as the organisation has grown, management may wish to consider addressing this issue in the mission statement, by including some reference to the importance of team working and treating employees well.

This will help reinstate staff's understanding of the company's values. It could be argued that Mr Z himself used to 'do the job of' the mission statement in this respect but with the growth in staff numbers, a mission statement is now needed to convey the fact that the company exists for customers and employees.

The basic values and beliefs of D – The management of D will need to consider exactly what these are so they can be included in the mission statement being created. Mr Z may be of the opinion that these values have been obvious to all in the past, but since this is no longer the case, they must now be identified and summarised in general terms.

The basic values are unlikely to still be related to D's use of innovative technology as they were in the past. Including past values (the importance of innovation) will show D up to be out of touch with the market and so careful consideration of new values must be undertaken. These are likely to include providing best value services and customer care given the mature stage of the industry.

Sustainable Competitive Advantage – where is D's distinctiveness? The mission must try and 'set D apart' from the competitors. Management will therefore need to carefully consider what it is that makes them distinctive. This may be difficult to pinpoint since there are many competitors operating in the same way. If D has a distinct brand name, or a wider product range than these other printing companies, this should be included in any mission statement created.

Main reasons for D's choice of approach – An appropriate mission statement needs to summarise the main reasons for D's choice of approach to conducting business (for example, valuing staff and customers, providing value for money etc.). This may be as simple as stating that the employees of D are a team who treat each other, and their clients with respect. Management will need to carefully consider the message they are trying to convey to stakeholders and make sure it is clearly set out in the mission.

(c) Characteristics of strategic objectives that would be appropriate for D at this stage of the industry life cycle

Strategic objectives possess four characteristics which set them apart from a mission statement:

The SMART framework could also have been used here as an answer structure.

1 A precise formulation of the attribute sought – so an appropriate objective for D may be to maintain their market share, which is only slightly above their main competitor.

2 An index or measure for progress towards the attribute – D may choose to measure market share in percentage points since this will be relatively easy to ascertain for both D and the competitors.

3 A target to be achieved – The management of D may choose a target similar or slightly above their current market share percentage, thus satisfying the objective of 'maintaining' their presence in the market

4 A time frame in which it is to be achieved – D may wish to maintain market share over the next 5 years, depending on the strategy time horizon management usually consider. The key issue is that there must be an exercise whereby at the end of the timeframe, a review of whether the objective has been achieved is carried out.

STRATEGIC CHOICE

52   HFH (SEP 13 EXAM)

Key answer tips

Requirement (a) should be a straightforward question which requires candidates to present a SWOT analysis. Candidates are expected to identify aspects within each of the four quadrants of the SWOT and to explain each of the points made. The answer must be from the point of view of HFH.

Requirement (b) requires candidates to apply their knowledge and understanding of change adept organisational characteristics to CFC. Clearly candidates must have the syllabus knowledge of change adept organisations to answer this question. However, a sound evaluation of the unseen material relating to CFC should provide the candidates with sufficient information to answer this question.

Requirement (c)(i) should be a straightforward question requiring candidates to discuss the benefits and difficulties of a merger between the two charities. Candidates should clearly present a separate discussion for the benefits and difficulties, and answers must be directly applied to the scenario context.

Requirement (c)(ii) requires candidates to present and justify a final recommendation. Candidates should use their answers in part (c)(i) to help to justify their final recommendation. It is important that candidates clearly and fully justify any recommendation made.

(a)   **SWOT analysis**

Strengths	Opportunities
• HFH is well respected in the charity environment and, therefore, in the current climate for mergers, this reputation is a positive factor for change.	• There are obvious opportunities for collaboration in the charities sector.
• HFH has an experienced Board of Trustees which is open and willing to embrace change and recognise the need for change.	• The Government of the country is positively encouraging this form of collaboration and is providing incentives for collaboration.
• Specialist skills with helping homeless people.	• HFH could develop and work on larger and more innovative projects by working in partnerships.
• Committed employees and volunteers.	• HFH may be able to gain access to new sources of funds and volunteers.
• Board of Trustees with vision to see the need to offer other services.	• Changing needs of beneficiaries opens up new opportunities for new services.
	• Merger with CFC.
	• Offer employment training services.

Weaknesses	Threats
• Limited fundraising capability. • Low profile in charity sector. • Declining donor base. • Inadequate resources to cope with rising demand. • Over reliance on limited sources of funding. • Employees and volunteers don't have employment training skills.	• Economic recession leading to a general lack of financial stability and reduced funding. • Loss of key personnel and volunteers due to pressure. • Greater demand putting pressure on scarce resources. • With recession, demand may continue to grow and HFH may struggle to provide adequate service and lose its good reputation.

Examiner's comments

This question was very well answered. Most candidates provided a good range of factors in all elements of the SWOT analysis. The only minor weakness of answers to this question was that some candidates confused some of the weaknesses and threats. Most candidates evaluated the scenario material very well and were able to successfully apply the SWOT framework to HFH

Common Errors:

• Some confusion of weaknesses and threats

(b) *Examiner note: The following introductory section is for tuition purposes only. Candidates are not expected to provide this definition of Kanter's characteristics of change adept organisations in their answers.*

According to Kanter, organisations which are change adept have the following characteristics:

• The imagination to innovate

• The professionalism to perform

• The openness to collaborate

CFC Board of Trustees demonstrates these characteristics in a number of areas.

It is innovative in continually enhancing its services, including helping people to learn new skills such as IT, and it also has always embraced technology and the use of a sophisticated website to advertise its services. Therefore, this fits Kanter's first characteristic of a change adept organisation, as having the 'imagination to innovate'.

The Board of Trustees of CFC has also been open and encouraged collaboration and partnerships with other organisations in Country Z, in order to develop and enhance the services it offers and to utilise the expertise and knowledge of other complementary organisations. This aspect of CFC's activities demonstrates a further characteristic of change adept organisations, in that it has 'an openness to collaborate'.

Examiner's comments

This question was not well answered. Most candidates clearly did not have any knowledge of Kanter's recommended attributes for change adept organisations. However, some candidates did make an attempt to answer the question using the information about CFC within the scenario. Many candidates did correctly identify the need to be innovative as a key characteristic but few could correctly identify a second attribute. Some candidates also incorrectly focused their answers upon HFH and not CFC.

Common Errors:

* Lack of knowledge of this syllabus area

* Discussion of HFH

(c)   (i)   **Benefits for HFH**

* Access to CFC's employees and volunteers and their greater knowledge of new service areas such as employment training.

* It should allow HFH to expand its services to customers thus improving its service levels.

* Merging should allow for staff retention and a wider access to volunteers.

* It should permit HFH better access to more secure funding.

* CFC provides help to people with IT skills and job interviews and these skills can be passed on to HFH's employees. The two organisations will have a shared common goal to provide help to people requiring IT skills and jobs.

* The two organisations would be part of a bigger charity and this may give all of HFH's employees and volunteers an opportunity to gain wider experience in their career and better job security.

* It should provide homeless people with access to a wider range of other services.

* It should allow both organisations to become more efficient and cut central overheads.

* A merger would help HFH survive in the longer term and be less dependent on its existing source of donations.

* It raises the profile of the need to provide shelter for homeless people.

Difficulties for HFH

* There is likely to be staff resistance to change and a fear that they may not be doing the work that they used to do and want to do - especially relevant for volunteers.

* When merging the two organisations, their IT systems and different cultures and working practices may cause difficulties in integration.

* CFC, as the larger charity, may appear to 'take over' HFH and HFH's employees and volunteers may feel less needed and lose focus and motivation.

* There may be loss of identity through a merger with a larger charity.

- The wider range of services provided by the larger organisations in the new charity, post-merger, may detract from HFH's main purpose of providing accommodation for homeless people.

- Management of the change process takes up time and may affect the management's ability to focus on the immediate problems of the growing demand for shelter in the current recession.

- Central Government funding usually comes with some form of central Government control meaning that HFH may lose some autonomy.

Examiner's comments

This question was very well answered. Most candidates provided an extensive range of both benefits and difficulties and there was evidence of a real depth of discussion in many answers. The only weakness of a minority of candidates' answers was that they were brief and lacked depth, in that they were presented in a bullet point format. The question asked for a discussion so it is important that candidates provide more than an unexplained bullet point list.

Common Errors:

- Some answers were very brief and poorly discussed

(c)   (ii)   It would seem to be highly beneficial for HFH to merge with CFC, therefore the recommendation is for the two charities to merge. In fact it may be the only option for HFH to survive.

In the context of the current climate for mergers and the government positively encouraging mergers it would appear sensible. The two charities are highly compatible in their areas of work and there appears to be a high degree of synergy. CFC is a good fit for HFH and both charities share common goals.

In addition, due to the funding and donations problem, if the merger is not agreed, then the combination of increased demand and falling funding for HFH, which has a low profile, will result in it failing in its fundamental purpose of providing shelter for the homeless. The access to funding provided by the merger is more likely to help HFH in its basic purpose of continuing to try to meet the growing demands of homeless people.

With the government favouring mergers of charities, and the possible mergers of other charities, rejecting this proposal now could ultimately lead to the failure and closure of HFH if it were to lose more funding.

This is a good opportunity and needs to be seized before CFC selects a different charity to merge with.

Examiner's comments

This question was very well answered. Most candidates made a sound recommendation of merging the two organisations and also fully justified their recommendation. It was encouraging to see that nearly all of the candidates that answered this question made a very good attempt at justifying their recommendation.

---

53   GGG (NOV 12 EXAM)

Key answer tips

Requirement (a) should be a straightforward question, requiring candidates to apply Ansoff's growth vector matrix directly to the scenario information. Candidates are not required to make any recommendations in this answer but are required to analyse the opportunities to GGG presented within the scenario information within the Ansoff framework. This question requires a high level of application, analysing the information from the scenario in order to apply this directly to the matrix.

Requirement (b) requires candidates to build upon their answers to part (a) to evaluate the opportunities they have identified within the Ansoff growth vector matrix, using the criteria of Suitability, Acceptability and Feasibility. This question once again requires a high level of application.

Requirement (c) requires candidates to demonstrate their ability to present a sound recommendation based upon their previous analysis of the scenario information. Candidates are expected to provide a sound judgement which is consistent with their analysis within the previous two requirements.

(a)   GGG could utilise the Ansoff growth vector matrix to analyse the possible future strategic directions it could follow.

		Products	
		Existing	New
Markets	Existing	Market Penetration	Product Development
	New	Market Development	Diversification Related/Unrelated

Market Penetration

GGG could attempt to increase its market share with its existing services to its current market or region. The market is a growing one; with the change in demographics, therefore, market penetration is a real option for GGG. As it currently has 25% of its region's market with the rest fragmented between local government run and privately owned care homes, there is potential for GGG to undertake promotional activities in order to obtain business from these competitors. In particular, the sale and closure of a number of the privately run care homes could be an opportunity to obtain a greater share of the market through targeting these care homes customers. GGG may have to consider its pricing strategies however, as its prices may well be higher than its competitors. It may need to consider a reduction of prices or some form of discounted offer to attract customers who are currently paying less than they would be charged in GGG's care homes.

Product Development

GGG could attempt to offer new services to its existing market or region.

Within the scenario, there is mention of a new 'relief package' facility that is becoming popular with customers. GGG could consider offering its facilities for customers within its region for this new service. This would have to be investigated further to ensure that GGG has the capacity and facilities to offer such a service. If there is clearly a growing need for this type of package, then GGG could try to gain early market entry in order to gain early mover advantage. The issue for GGG is likely to be capacity constraints and the need to weigh up the benefits and costs of the option against those of offering continued longer term care to its residents.

In addition, the additional services that could be offered by the qualified staff and nurses of GGG to its patients as an alternative to referral to hospitals could be a form of product development. However, this is likely to involve investment in re-training and facilities.

Market Development

GGG could attempt to increase its revenues by offering its current services to new customers or at a different geographical location.

One option would be to consider moving into another geographical region in its own country to offer its services to the elderly. This is a possibility as the national geographic trend suggests increasing demand nationally for elderly care. However, this is a riskier strategy as GGG currently has no experience of its competitive environment outside its own region and the competitive market may be very different. In addition, GGG would require heavy investment in facilities outside of the region. However, the market conditions are likely to be the same as in its own region and, therefore, it could consider buying or merging with another private care home outside of its current region. However, GGG must consider the rising costs of running care homes and the consequent need for it to price its services accordingly.

Diversification

GGG could consider offering new services to new customers. For example, the trained staff and nurses could be used to offer other nursing and rehabilitation services to individual customers, other care homes or to GP surgeries. These could be offered within the facilities of GGG or could be offered on site in customers' homes.

GGG's administrators are also highly experienced and GGG could consider utilising their experience to offer consultancy and management services to other care homes which might consider outsourcing their management and administration function to GGG.

Examiner's comments

This question was reasonably well answered. Most candidates used the information from the scenario well, but a number of candidates confused the different quadrants of the model. Markers were flexible in awarding marks for application of the strategic options for GGG to the Ansoff matrix, as long as candidates clearly explained and justified their classifications. Some candidates clearly did not know the model sufficiently well to apply it correctly. However, it was encouraging to see the level of application of candidate answers to this question. However, few candidates scored very highly on this requirement as few adequately analysed the opportunities, instead most merely identified and explained them.

Common Errors:

- Identification and explanation of the opportunities rather than analysis of the opportunities

---

(b)   According to the Johnson, Scholes and Whittington approach, an organisation's potential strategies can be evaluated against the following criteria:

- Suitability: whether a strategy fits with the organisation's operations and its strategic position.

- Acceptability: whether a strategy fits with the expectations of the stakeholders.

- Feasibility: whether the strategy can be implemented, taking into consideration practical considerations such as time, cost and capabilities.

GGG must consider if the proposed strategy is suitable to respond to environmental events and opportunities and whether it fits with the current strategic position. It would need to consider whether it had the right level of resources and competences. It would also have to consider its key stakeholders in terms of both risk and return. It is important to note that GGG must also consider 'who' their customers are, as customers will include not only the actual residents of the care home but also their families or their current carers. Reviewing each of the strategies identified in the Ansoff matrix, GGG should consider:

Market penetration

Suitability: This strategy would appear suitable as GGG has spare capacity and also this option builds upon GGG's current expertise so there is clear strategic fit.

Acceptability: The key stakeholders such as staff and management are unlikely to be opposed to this strategy as it is a mere development of the current activities of GGG. Existing customers should find it acceptable as long as current standards of operation are not affected if the care homes now take on more customers.

Feasibility: GGG has the resources in terms of capacity and competences to undertake this strategy. However, further growth could mean the need to invest in more facilities if spare capacity limits are exceeded. GGG would also need to consider the costs of advertising.

Product Development

Suitability: This strategy continues to fit with GGG's strategic position and would certainly exploit an obvious market opportunity. It will complement the existing long term care facilities and should help to balance GGG's portfolio. Therefore it is suitable.

Acceptability: Staff may find this strategy unacceptable if it requires additional training or detracts them from the care of GGG's existing long term care customers. Existing customers should be neutral in the decision as long as it does not affect the standard of their care and potential customers are likely to be positive towards the proposal.

Feasibility: Investment in facilities and training may make this option unfeasible but GGG would have to weigh up the long term benefits of building market share through subsequent conversion from short-term care residents into long-term residents and by improving quality of care by providing services in-house rather than necessitating referral to hospital.

Market Development

Suitability: There is certainly a potential for opportunities outside of its current geographical region. The national trend suggests increasing demand nationally for elderly residential care. However, GGG has no experience of its competitive environment outside its own region and the competitive market may be very different. GGG does not know whether its own service would be superior from that offered by competitors.

Acceptability: Staff and managers may not find this strategy acceptable as it might affect their own workloads, location and roles. However, current customers are likely to be neutral to the proposal.

Feasibility: Can GGG find the right facilities or a suitable partner to merge with or acquire? Costs of relocation of some staff or recruitment and training would need to be carefully considered. There might be some resistance from staff and competitors. Also, GGG needs to consider timescales and possible local Government resistance. Therefore, market development may not be feasible.

Diversification

Suitability: GGG has the necessary skills to undertake diversification although additional training may be required. In the present climate it would appear that the opportunities for this development may be limited. It would fit with the current activities of GGG and therefore has strategic fit.

Acceptability: The staff may find this acceptable as it would develop their skills and enhance their job roles. Existing customers are also likely to find this acceptable as it would not mean disruption to them assuming the new services do not detract from their own care. However, GPs and hospitals may not find this acceptable as they may not agree that the same level of care can be offered by GGG's staff.

Feasibility: GGG will have to invest heavily in training and facilities which may make this unfeasible. There may also be resistance to this from local GPs and hospitals. Therefore, GGG may find this strategy unfeasible.

Examiner's comments

This question was not well answered. It was disappointing that a large number of candidates clearly do not know the basic definitions of Suitability, Acceptability and Feasibility as there appeared to be much confusion and repetition between these criteria in many answers. In addition some candidates failed to adequately justify their evaluations, merely making statements such as 'Relief care packages are feasible' without any further comment. This is clearly insufficient and not worthy of any credit. Once again, candidates must make careful note of the verbs used and present answers which are of an appropriate depth to address the verb.

Common Errors:

- Lack of syllabus knowledge of Suitability, Acceptability and Feasibility

- Limited evaluation

(c)   In the current market and competitive environment, where GGG is managing to remain profitable despite other similarly businesses failing, the recommended options for GGG would be to follow a market penetration strategy with product development.

The current geographical market clearly has potential for GGG so there is no need for a market development strategy. A market penetration strategy would allow GGG to exploit the current trends and build upon its own strength and reputation. It is also the least risky option in a time when costs are clearly rising. Product development with the care relief packages should also be considered as it has clear potential for GGG to exploit its current spare capacity and to use its expertise to develop a clearly growing market need.

54   XZY (MAY 10 EXAM)

Key answer tips

In part (a) you are required to apply Ansoff's matrix to XZY. For twelve marks, you need to consider each of the four quadrants of the matrix and, most importantly, you had to apply them to XZY itself. That would involve deciding which strategy the company is currently pursuing and how it could adopt each of the other three approaches. Keep your answer applied to the scenario by trying to mention XZY in each point you make.

Parts (b) and (c) focus on change management. Part (b) examines the practical difficulties that XZY will face at downsizing its staff. The question is broad, so you don't need to just discuss resistance – make sure you discuss financial problems as well.

Part (c) asks for you to recommend how the change process should be managed in the company. There are other models you can use here, but Lewin's Three-Stage model is the easiest one to learn and apply.

(a)   **Evaluation of alternative strategies for XZY**

Ansoff's matrix is a common technique for developing business strategies by looking at where a business should compete. It examines whether a new or existing products should be sold to new or existing markets.

Market penetration (existing products to existing markets)

Give that the CEO describes XZY as "selling what we know to who we know," market penetration would appear to be the current strategy employed by the business.

XZY has a range of well-regarded products. Selling these to existing customers in Asia who already have a good working relationship with XZY is a low-risk approach and one that has produced good financial results so far.

However, by ignoring markets further afield and not developing new products, XZY is passing up on future growth potential. This is beginning to cause problems with the company's relationship with its investors.

Due to this, XZY may wish to investigate one of the other three strategies suggested by Ansoff's matrix.

Product development (new products to existing markets)

If XZY wishes to increase its sales growth, it may be advisable for it to launch new products in Asia. This would aim to increase its revenue earned from existing customers and markets.

XZY does have a proven track record of successfully launching good quality products, as evidenced by its current market position. Selling these products to the Asian customers that the company already works with and understands is likely to increase chances of success.

In addition, years of profitable trading mean that XZY is likely to have the funds needed for research and development of new products.

However, any new product launch is inherently uncertain. It may not be possible to find a new product with features that current customers will value highly enough to want to purchase.

In addition, any problems with the new products may damage the reputation of XYZ in its main markets and harm sales of existing products.

Market development (existing products to new markets)

XZY only operates in the Asian markets. Market development would involve selling its existing product range in new markets, such as Europe or America.

This approach has the advantage of using XZY's current strong product range and experience of selling. The good quality of XZY's product will increase the chances of such a strategy being successful.

This strategy will, however, be higher risk for XZY. It has no experience of selling outside of Asia. For example, XZY's products may not meet European customer's needs.

Finally, XZY may have problems with cultural or legal differences between Asian and non-Asian markets, which will increase the barriers to entry. For example, European countries may have different safety standards than Asian countries, which XZY's products would need to meet before they could be sold there.

Diversification (new products to new markets)

This would be the highest risk strategy of the four, requiring XZY to launch a new range of products into a new market that it has no experience of.

XZY could choose related diversification. This normally involves vertical integration – the expansion in either direction along the XZY's supply chain. This could enable XZY to secure its supply chain and access new markets. It may also streamline XZY's supply chain and reduce costs, helping to grow profits as demanded by investors.

XZY would need to ensure that such a move did not upset their existing suppliers or customers, who XZY may start competing with.

Alternatively, XZY could look for unrelated, or conglomerate, diversification. This would involve making and selling products which are totally unrelated to the current range and in doing so spreading the company's risk. Given XZY's lack of experience in this new area, chances of failure will be high.

XZY could choose to purchase another business that currently operates within the new market area and take advantage of their specialist knowledge. However the takeover of a successful company is likely to be expensive and XZY is unlikely to be able to add value to such a business as a parent.

Such a move may be resisted by investors as it is unlikely to add to their wealth and may simply take up a disproportionate amount of XZY's management time.

(b) **Difficulties in changing organisational structure and reducing employee numbers**

The proposed changes are likely to meet significant resistance from employees. This will be caused by the risk of unemployment as well as the reorganisation causing changes to working conditions.

Given the profitable nature of the business it may be difficult to convince staff of the need for redundancies.

If the XZY proceeds with the change of structure, they may see falling staff morale and, depending on whether the staff are unionised, strike action. Either may damage the results of the company and merely distract managers from the normal operations of the company.

Changing the organisational structure may, at least in the short-term, be confusing for staff. As staff members are learning new roles and responsibilities, XZY may see a fall in efficiency which may upset customers.

Any staff members with specialist skills or knowledge will need to be identified before the reorganisation process begins and will need to be retained. This can be difficult and XZY runs the risk of losing key staff members.

XZY is also likely to find that the cost or restructuring and reducing staff numbers may lead to short-term cost increases. Redundancy and retraining costs may be significant.

(c) **Recommendation of how the CEO can manage the change process**

The CEO could use a change management model, such as Lewin's 'organisational ice cube'. This suggests a three-stage approach to managing change within an organisation.

Unfreeze

This involves creating the initial motivation to change by convincing staff of the undesirability of the current situation.

The CEO could deal with this in a number of ways:

- Communicate with employees and explain the need to increase profitability. This is unlikely to be successful as the company is currently profitable. Staff are unlikely to accept the need for redundancies and restructuring on this basis.

- Create additional forces for change by showing the benefits of the restructuring. This could include pay rises or bonuses for remaining staff members as well as more responsibility and prospects for development.

- Allow staff to participate in the restructuring plans. Getting employees involved in the decision making process may not only generate useful ideas, but will also increase the chance employees will accept the reorganisation.

Change

This stage involves restructuring the company and making redundancies.

Staff should be kept informed throughout the process and support should be given to those who will be made redundant, for example advice on retraining or time off to attend interviews.

In addition, employees who have seen their roles changed should get full training and support to ensure they can be successful in their new position.

Re-freeze

This stage ensures that staff do not fall back into old ways. For XZY it will involve ensuring that employees do not slip back into their old roles.

Amongst other things, this could be accomplished by:

- New incentive systems for employees based on their new roles

- Promotion of employees who have supported the reorganisation.

If the CEO adopts this approach he will increase the chance of the reorganisation being successful.

55 TKC (SEP 11 EXAM)

Key answer tips

Part (a) is a relatively standard question examining Ansoff's matrix. As well as identifying the four potential strategies that this suggests, you needed to apply it to TKC. Any sensible suggestions should have scored here, but you should link it to the proposed BAB acquisition where possible.

Part (b) should have been seven relatively easy application marks. Make sure that you consider both advantages **and** disadvantages. Also, a generic list of disadvantages of acquisitions would not have scored well here – you must apply it to BAB and TKC.

Part (c) was a trickier requirement as it was rather broad. However, this could be an advantage! Anything reasonable that TKC would need to plan for would earn you credit here. In particular, think about any complex or high risk areas.

(a) Ansoff's product-market scope matrix (below) shows the possible future strategic directions available to a business.

	Existing Products	New Products
Existing Market	Market Penetration	Product Development
New Market	Market Development	Diversification

All the strategies within the four cells imply increased investment in products and markets and so are usually associated with growing markets where a reasonable rate of return can be earned.

The future direction of TKC is going to be influenced by two important factors:

1　TKC is going to dispose of two of its divisions to achieve 'a more concentrated business focus'.

2　Its potential new acquisition, BAB, has a substantial export business which TKC does not have.

If Ansoff's matrix is used to analyse the future strategic direction of TKC, opportunities could be identified in the following areas.

- **Market penetration**: TKC may be able to offer some BAB products to TKC's customers.

- **Market development**: TKC may be able to offer some of its products in BAB's export markets.

- **Product development**: The acquisition of BAB may lead to synergistic benefits in the area of product development. Any new products could be offered to both TKCs and BAB's customers.

- **Diversification**: TKC's Board wants to achieve 'a more concentrated business focus'. It is unlikely therefore that it would be interested in diversification.

Examiner's comments

Surprisingly, this question was not well answered. It should have been a straightforward knowledge demonstration question with application to the given scenario information. However, it was most disappointing to see how many candidates could not apply this model to the scenario information. The first mistake was that many candidates attempted to apply the model to the leisure and financial services divisions of TKC. However, candidates had specifically been informed in the scenario that these two divisions were to be divested. Therefore application of the model to these divisions was irrelevant and awarded no marks.

Secondly, many candidates failed to apply the model at all to the engineering division and instead provided a generic description of each area of the model. Candidates should know by now that there are few if any marks available for generic descriptions of syllabus theories and models.

Common Errors

- Generic answers with no application to TKC

- Discussion of the leisure and financial services division

(b) The factors in favour of TKC acquiring are:

- Post acquisition, TKC would have the largest engineering business in the UK.

- The acquisition would give TKC substantial export business which it does not currently have.

- Despite the recession and the severe downturn in consumer spending, TKC's engineering division is profitable. TKC claims it has 'exceptional management skills'. It could be that these could be applied to the new acquisition which could earn 'exceptional profits'.

Unfavourable aspects of the proposed acquisition relate to the current status of BAB which is in financial difficulties. The reasons for the failure are unknown but must relate to problems with its financing, performance or possibly both. The acquisition of up to 500 new employees would be a substantial management task for TKC.

TKC's decision to buy BAB will be largely influenced by the reasons for BAB's failure and whether TKC has the resources to remedy these.

TKC has no experience of export business, so it may not have the expertise to earn a profit from these.

(c) As a publicly listed company, TKC should be conscious of the effect that these changes will have upon its share price. TKC should plan a campaign to influence the wider financial community in favour of its proposals. It could be open to the criticism that, with a falling share price and little cash, this is not the time to be making a substantial acquisition. TKC needs to stress the positives which emanate from the acquisition of BAB: that it would become the largest engineering company in revenue in the UK, that it could make exceptional profits due to its exceptional management skills, that its engineering division is currently profitable and that the acquisition would bring a new aspect to its business; substantial exports. TKC should also stress that its divestment will mean its sheds its loss-making activities and will be an easier company to manage in the future with a sharper focus.

If TKC proceeds with its corporate reorganisation and the acquisition of BAB, it must recognise and plan for the complexity involved in its proposals. Currently, TKC employs 900 people in its three divisions which have similar sized revenues. It is reasonable to assume that their workforces are of a similar size which means they will be losing approximately 600 employees. At the same time, TKC will be acquiring up to 500 employees with the acquisition of BAB. Dealing with the Human Resource issues presented by such large movements of employees is a very substantial task and TKC is going to have to organise its Human Resources function to deal with this. It is likely to have to use outside help to deal with this sudden increase in work.

The divestment and acquisition are going to involve considerable financial outlays. TKC has exhausted its cash reserves and its share price has experienced a severe decline. This implies that TKC may have to rely substantially on debt financing for the divestment and acquisition. Therefore, it is going to have to secure credit for a suitable period if it is to proceed with these two strategies.

It is not stated which mechanism TKC will use to divest itself of its two divisions. TKC has a variety of ways in which it can divest itself of these two divisions, namely;

- Sale

- Management buy-outs

- Liquidation

Each of these methods will require substantial senior management time and commitment and specialist legal advice. This has to be planned and the costs budgeted for.

Beer and Nohria (B&N) have categorised changes where shareholder value is the main concern as 'Theory E change strategies' which include 'layoffs, downsizing and restructuring'. B&N believe that organisations using Theory E change strategies ignore the feelings and attitudes of their employees and therefore lose the commitment and creativity required for sustained competitive advantage.

It is very likely that TKC will encounter resistance to the proposed changes from a number of directions:

TKC existing employees: those employees in the two divisions which are to be divested may fear that they will lose their jobs, or that their employment under new owners will not be as enjoyable as under TKC, or that their working conditions/career prospects will suffer.

TKC's new employees: those people currently working for BAB may not wish to work for TKC and are likely to share many of the anxieties of TKC's existing employees.

Shareholders: their support will be necessary for such fundamental changes and TKC should not assume this will be given automatically. TKC will need to plan a campaign of information and persuasion to ensure its shareholders' support.

TKC will need to plan strategies to overcome the resistance to change which it is likely to encounter from a number of sources.

Examiner's comments

This question was reasonably well answered. Many answers correctly focused upon re-organisation activities such as planning for redundancies and the cost of re-organisation. Also, many answers also correctly discussed the main issues involved in acquisition of BAB, such as the planning of the necessary finance and the possible cultural and management issues. Many answers also correctly identified the need to plan for possible resistance to both changes. The main weakness of some answers was that some candidates provided only very brief list-based answers, with limited discussion of the points made. The question clearly asked for 'recommendations' which must always be justified and explained.

Common Errors

- Focus of answers only upon resistance to change issues

---

56   F PLASTICS (NOV 07 EXAM)

Key answer tips

In part (a) (i) you only have 5 marks for discussing F's many difficulties so be careful not to exceed the time allocation.

For part (a) (ii) you need to generate a range of strategies to discuss. Make sure you evaluate your strategies.

In part (c) the main problem lies in generating ideas but enough to pass should be fairly easy.

(a)   (i)   F has a deteriorating financial position as seen by falling market share and reduced profits. This is due to the following underlying difficulties:

Narrow product portfolio

F is over-reliant on two product ranges and heavily dependent on its domestic market. Any threats to these products thus have a much bigger impact on F as a whole.

Lack of a clear competitive strategy

F's main emphasis seems to be competing in markets where products are fairly standardised such as beer crates. This would suggest that a cost leadership competitive strategy is needed. However, it also sells more technologically sophisticated products and invests heavily in R&D, indicating a differentiation strategy.

This lack of a clear strategy could ultimately undermine both approaches, leaving F "stuck in the middle".

Threat from competitive forces

The combination of an increasing threat from cheap crate imports and industry consolidation is forcing down margins on crates.

Cultural deficiencies

F has a mechanistic, bureaucratic culture that has resulted in a lack of flexibility and confrontations with unions.

Lack of focus in R&D

F is not directing its R&D spend efficiently.

(ii)   F should consider the following strategies to address its difficulties:

When identifying strategies you could include competitive strategy (e.g. using Porter's generic strategies) and corporate strategy (e.g. using Ansoff's matrix) or you could brainstorm different possibilities for each of the current products mentioned.

Enhance a low cost strategy for crates by cost-cutting

F could try to enhance its competitive advantage by cutting back on unnecessary expenditure, such as R&D. This would improve margins and may discourage new entrants to F's domestic market.

The main disadvantage of this option is that F would have to give up its high technology products, thus limiting its future prospects to an even smaller portfolio.

On these grounds this proposal is rejected. As a compromise F should analyse its crate operations to see where efficiencies can be gained without compromising other product ranges.

Withdraw from the beer crate market

Some shareholders have suggested withdrawing from beer crates. The main argument in favour of such a move is that the current trend is of increasing competition and falling margins.

However, crates are one of F's main products. Profit may be falling but management need to see if F is still making positive contribution. If it is then closure should be rejected at least in the short run.

In the longer run it is recommended that F reduce its reliance on crates. This may involve a phased withdrawal but widening the product range would offer more opportunities for growth (see below).

Look for new markets for crates

Given that foreign competitors are exporting to F's domestic market, there may be scope for F to export to those foreign markets.

The main advantages of this are that it would enable F to utilise spare capacity lost over the last few years. There may be scope for F to use existing distribution channels for the crates.

The main problem is whether F can compete with foreign competition on cost once distribution costs have been incorporated. This is a major concern given F's experience in its domestic market. It is recommended that the directors assess neighbouring countries to see if the plan is viable.

Increase the development of electro-plastics and other high-technology products

F does currently sell more technologically sophisticated products and could seek to develop these further.

The main arguments in favour of this move are that

- this could be a high growth area with less competition,

- F already has a well established R&D function,

- F is ahead of the competition in the use of electro-plastics and

- F may be able to command higher margins through a strategy of differentiation.

The main problem is that R&D is currently lacking focus. This should be straightforward to rectify so this strategy is recommended.

(b)   Failure to keep shareholders informed is a serious weakness for the following reasons:

- A lack of information will make shareholders feel that their investment in F is more risky, resulting in a lower share price. The directors of F will thus be failing in their main objective of maximising shareholder value.

- At some stage F will be seeking to raise additional finance for investment. A failure to build good relationships with shareholders now will make them more reluctant to invest further. This will limit F's opportunities for raising finance.

- Any new ventures are likely to result in share price falls as shareholders will not have sufficient information to understand new proposals fully. Even if information is disclosed investors may be suspicious due to a history of a lack of details. This may discourage the directors of F from seeking new growth opportunities.

- Without regular detailed press releases, investors will place too much reliance on the published financial statements. There could thus be an over-reaction to the fall in profits and widespread selling of the shares with a corresponding fall in the share price.

- A combination of all of the above will result in F's share price being more volatile.

- Should a takeover bid be made for F, then shareholders will be less loyal to the current board and more willing to accept an offer. While a bid may be beneficial in terms of shareholder wealth, a lack of loyalty would be a concern for the directors.

- If profits continue to fall, then at some stage there may be a motion at the AGM to replace all or some of the directors. Failure to develop strong relations with major shareholders would make the likelihood of dismissal greater.

- The lack of disclosure may well be in breach of governance guidelines and relevant Stock Exchange regulations.

57 DDD BIOTECHNOLOGY (MAY 08 EXAM)

Key answer tips

Part (a) asks for a description of the SFA framework and should be straightforward for the well-prepared student.

Part (b) then requires the practical use of the framework for the 3 options identified in the scenario. A good structure with headings and subheadings is essential to keep this part from becoming long winded since only 4 marks will be available for each option's evaluation.

Part (c) requires the identification of another strategic option but it is imperative that the option chosen is evaluated using the SFA framework to keep it in line with the rest of the question.

Part (d) is finally the recommendation and can be brief for only 2 marks.

(a) The Suitability, Feasibility and Acceptability framework as used for evaluating strategic options:

Once an organisation has identified potential strategies, a decision needs to be taken as to which ones, if any should be adopted by the business. One method which can be used to evaluate a strategy is to appraise it under the three headings of suitability, acceptability and feasibility.

- **Suitability** – Management will need to know if the strategy fits with their circumstances. It will be suitable if it fits with the environment, allowing them to exploit opportunities and avoid threats. Suitability can also be assessed based on whether the strategy builds on strengths and remedies weaknesses or whether it is consistent with the mission and objectives of the business.

- **Feasibility** – A strategy is feasible if it is can actually be undertaken by the organisation. It will need to be affordable to the business (i.e. finance must exist or be easily raised in order to carry the strategy out). It will also be feasible if it uses the current resources and competences of the company.

- **Acceptability** – A strategy will be acceptable if it gives adequate returns to shareholders, has manageable risk and is not rejected by the key stakeholders in the organisation.

(b) **Evaluation of strategic options using the SFA framework**

Option 1 Allow the venture capitalists to take a 60% equity stake in the company in return for guaranteeing the cash flow until a successful drug launch is achieved.

- **Suitability** – The guaranteed cash flow will enable the company to continue to work towards their objective to launch a successful drug 2 years from now and then in most years after that for at least 6 years. This is therefore consistent with stakeholder expectations, namely those of the staff and the venture capitalists. The guarantee will assist the company in avoiding a reduction in activity caused by insufficient funds in around 9 months' time. It is therefore suitable since it remedies a weakness.

- **Feasibility** – The venture capitalists offer involves the founders being left with only 40% of the company's equity, significantly lower than their current 85% stake. The cost of the additional finance is therefore high but within the company's capabilities to offer.

- **Acceptability** – This option is likely to be unpopular amongst the other staff since any windfall they get on flotation will be reduced, the greater share going to the venture capitalists. Since all the staff, including the founders, have been working for low salaries, the floatation shares represent a significant factor in their motivation. However, they may need to accept this option since it reduces the risk of cash shortages going forward.

Option 2 Sell to a large pharmaceutical company and continue to work in research roles for them together with a few other staff.

- **Suitability** – This option will also remedy the cash flow weakness since the scientists will have the pharmaceutical companies' resources to draw on. It will not however, allow DDD to continue to pursue the development of innovative drugs; DDD will be 'swallowed' up by the bigger company which is not consistent with their objectives of successful drug launch and flotation. This option does not appear to be suitable.

- **Feasibility** – The current resources and competences of DDD will be underused by this strategy with not all staff being employed by the purchasing company. The strategy is also likely to be considered too expensive in that all the hard work put into DDD's products to date will be lost to the bigger company. It is therefore not feasible.

- **Acceptability** – The staff will resist this option since it threatens job losses. However, ultimately it will be the founders' decision as they hold 85% of the equity. As a new and innovative company very close to a successful drug launch, the idea of selling out so early (and so probably for a relatively low price) is likely to be unacceptable to them as well.

Option 3 Enter into a merger with a similar biotechnology company which has one upcoming drug launch.

- **Suitability** – There is no guarantee that the merged company will have the cash flow to continue DDD's work. The partner organisation has yet to launch a successful drug and the launch it has planned for 6 months time cannot be guaranteed due to the nature of the industry and the extensive clinical trials through which any new drug must pass. There seems to be few synergies obtained by going ahead with the merger. Any staff cost savings will be minimal given the low salaries paid.

- **Feasibility** – It is unlikely that DDD can afford this merger to go ahead. The combined organisation will require far more resources to operate, especially since the other companies drugs (apart from the imminent launch) appear to be at a much earlier stage of development to those in DDD.

- **Acceptability** – Again the staff will resist since this option is likely to bring job losses. The risks that DDD faces would seem to be heightened by this option, cash is likely to run out even quicker in the merged organisation.

In conclusion, only refinancing with the venture capitalist (option 1) seems to satisfy the criteria for strategic evaluation set out in the suitability, feasibility, acceptability framework.

(c) **Additional Strategic Option**

DDD could also consider scaling down investment on drugs at the early stages of development and concentrate on the one (or ones) most likely to reach the market in the shortest length of time. The business may then be able to survive on its cash reserves for 2 years (i.e. up until a possible commercial launch) rather than 9 months if current activity levels are maintained.

- **Suitability** – This option will allow DDD to prioritise its opportunities and still achieve a successful drug launch in 2 years time. The shortage of cash which is the main weakness will not be remedied but its impact will be minimised. There is a risk that opportunities may be missed on other drugs which have their investment cut but, this may just have a suspensory effect, as when a successful launch is achieved, investment can recommence.

- **Feasibility** – The founders of DDD will need to carry out careful analysis of their development portfolio in order to identify those drugs which are least sustainable. With 12 drugs in the research phase of development, it should be possible to streamline the portfolio.

- **Acceptability** – The innovative nature of DDD will make this option unpopular amongst staff. It is essential that drugs are developed continuously by pharmaceutical companies and the owners (including the VC's) may find any scaling down unacceptable.

(d) **Recommendation**

The owners of the company hold 85% of the equity. Since the speculative nature of the industry rules out bank loans on commercial terms, the owners must look to their equity share to realise the funds needed to guarantee cash flow in DDD.

They should therefore attempt to negotiate with the venture capitalists. The guarantee of cash flow until a successful launch may be secured for a slightly lower equity stake that will be more acceptable to the stakeholders.

58   JKL (NOV 10 EXAM)

Key answer tips

Section (a) should be a very simple requirement, asking for the advantages and disadvantages of organic versus acquisition growth. Be aware of the need to apply your points to the scenario. If you have just created a list of generic points, you are unlikely to score well.

Part (b) asked you to recommend what JKL could do to avoid the problems it has faced with the acquisition of LMN. The easiest way to handle this style of question is to first identify what the problems with the LMN acquisition were and then suggest improvements to fix these issues.

Part (c) looks at change agents. This has been a relatively popular examinable area. As well as defining what a change agent is, make sure you answer the question by looking at how having one would help JKL through the acquisition process.

(a) (i) **Organic growth**

JKL has chosen in its strategy to grow organically. It has been influenced in this choice because of its recent experience with an acquisition which resulted in failure. It could be argued that organic growth is less risky than growth by acquisition. This is substantiated by the empirical evidence which demonstrates in the majority of cases when a company is acquired, it is the acquired company that benefits financially to the detriment of the acquiring company. Organic growth is usually achieved by reinvestment of profit which is then applied to the development of the company's strengths. Therefore, organic growth will happen at a pace commensurate with the organisation's ability to absorb and benefit from it. However, if organic growth is achieved by reinvestment then the speed of growth will be constrained to an extent by the amount of profits available for reinvestment. Organic growth will be suitable for a company where the culture is one of gradualism rather than radicalism: Evolution rather than Revolution.

(ii) **Acquisition**

In many ways, an evaluation of growth by acquisition is the opposite of organic growth. Growth by acquisition can be fast, radical and transformational. It can offer opportunities to a company which otherwise would not be available. Thus, an acquisition target may have unique competences and capabilities, for example, it may own patents, licences and commercial and brand franchises, which are otherwise unavailable. Acquisition gives JKL the possibility of eliminating a competitor. However, the biggest downside to any acquisition is the empirical evidence which demonstrates that most acquisitions do not benefit the acquirer.

Examiner's comments

This question was well answered by most candidates. Most answers demonstrated a sound knowledge of organic growth and acquisitions and made a reasonable attempt at applying this to the scenario.

A number of answers did fail to adequately apply the theory to the scenario and some answers merely stated that the advantages of organic growth were the disadvantages of acquisitions and vice versa (e.g. a disadvantage of organic growth is that it is slow and an advantage of acquisition is that it is fast, or acquisitions are expensive and organic growth is less costly). This was awarded few marks.

A number of candidates also failed to correctly address the issues of moving into France, in that they failed to realise that some of the problems, such as language barriers, were exactly the same, whichever option of expansion was chosen.

Common Errors

*   Theoretical answers with limited application to JKL

*   Stating that the advantages of one method were the disadvantages of the other and vice versa

---

(b)   (1)   **JKL and LMN had very different accounting and control systems and these had not been satisfactorily combined**

Although at the start of the acquisition process the accounting and control systems of the two companies will be different they must be made to converge as soon as possible. This is necessary to preserve the integrity of the published financial statements, for example, it would not be acceptable for the two companies to value their stocks on different bases. If managers are subjected to different control systems in the two companies, for example, JKL pays a bonus if a manager meets her budget targets but XYZ does not, there would be motivational problems if this continued. JKL would need to review the two systems, identify the differences and plan for their convergence. The change agent could facilitate this with the help of the Management Accountant.

(2)   **JKL and LMN had very different corporate cultures and this had posed many difficulties which were not resolved**

In any acquisition JKL will encounter a different culture to its own in the target company. JKL needs to survey and explicitly recognise the cultural differences and categorise those which are vital for the success of the acquisition. It should then outline an operational strategy to reconcile or accommodate these differences. Achievement against the plan should be regularly reviewed. This process of reconciliation and accommodation could be managed by the change agent.

(3)   **JKL had used an autocratic management style to manage the acquisition and this had been resented by the employees of both companies**

An autocratic management style implies that there is no delegation of responsibility: everything is driven from the centre. JKL's use of this style had led to resentment and this, in turn, would probably lead to resistance. There are a number of alternative management styles that JKL could use, for example, participation, negotiation and facilitation. JKL should use a contingency approach and not assume that one management style will be suitable for all situations and all times.

Examiner's comments

This question was reasonably well answered, particularly by those candidates who correctly identified that their answer should be focused upon the three difficulties encountered by JKL as presented in the scenario. Most candidates made a reasonable attempt at identifying and discussing a good range of actions to prevent these three problems from arising again in future acquisitions. However, those answers which failed to focus upon the three difficulties identified in the scenario were largely not of a pass standard.

A number of candidates incorrectly took the approach of presenting a list of generic change management activities which should be undertaken, with little or no emphasis at all upon the question actually asked. Again, candidates are advised to read the question requirements more carefully

Common Errors

- Brief, theoretical answers based upon the change management process

- Incorrect approach taken – not focused upon the three difficulties identified in the scenario

(c)   A change agent is a person, or a group of people, who help an organisation to achieve strategic change. In the matter of JKL acquiring a French company, XYZ the change agent could carry out the following useful tasks:

(1)   **Define any possible difficulties presented by the proposed acquisition**

One obvious difficulty presented by the proposed acquisition consists of the potential problems in communication between the two companies as none of JKL's staff speak fluent French or are able to correspond in French. XYZ is in a similar position as only a small number of its staff speak English fluently: none are able to correspond in English. The change agent would be able to highlight this difficulty for the attention of JKL's management and to point to the areas of communication which are likely to cause the most problems: for example, phone conversations may be most problematic because of their ephemeral nature, e-mails a lesser problem because of their more permanent nature.

(2)   **Examine what causes the problem and diagnose how this can be overcome**

In this particular example, the change agent would have no difficulty in diagnosing the cause of the problem: it is the lack of complementary language skills in both companies. The solution would be to increase the language skills in both English and French in both companies.

The more creative role for the change agent in this situation is to propose ways in which this problem could be overcome. Depending on the background of the change agent he/she may have to seek expert advice from a linguist experienced in both the English and French languages. There are a variety of ways to achieve the desired solution that the change agent could propose. One possible way would be for JKL to employ a language tutor to work with both companies.

(3)   **Arrive at alternative solutions**

In order to give the management of JKL some alternative ways of overcoming the lack of relevant language skills in the two companies the change agent could suggest alternative solutions, such as:

- JKL could specify that all new appointments at senior management level are bi-lingual in French and English.

- JKL could use the English speaking members of staff at XYZ to coach their counterparts in JKL in the French language.

- JKL could send its senior managers at both companies to external language training.

(4)   **Implement solutions**

Once the management of JKL, after consultation with the change agent, have arrived at their preferred solution it will need to be implemented. The change agent could usefully take the lead in this process as he/she will be very well-informed about the preferred solution and the reasons why it has been chosen. If JKL's chosen solution is to employ a language tutor to work with both companies the change agent could draft the job specification and assist with the recruitment and induction of the tutor.

(5)   **Transmit the learning process that allows the organisation to deal with change on an ongoing basis by itself in the future**

The change agent should document the learning process and discussions which JKL has undergone whilst resolving the lack of foreign language skills in both companies. This experience should be disseminated throughout both companies and the change agent should take the lead in this by organising workshops for managers and information sessions for employees.

Examiner's comments

This question was generally well answered. Most candidates discussed a range of actions that would be appropriate for a change agent as part of the successful acquisition process. There was also evidence of some good application to JKL. However, some candidates failed to the answer the question set, focusing incorrectly upon listing and discussing the skills and attributes of a change agent. Again, candidates are reminded to read the question requirements carefully.

Common Errors

- Incorrect emphasis upon skills of a change agent rather than the actions he/she should undertake

---

59   CCC CONGLOMERATE (MAY 08 EXAM)

Key answer tips

Section (a) asks you to **explain** a term. A simple definition will not be enough to achieve 3 marks

Both sections in part (b) ask you to **evaluate**. This means give pros and cons, or both sides of an argument as well as a conclusion. For example in (b) (i) what evidence is there to support the comments? Is it reasonable? Have the board destroyed value?

Equally in (b) (ii) the pros and cons of the suggestion need to be presented and its reasonableness assessed.

Part (c) has two distinct parts. The first is to identify and evaluate methods of disposal. A list will not suffice given the use of the word evaluate again. Each method must be appraised for suitability. The second part is to make a recommendation of an appropriate method for CCC to use. This part of your answer needs to be clearly headed up as a recommendation and should flow from the evaluation already carried out in the first part.

(a)   **Conglomerate Diversification**

Conglomerate diversification may also be referred to as unrelated diversification and describes the expansion strategy of a company into a totally new area with no links to its current operations. The only synergy lies with the management skills, since it has a single board of directors. In CCC the areas of construction, engineering and real estate may be viewed as having distinct products and markets, and so CCC could be described as a conglomerate.

Ansoff's directions for growth model characterises conglomerate diversification as launching 'new products' into 'new markets'. As such it may be seen as the most risky of Ansoff's strategies. Management are unable to take advantage of operational synergies across subsidiaries and each division may therefore have no advantage over a much smaller firm.

Conglomerate diversification is often viewed as unattractive to investors who may wish to diversify their own share portfolio by investing in several companies without this being done for them by a corporation.

(b)   (i)   **Evaluation of Institutional Investors Comments**

The Institutional Investors have commented that the board have 'destroyed value'. They are likely to have reached this view because the stock market valuation of CCC seems low at $1,000 million when compared to the possible combined values of the three separate divisions.

Using the industry PE ratio's given and the previous year's earnings, the divisional values would be:

Construction and building $50m × 8 = $400m

Engineering and machinery $20m × 13 = $260m

Real estate $30m × 23 = $690m

Combined value $400m + $260m + $690m = $1,350m, considerably higher than CCC's market value of $1,000m.

However, it should be noted that these PE ratios are for companies within the relevant industries and not divisions. The divisions of CCC may not make these earning figures as standalone entities. The support in raising capital from group headquarters for example may be expensive to obtain independently.

It is therefore difficult to conclude that the board has definitely destroyed value, although it is clear why the investors hold this view.

(ii)   **Evaluation of institutional investor suggestions**

The institutional investors are suggesting:

1   Disposal of the real estate division

2   Closure of group headquarters and relocation of the board and treasury functions to one of the divisional headquarters.

The shareholders appear to be suggesting that both actions are taken, however taking each one in turn:

The suitability feasibility acceptability (SFA) framework could also have been used here.

Disposal of the real estate division

Disposal of the real estate division would raise a significant amount of cash (possibly in the region of $690m, see i) above) however it would also limit the growth prospects of the overall organisation.

Although not the most profitable division at the moment, the real estate arm of the company has provided profit growth of over 20% p.a. in the three years since it was formed and the management believe this to be at least sustainable. This level of growth is far higher than the other two divisions.

Assuming growth of 20% per year, in 3 years time the division could be earning in excess of $50m. The other 2 divisions seem to pose fewer risks however. The construction division is described as 'mature...with modest growth' and the engineering division offers growth of around 10% per annum. The lack of 'fit' of real estate with the risk profile of the organisation could be an argument to dispose of it and stick to the core competences of the company.

Closure of group headquarters

Closure of group headquarters will lead to significant cost savings in the longer term. The premises will presumably be sold and the staff (apart from the directors) given redundancy or relocated. If the board and treasury function can reasonably be located at one of the other divisions then this would seem like a feasible suggestion.

Currently, the headquarters are funded by a management charge on the divisions which will be considerably less should this go ahead.

As a key stakeholder in CCC, the institutional shareholders should expect their objectives to be considered when the company is devising its strategy. Their suggestions are linked to a desire for a large, one off dividend.

It is important that the directors consider the views of the other shareholders, who between them hold 80% of the company's shares (the institutional shareholders in question hold 20%). They may agree with the board that the strategy to date has served their best interests and not wish to see these changes made. They may have a different attitude to risk and prefer to see CCC keep the high risk real estate division.

In addition, there are other stakeholder groups to consider, for example the employees who may be at risk of losing their jobs.

(c) **Methods available to the Board for the disposal of the real estate division**

Sale to another company

The division could be sold to another company, for example a competitor in the real estate sector. The difficulty with this method will be reaching the correct price for the strategic business unit. A purchase based on share price is not possible and if CCC were to sell the division on the basis of the PE ratio valuation given in a) above, they may find potential buyers expect a significant discount since the division is not a listed company.

Any valuation based on the assets within the retail division is likely to be far too low, not taking into account the 'value' which has been added by the management team and the overall stewardship of CCC. The institutional shareholders may therefore be unhappy with this method of sale.

However, given the success of the real estate business, its presence in a fast growing market and the skills of the management team, it is likely that a competitor could be found to buy it, and in fact a competitive bidding situation may materialise.

This method is likely to lead to job losses as the purchasing company seeks to gain operational synergies, sharing resources across the enlarged organisation.

Management Buy Out

The real estate divisional management are described as 'the most dynamic management team within CCC'. They believe that the strong growth of the division can be maintained and even surpassed and therefore they may be interested in purchasing the division themselves.

If management do not have adequate personal wealth to do this, the success of the division is likely to allow them to attract investors and put together a leveraged buyout, with the bulk of the finance provided by a venture capitalist firm for example.

If the board does propose an MBO to the management team, the team will have a good idea of the divisions' value and may expect a favourable price in return for all of their hard work to date.

The board's responsibility is however to the shareholders and they must obtain the best deal possible on their behalf. This is particularly the case since the sale of the division is in response to shareholder calls for a one-off dividend. If the board are perceived to sell the division too cheaply to the management team, this could cause problems with future shareholder relationships.

Demerger

The real estate division could be incorporated and split off as a standalone company. The shares in the division could be allocated to CCC's existing shareholders in proportion to their existing shareholdings.

If CCC believe that head office no longer adds any value to the division, and its value is being 'hidden' within the overall conglomerate, then this is an appropriate course of action. The institutional shareholders could decide whether to sell or retain their shares in the new entity. If the growth prospects are as strong as the divisional managers seem to believe, there is a possibility the share price of the new entity will fast outstrip that of its old parent company.

Recommendation

Given the growth achieved by management in the 3 years since this division was formed, and their dynamic characteristics, the ethical thing to do would be to give them the option of an MBO, ensuring that independent valuations are sought and a fair price achieved for all of CCC's shareholders.

If this is not a feasible option, then the demerger option would seem the most commercially sound, and would give the institutional shareholders the windfall they demand.

60   Y TELECOMMUNICATIONS (MAY 09 EXAM)

Key answer tips

Part (a) asks you to simply explain the characteristics of a joint venture and as such should represent easy marks to the well prepared candidate.

In part (b) it is the benefits **to country C** of a joint venture which must be considered. Candidates who offer general benefits of joint ventures will not score well. The key to success here (and in part c) is to use the information in the scenario. What were the government trying to achieve through deregulation? Will they get it via a joint venture with C?

Part (c) asks for an **evaluation** of the risks that Y should consider. The verb 'to evaluate' means you must try and signal the importance of each risk rather than just describe it. Answers should be structured around the verb and not just be general drawbacks or problems with the JV for Y.

In summary, a straight forward question, definitely one to 'choose' in section B.

(a)   **Characteristics of a joint venture**

A joint venture is a method by which firms collaborate to jointly enter a market.

The partners in a joint venture form a separate company in which each holds an equity stake. Since this is a formal arrangement, a contract will need to be drawn up (called 'Heads of Agreement') to govern rights, responsibilities, dispute resolution procedures and any other relevant formal issues.

Usually management is provided by the parties to the agreement and is able to draw on the expertise within each organisation.

There are two possible joint venture structures which can be adopted. In the first, all of the companies play an active role in the operation of the company formed. In the other structure, one company provides expertise whilst others provide equity only. This second structure is more common in large, expensive projects. For example a consortium of banks may provide funding to build a tunnel connecting two countries under water.

The joint venture suggested between Y and the local company in country C is likely to involve both companies playing an active role in the new enterprise.

(b)   **Benefits of a joint venture to Country C**

Y is unlikely to have become a 'successful and well established international telecommunications company' without using the latest communications technology. A joint venture between one of the four telecommunications companies in C and Y will enable the country to access this technology, thus satisfying the government's main objective in opening up the market to foreign investment.

The national telecommunication company in C was 'using old equipment' and 'in need of considerable capital investment'. With Y's expertise and resources, the telecommunications infrastructure in C is likely to improve significantly.

The government of C is under pressure to ensure that the country benefits from any foreign investment. The joint venture structure will ensure that part ownership of new infrastructure resides within country C.

The joint venture will potentially give the residents of Country C access to jobs and training opportunities. Y is a growing company with a history of successful expansion and the residents of C, a developing country, may experience a significant improvement in their living standards through access to employment.

The residents of C will gain access to more sophisticated, reliable telecommunications services, much more quickly than they would if the joint venture did not go ahead. An acquisition of one of the four companies by Y would be slower, since Y would need to learn about the market.

The stakeholders who put up 'strong resistance' to the privatisation, may be happier and less likely to protest against a joint venture which retains some of the ownership of a new company in the hands of members of the public and institutional investors of Country C.

In summary, a joint venture with Y will allow Country C to share the risks involved in expanding and modernising their telecommunications industry with an established and successful company, only investing a proportion of the equity and gaining access to expertise as well as capital.

(c) **Evaluation of risks that Y should consider before entering into the Joint Venture**

Disputes over the amount of effort being put in, the allocation of partners' costs and the division of rewards

Company Y is clearly the most knowledgeable partner with respect to recent technology and market expansion. There is a risk that Y' stakeholders feel they are putting all of the effort in to the venture, paying for the infrastructure (the local company requires capital investment) and yet not getting all the rewards. If the company is successful, part of the profit will of course go to the shareholders of the local company.

This risk may however not be significant if Y's stakeholders recognise the benefits that quick access to country C will bring.

Possibility that partners will gain confidential information about each other which may be used to elsewhere or if the venture breaks down

Country C will gain a lot from a potential joint venture with Y. At the present time, it has four telecommunications companies with limited resources and out of date equipment. If Y's expertise is used to make the joint venture with one company a success, there is a significant chance the other companies will also benefit through monitoring the Joint Venture and perhaps paying for access to the new infrastructure.

The government of C may be particularly keen for this to happen and so not insist on confidentiality of operations. Whilst this may be beneficial for Country C, it would not benefit Y. If the venture breaks down, Y may have 'given away' significant knowledge about how to operate a successful telecommunications company, again with no benefit received.

This represents a significant risk to Y, particularly since neither party in the joint venture has experience of such an arrangement.

Disputes over operational matters such as the use of trademarks, pay levels and approach to markets

The management of Y will have a set method of overseas expansion, despite this being their first potential joint venture. Operational matters may be questioned by the management of the local telecommunications company who will not be used to competitive strategies and may find them 'over the top' or 'aggressive'.

This risk will need to be managed by Y to reduce its potential impact. Management strategies will need to include the education of local managers and communication, so that they feel part of decision making.

The risk of disruption to operations

There has been strong resistance to the privatisation of the telecommunications market in Country C. Those stakeholders who protested against allowing foreign investment in may cause problems for the new joint venture, seeing it as foreign investment rather than an opportunity for Country C to partake in economic growth.

There may be boycotts or physical attempts to prevent improvements of infrastructure. It should be noted however, that potential disruption would also be a risk of an outright purchase of a Country C telecommunications company.

The risk of failure

Ultimately, there is a risk the joint venture will fail, partly due to the materialisation of risks evaluated above.

Y has never taken part in a strategic alliance and will need to be considerate of their local partners, who may pull out if they perceive Y to be 'taking over' and treating this venture as one of their usual acquisitions.

A detailed 'heads of agreement' should reduce imbalance between the partners and make the venture less likely to fail.

IMPLEMENTATION OF STRATEGIC PLANS AND PERFORMANCE EVALUATION (30%)

THE PERFORMANCE MEASUREMENT MIX

61   ZZZ (NOV 11 EXAM)

Key answer tips

While it is split into three requirements, this past exam question links together to ask for a comprehensive analysis of ZZZ's performance management approach.

Part (a) asks you to evaluate the performance management system for H. As the question asks for an evaluation, you would need to ensure that you considered both good and bad points of the current system.

Any drawbacks you identify in (a) should help you to answer (b) – suggested improvements that ZZZ could make to its performance management system. Don't forget to justify your suggestions!

Finally, part (c) asked you to examine possible performance measures that could be used to help ZZZ see if it is likely to maintain preferred supplier status with MMM. Anything reasonable should have scored here but, as in (b), you needed to ensure that you justified your suggestions.

(a)   H has the following three objectives:

1   **Maintain ZZZ's preferred supplier status with MMM:**

In order to achieve this objective ZZZ has to achieve a number of different things:

(i)   ZZZ is guaranteed £2 million worth of business each week. This is the minimum, so that it could be that some weeks MMM wants a greater number of components. H has to ensure that ZZZ has the production capacity and flexibility to meet MMM's demand.

There is nothing explicit within ZZZ's performance management system (PMS) that addresses this aspect of MMM's requirements.

(ii)   MMM insists that ZZZ's prices will reduce by 4% year-on-year.

There is nothing explicit within ZZZ's (PMS) that addresses this aspect of MMM's requirements.

(iii)   ZZZ will lose its preferred supplier status if there are two reports of any of its components failing when they have been delivered to MMM.

There is nothing explicit within ZZZ's (PMS) that addresses this aspect of MMM's requirements.

2   **Keep ZZZ's expenditure within the limits set each year in the budget which is approved by its Board of Directors:**

H's PMS is based on budgetary control. Quarterly reports are prepared showing budget and actual expenditure. However the delay in the reporting system seems to militate against control and the operational managers are only shown aggregate amounts in the cost centres. H believes that the details of ZZZ's finances should not be shown to the operational managers. The operational managers are not involved in capital expenditure decisions for the same reason.

Therefore the PMS is too aggregated, too late and too restricted in its reporting scope to contribute much to the achievement of this objective.

3   **Develop the management skills of ZZZ's 32 operational managers:**

As alluded to in 2 above, the 32 operational managers are not involved in a meaningful way with ZZZ's budgetary control, neither are they involved in capital expenditure decisions. This would not be the case in most organisations and far from the PMS developing their management skills, it inhibits them.

Summary

With regards to all three of H's objectives, the PMS contributes little or nothing to the achievement of H's objectives. In these respects ZZZ's PMS is ineffective.

(b)   ZZZ's current performance management system produces three-monthly variances reports. It seems unlikely that these are sufficiently timely to contribute to effective control. This could be improved by making these reports more frequent; at a minimum, monthly. Some variance reporting might be appropriately done in 'real-time'.

ZZZ has 2,000 cost centres for which it produces reports. This could be improved by ZZZ reviewing the number of cost centres and future analysis could be assisted if this number was reduced. If H prioritised his cost centre review activities, this would make better use of his time than by trying to examine all of the current 2,000 cost centres. He could prioritise the cost centres by the size of their expenditures and also by only looking at exceptional items.

Currently, there is no obvious way of ensuring that the results of the cost centre reviews can influence future behaviour as ZZZ's operational managers are not shown the variance reports. The operational managers should be shown the results of the review of variances which could then form the basis of feedback and feedforward reporting and action. This would result in ZZZ being able to learn from past performance and so influence future performance. Unless the feedback loop is completed, control is uninformed and performance is not being managed.

ZZZ could widen the scope of its performance management system by reporting on non-financial aspects, for example, quality and reliability.

(c)   The following aspects of ZZZ's performance contribute towards the maintenance of its preferred supplier status and are suitable for the formulation of performance measures. In all cases regular reporting of achievement against these measures could demonstrate progress.

Weekly guaranteed minimum amount of business of £2 million

ZZZ has to be able to supply MMM with at least £2 million worth of components each week with the implication that some weeks MMM will require more than this. Therefore, a performance measure dealing with 'Reliability of Production' or 'Production Flexibility' or 'Production Achievement' would be appropriate.

Year-on-year reduction of 4% in the prices

This implies that ZZZ will have to reduce its costs year-on-year. Therefore, a performance measure relating to 'Cost Reduction' or 'Cost Improvement' would assist ZZZ in meeting the price reduction target.

Just-In-Time production system

ZZZ needs to ensure that it can continually successfully interface with MMM's JIT system. Therefore, a performance measure relating to 'Timeliness of Delivery' or 'Achievement' against MMM's demands would address MMM's requirements.

Component failure

If ZZZ's components fail on two occasions it will lose its preferred supplier status. Therefore, a performance measure covering 'Product Quality' or 'Product Reliability' or 'Product Durability' would be useful.

Examiner's note: more examples of performance measures have been given than asked for in the requirement to assist teachers and candidates. The candidates did not have to use the same titles for their performance measures but were given appropriate credit for performance measures that capture the sense of MMM's demands.

Examiner's comments

This question was not well answered. It is disappointing once again to see how many candidates appear to not understand what a performance measure is. Many candidates' answers were focused upon activities or processes such as 'undertaking customer satisfaction surveys' or 'introduce a balanced scorecard' which are clearly not performance measures. Many candidates also failed to focus their measures directly on maintaining the preferred supplier status and instead provided general measures of performance such as ROCE or profitability. These were not directly related to the requirement and therefore not relevant. This continues to be an area of weakness for candidates and needs to be addressed.

Common Errors

- Including processes and activities NOT performance measures

- Measures not relating to preferred supplier status

---

62 RCH HOTELS (MAY 10 EXAM)

Key answer tips

Part (a) is a slightly unusual question that examines how well you know the JSW model of strategy. Remember that JSW stated that each stage in strategic development depends on the other two stages.

Part (b) should be a straightforward requirement, asking for identification of CSFs and their appropriate KPIs. There are a large number of possible answers here – anything sensible will get credit. Make sure your CSFs relate to TDM, not the RCH hotel chain.

(a) **Explanation of why implementation is included in the JSW model**

Strategic implementation is the final stage of JSW's model of strategy. By the time a company has reached this stage, it has analysed its environment and selected a strategy that will best suit its objectives.

However, just because a business has carefully decided on which strategy it wishes to follow does not mean that the strategy will be accomplished successfully. The strategic implementation stage is designed to maximise the chances of this happening.

To do this, implementation involves:

- Formulation of detailed plans and budgets
- Target setting for KPIs
- Monitoring and control

These allow a business to identify the overall resources required for the project. It will also enable it to plan ahead and identify and solve any possible problems that may arise with its chosen strategy.

KPIs will allow a manager to continually check whether a new strategy is accomplishing its aims and, if it is not, to either take corrective action or abandon it.

(b) (i) **Identification of four CSFs appropriate for TDM**

- Critical success factors for TDM may include:
- Employee satisfaction – given that TDM is in a service industry, staff are likely to be key to its products and high levels of staff turnover are a concern.
- Course quality – given the competitive nature of the market, it is vital that TDM continues to offer appropriate courses that will attract students.
- Student satisfaction – in order to be successful, TDM must ensure students are pleased with their courses. If not, they may move to alternative suppliers and may dissuade other students from using TDM.
- Strong financial results – after the takeover, TDM will need to make sufficient profits to maximise the wealth of RCH shareholders.

(ii) **Recommended key performance indicators to support each of the CSFs**

TDM's performance can be measured by establishing key performance indicators for each CSF and measuring actual achievements against them.

Employee satisfaction

Number of staff leaving each period

This is the most direct measure of whether staff members are satisfied with their roles within the business. TDM is experiencing increasingly high staff turnover, which may mean they are losing valuable, skilled members of staff.

Sickness/absence per staff member per month

De-motivated or unhappy staff can tend to take more time off work due to sickness. TDM should monitor this as an indirect measure of staff satisfaction, especially as it is likely to cause disruption to courses.

Course quality

Pass rates compared to national average

TDM currently achieve exam pass rates that are comparable to the national average. Given the competitive nature of the market they operate in, this is likely to be something prospective students use as a way of choosing a tuition provider.

Number of students choosing not to complete the course compared to average

If a course is of poor quality (either poor materials or tuition), students may choose not to complete the course – either ceasing to study with TDM or moving onto an alternative course. If the number of students doing this is above average, it should be investigated and targets put in place to bring it down to average.

Student satisfaction

Percentage student approval rating

TDM could give students a questionnaire at the end of each course. This could ask them about how they rate the course, the tutor and the course material. This could be invaluable for identifying problem areas that the business needs to resolve. This would be likely to please RCH given their focus on customer research.

Percentage of students going on to further studies with TDM

TDM offers a range of courses, including degrees at both Bachelor and Masters level. If students feel that TDM have provided a good service, they will be more likely to take their studies further with the organisation.

Strong financial results

Market share

While TDM currently has the largest market share in its segment, large numbers of competitors are continually entering the market. If market share begins to fall, it will have a damaging effect on the profitability of the business.

Profit targets

Given that RCH has purchased TDM with the specific intention of increasing profitability, it is likely that they will have specific targets in mind for the business that TDM will need to work to achieve. For example, TDM may need to measure profit margins to ensure they meet the targets set by RCH.

63   DLC (NOV 10 EXAM)

Key answer tips

Part (a) asks for the usefulness and limitations of DLC's control system. DLC's controls are entirely financial and rely on budgets and ROCE calculations. While this financial focus can have benefits, remember that controls should monitor all important areas of the business. For DLC this would include innovation and customer service, which are currently ignored.

In part (b) you are asked to advise how non-financial performance measures could help DLC. The clearest way to discuss this would be to look at CSFs and KPIs. This would involve not only discussing what CSFs and KPIs are, but also illustrating how they would work for DLC itself. Try to give some examples!

Finally, part (c) looked at Customer Profitability Analysis. To answer this successfully you will need to have a good working knowledge of this model. Again, while a definition would potentially get you some credit here, it should be tied in to the circumstances of X and DLC to score well.

(a)   **DLC's control system's usefulness**

In order for DLC to operate a traditional budgetary control system it must engage in forecasting and, following on from this, planning. This then results in a system in which budgeted expenditure is compared to actual expenditure. The system imposes discipline within DLC as regards its future plans and also in the collection of data regarding actual expenditure and the monthly reporting thereon. In order to produce DLC's budgets there will be internal consultation and discussion which should result in a coherent and co-ordinated operating plan. The targets inherent within this system will also provide a degree of motivation for DLC's budget managers. DLC also computes its Return On Capital Employed (ROCE) monthly. ROCE attempts to capture the totality of the business's performance and provides a view of the effectiveness of DLC's investments.

DLC's control system's limitations

Traditional control systems have been widely criticised in recent years. Budgeting is frequently done on a 'Historic Cost plus inflation' basis which means that it is backward-looking. It is not clear how frequently, if at all, DLC revises its budget estimates, for example, by use of quarterly plans. Neither does DLC appear to flex its budget for actual levels of activity nor take account of seasonal variations in expenditure patterns. Although DLC reports on its sales achievement against budget in aggregate, given the size of DLC's revenue, $24 million, this is unlikely to yield sufficient information for detailed management control.

X relies heavily on the use of ROCE to reflect DLC's performance. However, a number of flaws are manifest within ROCE. It is arguable that ROCE is not suitable for an organisation like DLC which is not yet mature. DLC will have had start-up costs which would depress ROCE but which will not recur. Therefore, historic comparisons of ROCE achievement are liable to suffer distortion. Another problem arises because of DLC's substantial level of capital investment. New capital investment will also depress ROCE which might restrict managers' willingness to invest. However, this would be a mistake as DLC requires substantial and continued capital investment to be successful.

DLC has no system for reporting upon the two critical areas of Technological Innovation and Customer Service. This is a serious omission as these two areas are the basis of DLC's success. They, therefore, should be reported upon explicitly, regularly and contemporaneously. Although ROCE reflects DCL's success in the areas of Technological Innovation and Customer Service it too is aggregated and probably too late to act as a control measure.

The final omission concerns DLC's customers. DLC is now too large for X to know everything about every customer and contract and she has recognised that this is a weakness. It would be expected that a company like DLC would have systems to report contract and customer profitability. DLC's lack of these is a weakness.

Examiner's comments

This question was reasonably well answered by most candidates. Most candidates focused correctly upon the usefulness and limitations and recognised that, on balance, there were significantly more weaknesses in the current control system than strengths. Some candidates' answers were over focused upon lengthy discussions of budgets and ROCE, with limited emphasis upon application to the scenario. Some candidates also failed to recognise the less obvious weaknesses such as the lack of control measures relating to the key success factors and a lack of reporting on customers.

Common Errors

- Too much emphasis on theoretical discussions on budgets and ROCE with limited application to the scenario

- Answers which were too brief and only focused upon budgets and/or ROCE

- No discussion of the weakness relating to having no non-financial performance measures and no measures relating to key success factors and revenue segmentation

---

(b) Although X has not articulated a formal strategy she has an implicit one based upon the following objectives: expansion within the same market/business segment, personal enrichment and the provision of secure well paid jobs for DLC's staff. It is also implicit that DLC will endeavour to achieve these objectives by excellence in Technological Innovation and Customer Service. As DLC's control system is exclusively a financial one it is unable to capture the richness of DLC's business experience and enable it to maintain and improve its performance in the two areas critical for its success.

X would, therefore, be assisted in the achievement of her strategic objectives by formalising excellence in Technological Innovation and Customer Service as Critical Success Factors (CSFs) and then developing Key Performance Indicators (KPIs) which would indicate the extent to which the CSFs are being achieved. KPI's can be both financial and non-financial: a range of non-financial KPI's could provide a creative measure of feedback about DLC's performance which is not currently available from the financial control system.

The KPI's should be reported upon within a time-scale which is appropriate to the parameter which is being measured. Thus, for example, it may be appropriate to report against a KPI for customer complaints (which would be supporting the CSF excellent Customer Service) daily. However, a KPI measuring innovation in the installation time for a telephone exchange (which would be supporting the CSF excellent Technological Innovation) would be more appropriately reported upon against a longer timescale. The KPI's should not be too numerous otherwise X is likely to be overwhelmed by them: she should also continually keep their usefulness under review. If DLC is continually meeting or beating a KPI it may be appropriate to discard this one and introduce a new one so that X may make the best use of her time.

X has acknowledged that the lack of control information which she has about sales is a weakness. Non-financial performance measures could address this weakness and contribute towards X achieving her strategic objectives. KPI's could also be constructed for sales performance as they are for CSF's.

Examiner's comments

This question was generally not well answered. Too many candidates focused their answers upon discussion relating to the advantages and disadvantages of non-financial performance measures. Others provided lengthy discussions of the Balanced Scorecard, which was not required. Other candidates provided lists of possible non-financial performance measures for the two key success factors, but again, this was not asked for in the requirement.

Candidates were specifically asked HOW the measures could help DLC, not to provide a list of examples of performance measures. Candidates must make sure that they read the question requirements carefully and only answer the question that has been set.

Common Errors

- Discussion of the balanced scorecard with only limited application to the scenario
- Lists of non-financial performance measures which were unexplained

---

(c) Currently X does not know the profit which DLC makes from each customer. As the annual revenue in 2010 is $24 million, this is too large for one person to know every detail about it as she did when the business started.

One of X's aims is for her business to continue expanding within the same market/business segment: it is implicit that she wants this expansion to be profitable. In the present circumstances X is not aware which of her current customers are profitable and which ones unprofitable. When DLC expands there is a risk that some new customers will also prove to be unprofitable ones and, possibly, that she might turn away profitable business.

Customer Profitability Analysis (CPA) is defined by CIMA as the 'Analysis of the revenue streams and service costs associated with specific customers or customer groups'. If X introduces CPA to her company it will reveal which customers are profitable and, therefore, should be retained and nurtured. Conversely, CPA will suggest which customers DLC should consider ceasing to do business with. As X wants to expand her business within the same market segment CPA could give insights as to the attractiveness of this segment and guidance as to which new customers and contracts she should accept. CPA could also help X to evaluate whether other market segments may provide more attractive expansion prospects in the future.

Examiner's comments

This question was reasonably well answered. Most candidates provided an adequate definition of Customer Profitability Analysis and were able to apply their discussions of CPA directly to DLC.

Common Errors

- Theoretical answers which were not applied directly to DLC

---

64   E5E (MAY 05 EXAM)

Key answer tips

Overall a straightforward question. However, the main weaknesses shown by candidates in the real exam were a lack of depth (i.e. basic lists of notes, with little explanation.) and a lack of application to E5E.

(a)   **The advantages and disadvantages of benchmarking for E5E are as follows:**

Advantages

- A better understanding of the firm's position

- Highlights particular areas that need changing

- Can identify problem areas in advance

- Can be integrated into target-setting, performance appraisal and bonuses

- Could highlight areas where other charities are much more effective so perhaps E5E should stop those activities

- Can be used to overcome complacency

- Should be particularly useful in improving economy and, to some extent, efficiency – all charities have financial constraints and benchmarking would highlight areas for improvement

- Enables better information to be provided to stakeholders – particularly useful in supporting applications for government funds.

Disadvantages

- Time consuming and expensive to implement

- Finding suitable comparisons can be difficult

- Not so useful in improving effectiveness as the stated objectives are very difficult to measure:

  'To fund world class research into the biology and the causes of heart disease.' What is 'world-class'?

  'To develop effective treatments and improve the quality of life for patients.' How do you measure 'quality of life'?

  'To reduce the number of people suffering from heart disease.' Cause and effect can be difficult to match – can reductions in mortality rates be traced directly to E5E's work?

  'To provide authoritative information on heart disease.' How to measure what is 'authoritative'?

- Not a competitive industry – does it matter if another charity is more effective in certain areas?

- Danger of information overload

- Problems gathering information when so many staff are volunteers – there may be a need for extra training here as well

- Can be de-motivating if the organisation fails to meet benchmarks

In summary benchmarking may help the charity become more economic and efficient but will not aid effectiveness.

(b)   **Stages in conducting a benchmarking exercise**

There is no universally agreed set of steps to follow when conducting a benchmarking exercise. The following is just one suggested answer.

E5E could use the following steps to conduct a benchmarking exercise:

1   **Planning**

- Decide what you wish to benchmark – for example, fund raising, % of funds passed on to recipients, % of funds raised from government, % of staff who are volunteers, funds raised per person, etc.

- Decide against whom you want to benchmark – this could include internal benchmarks (difficult), competitive benchmarks (e.g. other health research charities such as cancer research), activity benchmarks (e.g. universities to assess the educational aspects of E5E) and generic benchmarks (e.g. other communications organisations such as newspapers).

- Identify outputs required – e.g. a breakdown of funds collected, feedback on talks given.

- Determine data collection methodologies – e.g. should volunteers record information, should standard forms be prepared for talks, etc.

2   **Data collection**

- Secondary/background research – getting comparators.

- Primary research – from the benchmark.

3   **Analysis**

- Of the gaps – are they significant?

- Of the factors that create the gaps (enablers) – E5E would need to discuss findings with the relevant staff to understand why there are differences. For example, the benchmarking charity may have been much larger than E5E.

4   **Implementation of improvement programmes**

- Implementation planning – for example, visiting best in class and observing their methods.

- Roll-out of new modus operandi (changes) – for example, setting up new training programmes for volunteer staff, designing new advertising, training speakers, etc.

5   **Monitoring results**

- The process should be continuous.

(c)   **Dealing with the concerns of staff**

In each of the above stages the concerns of voluntary staff should be taken into account:

- E5E should have meetings to explain to staff why benchmarking is being introduced, its benefits and potential problems.

- Staff should be reassured of senior management commitment to the process.

- They should be consulted when deciding what to benchmark and what measures to use.

- They should be asked to help design new forms if they will be using them.

- They should be asked if they have any experience of benchmarking – just because they are volunteers does not mean that they have not had jobs where such experience may be gained.

- Emphasis should be on improvements of the processes rather than criticising staff.

65   CCC (MAY 12 EXAM)

Key answer tips

This question focuses on a key performance measurement approach in E3 – the Balanced Scorecard. Be careful to read the question carefully – part (a) asked for a general analysis of how the Balanced Scorecard would help CCC, part (b) asked for you to suggest perspectives that could be used as part of the Balanced Scorecard and part (c) asked for drawbacks.

(a)   In a widely published model, Johnson and Scholes characterise the strategic management process as consisting of three inter-related elements:

- strategic analysis

- strategic choice

- strategic implementation.

CCC has developed both mission and vision statements and an overriding objective so they have dealt with the first two elements. However, the comments of the Corporate Affairs Director that 'our strategy and vision ..(are)..not happening' indicate that CCC has been unsuccessful in strategic implementation. This is not an unusual situation as firms often experience a disjunction between the three elements. This is one of the reasons that the Balanced Scorecard (BS) was developed by Kaplan and Norton 'to assist strategic policy formation and achievement'.

The BS (See diagram below) comprises four perspectives surrounding the organisation's vision and strategy. Each of these perspectives can be associated with an aspect of CCC's vision statement.

Vision and Strategy

Our **vision** aspires to:

- provide superior returns to our shareholders

- continually improve our trading methods

- delight our customers

- learn from our mistakes, work smarter in the future

Our strategy is to double the size of our revenue by 2015.

Customer perspective	Financial perspective
To achieve our vision how should we appear to our customers?	To succeed financially how should we appear to our shareholders?
Delight our customers	**Provide superior returns to our shareholders**
Learning and growth	Internal business process
To achieve our vision, how will we sustain our ability to change and improve?	To satisfy our shareholders and customers, what business processes must we excel at?
Learn from our mistakes and work smarter in future	**Continually improve our business processes**

Examiner's comments

This question was generally not well answered. Most candidates provided a largely descriptive answer of the four balanced scorecard perspectives, with little or no discussion of how it could assist in delivering the organisation's vision and strategy. Candidates were provided with a vision statement which contained four aspirational statements which corresponded directly to the four balanced scorecard perspectives. Disappointingly, very few candidates identified the link between CCC's vision statement and the balanced scorecard.

Common Errors

- Descriptive answer only.

- No discussion of the link between the balanced scorecard and an organisation's vision and strategy.

(b)   The Balanced Scorecard can be made operational by using:

- **Objectives**: what CCC wants to achieve

- **Measures**: these will express the progress made towards an objective

- **Targets**: these give specific values and timescales for the achievement of the measures

- **Initiatives:** these are the actions taken to achieve a target

Examples of these four aspects are given in the table below:

Perspectives	Objective	Measure	Target	Initiative
Financial	Provide increasing dividend returns	Dividend yield	6% dividend yield by end 2012	Cost cutting exercise to increase profits
Customer	Increase customer satisfaction	Customer complaints	Reduce customer complaints to 1% of transactions by mid 2013	Increased training for sales executives
Learning and Growth	Raise the educational level of staff	Number of graduates	50% of staff to be graduates by 2014	Sponsor staff on degree courses
Internal processes	Be at the forefront of the use of Information technology	Replacement rate for PCs	All PCs to be no older than 2 yrs by the end of 2012	Seek new PC suppliers

The examples given above are not exhaustive: candidates were given credit for other appropriate examples.

Examiner's comments

This question was reasonably well answered. Many candidates made a sensible attempt at a good range of objectives, measures and targets, based upon the information that was provided in the scenario. Some candidates incorrectly confused the measures with the targets and there was a degree of overlap between these two areas in many answers. For example, some candidates identified a financial measure as growth in dividend yield and a target as increased dividend yield. Similarly, some candidates identified objectives which were actually targets. The main weakness of most answers was the identification of appropriate initiatives, where candidates were required to identify the actions which could be taken to achieve the objectives. Most candidates did not do well in this area as they appeared not to understand what 'initiatives' were. However, the examiner had provided an example within the scenario information to assist candidates in understanding of initiatives but most appeared not to pick up on this.

Overall, most candidates performed reasonably well on this question, demonstrating a good degree of understanding of the balanced scorecard and an ability to make a sound attempt at application. Those who did not perform well mostly did so as a result of a basic lack of knowledge of the model.

Common Errors

- Overlap of targets and measures within each perspective.

- Poor understanding of initiatives.

(c) **Potential drawbacks**

It is possible that the pursuit of one perspective may adversely affect another one. For example, if customer satisfaction was to be increased by increased investment in inventory, the financial perspective could be damaged. In this case, CCC would have to prioritise one of the perspectives even though both of them were helping to deliver the vision and strategy.

As CCC has not used the BS before there may have to be a cultural change for it to work successfully: cultural change can be hard to achieve.

The BS may require substantial investment in dedicated software and training costs.

The BS does not provide a single overall view of performance. Managers and analysts often favour measures such as R.O.C.E. which capture overall performance.

Any other appropriate drawbacks identified by candidates would be given credit.

Examiner's comments

This question was reasonably well answered, with many candidates identifying the drawbacks relating to the complexity of the BSC and the possible management and cultural resistance. However, a number of answers only focused upon the drawbacks of performance measurement in general and the answers were not specifically focused upon those issues directly related to implementing a BSC. Yet again, many candidates used the regular and well used examples of 'costly and time consuming', which were awarded limited credit unless directly applied to the Balanced Scorecard specifically.

Common Errors

* General answers relating to performance measures and not the BSC directly.

---

66 SAH (SEP 11 EXAM)

Key answer tips

Part (a) asks for the strengths and weaknesses of SAH's existing controls. When deciding on the drawbacks, look for problems and weaknesses in the business that are mentioned in the scenario. These can often indicate control weaknesses.

Part (b)(i) asked for how the Balanced Scorecard could be applied to SAH. This should have been an easy requirement, but as usual you need to ensure that you fully answer the question set. Not only did the requirement ask for one possible measure under each category, but it also wanted a justification for the measure that you selected. Failing to justify your answer would have cost you valuable marks here.

Part (b)(ii) is a common style of question. Don't forget that most models within E3 have drawbacks and problems. You may be asked to discuss these and examine whether the model is actually appropriate for the organisation in the scenario.

(a) **Strengths**

* SAH has a control system based on standard costing.

* The control system covers manufacturing cost which is 60% of a yacht's total cost.

* The managing director, N, is familiar with the control system.

Weaknesses

- N has experienced difficulty in his role because the control system only reports financial results.

- Although the current system endeavours to control the majority of manufacturing cost this leaves some significant gaps: namely the other 40% of a yacht's total manufacturing cost and also all other costs, for example, marketing and finance.

- The control system is now 26 years old. Although it was effective in 1985, changes since may have impaired its effectiveness. It seems that it would benefit from a review.

- N, the managing director of SAH, would like a system that gives him 'integrated control over all aspects of the business'. The current system does not do this.

- SAH's customers value quality, reliability and performance. The current control system does not explicitly report on any of these attributes.

- SAH has been criticised by its customers for late delivery and by potential customers because its yachts look 'old-fashioned' and are 'too slow'. N has stated that the current Return on Capital Employed (ROCE) of 3% is unacceptable. SAH's cash flow is under pressure. All these, although not due exclusively to the control system, nevertheless suggest that it is not adequate for SAH's current needs.

Examiner's comments

This question was not well answered. Firstly, most answers failed to identify any strengths of SAH's current control system. Candidates should have been able to identify at least one relevant strength. The other more significant weakness of answers to this question was that many candidates failed to focus their answer directly upon the current standard costing control system in operation in SAH.

Many answers instead discussed the strengths and weaknesses of SAH as an organisation. This was not what was asked in the question requirement and therefore awarded no marks. Candidates must make sure that they only answer the question that has been set.

Common Errors

- Answers focused only upon weaknesses

- Discussion of organisational strengths and weaknesses rather than control system weaknesses

---

(b) (i) The Balanced Scorecard is designed to 'translate mission and strategy into measures and objectives'. Its purpose is to inform employees about the drivers of success and direct their attention towards actions that will help to deliver the organisation's Vision and Strategy. The Vision and Strategy should be made explicit within the Balanced Scorecard.

Financial perspective: Proposed measures

- Aggregate contribution margin: An improvement in this measure should improve ROCE which is currently unacceptably low.

- Receivables: Cash flow is very important for SAH and it has been under pressure recently. A reduction in receivables will improve SAH's cash flow.

Customer perspective: Proposed measures

- Performance against delivery dates: This was a weak area for SAH in 2010/2011. SAH would want to improve its performance here and so improve its image to its customers and potential customers.

- Order book: As each yacht is built to order and takes at least a year to build, it is important that SAH knows it has continuity of demand. SAH can gauge the popularity of its yachts by the number of people who have placed an order for one.

Learning and growth: Proposed measures

- Number of staff with advanced craft and academic qualifications: SAH has had a policy of developing its staff from within. However, it has experienced criticism because its yachts look 'old fashioned'. It may be that SAH's ability to change and improve has been inhibited by a lack of staff with advanced qualifications.

- Number of design innovations: This measure would demonstrate SAH's ability to change its manufacturing processes to improve efficiency and reduce cost and its product designs to meet customers' needs.

Internal business perspective: Proposed measures

- Materials price variance: This would focus attention on a current area of difficulty for SAH, which is having to deal with increasing material prices.

- Build time per yacht: If SAH could reduce its build time it might be able to avoid late deliveries, sell more yachts and use its working capital more efficiently. This could improve its profitability.

The introduction of Balanced Scorecard into SAH does not necessarily mean that it should abandon its standard costing system. As this deals with 60% of the total cost of a yacht, the standard costing can still give valuable control information.

Examiner's comment: Although only one measure was required there are a great deal of possible measures which SAH could use within a Balanced Scorecard. Two possible ones have been given for each perspective. Candidates who proposed alternative, credible measures were appropriately rewarded.

Examiner's comments

This question was reasonably well answered by many candidates. Most answers provided a sound overview of the BSC itself and many candidates were able to present a good range of measures for the four perspectives. The main weakness of answers to this question was the lack of justification of the measures. Some candidates correctly defined the perspective in general terms but failed to justify their chosen measure in the context of SAH. The question requirement clearly asked candidates to justify each measure and those that failed to do so were awarded a fail mark.

Common Errors

- No/poor justification of measures identified

- Limited application of measures to SAH

(ii)   N could encounter the following problems when he introduces the Balanced Scorecard:

Gaining management commitment to the concept of the Balanced Scorecard

Kaplan suggest that some managers prefer to be measured solely by financial measures because these are inaccurate and obscure individual's responsibility for performance. As the Balanced Scorecard does not link directly to profit, some managers believe it not to be relevant to them.

Congruency of measures

Although the measures proposed for the Balanced Scorecard are supposed to be congruent, i.e. mutually reinforcing, they may not be. Thus, for example, an initiative to improve the customer experience may adversely affect a financial measure, for example, Return on Capital Employed.

Measuring only the things that are easy to measure

This may occur because the business is unaware of the processes that add value to the business. Balanced Scorecard measures need to reflect aspects of the business operations that contribute towards the achievement of its vision. Such aspects may not previously have been measured and the formulation of new measures may be difficult, for example, measuring quality. This may lead managers to ignore these aspects and concentrate their attention on measurable but less important aspects of the business operations.

Allocating responsibility for developing the measures

The measures should be developed by staff with an all-round understanding of the business. These will not necessarily be from within the finance function. If the measures are developed within the different functions there is likely to be a variable degree of expertise available to perform this task. If the measures are developed centrally, they may be resisted by managers if they have not been consulted in the process.

Examiner's comments

This question was reasonably well answered, although many answers were rather thin. Most answers focused upon management issues such as resistance to change, commitment, cost and time constraints.

Few answers focused specifically upon the problems of introducing a BSC, such as developing appropriate measures and allocating responsibility within SAH. However, most candidates presented three relevant issues and were therefore awarded a pass mark. Higher marks were awarded to those candidates whose answers focused specifically upon BSC issues.

Common Errors

*   Too much focus upon issues such as cost and time rather than specific difficulties of implementing a BS

---

67   JIK (MAY 11 EXAM)

Key answer tips

Requirement (a) should not have been a surprise to a well-prepared student, asking for the appropriateness of JIK's current control system. Don't forget that if you are asked to **evaluate** something, you will have to examine both sides of the argument – in this case reasons why JIK's controls are appropriate and reasons why they are inappropriate. Failure to properly evaluate the controls will limit your marks.

Part (b) is a straightforward requirement to recommend two CSFs for JIK. Note that justification was required here. Merely stating a CSF would get you very few marks – you had to say why it would help JIK to be successful in the future.

A slightly trickier part (c)(i) asked you to make suggestions as to what JIK would need to change regarding its control system. Remember that CSFs are often not able to be directly measured. Instead, an organisation will create KPIs that will help them to measure whether the CSF is being met. Try to link your answer to whatever CSFs you suggested in (b), as the question directed.

The last requirement, (c)(ii), asked for improvements to JIK's costing, reporting frequency and information requirements. Use the requirement to break your answer into headings. Any reasonable comments, if justified, could have scored here.

(a)   **JIK's control system**

This is 'focused exclusively' on the manufacturing process even though JIK is also a retailer and installer of domestic kitchens. It is appropriate for the control system to monitor manufacturing efficiency by means of the three variances: Materials price, Materials usage and Manufacturing labour efficiency. No rationale has been given for concentrating on these three variances and there may be other variances which could provide useful control information which are not currently computed, for example, material yield and labour rate.

Although JIK uses standard costing it is not clear that it computes product costs. A lack of product costs may be the reason it was 'surprised' about its 2010 profit margin. Standard costing could be criticised for misdirecting management's attention. Thus, in the case of a 'Lux-Style' kitchen where the highest standards of materials are used it is important that the quality of the finished product is not compromised. Therefore, it might be appropriate to accept an unfavourable material price variance in order to maintain the product's standards. Variance analysis should not be used in isolation but a holistic view needs to be taken about JIK's operations and the current control system may not lead to this. JIK is not currently monitoring and controlling aspects which are vital for competitive success. It has not identified its Critical Success Factors.

There is weekly reporting of the variances and implicit is that there should be follow-up actions resulting from these reports. However, a week is not necessarily the appropriate reporting period for all aspects of JIK's business. If there is a production problem leading to excessive materials waste a week is too long a time to wait before remedial action can be taken. Therefore, real-time or contemporaneous reporting may be more appropriate for manufacturing operations.

A major deficiency of JIK's control systems is that they do not extend to retailing and installation activities. The Value installation teams are incentivised to complete kitchens which could be good for their productivity. However, there is a high level of complaints associated with their work. As there is no evident means of monitoring the installation teams' work, the causes of the complaints cannot be identified.

Examiner's comments

This question was not well answered. It was the least popular on the whole paper and by far the worst answered. It was most disappointing to see how few candidates had any real understanding of management accounting control systems and who failed to present a basic evaluation of what was clearly a limited control system. Most answers went little further than describing the current control system rather than evaluating it.

Strategic implementation, control, and business performance and appraisal are of fundamental importance both for the purposes of the E3 examination and for the work of management accountants. Candidates are strongly urged to better acquaint themselves with the theory relating to these topics and its application.

(b) CIMA has defined Critical Success Factors (CSF) as 'An element of the organisational activity which is critical to its future success. Critical success factors may change over time, and may include items such as product quality, employee attitudes, manufacturing flexibility and brand awareness'.*

There are a range of CSF's which could be helpful for JIK. They include:

CSF: Quality of installations

There are different quality expectations for the two kitchens and there has been different levels of quality achieved implicit in the historic pattern of complaints. This strongly implies that the quality of installation should be tracked as a separate CSF for each kitchen. This CSF is important for JIK because of the cost implications of rectifications and guarantee claims. It is also important because of the effect that poor quality will have on JIK's future business.

CSF: Customer satisfaction

Like quality, this CSF will need to be monitored separately for each kitchen. Customer satisfaction covers the entire life of a transaction starting with the initial enquiry about a purchase and continuing after installation for the life of the kitchen. Customer satisfaction will have an influence on JIK's future business which is dependent, in part, on repeat orders and recommendations. This CSF will also reflect the market's perception of JIK's brand.

CSF: Brand performance

JIK has two distinct brands. They are directed at different market segments and have different associated attributes. 'Value' kitchens offer limited choice to the customer and retail, on average, for £5,000. JIK would like to maintain this business at its present level (2,000 kitchens a year minimum) £10 million revenue. JIK needs to identify where this brand is situated in its life-cycle and what marketing activities may be required to support it.

The 'Lux-Style' brand is aimed at a different market segment and JIK would like to grow this aspect of its business which produces revenue of £2 million. The same considerations apply to this brand as to 'Value'.

The success of both brands is vital for the continued success of JIK and this CSF gives a holistic view of performance.

CSF: Manufacturing excellence

JIK manufactures all the kitchens which it sells and installs. Manufacturing will be a significant aspect of JIK's total costs and an important contributor to profitability. Currently, JIK monitors some limited aspects of manufacturing through its control system. However, there are many other aspects which are not reported upon: for example, manufacturing flexibility, innovation, absenteeism and investment in technology. This CSF has a much wider scope than the current control system and should assist in the quest for competitiveness.

*CIMA: Management Accounting: Official terminology, 2005, p 47 quoted in CIMA Learning System, E3, page 19.

Candidates were only required to provide two CSFs. These others have been given for completeness. Any other sensible CSF provided by candidates were rewarded appropriately.

Examiner's comments

This question was very badly answered. It was most disappointing to see how few candidates were able to identify any relevant CSFs and it would appear that most candidates who answered this question did not in fact, understand what CSFs are. This is an important part of the syllabus but clearly a weak area of knowledge and understanding by many candidates. This is an area which must be improved upon.

(c) (i) JIK's current control system is one dimensional focusing on the efficiency of its manufacturing process. The introduction of Critical Success Factors means that the control system will have to become multi-dimensional as CSFs are by their nature holistic. They are not confined to financial data arising from the accounting system. Therefore, the introduction of CSF's will necessitate the synthesis of quantitative and qualitative information. As the CSFs are broad in scope, for example, Brand performance, there will be a need to incorporate and report upon external information such as market share.

In order to implement, or operationalise, the CSFs JIK will need to introduce supporting Key Performance Indicators (KPIs). For example, for the CSF Manufacturing performance, JIK will need to establish and report on a range of KPI's which inform on the extent to which excellence has been achieved: wastage, downtime, set-ups, stock-outs, cycle time.

Examiner's comments

Once again, this question was not well answered, largely due to the fact that the answers to part (b) of the question were so poor. However, even if the candidate had provided incorrect CSFs in the previous answer they still should have identified that any CSF requires comprehensive and multi-dimensional evaluation and therefore should have been able to present a discussion around these issues. However, most candidates did not.

(ii)   **Standard Costing**

JIK may have to abandon or modify its standard costing and reporting system. This is because the current system could lead to an inappropriate emphasis being placed on certain aspects of performance, for example, labour efficiency to the detriment of the achievement of a CSF, for example, customer satisfaction. It is remarkable that the installations for Value kitchens generate a substantial level of complaints whereas there has never been a complaint made about a Lux-Style kitchen. It could be that the different remuneration arrangements for the installation teams have led to this and as the complaint level will be an important aspect of the CSF, Customer Satisfaction, JIK may need to change its remuneration arrangements. It should also consider whether it would benefit from a wider range of variance reporting: for example it may find it useful to report on material yield and labour rates.

Reporting frequency

For all CSFs JIK will need to decide upon appropriate reporting intervals. Although it is convenient to synchronise this with the accounting reporting cycle, CSFs and KPIs do not necessarily coincide with accounting period ends. Some KPI's may need to be reported in real-time, for example, material wastage, others may be of a much longer duration such as Customer Satisfaction. There is a strong argument for de-coupling the reporting of CSFs from the financial reporting cycles.

Information requirements

The introduction of CSFs and KPIs will require collection of a new range of information. Although some of this will be internally generated, for example, labour absenteeism, others will be external, for example, market share. JIK will be able to collect some of this new information from external sources and databases. These external sources could enrich the quality of JIK's decision-making and strategy formation. For example, the Internet could assist JIK in its understanding of social trends required for a PEST analysis.

It may also be appropriate to allow JIK's internal information systems to interface with external users. JIK could solicit customer feedback which the customers could enter directly into JIK's system, for example, by means of an on-line survey.

Internally, JIK's information systems could be decentralised to allow users at all levels to contribute information and to use it. These privileges could also be extended to some external users, such as key suppliers, where appropriate. The information systems will need to set appropriate authorisation levels for access for the various users.

With the enhanced collection and dissemination of information, the wider levels of access and the interface with the external environment, JIK may also have to modify its hardware and software resources.

> **Examiner's comments**
>
> This question was not well answered. Again, this was largely due to the poor standard of answer throughout the rest of this question. Standard costing/control systems appears to be a recurring weakness for many candidates and the fact that most candidates chose not to answer this question suggests that many are not confident in their abilities to answer a question on this topic. Those who did presented clear evidence of a lack of knowledge and understanding of this syllabus area. Candidates must be aware that this is an important aspect of the E3 syllabus and should not be avoided.

BUSINESS UNIT PERFORMANCE AND ORGANISATIONAL STRUCTURE

68   DDD (NOV 12 EXAM)

Key answer tips

Requirement (a) should be a straightforward question requiring candidates to demonstrate their knowledge and understanding of divisional structures and functional structures. Candidates must apply their answers directly to DDD to be awarded a pass mark.

Requirement (b) requires candidates to demonstrate their knowledge and understanding of centralised versus decentralised decision making. It is important that candidates do not merely discuss centralisation and decentralisation in general. The question specifically focuses upon the decision making process and the current challenges faced by DDD in decision making.

Requirement (c) requires candidates to demonstrate their knowledge and understanding of alternative organisational structures and their importance and relevance to DDD. Candidates need to consider specifically the recent contract won by DDD and the most appropriate organisational structure to ensure that it will be undertaken successfully. Specifically, candidates are expected to consider matrix or project based structures and their benefits to DDD.

(a)   An organisation's structure is necessary to ensure the successful implementation of its objectives and strategies. It can be defined as 'the established pattern of relationships between individuals, groups and departments within an organisation'. It is important that an organisation chooses the right structure in order for it to successfully manage both its internal and external relationships and to ensure that its business is conducted as effectively as possible.

    (i)   **Functional Structure**

        A functional structure divides the organisation into functions or activities such as finance, HR, production and IT. The main reason for this type of structure is to allow the exploitation of specialisation.

        Evaluation of the benefits to DDD

        A functional structure will allow the grouping of specialist skills and activities. This grouping of expertise may give DDD a competitive advantage against larger, more divisionalised organisations.

This will allow for the elimination of duplication of activities across projects and therefore should help to keep costs down for DDD. As a medium sized organisation likely to be competing against similar or larger sized organisations, elimination of unnecessary duplication of costs could be a key factor in its competitiveness.

In a centralised organisation, such as DDD, a functional structure facilitates the management and control of functional specialists.

Evaluation of the drawbacks to DDD

Often, in functional structures, there are barriers between functions that may affect co-ordination and the flow of information. This could mean that for DDD communication between members of project teams is affected and the co-ordination of project team members may result in delays or mis-communication. Overall, this could affect the quality of the project output.

A functional structure may cause DDD to focus more upon its internal processes rather than on the quality of is outputs and customer satisfaction. As stated in the scenario, the lack of integration of the functions is seen as a key problem for DDD.

Functional structures can struggle to cope with growth and change. DDD has just won a major contract for a large sporting event and this may mean a degree of change is essential. However, the current structure would seem inappropriate to manage this.

(ii) **Divisional Structure**

A divisionalised structure subdivides the organisation into smaller units based upon, for example, either a product or market focus. DDD could divisionalise on the basis of type of product/customer or by geographical location.

Evaluation of the benefits to DDD

- DDD's staff could be located by project expertise in one location. The expertise in one location should encourage quicker, better quality decision making and a better customer focus.

- DDD's managers would be given greater empowerment and motivation through divisionalisation because they would have the power to make decisions within a delegated level of authority.

Evaluation of drawbacks to DDD

- Divisionalisation can result in more duplication and thus increase costs for DDD. In a highly competitive market this may make DDD less competitive. Costs associated with additional administration, management and control activities may be incurred.

- There is a potential for sub-optimisation in DDD, as highlighted by the Finance Director, who has experience of divisionalised structures.

- Divisionalisation may result in more formalised central policies and control procedures imposed by DDD's Board which will negate any benefits of improved potential empowerment for managers.

Examiner's comments

This question was not well answered. This was very disappointing as this syllabus area builds upon knowledge from subjects earlier in the Enterprise pillar. This should have been a straightforward question, yet most answers were confused and lacked real depth of understanding of functional and divisional structures. Many answers were repetitive, with the benefits of one structure being used as the drawbacks of the other. In addition most answers were generic and not applied sufficiently to DDD. In fact, most answers largely ignored the scenario information relating to DDD's current structure.

Common errors:

- Limited application to DDD
- Lack of depth of syllabus knowledge

(b)   In a centralised organisation, the senior managers (normally the Board of Directors) will retain the authority over strategic decision making and most of the organisation's management and control activities.

In a decentralised organisation, authority to make decisions is given to managers of divisions/ units/ projects lower down in the organisation hierarchy. Decentralisation allows the front line managers and staff to make decisions in response to customer and environmental demands and allows better management of local issues by local managers who are closer to the decision being made.

Evaluation of centralisation in DDD

As the organisation is currently run with a functional structure, a centralised approach is likely to be appropriate. However, the functional structure of DDD could be inappropriate and therefore DDD must question the appropriateness of a centralised decision making and control system.

Advantages of centralisation to DDD

- If DDD were to allow more decentralised decision making this may result in sub-optimisation and poorer overall performance of DDD.

- Having centralised strategic decision making and control will ensure one overall objective for DDD, leading to improved conformity and goal congruence.

- DDD's costs should be minimised as there is less duplication of decision making and management activities.

- The senior managers of DDD can remain as the specialists in strategic management which allows all of the other managers to focus upon their own functional specialisms.

However, the **drawbacks** of a centralised structure to DDD are as follows:

- The senior engineers of DDD would appear to be highly frustrated with their lack of input into strategic decisions, which will lead to demotivation and low morale.

- This in turn will lead to good and talented staff leaving the organisation, which is in evidence from the scenario. This is clearly not acceptable for DDD, as these staff not only leave, taking valuable knowledge and experience with them, but they are also likely to take this to rival organisations.

- The senior managers and Board of DDD are unlikely to have all of the knowledge required to make every decision needed to operate DDD successfully and therefore sub-optimal decisions may be made as a result of this lack of knowledge.

- Other managers in DDD will have less opportunity to learn and develop and gain experience which will be detrimental to DDD. Again, this is likely to result in these managers leaving DDD to seek better managerial experience elsewhere.

- Time taken for decisions lengthens in a centralised structure causing delays and missed opportunities.

Therefore, a decentralised approach to DDD is likely to result in the following benefits for DDD:

- Greater staff motivation with greater responsibility and autonomy which should result in reduced staff turnover.

- More experienced staff who will become future senior managers in the organisation. If DDD is spending time and money in developing staff then it is cost effective if it retains these staff within its business instead of training them for the benefit of other rival organisations.

- Better, more focused decisions made closer to the customer thus increasing speed of response and hopefully reducing late payment charges to DDD.

- Improved customer satisfaction due to increased responsiveness as better informed decisions will be made more quickly.

Examiner's comments

This question was reasonably well answered. Most candidates demonstrated a good level of knowledge and understanding of centralised decision making and many answers were applied directly to DDD. Again, those candidates who performed badly on this requirement did so due to either poor syllabus knowledge or because of lack of application to DDD.

Common Errors:

- Poor application to DDD

(c)   DDD is operating in a number of different product and customer types and in different geographical locations. Its current functional structure appears not to provide a sufficient level of co-ordination and integration and is clearly a source of frustration for senior engineers in DDD. It is recommended that a matrix or project based structure be applied to DDD, based upon the focus of multi-functional project teams.

A matrix or project based structure is based upon teams which are flexible and often temporary. For DDD, a project team could be set up for each contract won which would maintain and exploit the basis of the organisations functional specialism but would allow for better co-ordination and co-operation of the functions within one team environment.

A matrix or project based structure would normally have two reporting lines; one to the functional manager and one to the project manager. For DDD this would mean a team focused structure where each CHP project would have a team with members from all of the functional areas, led by a project manager or senior engineer. The team would work together on the project until it is complete and then return to the main functional activities or move to another project.

It is widely recognised that in the modern business organisation the need for flexibility will be a key determinant of organisations' ability to survive. Many writers suggest that organisations will have to work more flexibly, use team based structures, allow greater delegation of decision making and rely more frequently on operating in network or collaborative arrangements with other organisations.

DDD's need for a flexible structure following the recent contract won

The new contract for DDD to design and install a range of innovative products in collaboration with other organisations is going to involve working with a number of different organisations over a long period of time to present one final outcome (a successful sporting event delivered on time).

Interaction with a range of partners with different skills and experience will require DDD's staff to take a more flexible approach in its activities and work in a more collaborative way. Working with external partners will require different communication methods and different management and control methods.

If DDD cannot work flexibly with its partners in terms of work arrangements, use of technologies and skills development, then DDD may find that it could lose the contract or face heavy penalties for late project deliverables throughout the life of the project.

The benefits to DDD of a matrix structure would be:

- Increased integration and co-ordination of the functional specialists, overcoming a current criticism of the organisation.

- Team members becoming multi-skilled and multi-disciplinary which would benefit both the individuals and DDD as a whole.

- Greater cohesion and communication should result in better decision making and improved customer satisfaction. A more flexible approach to organisation should allow DDD to be more innovative and reactive to the demands of the market and its customers and should make it more competitive.

However DDD would still have to consider some of the potential problems with a matrix structure, such as the potential conflict that may occur between the dual authority roles of project manager and functional manager, which may cause internal disputes and also result in problems for the individual team members in terms of understanding where their responsibilities lie. Also, a matrix structure could add additional costs for DDD in terms of additional requirements for project managers to be employed.

However, DDD may still face the problem of a centralised management and control structure which could inhibit the freedoms associated with a matrix structure. If DDD is to truly make the most from a matrix structure the organisation also has to reconsider its centralised approach to management and control.

Examiner's comments

This question was not well answered. It was very disappointing to see how few candidates recommended a matrix or project team structure for the new contract. Most candidates recommended a divisional structure or a functional structure, despite the weakness of these highlighted in the scenario information. It appeared that many candidates just had little or no knowledge of matrix structures. Those that did recommend matrix structures often provided only descriptive answers, with little real justification in relation to the large contract won by DDD. It would appear that syllabus knowledge is weak in this area and must be addressed.

> Common Errors:
>
> - Poor recommendations
> - Lack of application to DDD

69 NGV (MAR 11 EXAM)

Key answer tips

Part (a) was a rather tricky requirement, asking for how far ratio analysis would help NGV achieve financial control and achieving an adequate ROI. The key to this was remembering that NGV is a government department, so it lacks several key features of a business organisation (such as the ability to earn revenue) which will limit the value of ratio analysis. Remember that not all organisations in your exam will be commercial!

NGV also lacks a strong management accounting function. If the financial information is unreliable or is not in a useful format, this will limit the value of ratio analysis.

Part (b) then asks for how NGV should implement a knowledge management strategy. Note that the requirement is not asking for you to look at the stages of knowledge management or the benefits – the focus is practical. What would be needed for the knowledge management strategy to be a success?

(a) NGV employs 320 staff and has forecasted annual expenditure in 2011 between £20 and £25 million and has 180 cost centres. This implies it is the sort of complex organisation which would benefit from a system of financial control based on financial ratio analysis. However, this normally takes place against a background of budgetary reporting where actual expenditure is compared to budget expenditure. This is usually reported both on a period and year-to-date basis. It is also common for the periodic reporting, which is usually done monthly, to be accompanied with forecasts of expenditure for the remainder of the budget year. Budgets may be modified during the budget year if a fundamental change has occurred and they are often kept continually up-to-date by the use of 'rolling' budgets.

However, many of the components required for a system of budget reporting are not in place in NGV. NGV does not have a management accounting function and only knows 'approximately' the aggregated spending which has taken place. For effective control to take place there would need to be disaggregation of the total budget and this would be normally analysed within responsibility centres which reflected NGV's organisational structure. Neither, does NGV have a formal system for forecasting expenditure and, as it normally has a deficit at the year end, there is a weakness here which needs to be rectified.

Financial control based on ratios encapsulates the financial performance of an organisation summed up by the ratio: Percentage Return on Investment (ROI). ROI is usually analysed into its components which examine Income: Sales and Sales: Investment. These ratios are then analysed in their turn. However, little of this analysis could be performed within NGV at present, as it has no sales revenue and the value of its assets is not recorded within NGV.

NGV does not generate any income and does not receive the benefits of the commercial exploitation of its innovations. Bringing the process for patenting innovations and exploiting them within NGV would be a major contribution towards NGV becoming commercial. However, this is a separate issue to the introduction of financial ratio analysis.

If NGV was to earn income from its innovations, it would be more appropriately constituted as a profit centre or, possibly, an investment centre.

Summary

Financial ratio analysis will be able to make a contribution towards NGV becoming commercial. However, this will be limited as many of the aspects of a commercial business are missing within NGV.

Examiner's comments

This question was not well answered. It was the least popular question on the paper and by far the most poorly answered. Those candidates who attempted this question appeared to have very limited understanding of financial ratio analysis and most answers were largely based upon very brief and unnecessary descriptions of return on investment. Very few candidates identified the current weaknesses in the financial information reporting structure of NGV and how this impacted upon the extent to which it could make use of financial ratio analysis in producing an adequate ROI.

Common Errors

- Lack of focus upon financial ratio analysis

- Too much emphasis of answers upon ROI

(b)   NGV currently employs 80 staff who are regarded as being world leaders in their research expertise. These staff often produce innovations with great commercial potential but frequently leave for better paid jobs in the private sector. Another problem which NGV faces is that of staff who leave before the completion of their research project which cannot then be completed because their expertise has been lost. In addition to the knowledge of the research projects which NGV is losing, it is also losing the tacit knowledge, or 'know-how' of the staff who leave. Tacit knowledge is informal knowledge and personal to the individual but it represents a significant organisational asset. The 'brain drain' to which the Director of NGV refers is inhibiting his organisation's success and it would be the aim of a knowledge management strategy to secure for NGV a richer 'knowledge stock' which would assist it in its quest to become commercial. NGV also has many staff who have not produced any significant research 'break-throughs'. It could be that these staff would be enabled to be more creative and productive if NGV implemented a knowledge management strategy.

In order to implement a knowledge management strategy, like so many other strategies and initiatives, there needs to be support for it at the highest level of the organisation. One reason for this is that the implementation of the knowledge management strategy will cost money and might lead to changes in organisational structure and procedures. Thus, for example, there may need to be appointed knowledge managers who are responsible for the strategy's implementation.

This high level support should not be too difficult to achieve as the Director has articulated his concern at the number of staff who leave and this concern is strengthened by the pressure he is being put under to become commercial. One practical measure the Director could instigate is a review of the pay structures at NGV, as inadequate pay may be exacerbating the loss of institutional knowledge.

As NGV has 320 staff there will need to be some technological infrastructure designed to assist in the capture and storage and distribution of knowledge. This could take the form of an Organisational Management System (OMS) which could include e-mail, databases, intranets and data mining tools. The OMS should aim to deal with both 'explicit knowledge'; that which is already known within the organisation, for example, research reports, and tacit knowledge; that which is contained within peoples' heads.

The next step towards implementing the knowledge management strategy would be to build 'repositories of knowledge' appropriate for NGV which would consist of a network of contents pages giving links to other databases where the actual knowledge is stored. This step is most important as knowledge is of no use unless it can be located by any legitimate user. The services of an information specialist, such as a librarian may be very useful in building the repository.

There would be a need to foster a culture of sharing knowledge within NGV so that it can be captured, stored and used. There may be resistance to this from some staff, particularly with respect to their own tacit knowledge, as this is usually regarded as a personal possession. This may prove to be the most difficult part of the implementation for NGV. The staff would need to be convinced that the knowledge management strategy provided mutual benefits for NGV and for the individual.

Finally, the various databases would need to be populated and the staff trained and encouraged to use their contents. The operation of the OMS would need to be kept under review and up-dated as necessary. If the system is working well this should provide a source of motivation for NGV's staff. This motivation could be reinforced by linking individual's participation in the culture of sharing of knowledge to NGV's staff appraisal system, if it has one.

Examiner's comments

This question was not well answered. Very few candidates demonstrated an understanding of knowledge management within the context of NGV and it was most disappointing to see how few of the answers focused correctly upon the implementation of a knowledge management strategy relevant to NGV. Most answers went little further than a description or definition of knowledge management or descriptions of the possible technology requirements. It would appear that most candidates failed to read the question requirement carefully as few answers focused upon the process of KM strategy implementation.

Common Errors

- Answers not focused upon KM strategy implementation

- Description of technology requirements only

---

70   FIVE FORCES MODEL (NOV 05 EXAM)

Key answer tips

Surprisingly at this level, this question is essentially bookwork. The main problem for students in the exam was whether they felt they knew the topics in sufficient depth to pass.

The main difficulty lies in applying Porter's five forces model to transfer pricing in part (b)

(a)   **Competition**

Over the last three decades, business has focused on one fundamental idea – the pursuit of sustainable competitive advantage. While the idea of competition is not new, Michael Porter in particular has expanded the concept from competing with rivals to incorporating the struggle for power between the firm and five competitive forces.

Porter argued that each of these forces can reduce overall industry profitability and the individual firm's share of that profit – their 'profit potential' – because they can influence prices, costs and the level of investment required. One of the forces is competitive rivalry – suppliers and customers are also included.

Customers/Buyers

Porter argued that buyers can reduce profits in an industry by exerting their market power, usually through demanding higher quality and/or lower costs. In principle this is no different from profits being competed away by other rivals.

For example, the UK grocery business has been concentrated into the hands of a small number of large powerful retailers, resulting in dramatically reduced profitability in agricultural markets.

The power used by buyers can also have the secondary effect of increasing competitive rivalry by forcing down prices, bargaining for higher quality or improved services and by playing competitors against each other. All three of these are at the expense of industry profitability.

Not everyone agrees with Porter – some would argue that the idea of satisfying customer needs should not be abandoned in favour of a view that sees customers either as direct competitors or as means to the firm's end. Customers are not objects whose reason for being is to be fought over by competitors seeking 'sustainable competitive advantage'.

Suppliers

In a similar way Porter argued that suppliers can exert bargaining power over companies within an industry by threatening to raise their prices and threatening to reduce the quality of their goods and services.

The effect of this power is to squeeze profitability out of an industry unable to recover cost increases by raising its own prices.

This can be seen in the PC business, where software and processor suppliers make great profits, but PC manufacture remains relatively less attractive.

(b)   **Transfer prices**

The requirement does specify that Porter's five forces should be part of your discussion. However, there are many easy marks for talking about the "usual" factors involved in transfer pricing

There are four specific criteria that a good transfer pricing policy should meet:

- it should provide motivation for divisional managers

- it should allow divisional autonomy and independence to be maintained

- it should allow divisional performance to be assessed objectively

- it should ensure that divisional managers make decisions that are in the best interests of the divisions and also of the company as a whole.

This final feature is usually referred to as goal congruence and is perhaps the most important of the four.

Given this, the following issues should be considered when setting transfer prices within a large, complex organisation.

Relative buyer/supplier power

Porter's views on buyer and supplier power are particularly relevant for transfer pricing.

High buyer power can occur if, for example, the receiving division has a choice of alternative supplies but the supplying division has no external market for its product. In such a case, the negotiated transfer price is likely to be very low with the following consequences:

- The profit of the receiving division is overstated and that of the supplying division understated. Both profit figures fail to reflect the true performance of the divisions.

- The supplying divisional manager may become de-motivated as they will be less likely to hit their targets.

- The supplying division may elect not to supply the receiving division and instead seek more outside sales or even halt production. This might force the receiving division to outsource with the consequence of an overall higher cost for the group or compromised quality if outsourced items are inferior.

High supplier power could occur if the supplier produces a high quality product that is unmatched in the market place. It could thus sell these in the outside marketplace, whereas the receiving division would struggle to find alternative supply. High supplier power would result in a very high transfer price with the following results:

- The profit of the supplying division is overstated and that of the receiving division understated. Again, both profit figures fail to reflect the true performance of the divisions.

- The receiving divisional manager may become de-motivated as they will be less likely to hit their targets.

- The receiving division may elect to outsource with the consequence of an overall higher cost for the group or compromised quality if outsourced items are inferior.

The degree of decentralisation

Buyers and sellers should be completely free to deal outside the company. If this autonomy is restricted, then the bargaining power of the two parties will be affected and the objectives of transfer pricing compromised.

Negotiation

Prices of all transfers in and out of a profit centre should be determined by negotiation between buyers and sellers. Head office interference with the transfer price could compromise the objectives set out above.

Information

Negotiators should have access to full data on alternative sources and markets and to public and private information about market prices to try to balance the power between them.

Negotiators should also be fully informed on the significance of the transaction in relation to the profitability of the company as a whole. This is an attempt to guarantee goal congruence but could compromise negotiations if managers feel under pressure to arrive at the 'right answer' for the firm as a whole.

Market prices

Most negotiated transfer prices rely on the existence of market prices to act as a reference point. However, there are a number of problems with using market prices:

- There may be no intermediate market price. The product or service might not be readily available on the open market (an example might be a partly completed car being transferred from one division to another).

- The market price might not be independent. This would occur if the transferring division were in the position of a monopolist both within the company and in the outside market.

- Difficulty in agreeing a source of market prices. Debates will occur over the size, quality, timing and location of internal transfers compared with a range of published prices.

- The need to adjust prices for different volumes. Prices quoted may well not relate to the levels of transfers that are likely to take place; in the same way, the extent of reductions due to saved selling costs will be difficult to estimate.

- Published prices may be fictitious. This is a variation on the previous problem but is typified by those products for which it is customary for a seller to publish a price then the buyer to negotiate a lower figure.

71   EEE DIVISIONALISED COMPANY (MAY 08 EXAM)

Key answer tips

Part (a) – Make sure you talk about the **information** required rather than 'how to assess an acquisition'. Frameworks like PESTEL and 5 forces will be useful for structure but must be related to the question – we are assessing the **acquisition** not the market it operates in, although the two are linked.

Part (b)(i) Again, you need to make sure you talk about the difficulties EEE may experience post acquisition and not just the problems with measuring divisional performance in general.

(ii) Discussing the disadvantages of ROI should be straightforward – you just need to make sure enough points are made to secure 4 marks.

(a)   Information required assessing the suitability of an acquisition target.

EEE wish to acquire a competitor in a neighbouring country with a view to moving all production there. The new company will be classed as a division. In assessing the suitability of acquisitions, EEE will require the following information:

Environmental Analysis – although the potential acquisitions are electrical equipment producers like EEE, they will be subject to different environmental constraints due to their geographical location. The PESTEL framework could be used to generate the information required to assess the suitability of targets.

- Information on government stability and political intervention in business will be required. Since the neighbouring countries are not as developed as country F, their governments may be protective of 'home grown' industry and reject any attempts to acquire companies by EEE. Equally they may make it difficult for EEE to operate in their country. Taxes on foreign firms may be high for example.

- EEE will need to know information about the economy of the target countries. If they are growing economies, they may be very attractive to EEE with cheap labour and infrastructure which will allow EEE to cut costs and lower prices.

- EEE will need to understand the culture of the target acquisitions, in terms of working styles and attitudes. It will be very important to find a company with a 'good fit' to EEE's working practices since it will become such an important part of the value chain replacing EEE's current manufacturing division entirely.

- EEE will need to know whether technological development within the target countries is sufficient to allow it to operate a manufacturing division there. Information will need to be communicated efficiently to head office in country F.

- Information on employment law and health and safety legislation in target organisations will also be needed. Compliance with onerous domestic laws could make an acquisition prohibitively expensive for EEE.

The board will also require information to satisfy Porter's tests for acquisitions:

- The attractiveness test. Since each potential acquisition will need to be assessed for attractiveness, information will be required on any barriers to entry (government disincentives as mentioned above, for example), bargaining power of suppliers and customers and local competition. Since EEE is looking at targets in its own industry, this information should be easy to obtain. EEE has a reputation for producing high quality products so a target which has good quality local suppliers with modest power is likely to be the most attractive to the board.

- The cost of entry test. EEE will require information on the cost of purchasing a competitor in a neighbouring country. The target's financial performance and growth prospects will need to be taken into account when negotiating any purchase. Since the potential acquisitions are all privately held, EEE will not be purchasing shares from the market and so will need information on the owners of each company and their willingness to sell.

- The better-off test. Ultimately EEE will need to gather information to assess whether they will benefit as a company from any acquisition. The acquisition must do something for shareholders that they cannot do for themselves. In this case, EEE will need to prove that the extra sales and the cost savings from moving production abroad will add value to the company. The board will therefore require information on cost structures and sales from the target companies.

In conclusion, EEE will need to ensure that any potential synergies that a target acquisition could bring to the company are properly researched and sufficient information is gathered to enable the board to make an informed decision on which company to acquire.

(b) (i) Difficulties EEE may experience with the performance measurement of divisions, post acquisition.

EEE intends to maintain its divisionalised structure and treat the acquired company as a new division. Issues with divisional performance measurement may include:

Problems with goal congruence – within the new division, performance in line with EEE's company objectives will need to be promoted. This may be a problem particularly where quality is concerned. Any acquisition is likely to be used to making poorer quality products so the board of EEE will need to ensure that performance is measured in terms of good quality output rather than simply output. This will ensure that EEE's objectives are maintained.

EEE may face difficulties motivating employees of the new division. They may feel that any new performance measures put in place are unfair and they are likely to resist changes to working practices. They may not supply the information required to assess performance.

The board may find that it is difficult to establish uniform performance measurement across all divisions, particularly where the acquisition is concerned. The new company will have different accounting systems which may take some time to bring in line with the rest of EEE.

The new division is geographically separate and EEE may find that it continues to operate as an isolated unit, unwilling to share information or not perceiving itself to be part of a bigger organisation. Performance measures will need to counter this, making sure they are designed with the whole organisation in mind.

In order to make a good impression on its new owners, management of the division may even be tempted to manipulate the figures they report. This will be particularly likely if individual bonuses are dependent on financial performance. Given the geographical location of the new division and the potential lack of technology to enable effective communication, this would be difficult to remedy.

(ii) ROI is a profit based performance measure. The disadvantages of using it are:

It may not lead to goal congruence. A division with a particularly high ROI may not accept a project with a lower ROI because it will lower overall divisional ROI and any bonuses based on it. It may be however that the company as a whole is operating at a lower ROI and so the project should be accepted.

Since ROI is a measure of profit relative to divisional capital employed, if a division cannot increase profits they may instead seek to keep capital employed as low as possible, not investing in new machinery when needed, for example.

ROI is a short term measure and divisions may therefore forget longer term strategic objectives. They may cut 'discretionary costs' like training, for example, which benefit the organisation in the long term and are essential to overall strategic success.

Using ROI as the primary performance measure ignores the non financial performance of the division. The new manufacturing division may improve quality, for example, to bring its production in line with that expected by EEE. In the short term, this may increase costs and under ROI, management would be penalised for it.

OTHER IMPLEMENTATION ISSUES

72 SSS (SEP 13 EXAM)

Key answer tips:

Requirement (a) should be a straightforward knowledge demonstration question, requiring candidates to demonstrate their understanding of the two key syllabus areas of BPR and PI.

Requirement (b) requires candidates to demonstrate their ability to apply the knowledge of BPR demonstrated in their answers to requirement (a) to the scenario organisation. Candidates must only use the processes mentioned in the scenario to base their answers upon. It is also important that answers should focus upon the application of BPR only.

Requirement (c)(i) examines the candidates' understanding of the impact of BPR upon organisational culture. Candidates should ensure that their answers focus directly upon the possible cultural impact of implementing BPR within SSS. A generic discussion of culture or a description of the cultural web of SSS will not be awarded a pass mark.

Requirement (c)(ii) requires candidates to identify and justify the solutions to the cultural problems identified in part (c)(i) of the answer.

(a)   Business Process Re-engineering and Process Innovation are similar concepts in the area of business process re-design and innovation. Both aim to improve the processes to make a business run more efficiently with the use of technology to help deliver business effectiveness. In the context of the case scenario, these changes should be focused on improving the quality and level of customer service to meet the demands of customers who now have a choice of bank in Country W.

Business Process Re-engineering (BPR)

BPR is the fundamental re-design of the existing business processes in order to achieve dramatic improvements in performance to meet the needs of the customers and to eliminate inefficient processes. BPR tries to identify each of the required steps in a particular process and to define a better system to achieve this service delivery. It often involves the use of technology innovatively to carry out business processes in new ways. For SSS it is likely to involve a radical re-think of its existing business transactions and customer service activities and a review of its current use of technology, particularly in undertaking basic customer transactions and the use of its website. BPR needs to link into SSS's agreed strategy for the future and how that strategy can best be achieved in the long-term. It should not be seen as a short-term fix or way of cutting costs.

Process Innovation (PI)

PI focuses upon the invention of completely new processes, rather than re-designing existing ones and it involves the creation of totally innovative ways to do business and nearly always involves the use of new high tech solutions. This approach is likely to involve SSS re-thinking the entire business and its mission rather than upon individual banking processes and activities that it currently undertakes. Therefore, its impact upon SSS is likely to be much more radical and far reaching than BPR, in that it is likely to involve a complete re-think of the whole mission of the bank and lead to changes in structure and total re-design of processes. An example in the banking business would be the installation of finger print recognition readers at cash machines to identify the customer rather than the use of a magnetic strip on a cash withdrawal plastic card. The use of this new technology would reduce fraud and differentiate SSS from its competitors. Therefore, for each business process, PI would look to see how the use of technology could deliver a better service for customers. This may be through the use of internet banking to save SSS's branch staff processing each of the transactions, or for customers to be able to download their transactions to their computers for further analysis, which could be an attraction for business users.

Examiner's comments

This question was reasonably well answered. Most candidates were able to provide a very good definition of both BPR and PI. However, some candidates clearly did not know what PI is and either ignored this part of the question or provided a poor definition. The main weakness of answers to this question was the explanation of the impact that these two methodologies would have on SSS. Many answers failed to answer this part of the question at all, providing only a basic definition of the two terms in the requirement. Again, candidates are reminded that they must answer the question that has been set.

Common Errors:

- Poor knowledge of Process Innovation
- Limited application of answers to SSS

(b) Each business process performed by SSS needs firstly to be broken down into a series of processes. Each process then needs to be recorded and analysed to find out whether it is necessary, whether it is adding value and whether it provides support to other value adding processes. Any process which is not adding value or which is not providing essential support to the value adding activities needs to be eliminated. Those processes that remain need to be re-designed so that they are as efficient as possible. For SSS this is likely to involve the introduction of new technology to improve these processes. However, SSS must ensure that the statutory processes are not compromised.

The benefits that SSS is likely to obtain from BPR are as follows:

In-branch cash deposits and withdrawals

The activity of depositing and withdrawing cash from the bank is a vital one for customers and therefore must be retained, but clearly there are inefficiencies in the current way of operating this process. Deposits and withdrawals currently are carried out manually in-branch, resulting in long waiting times for customers. BPR would be likely to involve the review of branch staff processing activities to see if there are any unnecessary or duplicate processes taking place and to eliminate these if they do not add value to the customer. In addition, BPR will involve the review of each process to determine whether it could be improved or eliminated through the introduction of technology. The introduction of automated deposits and withdrawals would drastically reduce the manual input of staff and reduce waiting times for customers but would require investment in the installation of Automated Teller Machines (ATM's) into branches.

Loan applications and account opening

Loan applications and opening of new accounts are complex processes, requiring multiple forms to be completed and an interview process. These are likely to be more complex processes than deposits and withdrawals, but nevertheless, there is likely to be room for improved efficiency. BPR would involve the analysis of the whole process and all of the activities involved. It is likely that BPR would identify the need for only one form that captures all of the necessary customer information and it is likely that this could in fact be improved or indeed eliminated through the development of an online application form through SSS's website. Online entry should eliminate the possibility of forms being mislaid, lost or completed incorrectly, again enhancing customer service. Online processing checks, ensuring that data fields are correctly entered by customers should reduce errors and eliminate unnecessary staff activities in checking and re-processing forms.

Customer service activities

Customer relationship management is not a factor that SSS considers to be necessary, as customers have traditionally been loyal. However, this is largely driven by lack of competition, rather than because of high levels of customer satisfaction. Now that customers of Country W have alternative banking opportunities this has now highlighted the need for SSS to focus attention on managing its relationship with its customers. This is evident from the number of customers now leaving SSS and moving to the foreign banks. BPR activities would assist SSS in understanding those processes which SSS's customers value the most and eliminate those which are not valued. The foreign banks have introduced a range of new products, including online banking and mobile and telephone banking facilities, as well as much higher levels of customer service. Clearly these are valued by the customer. As discussed above, in- branch transactions by SSS should be reduced or eliminated completely in favour of online banking facilities. Use of mobile and internet technologies to undertake its business processes and activities should increase customer satisfaction and customer service levels. Also, they will save time and improve efficiency whilst retaining effectiveness.

Overall, it is likely that BPR may increase costs within SSS in the short-term as investment in technology is likely to be required. However, this should have the effect of reducing costly levels of wasted manual activities and processes. In the long-term the benefits should be increased levels of efficiency, profitability and high levels of customer service and retention.

Note: The question only requires candidates to analyse two different business processes of SSS.

Examiner's comments

This question was generally not well answered. Some candidates failed to apply BPR to two different processes undertaken by SSS. However, most were able to identify and discuss the weaknesses of the current deposit and withdrawal process and the loan application process of SSS. Most candidates were able to discuss the impact of BPR on simplifying the processes and reducing non value-adding elements but few answers considered or evaluated the application of technology in both of these processes. Many answers were very brief and lacked any real depth of discussion or understanding of the possible improvements that BPR could make to these processes. Candidates were not expected to have a detailed knowledge or understanding of these individual banking processes, but should have been able to discuss the role that BPR, and the application of technological solutions, could make in the elimination of the non-value-adding elements.

> **Common Errors:**
>
> - A description of the BPR process with limited application to SSS
>
> - Brief and poorly developed answers with limited focus upon the improvements that BPR could make

(c) (i) BPR will be a major change in SSS and is likely to have an impact upon the culture of the business. Culture can be generally defined as 'the way we do things around here' (Charles Handy).

Currently, the culture of SSS appears to be highly bureaucratic and process driven, with staff having to follow rigid procedures and rules, regardless of whether those processes are actually necessary or not. The current structure of the organisation is rigid and inflexible and staff are not encouraged to think of new ideas or ways of operating.

This has resulted in a culture where staff follow these rules and procedures, taking them for granted and not questioning the status quo. This has led to a culture of merely 'doing', which has resulted in low morale, especially as frontline staff receive the brunt of customer complaints.

There is no cultural focus upon the importance of the customer as customer reviews have never been undertaken. Therefore, culturally, the customers experience is not considered to be an important aspect of the business.

It is likely that this culture is deeply embedded in the staff and therefore will be difficult to change. Therefore, it is likely that any initiative such as BPR will lead to resistance to change from staff.

Managers are also likely to find change difficult due to their lack of experience of change in the bank's systems and procedures in the past.

Therefore, a change agent may be necessary to lead the process and to direct both staff and management. This in itself may be problematic as the staff will never have had experience of working with change agents and may resist what could be seen as interference, particularly if it is an external change agent.

> **Examiner's comments**
>
> This question was well answered. Most candidates recognised the limitations of the deeply embedded bureaucratic culture and its possible effect upon the change process in SSS. Most candidates also adequately considered the possible resistance to change by the staff due to their lack of experience of change and their lack of understanding of the need for change. Most answers were very well applied to the scenario information. However, some candidates spent too long in their answer focusing upon a discussion of the elements of the cultural web. This was not asked for nor was it necessarily an appropriate structure for the answer. Therefore, candidates are advised to only use models and theories when it is appropriate to do so. It would appear that sometimes candidates will use a model or a concept to answer a question merely because it was examined in a previous examination. Each examination question is different and therefore candidates must learn that a 'one model answers all questions' approach is not acceptable.

Common Errors:

- Over focusing upon the cultural web without suitable application to the scenario information

- Answering part (c)(ii) in this answer

(c) (ii) The use of the Kotter and Schlesinger 6 stage change model or Lewin's unfreeze/move/re-freeze model may be useful for SSS to adopt to help in the change management process within SSS. It will be necessary for the 'tone from the top' to be set and for the SSS Board to be fully committed to change as a way to improve the customer experience. Any cost savings that occur are incidental and a favourable side-effect of change – but the whole focus needs to be on delivering a better service to customers.

It will be necessary to hold road shows and communicate the ideas for change with staff at all of its 100 branches. This could be done by posters, email, newsletters as well as regular staff briefings at all branches.

This change process takes time, but it is a necessary step in order to achieve employee 'buy in' and for all employees to participate in helping to bring about change and to focus on what customers want.

It may also be necessary to introduce performance related pay (PRP) which links SSS's new business objectives into employees' bonus payments. This will help motivate both employees and managers to achieve the business objectives.

Employees will resist change but emphasis and time needs to be put in by change agents to help overcome this resistance. Tesco has change agents and 'Champions for change' employees at all stores to help bring about business efficiencies and to focus on the customer.

Employees may fear for their jobs and are not familiar with the extensive use of technology, especially very high technology methods, and training will be required. To reassure them, all employees need to be educated that these actions are for the long-term growth of SSS rather than simply for short-term cost savings.

BPR has a reputation for being seen only as a way of cutting costs and achieving staff reductions / redundancies, so it is natural for employees to be concerned.

However, all employees should be briefed about SSS's current loss of customers and its market share and what impact the new foreign banks have had on SSS's performance. It should be explained that the BPR review is being undertaken to enable SSS to grow and develop a long-term strategy to enable it to better serve its customers. Structures will need to be considered and new ways of working will have to be set up. Involvement and participation will be new to staff and training must be undertaken. However, if redundancies are a likely outcome, the Board needs to be transparent and clearly and unambiguously explain this to staff to obtain their confidence.

73   MC (MAR 13 EXAM)

Key answer tips:

Requirement (a) requires candidates to evaluate how the features of the new information system, as presented in the scenario, would help to improve the services of the medical centres and hospitals. Therefore candidates are required to review each of the features listed and consider how it would improve the current services.

Requirement (b) requires candidates to assess the project management problems that might occur during the project, specifically relating to allowing each individual medical centre and hospital to discuss its own needs with the project team. Candidates are expected to apply their knowledge and understanding of project management to this particular aspect of the project. A general discussion of project management problems is not required.

Requirement (c) requires candidates to recommend four performance measures which could be used to measure the achievement of the project team objectives. This should be a straightforward question to identify and justify a number of suitable performance measures appropriate to the objectives. Candidates are only required to recommend and justify four measures.

(a)   **Administrative uses:**

• Patient notes, organisation and management

• Messages and emails instantly sent and received and copies kept

• Ease of transmission of records and files

Improvements to administrative services:

• There will be significantly less time spent administering a computer-based system. Therefore more time can be spent on patient management and value adding activities such as patient care.

• There will be a reduction in the time spent on the telephone with no record kept of phone conversations and therefore less room for error in communication.

• There should be more timely and likely critical receipt of results and patient records. This will cut down on the time of worry for patients waiting for test results.

- Quicker and more accurate access to patients' medical records and medical history. This will enable doctors, especially in a medical emergency, to be aware of all factors and any special circumstances or allergies.

- Convenient and more reliable method to leave messages rather than phone or fax. Again this will give patients and staff more confidence in the communication process.

- Permanent record by email will allow for all recipients to receive the same message and therefore avoids the need for duplication and possible incorrect or inaccurate information. This is particularly critical in diagnosis and communication of results.

- Opportunity to send information to multiple recipients at once. Multiple recipients to receive the same message and therefore avoid the need for duplication and possible mis-communication. More efficient, less prone to human error and everyone concerned gets access to the transfer of the data.

Medical uses:

- Test results can be sent directly and immediately to doctors and patients, allowing for speedier medical response.

- Medical knowledge can be shared throughout Country Q through the use of databases and diagnostic systems, resulting in improved national healthcare. This can be extended to share medical knowledge, diagnosis and discoveries throughout many countries and Country Q could benefit significantly from input from medical experts throughout the world.

- Best practice can be shared across the country.

Improvements to medical staff services:

- The MC system will enable access to up to date medical research and the latest information for diagnosis and treatment, leading to improved decision support and improved diagnostics and treatment.

- It should result in quicker delivery of test results to patients, meaning patients are more satisfied and receive treatment more responsively. This in turn will provide a better health care service for patients, especially if the patient attends more than one medical centre or is repeatedly in hospital. The system would enable all health care professionals to access up to date information.

- There will be a greater ability to share medical knowledge via peer communication helping to increase and share medical knowledge. This should improve the confidence in diagnosis.

- The system will enable 'best practice' to be shared between medical centres and hospital doctors and administrative staff.

- It should lead to increased reliability of medical data held within the system.

- This system may assist in remote consultation, which may be necessary in Country Q if patients have to travel long distances to see doctors.

(b) **Project management problems**

Allowing individual medical centres and hospitals to determine their own individual method of connection and operation will inevitably lead to problems of control for the project manager.

Allowing each medical centre to discuss usage or its specific needs for the MC information system with the project team could lead to the project team losing focus on the key objectives and diverting away from the original objectives. Although this allows individual fears and concerns to be addressed and overcome, it could result in the project team digressing from the project timetable to address minor needs of only a few users. This could confuse the project team and ultimately lead to cost over runs and loss of control of the project. There could be a duplication of effort if different members of the project team are dealing with similar queries from different groups of end users.

Individual contact between 100 medical centres and 30 hospitals will increase project costs and cause delays to the planned implementation timescales.

However, it could allow for greater input from the end users which could help the project team to better understand their needs.

Hardware and software requirements

It is likely to add significantly to project costs to purchase individually, rather than in bulk, the hardware, software and installation equipment. This is all also likely to increase project time and will require significant additional team effort.

Choice of which aspect of the MC information system to connect to

The project team will lose the synergy of one approach across many sites. Obviously, each site will have different connection needs, because of differences in size, location, needs of patients and medical staff. However, a consistent, core approach for connection is critical if control is to be maintained and if costs are to be kept to a minimum (economy of the VFM concept). It will be very difficult to ensure consistency of connection if each individual site has its own discretion. It may also lead to a loss of goal congruence in the overall achievement of the project objectives.

Timing of connection

Most hospitals and medical centres are not likely to want to be the first to adopt connection to the network - most are likely to prefer to transfer later. This too is likely to cause project management problems, as the project team needs to plan for a gradual changeover.

Technically, it would be preferable to make connections gradually and phased over the period. If left to the hospitals and medical centres, the project team will lose control over resource smoothing and this may place excessive demand upon the project team in the later stages of the project life.

Examiner's comments

This question was not well answered. It would appear that most candidates were not expecting a question relating to project management, even though it is part of Section D of the E3 syllabus (Project Management: monitoring the implementation of plans). In addition to this, the E3 examination may examine any material which has been previously examined within the Enterprise pillar. Project management is a key aspect of the E2 syllabus and therefore candidates must be aware that this can, and will be, examined within in E3. However, it would appear that most candidates had remembered very little of their previous E2 studies of project management. Many answers failed to focus upon the specific project management problems of loss of control, increase in project costs, lack of goal congruence and lack of consistency. Instead many answers focused upon issues such as lack of staff experience within the hospitals and medical centres and lack of motivation and possible resistance to change by staff. These issues did not address the question set as this was not a question about change management problems. Candidates must make sure that they clearly read each question requirement and only answer the question that has been set.

Common Errors:

- Lack of focus upon specific project management problems.

- Answers focused upon change management problems and not project management problems.

(c)   **Possible performance measures:**

(Note candidates only have to present 4 performance measures)

1   **Access and usage times of the system compared to original project plan for access and usage rates.**

Regular measures of access and usage will be important measures. The Government will also be interested in the achievement of successful access and usage compared to the plan to ensure that the project is seen to be a success and not a waste of valuable resources.

2   **User satisfaction rates.**

This could be provided by regular questionnaires and feedback to the project team by the users and potentially the patients themselves.

Ultimately, the success of the system will be determined by the users themselves and whether they find the system beneficial and usable. Therefore it is vital to ensure that user satisfaction is monitored and reviewed regularly to ensure that the system continually meets the users' needs.

3   **Number of staff trained per hospital/ medical centre**

and

4   **Number of training days per member of staff.**

The direct users of the MC information system will be most interested in training measures and usage and access measures, as their main concern will be with their ability to use the system effectively and how the usage of the system will affect their day-to-day workload. The Government will be interested in training courses (it will want to ensure that users will be accessing the system correctly, so as to avoid future maintenance and support costs)

5   **Comparison of administrative staff usage versus medical staff usage times.**

and

6   **Number of times doctor/ medical practitioners access the diagnostic system**

Measures of the actual usage of the system will provide valuable information to the Government of the Value For Money of the final system in operation. In particular, the medical diagnostic system is likely to be a highly expensive system to operate and maintain and therefore the Government will need to assess and monitor its usage to ensure that the resources are not being wasted or under used.

7   **Number of connections per month and in total - this could be in the form of staged targets set per month leading to 80% of medical centres and 90% of hospitals connected by July 2014.**

As this is likely to be a highly political project and one which is very high profile, it is important for the government that the project is seen to be a success and, therefore, successful connections will demonstrate that public funds are not being wasted.

8   **Monthly Cost per connection versus budget.**

The Government will also be monitoring the overall cost of the project to ensure that it is economical and that the technology fund is not being wasted. Regular measures of connection progress and the cost of connections will be important measures.

Examiner's comments

This should have been a very straightforward question, merely requiring candidates to take the Government objectives as listed in the scenario and identify only four possible measures which could be used to identify whether these objectives were being met. However, this question was not well answered. Candidates must not think that every time they are asked a question on performance measures then they must automatically produce a balanced scorecard! The question specifically asked for performance measures relating directly to the objectives set by the Government, which were clearly presented in the scenario information. Yet so many candidates completely ignored these and instead prepared a balanced scorecard with measures relating to patient satisfaction surveys and internal development measures which were largely irrelevant to the objectives specifically and directly presented in the scenario. The scenario information is there for a reason and candidates must use it and not completely ignore it. A balanced scorecard could have been reasonably used, but the measures must have been directly related to the Government objectives in the scenario. Far too many candidates completely ignored these and therefore failed to answer the question that had been set.

Common Errors:

- Ignoring the objectives set by the Government and listed in the scenario

- Not presenting performance measures at all - rather CSFs

- Use of a balanced scorecard which contained inappropriate measures for the objectives set

74 4D TEACHING HOSPITAL (MAY 06 EXAM)

Key answer tips

Part (a) is tricky because there are no universally accepted definitions of BPR and PI and some involve considerable overlap. If necessary the definition of PI could be invented! In part (ii) make sure you justify your classification by reference back to your definitions in part (i). Also in part (i) make sure you discuss the **role of IT** in each as this was explicitly asked for.

In part (b) ensure that you explain and **evaluate** each benefit.

(a) (i) Business Process Re-engineering (BPR) is the fundamental re-thinking and rational re-design of existing business processes to achieve improvements in performance measures such as cost, quality, service and speed.

Process Innovation (PI) is the invention of entirely new processes.

The main differences between BPR and PI are as follows:

- BPR focuses on existing processes whereas PI emphasises the invention of new processes.

- There is a much greater emphasis on human resource management in PI. BPR has often been criticised for neglecting HR issues.

- PI may involve rethinking the entire business and its mission rather than focusing on individual processes as is the case with BPR.

- With BPR the role of IT is generally as an implementation tool, for example to improve the speed of information processing. With PI, IT is often a change trigger allowing the development of new processes due to technological advances.

  For example, improvements in the technology surrounding wireless LAN has allowed hospital consultants to refer to and update detailed patient records while doing ward rounds, completely changing the previous process of writing up notes later.

(ii) The new OTIS system could be viewed as an example of BPR on the grounds that:

- The new process is still one of linking students, lecturers and surgeons but on a larger scale. As such it is a development of an existing system.

However, it is more likely to be viewed as PI because:

- The inclusion of remote students to participate in the system could be argued to be an entirely new process.

- Developments in web technology have triggered the change.

On balance the new system should be viewed as PI.

(b)   The benefits of OTIS are as follows:

To 4D

- The new system will improve 4D's already good reputation. This could be significant as it might result in greater success in raising funds and reduce the chance of closure if local government decides that it has too many hospitals.

- The new system will considerably reduce the training cost per student, freeing up funds for other areas.

- The new system could also allow 4D to raise additional funds by charging remote students to participate. This could be a significant injection into the hospital finances, facilitating further expansion of the teaching side.

- The extra possibilities that the new system presents could allow 4D to attract and keep the very best professors, lecturers and consultants. Given the existing excellence, this is unlikely to be a major benefit.

To society

- The improved training should mean that the level of expertise among surgeons will be higher, improving the likelihood of a healthy recovery of patients undertaking surgery. In the local community the standard of clinical excellence was already very high so the improvement will not be significant.

- However, the possibility of receiving high level training and supervision for surgeons in more remote locations could give a dramatic improvement in patient prognoses.

- The new system should also mean that surgeons can be trained more cheaply and efficiently. Given that some finance is likely to come from public sources, this should free up funds for other services (e.g. social care) to be provided. This benefit will be less significant due to the sums involved.

Section 5

SPECIMEN PAPER QUESTIONS

E3 – ENTERPRISE STRATEGY

1   Pre-seen Case Study

Background

Power Utilities (PU) is located in a democratic Asian country. Just over 12 months ago, the former nationalised Electricity Generating Corporation (EGC) was privatised and became PU. EGC was established as a nationalised industry many years ago. Its home government at that time had determined that the provision of the utility services of electricity generation production should be managed by boards that were accountable directly to Government. In theory, nationalised industries should be run efficiently, on behalf of the public, without the need to provide any form of risk related return to the funding providers. In other words, EGC, along with other nationalised industries was a non-profit making organisation. This, the Government claimed at the time, would enable prices charged to the final consumer to be kept low.

Privatisation of EGC

The Prime Minister first announced three years ago that the Government intended to pursue the privatisation of the nationalised industries within the country. The first priority was to be the privatisation of the power generating utilities and EGC was selected as the first nationalised industry to be privatised. The main purpose of this strategy was to encourage public subscription for share capital. In addition, the Government's intention was that PU should take a full and active part in commercial activities such as raising capital and earning higher revenue by increasing its share of the power generation and supply market by achieving growth either organically or through making acquisitions. This, of course, also meant that PU was exposed to commercial pressures itself, including satisfying the requirements of shareholders and becoming a potential target for take-over. The major shareholder, with a 51% share, would be the Government. However, the Minister of Energy has recently stated that the Government intends to reduce its shareholding in PU over time after the privatisation takes place.

Industry structure

PU operates 12 coal-fired power stations across the country and transmits electricity through an integrated national grid system which it manages and controls. It is organised into three regions, Northern, Eastern and Western. Each region generates electricity which is sold to 10 private sector electricity distribution companies which are PU's customers.

The three PU regions transmit the electricity they generate into the national grid system. A shortage of electricity generation in one region can be made up by taking from the national grid. This is particularly important when there is a national emergency, such as exceptional weather conditions.

The nationalised utility industries, including the former EGC, were set up in a monopolistic position. As such, no other providers of these particular services were permitted to enter the market within the country. Therefore, when EGC was privatised and became PU it remained the sole generator of electricity in the country. The electricity generating facilities, in the form of the 12 coal-fired power stations, were all built over 15 years ago and some date back to before EGC came into being.

The 10 private sector distribution companies are the suppliers of electricity to final users including households and industry within the country, and are not under the management or control of PU. They are completely independent companies owned by shareholders.

The 10 private sector distribution companies serve a variety of users of electricity. Some, such as AB, mainly serve domestic users whereas others, such as DP, only supply electricity to a few industrial clients. In fact, DP has a limited portfolio of industrial customers and 3 major clients, an industrial conglomerate, a local administrative authority and a supermarket chain. DP finds these clients costly to service.

Structure of PU

The structure of PU is that it has a Board of Directors headed by an independent Chairman and a separate Managing Director. The Chairman of PU was nominated by the Government at the time the announcement that EGC was to be privatised was made. His background is that he is a former Chairman of an industrial conglomerate within the country. There was no previous Chairman of EGC which was managed by a Management Board, headed by the Managing Director. The former EGC Managing Director retired on privatisation and a new Managing Director was appointed.

The structure of PU comprises a hierarchy of many levels of management authority. In addition to the Chairman and Managing Director, the Board consists of the Directors of each of the Northern, Eastern and Western regions, a Technical Director, the Company Secretary and the Finance Director. All of these except the Chairman are the Executive Directors of PU. The Government also appointed seven Non Executive Directors to PU's Board. With the exception of the Company Secretary and Finance Director, all the Executive Directors are qualified electrical engineers. The Chairman and Managing Director of PU have worked hard to overcome some of the inertia which was an attitude that some staff had developed within the former EGC. PU is now operating efficiently as a private sector company. There have been many staff changes at a middle management level within the organisation.

Within the structure of PU's headquarters, there are five support functions; engineering, finance (which includes PU's Internal Audit department), corporate treasury, human resource management (HRM) and administration, each with its own chief officers, apart from HRM. Two Senior HRM Officers and Chief Administrative Officer report to the Company Secretary. The Chief Accountant and Corporate Treasurer each report to the Finance Director. These functions, except Internal Audit, are replicated in each region, each with its own regional officers and support staff. Internal Audit is an organisation wide function and is based at PU headquarters.

Regional Directors of EGC

The Regional Directors all studied in the field of electrical engineering at the country's leading university and have worked together for a long time. Although they did not all attend the university at the same time, they have a strong belief in the quality of their education. After graduation from university, each of the Regional Directors started work at EGC in a junior capacity and then subsequently gained professional electrical engineering qualifications. They believe that the experience of working up through the ranks of EGC has enabled them to have a clear understanding of EGC's culture and the technical aspects of the industry as a whole. Each of the Regional Managers has recognised the changed environment that PU now operates within, compared with the former EGC, and they are now working hard to help PU achieve success as a private sector electricity generator. The Regional Directors are well regarded by both the Chairman and Managing Director, both in terms of their technical skill and managerial competence.

Governance of EGC

Previously, the Managing Director of the Management Board of EGC reported to senior civil servants in the Ministry of Energy. There were no shareholders and ownership of the Corporation rested entirely with the Government. That has now changed. The Government holds 51% of the shares in PU and the Board of Directors is responsible to the shareholders but, inevitably, the Chairman has close links directly with the Minister of Energy, who represents the major shareholder.

The Board meetings are held regularly, normally weekly, and are properly conducted with full minutes being taken. In addition, there is a Remuneration Committee, an Audit Committee and an Appointments Committee, all in accordance with best practice. The model which has been used is the Combined Code on Corporate Governance which applies to companies which have full listing status on the London Stock Exchange. Although PU is not listed on the London Stock Exchange, the principles of the Combined Code were considered by the Government to be appropriate to be applied with regard to the corporate governance of the company.

Currently, PU does not have an effective Executive Information System and this has recently been raised at a Board meeting by one of the non-executive directors because he believes this inhibits the function of the Board and consequently is disadvantageous to the governance of PU.

Remuneration of Executive Directors

In order to provide a financial incentive, the Remuneration Committee of PU has agreed that the Executive Directors be entitled to performance related pay, based on a bonus scheme, in addition to their fixed salary and health benefits.

Capital market

PU exists in a country which has a well developed capital market relating both to equity and loan stock funding. There are well established international institutions which are able to provide funds and corporate entities are free to issue their own loan stock in accordance with internationally recognised principles. PU is listed on the country's main stock exchange.

Strategic opportunity

The Board of PU is considering the possibility of vertical integration into electricity supply and has begun preliminary discussion with DP's Chairman with a view to making an offer for DP. PU's Board is attracted by DP's strong reputation for customer service but is aware, through press comment, that DP has received an increase in complaints regarding its service to customers over the last year. When the former EGC was a nationalised business, breakdowns were categorised by the Government as "urgent", when there was a danger to life, and "non-urgent" which was all others. Both the former EGC and DP had a very high success rate in meeting the government's requirements that a service engineer should attend the urgent break-down within 60 minutes. DP's record over this last year in attending urgent breakdowns has deteriorated seriously and if PU takes DP over, this situation would need to improve.

Energy consumption within the country and Government drive for increased efficiency and concern for the environment

Energy consumption has doubled in the country over the last 10 years. As PU continues to use coal-fired power stations, it now consumes most of the coal mined within the country.

The Minister of Energy has indicated to the Chairman of PU that the Government wishes to encourage more efficient methods of energy production. This includes the need to reduce production costs. The Government has limited resources for capital investment in energy production and wishes to be sure that future energy production facilities are more efficient and effective than at present.

The Minister of Energy has also expressed the Government's wish to see a reduction in harmful emissions from the country's power stations. (The term harmful emissions in this context, refers to pollution coming out of electricity generating power stations which damage the environment.)

One of PU's non-executive directors is aware that another Asian country is a market leader in coal gasification which is a fuel technology that could be used to replace coal for power generation. In the coal gasification process, coal is mixed with oxygen and water vapour under pressure, normally underground, and then pumped to the surface where the gas can be used in power stations. The process significantly reduces carbon dioxide emissions although it is not widely used at present and not on any significant commercial scale.

Another alternative to coal fired power stations being actively considered by PU's Board is the construction of a dam to generate hydro-electric power. The Board is mindful of the likely adverse response of the public living and working in the area where the dam would be built.

In response to the Government's wishes, PU has established environmental objectives relating to improved efficiency in energy production and reducing harmful emissions such as greenhouse gases. PU has also established an ethical code. Included within the code are sections relating to recycling and reduction in harmful emissions as well as to terms and conditions of employment.

Introduction of commercial accounting practices at EGC

The first financial statements have been produced for PU for 2008. Extracts from the Statement of Financial Position from this are shown in Appendix A. Within these financial statements, some of EGC's loans were "notionally" converted by the Government into ordinary shares. Interest is payable on the Government loans as shown in the statement of financial position. 'Reserves' is a sum which was vested in EGC when it was first nationalised. This represents the initial capital stock valued on a historical cost basis from the former electricity generating organisations which became consolidated into EGC when it was first nationalised.

Being previously a nationalised industry and effectively this being the first "commercially based" financial statements, there are no retained earnings brought forward into 2008.

APPENDIX A EXTRACTS FROM THE PRO FORMA FINANCIAL STATEMENTS OF THE ELECTRICITY GENERATING CORPORATION

Statement of financial position as at 31 December 2008

	P\$ million
ASSETS	
Non-current assets	15,837
Current assets	
Inventories	1,529
Receivables	2,679
Cash and Cash equivalents	133
	4,341
Total assets	20,178
EQUITY AND LIABILITIES	
Equity	
Share capital	5,525
Reserves	1,231
Total equity	6,756
Non-current liabilities	
Government loans	9,560
Current liabilities	
Payables	3,862
Total liabilities	13,422
Total equity and liabilities	20,178

1   **Unseen material for Case Study**

Background

EGC was privatised just over a year ago and is now Power Utilities (PU). The new Board of Directors of PU is accountable to the shareholders, the major one being the Government which holds 51% of the shares.

In an early move by PU, it has taken over two of the private electricity distribution companies. One of these, DP, located in the Eastern Division of PU, serves a limited portfolio of industrial customers and three major clients. The takeover was not disputed with DP's Board recommending to its shareholders acceptance of the bid. PU now holds 90% of DP's shares.

The Board of Directors of PU has established a Management Board at DP which is independently chaired by a nominee from PU's Board. The previous Executive Directors on DP's board have all retained their posts and their remuneration includes a performance bonus based on DP's overall profitability. The previous Chairman of DP has retired.

Customer service

During the time when EGC was nationalised, customer break-downs had been categorised by the Government as Urgent (when there was a danger to life) and Non-urgent (all other breakdowns).

There was a requirement for Urgent break-downs that a service engineer should be with the customer within 60 minutes or less. Before privatisation the electricity distribution industry had a very high success rate in meeting this requirement with 99.9% of customers being attended within 60 minutes and nobody ever waited longer than 90 minutes for attention.

Non-urgent break-downs were attended to in turn but there was no maximum time requirement for an engineer to attend. There were always a significant number of Non-urgent break-downs to attend to and customers might wait as long as six months for attention.

During the last year there have been an increasing number of complaints to DP from its customers regarding the slow attendance of service engineers following a reduction in their numbers. It was often now the case that customers with Urgent break-downs had to wait for up to a day for attention and the situation for customers with Non-urgent break-downs also had got worse.

Options for change

The Technical Director (TD) of DP has been investigating the deteriorating standards of customer service. He believes that there are two possible ways forward which he proposed to put to the Board of Directors of DP.

The first would be to invest a considerable amount of resources to improve the existing in-house customer service carried out by DP's service engineers. The other response would be to outsource customer service. The financial data relating to both these options is given below:

Financial implications

In-house

If the customer service is kept in-house, DP will have to spend money recruiting additional engineers and training and equipping all the engineers to a very high standard. In order to meet the service targets of 100% attendance within 60 minutes for Urgent break-downs (which it is estimated will amount to 6,000 each year) and also that up to 2,000 Non-urgent break-downs are resolved each year, DP will employ 75 engineers. The cost of establishing this new service network together with infrastructure, recruitment, training and equipment set-up costs in the first year only will amount to P$50,000,000. In addition, there would be an annual running cost of P$8,000,000.

Outsource

DP has had a quote from a reputable service company, RSC. RSC would employ 38 service engineers and would charge DP P$250 for each Urgent break-down which it attended and P$150 for each Non-urgent break-down which it attended. It has enough capacity to attend all the break-downs which DP estimates will occur each year. However, it cannot commit to attending 100% of Urgent break-downs within 60 minutes: RSC estimates it will only be able to attend 99% of Urgent break-downs within 60 minutes. The remainder will take between 2 and 4 hours before RSC can get its engineers to the customer.

As a condition of RSC accepting the contract it will require a 'one off' payment of P$30,000,000 when the contract is signed.

Other information

Industry history shows that there is a probability of fatality or serious injury when the response to an Urgent break-down is delayed. In the case of DP, it is estimated that every urgent break-down not attended by a service engineer within 60 minutes carries a 0.1% chance of a fatality or serious injury.

Investments such as the one proposed by the TD are regarded by DP as having an opportunity cost of capital of 10%.

The TD and the Management Accountant (MA)

In their discussions about the outsourcing of the customer service the MA had asked the TD if it was possible to quantify the financial cost of fatality or serious injury caused by the nonattendance of an engineer within 60 minutes to an Urgent break-down. The TD said it was not worth doing this as the chance was so small and he did not want to distract the Board in its decision making with irrelevant data. The MA agreed that the probability of a fatality or serious injury was low but nevertheless as DP aspired to being a good corporate citizen and in the interests of transparency this information should go before the Board.

The TD stated that these forecasts were his, he took responsibility for them and he would not be placing the information about fatality and serious injury before the Board. The TD stated that he would answer any question put to him by the Board but that the MA should concentrate on his own job and let the TD get on with his.

Required:

(a) (i)   Compare and contrast the rational planning model with the Incrementalist approach to strategic planning. **(6 marks)**

     (ii) Advise the Board of Directors of DP of another approach to forming strategy which would be most suitable for its organisation's changed circumstances as a privatised company. **(4 marks)**

(b) (i)   Analyse the two alternative methods of servicing DP's customers. Note: All 10 marks are for calculation in this requirement. **(10 marks)**

     (ii) Discuss the consequences of the two methods of servicing DP's customers. **(5 marks)**

(c) Evaluate the extent to which the views of the Technical Director regarding the disclosure of information about non-attendance at Urgent break-downs within 60 minutes represents an ethical dilemma for the Management Accountant. **(10 marks)**

(d) In the light of the changed circumstances of DP, and your findings and evaluation above:

     (i)   recommend, with reasons, four Critical Success Factors (CSFs) which would be appropriate for DP as a company **(8 marks)**

     (ii) discuss the main attributes for an effective Information System by which DP would be able to manage the Urgent and Non-urgent breakdowns. **(7 marks)**

(Total: 50 marks)

2 ZZM is a multinational company which buys agricultural products for use in its manufacturing process. ZZM has committed to observe all guidelines and codes of conduct for multinationals. This policy was prompted by ZZM's desire to be a good corporate citizen.

ZZM has been trading profitably for ten years with farmers' co-operatives in Agriland, an agricultural country. ZZM's business is an important part of Agriland's economy. ZZM has made efforts to improve both the production techniques of the farmers and the living conditions of farm workers and their families. ZZM has built a number of schools and also a district hospital in Agriland.

The farmers' co-operatives have freedom to trade with anyone but have chosen to deal exclusively with ZZM. ZZM has enjoyed harmonious relationships within Agriland but this now seems threatened by a number of factors.

The Government of Agriland has been under the control of the same political party for the previous 15 years. Recently there have been allegations of corruption made against the Government and its popularity has decreased: some analysts think it might lose the next general election. The main opposition party is very nationalistic and opposed to free trade. It has stated that if it is elected it will nationalise all foreign owned businesses without compensation.

The farm workers' union in Agriland has asked for an immediate 10% pay rise as farm workers' pay has not increased for two years although prices have increased by 20%. The farm workers have never been militant but this is changing. In some areas of Agriland, farm workers have gone on strike.

At a recent meeting between the President of Agriland and ZZM, the President said there was a common interest in preventing the main opposition party from winning the next general election. The President suggested a number of strategies which could be followed:

1   ZZM could give a substantial donation to the President's party for its election funds.

2   ZZM could agree to an extra tax on its Agriland operations. This could be used to increase the national minimum wage for farm workers.

3   ZZM could open an agricultural processes factory within Agriland to assist economic development.

The President stated his strategies were not mutually exclusive. He added that if ZZM was not able to help him, then he would seriously consider nationalising ZZM's operations without any compensation.

Required:

(a)   **Advise how stakeholder mapping could assist ZZM in deciding the options to pursue with respect to Agriland.**

   Note: **You are not required to draw Mendelow's matrix**   **(4 marks)**

(b)   **Construct a stakeholder analysis for ZZM's business in Agriland.**   **(9 marks)**

(c)   **Evaluate the options suggested by the President and one other option which you have identified.**   **(8 marks)**

(d)   **Recommend the option which you consider ZZM should follow. Explain the reasons(s) for your recommendation.**   **(4 marks)**

(Total: 25 marks)

3 RTF is an architectural practice owned by 3 partners and employing 20 other staff. Its vision has been stated as: 'Your future designed by RTF: Today!' Its business is focused on designing housing schemes for local governments and also individual houses for wealthy clients. The emphasis in the housing schemes has been to produce high-quality homes to standard designs and ensuring that the schemes were completed on time and within budget. RTF has established a library of designs which it has successfully used and which can be reused. The relationships which RTF has established with local government employees have been important for the successful completion of its contracts. RTF has a corporate contacts database where every local government employee it has dealt with is recorded. This has proved invaluable to RTF.

RTF's other main income stream comes from the design of individual, 'one-off', houses for wealthy clients. The partners have always enjoyed this work as it gives them the opportunity to express their professional talents. However, the recently appointed Management Accountant has concerns about this business as she believes the partners spend a disproportionate amount of their time on this work. One fundamental control system within a professional practice is the system for recording time which forms the basis for costing work. Unlike most of its industry which uses proprietary software, RTF relies upon a manual system for recording time spent on each project and the results are often inaccurate.

The partners have always believed that a staff development policy is important for success. They have invested in improving the educational and technical background of their staff. RTF has a strong relationship with its local university. One result of this relationship is a computerised design package, '2020Design', which RTF and the university jointly developed and own. The package speeds up the design process and offers the possibility of significant cost savings. If this package is applied within RTF it could result in either a greater throughput of work from the existing staff, staff reductions or some combination of both of these.

RTF has carried out market research regarding the potential demand for 2020Design. This research indicates that 2020Design will be a viable commercial product. In what will be a significant strategic and cultural change for RTF it intends to market 2020Design and has employed a Marketing Manager. The Marketing Manager intends to licence agents to sell 2020Design in RTF's home country and abroad.

RTF does not have any systematic way of relating its operations to its vision or of measuring performance. However, one of the partners has heard of the Balanced Scorecard and has suggested that this might be an appropriate model for RTF to use.

Required:

(a) Explain the four different perspectives of the Balanced Scorecard model. **(4 marks)**

(b) For each of the four perspectives, discuss and recommend two appropriate measures which would assist RTF. **(8 marks)**

(c) Recommend how RTF could introduce and use the Balanced Scorecard to help it achieve the required changes in strategy and culture. **(13 marks)**

(Total: 25 marks)

4   GHK is a restaurant chain consisting of eight restaurants in an attractive part of a European country which is popular with tourists. GHK has been owned by the same family for the previous 15 years and has always traded at a profit. However, a number of factors have meant that GHK is now in danger of making a trading loss. There has been a substantial drop in the number of tourists visiting the region whilst, at the same time, the prices of many of the foodstuffs and drinks used in its restaurants has increased. Added to this, the local economy has shrunk with several large employers reducing the size of their workforce.

The owners of GHK commissioned a restaurant consultant to give them an independent view of their business. The consultant observed that the eight restaurants were all very different in appearance. They also served menus that were very different, for example, one restaurant which was located on a barge in a coastal town specialised in fish dishes, whereas another restaurant 20 miles away had a good reputation as a steak house. The prices varied greatly amongst the restaurants; one restaurant in a historic country house offered 'fine dining' and was extremely expensive; yet another located near a busy railway station served mainly fast food and claimed that its prices were 'the cheapest in town'. Three of GHK's restaurants offered a 'middle of the road' dining experience with conventional menus and average prices. Some of the restaurants had licences which enabled them to serve alcohol with their meals but three restaurants did not have such licences. One restaurant had a good trade in children's birthday parties whereas the restaurant in the historic country house did not admit diners under the age of 18.

The consultant recommended that GHK should examine these differences but did not suggest how. The owners responded that the chain had grown organically over a number of years and that the location, style and pricing decisions made in each restaurant had all been made at different times and depended on trends current at that time.

Required:

(a)   **Advise the owners of GHK how the application of Porter's Three Generic Strategies Model could assist them in maintaining or improving the profitability of their restaurants.**

   Note: **You are not required to suggest individual generic strategies for each of GHK's restaurants.**   **(10 marks)**

(b)   **Advise how GHK could employ a range of organisational information systems to support whichever generic strategy it chooses to adopt.**   **(15 marks)**

(Total: 25 marks)

Section 6

ANSWERS TO SPECIMEN PAPER QUESTIONS

E3 – ENTERPRISE STRATEGY

1   DP

(a)   (i)   The rational planning model (RPM) is arguably the model most associated with the formation of strategy. CIMA has defined aspects of this model in the following ways:

'Planning: the establishment of objectives and the formulation, evaluation and selection of the policies, strategies, tactics and action required to achieve them. Planning comprises long-term strategic planning, and short-term/operational planning.'

'Strategy: a course of action, including the specification of resources required, to achieve a specific objective.'

'Strategic plan: a statement of long-term goals along with a definition of the strategies and policies which will ensure achievement of these goals.'

RPM has the advantage of being well-known and it offers a procedure to enable organisations to construct their strategies which articulate the organisation's desired relationships with its external environments. Added to this, the rational planning model when viewed at its short-term perspective has an obvious interface with accounting constructs such as annual accounts and budgets.

The use of RPM is often a requirement for organisations receiving funds from central government such as hospitals and universities who are asked to produce, for example, one year and five year plans.

RPM has as an underlying tenet the concept of maximization derived from classical economic theory. In contrast, H Simon suggested that managers were more likely to pursue satisfactory goals: that they were 'satisficers'. This is associated with the idea of incrementalism: making small and slow changes to strategy rather than radical changes, 'Evolution not Revolution'. Quinn described the process of logical incrementalism whereby strategy is made not by planning but rather by gradual discrete changes allied to an underlying logic.

The two approaches represent different philosophies regarding the formation of strategy. Arguably, there is no right way of formulating strategy; what is most suitable for an organisation is contingent upon its individual circumstances.

Other approaches which have been observed in practice include, Mintzberg's 'crafting' strategy and the antithesis of planning, 'freewheeling opportunism'.

(ii)   In the circumstances of DP having newly emerged from state control it is most likely that RPM is the most familiar approach for them. If the contention that there is no right way of approaching strategy is valid DP could continue with its RPM but adapt it and make it more flexible by admitting the emergent. Thus, for example, it might shorten its planning period and be willing to continuously monitor and change its strategy, if that should prove beneficial.

(b)   (i)

Option 1		P$000s	Option 2		P$000s	
In-house			Outsource			
Capital cost		**50,000**	Capital cost		30,000	
Yearly running cost		**8,000**	Yearly running cost			
Urgent visits	6,000		Urgent visits	6,000	1,500	P$250 a visit
Non-urgent visits	2,000		Non-urgent visits	2,000	300	P$150 a visit
			Yearly running cost		**1,800**	
No. of engineers	75		No. of engineers	38		
Service standard			**Service standard**			
Urgent	100%		Urgent	99%		
Non-urgent	Within 1 month		Non-urgent	ASAP		

10 year period				10 year period		
Year	P$000s	P$000s		**Year**	P$000s	P$000s
0		−50,000		0		−30,000
1 to 10	8,000			1 to 10	1,800	
Annuity factor 10 years/10%	6.145	−49,160			6.145	−11,061
Total		**−99,160**				**−41,061**

(ii)   The financial aspect of this decision indicates the adoption of outsourcing which is only 41% of the cost of the in-house operation. However, the service attainment projected for this option is inferior to that of the in-house: only 99% of the Urgent break-downs are attended to within 60 minutes and it is not clear when the Non-urgent break-downs will be attended to. This lower standard of customer service is, presumably, a result of employing only half the number of service engineers as compared to the in-house option.

The lower customer service standard also carries a small but arguably significant risk of a fatality or serious injury due to non-attendance within 60 minutes:

6,000 break-downs × 1% = 60 breakdowns not attended to within 60 minutes
60 break-downs × 0.1% = 0.6 fatalities or serious injury.

The consequence in terms of human life of this lower service standard is that 0.6 or 1 person could die each year. This could have serious financial consequences for DP and the image of the company would be damaged if it was known that it had implemented a service policy with this attendant risk of fatality and serious injury.

It is also possible that this risk may conflict with corporate values and it would certainly conflict with the personal values of some of the employees of DP, for example, its service engineers.

(c) The Chartered Institute of Management Accountants (CIMA) has adopted a Code of Ethics (hereafter the Code) to give guidance to its members with regard to their behaviour.

CIMA has established fundamental principles of professional ethics for professional accountants which include:

Integrity 'A professional accountant should be straightforward and honest in all professional and business relationships'.

CIMA further state that 'A professional accountant should not be associated with reports etc. where they believe that the information:

Omits or obscures information required to be included where such omission or obscurity would be misleading'.

It is arguable that not telling the Board of Directors of DP about all the consequences of the outsourcing service option, namely the likelihood of a fatality or serious injury conflicts with corporate and ethical values and is not behaviour that is 'straightforward and honest'.

Objectivity 'A professional accountant should not allow bias, conflict of interest or undue influence of others to override professional or business judgements'.

The principle of objectivity imposes an obligation on all professional accountants not to compromise their professional or business judgement because of bias, conflict of interest or the undue influence of others.'

It is arguable that the Technical Director is using his position and personality to keep the Management Accountant silent, on the aspect of safety, which is a conflict under the Code.

The situation in which the Management Accountant is in with regards to the non-disclosure of the information about a potential fatality or serious injury should the out-sourcing service option be followed is potentially in conflict with two of the fundamental principles of the Code.

As such the Management Accountant has an ethical dilemma to resolve and should seek further guidance from the Code as to how to proceed.

All the quotations in this section are from the CIMA Code of Ethics for Professional Accountants, October 2007.

(d) (i) CIMA defines Critical Success Factors (CSFs) as: 'CSFs are elements of the organisational activity which are central to its future success. CSFs may change over time and may include items such as product quality, employee attitudes, manufacturing flexibility and brand awareness'.

Product quality

DP's product is electricity and its supply should be fit for purpose. This implies continuity of supply and that means that DP must work to ensure that power fluctuations and interruptions are kept to a minimum. DP would need to specify CSFs to monitor these aspects which would be amenable to ratio analysis and also variance analysis. Examples would be:

- % number of minutes supply was interrupted
- Cost of interruptions in penalty payments

Employee attitudes

DP's employees have undergone a significant change in their working lives due to change in ownership structure. This change from nationalised industry to private sector company has many cultural implications. These changes will have impacted upon employee morale and DP would be concerned whether the changes have had beneficial or detrimental effects.

Examples of CSFs in this area would include:

- Employee turnover
- Absenteeism

Manufacturing flexibility

Not discussed as it would require specialist knowledge of the electricity distribution industry.

Brand awareness

In a free market environment and given that electricity is an homogenous product, from the point of view of the customer, it is comparatively easy for customers to change their suppliers. Suppliers will try to reduce the rate at which customers move between them, the churn rate, by offering loyalty incentives and by competing on price.

A further competitive option which is available to producers of homogenous products is to try to establish some form of brand identity. An example of this in the UK is the energy company E.ON which sponsors a major English sporting competition, the FA Cup.

DP could establish CSFs such as:

- % of market aware of the DP brand
- Number of customers moving to DP in the previous period
- Number of customers moving from DP in the previous period

Note: The CSFs given in this section are examples and not an exhaustive list. Candidates would also be rewarded for other appropriate examples.

(ii)   DP needs to manage breakdowns which have important implications for customer service and safety. Whatever system it employs it must have the characteristics of being robust, flexible and comprehensive.

An essential element of such a system is a database with its allied database management system. The database should hold, and allow access to, for example, details of all of DP's customers including their service histories, geographic and contact details. The database should also include, for bigger/industrial customers, layout plans of their electrical equipment and have the ability to access and transmit to the service engineers fault-finding information and manufacturers' drawings and information.

The service engineers would need to be equipped with wireless computers which could communicate with the database whilst the service engineer is attending a break-down and provision should be made for alternate communication in areas of poor wireless reception. They will also require a suitable GPS device to assist in locating the break-downs.

The information system should also incorporate software to identify where each service engineer is located and their current status. The software should also incorporate algorithms to optimise the responses of the service engineers to break-downs.

2   ZZM

(a)   A stakeholder analysis for ZZM's operations within Agriland would enable ZZM to identify the degree of interest and power possessed by each group or stakeholder. As an example, consider both the President of Agriland and a farm worker in one of the co-operatives. Both have an interest in ZZM's business but that of the President is very great whilst the farm workers' is much smaller. Similarly, the power to affect ZZM's business is very high in the case of the President but would be negligible in the case of the farm workers.

Having identified the stakeholders, it would be clear to ZZM whose support it will need in order to be successful. It will also identify any stakeholders who may have the power or potential power to disrupt its business.

Having categorised the stakeholders, ZZM then has guidance as to how it should manage these and their expectations in the future. Mendelow's suggested stances are:

- Minimal effort
- Keep informed
- Keep satisfied
- Must secure agreement

(b)   Using Mendelow's model the following stakeholders are present for ZZM's operations within Agriland:

High power/High interest

These would include the President of Agriland and also the Government of the country. The main opposition party has the potential to also be included in this category. However, unless and until it wins the general election it does not possess high power. The farm workers' union is in a similar position to the main opposition party as its power seems low at present but could grow with increased militancy.

High power/low interest

ZZM's shareholders have ultimate power over the company should they choose to exercise it. However, as Agriland represents only one of the many countries where ZZM does business the shareholders are unlikely to have a high level of interest in it.

Low power/High interest

The main opposition party and the farm workers' union both have high levels of interest in ZZM's business but, at present, have little power.

Other groups

The farmers' co-operatives, the farmers and the farm workers and their families would all probably have interests ranging from medium to high. The amount of power which they possess is not clear. It could range at its highest for the co-operatives if they were to take combined action with respect to ZZM, to low to non-existent in the case of an individual member of a farm worker's family.

Low power/low interest

There are no groups mentioned in the scenario which fall into this category.

(c) **ZZM could give a substantial donation to the President's party for its election funds.**

Given the concerns about corruption this option seems questionable and it may conflict with the codes of conduct which ZZM supports. It would create a definite association between ZZM and the President so that, if the President did not win the election, it could prove very difficult for ZZM to carry on business within Agriland. However, if the main opposition party wins the election ZZM will be nationalised without compensation.

ZZM could agree to an extra tax on its Agriland operations. This could be used to increase the national minimum wage for farm workers.

The effect of this tax may make ZZM's business in Agriland uneconomic. Although ZZM is an important part of Agriland's economy, it does not directly employ the agricultural workers. ZZM may consider that this proposal is unreasonable and, if agreed to, may create a bad precedent both within Agriland and also in other countries where ZZM trades.

ZZM should open an agricultural processes factory within Agriland to assist economic development.

The economic viability of this proposal needs to be examined. It could prove to be a realistic option and the contribution which it makes to the development of the economy of Agriland is important.

The President stated that his strategies were not mutually exclusive. He added that if ZZM was not able to help him then he would seriously consider nationalising ZZM operations without any compensation.

Of the three options proposed by the President only the last one seems to be potentially acceptable. The President's further comments suggest that he may be requiring that ZZM agrees to all three proposals and he has also threatened ZZM with nationalisation without compensation.

Taken as a whole, the President's views could lead ZZM to a strategy of its own; withdrawal from Agriland. This would have the disadvantages of the loss of profits from the business in Agriland and the effects upon the economy and people of Agriland. However, depending upon the results of the next general election, or even earlier depending upon the President's actions, ZZM may lose its business anyway.

(d)   It is not obvious which option ZZM should follow. It will depend upon a number of factors, including an assessment of the likely results of the next general election and also how much the President's suggestions represent a bargaining stance and how much they are definite plans. ZZM also needs to evaluate changes in social conditions; the rise in militancy within the farm workers and the climate of corruption within Agriland. ZZM should also always have the interests of its shareholders in mind. Against these factors must be set the damage which will be incurred to ZZM's profits and also to the people and economy of Agriland should ZZM withdraw. Based on current information it is recommended that ZZM prepares to withdraw from doing business in Agriland.

3   RTF ARCHITECTS

(a)   The Balanced Scorecard model was developed by Kaplan and Norton (1992, 1996) as a means to integrate an organisation's vision, strategy and operations. It is a multi-dimensional model which contains four perspectives which embrace both financial and non-financial control measures.

The four perspectives are:

Financial: where the question posed is 'To succeed financially how should we appear to our shareholders?'

Customer: similarly asks, 'To achieve our vision how should we appear to our customers?'

Learning and growth: demands, 'To achieve our vision, how will we sustain our ability to change and improve?'

Internal business process: asks, 'To satisfy our shareholders and customers, what business processes must we excel at?'

The inclusion of the organisation's vision is central to the model.

(b)   The following are sample measures which would be appropriate for RTF to use within the Balanced Scorecard model.

Financial measures:

Gross profit: it is expected that RTF already calculates this but it is an important measure which should be reported upon regularly.

Net profit: the same comment applies as for gross profit.

Profit per contract: as RTF undertakes a variety of work it should be able to identify the profitability of each of these aspects.

Return on Capital employed: an important and well-known measure which captures the totality of the business.

Customer measures:

Number of new customers in period: it is important for RTF, as with any company, that it continues to attract new business.

Number of customer complaints: this measure gives an indication of the quality of the work produced by RTF.

Amount of repeat business: RTF has built up relationships with local government and also spends time and money maintaining its corporate contacts database. This measure will give an indication if this effort is worthwhile.

Market share: RTF operates in a competitive market and needs to know the size of its market share and the trend in its growth or decline.

Learning and growth measures:

Number of academic and professional qualifications possessed by staff: in what is essentially a knowledge and craft industry, it is important that RTF maintains a high level of academic and professional ability within its personnel.

Number of technical qualifications possessed by staff: this measure demonstrates the level of technical expertise possessed by the business.

Number of new designs added to library: this measure indicates directly one aspect of RTF's creativity.

Number of 'one-off' houses designed in period: these houses give opportunity for RTF to express their creativity. This measure indicates the degree of innovation within the business.

Internal business process measures:

Average design time spent per contract: it is important that the time of the business's staff is used efficiently. This measure gives an indication of staff efficiency.

Time spent each week by partner on design work: it is important to utilise the design skills of the partners to best advantage.

Number of contacts in corporate database: relationships are important in this business and this measure shows how extensive these relationships are.

Number of contacts added to database in period: this measure supplements the one immediately above and it shows the rate at which the corporate contracts are growing.

(c) The use of the Balanced Scorecard is a departure from RTF's previous practice. It will now have a systematic way of reporting on its performance from four different perspectives which are linked to the achievement of its vision. It is also going to be transformed from a purely architectural practice to one that has a valuable commercial computerised design package to market and sell. Furthermore, it will be bringing people into the business that may not necessarily have a background in architecture.

Although there is not a single right way to help RTF successfully make the transition, a number of elements can be identified which are important:

Translating the vision

Vision is at the centre of the Balanced Scorecard. With the developments that are taking place within the company it may be that the vision, 'Your future designed by RTF: Today!' should be re-negotiated. There needs to be an opportunity for this to be discussed and for a consensus to be formed within RTF about what their vision should be. The implications of the (new) vision need to be understood by all the participants in the business.

Communication and linkage

An important part of the cultural change introduced by the Balance Scorecard is the system of performance management which has not existed within RTF previously. The essence of the Balanced Scorecard is one of integration of vision with strategy and operations. Therefore, the aspirations of the vision should find expression in both departmental and individual objectives. Some organisations have associated the achievement of these objectivises with reward systems and introduced performance related pay. RTF would have to evaluate if performance related pay is appropriate for the type of work carried out by its staff.

Business planning

RTF now has the opportunity to develop a business plan, or plans, which should be integrated with the staffs' individual plans as well as the departmental ones. The Marketing Manager will have an important role in identifying the potential sales for the 2020Design package

Change and learning

There is going to be a period of change and learning for RTF as it adjusts to the development and implementation of the Balanced Scorecard and also to its new commercial venture the 2020Design package. RTF should actively encourage its staff to embrace this opportunity for learning. There may also be an opportunity to involve stakeholders outside the business, such as customers and suppliers, who are in a good position to offer feedback.

4   GHK RESTAURANTS

(a)   Porter's 'Three Generic Strategies Model' was developed in 1980 and since then has gained international dissemination. The model analyses how firms can achieve competitive advantage which Porter suggests can come about by adopting one of the following policies:

Overall cost leadership: the firm is the lowest cost producer relative to its competitors.

Differentiation: the firm can create something which is unique and for which consumers will pay a premium.

Focus: the firm serves a narrow strategic target more effectively than its competitors who are competing more broadly.

Porter asserts that each generic strategy requires different attributes and, therefore, it is unlikely that any firm can pursue more than one generic strategy simultaneously and be successful. He cautions against firms becoming 'stuck in the middle'.

As well as Porter's model being used analytically, it can also be used pro-actively to help a firm design its competitive strategy. In the case of GHK no coherent strategy has been followed with respect to its eight restaurants. A preliminary analysis suggests that the following strategies are being followed:

Overall cost leadership: (the firm is the lowest cost producer relative to its competitors), at the restaurant near the busy railway station.

Differentiation: (the firm can create something which is unique and for which consumers will pay a premium) at the 'fine dining' restaurant in the historic country house.

Focus: (the firm serves a narrow strategic target more effectively than its competitors who are competing more broadly) at the fish restaurant, the steak restaurant, the restaurant offering children's birthday parties.

Stuck in the middle: three 'middle of the road' restaurants with conventional menus and average prices.

The generic strategy which GHK decides to follow will be linked to a marketing strategy. It is not necessarily the case that GHK is wrong to follow a number of generic strategies because if each restaurant is taken as a strategic business unit it will have a particular catchment area from which it draws its customers and looked at in isolation that strategy might be the optimal one for that restaurant. However, a systematic examination of each restaurant using the logic of Porter's model and examining the basis by which that restaurant competes and whether this will yield a long-term competitive advantage will be invaluable.

With respect to the restaurant near the busy railway station, if this is attempting to compete on the basis of being the lowest cost producer and, therefore, charging its customers the lowest prices, it is doubtful that this can give a long-term competitive advantage. The prices of a restaurant's inputs, mainly food and labour, are set within their local markets and available to any competitor. The technology and processes of restaurants are mature ones and it is unlikely that GHK could innovate in this area to secure competitive advantage.

The three restaurants which are 'stuck in the middle' should be given immediate attention as Porter's model suggests they are unlikely to be successful.

If the owners of GHK use Porter's 'Three Generic Strategies Model' it will give them an appreciation of the basis upon which their various restaurants compete and should prompt them to make modifications to their strategy and attempt to secure long-term competitive advantage.

It may be the case that GHK treat each of its restaurants as a strategic business unit and, therefore, employ a number of different generic competitive strategies. Alternatively, GHK may wish to trade as a homogenous entity which would imply it would use only one of the three generic competitive strategies to avoid being 'stuck in the middle'.

(b)   Information systems could support GHK's chosen strategy in the following ways:

Strategic

In order to decide which of the generic strategies would be appropriate, GHK will require information to construct a PEST analysis. It will need detailed market and demographic information, for example, to decide whether a particular restaurant has access to a hinterland of customers who are willing to pay a premium price. This would then indicate the suitability of a differentiation strategy. Marketing research could then indicate the type of differentiation for which these customers are willing to pay a premium. It could be the case that the differentiation strategy would be suitable not only for the restaurant in the historic country house but also for the fish and the steak restaurants. Statistics of market share would demonstrate GHK comparative position. The degree of success of the strategy it was following would be monitored by periodic reporting of market share.

GHK owners could utilise an executive information system to help them in their decision-making. Inputs to this system would include both their own researches and data and also data from specialist external databases.

If GHK wanted to pursue a strategy of overall cost leadership (although the answer in (a) suggests that this is unlikely to be successful) an information system which tracked market prices for restaurant supplies would be required.

GHK could use information systems to help it determine the most appropriate generic competitive strategy for its business. However, it should also recognise that the information systems which it chooses to deploy can, of itself, be a source of competitive advantage for its business. An example of this could be that GHK, through its PEST and market research, may identify profitable groups of customers whose needs are not being met at present, such as vegans. GHK may be able to construct a website offering a booking service for restaurants in its regions and link this with an affinity or loyalty card. This would then generate valuable current data about the restaurant which GHK could incorporate in its strategic review processes.

Operational

At the operational level there is much that good information systems and management accountancy can contribute to a successful generic strategy for GHK. Porter's 'Three Generic strategies model' is essentially about achieving and maintaining competitive advantage: that is out-performing its rivals. For its basic requirements GHK would require a comprehensive database, allied to a system for capturing real-time operational data, and a reporting package.

Given these requirements, GHK could address such important parameters as its capacity utilisation. The management accountant using real-time information could provide timely information about the number of customers served each day. This information could be further analysed to reveal variations in demand by both day and time: Which day are we busiest? What time of day is the quietest? Such analysis could be presented in management accounting reports and would assist in decisions such as: At what times should the restaurants be open? Is it worth opening every day of the week?

The restaurants could also equip its waiters with PDA's (Personal Digital Assistants)to record orders and 'Smart-tills' to record and analyse its sales receipts. At the operational level GHK could use proprietary industry software to cost and plan its menus. These functions could be integrated to order ingredients and monitor stock levels. This information allied to the real-time information about orders and sales would enable real-time profitability information to be generated by the management accountant.

The results emanating from the operational level would indicate the degree of success of the generic strategy. It would also indicate either the continuance of that strategy or could suggest that it was time for a strategic review and a possible change of strategy.

DO NOT OPEN THIS QUESTION PAPER UNTIL YOU ARE TOLD TO DO SO

Enterprise Pillar

E3 – Enterprise Strategy

19 November 2013 - Tuesday Morning Session

Instructions to candidates

You are allowed three hours to answer this question paper.
You are allowed 20 minutes reading time **before the examination begins** during which you should read the question paper and, if you wish, highlight and/or make notes on the question paper. However, you will **not** be allowed, **under any circumstances**, to open the answer book and start writing or use your calculator during this reading time.
You are strongly advised to carefully read ALL the question requirements before attempting the question concerned (that is all parts and/or sub-questions).
ALL answers must be written in the answer book. Answers written on the question paper will **not** be submitted for marking.
You should show all workings as marks are available for the method you use.
The pre-seen case study material is included in this question paper on pages 2 to 6. The unseen case study material, specific to this examination, is provided on pages 8 and 9.
Answer the compulsory questions in Section A on page 11. This page is detachable for ease of reference.
Answer TWO of the three questions in Section B on pages 14 to 19.
Maths tables and formulae are provided on pages 21 and 22.
The list of verbs as published in the syllabus is given for reference on page 23.
Write your candidate number, the paper number and examination subject title in the spaces provided on the front of the answer book. Also write your contact ID and name in the space provided in the right hand margin and seal to close.
Tick the appropriate boxes on the front of the answer book to indicate the questions you have answered.

E3 – Enterprise Strategy

TURN OVER

© The Chartered Institute of Management Accountants 2013

Introduction

The Games is an international multi-sport event that is held within a region of the world every four years. It attracts competitors from 10 different countries within the region and is held at a different time from the Olympic Games. The Games are held in each of the countries within the region in turn. The next Games are scheduled to take place in Country C in October 2015. There are 25 sports included within the Games ranging from archery through to weightlifting. The Games were first held in 1979 and this is the first time that Country C has hosted them.

Games Co-ordinating Committee (GCC)

The Games Co-ordinating Committee was established to set out the framework within which the individual country organisations should work in delivering the Games. Membership of the GCC is drawn from all the countries within the region which take part in the Games. Its aim is to promote the Games throughout the region of the world in which the Games take place. It is also responsible for setting out the mission under which the Games are established in each country.

Mission of the GCC

The mission of the GCC is to:

- Encourage and promote ethical competition in sport;
- Encourage and co-operate with public and private organisations in the preparation for and staging of the Games;
- Achieve high levels of sustainability for the infrastructure of the Games and the environment in which they take place;
- Promote sport and healthy lifestyles amongst young people;
- Promote the Games' values of excellence, unity and achievement.

The mission of the GCC is untouchable in the sense that all who are involved in the Games, in whatever role, must adopt and promote it.

Organisation of the Games within Country C

In 2010, the Parliament in Country C passed an Act creating GAMESCO, a company limited by guarantee to organise and deliver the Games on time and within budget. GAMESCO also has responsibility for disposal of assets after the Games and selling any surplus land which is not retained for sporting purposes.

The Minister of Sport in Country C and the elected Mayor of the city in which the Games are due to take place are the only two shareholders of GAMESCO. Governance of the Games is carried out entirely by GAMESCO. In carrying out this role, it co-ordinates the activities of all people and organisations engaged in preparing for and operating the Games and it is responsible for the subsequent liquidation of all the Games' assets.

The Government of Country C believes that the Games will provide a major boost to Country C by providing commercial opportunities for enterprises such as hotels and retail outlets and enabling the re-generation of the current dilapidated land on which the Games will take place. It is expected that the prosperity of Country C and, in particular, the whole area in which the Games will take place, will increase.

Mission, Vision and Values of GAMESCO

The Board of GAMESCO is committed to meeting the mission of the GCC. It has established its own mission and values as follows:

Mission:
"To deliver the Games successfully on time and on budget in accordance with the expectations of our stakeholders and in accordance with the mission of the GCC."

GAMESCO is responsible for preparing, operating and winding up the Games, all within its budget. Country C's Government provided capital to GAMESCO for building work to proceed. However, Country C's Government is clear that it does not intend to support the Games beyond the funding it has already invested. This places a large responsibility on GAMESCO to ensure that its overall expenditure does not exceed the revenue it generates from its activities and the government grants it has received.

Values:
"GAMESCO will work tirelessly towards achieving the mission set out by the GCC. In striving to achieve the GCC's mission, GAMESCO will act fairly and responsibly with all its stakeholders, in particular its employees and partners, in order to generate trust and transparency."

GAMESCO's organisational structure

GAMESCO has a Board of Directors comprising: Chairman, Chief Executive, Directors for Finance, Sponsorship, Operations, Marketing, Commercial Activities, Estates, Communications, Human Resources, Information Systems, Venues, Athletes' Services, a representative from each of the Minister of Sport and the Mayor, a sports representative drawn from each of the sporting activities which will be competed in during the Games and a representative of the GCC.

GAMESCO's financial structure and budget

Country C's currency is C$. GAMESCO's financial structure is different from most commercial organisations. Under the Act of Parliament which set the company up, a provision was made that GAMESCO would not be subject to corporate tax.

Revenue is generated by a mixture of government grants, sponsorships, ticket sales for the Games, rental of accommodation and broadcasting and other commercial fees. All capital works relating to the Games themselves, such as the athletics stadium, the cycling velodrome, the gymnastics arena and the swimming pool, are funded by government grants. However, construction of buildings for commercial activities such as cafes and restaurants is funded by the commercial organisations themselves and is not the responsibility of GAMESCO. The budget for the expected final cost of the Games is shown at Appendix 1.

Project management

An overarching supervisory consortium of experts in project management has been engaged by GAMESCO as an outsourced service. The role of the consortium is to prepare and monitor construction work on the whole of the Games Park site. The Games Park site will accommodate such buildings as the athletics stadium, the cycling velodrome, the gymnastics arena and the swimming pool. In addition, the consortium will ensure that utilities are installed, plans for construction works are approved, construction work progresses according to schedule and that contractors are able to access the site when building work takes place.

GAMESCO employs independent project management teams with project managers responsible for each major building construction on-site. These project managers report directly to the consortium on the progress of the construction project for which they are responsible. An Information Systems Project Manager has been appointed by GAMESCO, whose role is to co-ordinate the provision of information systems on the site and to liaise with all the project managers on their information systems requirements for the construction projects for which they are responsible.

A project management team has also been established to market the Games. All GAMESCO's marketing staff, with the exception of the Marketing Director, are attached to this project team.

Service provision

Professional architects, engineers and building companies are all engaged in developing the Games Park. In addition, land on which buildings will be erected must be clear of pollution. Utility services, such as water and electricity supplies to all venues involved with the Games are in the process of being provided.

On the Games Park site itself, there will be a number of fast-food outlets, cafes and restaurants as well as ice cream parlours, sweet stores and souvenir shops. Hygiene facilities, such as toilets, will need to be provided. All of these will remain on-site for the duration of the Games and will be demolished afterwards. Some parks and gardens will be constructed within the Games Park. The parks and gardens will not be demolished but remain as amenities for the local population after the Games have finished.

Security for the Games will be tight. It is proposed that GAMESCO will engage a highly reputable security services contractor to provide security at all the Games' venues, around the perimeter as well as within the grounds of the Games Park. It will be essential for the security contractor to engage sufficient staff to carry out this very large security service.

Staffing
While GAMESCO does employ its own staff, the majority of people working on-site are contractors. At present most of the activity being undertaken on-site is construction work. GAMESCO does employ its own Human Resource Management, Information Technology support and accounting staff.

Senior staff and project managers are contracted for the duration of the Games and in some cases beyond. They are paid at a competitive rate. However, most staff are employed on temporary contracts on a month-to-month basis and generally receive relatively low pay compared with unskilled labour in Country C which has a high level of unemployment.

When the Games begin, it is expected that most ancillary staff on-site, who will direct spectators to venues and facilities, will be volunteers. Many of these volunteers will take annual leave from their places of work in order to carry out this task.

Sponsorship
A major source of revenue for GAMESCO is sponsorship deals with major business organisations and this is therefore crucial to the successful staging of the Games. Sponsors are required to provide a guarantee of a minimum payment of C$ 1 million to GAMESCO. For this, sponsors become official partners of the Games and acquire marketing rights. This enables sponsors to build their brands and customer relationships, increase their revenue and enhance their own commercial reputation. Sponsorship can be divided into two types, direct and indirect.

Direct sponsorship - gold sponsorship
There are two levels of direct sponsorship, gold and silver. Gold is the highest level of sponsorship and gives sponsors major marketing rights. Gold sponsors are drawn from businesses such as electronic equipment suppliers, soft drink manufacturers and fast-food chains which can provide products and services to support the staging of the Games, in addition to providing a financial contribution. Gold sponsors are also expected to promote the Games by engaging in the development of sporting events across the region of the world in which the Games take place. For this, gold sponsors are entitled to use the Games logo on their products and services.

Gold sponsors are required to engage in a range of activities to support the mission of GCC at the Games. See page 2 for details of the mission of the Games.

Direct sponsorship - silver sponsorship
Silver sponsors are only required to make a financial contribution to the staging of the Games. However, they too, are able to use the Games logo.

Indirect sponsorship
A form of indirect sponsorship which takes place when the Games are in progress is hospitality. Hospitality sponsorship relates to large businesses hiring facilities on-site in the Games Park to entertain their own customers and clients while the Games are in progress. These facilities mainly consist of hospitality rooms and boxes. The hospitality rooms and boxes in prestige venues, such as the athletics stadium, the cycling velodrome, the gymnastics arena and the swimming pool, will command a higher price on days when popular Games events are being held and also when medals are being awarded.

Brand Leases
One significant area of revenue generation is the opportunity for GAMESCO to lease its brand to all organisations engaged in supplying products and services to the Games. It is a condition for all goods and service suppliers that they must display the Games brand in all the venues in which they operate and in doing this, they incur a leasing charge which is directly payable to GAMESCO. In addition, any other organisation wishing to use the Games brand must also pay a leasing charge to GAMESCO for permission to do so.

Marketing
GAMESCO has carried out considerable press and television advertising and intends to increase this as the Games draw closer in order to stimulate public enthusiasm and ticket sales. Television rights to broadcast the Games have been agreed and GAMESCO has invested in stocks of merchandise which it has distributed to retailers around Country C.

Games Village
The athletes will be accommodated in the Games Village which is located in the Games Park. The Games Village will consist of several purpose built blocks of accommodation which provide hotel services in respect of individual bedrooms with en-suite toilet and shower facilities. The Games Village will also have its own catering and laundry facilities, using locally contracted staff. The daily cleaning of the rooms will also be contracted out to a local company.

The Games Village will provide a regular bus shuttle service for the use of athletes to and from the city centre in which the Games are being held and also to and from the airport.

After the Games, the Games Village will be converted into apartments to house local people.

Drug testing and medical facilities
A specific building will be constructed to enable appropriately qualified experts to carry out internationally approved drugs tests on athletes. The drug testing facility will be located close to the medical centre which will be specifically built for treating the athletes. If any spectator requires medical attention beyond basic first-aid, he or she will be taken to the nearest hospital as will any athlete if he or she requires treatment which cannot be provided at the medical centre. After the Games have finished, it is expected that the medical centre will be converted into a health clinic which will provide services to local residents.

Business opportunities and legacy
Much has been made in Country C about the huge opportunities for local businesses and the legacy of the Games. There is a range of contracts and work being done or still to be undertaken by businesses in Country C. These include construction, land regeneration, the provision of utility supplies and catering facilities before and during the Games. After the Games have finished, there will still be much work particularly for construction companies in reinstating land and undertaking buildings alteration work.

Construction works including hotels and shopping facilities are now planned to be built on derelict land and all will be within easy reach of the Games Park. The hotels and shopping facilities are particularly attractive to developers as it is expected that the regeneration of the land, parks, gardens and sports facilities which remain after the Games will attract visitors and tourists.

A major legacy is that many new homes and amenities will become available after the Games. For example, the athletes' accommodation in the Games Village will replace much sub-standard accommodation in which many local people are currently housed. The Government thinks that the Games, which will be televised across the region and in other parts of the world, will showcase the country in general, attracting visitors and businesses not just for the duration of the Games but afterwards as well.

In addition to the economic benefits, the Government hopes that the Games will inspire the public in Country C to take more physical exercise which it anticipates will bring health benefits to the population. Some of the facilities which will be constructed for the Games, such as the cycling velodrome, the gymnastics arena and the swimming pool, will become available for public use after the Games, enhancing the amenities for the local population.

Budget for the delivery of the Games

	C$million
Preparation of the Site and Infrastructure	
Power and utilities	550
Preparatory construction work	370
Structural work including access roads	760
Landscaping	250
Other preparation and infrastructural works	185
Total preparation of site and infrastructure	**2,115**
Venues	
Athletics stadium	500
Swimming Pool	260
Cycling velodrome	50
Gymnastics arena	45
Venues operations control centre	20
Other Games Park venues	100
Total venues	**975**
Transport	
Transport capital projects	300
Transport operating costs	350
Total transport	**650**
Games Park Operations and Security	
Games Park Operations	220
Security for Games Park construction	240
Security during Games	70
Insurance	80
Total Games Park operations and security	**610**
Games Village and Media Centre	
Games Village construction	750
Media Centre construction	300
Total Games Village and Media Centre	**1,050**
Total expected final cost before contingency	**5,400**
Contingency	540
Total expected final cost	**5,940**

End of pre-seen material

The unseen material starts on page 8

This page is blank

Question One

Unseen case material

The Games Information System

A key feature of marketing the Games will be the Games website. The previous two Games both had a dedicated Games website to advertise and promote the Games and also to sell tickets and merchandise. However, there were criticisms of the websites of previous Games. Many customers complained about the lack of relevant information and the number of errors which occurred when purchasing tickets online.

The Information Systems (IS) Project Manager, responsible for the development and management of the overall information systems for the whole Games, believes that the main weakness of previous Games' information systems was the lack of integration of the websites with the overall strategy of the Games. Furthermore, the previous Games organisers did not regard the development of information systems as strategically significant to the successful delivery of the Games.

The Velodrome Project

Cycling will be one of the most popular sporting activities within the Games. However, the city which is hosting the Games does not currently have a cycling arena. Therefore a cycling arena, called the Velodrome, needs to be built. This facility will be retained after the Games with the intention that it will be used by the local community and also become a national training centre for track cycling in Country C. The Government's aim is that this will assist in the development of Country C's future sporting aspirations and increase the level of sports participation for many years to come.

Project Management of the Velodrome project

A project team was set up at the start of June 2013. The aim of the project is to construct a high quality, world-class Velodrome which must be complete by the 31st May 2015 within a budget of C$50 million. Construction of the Velodrome is due to begin on the 1st December 2013.

A Project Manager, Z, has been employed by GAMESCO to manage the Velodrome construction project. This will be a highly complex project involving many external contractors, including key building suppliers and contractors, utility suppliers, and track and seating component suppliers. The successful construction of the Velodrome will rely upon the effective collaboration of a multi-disciplinary project team made up of GAMESCO staff and staff members of the external organisations responsible for the construction project. Z has the highly complex job of co-ordinating the work of team members within a highly flexible project environment and scheduling, planning and managing the key project activities.

GAMESCO has set three key targets for the delivery of the Velodrome. These are:

(i)   meeting the final deadline of the 31st May 2015;
(ii)   meeting the expected level of quality; and
(iii)   not exceeding the budgeted cost allowed.

The Project Manager must ensure that these key project targets are planned and controlled effectively throughout the whole life of the project. GAMESCO has set a number of targets for sustainability of the infrastructure of the Games in line with the Games Co-ordinating Committee's mission. The Government of Country C is keen to encourage the use of local staff and suppliers based in Country C wherever it is possible.

Supplier Management in the Velodrome project

A key decision needs to be made between two potential suppliers of the wooden track boards for the Velodrome. The track boards make up the track racing surface and the quality of the material chosen for this critical component of the Velodrome is very important. The timing of delivery of the wooden track boards is critical as they must be installed within the facility six months before final completion of the Velodrome. This is because the wooden track boards need to acclimatise to the atmosphere in the Velodrome and to settle into place. (The wood used is likely to move fractionally and require minor adjustments before the track can be used). The Project Manager is aware that the construction of velodromes in other countries has shown that the track boards should cost (including installation) on average, 5% of the total budget for the Velodrome construction.

The two potential suppliers of the track boards are Supplier A and Supplier B. A decision must be made and an order placed with one of these two suppliers within the next two weeks in order to meet the deadline for the completion of the Velodrome. The following information is available relating to each supplier:

Supplier A
- Supplier A is based in Country C.
- Supplier A has not undertaken work on this scale before. However, it has a good reputation for quality in Country C. The material it proposes to use will be sourced from the region within which the Games are being held.
- The price which Supplier A has quoted for only the cost of the track boards is C$2 million. However, it has stated that there will be an additional cost for a specialist installation company to lay the track boards within the Velodrome as Supplier A does not possess this expertise itself. The installation company, used regularly by Supplier A, which is also based in Country C, has stated it will require 4 weeks from the delivery date quoted by Supplier A to lay the track. The quoted price for this is C$125,000 per week in addition to Supplier A's quotation of C$2 million for the track boards.
- Supplier A expects to deliver the track boards to site in the first week of November 2014. However, should Supplier A not meet this deadline, then installation would have to be put back by a further 4 weeks, due to other contract commitments of the installation company during November 2014.
- Supplier A estimates that the track boards will have a life of 10 years before it is necessary to replace them. Supplier A cannot provide the on-going maintenance required to maintain the quality of the track boards after the Games are completed.

Supplier B
- Supplier B provided the track boards on time and of sufficient quality for the Velodrome which was built for the last Games. The total price quoted by Supplier B is C$3 million.
- Supplier B is based outside of the region of the world in which the Games are being held and the wood it would use is sourced from a different country, over 1,000 miles away from its factory. The wood is shipped to Supplier B, which then undertakes a complex refining and treatment process. It is then transported, normally by air, to its final destination. Supplier B invests heavily in re-forestation programmes (that is, planting new trees to replace each tree cut down) within the regions from which it sources its wood.
- Supplier B employs its own specialist installation team and this is included in the price it has quoted. However, during the last Games, the final cost of the track boards and installation was 4% higher than Supplier B's original quoted price. The track boards are guaranteed to be delivered by the 1st November 2014 and be fully installed within 3 weeks. The track boards will have a guaranteed life of 15 years.
- Supplier B could maintain the track boards it supplies for an annual fee of C$80,000 for 15 years after installation. Supplier B has stated that should it not win the contract it could still provide the on-going maintenance of the track boards supplied by a different supplier but this would cost an estimated C$120,000 per year for the expected life of the track boards.

End of unseen material

The requirement for Question One is on page 11

This page is blank

Required

(a) **Discuss** the importance of an effective Information Systems (IS) strategy in order to successfully deliver the Games in 2015.

(7 marks)

(b) In respect of the Velodrome project:

   (i) **Discuss** the challenges faced by the Project Manager, Z, in planning and managing the project.

(8 marks)

   (ii) **Recommend**, with reasons, a range of management control actions which should be implemented to reduce the potential risks which could endanger the successful delivery of the Velodrome project in respect of the three targets set by GAMESCO.

(12 marks)

(c) (i) **Evaluate** the proposals put forward by the two potential suppliers of the track boards for the Velodrome project against the project constraints of

   - Time
   - Quality
   - Sustainability and locality

(13 marks)

   (ii) **Discuss** the difficulties that the Project Manager, Z, will face in evaluating the installation and on-going maintenance costs of the track boards quoted by each of the suppliers.

(10 marks)

(Total marks for Question One = 50 marks)

(Total for Section A = 50 marks)

End of Section A
Section B starts on page 14

Section B starts on page 14

This page is blank

This page is blank

TURN OVER

Question Two

XXA is a bakery business which was established in 1982 by J, the current Chief Executive. XXA has grown from operating within J's kitchen in his own home, to now operating 12 bakeries located throughout Country Q. Last year XXA generated revenues of Q$25 million. XXA is listed on Country Q's alternative stock exchange (which is similar to the Alternative Investment Market in the UK). J leads a Board of Directors which runs the business from a central head office. XXA currently uses Shareholder Value Analysis (SVA) as a measure to evaluate the overall performance of the business. For the last five years, the business has seen significant growth but a number of the directors have expressed concern that the current centralised approach to organisation and performance management of XXA will stifle future growth of the business.

The Board of Directors of XXA recently met to consider the re-organisation of the business into divisions, based upon regional location. It was proposed that XXA establish four divisions, North, South, East and West and these would be headed by new divisional directors from the current Board. It is proposed that these four divisions would operate as investment centres and the divisional directors would be responsible for all of the divisional activities relating to their region. If the proposed divisions were to be established, the directors have suggested that bonuses for divisional directors should be based upon the divisional performance achieved in each director's division. One of the current directors has stated that Return on Investment (ROI), based upon the original (initial) investment, is an appropriate method of performance measurement, and he proposes this should be adopted by XXA. However, J has concerns about linking divisional directors' bonuses to divisional performance.

He does not consider that ROI is the best measure of divisional performance and believes that Residual Income (RI) is a better measure of divisional performance. At a recent meeting, J provided the Board with examples of two recent investment decisions undertaken by XXA to illustrate his concerns.

Investment 1: Last year, a factory based in the Northern region of Country Q was considering investing in a new range of ovens. These ovens cost Q$2 million. The controllable profit estimated to be earned from the ovens was Q$400,000 each year. If XXA had been set up in a divisional structure at this point in time, it was anticipated that the Northern divisional ROI (based upon all of the factories within the proposed Northern region) would have been 22%. The decision was made by the Board to accept the investment based on a capital investment appraisal showing that it provided a positive net present value. Since investing in the ovens, the factory has been able to produce a wider range of products and a number of XXA's customers have indicated that they will be increasing their orders in the future.

Investment 2: Last year, a factory based in the Southern region, was considering investing in a new high technology production line to speed up and improve the quality of specific products and to reduce staff costs. This was proposed to cost Q$5 million. The controllable profit estimated to be earned from the new production line was forecast to be Q$450,000 each year. If XXA had been set up in a divisional structure at this point in time it is anticipated that the Southern Divisional ROI (based upon all of the factories within the proposed Southern region) would have been 8%. The Board decided to reject this proposal based upon its negative net present value.

XXA's pre-tax cost of capital is 15%.

The requirement for Question Two is on the opposite page

(a) **Explain** the benefits to XXA of using Shareholder Value Analysis as an overall business performance measure before the adoption of a divisional structure.

(6 marks)

(b) **Discuss** J's concern about linking divisional directors' bonuses to divisional performance.

Note: Candidates are NOT required to undertake any calculations in this answer

(5 marks)

(c) **Evaluate** the relative merits and disadvantages of using both ROI and RI to measure divisional performance in XXA.

You should use the two investment examples provided by J to the Board in support of your answer.

Note: There are 6 marks available for calculations

(14 marks)

(Total for Question Two = 25 marks)

Section B continues on page 16

TURN OVER

Question Three

VVT is based in a small southern European country and has been trading for 12 years. It imports electronic consumer products, such as televisions, home entertainment systems, computers and printers from one supplier, MMM, which is based in an Asian country. VVT re-brands and re-packages these products as VVT 'own brand' and then sells them to customers within its own country.

Most customers pick up their products directly from VVT's stores and set them up themselves. However, for more complex products such as large home entertainment systems, VVT offers a home set-up service, for which VVT makes a small charge. VVT's technicians will also visit customers' homes to solve technical problems with equipment if it is still within the warranty period. VVT offers an online helpline and also a warehouse-based repair facility for its customers if the products VVT sold to them are out of the warranty period. Feedback from customers suggests that this customer support is highly valued as VVT's larger competitors don't offer such extensive product support.

VVT has a website which provides a comprehensive display of its products, product specifications and prices. However, customers cannot order or pay for products online. Orders are placed through a dedicated phone number clearly identified on the website. Trained technicians are on hand to help customers decide on the product which best meets their needs. Customer feedback indicates that this support is highly valued. As well as using the website to advertise its products, VVT advertises in the national newspapers and undertakes direct mailing by post. VVT also maintains a customer and product database, which holds customer details and records their buying history. VVT uses this database solely to help with its direct mailing activities. However, the marketing managers of VVT are aware that this database could be more effective if it employed more sophisticated analysis.

VVT places its orders for products through MMM's website and pays by bank transfer. VVT is not committed to a long-term contract with MMM and therefore MMM does not offer credit terms to VVT. When the payment is authorised, MMM sends an automatic e-mail to VVT to confirm the order, to provide an order reference number and a proposed shipping date. A further email is sent to VVT once the order has been despatched. A logistics company based in Europe, but not in VVT's home country, delivers the order from the shipping port to VVT. MMM organises the whole supply process, from initial product despatch right through to the delivery of the order to VVT's warehouse.

This supply process has, in the past, caused a number of problems for VVT. First, missing or delayed shipments can only be tracked by going through MMM, which has often been slow to respond to queries. Second, MMM cannot always provide reliable shipping dates and does not track the progress of shipments carefully. Third, the European logistics company has not always been reliable which has resulted in delays to deliveries which are quite unpredictable. This can cause congestion in VVT's delivery bay or lead to VVT being out of stock of some products. As a result, VVT tends to order more products than is necessary to ensure that it is not left short, but this adds to its warehousing and inventory holding costs.

On arrival of the order at VVT's factory, the products are quality inspected. This is a rigorous process and only those products which are 100% defect free are re-branded and re-packaged with VVT's recognised logo. Products which fail VVT's quality inspection are returned to MMM for a refund.

The requirement for Question Three is on the opposite page

Required

(a) **Evaluate** the primary activities of VVT. Your answer should clearly explain the significance of each of these primary activities in adding value to VVT's customers.

Note: You should use Porter's Value Chain to structure your answer, but you are NOT required to draw the value chain as part of your answer.

(10 marks)

(b) **Discuss** the potential benefits to VVT of carrying out more sophisticated analysis of its customer database through the use of data warehousing and data mining.

(6 marks)

(c) **Recommend**, with reasons, THREE ways in which VVT could improve its supply chain activities to remove non value-adding activities.

(9 marks)

(Total for Question Three = 25 marks)

Section B continues on page 18

Question Four

PPP is a publisher of books, founded in 1960 by family X. PPP's success over its first 40 years of trading demonstrated that large demand existed for books covering different topics and suiting many different readers' tastes. The Board of Directors of PPP has always been very proud of its reputation in the market place for the high quality of books it publishes to a wide reading audience.

There is a strong family ethos in PPP with a number of the founding family members still working for the company. PPP's staff take great pride in the reputation of the company and in its traditional values. This is demonstrated by low levels of staff turnover and low absenteeism.

In the last 10 years, PPP has seen a steady decline in its sales of paper-based books. Eight years ago, PPP installed new state-of-the-art printing technology in its two print factories in order to improve efficiency. However, the volume of sales continued to decline. In 2010, PPP made 50 staff redundant. These redundancies followed the closure of one of its major customers, a chain of high street bookshops.

PPP now employs over 250 staff. The staff are based in two locations in PPP's home country. Half of PPP's staff have never worked for another organisation.

PPP set up a website in 2011 in order to sell its books, in the traditional paper format, direct to the public. Although initially the website was successful, sales in terms of both volume and value, failed to grow after the first year of the website's operation. The Board of PPP is seriously concerned for the future of the company.

The market for books is rapidly changing. The Board of PPP recognises that it does not have the skills or the resources to convert its business operations to meet the changing requirements of its customers.

The Board has recently been approached by a large international publishing group QZZ which is proposing to acquire PPP. QZZ is keen to retain the staff of PPP. After acquisition, a greater focus will be placed upon e-business and the development of electronic books. QZZ also intends to reduce the topic range of PPP's published books. The staff of PPP may have to relocate to other business units within QZZ and all of PPP's staff will have to be re-trained so that they can work within a high technology-based environment. Any staff refusing to undertake re-training or relocation could legally face redundancy due to technical or organisational reasons. PPP would retain its name, as QZZ recognises the strong reputation of the PPP brand in the marketplace. However, it is likely that the strong family ethos built up over many years will be lost after acquisition. QZZ has also stated to the Board of PPP that in the longer term, it may also need to consider closing one of PPP's print facilities as it reduces the range of published books.

The Board is currently evaluating the proposed acquisition by QZZ and is considering the appropriate actions it must take to manage the potential effects of the proposed acquisition.

The requirement for Question Four is on the opposite page

End of Question Paper

Maths Tables and Formulae are on Pages 21 and 22

This page is blank

MATHS TABLES AND FORMULAE

Present value table

Present value of $1, that is $(1 + r)^{-n}$ where r = interest rate; n = number of periods until payment or receipt.

Periods (n)	Interest rates (r)									
	1%	2%	3%	4%	5%	6%	7%	8%	9%	10%
1	0.990	0.980	0.971	0.962	0.952	0.943	0.935	0.926	0.917	0.909
2	0.980	0.961	0.943	0.925	0.907	0.890	0.873	0.857	0.842	0.826
3	0.971	0.942	0.915	0.889	0.864	0.840	0.816	0.794	0.772	0.751
4	0.961	0.924	0.888	0.855	0.823	0.792	0.763	0.735	0.708	0.683
5	0.951	0.906	0.863	0.822	0.784	0.747	0.713	0.681	0.650	0.621
6	0.942	0.888	0.837	0.790	0.746	0.705	0.666	0.630	0.596	0.564
7	0.933	0.871	0.813	0.760	0.711	0.665	0.623	0.583	0.547	0.513
8	0.923	0.853	0.789	0.731	0.677	0.627	0.582	0.540	0.502	0.467
9	0.914	0.837	0.766	0.703	0.645	0.592	0.544	0.500	0.460	0.424
10	0.905	0.820	0.744	0.676	0.614	0.558	0.508	0.463	0.422	0.386
11	0.896	0.804	0.722	0.650	0.585	0.527	0.475	0.429	0.388	0.350
12	0.887	0.788	0.701	0.625	0.557	0.497	0.444	0.397	0.356	0.319
13	0.879	0.773	0.681	0.601	0.530	0.469	0.415	0.368	0.326	0.290
14	0.870	0.758	0.661	0.577	0.505	0.442	0.388	0.340	0.299	0.263
15	0.861	0.743	0.642	0.555	0.481	0.417	0.362	0.315	0.275	0.239
16	0.853	0.728	0.623	0.534	0.458	0.394	0.339	0.292	0.252	0.218
17	0.844	0.714	0.605	0.513	0.436	0.371	0.317	0.270	0.231	0.198
18	0.836	0.700	0.587	0.494	0.416	0.350	0.296	0.250	0.212	0.180
19	0.828	0.686	0.570	0.475	0.396	0.331	0.277	0.232	0.194	0.164
20	0.820	0.673	0.554	0.456	0.377	0.312	0.258	0.215	0.178	0.149

Periods (n)	Interest rates (r)									
	11%	12%	13%	14%	15%	16%	17%	18%	19%	20%
1	0.901	0.893	0.885	0.877	0.870	0.862	0.855	0.847	0.840	0.833
2	0.812	0.797	0.783	0.769	0.756	0.743	0.731	0.718	0.706	0.694
3	0.731	0.712	0.693	0.675	0.658	0.641	0.624	0.609	0.593	0.579
4	0.659	0.636	0.613	0.592	0.572	0.552	0.534	0.516	0.499	0.482
5	0.593	0.567	0.543	0.519	0.497	0.476	0.456	0.437	0.419	0.402
6	0.535	0.507	0.480	0.456	0.432	0.410	0.390	0.370	0.352	0.335
7	0.482	0.452	0.425	0.400	0.376	0.354	0.333	0.314	0.296	0.279
8	0.434	0.404	0.376	0.351	0.327	0.305	0.285	0.266	0.249	0.233
9	0.391	0.361	0.333	0.308	0.284	0.263	0.243	0.225	0.209	0.194
10	0.352	0.322	0.295	0.270	0.247	0.227	0.208	0.191	0.176	0.162
11	0.317	0.287	0.261	0.237	0.215	0.195	0.178	0.162	0.148	0.135
12	0.286	0.257	0.231	0.208	0.187	0.168	0.152	0.137	0.124	0.112
13	0.258	0.229	0.204	0.182	0.163	0.145	0.130	0.116	0.104	0.093
14	0.232	0.205	0.181	0.160	0.141	0.125	0.111	0.099	0.088	0.078
15	0.209	0.183	0.160	0.140	0.123	0.108	0.095	0.084	0.079	0.065
16	0.188	0.163	0.141	0.123	0.107	0.093	0.081	0.071	0.062	0.054
17	0.170	0.146	0.125	0.108	0.093	0.080	0.069	0.060	0.052	0.045
18	0.153	0.130	0.111	0.095	0.081	0.069	0.059	0.051	0.044	0.038
19	0.138	0.116	0.098	0.083	0.070	0.060	0.051	0.043	0.037	0.031
20	0.124	0.104	0.087	0.073	0.061	0.051	0.043	0.037	0.031	0.026

Cumulative present value of $1 per annum, Receivable or Payable at the end of each year for n years

$$\frac{1-(1+r)^{-n}}{r}$$

Periods	Interest rates (r)									
(n)	1%	2%	3%	4%	5%	6%	7%	8%	9%	10%
1	0.990	0.980	0.971	0.962	0.952	0.943	0.935	0.926	0.917	0.909
2	1.970	1.942	1.913	1.886	1.859	1.833	1.808	1.783	1.759	1.736
3	2.941	2.884	2.829	2.775	2.723	2.673	2.624	2.577	2.531	2.487
4	3.902	3.808	3.717	3.630	3.546	3.465	3.387	3.312	3.240	3.170
5	4.853	4.713	4.580	4.452	4.329	4.212	4.100	3.993	3.890	3.791
6	5.795	5.601	5.417	5.242	5.076	4.917	4.767	4.623	4.486	4.355
7	6.728	6.472	6.230	6.002	5.786	5.582	5.389	5.206	5.033	4.868
8	7.652	7.325	7.020	6.733	6.463	6.210	5.971	5.747	5.535	5.335
9	8.566	8.162	7.786	7.435	7.108	6.802	6.515	6.247	5.995	5.759
10	9.471	8.983	8.530	8.111	7.722	7.360	7.024	6.710	6.418	6.145
11	10.368	9.787	9.253	8.760	8.306	7.887	7.499	7.139	6.805	6.495
12	11.255	10.575	9.954	9.385	8.863	8.384	7.943	7.536	7.161	6.814
13	12.134	11.348	10.635	9.986	9.394	8.853	8.358	7.904	7.487	7.103
14	13.004	12.106	11.296	10.563	9.899	9.295	8.745	8.244	7.786	7.367
15	13.865	12.849	11.938	11.118	10.380	9.712	9.108	8.559	8.061	7.606
16	14.718	13.578	12.561	11.652	10.838	10.106	9.447	8.851	8.313	7.824
17	15.562	14.292	13.166	12.166	11.274	10.477	9.763	9.122	8.544	8.022
18	16.398	14.992	13.754	12.659	11.690	10.828	10.059	9.372	8.756	8.201
19	17.226	15.679	14.324	13.134	12.085	11.158	10.336	9.604	8.950	8.365
20	18.046	16.351	14.878	13.590	12.462	11.470	10.594	9.818	9.129	8.514

Periods	Interest rates (r)									
(n)	11%	12%	13%	14%	15%	16%	17%	18%	19%	20%
1	0.901	0.893	0.885	0.877	0.870	0.862	0.855	0.847	0.840	0.833
2	1.713	1.690	1.668	1.647	1.626	1.605	1.585	1.566	1.547	1.528
3	2.444	2.402	2.361	2.322	2.283	2.246	2.210	2.174	2.140	2.106
4	3.102	3.037	2.974	2.914	2.855	2.798	2.743	2.690	2.639	2.589
5	3.696	3.605	3.517	3.433	3.352	3.274	3.199	3.127	3.058	2.991
6	4.231	4.111	3.998	3.889	3.784	3.685	3.589	3.498	3.410	3.326
7	4.712	4.564	4.423	4.288	4.160	4.039	3.922	3.812	3.706	3.605
8	5.146	4.968	4.799	4.639	4.487	4.344	4.207	4.078	3.954	3.837
9	5.537	5.328	5.132	4.946	4.772	4.607	4.451	4.303	4.163	4.031
10	5.889	5.650	5.426	5.216	5.019	4.833	4.659	4.494	4.339	4.192
11	6.207	5.938	5.687	5.453	5.234	5.029	4.836	4.656	4.486	4.327
12	6.492	6.194	5.918	5.660	5.421	5.197	4.988	4.793	4.611	4.439
13	6.750	6.424	6.122	5.842	5.583	5.342	5.118	4.910	4.715	4.533
14	6.982	6.628	6.302	6.002	5.724	5.468	5.229	5.008	4.802	4.611
15	7.191	6.811	6.462	6.142	5.847	5.575	5.324	5.092	4.876	4.675
16	7.379	6.974	6.604	6.265	5.954	5.668	5.405	5.162	4.938	4.730
17	7.549	7.120	6.729	6.373	6.047	5.749	5.475	5.222	4.990	4.775
18	7.702	7.250	6.840	6.467	6.128	5.818	5.534	5.273	5.033	4.812
19	7.839	7.366	6.938	6.550	6.198	5.877	5.584	5.316	5.070	4.843
20	7.963	7.469	7.025	6.623	6.259	5.929	5.628	5.353	5.101	4.870

FORMULAE

Annuity

Present value of an annuity of $1 per annum, receivable or payable for n years, commencing in one year, discounted at r% per annum:

$$PV = \frac{1}{r}\left[1 - \frac{1}{[1+r]^n}\right]$$

Perpetuity

Present value of $1 per annum, payable or receivable in perpetuity, commencing in one year, discounted at r% per annum:

$$PV = \frac{1}{r}$$

LIST OF VERBS USED IN THE QUESTION REQUIREMENTS

A list of the learning objectives and verbs that appear in the syllabus and in the question requirements for each question in this paper.

It is important that you answer the question according to the definition of the verb.

LEARNING OBJECTIVE	VERBS USED	DEFINITION
Level 1 - KNOWLEDGE What you are expected to know.	List State Define	Make a list of Express, fully or clearly, the details/facts of Give the exact meaning of
Level 2 - COMPREHENSION What you are expected to understand.	Describe Distinguish Explain Identify Illustrate	Communicate the key features Highlight the differences between Make clear or intelligible/State the meaning or purpose of Recognise, establish or select after consideration Use an example to describe or explain something
Level 3 - APPLICATION How you are expected to apply your knowledge.	Apply Calculate Demonstrate Prepare Reconcile Solve Tabulate	Put to practical use Ascertain or reckon mathematically Prove with certainty or to exhibit by practical means Make or get ready for use Make or prove consistent/compatible Find an answer to Arrange in a table
Level 4 - ANALYSIS How are you expected to analyse the detail of what you have learned.	Analyse Categorise Compare and contrast Construct Discuss Interpret Prioritise Produce	Examine in detail the structure of Place into a defined class or division Show the similarities and/or differences between Build up or compile Examine in detail by argument Translate into intelligible or familiar terms Place in order of priority or sequence for action Create or bring into existence
Level 5 - EVALUATION How are you expected to use your learning to evaluate, make decisions or recommendations.	Advise Evaluate Recommend	Counsel, inform or notify Appraise or assess the value of Advise on a course of action

Enterprise Pillar

Strategic Level Paper

E3 – Enterprise Strategy

November 2013

Tuesday Morning Session

Strategic Level Paper

E3 - Enterprise Strategy
November 2013 Examination

Examiner's Answers

SECTION A

Answer to Question One

Rationale

This question examines learning outcomes from across the syllabus. Requirement *(a)* examines learning outcome A2(b) *'evaluate the strategic and competitive impact of information systems '* and is designed to test candidates' understanding of the importance of effective Information Systems in delivering the Games. Requirement *(b)*(i) examines learning outcome D1(a) *'recommend appropriate control measures'* and is designed to test candidates' understanding of the project management environment. Requirement *(b)*(ii) examines learning outcome D1(a) *'recommend appropriate control measures'* and is designed to test candidates' understanding of effective control within the project management environment. Requirements *(c)*(i) and *(c)*(ii) examine learning outcome C1(b) *'evaluate strategic options'* and are designed to test candidates' knowledge and understanding of the complexities of supplier choice and management within a project environment.

Requirement (a)

The Information Systems strategy should be concerned with aligning the IS development with the needs of the whole Games. It is important to have an effective IS strategy for the Games as the information systems used must support the overall successful delivery of the Games. The IS strategy should have been developed alongside the overall Games strategy as the two will be directly linked. Without an effective IS strategy, the Games are less likely to be successfully managed, co-ordinated and communicated. As Country C and GAMESCO have the ultimate deadline of delivering the Games in October 2015, there is no room for slippage or cost over-runs. Therefore it is imperative that the IS strategy monitors and reports on all aspects of the Games so that GAMESCO can deliver the Games on time and on budget.

The IS strategy needs to identify what information is required, and by whom, in order to maintain the ability to monitor and communicate progress and to identify all aspects of each of the many construction projects within the overall project of delivery of the Games.

An IS strategy for the Games would involve identifying what information is needed by the Games organisers, staff and key markets to enable GAMESCO to meet its overall objectives. This will include consideration of the information which would be needed at strategic, tactical and operational levels of the project. The IS strategy for the Games must be focused upon the delivery of the key information requirements of the organisers, project teams and external clients and it should help these users to increase their productivity and assist in the optimum delivery of the Games.

An effective Games information system stategy would focus upon the following key areas:

Project reporting and management
The successful delivery of the Games is reliant upon the successful delivery of the main construction projects which will make up the Games. These projects will need to ensure successful delivery against the project constraints of time, cost and quality. An effective IS strategy should ensure that all of the projects have effective project reporting and management systems which provide thorough and regular feedback to the project teams. In addition, effective Information Systems should integrate this information from projects to allow the overall progress of the project to be monitored by the organisers and key stakeholders. Therefore an effective Information System strategy will ensure that stakeholders are provided with key project progress information.

Customer Information and e-commerce
There has been some criticism of previous Games by customers in that information was not correct, in particular there were weaknesses in previous Games websites. An effective Information System strategy for the Games should recognise the critical importance of the website to the successful delivery of the Games, both as an informational tool and also as an e-commerce tool. Clearly this was not the case in the past. The website for the Games should be an integral part of the overall successful delivery, both in terms of advertising and a key communication tool throughout the region and the wider public but also as an e-commerce tool to sell tickets and merchandise. An effective Information Systems strategy will build in the need for effective communication and e-commerce, using the website within the overall Games strategy.

Stakeholder expectations
Effective information systems will be expected by key stakeholders. It is likely that stakeholders such as customers, ticket agents, television companies and advertising partners will expect the Games to operate an effective website. Therefore development of an effective information systems strategy will satisfy the expectations of key stakeholders and encourage greater acceptance and satisfaction with the Games.

Summary
In summary, the Information System will help the GAMESCO management team deliver the Games. If the Information System does not provide the information required to the many users in the right format at the right time, it will have an adverse impact on the delivery of the Games. Therefore, as many organisations recognise, the Information System strategy is key to the success, or the failure, of the organisation. GAMESCO must ensure that the Information System will support the management team and enable it to make the right decisions based on accurate and timely information.

Requirement (b)(i)

The flexible project management environment of the Velodrome project brings with it a number of key challenges for the Velodrome Project Manager. The need for flexibility normally arises from the need to remain adaptive when operating in a volatile or fast moving external environment. Also, the working practices within the Velodrome project environment, where high levels of collaboration are needed between internal project staff and external partners who come in and out the project at different times, requires a high degree of flexible project planning and management arrangements.

Planning
Effective project planning in this environment is critical as there will be no scope for slippage in time, in particular, as there is an unmoveable project deadline. Planning the deliverables of the many external contractors will be highly complex as their activities will need to integrate and logically follow on from each other. However, getting external contractors to fit in with the overall plan will be difficult and costly. To avoid this potential loss of control, it will require careful and detailed project planning and contract negotiations.

Time planning and initial budget planning are critical and it will be important for the Project Manager to co-ordinate and communicate closely with external contractors prior to commencement of the project. It is likely that there will be a complex arrangement of staff from internal and external sources. Planning for and integrating these staff to co-ordinate effectively for overall delivery will be a key task of the Project Manager. Planning will require a degree of flexibility and contingency and it is likely that within the initial planning stage a number of key risk factors to the project will need to be identified and evaluated. Project planning is likely to be one of the most important stages of the Velodrome project in order to assess the degree of flexibility required, to identify the risks and determine a range of appropriate controls prior to the commencement of the project.

A further challenge to the Project Manager lies in forecasting the timing of the peaks of the project and ensuring that there is available experienced staff from the 'pool of non-project specific' people, or indeed borrowing certain people from other projects, when they are required. For example, during the delivery of the wood for the track and during the installation period of the track, the Project Manager may want a large team of quality control supervisors to ensure that the wood is correctly prepared before the track is laid and that the boards are laid correctly. Involving a team of quality control people during the process should ensure that problems do not occur at a later date. The Project Manager will need to plan the timing and manpower requirements and 'book' this quality control expertise at an early stage to secure the necessary resources. However, if project timing slips, then the required manpower may not be available. It is imperative that project planning and manpower resource planning is continually updated to ensure availability of resources when they are required.

Managing

There are likely to be complex staff relationships both internally and externally. A culture which encourages collaboration and participation is therefore needed. Regular and detailed communication internally and externally is vital to ensure that all parties have all of the relevant information they need to operate effectively. The cultural challenges are likely to be significant, as the Project Manager will have to manage a number of different project team members from differing backgrounds and experience all working together towards one common project objective.

It may be necessary to have more people allocated to the project as a core team, so as to overcome small peaks and troughs due to the strict deadline for project delivery. The project cannot be 'lean' in manpower terms as this would probably result in delays. There is no room for slippage. There is also a need to communicate with staff joining and leaving the project to make sure that relevant information has been recorded and understood by all, in order to reduce the chance of error and omissions or duplication of work. The project plan needs to be communicated to employees on a very regular basis; often a meeting at the start of each day.

To instil this common objective into such a diverse range of team members is likely to be a significant challenge for the Project Manager. However, regular team briefings and regular communication should help to overcome this and build team spirit. Team building events prior to commencement of the project may assist in more effective project management later in the life of the project. As this is such a high profile project, it is likely that motivation levels will be high and the key participants will be focused upon the successful delivery of the project. The Project Manager must instil this within the team throughout its life.

Requirement (b)(ii)

Controls are normally focused upon the three critical project constraints of time, quality and cost.

Time

- The progress of the project towards meeting its completion deadline of the 31st of May 2015 must be managed and controlled effectively and frequently. The main control methods of achieving this would be to undertake regular project progress reporting. Initially the Project Manager will undertake critical path analysis and set key milestones for the achievement of the project. These milestones and critical path activities will then be monitored by the team on a regular basis to ensure that these are being reached.

- Regular project status review meetings with key project staff, both internally and externally, should be held, either weekly or monthly. This ensures that a constant review of progress towards achieving deadlines is being undertaken and that any slippages in time are being monitored and controlled regularly.

- To ensure on time delivery, the Project Manager needs to prepare and update the critical path for the construction of the Velodrome and identify key dates on the critical path.

- It is recommended that the project plan should be updated every day so that everyone involved with the project has access to the latest data, such as the contract with supplier X was placed on xx date or that contract variation number was agreed with supplier Y on xx date. All contract variations should be signed off by the Project Manager, as even minor changes with suppliers could have a knock-on effect on delivery dates or costs.

- There should be a dedicated manager controlling the critical path and updating the project plan for events that occur and identifying events that have not yet occurred which could adversely impact future critical dates. By having a dedicated manager to monitor the critical path closely this will reduce the risk of late delivery.

Quality

- Material inspections should be carried out regularly and frequently to ensure that substandard materials are eliminated and replaced as soon as delivery takes place. The project is working to a tight deadline so re-works are unlikely to be feasible. A 'right first time' approach in terms of quality management must be at the forefront of project development of the Velodrome project.

- Monthly reviews should also be supplemented by 'Deep Dive' quality assurance reviews. These will be scheduled to review the project once every six months, although for a high profile project such as the Velodrome, additional reviews may be held. These reviews will involve government, GAMESCO and delivery partner executives, and the relevant project teams.

- It may be suitable to have a quality control manager who is a 'floating' project member and not dedicated to the project. This manager would be responsible for visiting suppliers and outsourced contractors before contracts are placed to assess whether the supplier has the capability of delivering to the proposed contract specifications. Preventative inspection before placement of contracts and further inspection during the manufacturing process (such as the manufacture of the wood for the track) would save time, which is critical, and will hopefully prevent poor quality work or materials being used on the Velodrome project.

Cost

- Due to the level of expenditure expected to be incurred by the Velodrome project it is recommended that there should be a dedicated accountant as part of the project team to monitor costs in order to alert the Project Manager to potential cost over-runs. It is recommended that all purchase orders for equipment, outsourced suppliers and all other contracts should be counter signed by the project accountant before orders are placed to ensure that costs are controlled before they are incurred.

- The Velodrome project has a budget of C$50 million. An initial project Anticipated Final Cost (AFC) needs to be set up to manage this budget and must be reviewed regularly.

- The Original Budget must be allocated to each cost centre as the starting point for all cost reporting.
  These are likely to comprise the following:
    - construction contracts
    - design contracts
    - project management and assurance costs
    - project contingency

- A Cost Report will need to be provided on a weekly/ monthly basis against the original budget cost reports. For each contract/line item the report should identify:
    - budget
    - forecast price (based on anticipated variation to contracts plus an assessment of risk); and
    - actual cost to date and forecast cost to completion.

- Trend reviews could be held to investigate delivery cost pressures and identify ways they may be mitigated. These meetings should involve project teams, delivery partner staff and sponsors. Trends reviews will ensure that senior management can quickly focus on the issues which are most likely to mitigate cost pressure.

- Quarterly Funders AFC. Every quarter, a report to funders should be presented which includes the project's current forecast of the AFC.

Requirement (c)(i)

Project Constraint	Supplier A	Supplier B	Evaluation against project constraints
Time	1st week of November 2014 delivery. Installation of 4 weeks which is 1 week longer than Supplier B, but if completed on schedule should allow for the final project completion date to be met. However, there is a high potential risk that any delay to this delivery date could mean that installation gets put back by 4 weeks (to the first week of Dec 2014) which would mean the track would not be in place for the required 6 months for acclimatisation in order to meet the projrct deadline of 31st May 2015. This is a major risk to the project.	1st November 2014 delivery. Installation of 3 weeks. Supplier B's schedule, if met, will mean that the project will meet the deadline for installation of the track boards 6 months prior to the Velodrome opening.	There is a clear potential risk of Supplier A not delivering on time resulting in the velodrome not being ready for May 31st 2015 Supplier A is therefore a high risk unless it can provide a guaranteed delivery date. The timing of this project is the critical project constraint and therefore any delay in any of the components could severely risk the final delivery of the overall project. This must be the major consideration for Z as it is clearly the critical project target as set by GAMESCO.
Quality	Supplier A has not undertaken work on this scale before but it does have a high reputation for quality in Country C. The track boards only have a 10 year estimate life cycle. This is 33% less than Supplier B (15 years). Supplier A does not provide its own maintenance facility so it cannot guarantee long term quality management.	Supplier B has a proven track record in previous Games velodrome developments. Supplier B provides a guaranteed life cycle of 15 years with regular maintenance provided.	The quality of the track boards is a critical aspect of the Velodrome construction as the racing surface is the key component of the Velodrome facility. Therefore, Supplier B would be preferable as it also provides a long-term maintenance facility and has a proven track record of quality delivery.
Sustain-ability	Supplier A is based within the region where the Games are being held. Therefore, it is not likely to emit high levels of emissions in transportation of the materials. However, no information is given about production methods or technologies,	Supplier B ships raw materials over long distances and then air transports to their final destination. All of this is likely to result in high levels of carbon emissions. However, Supplier B does undertake carbon off-setting with reforestation,	More information is needed from Supplier A on its production and transportation methods as they may not be sustainable. Supplier B likely to be preferable due to its clear sustainability activities and its quality standards.

	which could in themselves be harmful and dangerous.	so it appears to be an organisation which takes its sustainability responsibilities very seriously, which is a key consideration of the Government.	
Locality	Supplier A is based in Country C. The installation team used would also be from Country C. This is likely to be encouraged by the Government of Country C as it is keen to use local suppliers within the Games projects.	Supplier B is based in another region of the world and uses its own installation team. No local staff will be used. It is known that the Government of Country C is keen to use local staff and suppliers and therefore it is likely to be less favourable towards Supplier B.	Supplier A is preferable from the point of view of the Government due to its location and the fact that the Government is encouraging optimisation of local suppliers and staff. However, this is not likely to be a major deciding factor for the Project Manager as the other project factors are more critical to the successful delivery of the project.

Requirement (c)(ii)

The evaluation of the costs of the track boardsfor each supplier is likely to be complex. Although the cost of the track boards including installation is estimated to be only 5% of the overall cost of the project, cost is one of the key project targets as set by GAMESCO. Any mistakes made in choosing the supplier could have serious consequences on the final delivery of the project and upon the overall quality of the project. Therefore the cost of the track boards must also be evaluated in terms of both quality and timing considerations.

The cost quoted by supplier A is C$2 million plus an additional $0.5 million installation cost. The total cost associated with using Supplier A is therefore C$2.5 million. On a pure cost basis, the Project Manager would consider this as acceptable as it meets the 5% estimate of the total budget for the Velodrome. However, the evaluation of supplier A would be far more complex than the mere evaluation of the total cost itself. The total cost of C$2.5 million is significantly lower than Supplier B but this tender would mean two suppliers to be managed which could bring higher risks to cost control and cost management of the project, let alone the risk of delays and slippage.

The cost of supplier B is C$3.0 million, possibly rising to C$3.12 million, should Supplier B's costs increase by 4%, as happened in the previous Games. Both of these costs exceed 5% of the budget for the Velodrome. However, the project is likely to have contingent funds which would cover this difference but it would need to be closely managed by the Project Manager. Importantly, this cost needs to be evaluated alongside the other key project targets of timing and quality of the track boards supplied by Supplier B.

The Project Manager may also consider using an average annual cost approach to evaluate the costs of each supplier. For Supplier A, the average annual cost would be C$250,000 per year for the 10 year life of the track board installed. For Supplier B there would be an average annual cost over the 15 year life of the track boards of C$200,000, which is 20% lower than Supplier A on an annual basis. However, the Project Manager should also consider the risk that Supplier B could again potentially exceed the estimated cost by 4%. This would result in a total cost of C$3.12 million and therefore an annual average cost of C$208,000. However, this is still lower than Supplier A's annual average cost.

However, it must be recognised that average annual cost is a simplistic method of evaluation and in theory it would be better to evaluate the quotations from the suppliers based on their NPV's and then on their equivalent annual costs. The scenario does not enable such an analysis as the cost of capital for the project (or for the Games as a whole) is not provided.

A further complexity of evaluting the project costs is that the Project Manager must also consider the legacy of the Velodrome.and the Project Manager must therefore also take into consideration the on-going maintenance costs of the Velodrome to provide for its continued use after the Games.

For Supplier A, if the maintenance costs are taken into account, then the average annual undiscounted cost is C$370,000 based on maintenance costs supplied annually by Supplier B at C$120,000 per year for 10 years. For supplier B, assuming a 4% over-run on the quotation, the average annual undiscounted cost is $288,000 based on maintenance costs supplied annually by Supplier B at C$80,000 per year for 15 years. Therefore Supplier B is still cheaper than Supplier A, based on an annual average cost basis. However, again this is a simplistic analysis as it does not take into account the discounted on-going costs. The Project Manager would have to take into account other variables such as the management of the maintenance contracts and other potential unforeseen on-going costs.

In summary, there are a number of complexities in evaluating the cost of the project. However, it must be noted that the evaluation of the cost should only be considered in the context of the other two key project targets. To make a decision upon the suppliers based upon cost alone would ignore the fact that in terms of this specific project, cost is of lesser importance than ensuring the Velodrome is delivered on time and is entirely fit for purpose.

Answer to Question Two

Requirement (a)

The current performance measure used by XXA is Shareholder Value Analysis (SVA).

Shareholder value is a term that suggests that the decisive measure of a company's success is how much it increases the value of its shares to its shareholders. Shareholders only recognise the benefits of future cash flows. Therefore NPV analysis, which calculates the discounted value of future cash flows and compares this with the initial investment based on a suitable risk adjusted cost of capital, will help ensure that the focus of investment is such that only projects providing a positive NPV are approved.

Essentially, shareholders' funds should be used to earn a higher return than could by earned by investing in the next best alternative with the same or very similar level of risk. The basic rule of SVA is that a company adds value for its shareholders only when equity returns exceed equity costs. When that value has been calculated, the company can take steps to improve its performance and also use SVA to measure the success of those actions.

The principle is that the management of any company should first and foremost consider how the interests of its shareholders will be affected by any decisions it takes.

However, there is no agreed way of determining how to calculate SVA. Therefore, before deciding to implement it, the Board must first define how it intends to calculate SVA and what it should include, and follow this consistently.

Benefits of SVA to XXA

- SVA holds that the Board of XXA should first and foremost consider the interests of shareholders in its business decisions.

- SVA takes a long-term view and is about measuring and managing cash flows over time. It would provide XXA with a clear understanding of value creation or degradation over time within each business unit.

- SVA offers a common approach, which is not subject to the particular accounting policies that are adopted. It is therefore globally applicable and can be used across most sectors.

- SVA will force XXA to focus on the future and its customers, with specific attention to the value of future cash flows.

- SVA can set a minimum time period for discounted cashflows to payback an investment in order to minimise the risks of not forecasting future cashflows accurately.

However, shareholder value does not take into account societal needs. Shareholder value financially benefits only the owners of a business; it does not provide a clear measure of social factors such as employment, environmental issues, or ethical business practices. Therefore, a management decision can maximize shareholder value while adversely affecting third parties, including other companies.

Requirement (b)

Should XXA decide to establish four divisions and link managerial performance to divisional performance, this could result in lack of goal congruence, if divisional directors work towards optimising the results of their own division, which could be to the detriment of XXA as a whole. Sub-optimisation can occur when managers take actions to improve the divisional situation at the expense of XXA. For example, divisional managers may undertake short-term actions in order to improve short- run divisional performance at the expense of the long-term opportunities and development of the whole businesses.

Divisional directors of XXA may be incentivised towards dysfunctional decision making if rewards are based on short-term divisional profits. The effect of this is that directors will take decisions that will enable them to achieve bonuses that may not be in the long-term interest of their division. Furthermore, even if the division's interests are fully considered, it may not be in the overall company's interest. This may discourage XXA's divisional managers from making the decision to invest, particularly where the benefits may not materialise quickly.

Divisions within XXA may be different sizes, with different levels of revenues and differing risk profiles. Therefore using a standard cost of capital of 15% (pre-tax) may need to be adjusted to reflect the risk profile of the division or the individual investment. A large investment with long-term cash flows that is expected to produce a positive net present value is usually considered to be more risky than a small investment with short-term cash flows that also produces a positive net present value. Generally speaking, the longer the term of the payback period, the more risky is the project due to uncertainty about the future cash flows. For large scale investments, to use a standard cost of capital which ignores the specific risks relating to different projects is naïve and too simplistic, particularly in today's changing and fiercely competitive marketplace. A standard cost of capital may be appropriate for small scale investments which do not have a large impact on the overall weighted average cost of capital of the company.

Another factor to be considered is that XXA as a whole may not be able to afford to provide the finance to undertake all investment proposals. It is usual to review all positive NPV projects and then make a decision on which projects should be approved, due to the absolute limit on capital funding, a process referred to as capital rationing. Perhaps projects under a specified value could be approved by divisional directors, whereas larger investment projects would need central authorisation from the Board or J. After all, XXA has not got access to unlimited investment funds.

A further criticism of basing rewards on divisional performance is the potential stress that the divisional directors may feel if their remuneration is based upon performance. This may encourage them to make decisions with which they are unhappy, resulting in increased stress.

Requirement (c)

	Investment 1 Q$	Investment 2 Q$
Original Investment cost	2,000,000	5,000,000
Controllable profit	400,000	450,000
ROI (Controllable Profit / Original Investment cost)	20%	9%
Expected Divisional ROI	22%	8%
Current cost of capital for XXA	15%	15%
Divisional director's likely motivation based on divisional ROI	Reject	Accept
Goal congruent motivation of the divisional director as desired by XXA based on the NPV of the investment	Accept	Reject

Residual Income

	Investment 1	Investment 2
Investment cost	2,000,000	5,000,000
Controllable profit	400,000	450,000
Cost of capital charge (15% of investment cost)	300,000	750,000
Residual Income	100,000	(300,000)
Divisional director's likely motivation based on divisional RI	Accept	Reject
Goal congruent motivation of the divisional director as desired by XXA based on the NPV of the investment	Accept	Reject

For XXA, if ROI had been used as a measure of divisional performance, then the divisional directors may have made the wrong decisions in rejecting Investment 1 and accepting Investment 2. This is because for Investment 1, the proposal would have impacted negatively upon the divisional return as, at 20%, it would have the effect of reducing the divisional ROI below the current level of 22%. However, the current organisational cost of capital stands at 15%, so the goal congruent decision would have been to accept the proposal which was the decision actually taken by XXA based on its positive NPV.

Likewise, for Investment 2, the divisional manager would have accepted this proposal as the divisional ROI would have increased as the proposal earns 1% above the current divisional ROI of 8%. However, the return of the proposal fell short of the current cost of capital of the organisation and the goal congruent decision would have been to reject the proposal which was the actual decision reached by XXA based on its negative NPV.

Merits of ROI as a divisional performance measure

- It is widely used and accepted in practice. However, this does not mean that it should be used by XXA if better alternatives are available.

- A minimum company-wide ROI can be set for an organisation as a benchmark for project evaluation. This would be a useful measure for an organisation such as XXA with only 4 potential divisions.

- As a relative measure, it allows for easy comparison of divisional performance and therefore offers an easily understood control measure for the directors of XXA.

- As it is based upon capital employed, it encourages divisional managers to reduce or to optimise the level and usage of assets such as divesting obsolete equipment and excessive use of capital employed. This results in greater efficiencies and less wastage, which for an organisation such as XXA, where competition is likely to be high and customers price sensitive, then minimising excessive investment costs to retain profit margins and competitive prices will be paramount.

Disadvantages of using ROI as a divisional performance measure

- As can be seen from the calculations above for XXA, it can lead to dysfunctional decision making, which is likely to be to the detriment of XXA as a whole.

- Due to differing asset replacement approaches used, it could make comparisons difficult and ROI also may increase with the age of assets. Therefore if one division in XXA operates with older assets than another then its ROI may look superior, but in fact it may well be operating with worn out and old assets which are not efficient and may result in expensive replacements further down the line.

- ROI can be a disincentive to invest. A divisional manager will not choose to invest in a proposal which may reduce his or her own ROI but in fact would increase organisational ROI (see above).

- ROI can be calculated in a number of ways, which can lead to different decisions. In XXA, ROI was calcuated on the basis of original investment but the commonly used approach would be to use an average investment. For example, for Investment 1, ROI based upon an average investment would have been 40% which would have resulted in the divisional director making a goal congruent decision.

Merits of RI as a divisional performance measure

- It overcomes the potential problems of under-investing discussed in ROI above.

- It makes it quite clear to the divisional managers of XXA what the financing costs of projects are.

- As can be seen from the example above, RI is more consistent with the objective of trying to maximise the total profitability of the organisation and not the individual divisions. This would seem to be something that the current Board, as a centralised organisation, would be keen to ensure continues.

- Residual income is more flexible as the cost of capital applied to different projects can be adjusted to reflect the appropriate level of risk associated with them.

Disadvantages of using RI as a divisional performance measure

- It is an absolute measure which means that it is difficult to compare the performance of divisions of differing sizes. For example, one division may be much larger than the others and may therefore be viewed as having superior performance. This may cause resentment between the divisional directors.

- RI does not take into consideration the relative size and cost of the investment to the organisation.

In summary, ROI's biggest shortcoming is that it ignores the cost of finance entirely. Furthermore, the overall ROI of a division will increase over time simply because of the depreciated value of the cumulative assets. RI's significant disadvantage is that it ignores the length of time in which future cash flows from a project will arise and the relative size of the investment. There is no gauge on the length of payback or discounted payback. From the perspective of XXA, both methods are simplistic and contain flaws.

Answer to Question Three

Rationale

This question examines Sections A and C of the syllabus. Requirement *(a)* examines learning outcome C2(c) *'produce an organisation's value chain'* and is designed to test candidates' ability to apply the value chain to a scenario context. Requirement *(b)* examines learning outcome A2(b) *'evaluate the strategic and competitive impact of information systems* and is designed to test candidates' understanding of the use and benefits of databases and data warehouses. Requirement *(c)* examines learning outcome A1(e) *'recommend how to interact with suppliers and customers'.*

Suggested approach

For requirement *(a)* candidates are required to evaluate the primary activities of VVT, using Porter's Value Chain model. This should be a straightforward question, requiring candidates to analyse the scenario information and evaluate those aspects which are relevant to VVT's value chain.

For requirement *(b)* candidates are required to demonstrate their knowledge and understanding of data warehousing and data mining in relation to VVT. This should be a straightforward question but importantly any benefits of data warehousing and data mining must be directly related to VVT.

For requirement *(c)* candidates must evaluate the current supply chain activities identified in the scenario material and then recommend improvements to these. Therefore it is important that any recommendation made is fully justified in relation to the weakness identified in the supply chain. This should be a straightforward question as there are several possible examples of weakness which can be identified from the scenario information provided.

Requirement (a)

INBOUND LOGISTICS	OPERATIONS	OUTBOUND LOGISTICS	MARKETING AND SALES	SERVICE
Rigorous Quality inspection of all goods delivered by MMM.	VVT logo used to re-brand all products received from MMM.	VVT offers in-home set up by trained technicians.	National advertising in the newspapers.	In-home technical installation and support at a small charge.
Fully configured products delivered to the warehouse.	VVT re-packages products in own designed packaging.	Customers can talk to trained technicians at point of sale to ensure that they order the product that suits their needs.	Website promotes its range of products and allows for web-based enquiries.	Back to warehouse repair support for out of warranty products.
			High inventory held in the warehouses to ensure customers can take quick delivery of products.	Dedicated phone line to assist with customer queries and questions when ordering.
High inventory held in the warehouses to ensure products are available to customers.			Direct mail from customer database used encouraging brand loyalty.	

Inbound logistics:

Rigorous quality inspections undertaken by VVT results in 100% defect-free products. This is likely to be very important to customers who will have expectations of reliability and quality for pre-configured equipment. This should help to increase customer satisfaction levels and also reduce service costs for VVT.

High stocks held will mean that VVT's customers will benefit from immediate delivery and not have to wait for products to be shipped. This again should increase customer satisfaction levels. However, this is likely to add significant costs to VVT in terms of stock holding and warehousing costs, to a large extent due to MMM's inadequacies.

Operations:

This is a relatively small aspect of VVT's business activities, as it merely rebrands the products with its own logo and places them into its own designed packaging. No further additions or configurations take place. Therefore, within operations, VVT adds little value to the customer.

Outbound logistics:

Trained VVT technicians are used to installing some systems within customers' homes. With complex technology this is likely to be highly valued by customers. Also trained technicians are used at the point of sale to assist customers in buying the most suitable products. It would appear that VVT's competitors do not offer the same level of support and assistance to customers. This service helps VVT's customers make informed choices of products and is more likely to secure a sale and a satisfied customer. This is also highly valued by the customers.

Marketing and Sales:

Direct marketing to existing customers makes customers feel wanted and valued and encourages loyalty.

The limited use of the website in terms of product ordering and payments is a key weakness of the primary activities and is likely to need significant development if VVT wishes to grow the business. Although it adds value in terms of providing an information source to customers, it could be exploited more usefully by VVT to add value to the business. VVT does use its customer database to undertake direct marketing which could be of value if it is used specifically to target particular customers and particular products.

Dedicated phone lines for customers' queries and the ability to talk to trained technicians ensures that VVT offers a high quality of customer service and a positive experience for customers. This adds value as it provides a service which customers recognise as important in the selection and subsequent order for VVT products.

High inventory levels ensure that customers can obtain any product that is advertised or is shown on VVT's website without a long delay from order to delivery. The ability of VVT to meet customer orders is an important added value activity.

National advertising takes place through national newspapers, although this is unlikely to add significant value as VVT's main competitors are also likely to undertake a similar form of advertising.

Service:

These are key 'added value' activities that many of VVT's larger competitors do not offer and these services may play an important role in customers' decisions to buy VVT's products.

The home installation service is clearly a huge help to customers who buy complex products from VVT. This service may make the difference between a dissatisfied customer if the customer had set up the product himself, perhaps incorrectly, and a satisfied customer with a correctly set up product. This adds value as the product can be used quickly and correctly by the customer gaining improved levels of customer satisfaction. This is likely to lead to further orders of other VVT products or recommendations benefitting VVT.

The technicians' visits to homes to sort out problems for warranty products is clearly more appealing to customers than being required to take the faulty product into a VVT shop. Even though this service costs VVT money to provide, it is another unique selling point which appeals to customers and differentiates VVT from its competitors and therefore adds value.

Warehouse based repairs are a good solution for customers with products out of the warranty period, as a minor repair may only be required. This service prevents customers having to buy a new product at a far greater cost if it can be repaired in the factory. This encourages brand loyalty and adds value to the customers' experience with VVT.

Feedback indicates that the services offered by VVT are highly valued by its customers. Its larger competitors cannot offer a similar level of customer service which is therefore a key source of competitive advantage for VVT. This must be retained and developed as much as possible, even if the business grows.

Requirement (b)

Currently VVT uses its customer database purely as an information source to undertake direct mailing activities. However, if VVT were to use it more as a data warehouse, it may benefit significantly.

A data warehouse is a subject based, integrated collection of data that helps management in its decision making process. It collects information from various sources, both internal and external to the organisation, and makes it available to the end-users in an understandable and usable format to assist them in decision making.

VVT could benefit from using its customer database more effectively in the following ways:

- A data warehouse would enable VVT's managers to make comparisons between different factors within its database. For example, have customers buying habits changed over a number of years? Comparisons of sales in particular areas or age groups for specific products could be made. This would allow VVT to understand potential areas of growth and development or areas where products are less popular than they were previously. This could assist VVT with stock management and ensuring the correct products are available.

- A key benefit of using a data warehouse is the ability to undertake data mining. This involves using advanced analytical tools to discover useful relationships in databases. Data mining turns data into information for decision making. For example, the sales records of a particular model of television might indicate a correlation with a particular age group or location of buyer which could assist VVT in directing its advertising more effectively.

- Data mining might also assist VVT with identifying associations, such as computers being bought at the same time as printers or sequences such as the purchase of a television often results in the later purchase of speaker systems. This will then allow VVT to predict potential customer buying behaviour patterns and allow VVT to be more responsive to customer needs.

- If the database is linked to the website, then VVT could exploit this by using direct e-mail adverts to customers, specifically tailored to their buying patterns and the associations identified from data mining. This could reduce the costs of traditional direct mailing by post.

Requirement (c)

Examiner's Note: Candidates were only expected to provide three recommendations.

VVT's main weakness is its reliance on one supplier with no long-term contract in place. It also has a supply chain which appears to be inefficient and error prone. VVT may wish to consider the following methods of improving its supply chain and remove some of the non-value adding activities:

- VVT should sign a formal 1 year rolling contract with MMM. There is an urgent need for VVT to sign a long-term supply contract with MMM to secure continuity of supply, on which at present VVT business is totally dependent. However, VVT could also consider widening its supply base by looking for other suppliers. However, this could increase costs for VVT in sourcing and managing a number of different suppliers but this must be weighed against the reduction of the risks associated with having only one supplier. Other suppliers may have better systems in place to monitor and control deliveries which would benefit VVT.

- VVT should also establish a secure online ordering and tracking system which links through to VVT's inventory system, so that as products are sold it triggers either an automatic order with MMM or a reminder to VVT's procurement department to place an order for specified products. All despatches from MMM should be updated on this tracking system, in real time, to enable VVT to track all orders from leaving MMM through to delivery at VVT's warehouse. This would enable VVT to know where all orders are at any specific point and prevent over-ordering. VVT uses only one supplier, MMM, which could be considered to be a weakness of the supply chain.

- The use of the logistics company to deliver orders from the port in the neighbouring country is another 'weak link' in VVT's supply chain. If VVT could track each order then it would be able to ensure that the courier collected the goods as soon as they arrived in the shipping port. Also, the contract with the logistics company should include penalties for late delivery, to ensure deliveries are made to VVT within a specified period of time, such as 48 hours or 72 hours, from arrival in the port. VVT should consider replacing the logistics company used by MMM from a neighbouring country with a logistics company of its own choice. If VVT had better information relating to the shipping delivery dates then VVT could organise the pick up from the port using a logistics company over whom it has control, rather than being organised at a distance by MMM. This has clearly been a problem in the past as orders have gone missing with the logistics copmany and this could be reduced if VVT had a contract with a local company which it could monitor and exercise some degree of control over.

- As the business involves electronic consumer products such as TVs and computers, it is important that VVT does not hold large inventories of these products as they could quickly become obsolete and the inventory would need to be written down and the products sold off cheaply or even disposed of. A small inventory should be held which satisfies the need to meet customers' orders with minimum delay but prevents large inventory holding of these products. It would be better for VVT to place smaller but more regular orders with MMM. However, this needs to be balanced with the increased order and shipping costs associated with more frequent deliveries.

- VVT should consider identifying suppliers which can provide superior information about delivery and shipping dates. Most suppliers should be able to provide shipping information through their website using internet based order tracking systems. This will provide VVT with much better information in terms of supply dates and should hopefully reduce the impact of potential stock outs or the need to overstock – thus reducing costs. In fact VVT should consider identifying and using suppliers which could re-brand and re-package their products at their own production sites, reducing the costs of VVT having to undertake this at its own warehouse. This could significantly reduce its costs, particularly if the supplier is operating in a location where labour costs are lower than in VVT's own country. However VVT would have to consider the impact that this could have on its own reputation as it would have to make redundancies and also bad publicity may follow if it is considered that VVT is cutting costs through using cheap overseas labour. The elimination of re-packaging would remove non-value adding activities of VVT.

Answer to Question Four

Requirement (a)

- PPP staff will be affected by the change of ownership as they may have to re-locate and undertake additional training. Thus, their location and responsibilities may change and therefore this could be a source of resistance.

- QZZ is proposing to move towards more online production and delivery of books and many staff will be unfamiliar with this type of product. PPP currently operates very traditionally and therefore this will have a significant impact upon the jobs and roles of the remaining staff. They are likely to resist this.

- The changes to the methods of operating may seem to be implied criticisms of the current family ethos of the business and this may cause resentment by the staff and the family members still working in the business. This may cause resistance.

- Re-location of employees has implications for each employee's family, housing and children's schooling. Is the relocation within reasonable commuting distance or is it to another part of the country? This impact on the wider family will likely be highly resisted.

- Potentially, there could be redundancies in the long term if QZZ acquires PPP and clearly all of the staff in PPP will be resistant to this. Many of the staff of PPP will resist change due to the obvious concerns about their jobs.

- The Board of Directors is very proud of its wide readership but QZZ intends to re-focus this to a much narrower audience. This proposal to reduce the readership is likely to be resisted by the Board and the staff.

- The work of the staff may now become less interesting if the business moves towards electronic delivery of books. This will affect morale and thus will create resistance.

- The break-up of the 'family ethos' is likely to meet with strong resistance from staff. Staff have valued the family ethos in PPP and are used to the company culture and have helped to establish PPP's good reputation. Now all of their hard work and commitment to the company, shown through low staff turnover and low absenteeism, will not count at all in the future.

Requirement (b)

QZZ intends to re-organise PPP and to change its methods of operating. This is not unethical as it would appear necessary to safeguard the long-term survival of PPP. However, the way in which QZZ manages this acquisition could have ethical implications. In the UK, TUPE (Transfer of Undertakings/ Protection of Employment) provides legal protection to employees in relation to transfer of their employment contracts to a new employer. It can be assumed that the country in which PPP operates will have a similar legal protection for employees. As well as following its legal obligations, QZZ must also consider its ethical obligations to the employees of PPP.

QZZ should insist that the staff of PPP are informed by the Board of PPP prior to acquisition. Staff should be informed of the potential acquisition so that they can have a full understanding of the acquisition process and have a better opportunity to make the correct decision for themselves. If they wish to leave prior to the acquisition to improve their own job prospects then they should be allowed to do so even if this means breaking a contractual agreement between the employer and employee. It could be considered unethical to not inform staff in appropriate time for them to make the best decisions for themselves. Therefore, staff must be informed immediately that a potential acquisition is being considered by the Board.

QZZ must treat employees with consideration for the potential stress that they are likely to be going through. Some staff may be fearful of using new technology. Employees should be offered appropriate re-training in e-business, with which they may not be familiar. This must be handled sensitively and with care. Staff should be encouraged to participate as this gives them new skills. They must not be forced to re-train with the threat of re-location or redundancy as this will not encourage them to embrace these new skills. This could result in stress-related illness causing them to take time off work and cost QZZ more and may be considered unethical behaviour. Staff should be encouraged and rewarded for a positive attitude to re-training and offered incentives. QZZ should consider offering incentives such as flexible working arrangements or bonus payments for training courses attended.

QZZ should consider its ethical obligations to the staff of PPP, many of whom have only ever worked for PPP and will have no other working experience. Therefore they may find it difficult to work within a new environment for new employers. Training in the culture of QZZ may be required in order to familiarise PPP's stafff with the new working culture required.

QZZ has stated that if staff refuse to re-train or relocate then they could face redundancy. It could appear to be acting unethically if it offered staff no alternative options before redundancy. For example, QZZ should consider offering incentives such as flexible working arrangements or additional payments for travelling costs. It is likely that staff will be resistant to such major changes to working arrangements and therefore QZZ must try to incentivise the staff. Volunteers for re-location could be identified as a starting point. Also assistance with re-location both financial assistance and support during the move such as finding housing, temporary accommodation, schools etc would be an appropriate approach.

However, it is important to remember that QZZ is making a rational business decision and difficult decisions regarding employees sometimes have to be made. This does not necessarily make them unethical but QZZ must ensure that any actions it undertakes which affect employees are sensitively handled.

Requirement (c)

It is recommended that staff are notified that an acquisition is being negotiated as soon as possible. Any changes which will impact upon them should be communicated so as to keep them informed, as speculation, gossip and fear of what is about to occur is often worse than the actual truth about the changes. Therefore QZZ needs to be mindful of the commitment of PPP's employees and recognise that they are key assets to the company. Staff need to be motivated and encouraged to change and re-train in order to make the acquisition a success.

Unfreeze
It is recommended that the Board of PPP must communicate immediately with the staff regarding the reasons for change. It must make it clear that PPP does not have the resources or the skills to operate in the current environment and that if PPP does not change through acquisition then it is likely that the company will close. The Board needs to clearly demonstrate to staff the changing market conditions and the clear change in the buying behaviour of customers for books. PPP can use the closure of the chain of book stores as clear evidence of this.

Change
Changing the behaviour of staff is likely to be complex and a range of methods will be needed. It is recommended that effective and regular communication must be carried out with staff regarding not only the redundancy process but also the opportunities the acquisition will bring. Meetings must take place with all staff to discuss the potential impact on them of the closure of the printing facility and the process of taking up new appointments.

Those staff who could be made redundant should be offered counselling. The Board of PPP must try to persuade QZZ that it must offer appropriate redundancy terms and should also invest in some form of assistance for staff. These staff have been highly loyal to PPP and if QZZ wishes to maintain a feeling of loyalty it must prove that it intends to treat its staff well. Morale is going to be a major driver of whether the acquisition will succeed or not and therefore encouraging up-beat morale should be a key consideration during the change process.

Re-training and re-location should be carefully managed. Staff may fear new technologies and methods of operating and therefore regular training must be carried out. Incentives and assistance should be provided for re-locating staff.

Re-freezing
It is recommended that incentives must be offered to those staff accepting the change. Bonuses should be offered to those staff who clearly accept the change.

It is recommended that regular communications with staff regarding acquisition negotiations should be carried out so that staff are fully informed throughout the process and commitment and motivation is maintained. After the acquisition, further communication should be carried out regularly to highlight improvements which have occurred.
